The Edge *of the* Woods

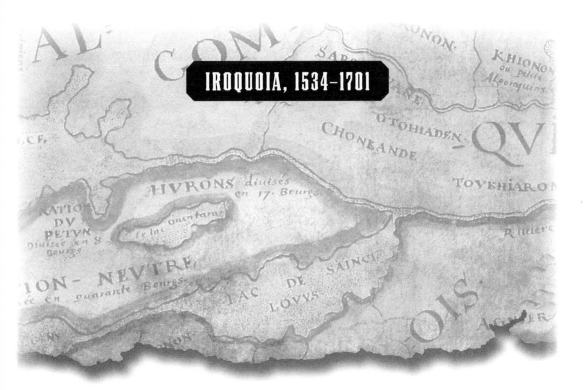

IROQUOIA, 1534–1701

The Edge *of the* Woods

JON PARMENTER

MICHIGAN STATE UNIVERSITY PRESS • EAST LANSING

⊗ The paper used in this publication meets the minimum requirements
of ANSI/NISO z39.48-1992 (R 1997) (Permanence of Paper).

This publication was made possible by the generous support
of the Hull Memorial Publication Fund of Cornell University.

Michigan State University Press
East Lansing, Michigan 48823-5245

Printed and bound in the United States of America.

20 19 18 17 16 15 14   1 2 3 4 5 6 7 8 9 10

ISBN: 978-1-61186-139-6 (pbk.)
ISBN: 978-1-60917-214-5 (ebook: PDF)

The hardcover edition of this book was catalogued by the Library of Congress as follows:

LIBRARY OF CONGRESS CATALOGING-IN-PUBLICATION DATA
Parmenter, Jon.
The edge of the woods : Iroquoia, 1534–1701 / Jon Parmenter.
p. cm.
Includes bibliographical references and index.
ISBN 978-0-87013-985-7 (cloth : alk. paper) 1. Iroquois Indians—Social life and
customs. 2. Iroquois Indians—Social conditions. 3. Social structure—North
America—History. 4. Social mobility—North America—History. 5. Spatial
behavior—North America—History. 6. Power (Social sciences)—North America—
History. 7. Community life—North America—History. 8. Human geography—
North America—History. 9. North America—Social life and customs. 10. North
America—Social conditions. I. Title.
E99.I7P26 2010
970.01—dc22
2009031982

Cover and book design by Sharp Des!gns, Lansing, Michigan
COVER: Detail from "Novvelle France," ca. 1641.
Courtesy of the UK Hydrographic Office, Taunton.

Michigan State University Press is a member of the Green Press Initiative and is
committed to developing and encouraging ecologically responsible publishing
practices. For more information about the Green Press Initiative and the use of
recycled paper in book publishing, please visit *www.greenpressinitiative.org*.

Visit Michigan State University Press on the World Wide Web at *www.msupress.org*

CONTENTS

MAPS & FIGURES

MAPS

FIGURES

PREFACE

On March 12, 1697, a delegation of Onondaga headmen visiting Albany met with Robert Livingston, the town clerk and "Secretary to the Indians" who was responsible for translating and recording all "intelligence or propositions" communicated between Native American diplomats and New York authorities. Although this process usually involved Livingston transcribing words spoken aloud, on this day the Onondagas did the writing. Using a red wax crayon, the Onondagas sketched an outline map of interconnected lakes and rivers. A rather nondescript drawing at first glance, its significance was revealed in the key to the map, which the Onondagas dictated to Livingston. Represented on the Onondagas' "Drafft of this Countrey" (see figure 1) were elements of five major drainage systems in northeastern North America (the lower Great Lakes basin, and the St. Lawrence, Susquehanna, Connecticut, and Hudson rivers) in an area spanning approximately 150,000 square miles. Within this immense region the Onondagas had also mapped the spatial relationships among these linked water routes (portages, neighboring Iroquois towns, and English and French colonial settlements) in a manner that indicated their intimate, direct knowledge of this vast extent of territory.[1]

How had the Onondagas acquired such an extensive spatial consciousness? Oral, archaeological, and documentary evidence attests to the highly mobile character of Iroquois people in pre- and early post-contact times. At the moment of their first encounter with Europeans, Iroquois people possessed centuries of experience with building reciprocal relationships between people and communities that extended over spatial distances and that were sustained by frequent human movements for political, ceremonial, and economic purposes. Exotic lithics, ceramics, and goods such as shell wampum and native copper in the archaeological record of pre-contact Iroquoia reveals abundant evidence of extensive Iroquois mobility. Early European observers noted a particular flair for travel among the Iroquois, describing trail systems, shelters, signage, maps sketched on bark or plotted with kernels of maize, water travel in bark canoes, prepared travel foods, and an overarching cultural ethic of hospitality that sustained it all. During the sixteenth and seventeenth centuries, Iroquois people

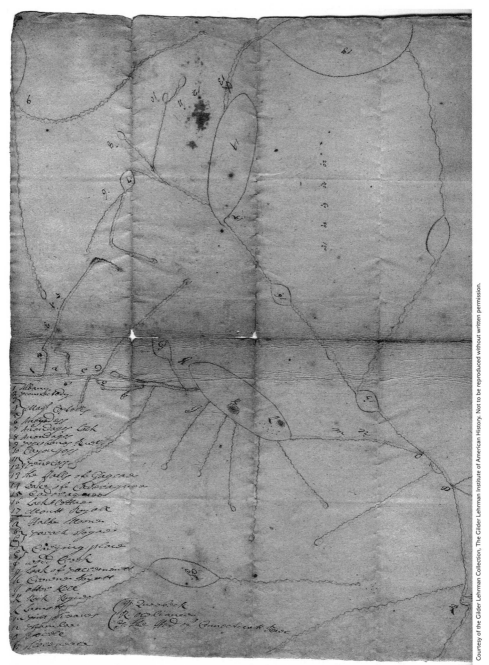

"Drafft of this Countrey," 1697. GLC03107.02046. [Northern New York and part of Canada, map].

regularly traveled hundreds of miles in all directions from their homelands, and by 1697 they possessed an unsurpassed level of geographical knowledge of northeastern North America.

What did such knowledge do for the Iroquois? Far from representing a disintegration of core Iroquois cultural values, mobility provided a means of strengthening those values and of extending them to other peoples living at the constantly-shifting "edge" of Iroquoia's "woods." Pre- and post contact Iroquois movements changed the geographical reckoning of Iroquois homelands to encompass an increasingly larger geographic space while simultaneously accommodating relations between increasing numbers of Iroquois people living at ever-greater distances from one another. Cycles of spatial dispersal and convergence generated by Iroquois people in accordance with seasonal, strategic, or sacred exigencies sustained ties between kin and thus a coherent sense of community over considerable geographic distances. Free Iroquois movement through extensive spaces also negated colonizers' efforts to fix Iroquois nations into predictable administrative units and yielded an enhanced repertoire of empirical knowledge of geographical, political, and economic circumstances that Iroquois people eventually employed to contest settler encroachments on Iroquois space.

This book explains how Iroquois people translated spatial concepts embedded in their traditional philosophy into actions that engaged new challenges and opportunities brought about by early European intrusions on the borders of their homelands from 1534 to 1701. Departing from scholarship that has long identified fixed localities in clearly bounded spaces as the fundamental analytical units of Iroquois culture, this study contends that extensive mobility on the part of Iroquois people from 1534 to 1701 established a geography of solidarity. Through strategic uses of mobility, the Iroquois were able to link supposedly "scattered" and "fragmented" communities in a wide-ranging, often fluid, yet interconnected indigenous polity.

Drawing on multilingual archival and published documents, archaeological data, and Iroquois oral traditions, this book demonstrates how Iroquois society, as it expanded spatially after 1534 to include new places and new peoples, balanced core cultural values against the imperatives of lived experience and sustained a hitherto-unrecognized degree of cohesion while engaging the opportunities and impositions of North American settler colonialism. Mobility not only embodied Iroquois values of hospitality and attentiveness to renewals of reciprocal human relationships, it created a vital spatial context for the exercise of Iroquois power.

Focusing on the changing conceptions, usage, and structures of space during the late precolonial period of Iroquois history (defined in this study as the era between the arrival of Europeans and the confinement of Iroquois people on reservations after the American Revolutionary War) illustrates the fundamentally geographical nature of the entangled relationship of the Iroquois with neighboring settler colonies after 1609. The analytical framework of cross-cultural entanglement, recently articulated by historical archaeologists, facilitates an appreciation of history-as-lived for all parties in contact situations and illuminates how these contacts occurred in a context of incomplete colonization.[2] Contested views of space and its proper use were manifest in the earliest of Iroquois disputes with settlers over conflicting jurisdictional constructions of territoriality and property rights, especially the extent of Iroquois rights to freedom of movement for settlement, procurement, and communication purposes.

This history of precolonial Iroquoia is not a study of Iroquois "resistance." Rather, it is an effort to analyze innovative change over time in Iroquois spatial practices. The book seeks to comprehend the ways in which spatial mobility represented the geographic expression of Iroquois social, political, and economic priorities. By reconstructing the late precolonial Iroquois settlement landscape, and the paths of human mobility that constructed and sustained it, this study challenges the persistent synechdocal linkage between Iroquois "locality" and Iroquois "culture," and more fully maps the extended terrain of physical presence and social activity that Iroquois people inhabited. Studying patterns of movement through and between the multiple localities in Iroquois space, the book offers a new understanding of Iroquois peoplehood during this period: rather than eroding, Iroquois identities adapted, even strengthened, as the size and shape of Iroquois homelands changed dramatically during the seventeenth century (see figure 2).[3]

Additionally, the book analyzes how the Iroquois transformed their late precolonial space by creating new communities, modifying local settlement patterns, establishing new routes of commercial and social exchange, and asserting the legitimacy of indigenous constructions of territory and property vis-à-vis those of the colonizers. Iroquois ordering of spatial movements and their attendant communication flows made for efficient information processing. Eventually, this cultural facility for optimizing mobility enabled Iroquois people to assert control over information conduits both within Iroquois space and between Iroquois people and others on the peripheries of Iroquoia. If we accept the idea of knowledge as a resource, we can appreciate the ways in which diversified networks of human contacts obtained and maintained through spatial mobility constituted social power for Iroquois people, insofar as the nature and extent of those contacts provided valuable, actionable information about other people, places, and things.[4]

Similarly, a view of knowledge as a resource enables us to grasp the significance of the conceptual diffusion of Iroquoian ideas about mobility embedded in the "Edge of the Woods" ceremony (as depicted by various European observers of the ritual). Some indigenous American societies erected large-scale communal public structures as a form of "mass media" to communicate and reinforce their normative sociopolitical models: among the Iroquois, the ideological "mass media" or code appears in rich spatial metaphors and ceremonies associated with movement, which eventually became integral components of the traditions and rituals of the Iroquois League. Spatial

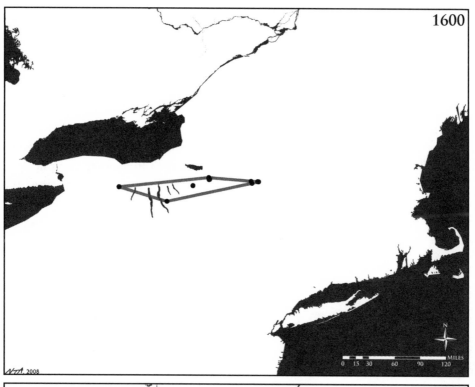

1600

1641

The Changing Shape of Iroquoia, 1600–1701

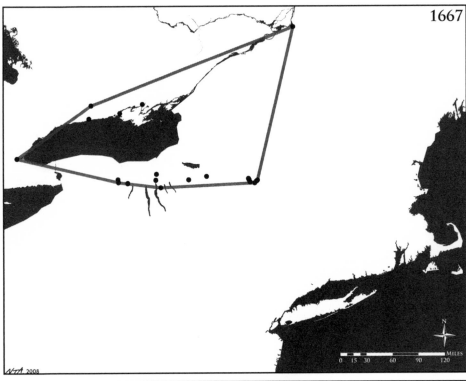

1667

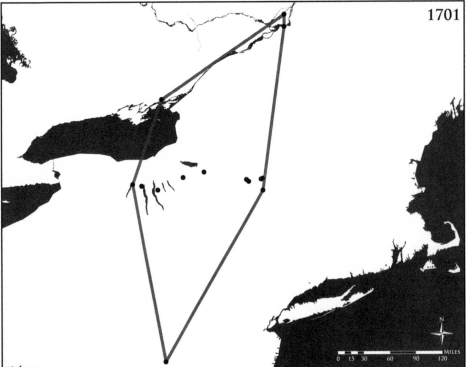

1701

The Changing Shape of Iroquoia, 1600–1701, *continued*

metaphors were conveyed verbally and nonverbally in ceremonial speeches, dances, greetings, hospitality, and exchanges of exotic material objects procured from afar (such as copper and shell wampum). Such "sensuous performances" exposed these ideas and objects to communal perception and collective deliberation regarding their meanings and significance. Collectively, they testify to the central role of mobility as a source of power and cohesion in Iroquois culture.[5]

By assessing the ways in which the Iroquois engaged the pressures and opportunities presented by the development of European settler colonies on the periphery of their homelands, this book relates the Iroquois experience to larger critical conversations concerning colonialism's impact on human cultures, polities, and economies, a discourse from which Native Americans are often excluded as agents of change. Recognizing that North American settler colonialism has not only invaded and conquered territorial space but that it has also colonized indigenous epistemological spaces, the book also attempts to tell the story of sixteenth- and seventeenth-century Iroquois history from the "inside out." That is, it compares multiple European accounts of the Iroquois during this period, draws on the physical evidence of the archaeological record, and then casts all this information through the sieve of textualized Iroquois oral traditions (the only versions accessible to those outside contemporary Iroquois society). In so doing, it aims to render articulate some of the many silences of the Iroquois past.[6]

TECHNICAL NOTES ON TERMINOLOGY, DATING, AND CITATIONS

This study employs the term "Iroquois" to denote individuals and communities of the five founding nations of the Iroquois League (Mohawks, Oneidas, Onondagas, Cayugas, and Senecas), "Iroquoian" as a collective reference to the members of the Iroquoian language family (which extended beyond the Five Nations of the League), and "Iroquoia" to refer to the territorial space inhabited and used by Iroquois people. For spellings of individual names, this book follows standardized versions in the *Dictionary of Canadian Biography* unless otherwise noted.

The English used the Julian (Old Style, or O.S.) calendar during the time period encompassed by this study, although the French and Dutch had adopted the modern Gregorian calendar (New Style, or N.S.) in 1582. In order to provide the most accurate historical reconstruction of Iroquois activities, I have adjusted all dates discussed in the text to N.S. by silently adding ten calendar days to O.S. dates between 1500 and February 18, 1700, and eleven calendar days to O.S. dates after February 19, 1700. Thus an event dated in O.S. as March 22, 1676/77 (New Year's Day on the Julian calendar was March 25) would be discussed in the text as occurring on April 1, 1677. Following standard historical practice, I have indicated O.S. dates cited in manuscript sources.[7]

Each note contains citations to sources listed in an order roughly corresponding to the sequence of information conveyed in the related section of text. Notes also provide page-level references to all quoted passages in the text. In the event that a single source provides all direct quotes in a particular note, the note supplies the page range within that source where the quotes may be found. Published primary sources are cited by volume and page references only, while manuscript sources are cited with descriptions and dates. I have cited French sources in translation when possible. Translations from French-language sources are my own unless otherwise noted.

ACKNOWLEDGMENTS

This book began its life as a chapter I planned to add to a revision of my 1999 University of Michigan dissertation on eighteenth-century Iroquois history. Now, one decade later, I am delighted to have the opportunity to thank the many people who helped make it possible.

Ian Steele at the University of Western Ontario and John Shy at the University of Michigan provided examples of scholarship and professionalism that continue to motivate and inspire me to the present day. I can never repay the faith they placed in me. David Lloyd at St. Lawrence University took a chance and hired me as a newly minted Ph.D. in 1999. Both David and Len Moore (now at McGill University), remain great friends and key professional advocates. I had the good fortune to join the History Department at Cornell in 2003, a wonderful place in which to think, teach, and write. My departmental colleagues encouraged me to rethink the monograph I had planned to write, and their questions, critiques, and insights have proven enormously influential over the past six years. Among them, I thank especially Ed Baptist, Derek Chang, Sherm Cochran, Ray Craib, Maria Cristina Garcia, Durba Ghosh, Sandra Greene, Itsie Hull, Michael Kammen, Holly Kase, Vic Koschmann, Fred Logevall, Tamara Loos, Larry Moore, Barry Strauss, Eric Tagliacozzo, Robert Travers, Maggi Washington, and Rachel Weil. My senior colleague in early American history, Mary Beth Norton, has been a true mentor in all aspects of my professional life from the moment of my arrival at Cornell, and I am deeply grateful for all that she has done on my behalf. I also thank the Department for its many years of financial support from the Faculty Research Fund and the Return J. Meigs Fund.

In addition to my departmental colleagues, I have also received help and support from many colleagues in the wider Cornell University community. Jane Mt. Pleasant of the American Indian Program (AIP) provided generous junior faculty research funds that supported my work on this book. Eric Cheyfitz and Audra Simpson (now at Columbia University), read my work and offered their advice. Kurt Jordan, my colleague at Cornell, was most influential in getting me to take historical archaeology seriously—this book would look very different without the near-daily conversations we have shared for the past five years. I thank him for his longstanding patience with a disciplinary outsider. Several undergraduate research assistants at Cornell (Becca Wall, Erica Hartwell, and Jess Herlich) helped me get all my "data" organized for efficient analysis. Bob Kibbee of the Maps and Geospatial Information Collection at Olin Library introduced me to Nij Tontisirin, a graduate student in City and Regional Planning at Cornell. Nij worked tirelessly to produce all the maps in the book and ran all the GIS analyses used in Appendix 1. Greg Tremblay extricated me from innumerable hardware snafus and introduced me to the world of dual-screen computing. The staff at the Olin Library (especially David Block, Peter Hirtle, Anne Kenney, and the Interlibrary Loan Department) ensured that I had not only an outstanding collection but also a treasured faculty study in which to write in peace and quiet. Tom Bollenbach and Peter Holquist persuaded me in late 2005 to return to active participation in ice hockey, and I have been "between the pipes" on a weekly basis ever since.

Beyond Cornell, a number of colleagues answered questions and offered feedback on my ideas. I hasten to add that they bear no responsibility for any mistakes or omissions that may appear below. My thanks to Gerald Taiaiake Alfred, Salli Benedict, Wallace Chafe, Neal Ferris, Jim Folts, Charles Garrad, Charly Gehring, George Hamell, Lawrence Jackson, Jaap Jacobs, Jordan Kerber, Tobi Morantz, Paul Otto, Kees-Jan Waterman, and Hanni Woodbury. I also benefited from the expertise and intellectual generosity of the following professional and avocational archaeologists: Monte Bennett, Bill Engelbrecht, Wayne Lenig, Martha Sempowski, and Greg Sohrweide. Douglas Mackey of the New York State Historic Preservation Office, Dr. Christina Rieth of the New York State Museum, and Sheryl Smith of Parks Canada's Ontario Service Center made critical archaeological data available for my research, for which I thank them.

I received external funding for the research and writing that produced this book from the New York State Archives Partnership Trust (Larry J. Hackman Research Residency Fellowship), the American Philosophical Society (Philips Fund Grant for Native American Research), and the Huntington Library (Robert L. Middlekauff Fellowship). Additionally, I gratefully acknowledge the support of the National Endowment for the Humanities (Fellowship FA-53273-07). Any views, findings, conclusions, or recommendations expressed in this publication do not necessarily reflect those of the National Endowment for the Humanities. A generous subvention from the Hull Memorial Publication Fund of Cornell University helped to defray the production costs of this book.

Sheri Englund, Kurt Jordan, Mike Oberg, Mary Beth Norton, Erik Seeman, David Silverman, and Ian Steele read the entire manuscript in draft and their incisive commentary greatly improved the final product. Martha Bates at Michigan State University Press never gave up on this monograph. I would also like to thank Kristine Blakeslee, Robert Burchfield, and Annette Tanner at the Press for all their help in seeing the project through to completion. Margie Towery of Towery Indexing Service prepared the index in an expert and timely manner.

My family did the most to help me complete this book. I thank my in-laws, the Boyces, for their understanding of my hectic schedule, for numerous rides to and from various points in the Midwest, and for making sure that the rest of my immediate family had summer vacations even when I could not. My parents and sister tolerated infrequent visits and provided all manner of emotional and fiscal support for my professional development over the years—thanks Mom, Dad, and Sara! Brendan, Claire, and Ryan have taught their Dad many lessons about the human condition and collectively they ensured that his book was not rushed into print. My lovely wife Peggy, a literary scholar who entered my life in the reading room of the American Philosophical Society Library twelve years hence, has been a partner in every sense of the word. Her love and support, more than anything else, enabled me to finish this book.

ABBREVIATIONS

A1894   New York (Colony) Council Papers, 1664–1781. 103 vols., NYSA

A1895   New York (Colony) Council Minutes, 1668–1783. 31 vols., NYSA

AENA   *Archaeology of Eastern North America*

AICRJ   *American Indian Culture and Research Journal*

AIQ   *American Indian Quarterly*

AMD   William H. Browne et al., eds. *Archives of Maryland.* 72 vols. to date. Baltimore: 1883–.

APC   W. L. Grant and J. Munro, eds. *Acts of the Privy Council of England, Colonial Series.* 6 vols. Hereford: Her Majesty's Stationery Office, 1908–12.

APSP   American Philosophical Society *Proceedings*

ARMA   *The Acts and Resolves, Public and Private, of the Province of the Massachusetts Bay.* 21 vols. Boston: Wright & Potter, 1869–1922.

ASCNYB   Archaeological Society of Central New York *Bulletin*

BJNYSAA   *Bulletin: Journal of the New York State Archaeological Association*

BL   William Blathwayt Papers, HEHL

BP-CW   William Blathwayt Papers, Archives Department, Colonial Williamsburg, Williamsburg, Va. Microfilm copy in HEHL.

BRH   *Bulletin des Recherches Historiques*

CHR   *Canadian Historical Review*

CJA   *Canadian Journal of Archaeology*

CJVR   A. J. F. van Laer, ed. *Correspondence of Jeremias van Rensselaer, 1651–1674.* Albany: University of the State of New York, 1932.

CMRNF   *Collection de Manuscrits contenant Lettres, Mémoires, et autres Documents Historiques Relatifs a la Nouvelle-France.* 4 vols. Quebec City: A. Coté, 1883–85.

CNYCM   *Calendar of New York Council Minutes, 1668–1783.* Albany: University of the State of New York, 1902.

CSPC   W. N. Sainsbury et al., eds. *Calendar of State Papers, Colonial Series: America & West Indies.* 45 vols. to date. London: Her Majesty's Stationery Office, 1860–.

DCB   Frances Halpenny et al., eds. *Dictionary of Canadian Biography.* 15 vols. to date. Toronto: University of Toronto Press, 1966–.

DHNY   E. B. O'Callaghan, ed. *Documentary History of the State of New York.* 4 vols. Albany, N.Y.: Weed, Parsons, 1849–51.

EFWSI   *Explorations and Field-Work of the Smithsonian Institution.* Washington, D.C.: Smithsonian Institution, 1912–.

ERNY   *Ecclesiastical Records of the State of New York.* 7 vols. Albany, N.Y.: J. B. Lyon, 1901–16.

FOCM   Charles Gehring, ed. *Fort Orange Court Minutes, 1652–1660.* Syracuse, N.Y.: Syracuse University Press, 1990.

HEHL   Henry E. Huntington Library, San Marino, Calif.

IHC   *Collections of the Illinois State Historical Library.* 32 vols. Springfield, Ill.: State Historical Library, 1915–40.

IMC   Dean R. Snow, Charles T. Gehring, and William A. Starna, eds. *In Mohawk Country: Early Narratives about a Native People.* Syracuse, N.Y.: Syracuse University Press, 1996.

JDCSNF *Jugements et Déliberations du Conseil Souverain de la Nouvelle-France.* 6 vols. Quebec: A. Coté, 1885–91.

JJ   *Le Journal des Jesuites, Publié d'après le Manuscrit Original Conservé aux Archives du Seminaire de Québec.* 1871. Reprint, Montreal: Éditions François-Xavier, 1973.

JR   Reuben G. Thwaites, ed. *The Jesuit Relations and Allied Documents: Travels and Explorations of the Jesuit Missionaries in New France, 1610–1791.* 73 vols. Cleveland: Burrows Brothers, 1896–1901.

LAC   Library and Archives Canada, Ottawa

LIR   Lawrence H. Leder, ed. *The Livingston Indian Records, 1666–1723.* Gettysburg: Pennsylvania Historical Association, 1956.

MaHSC   *Massachusetts Historical Society Collections*

MCARS   A. J. F. van Laer, ed. *Minutes of the Court of Albany, Rennselaerswyck, and Schenectady, 1668–1685.* 3 vols. Albany: University of the State of New York, 1926–1932.

MCR   A. J. F. van Laer, ed. *Minutes of the Court of Rensselaerswyck, 1648–1652.* Albany: University of the State of New York, 1922.

MeHSC   *Maine Historical Society Collections*

MIN   *Man in the Northeast*

MNF   Lucien Campeau, S.J. ed. *Monumenta Novae Franciae.* 9 vols. to date. Rome: Institutum Historicum Societatis Iesu, 1966–.

MPCP   Samuel Hazard, ed. *Minutes of the Provincial Council of Pennsylvania.* 16 vols. Harrisburg, Pa.: Theo. Fenn, 1838–53.

MPHSC   *Michigan Pioneer and Historical Society Collections.* 40 vols. Lansing, Mich.: Robert Smith, 1874–1929.

MVHR   *Mississippi Valley Historical Review*

NAA   *North American Archaeologist*

NNN   J. Franklin Jameson, ed. *Narratives of New Netherland, 1609–1664.* 1909. Reprint, New York: Barnes and Noble, 1959.

NYCD   E. B. O'Callaghan and Berthold Fernow, eds. *Documents Relative to the Colonial History of the State of New York.* 15 vols. Albany, N.Y.: Weed, Parsons, 1853–87.

NYHSC   *Collections of the New-York Historical Society.* Third Series. 64 vols. New York: New-York Historical Society, 1869–1931.

NYSA   New York State Archives, Albany

NYSL   New York State Library, Albany

NYSM   New York State Museum, Albany

OA   *Ontario Archaeology*

OH   *Ontario History*

PA   Samuel Hazard et al., eds. *Pennsylvania Archives.* 9 series, 138 vols. Phila-
            delphia and Harrisburg: Joseph Severns, 1852–1949.

PAA   *Pennsylvania Archaeologist*

PMHB   *Pennsylvania Magazine of History and Biography*

PP   Carl Bridenbaugh, ed. *The Pynchon Papers.* 2 vols. Colonial Society of
            Massachusetts *Publications* Nos. 60–61. Boston, 1982–85.

PRCC   J. H. Turnbull and C. H. Hoadly, eds. *Public Records of the Colony of
            Connecticut.* 15 vols. Hartford, Conn.: Case, Lockwood, and Brainard,
            1850–1890.

PWP   Mary Maples Dunn and Richard S. Dunn, eds. *The Papers of William Penn.*
            5 vols. Philadelphia: University of Pennsylvania Press, 1981–87.

RAPQ   *Rapport de l'Archiviste du Province de Québec*

RAQ   *Recherches Amérindiennes au Québec*

RCNP   Nathaniel B. Shurtleff and David Pulsifer, eds. *Records of the Colony of
            New Plymouth in New England.* 12 vols. Boston: William White, 1855–1861.

RFF   Leopold Lamontagne, ed., and Richard A. Preston, trans. *Royal Fort Fron-
            tenac.* Toronto: Champlain Society, 1958.

RGCMB   Nathaniel Shurtleff, ed. *Records of the Governor and Company of the
            Massachusetts Bay in New England.* 5 vols. Boston: William White,
            1853–54.

RHAF   *Revue d'Histoire de l'Amérique Française*

RMSC   Rochester Museum and Science Center

RSCPT   Royal Society of Canada *Proceedings and Transactions*

VECJ   H. R. McIlwaine, ed. *Executive Journals of the Council of Colonial Virginia.*
            6 vols. Richmond, Va.: D. Bottom, 1925–1966.

VRBM   A. J. F. van Laer, ed. *Van Rensselaer-Bowier Manuscripts, Being the Letters
            of Kiliaen van Rensselaer, 1630–1643.* Albany: University of the State of
            New York, 1908.

WA   Peter Wraxall. *An Abridgment of the Indian Affairs Contained in Four
            Folio Volumes, Transacted from the Colony of New York, from the Year
            1678 to the Year 1751.* Ed. C. H. McIlwain. Cambridge, Mass.: Harvard
            University Press, 1915.

WHSC   *Collections of the State Historical Society of Wisconsin.* 20 vols. Madison: State Historical Society of Wisconsin, 1854–1915.

WJP   James Sullivan et al., eds. *The Papers of Sir William Johnson.* 14 vols. Albany: University of the State of New York, 1921–1965.

WMQ   *William and Mary Quarterly,* Third Series. 1943–present.

WP   *Winthrop Papers.* 6 vols. to date. Boston: Massachusetts Historical Society, 1929–.

INTRODUCTION

How then can your mind continue to be well?
You were seeing here and there the footprints of our ancestors;
and people are sorrowful as long as the smoke continues to rise.
How then can your mind continue to be well
when you are going along in tears?

—Excerpt from translated Mohawk text
of the "Edge of the Woods" ceremony

At the "Edge of the Woods," visitors to an Iroquois community are greeted, ritually cleansed and healed, and escorted from the "forest" (the space of warfare, hunting, spirits, and danger) to the "village" (the space of residence, agriculture, security, and peace councils). Originating prior to European intrusion as a component of the Iroquois Condolence ceremony, the "Edge of the Woods" occurs when "clear-minded" people travel to towns mourning the death of a leader. There, after a formal reception from the mourning community's representatives, the visitors initiate procedures of grieving and reviving the leader's title in the person of a living successor. Considered historically, the ceremony represented a rite of passage that at once remade individuals through acts of physical, social, and spiritual purification and restored order to the larger collective polity. On a pragmatic level, it worked to reassert structures of affiliation between Iroquois people while also allowing them to dictate the terms of movement between different communities. The ritualized regulation of the human movement in space manifested in the "Edge of the Woods" phase of the Condolence ceremony (twentieth-century observers documented as many as forty-five separate acts of reciprocal movement by its participants) demonstrates just how crucial the Iroquois considered spatial mobility to the maintenance of balanced human relationships.[1]

This book analyzes the history of Iroquois movement from 1534 to 1701 in an effort to explain the dramatic growth in the spatial domain of Iroquoia during this time and to understand how Iroquois people perceived their changing spatial environment and functioned within it. The book's structure follows that of the Iroquois

Condolence ceremony as a means of demonstrating the centrality of that ritual event to the sixteenth- and seventeenth-century Iroquois experience. The "Edge of the Woods," as a public social drama that at once recognized and contained a moment of formal transformation in Iroquois polities, constituted a critical symbolic prototype for innovative cultural change insofar as it rationalized and legitimized the creation of new practices from extant patterns of human movement. The six chapters that follow offer a new interpretation of this vital era of Iroquois history, one that illuminates the conceptual structures that informed the actions of Iroquois people and emphasizes the role of spatial mobility in precolonial Iroquois culture in order to elucidate processes of cultural innovation and transformation.

Reconstructing Iroquois movements through a vast extent of space during almost two centuries of time represents an undeniably complex exercise, and problems with the nature of the available evidence persist. We have only fragments available to us: documentary sources written by European cultural outsiders, material remains analyzed by archaeologists, and a limited amount of Iroquois oral tradition. In order to recover the experience of the Iroquois as historical actors in their own right, *The Edge of the Woods* combines an unprecedented comprehensive examination of new and in some cases overlooked historical data, archaeological and ethnographic evidence, as well as social theory pertaining to research questions on human mobility, settlement patterns, sociopolitical organization, and interregional exchange. Taken together, this expanded evidentiary base facilitates a systematic study of the patterns and contexts of historic Iroquois spatial mobility. Representations of Iroquois movement in these diverse sources—previously considered in isolation as random, fleeting, and incoherent—when subjected to comprehensive and integrative analysis, yield a picture of Iroquois movements that are deliberate, strategic, and often very clever.[2]

Employing an understanding of the Condolence ceremony as a "rite of passage" at once spiritual and spatial, the book argues that mobility enabled successful Iroquois engagements with the pressures and opportunities generated by settler colonialism on the borders of their homelands. By reassessing the history of Iroquois spatial mobility, this study offers new insights into the history of Iroquois identity construction and the structure and function of Iroquois governance. By emphasizing the experience of Iroquois historical actors in the context of their own times rather than as harbingers of a known future, it restores complexity and contingency to historical analysis of sixteenth- and seventeenth-century North American history. By attending to meanings and metaphors associated with movement in Iroquois epistemology, it challenges existing narratives of authenticity and inevitable decline in historical and anthropological scholarship on the Iroquois.[3]

• • •

Despite significant methodological interventions during the second half of the twentieth century, much of colonial-era North American historiography continues to anticipate the inevitable conquest of the continent's indigenous population by settler society.[4] In the case of Iroquois studies, this tendency derives from a long-standing association with evolutionist anthropology and its interest in reconciling the pre-Columbian Iroquois past with the postcolonial present by tracing the survival of "authentic" fragments of precontact "traditional" Iroquois culture through time.[5] Historians of the Iroquois have tended to evaluate ethnographic information obtained from informants or via participant observation in the nineteenth- or twentieth-century "ethnographic present" against earlier, documented examples of similar practices and customs. By emphasizing only those elements deemed impervious to change over time, these representations render Iroquois culture in extra- or even antihistorical terms.

Scholars have long identified fixed localities in clearly bounded spaces as the fundamental analytical units of authentic Iroquois culture. Such a construction of Iroquois authenticity derives from a research process in which ethnographers observing post-Revolutionary Iroquois reservations identified the spatial conditions and practices they witnessed as normative and subsequently projected them back in time. So-called authentic constructions of Iroquois culture stress the sedentary, agricultural component of Iroquois spatial practices as the most enduring, legitimate, and "civilized" form, thus explaining the survival of Iroquois culture into the postcolonial ethnographic present. The fundamental problem with this approach is that spatial mobility on the part of Iroquois people has been greatly constrained under circumstances of settler colonialism since 1800; as a result, Iroquois uses of mobility prior to 1800 became largely invisible in the ethnographic present. The "sedentarist metaphysics" bound up in this interpretive bias, which dates from the nineteenth-century studies of Lewis Henry Morgan, have precluded an appreciation of the extent to which freedom of movement contributed to Iroquois agency in engaging sixteenth- and seventeenth-century settler colonialism on the borders of their homelands. When presented with a picture of the "authentic" Iroquois as a sedentary, agriculturally settled people, the descent of the Iroquois to their contemporary status as colonized peoples within North American nation-states seems inevitable, even natural and necessary.[6]

In order to recover the history of the Iroquois people from such narratives of inevitable declension, we must first scrutinize the evolution of Iroquois historiography. While the Iroquois have been characterized as one of the "most studied" of all Native North American societies since at least 1940, very little attention has been paid to precisely *how* they have been studied over time.[7] This is significant, because modern anthropologically derived constructions of Iroquoian cultural patterns have persisted without substantial revision for more than 150 years. Anthropologist Elisabeth Tooker, writing in 1985, asserted that most of the cultural research conducted since the appearance of pioneering ethnologist Lewis Henry Morgan's *League of the Iroquois* in 1851 "merely added details to Morgan's synopsis." Notions of inevitable postcontact Iroquois cultural decline therefore remain deeply entrenched, owing in no small part to historians' failure to consider the problems inherent in relying uncritically on nineteenth-century ethnographic representations of Iroquois society and cosmology (obtained only *after* the United States and Canada had confined Iroquois people on reservations and reserves) to inform analyses of prior eras.[8]

Morgan researched and wrote *League of the Iroquois* in collaboration with Ely S. Parker, a Seneca from the community of Tonawanda, whom he met in an Albany bookstore in 1844. Parker, then sixteen years old, had been selected by Tonawanda leaders to acquire an education with the eventual goal of assisting in their legal struggle against efforts by New York State officials to impose the terms of an 1842 removal treaty on the Senecas. As both Morgan and Parker were concerned with presenting a particular version of Iroquois cultural history during a time of Seneca land loss and internal political crisis, *League of the Iroquois,* a product of what Morgan called their "joint researches" over the next seven years, cannot be characterized as disinterested cultural inquiry.[9]

While their objectives for the manuscript were not identical, Morgan and Parker found common ground in a narration of Iroquois cultural decline. Both Morgan and Parker defined as traditional the elements of Iroquois culture history that accorded with key tenets of the Gaiwi'io (also known as the Longhouse Religion), an innovative, syncretic series of spiritual teachings associated with the Handsome Lake revival movement that originated among the Senecas after 1799. By 1820, Parker's home community of Tonawanda served as the spiritual center of Gaiwi'io.[10] The movement arose during an era of extensive land loss following the end of the American Revolutionary War in 1783, when Iroquois people were forced to reorient their spatial thought and practices to adapt to extensive constraints on their usage of land. They left behind precolonial patterns that involved extensive freedom of movement, and instead concentrated on the optimal ways and means of occupying the internal space of fewer, smaller, and more isolated communities.[11]

Significant changes prescribed by Gaiwi'io included the adoption of male plow agriculture, raising livestock for meat no longer available via hunting, residence in nuclear-family households, and a prohibition on interracial marriage. Threatened by the prospect of removal from ancestral homelands, Gaiwi'io also radically revised Iroquois concepts of space and mobility. In the unprecedented context of Iroquois residence on bounded reservations surrounded by settler society, the narrative renders pathological any extensive spatial movement beyond the reservation community as detrimental to Iroquois cultural integrity.[12]

Ely Parker, a great-great-great-grandson of Handsome Lake, elaborated his own views on Iroquois cultural decline in writing shortly after beginning his extensive collaboration with Morgan. The Iroquois conflict with settler society, in Parker's view, was all but over by the mid-nineteenth century. He described his fellow Iroquois contemporaries as mere "remnants" who were "patiently waiting for that fatal and final storm, which seems to be their inevitable doom." Parker's apparent ironic nod to the ascendant contemporary trope of the "vanishing Indian" notwithstanding, it is clear that he used his collaboration with Morgan to craft an Iroquois past that would serve his two, related contemporary imperatives: garnering popular sympathy for the struggles of the Senecas to resist removal from what was left of their homelands, and asserting the "traditional" character of the Gaiwi'io-based Iroquois culture at Tonawanda in contrast to all other Seneca communities in New York State, who had adopted elective systems of governance modeled on those of their non-Native neighbors after 1848.[13]

Morgan, for his part, sought an understanding of Iroquois culture history that would resolve nineteenth-century American settler society's anxieties about the longevity of the Iroquois presence on the land in comparison to its own. Though confident that it was "well understood that the decline of the Iroquois commenced with their first intercourse with Europeans," Morgan set out to prove this point conclusively. First, he circumscribed the limits of "authentic" Iroquois space by identifying it as coterminous with the boundaries of New York State (see figure 3).[14] Morgan's geography of exclusion thus eliminated precisely half of the then-extant Iroquois communities in Canada, Wisconsin, and Kansas, where Gaiwi'io was largely unknown and where more than two-thirds of the Iroquois population then resided.[15]

Next, Morgan assigned this spatial fragment of Iroquois culture to the evolutionary category of "barbarism," which characterized Iroquois institutions as possessing only fragile, precarious links to the soil that could not withstand competition from "civilized" society. Although Morgan acknowledged the "genius" of Iroquois social organization in its preservation of individual freedom and national sovereignty among the constituent nations of the Iroquois League, his portrayal of the Iroquois "habit of traveling" and his assignment of Iroquois culture to the "hunter state" also, crucially, depicted the Iroquois as incapable of independent cultural innovation and progress. Morgan's *League,* which cast the Iroquois as a people "destined to fade away," thus naturalized the erasure of the remnant Iroquois as independent nations from the landscape of the early national New York and opened the way for their assimilation and replacement by a new American successor culture with supposedly more legitimate claims to the land.[16]

For much of the twentieth century, anthropologist William N. Fenton, a self-conscious successor of Morgan, exerted a great deal of influence over the direction and emphases of Iroquois studies as the subfield's acknowledged "dean."[17] The "upstreaming" methodology pioneered by Fenton during the 1950s involved the interpretation of historical sources in light of ethnographic materials collected via participant observation and informant interviews. According to Fenton, students of a particular culture may move "up" that culture's "stream" by projecting information from ostensibly better-documented eras into the distant past. Descriptions of the society that "ring true" at both ends of the time scale are regarded as the most valid

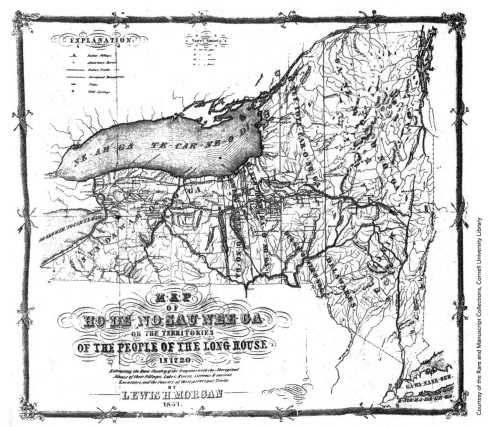

Morgan's 1851 Map of Iroquoia

indicators of "authentic" cultural aspects. Thus, in Fenton's view, the cultural heritage of the Iroquois consisted solely of "patterns identified in early sources that have persisted for the observation of ethnologists."[18]

The principal effect of "upstreaming" scholarship produced by Fenton and others during the twentieth century has been to further reduce the inventory of "authentic" Iroquois culture by emphasizing only those aspects deemed to manifest stability or continuity over time. Although there is an abundance of rich archival sources that reflect the complexity of the precolonial Iroquois past, these sources are often discounted as ancillary to what has been defined as "authentic" Iroquois culture. Instead, information obtained from or validated by a select group of "knowledge-able, intellectual, and communicative" senior male ritual specialists (predominantly followers of Handsome Lake) has come to serve as the principal metric of traditional-ism and authenticity in the eyes of outside researchers. Any cultural elements that cannot be (or have not been) "upstreamed" from an ethnographic present to pre-contact times have been ignored, discredited, or pathologized as deviant, degraded, or contaminated. By privileging Iroquois cultural characteristics deemed to manifest stability over time, "upstreaming" methodology renders broad swaths of the historic and contemporary Iroquois experience "inauthentic."[19] The "authentic" Iroquois are relegated to the distant, precontact past and to select, isolated pockets of contemporary Iroquoia, principally those communities remaining within the normative spatial boundaries of the modern-day state of New York.[20]

While the inventions of "authentic" and "inauthentic" Iroquois identity are certainly understandable in light of the extreme geopolitical pressures that the Iroquois confronted during the nineteenth century, it is time to set aside these inaccurate rubrics and to establish new terms for understanding Iroquois culture—past and present. Limited constructions of Iroquois cultural authenticity have engendered an interpretive blindness to the range of latent possibilities for cultural expression and effective, coordinated, and innovative action available to Iroquois historical actors at given moments in history. Even the standard discussions of the ways in which the geographic location of the Iroquois conveyed power and influence to the League during the colonial era imply spatial fixity and minimize Iroquois agency in making their own history. The notion of "authentic" Iroquois culture as solely a spatially localized and bounded phenomenon also compromises our understanding of Iroquois people as human actors in the past by denying them the capacity for internal complexity, debate, disagreement, and innovation. History written in this manner has the further effect, intentional or not, of sustaining contemporary rationales for the ongoing colonization of Iroquois people and spaces.[21]

This book's portrayal of the Iroquois as a formidable political power in sixteenth- and seventeenth-century North America stands in stark contrast to the dominant scholarly narrative of precolonial Iroquois history, which provides an autopsy of an Iroquois League surrounded and submerged by European nations shortly after first contact. For many historians and archaeologists, the seventeenth century witnessed the "disintegration of traditional Iroquois culture" in a series of "disasters" brought about by the arrival of Europeans: depopulation (from introduced European diseases and increased warfare), abandonment of settlement patterns deemed to reflect stable matrilocal residence (with an attendant decline in women's social authority), economic dependency on European material culture (with attendant "disorder inherent in chronic alcoholism" and loss of traditional skills related to craft production), dilution of core ethnic values as the result of mass adoptions of foreign peoples, and spiritual crises brought about by French Jesuit missionaries (with attendant political factionalism and out-migrations of people to New France). If, for some scholars, the seventeenth century brought too much cultural change, for others the "failure" of the Iroquois to "change enough" spelled their doom. The Iroquois people neither created "state"-level governance to compete with "more centralized political entities" nor adopted "European materialist values" in order to acquire sufficient "economic clout to withstand the pressures put on them by their European neighbors."[22] Even the traditional hereditary "League" governance, a system with roots in the precontact period, could not withstand a few decades of Europeans' presence in the view of scholars arguing for its replacement by a "Confederacy" composed of leaders of independently achieved status by circa 1660.[23]

These retrospective and dismissive views of the Iroquois as fragmented spatially and factionalized politically—so widely held and promoted today as a result of upstreamed histories of "authentic" Iroquois culture—would have greatly surprised the European settler population of seventeenth- and eighteenth-century North America. Close examination of the written and archaeological record reveals the degree to which the Iroquois occupied the attention of settlers and officials in New France and the Anglo-American colonies, as well as in London and Versailles. Documented European views of the Iroquois indicate a wide range of attitudes toward them: from a desire for their highly valuable military and political allegiance, to a concerted solicitation of economic trade partnerships they offered, to respect for the "intimately linked" character of their polity, to a very real fear of their potentially lethal military capacities. One attitude European settlers never expressed about the Iroquois prior to 1701 was contempt for them as mere colonized peoples. If we understand colonization to represent the conquest of physical space by an alien polity and that polity's ability to set the terms by which conquered space is defined, one cannot refer to Iroquoia as colonized in 1701.[24]

By abandoning the methodology and assumptions that have yielded histories of Iroquois spatial fixity, cultural fragmentation, and inevitable postcontact decline, we gain new perspectives on Iroquoia from 1534 to 1701. For example, assumptions of steady, irreversible postcontact Iroquoian demographic decline after the appearance of introduced European epidemic diseases in 1634 may be overturned by documentary evidence that indicates that the Iroquois managed a substantial population recovery by 1701. The Iroquois accomplished this recuperation via the incorporation of adoptees from other Native nations and through the deliberate, voluntary movement of individuals, families, clans, and even entire villages from early contact-era homelands in modern-day upstate New York to affiliated communities in precontact areas of use and occupancy in the St. Lawrence River valley as well as the north shore of Lake Ontario (see appendixes). Scholars have portrayed these movements almost exclusively in terms of permanent exodus with evasive intent, viewing the residents of these communities as "lost forever to the home population" of the Iroquois League. Yet by reading French and English colonial records against one another, one finds that Iroquois movement over time *toward* settler-contested spaces represented an effort to engage with colonizers and to turn their presence to Iroquois advantage. These movements also enhanced opportunities for hunting and trade, which, rather than corroding traditional values, actually reinforced communal ties through the redistribution of meat, peltry, and trade goods. By moving to appropriate the spatial "center" between competing European colonial empires, the Iroquois positioned themselves to take advantage of the military, economic, and especially the communications links provided by these new, affiliated communities. Far from representing a disintegration of core Iroquois cultural values, mobility provided a means of strengthening those values and of extending them to other peoples living at the constantly shifting "edge" of Iroquoia's "woods." Seen in this light, the Iroquois resemble a polity on the rise rather than a people in decline.[25]

The spatial history of precolonial Iroquoia presented in this study reassesses the Iroquois experience from 1534 to 1701 in terms of rational innovation on the part of Iroquois people. Consideration of precolonial Iroquois culture as a reflection of the constant negotiation of the social networks that sustained a sense of community reveals the extent to which Iroquois people, in the process of maintaining their distinct identity, undertook substantial reorganization and restructuring of elements of their cultural repertoire. As Iroquoia expanded spatially after 1534 to include new places and new peoples, the Iroquois balanced their core cultural values against the imperatives of lived experience, and modified their inventory of social mechanisms to sustain cohesion vis-à-vis the opportunities and impositions of settler colonialism. Thus, "traditional" Iroquoian culture need not be viewed as an ossified relic of the mythic past but rather as the ways in which a group of people, in a discrete historical moment, worked to limit and define the terms by which change took on meaningful form.[26]

• • •

This study, in addition to employing integrative analysis of a wide range of evidence, orients its analysis "downstream," beginning not with an ethnographic overview of "traditional" cultural patterns but rather with an examination of two foundational texts of Iroquois cultural tradition, the Creation Story and the Deganawidah Epic. More than just "confused fables" described by early European observers, these narratives provide crucial windows into core Iroquois cultural premises, representing otherwise inaccessible ideas about time, space, and historical process. The narratives are more than merely epiphenomenal to social relations; they not only reflect patterns of human action but also provide frameworks for their perpetuation over time. The overarching trend in these narratives (hitherto largely overlooked as a result of "upstreamed" reconstructions of "authentic" Iroquois culture as confined to fixed localities) reflects the normative character of spatial mobility in the matrix of Iroquois cultural identity. Analysis of these texts, undertaken in tandem with an investigation of material and written evidence, facilitates an understanding of how Iroquois people organized space within their physical world, and also an appreciation of how they worked actively to maintain unity on fundamental cultural values essential to their successful engagement with the pressures of colonialism.[27]

Iroquois epistemology considers the time of Creation, the origin of the physical world inhabited by human beings, as at once primordial and perennial. Oral recitations of the Creation Story, in other words, not only describe the origins of the world but also perpetuate the moment of Creation in the present. The generative power of movement permeates the Creation Story, which begins with Sky Woman's fall to earth, follows with the animal "earth-divers'" creation of the world on a turtle's back, and concludes with the creative movements on Earth of her twin grandsons, Flint and Sapling. These movements, in the opinion of the late Mohawk historian Deborah Doxtator, are balanced and cyclical in character, but rather than producing stasis, the "result of varied repetition of cycles is the gradual growth, layering, and development of the earth—a continual state of change and transformation brought about by balanced forces [Flint and Sapling] interacting with one another."[28]

Precolonial Iroquois spatial mobility is best understood as nonlinear in nature. Movements subsequent to Sky Woman's fall in the Creation Story retain Turtle Island (Iroquois homelands), as their central point of reference. Movement inward and outward from the center of Turtle Island by Flint and Sapling reflects the potential for the expansion and contraction of culturally appropriated Iroquois space. The Creation Story provides a further rationale for human mobility in its depiction of the world as composed of multiple reciprocal relationships between paired entities (for example, elder/younger, male/female, people/environment). This fundamental duality appears in the Creation Story's treatment of the "first times," when people were divided into two groups living on either bank of a river. This pattern of human relationships reflected the establishment of clans and moieties, in which kinship relations and reciprocal obligations provide a means to unite groups of people into a larger collective while also facilitating their individual autonomy and spatial separation at other times. Movement, in the Iroquois Creation Story, sustains a process of accumulative and innovative cultural change.[29]

The archaeological perspective, too, contributes an important account of how mobility figured in the lives of precolonial Iroquois people. The weight of material evidence now indicates that the Iroquois nations first encountered by Europeans during the sixteenth century in what is now Quebec and during the seventeenth century in modern-day New York State developed in situ after about A.D. 600, with the final formation of the League of the Iroquois accomplished about 1,000 years later. In situ development did not occur in vacuo. Rather than assuming that historically known Iroquois nations represented static, bounded, ethnic entities, they are better understood, as archaeologist William J. Engelbrecht has argued, as "the product both of multiple ancestral groups and of diverse contacts."[30]

Precolonial Iroquois mobility encompassed long- and short- distance interactions over land and via water routes with other Iroquoian and non-Iroquoian peoples in friendly contexts of trade and exchange as well as hostile contexts of warfare and captive-taking. Much of our knowledge of precolonial Iroquois movement stems from archaeological analysis of exotic lithics, ceramics, and goods such as marine shell and Native copper from distant regions on sites in Iroquois homelands. Iroquois women are universally regarded as the producers of ceramic cooking pots, while men are thought to have made pipes. Stylistic patterns on recovered pipes and potsherds are considered a direct reflection of group affiliation. Thus, nonlocal stone tools, ceramic pipes, and other items are presumed to occur as a result of male-dominated travel and trade, and the occurrence of types of pottery outside their identified homelands is viewed as indicative of "captive brides," stylistic copying, or, rarely, evidence of women's involvement in trade.[31]

These analyses of precontact movement rely on assumed patterns of gendered mobility that derive from matrilineal descent practices in Iroquois culture as well as from the matrilocal character of Iroquoian settlement patterns. Matrilineality involves the recognition of kinship affiliation through an individual's maternal ancestry, and in matrilocal settlement patterns men, upon marriage, leave their natal households for those of their wives. Thus, in precolonial Iroquois society, a given household could be expected to consist of several nuclear families: a senior woman and her husband, her daughters and unmarried sons, her daughters' husbands, and her daughters' children. While the use of ceramic analysis as a means of identifying postmarital residence patterns assumes that women within Iroquois societies received passively and then reproduced stylistic patterns, current archaeological and linguistic evidence suggests a correlation between shared pottery style and precontact matrilocal residence.[32]

More significantly, new research on the longevity of maize agriculture in Iroquois homelands indicates that matrilocal residence patterns played a critical role in the development of the "Three Sisters" (maize, beans, and squash) farming among the Iroquois during the millennium prior to European contact, as intra- and intergenerational continuity provided opportunities for sharing information on techniques, seed stock, and innovative tools and practices. The greater predictability of agricultural production by coresident matrilineal families offered a hedge against poor production in other areas of subsistence procurement for their members, which encouraged the perpetuation of this pattern in precontact Iroquoian societies. Multigenerational matrilocal residence also provided stability, security, and child care for people remaining in villages during periodic adult absences for hunting, trade, diplomacy, and warfare, as well as providing an important context for socialization and information exchange between in-marrying men and women, adopted refugees and captives, and their host families and clans.[33]

Yet three critical problems for the historical understanding of Iroquois spatial movement result from the analysis of gendered Iroquois mobility in the context of static notions of matrilineality and matrilocality. First, the idea of a stark, gendered dichotomy between the "forest" and the "clearing" as exclusively "male" and "female" domains (respectively) engenders overly rigid notions of male mobility juxtaposed to female fixity.[34] Second, an overemphasis on sedentary farming in the precolonial Iroquois economy obscures understanding of the mixed, seasonally mobile character of Iroquois food procurement.[35] Third, an overt stress on the "classic" precontact multihearth longhouse as the primary index of Iroquois sociopolitical structure and cultural identity leads to interpretations of any postcontact changes in housing and settlement patterns as evidence of decline and loss.[36]

Precolonial Iroquois subsistence patterns relied to a far greater extent on human movement than is usually recognized by scholars anxious to label Iroquois people as sedentary agriculturalists. Between 1300 and 1600, Iroquois town sites became larger and shifted from floodplains and river valleys to hilltop locations, partly in response to endemic conditions of regional warfare. The Iroquois built their settlements at this time in carefully selected locations offering abundant rainfall, long frost-free periods, lime-rich soils (which supported "Three Sisters" agriculture while also yielding abundant chert for the fashioning of stone tools), and often proximity to good fishing. Palisaded towns containing longhouses encompassed areas of up to ten acres, and in some cases represented home for up to 2,000 individuals. The entire spatial extent of a prototypical late precontact Iroquois settlement, including its residential area, crops, gathering and hunting areas, and a "defensive perimeter," has been estimated at 600,000 acres.[37]

Yet the classic palisaded Iroquois town surrounded by its agricultural fields, long viewed by evolutionist-influenced research as a hallmark of an increasingly sedentary residency pattern, was in fact a mobile phenomenon in precolonial Iroquois society. Iroquois individuals living between 1534 and 1701 could have expected to live at two or three different town sites over the course of their lives. These relocations did not derive from aimless wandering; Iroquois people retained clear knowledge and a strong sense of affiliation to former places of residency and sites of ancestral burials.[38] Rather, town movements resulted from careful planning, most often undertaken by the women of a given community, approximately every ten to twenty years on average (though smaller towns of fewer than 500 individuals probably moved less frequently). Documentary evidence and recent scholarship challenge prior scholarly assumptions of soil and game depletion as the primary factors driving Iroquois town relocations, and these moves appear now to have been motivated by the declining availability of local building materials and firewood, physical deterioration of bark longhouses and log palisades, the accumulation of refuse, and possible infestation by rodents and insects.[39]

During the fifteenth and sixteenth centuries, the "Little Ice Age" created unreliable climactic conditions for intensive agriculture in northeastern North America. Adapting patterns of their already mobile seasonal subsistence cycle enabled Iroquois people to maintain intensive agricultural practices in these suboptimal circumstances. These innovative strategies included, first, efforts to form relationships with alien peoples bordering their homelands in order to diversify and extend resource procurement zones. Such overtures occasionally evolved into broader endeavors either to displace these peoples from their territory or to incorporate them by persuasion or by force into an Iroquois nation. A striking example of the latter phenomenon is found

Courtesy of the Rare and Manuscript Collections, Cornell University Library

Native Women on the Move, Detail from Bressani's Map, ca. 1657

in the archaeological record of an early-sixteenth-century attack on an Iroquoian community in modern-day western New York (known to archaeologists as the Alhart site, located in Monroe County). Patterns of human remains at the site suggest that the attackers, likely Senecas, killed and beheaded many of the town's male defenders and then removed many of its women and children for integration into their own community. Second, the Iroquois benefited from a cultural premium on the ethics of reciprocity and hospitality, which promoted equitable, clan-based distribution of agricultural, hunted, and gathered food. Third, the Iroquois increased exploitation of aquatic and animal resources as a supplement to "Three Sisters" crops.[40]

Assertions of a stark, gendered division between the mobile male domain of the "forest" and the fixed female domain of the "clearing," while of considerable significance in Iroquois symbolic thought, are not supported by evidence of every-day precolonial Iroquois activity, which encompassed a far greater degree of spatial mobility and intergender cooperation than hitherto assumed.[41] The mixed, seasonal character of precolonial Iroquois subsistence practices involved a substantial degree of spatial movement by men and women in both the "forest" and the "clearing." Cooperative work groups of men and women maintained seasonal fish weirs and harvested passenger pigeons shortly after their annual spring hatch. Men also played significant roles in agricultural work, clearing and preparing fields for cultivation, and assisted with harvests. Men cut down trees while women split the logs and carried the firewood back to villages.[42] Up to three generations of matrilineally related males (unmarried boys and young men, their maternal uncles and great-uncles) assembled from different households and villages for early autumn "men's clan" hunting expeditions that ranged several hundred miles from town sites, and similarly constituted war parties often traveled farther still.[43] Far from being confined to towns or their affiliated "clearings," Iroquois women regularly took to the "forest" for a variety of purposes. Clan-affiliated women accompanied hunting expeditions, helping to butcher the meat and hauling it back to villages in pack baskets carried by burden straps lain over their foreheads.[44] Women also traveled independently—occasionally alone, often in small groups—for purposes of trade and visiting kinfolk.[45] They participated in military expeditions, carrying provisions, guarding canoes, and occasionally engaging in battle.[46] Women also traveled abroad with diplomatic embassies and spoke in the "great councils of the [Iroquois] nation."[47]

Historical documents reveal that these practices endured over long time spans among the constituent Iroquois nations. Evidence of mythical validation;[48] spatio-temporal patterns in place-naming,[49] trail systems, shelters, and signage;[50] "geographical" maps sketched on bark or beaver skin, or plotted on the ground with kernels of maize,[51] and other means of field communications (including bark and rock paintings, piles of cut rushes, pictographic sketches, and marked war clubs or tomahawks left at the scenes of raids);[52] water travel in elm bark and dugout canoes;[53] prepared travel foods such as parched cornbread and smoked eel;[54] and material culture innovations related to mobility (such as deerskin moccasins, wooden snowshoes, pack baskets, cradleboards, carrying frames, work satchels, burden straps, and mineral salves for fatigued limbs) all attest to the highly mobile character of precolonial Iroquois people.[55]

Consideration of the kinship, settlement, and gender patterns of precolonial Iroquois culture in processual terms, attempting to reconstruct the practices and understandings by which the Iroquois constructed these relations in everyday life rather than projecting back in time abstract, idealized behavior patterns derived from postcolonial-era classificatory studies or participant observation, indicates the ways in which matrilineal and matrilocal Iroquois social organization contained an inherent capacity for spatial movement. The imperative of clan exogamy among the Iroquois, which banned marriages between men and women of the same clan, provided a means for extending kinship relations over a large geographical area. Since these marriages were not restricted by local endogamy, exogamous Iroquois clans overrode national and territorial boundaries. Members of the same exogamous clan, in other words, could be found in a number of different Iroquois towns and nations (see table 1).[56]

Understanding the clan-based nature of Iroquois social structure is crucial to grasping the ubiquity of spatial mobility in precolonial Iroquois society. Adult men had responsibilities to the communities of their wives and to those of their parents,

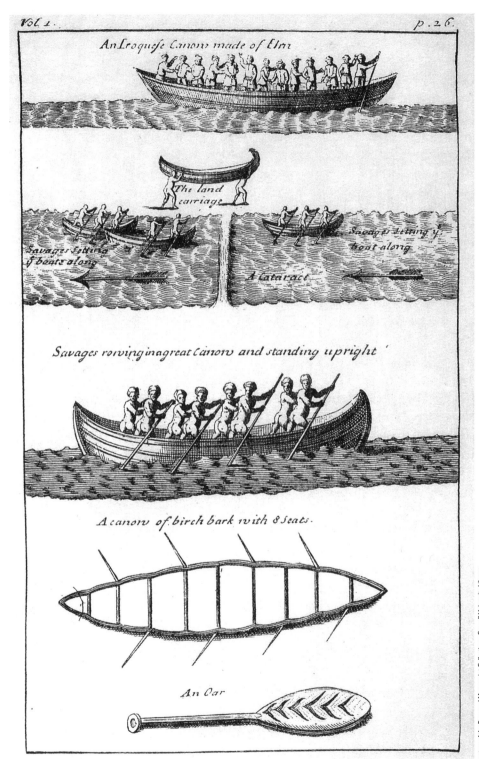

An Iroquese Canow made of Elm

The land carriage

Savages letting y bents along

Savages letting y boat along

A Cataract

Savages rowing in a great Canow and standing upright

A canow of birch bark with 8 seats.

An Oar

Lahontan's Drawing of Iroquois Canoes, from *New Voyages*, ca. 1703

TABLE 1. HISTORICALLY RECORDED CLANS AMONG THE FIVE IROQUOIS NATIONS

	MOHAWK (3)	ONEIDA (3)	ONONDAGA (9)	CAYUGA (7)	SENECA (8)
Turtle (5)	✖	✖	✖	✖	✖
Wolf (5)	✖	✖	✖	✖	✖
Bear (5)	✖	✖	✖	✖	✖
Deer (3)			✖	✖	✖
Beaver (3)			✖	✖	✖
Snipe (3)			✖	✖	✖
Eel (2)			✖	✖	
Hawk (2)			✖		✖
Ball (1)			✖		
Heron (1)					✖

SOURCE: Tooker, "Northern Iroquoian Social Organization," 94; Tooker, "The League of the Iroquois: Its History, Politics, and Ritual," 426–28.

as well as to those into which their sisters had married, given their role in educating and socializing their sisters' sons (who shared their clan identity). During the precolonial period, Iroquois women spent nights in their husbands' maternal households immediately after marriage, assisting their husbands' maternal kin with field labor and firewood collection (in addition to everyday responsibilities to their own maternal longhouses), until they bore children of their own and the family relocated to the mother's natal longhouse.[57] Frequent mobility on the part of these young childless women may have provided grounds for the precolonial Iroquois practice of burying a deceased infant along pathways in the hope that the infant's soul might more easily enter the womb of a woman passing by.[58] Women who married men of chiefly lineages may have maintained long-term residence in the longhouses of their husbands, given the need of these men to be attuned to the opinions of the members of their clan, whom they represented. The abundant evidence of precolonial spatial mobility is at odds with reservation-era ethnographic research, which characterizes Iroquois communities as largely autonomous localities through time. On the contrary, precolonial Iroquois society required frequent spatial movement by both women and men to sustain its sociocultural systems.[59] Traditions of clan hospitality buttressed mobility, as visiting members of a given clan received food and lodging from families of the same clan in other towns (a practice later extended to, and remarked upon, by Europeans).[60]

The mobility-based social, cultural, and economic systems revealed in the Iroquois archaeological and documentary record buffered short-term imbalances between population and resources and not infrequently, as we shall see, provided for more permanent adjustments and innovations. The success of mobility as an Iroquois strategy depended on ready access to reliable sources of information; thus, a symbiotic relationship between mobility and information existed in the precolonial Iroquois world. Information conduits—generated by "public criers," reports of parties returning from journeys, and everyday conversations between kinfolk, friends, visitors, and adoptees in Iroquois communities—are clearly discernible in oral tradition, in the European documentary record, and archaeologically through the patterning of interregional material culture flows (especially of ceramics and items of nonlocal origin). Supported and facilitated by social structures encouraging and validating movement (such as the ethic of hospitality and the ritual practices that eventually came to constitute the Condolence ceremony), these information conduits, in conjunction with Iroquois familiarity with specific routes of travel and associated technologies facilitating mobility, reduced the problem of distance for Iroquois societies.[61]

Facilitated by a cultural premium on hospitality, clans and moieties enabled spatially distant members of Iroquois society to come together into larger wholes. Affinal ties and their concomitant familial obligations and benefits facilitated the maintenance of group cohesion at increasing spatial scales (from clan to town and nation).[62] Given the evidence of spatial mobility and gender complementarity in Iroquois culture, the image of the kettle suspended over a fire containing a simmering soup of corn, with fish and/or meat and gathered foods, at once combined the collective subsistence contributions of women and men and constituted the basis of hospitality.[63]

Far from being a static, bounded entity, precolonial Iroquois space underwent constant reshaping through negotiations of power and identity. Movement played a crucial role in the Iroquois conceptual production of space, which integrated the cosmological and the quotidian in both thought and practice, and entailed not only a capacity for spatial organization but also for appropriating cultural space through networks of communication. Metaphors of mobility organized daily activity, and they also helped to define and represent concepts of the individual, society, and nature, as well as the matrix of relationships between these entities. Iroquois movement thus provided a symbol of group pride and contributed to the integration of the broader Iroquois League polity during the early contact era. The inherently flexible, nonhierarchical Iroquois view of power bound up in their ritual representations of spatial mobility thus contained a considerable capacity for innovation and adaptation.[64]

What distinguished the five Iroquois nations that formed the League was the primacy and extent of their success during the precolonial era, vis-à-vis even their Iroquoian neighbors, in formulating the ritual components associated with the "mourning-war" complex into a means of mitigating the potential for internal strife. "Mourning wars," which arose from a cultural mandate to replace deceased relatives and involved raids on rival Native nations (occasionally far-ranging and often large scale) to procure captives either to adopt or to interrogate, ritually torture, and execute, represented a common military practice throughout north-eastern North America prior to the arrival of Europeans.[65] Once the constituent nations of the League transformed former practices of blood revenge into a stable system of mutual defense and orderly political succession, the death of a leader no longer sent aggrieved young men into the field to commit hostilities against neighboring (now-allied) nations. The Condolence ceremony redirected such grief, ensuring that "mourning wars" were channeled toward alien peoples. Thus, the Mohawks, Oneidas, Onondagas, Cayugas, and Senecas secured extensive freedom of movement and communications among themselves.[66] This facilitated an increased range of external interaction through which the Iroquois enhanced their "spatial awareness" with information about other peoples and places (derived from adopt-ees' knowledge and connections as well as statements offered by and elicited from tortured war captives) and goods from multiple directions for redistribution within their collective polity.[67]

While the discourse of authenticity demands a pristine, fully formed and func-tioning Iroquois League in existence at the time of first contact and rejects the notion of any possible influences on its formation derived from European contact, archaeo-logical evidence suggests otherwise. The development of locally distinct stylistic pat-terns in female-crafted pottery indicates increased ties of specific women to increas-ingly large Iroquois communities, reflecting the clustering of formerly dispersed settlements in precolonial times (1400–1600) into the historically recognized League nations. Contemporaneous evidence of the movement of male-produced pipes and exchanges of marine shell and (after 1525) European trade goods reflects increased intercommunity movement by men. The concurrence of these two gendered spatial processes, in the view of archaeologists, facilitated the completion of the "classic" Iroquois League during the first three decades of the seventeenth century.[68]

The history of the formation of the League during the late sixteenth and early seventeenth centuries entailed a dramatic sociopolitical innovation on the part of the participating Iroquois nations. By elaborating practices each nation had refined during its own ethnogenesis to a larger scale and by drawing on existing rationales for spatial mobility in their cosmology and daily life, the members of the incipient League laid the foundation for a transnational cooperative polity. Occurring at a time when the Iroquois possessed more information about and evidence of the intru-sion of Europeans and their goods on the Atlantic coast, completion of the process of League formation reflected an increasing concern by Iroquois people for effec-tive engagement with these unprecedented, revolutionary, and spiritually powerful phenomena.[69] The ritual of the League, centered on the Condolence ceremony and the requickening of deceased leaders, defined new social rules in its performance, and, through its very redundancy (achieved via public recitations of League tradi-tion, which included the patterned repetition of key ideas and the visual encoding of messages in wampum strings and belts) facilitated communication of core structural principles to current (and future) members of the League.[70]

Oral tradition of the League's founding, also known as the Deganawidah Epic, exists in literally dozens of versions. Yet a consistent theme of the profound transformative power of spatial movement in this story of "nation formation," enacted in the Condolence ceremony, allowed Iroquois people to apprehend the ideas embedded in the League's founding narrative, to take them to heart, and to put them to work. In its relation of the processes of League formation, the Deganawidah Epic establishes crucial protocols for the regulation and inspiration of Iroquois behavior. Building on the notions of duality, complementarity, and reciprocity prevalent in the Creation Story, narratives of the League's formation promote the idea of the inherent transformative power of people to effect positive change through movement in space.[71]

Throughout the Deganawidah Epic, protocols pertaining to the transformation of a cultural context of intergroup hostility and suspicion to one in which freedom of movement and peaceful communication prevail assume imperative significance. The two heroes of the narrative, Deganawidah (the Wendat Peacemaker) and Hiawatha (his first Iroquois follower, usually identified as a Mohawk), are travelers who carry their message of peace, power, and righteousness to the five Iroquois nations. Throughout the narrative, Deganawidah, an outsider, approaches Iroquoia by canoe and delivers his message. Jigonsaseh, the Neutral Iroquoian "mother of Nations," agrees to Deganawidah's request to stop feeding warriors, changing the warpath between nations into a trail of unity. After accepting Deganawidah's message, Hiawatha emulates his practice of peaceful movement by stopping at a distance from his home village and building a fire to announce his arrival, rather than risk being mistaken for possessing hostile intent. Hiawatha employs strings and belts of shell beads (wampum) as a means of both facilitating and validating communications and recording and transmitting the principles and agreements of the League. Hiawatha must remove obstructions in the path caused by Tadodaho, a deformed, malevolent Onondaga wizard, to ensure clear communications between all the nations. Transformative boundary crossings facilitate three critical symbolic changes in the narrative: Hiawatha's first transformation from a cannibal warrior to a messenger of peace, Hiawatha's second transformation from a grieving wanderer to a powerful lawgiver, and the climactic joint effort by Deganawidah and Hiawatha to straighten the twisted mind and body of the fearsome Tadodaho by combing the snakes from his hair.[72]

Ethnographic research on the Condolence ceremony, the ritual enactment of the narrative of the League's founding, describes it as "structurally the most complex" of all Iroquois ceremonies. Recorded versions are said to last between six and eight hours, with numerous speakers participating and employing multiple narrative devices and frequent reciprocal gestures to create an episodic sequence. The five key stages of the Condolence ceremony are identified as:

1. *On the Journey* (or the Roll Call of Chiefs). Singers of the "clear-minded" or "condolers" moiety enumerate the hereditary titles of the League chiefs on their approach to the "grieving" or "mourners'" village.
2. *The Edge of the Woods* (or Near the Thorny Bushes). The mourners, having kindled a fire at the outskirts of their village, welcome the arriving condolers with a Requickening Address, which acknowledges the perils of the condolers' journey and works to restore their communicative powers by clearing away obstructions in their eyes, ears, and throats.
3. *The Requickening Address* (or Wiping Their Tears). The condolers reciprocate the mourners' initial gesture, clearing their eyes, ears, and throats from grief-induced stoppages and restoring them from a bereaved state to one in which they can resume normal social relationships.
4. *Six Songs.* One of the most sacred of all Iroquois rituals, it involves an invocation and offering of thanksgiving for social institutions embodied in the Condolence ceremony.
5. *Over the Forest.* The final stage of the ceremony consists of two distinct episodes: the first laments of the loss of ritual knowledge and calls on the original League founders to guide their descendants as they execute their obligations, and the second delivers rules governing succession to chiefly office and the rituals of the Condolence ceremony itself.[73]

Enactments of the "Edge of the Woods," as a rite of passage essential for requickening deceased leaders in the Condolence ceremony, do not merely replicate what came before; they create something new. Considered in the literal sense of replacing a deceased leader with a successor, the ceremony yields an individual embodying both ancient wisdom and new hope. This is not reincarnation; the successor, and the League into which he assumes his position, represent something necessarily different from what came before. Understanding the "Edge of the Woods" as part of an innovative cultural process of remaking, rather than as a restoration or perpetuation of past reality, enables a better grasp of spatial and temporal changes in Iroquois history. Such an approach also eludes the "authenticity" trap (or the insistence on stable, even static Iroquois cultural practices) by examining change over time in the documented enactments, uses, and regenerative functions of the "Edge of the Woods." These ceremonies functioned as crucial moments of Iroquois cultural expression that appealed to tradition and yet were also original insofar as they arose in and spoke to new contexts and contingencies in the late precolonial period.[74]

Widespread consensus among Iroquois people on the fundamental concepts and values reflected by the "Edge of the Woods" provided the philosophical and normative base for their unity across geographic space. The strength of the League rested on the capacity of its symbolic structure for innovation, enabling Iroquois people to engage novel political circumstances and to shape them for their own benefit. As a fundamentally creative cultural moment, the "Edge of the Woods" did not require unified adherence to a single, "orthodox" vision, which would have been far too limiting for Iroquois people living in the context of colonial entanglement. Instead, the practice of the "Edge of the Woods" from 1534 to 1701 served inventive ends. Beneath the symbolic spatial rhetoric evoking an image of Iroquois space as concentric zones ("clearings" surrounded by a "forest") lay a more complex cultural cartography, an ethnogeographic organization of space as structured by networks of sites linked by footpaths and canoe routes. The public, chanted songs and recitations and complex choreography of movements characteristic of the "Edge of the Woods" embodied and confirmed the culturally transmitted Iroquois sociopolitical system for participants and observers. The ceremony also set the stage, in a metaphorical sense, for "good correspondence and understanding" between people with cleared eyes, ears, and throats (the principal organs involved in the perception and production of speech), with the ultimate goal of attaining unity, consensus, and goodness of mind. These processes not only reminded participants of their cultural traditions, they also facilitated creative transformations in the patterns and organization constituting the cultural system itself. The "Edge of the Woods," in other words, at once facilitated Iroquois cultural change while retaining the vital cultural framework and context in which those changes occurred.[75]

The "Edge of the Woods" ceremony, as a reflection of considerate social relations aimed at perpetuating cultural connections, mediates and orders the movements of Iroquois people through space. Since the terrestrial space defined by the "Edge of the Woods" marks the metaphorical boundary between the secure/civilized/home and the dangerous/uncivilized/outlands in Iroquois symbolic thought, enactments of the "Edge of the Woods" from 1534 to 1701 were at once spiritual and spatial rites of passage that established and maintained social relations between individuals and groups and thereby facilitated the incorporation of newly created, or resettled, geographically distant places (and their residents) into the Iroquois polity. As the spatial narrative embodied by the "Edge of the Woods" engaged Iroquois experience with their surrounding landscape over time, the narrative and the landscape worked dialectically to construct and reproduce each other.[76]

Iroquois movements from 1534 to 1701 occurred over a vast range of eastern North America—from the shore of Hudson Bay to the palm groves of South Carolina, and from the coastal waters of Newfoundland to the lower Mississippi River valley. This extensive mobility, at once rationalized and regulated by the "Edge of the Woods" ritual, changed the geographical reckoning of Iroquois homelands to encompass an increasingly larger geographic space while simultaneously accommodating relations between increasing numbers of Iroquois people living at ever-greater distances from one another. The constituent nations and communities of the League grew, to paraphrase historian James Brooks, further and further together. The "Iroquois trail," made famous by Morgan as a land and water route connecting all Iroquois nations in the metaphorical "longhouse" from the Mohawk River to Seneca Lake, actually developed significant new lines and spurs reaching far beyond the bounds of modern-day New York State during the League's precolonial history.[77] From 1534 to 1701, Iroquoia became truly *kanonsionni* (an "extended lodge"), and the movement of people conferred distinct material, social, and political benefits on the Iroquois League as a whole.[78]

The Iroquois enjoyed extensive freedom of movement during their precolonial history, which they asserted and attempted to communicate in their relations with European intruders via the concepts of *kaswentha* ("Two-Row" diplomacy), and the Condolence ceremony.[79] Movements from and to precontact Iroquois homelands in modern-day upstate New York and beyond generated detailed awareness of an extent of space that bewildered European contemporaries and facilitated expressions of Iroquois spatiality that not only contested settler encroachment but also confounded colonizers' equation of spatial fixity with cultural stability.[80] The spatial dispersal and convergence of Iroquois people in accordance with seasonal, strategic, or sacred exigencies sustained ties between kin and thus a coherent sense of community over considerable geographic distances and rendered impossible efforts by colonizers to fix the Iroquois in predictable administrative units. Mobility thus created a vital spatial context for the exercise of Iroquois power.[81]

In addition to asserting freedom of movement for themselves, the Iroquois simultaneously assumed control over key nodes of transport in, through, and around Iroquoia. These included the Niagara portage (at modern-day Lewiston, New York), which skirts the famous falls and connects the upper and lower Great Lakes, and the Lake Champlain–Richelieu River corridor linking Albany and Montreal.[82] The Iroquois also kept close watch on all personnel movements within and around Iroquoia. They escorted allied Native nations seeking trade at Albany as well as European traders and diplomats into their homelands. They discouraged surveillance and mapping of their homelands. They established settlements near European outposts and reinforced their status as hosts by exchanging provisions with the garrisons. They agreed to occasional leases of their land, but retained usufructory rights rather than alienating them outright. Although settlers drew up many notoriously fraudulent patents to Iroquois lands beginning in the seventeenth century, these vast paper claims did not translate, prior to the 1770s, into a flood of settlers toward the periphery of Iroquoia. Through these patterns of spatial mobility, surveillance, and exclusion, the Iroquois came to monopolize flows of information through their homelands.[83] Effective internal communications, sustained by a relay system of "very fast messengers" reputedly capable of traveling eighty miles per day, and by canoes traveling more quickly still, enabled Iroquois leaders to generate an enhanced base of empirical knowledge of their circumstances vis-à-vis their colonial neighbors and to calibrate their foreign relations to a very fine degree.[84] Iroquois use of their wide network of communications links culminated in the crafting of a policy of diplomatic neutrality in 1701 that sustained patterns of mobility and promoted social and political stability within their homelands for the next eight decades.

This book provides a new appreciation of the extent of Iroquois initiative and success in their engagements, adaptations, and responses to the circumstances of colonial intrusion during a distinct period of their history. In contrast to recent scholarly claims that literate European colonizers supposedly capable of monopolizing information and imposing executive authority in their relations with Native peoples via quick, concerted action held a crucial political advantage over the Iroquois and other Native peoples, integrative analysis of multiple lines of evidence (documentary, archaeological, and oral tradition) indicates that the opposite was true during precolonial Iroquois history.[85] Innovations in spatial movement, in relationships with neighboring peoples (Native and non-Native), and in internal decision-making methods from 1534 to 1701 allowed Iroquois people to retain a far greater degree of external political influence and internal social cohesion than historians have hitherto acknowledged or understood. Mobility not only embodied core Iroquois social values of hospitality, condolence, and the renewal of reciprocal relationships, it also supported a broad repertoire of Iroquois cultural tools to engage successfully the challenges and opportunities posed by settler colonialism in ways that would become substantially more difficult after the American Revolution, when spatial confinement on reservations severely constricted the creative role of mobility in Iroquois society. From 1534 to 1701, however, spatial mobility enabled the Iroquois to deny outsiders' efforts to appropriate their extended homelands and to focus their energies instead on the assertion and defense of the "Edge of the Woods," the expanding outer limits of Iroquois space, vis-à-vis the would-be colonizers on their periphery.

The Edge *of the* Woods

1.

ON THE JOURNEY
1534–1634

There is nothing so difficult to control as the tribes of America. All these barbarians have the law of wild asses—they are born, live, and die, in a liberty without restraint; they do not know what is meant by bridle and bit.

—PAUL LE JEUNE, S.J., 1637

On October 3, 1535, Dieppe navigator Jacques Cartier donned protective armor and departed from his ship anchored in the St. Lawrence River for a formal visit to the Laurentian Iroquois town of Hochelaga. After marching about four and one-half miles, Cartier's party of twenty-five men met "one of the headmen of the village of Hochelaga, accompanied by several persons, who made signs" directing the French to stop at a "spot near a fire they had lighted on the path." The French complied, and the Hochelagan leader then offered a "harangue," which Cartier interpreted as a display of "joy and friendliness" and a means of "welcoming" guests. After an exchange of gifts, Cartier's entourage continued their escorted approach to Hochelaga for another one and one-half miles, passing through the Hochelagans' impressive agricultural fields until they reached the palisaded settlement, home to as many as 1,000 people.[1]

Though we have only a glimpse of the elaborate and formal proceedings that accompanied Cartier's entry into Hochelaga in 1535, the French explorer's description reflected the clear significance precolonial Iroquoian peoples attached to human movement. The official escort and ceremony at the edge of Hochelaga's woods served at once to remind Laurentian Iroquois observers of that community's control over the movement of outsiders into their space and to communicate that power to the armor-clad French explorer and his entourage. By formalizing spatial movement through such highly visible public representations, the Hochelagans protected their own freedom of movement within their homelands.

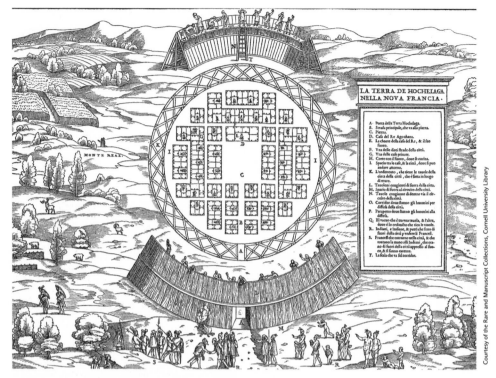

Ramusio's Stylized Drawing of Hochelaga, ca. 1556

One hundred years after the first encounters of the Laurentian Iroquois with Cartier, formal protocols governing spatial mobility had enabled five Iroquois nations (the Mohawks, Oneidas, Onondagas, Cayugas, and Senecas) to complete the development of a novel, overarching collective polity known as the Iroquois League. The League's structure manifested the centralizing tendencies of common membership in a confederation of nations while also recognizing the value of existing affiliations of individuals and groups to particular ideas, nations, and geographical spaces. The achievement of unity (not uniformity) among League nations represented its foremost rationale, and the process of League formation that occurred from 1534 to 1634 reveals that the League's constituent nations realized that such unity could best be attained through diversity. In other words, the Five Nations (as the League was known to contemporary Europeans) sought to integrate and accommodate differences and novel phenomena, rather than annihilate or ignore them.

Analysis of the often overlooked sixteenth century in Iroquois history is crucial to understanding the origins, nature, and magnitude of better-documented seventeenth-century Iroquois movements and their attendant impacts on Iroquois society, politics, and culture.[2] Following initial, episodic contacts with Europeans

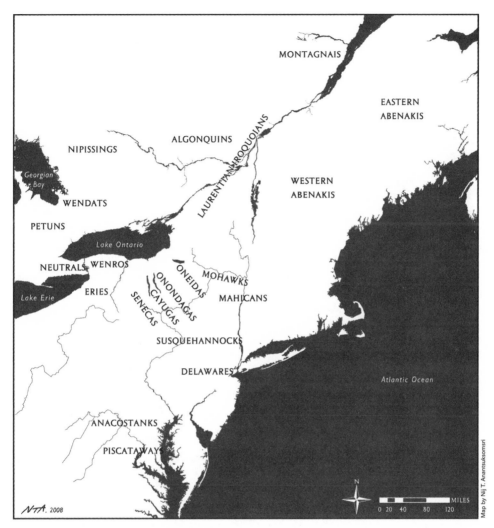

The Iroquois World, 1534–1634

during the early sixteenth century, Iroquois people went "on the journey," under-taking multiple new ventures throughout northeastern North America in order to gain access to European material goods and their attendant flows of information, ideas, and peoples. New postcontact patterns of Iroquois movement enabled the Mohawks, Oneidas, Onondagas, Cayugas, and Senecas to assimilate unprecedented numbers of captives from a variety of indigenous nations. The process of seeking out and integrating newcomers into Iroquois nations inaugurated a pattern of political innovation in which these five nations refined cultural systems for engaging others beyond communal boundaries. In so doing, they embodied the first ritual phase of the Condolence ceremony, "on the journey," which signifies a time of people coming together and consecrating relationships with one another.[3]

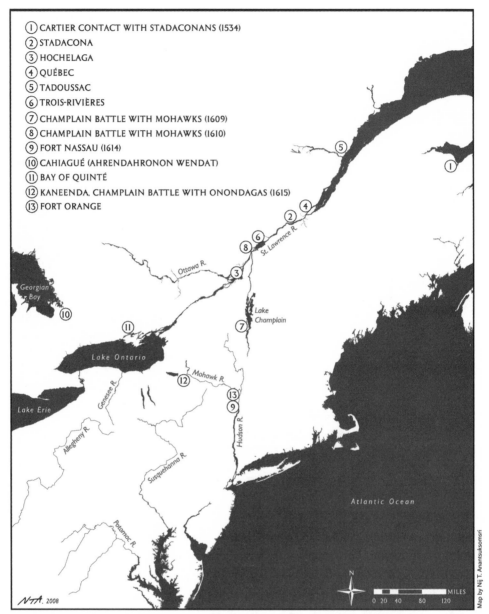

① CARTIER CONTACT WITH STADACONANS (1534)
② STADACONA
③ HOCHELAGA
④ QUÉBEC
⑤ TADOUSSAC
⑥ TROIS-RIVIÈRES
⑦ CHAMPLAIN BATTLE WITH MOHAWKS (1609)
⑧ CHAMPLAIN BATTLE WITH MOHAWKS (1610)
⑨ FORT NASSAU (1614)
⑩ CAHIAGUÉ (AHRENDAHRONON WENDAT)
⑪ BAY OF QUINTÉ
⑫ KANEENDA, CHAMPLAIN BATTLE WITH ONONDAGAS (1615)
⑬ FORT ORANGE

Iroquois Places of Interest, 1534–1634

Earliest Contacts

Iroquoian peoples residing in the St. Lawrence River valley experienced initial encounters with Europeans during the first four decades of the sixteenth century. The few French explorers and fishermen who intruded into these waters posed no immediate threat to the Laurentian Iroquois communities; indeed, they, not the indigenous people, experienced greater suffering from disease at that time. Yet the nature of the interactions assumed a confrontational character after 1534, when Jacques Cartier's ambitions revealed European colonizers' lack of respect for Iroquoian control over freedom of movement in and on the periphery of their homelands.

Contact between Iroquoians and Europeans may have begun as early as 1508, when French mariner Thomas Aubert sailed eighty leagues up the St. Lawrence River and returned to France with a "Canadian savage." Between 1510 and 1520, two more Dieppe-based sailors, Jean and Raoul Parmentier, appear to have met Laurentian Iroquois engaging in summer hunts of seals, porpoises, and "certain sea birds" in the Strait of Belle Isle between Newfoundland and the Labrador coast. The Parmentiers described the people they encountered there as rendering oil from these animals until the approach of winter, when they departed "with their catch in boats made of the bark of certain trees called birch, and go to warmer countries, but we know not where." The Parmentiers did not identify these people explicitly as Laurentian Iroquois; indeed, they could not have, given their lack of familiarity with these peoples' homelands, but other, more knowledgeable European observers documented the presence of Laurentian Iroquois hunters and fishermen through-out the St. Lawrence River valley and estuary, as well as in the Strait of Belle Isle, less than two decades later. Evidence of seal oil use for ceremonial and military purposes in Laurentian Iroquois culture further supports the likelihood of the Parmentiers' early contact.[4]

The significance of these potential early contacts lies in their location far outside what are traditionally viewed as Laurentian Iroquois homelands, thus indicating the capacity of these people for long-distance movement at the time of their first en-gagement with Europeans. The first conclusively documented instance of Laurentian Iroquois contact with Europeans occurred on July 21, 1534, when Cartier happened upon a large group of these people fishing for mackerel on the Gaspé Peninsula, approximately 400 miles from their hometown of Stadacona. The story of Cartier's subsequent interactions with the Laurentian Iroquois from 1534 to 1541 yields critical information about patterns of Iroquoian mobility during the early contact era.[5]

In 1534, Cartier counted over 300 Stadaconan men, women, and children who reached the Gaspé Peninsula in a convoy of forty canoes. They manifested prior ex-perience with Europeans by coming "very familiarly" to the sides of Cartier's ships in their boats, where Cartier's men gave them "knives, glass beads, combs, and trinkets of small value, at which they showed many signs of joy, lifting up their hands to heaven and singing and dancing in their canoes." Cartier described the Stadaconans as impoverished, noting derisively how they slept under their canoes and ate their meat and fish almost raw. But other evidence indicates that this expedition was multipurpose in character: the Stadaconans also carried a "large quantity" of corn and dried fruits and nuts. Cartier later learned that this group was out to avenge an attack made by the "Toudamans" (most likely the historically known Micmacs) on members of their community on an island in the St. Lawrence River near the mouth of the Saguenay River in 1533.[6]

Three days after Cartier's initial contact with the Stadaconans, the first clash between European and Iroquoian notions of space took place. Cartier's men erected a thirty-foot cross at the entrance of modern-day Gaspé Harbor, to which they affixed "a shield with three *fleurs-de-lys* in relief, and above it a wooden board, engraved in large Gothic characters, where was written LONG LIVE THE KING OF FRANCE." The French then commenced public worship of the cross, attempting to explain to Stadaconan observers by pantomime that "by means of this we had our redemption, at which they showed many marks of admiration, at the same time turning and looking at the cross."[7]

The Stadaconans' subsequent behavior suggested skepticism of the intruders' claimed rationale for their behavior. Immediately after the conclusion of this ceremony, Donnacona, the "captain" of Stadacona, approached Cartier's ships in a canoe, accompanied by three of his sons and his brother. Clad in an "old black bear-skin," Donnacona pointed to the cross and gave the French "a long harangue, making the sign of the cross with two of his fingers; and then he pointed to the land all around about, as if he wished to say that all this region belonged to him, and that we ought not to have set up this cross without his permission." In response, Cartier's men lured Donnacona nearer to one of their ships by holding up an ax, "pretending we would barter it for his skin," and then seized the Stadaconans as they came within reach. Cartier then tried to pass off the cross as a mere "landmark and guidepost" that would facilitate his return to the region "with iron." He detained two of Donnacona's sons (Domagaya and Taignoagny) as hostages and sent back Donnacona, his remaining son, and his brother (each bearing a hatchet and two knives) to the shore camp. A few hours later six Stadaconan canoes approached the French vessel, "each with five or six men who had come to say goodbye to the two we had detained and to bring them some fish. They made signs to us that they would not pull down the cross, delivering at the same time several harangues which we did not understand."[8]

Cartier's hostile encounter with the Stadaconans in 1534 inaugurated a pattern of fundamental disputes between Iroquois and European peoples about space and its use. Donnacona's canoe-borne speech, which Cartier interpreted as a claim of Stadaconan possession to the Gaspé Peninsula, is more likely to have been an assertion of the right of freedom of movement for his people in that region. Cartier's lie about the character of the cross as a mere guidepost masked his own intention to appropriate that space for France, an act that Donnacona, a man who "from his childhood had never left off or ceased from travailing into strange Countreys as well by water as by land," may well have perceived as a threat to Stadaconan mobility. Many subsequent conflicts in postcontact Iroquois history would replicate such incidents of mutual suspicion and miscommunication.[9]

Wasting little time in his effort to capitalize on information about the St. Lawrence valley's people and resources relayed by his Stadaconan detainees, Cartier departed St. Malo on May 19, 1535, hoping to discover the Northwest Passage to Asia. Delayed by storms, the French ships did not reach the St. Lawrence estuary for nearly three months. On August 13, 1535, passengers Domagaya and Taignoagny began actively guiding Cartier down the St. Lawrence, after passing Anticosti Island. The captives' assistance may have been more essential than Cartier admitted in the account of his second voyage, which contains no mention of the cross erected in 1534. On September 8, 1535, Domagaya and Taignoagny reached their home village of Stadacona.

Not content to tarry at Stadacona, Cartier made known his desire to push up-river to Hochelaga, another Laurentian Iroquois settlement, but he found no willing guides among his Stadaconan hosts. After a preliminary discussion with Donnacona on September 15, 1535 (which Cartier believed had established "a marvelous sted-fast league of friendship"), Donnacona clarified the nature of the arrangements in a formal ceremony two days later at the site of Cartier's anchored vessels. Following a round of singing and dancing, Donnacona moved all his people to one side, then drew "a ring in the sand, [and] caused the Captain [Cartier] and his men to stand in it." He then presented Cartier a gift of three Stadaconan children, which Taignoagny explained were offered to Cartier (as a sign of alliance) on the condition that he not travel to Hochelaga. The spatial gesture represented by the ring drawn in the sand, combined with the offer of children, represented the Stadaconans' conditional offer of allegiance, an offer that depended on Cartier accepting their power to control his freedom of movement and binding himself as an ally of the community with kin-based obligations of reciprocity.[10]

To such limitations Cartier refused to agree. He departed Stadacona for Hochelaga with fifty men on September 19, 1535, rejecting Donnacona's demand that he leave a hostage at Stadacona and ignoring Taignoagny's prediction of supernatural evil awaiting him upriver. Cartier reached his intended destination on October 2, 1535, but after a thirty-minute exchange of food, touching, and "mirth and gladnesse" with the Hochelagans, he and his men spent the night on their boats. After Cartier's formal entry into Hochelaga the next day, described at the beginning of this chapter, he took note of their defensive architecture and extensive agricultural fields. These observations led Cartier to conclude that the Hochelagans "do not move from home and are not nomads" like the Stadaconans. Yet later that day several Hochelagans escorted the French explorer to the summit of "Mount Royal," where they advised Cartier by "signs" of their ability to navigate waters beyond the Lachine Rapids "for three more moons [months]," and described their ongoing conflict with the "Ago-jouda" (likely Iroquois) people living to their west.[11]

Unable to obtain passage over the Lachine Rapids, Cartier and his party returned downriver and spent an uneasy winter in the vicinity of Stadacona. Early episodes of peaceful trading sessions and exchanges of "familiaritie and love" between the French and Stadaconans were gradually replaced by incidents of "strife and contention." Nutritional deficiencies among the French after December 1535 pushed the intruders to the brink of disaster. Indeed, the desperate French sailors suffering from scurvy received a remedy only after Domagaya himself contracted the disease in March 1536 from the steady diet of French maritime provisions he endured while wintering with (and likely spying on) the French. Once he received a cure at Stadacona, the majority of Cartier's men followed suit. They overcame their symptoms just in time to confront a new Stadaconan initiative.[12]

Taignoagny, who had returned home from a two-month-long winter hunt in late April 1536 with an indeterminate but sizable number of "foreign Indians," informed Cartier that Donnacona wanted to have Cartier take an elderly "Lord of the Country" back to France with him. Cartier, suspecting that the Stadaconans had "gone to raise the country to come against us," elected to circumvent that possibility by once again kidnapping Donnacona, Domagaya, Taignoagny, and seven other Stadaconans during feigned negotiations aboard one of the French ships. Cartier and his detainees departed Stadacona on May 6, 1536, with a cargo of wampum and food supplied by the Stadaconans on the promise of a return in ten to twelve months.[13]

Cartier experienced difficulty in persuading French officials about the value of his enterprise and did not return to North America until 1541. None of the ten kidnapped Stadaconans returned to their homelands; all but one ten-year-old girl had died in France by 1540. But prior to their deaths in captivity, the Stadaconans had persuaded French authorities of their juridical status as nations. The testimony of Cartier's Laurentian Iroquois captives, combined with evidence of their behavior in written reports of Cartier's first two voyages, influenced the royal commission for Cartier's third voyage. King Francis I instructed Cartier to consider North America as occupied by independent peoples who had the capacity to enter into nation-to-nation relations with France via treaties of alliance, peace, friendship, and commerce.[14]

Notwithstanding his failure to return the prisoners he had taken in 1536, Cartier received a warm welcome from Agona, Donnacona's apparent successor, at Stadacona in August 1541. Cartier traveled upriver to the Lachine Rapids, where he conversed with four Hochelagan men about the route beyond those rapids to the reputed indigenous kingdom of "Saguenay" located somewhere in the continental interior. The Hochelagans depicted the route to Saguenay "with certaine little stickes" spread on the ground to map rivers and portages.[15]

Following the communication of this spatial knowledge, Cartier's narrative of events during his final voyage is incomplete, although it suggests increasing hostility among the Laurentian Iroquois toward Cartier's presence. After noting mutual discussions among several communities about "what they should doe against us," Cartier gathered his self-described cargo of gold and diamonds (actually worthless iron pyrites and quartz) and retreated to Newfoundland by June 1542, en route to

France. A hint of intervening events appears in a Spanish Basque sailor's report of his summer 1542 voyage to Grand Bay, in Newfoundland. There he met with "many Indians," among them the "Chief in Canada" (possibly Agona), who claimed to have "killed more than thirty-five of Jacques's [Cartier's] men" while trading deer and wolf skins for axes and knives brought by the Basques.[16]

In Cartier's Wake

The years between Cartier's sixteenth-century departure and the early-seventeenth-century arrival of Samuel de Champlain, Henry Hudson, and Captain John Smith have received little attention from historians to date, owing primarily to a paucity of written records. Far from representing a historical vacuum, however, the second half of the sixteenth century witnessed a number of crucial developments in Iroquois spatial history essential for understanding the nature of Iroquois peoples' first sustained engagement with settler colonialism on the periphery of their homelands during the seventeenth century. Integrative analysis of archaeological research, Native oral sources, and fragments of documentary evidence reveals the ways in which indigenous conflicts over access to exchange routes engendered massive rearrangements of the human geography of northeastern North America. One such reconfiguration was that the Five Nations redefined their homelands as centrally located spaces with ready access to an extensive communications network. These vital developments enabled Iroquois people to advance preexisting processes of political and economic alliance formation before they engaged with the French, Dutch, and English colonizers who returned to North America after 1608.

The Laurentian Iroquois did not permit their negative experience with Cartier to deter them from maintaining patterns of long-distance exchange with Europeans in waters off Newfoundland. Basque whalers and fishermen from Spain and France constituted the dominant European presence in this region between 1540 and 1580. Archaeological and linguistic evidence helps to flesh out the picture of Basque-Iroquois interaction in Newfoundland during the middle decades of the sixteenth century. The discovery of a potsherd with diagnostic Laurentian Iroquois stylistic markings in a collapsed Basque structure on Red Bay in the Strait of Belle Isle, dating to approximately 1550, strongly suggests the presence of Laurentian Iroquois women. These Iroquois women regularly accompanied such long-distance expeditions and may have carried food to Red Bay in that pot and/or traded it there for Basque ceramics. Recent scholarship has established the cooperative, even seasonally coresident nature of Basque relations with Laurentian Iroquois (and other Native) inhabitants of the St. Lawrence valley, with the Basques providing payment (in the form of trade goods and possibly foodstuffs) in exchange for Native expertise and assistance in whale-oil rendering. In addition, important new linguistic research indicates that

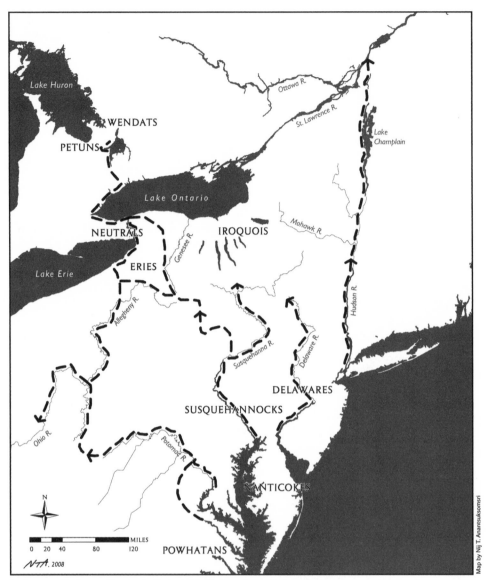

Indigenous Exchange Routes in Eastern North America, ca. 1520–1613

the long-assumed Basque origin of the word "Iroquois" is much more likely to have derived from direct Basque contact with Iroquois people, rather than having been obtained indirectly via Algonquian-speaking peoples.[17]

Trading relationships between the Mohawks, Oneidas, and Onondagas (and possibly some of the Laurentian Iroquois communities), augmented by the regular European presence at Tadoussac after 1550, constituted one of the two key axes of human, material, and informational movement during the early contact period of Iroquois history; the other axis extended into the continental interior from Chesapeake Bay, where Europeans engaged in direct trade with neighboring Algonquian peoples after 1546. The flow of trade goods along the Laurentian and Mid-Atlantic axes is reflected in archaeological evidence of increasing amounts of marine shell beads (of both North American and European origin), as well as European copper and iron, on Mohawk, Onondaga, and Seneca sites between approximately 1500 and 1540. Yet the rough parity in volume of these exotic items in the material record appears to shift after approximately 1560, with a continued presence of copper, brass, shell, and iron objects on Seneca, Onondaga, and Susquehannock sites and a relative scarcity of similar inventories on Mohawk sites until approximately 1580. These changing patterns of material evidence suggest the greater vitality of the Mid-Atlantic exchange axis vis-à-vis the Laurentian axis, and the increasing isolation of the Mohawks from the former. Evidence of this crucial shift in the material record, analyzed in conjunction with fragmentary documentary evidence from European voyagers and Native oral histories recorded by Europeans in the seventeenth century, facilitates historical reconstruction of the series of large-scale regional population shifts in northeastern North America after circa 1570.[18]

Critical new avenues of information, ideas, and personnel opened up to Iroquois nations after 1570. These changes in turn stimulated new spatial initiatives. Indeed, innovative patterns of movement related to exchange, resource procurement, and the assimilation of captives taken on distant military campaigns resulted in dispersals, assimilations, and relocations of indigenous nations throughout a vast arc of territory spanning the St. Lawrence valley, Georgian Bay on Lake Huron, the Ohio River valley, and the Susquehanna River valley (in modern-day Pennsylvania). These external spatial initiatives developed in tandem with individual Iroquois nations, yielding an increasing degree of local autonomy in favor of collective unity with their neighbors. These two mutually reinforcing processes, which began prior to European contact, would ultimately produce the historically known Iroquois League.[19]

Mohawk efforts to gain direct access to European fishermen and traders in the St. Lawrence River valley (over 400 miles from their home villages) during the 1570s offer one glimpse into innovative patterns of Iroquois movement during the early contact era. Tadoussac, located in Montagnais homelands, represented a crucial node in the Laurentian exchange axis. As the only place on the St. Lawrence River that offered Europeans an opportunity to combine whaling, inshore cod and salmon fishing, and trade with Native peoples, Tadoussac attracted a regular, multinational European presence (estimated at approximately 100 ships per year) during the latter half of the sixteenth century. The local Montagnais allowed their Algonquin neighbors to trade there freely in exchange for defensive cooperation against the increasingly aggressive Mohawk presence in the St. Lawrence valley at this time.[20]

The northward movement of Mohawks during the last three decades of the sixteenth century, motivated by their recent marginalization from the Mid-Atlantic exchange axis and possibly also by social repercussions stemming from severe drought and famine in northeastern North America during the late 1560s, affected not only the Montagnais and Algonquins near Tadoussac but also as many as 10,000 Laurentian Iroquois people residing in settlements spanning from modern-day Jefferson County, New York, to Quebec City. No Laurentian Iroquois communities survived as discrete entities after 1600. Scholars have advanced numerous explanations for their dispersal, all stressing to some degree escalated indigenous warfare associated with the intensification of European fur-trading activity in the St. Lawrence valley after 1580.[21]

Determining the fate of the indigenous Iroquoian population of the St. Lawrence River valley demands an imaginative and integrative treatment of the available evidence. An Iroquois oral history, which exists in several published eighteenth-century versions, describes the experience of a joint Iroquois-Algonquin hunting party during the latter half of the sixteenth century, prior to direct contact between the Iroquois nations that would later form the League and Europeans. The "Iroquois" in this story are taken to represent Mohawks. They are depicted in a subaltern role, accompanying the Algonquins in order to carry provisions and haul back the Algonquins' kill in exchange for a portion of it. But the hunters fared poorly, and the Algonquins permitted the Iroquois to go off on their own in search of game. Reconnoitering some time later, the Iroquois hunters reported great success, while the Algonquins remained empty-handed. In gratitude for the opportunity to partake in the hunt, the Iroquois shared "the best pieces" of their meat with their Algonquin hosts, but notwithstanding this gesture, jealous Algonquins murdered the Iroquois hunters. Upon their return to their home village, the Algonquins claimed that their Iroquois companions had disappeared. Suspicious Iroquois relatives of the deceased investigated the Algonquins' account by retracing the hunters' tracks. Upon discovery of the corpses of the Iroquois hunters, which had been exhumed by animals, the Iroquois realized that the Algonquins had murdered their countrymen. They subsequently terminated their association with the Algonquins, retreated southward, and commenced a mourning war that continued intermittently into the latter half of the seventeenth century.[22]

Even allowing for the possibility of pro-Iroquois bias in this account, it offers remarkable insight into the character of precolonial interindigenous relations. More important, it aligns well with other lines of available evidence about events in the late-sixteenth-century St. Lawrence valley. The earliest documentary evidence ascribes responsibility for the sixteenth-century dispersal of Hochelaga to the "Iroquois," which in French accounts prior to 1640 almost always meant "Mohawks." This data suggests the degree to which the Laurentian Iroquois became entangled in Mohawk (and possibly other Iroquois national) advances into the St. Lawrence valley after 1570. Other oral accounts, most notably an extensive and detailed narrative related by a group of Algonquins (known to the French as "Iroquets") in 1642, claimed that the Wendats had dispersed the Hochelagans. We need not necessarily regard these versions of events as mutually exclusive. Archaeological evidence indicates a widespread movement of Laurentian Iroquois people throughout Algonquian- and Iroquoian-speaking communities all across the Northeast—in voluntary, captive, and refugee contexts. Such evidence suggests that the Laurentian Iroquois were gradually dispersed by multiple adversaries rather than decimated in a one-time event traceable to a specific perpetrator.[23]

Such an interpretation accommodates other evidence of the Laurentian Iroquois presence among the Ottawa River valley Algonquins, Wendats, and Abenakis in the latter decades of the sixteenth century.[24] The lack of documentary or archaeological evidence of large-scale massacres in the St. Lawrence valley and the considerable spatial extent over which Laurentian Iroquois people moved as captives and refugees at that time suggest that host communities strongly desired their presence as live adoptees. In addition to providing replacements for deceased relatives, the Laurentian Iroquois brought many other potential benefits to host communities: early experience with Europeans, knowledge of travel routes and resource areas in the St. Lawrence valley, a capacity for long-distance mobility, kin-based connections with other communities, and possibly some linguistic expertise and novel subsistence practices (most notably an expertise in eel fishing). The similarities between Laurentian Iroquois cultural patterns and those of their Iroquoian neighbors would certainly have eased their transition into Iroquois and Wendat clans, especially given the latter groups' exogamous marital arrangements, which one scholar has identified as the "quickest way to cement" a core group and newcomers together.[25]

We need not assume, however, that that adopted Laurentians represented merely human stock integrated with an eye toward replicating the culture of their adoptive communities. Commonly "scattered" throughout diverse Iroquois clans and villages, they can be more fruitfully understood as "cultural seeds" that expanded their hosts' technological, cultural, and spatial repertoires of action. Once integrated into the kinship structure of their adoptive community, the diverse life experiences and histories of adoptees, rather than being obliterated or submerged, often had a profound and enduring impact on their hosts, given the adoptees' physical presence as lifelong community members following their adoption and assimilation and their role in producing and raising subsequent generations.[26]

Between 1570 and 1600, intense competition between the Iroquois, Wendats, and northeastern Algonquians for Laurentian Iroquois adoptees had important spatial consequences for Native peoples throughout northeastern North America. These conflicts caused the relocation of at least two Ontario Iroquoian populations (the Ahrendahronons and Tahontaenrats) from the north shore of Lake Ontario to the indigenous homelands of the Attigneenongnahac and Attignawantan Wendat nations in the vicinity of Georgian Bay.[27]

Simultaneously, intergroup dynamics related to the early contact Mid-Atlantic exchange axis led to three other significant shifts of indigenous population: first, the southward movement of the Susquehannocks from the headwaters of the Susque-hanna River in what is now New York State to sites in the lower Susquehanna River valley in modern-day Lancaster County, Pennsylvania, and an outpost at modern-day Romney, West Virginia; second, the southwestward movement of peoples from the southern shoreline of Lake Erie to the central Ohio River valley; and third, the east-ward movement of the Iroquoian-speaking Neutrals in southwestern Ontario toward the Niagara River valley.[28] The Neutrals' relocation may have affected the access of the Senecas, Cayugas, and Onondagas to the Mid-Atlantic exchange axis, but evidence of an adult African woman's remains on the Seneca Tram site (occupied circa 1585–1600) and a 1697 description of Onondagas hunting in proximity to their "ancient village" in the upper Susquehanna River valley suggest that these three nations retained at least some access to this key communications route.[29]

By 1600, all of these indigenous population movements had left the Mohawks, Oneidas, Onondagas, Cayugas, and Senecas in a spatially central location with a wide buffer zone vis-à-vis their Native neighbors. With direct access to the headwaters of five major waterways (St. Lawrence, Delaware, Allegheny, Susquehanna, and the confluence of the Mohawk and Hudson rivers), the Five Nations enjoyed unprec-edented freedom to move throughout an extensive range of geographic space, facili-tated by widening networks of external exchange contacts.[30]

In a context of dynamic mobility at the turn of the seventeenth century, the Mohawks, Oneidas, Onondagas, Cayugas, and Senecas completed the founding of a collective, overarching polity known historically as the Iroquois League. Archae-ologists, as William Engelbrecht has pointed out, "cannot dig up the League," but evidence of dramatic changes in mourning rituals (the core expression of League identity) strongly suggests the interest of Iroquois people in creating a context for peaceful movement among the five constituent nations. It is crucial to note that this evidence reflects not the origin but rather the completion of processes that had begun prior to direct sixteenth- and seventeenth-century Iroquois contacts with Europeans. Archaeologists have argued for the existence of a precontact Mohawk/Oneida/Onondaga "proto-League" (functioning during the fifteenth and early six-teenth centuries), which the Cayugas and Senecas subsequently joined.[31]

The emphasis on free, peaceful movement in the traditional story of the League's founding aligns well with what archaeological and documentary sources tell us of sixteenth-century events in Cartier's wake: the origins of Deganawidah (the Wendat Peacemaker in League tradition) at the Bay of Quinté (suggesting a possible Ahren-dahronon or Tahontaenrat affiliation); his subsequent canoe journey southward to Iroquoia to spread his message of peace via condolence; his initial effort to convince the Neutral Iroquoian woman Jigonsaseh to end her practice of supplying food to traveling warriors; the clear associations with spatial centrality bound up in Degana-widah's efforts to plant a "Tree of Peace" at Onondaga with roots extending in the four cardinal directions (with an eagle perched atop to warn against distant threats);

his use of exotic shell wampum as a mnemonic device and as material validation of messages (which underscored the fundamental significance of exchange and communications in League formation); and finally his emphasis on the idea of a "dish with one spoon," or the importance of free movement to shared hunting grounds among allied nations.[32]

Archaeological evidence of the performance of ritual condolences for deceased Senecas by members of other constituent nations of the Iroquois League after 1600 currently provides our best material validation of the enactment of the collective, reciprocal functions central to the Wendat Peacemaker Deganawidah's message of peace, power, and righteousness. Important recent studies by Martha L. Sempowski, Lorraine P. Saunders, and Robert D. Kuhn demonstrate that the Senecas, traditionally held to be the last of the five nations to join the League, undertook a dramatic alteration of their exchange patterns during the first two decades of the seventeenth century—replacing their former Susquehannock suppliers of shell artifacts and European goods from the Mid-Atlantic with goods originating in the Hudson River valley. Sempowski, Saunders, and Kuhn suggest that this comprehensive reorientation of Seneca trade required safe Seneca travel through the homelands of, or reliable exchange with, their Cayuga, Onondaga, Oneida, and Mohawk neighbors to the east. This evidence, combined with indications of increasing stylistic similarity in ceramic patterns among League nations at this time and relative parity in the volume of European (primarily Dutch) trade goods among the different Iroquois nations during the early seventeenth century, suggests that constituent nations of the emerging League had established peaceful internal relations. They did so by means of international "embassies," which included ceremonial exchanges of wampum and other material goods; public recitations of what one Jesuit observer later described as "fables, genealogies, and stories;" reciprocal performance of Condolence ceremonies; and discussions of "current affairs."[33]

At the time the constituent nations of the Iroquois League commenced direct contact with Europeans in the first decade of the seventeenth century, these nations had long possessed experience of intense conflicts with their Wendat and Algonquian neighbors, which derived from competition for access to trade routes and Laurentian Iroquois adoptees over the previous three decades. Documentary and material sources provide occasional glimpses into the nature and extent of these hostilities. In 1640, for example, an elderly Algonquin "widow" appeared at the French settlement of Trois-Rivières and related her life story to the Jesuits. Captured by the Onondagas as a child, she was raised among them to adulthood and recognized as one of their "women." Iroquet Algonquin warriors recaptured her from the Onondagas in 1615; she subsequently raised another family among the Algonquins only to lose them all to epidemic disease during the 1630s. In 1640, she settled near Trois-Rivières with five Algonquin orphans, intending to use her knowledge of Onondaga agricultural techniques to clear land and plant crops for her youthful charges. In June 1644, Mohawk leaders gave Jesuit captive François-Joseph Bressani "to a poor old woman whose grandfather had been killed in battle by the Hurons." A similar story is related by a French captive, who in the early 1650s described his adoptive Mohawk "mother" as an ethnic Wendat who had been captured in her youth and fully integrated into Mohawk society. These cases testify to the dynamic, intensely personal, occasionally violent, and ultimately far-reaching consequences of interindigenous conflict during the late sixteenth and early seventeenth centuries. Such conflicts forged close ties between different Native nations yet simultaneously sharpened consciousness of distinct indigenous national identities. Awareness of these early precolonial events and processes helps us to better understand how the five nations of the emergent Iroquois League came to fit European intruders into their pattern of spatial relationships after 1600.[34]

INTEGRATING EUROPEAN INTRUDERS INTO AN INDIGENOUS CONTEXT

Europeans arriving on the periphery of Iroquoia during the early seventeenth century found themselves quickly enmeshed in preexisting indigenous conflicts ranging from the St. Lawrence River valley to Chesapeake Bay. Following the pattern established between Cartier and the Stadacononans during the sixteenth century, first contacts between the Iroquois and the French (in 1603), the English (in 1608), and the Dutch (after 1611) occurred when Iroquois people were on journeys beyond their traditional homelands. The establishment of a regular Dutch presence in the Hudson River valley after 1613, however, represented a crucial turning point in Iroquois spatial history, insofar as it enabled the Five Nations to reorient patterns of mobility and thereby to articulate a coherent new geography of solidarity in which the sentient branches and roots of a metaphorical "Tree of Peace" at once encompassed the Five Nations and provided a means of engaging the new European presence on Iroquois terms.[35]

Officially granted freedom to cross the Atlantic to the Americas by the 1598 Treaty of Vervins with Spain, French traders affiliated with Protestant merchant Pierre Chauvin erected a trading post at Tadoussac in 1600 and returned there on voyages for the next two summers. In 1602, French traders brought two Montagnais men to the court of King Henri IV, where they discussed the possibility of an alliance to drive Mohawk competitors out of the St. Lawrence valley. Achieving the defeat of the Mohawks would enable the allied French and Algonquins to assert control over the Laurentian exchange axis with the nations of the continental interior, known for the remainder of the French colonial period as the *pays d'en haut,* or upper Great Lakes country. The two Montagnais diplomats traveled back to Canada with Samuel de Champlain in 1603 to communicate news of the French Crown's intention to assist in brokering a peace between the Algonquins and the Mohawks. In the event such negotiations failed, however, the French pledged to "send forces to vanquish" the Algonquins' "Iroquois" enemies.[36]

On May 27, 1603, Champlain witnessed a victory celebration of "Etchemins" (eastern Abenakis [Maliseets or Penobscots]), Algonquins, and Montagnais people at Tadoussac. Warriors from these nations reported having surprised and killed 100 members of a 1,000-man Iroquois war party near the mouth of the Richelieu River. This celebration inaugurated nearly two weeks of French negotiations with an estimated 1,000 members of these three nations, which resulted in the conclusion of a formal treaty of alliance. Champlain's 1603 promise of allied military assistance to Montagnais headman Anadabijou and Algonquin headman Besouat at once secured locally unhindered French settlement at Tadoussac and, echoing Cartier's inscribed cross, placed the French presence once more in a posture of hostility toward Iroquois peoples' freedom of movement in that region.[37]

Champlain perceived the Algonquians' 1603 offensive in terms of indigenous competition for access to European traders. The Iroquois, reportedly "in greater number" than their Algonquian neighbors, regularly "infest[ed] the banks all along the said River of Canada [the St. Lawrence]" and hindered direct Algonquian access to Tadoussac. Given the evidence of Laurentian Iroquois dispersal described above, however, we cannot rule out the possibility of ongoing competitive efforts between the Mohawks and their rivals for Laurentian Iroquois personnel as a potential motivating factor in this incident. In any event, Champlain devoted the remainder of his summer 1603 sojourn in the St. Lawrence valley to collecting geographic information from his new allies, much of which pertained to descriptions of war routes between their homelands and Iroquoia, and witnessing the return of Algonquian war parties with Iroquois "heads" and prisoners, as well as preparations for other anti-Iroquois military expeditions—preparations that featured ceremonial dancing by "stark naked" Montagnais women. Champlain returned to France in August 1603.[38]

After several years of exploration in what is now Nova Scotia and New England, Champlain returned to the St. Lawrence valley in 1608. He established Quebec at a highly defensible location near the former site of Stadacona in an effort to protect a Crown-authorized fur trade monopoly from Basque, Dutch, and illicit French competition. Champlain also pledged in 1608 to join the Iroquet Algonquins in an expedition against their Iroquois enemies, with whom "they had long been at war, on account of many cruelties practised against their tribe under the colour of friendship."[39]

Champlain's expeditionary force departed from Quebec with a number of Montagnais warriors in June 1609. En route, a mixed body of 200 to 300 Ahrendahronons (a newly incorporated member nation of the Wendat Confederacy) under Ochasteguin and Iroquet Algonquins under their eponymously named leader Iroquet joined the expedition, which traveled down the Richelieu River to Lake Champlain. On July 29, 1609, the allied Native-French force encountered a Mohawk war party on Lake Champlain near present-day Ticonderoga, two or three days' journey out from

Champlain's Battle with the Mohawks, 1609

the latter's home villages. Following an exchange of shouted threats, the two bodies of warriors erected barricades, and the Mohawks sent an advance embassy of two canoes to the Wendat and Algonquian encampment to see if they would be ready to fight at dawn. Having concealed the presence of Champlain and twelve other Frenchmen in their party, the Wendats and Algonquians readily accepted the invitation, and both sides spent the night dancing, singing, and exchanging verbal insults.

On the morning of July 30, 1609, Champlain remained hidden in a Montagnais canoe while an estimated 200 Mohawks, led by three headmen wearing headdresses with "three big plumes," approached. According to Champlain's account, the Mohawks "caught sight of me, halted and gazed at me, and I at them." Following this momentary pause, the Mohawks drew their bows, and Champlain opened fire. The four balls that flew from his musket killed two of the headmen on the spot and mortally wounded the third. The Mohawks, however "astonished" by the impact of Champlain's gun, nevertheless returned their own volley of arrows until another musket shot from one of Champlain's French companions scattered them. Pursuing Montagnais and Algonquin warriors secured ten or twelve Mohawk prisoners, killed several more, and collected the supplies and weapons the Mohawks had abandoned in their flight.[40]

Champlain hoped to use the diplomatic leverage gained from the 1609 victory over the Iroquois to secure Native assistance and escorts for explorations of the upper St. Lawrence valley and Great Lakes. However, he faced significant resistance to these plans from those he aimed to employ as guides. They, like their Stadaconan predecessors, sought to restrict French freedom of movement. Champlain had also inherited a legacy of broken promises by Basque fishermen to assist the Montagnais and Algonquins against the Iroquois (presumably with firearms). He would have to prove himself again.[41]

Champlain departed Quebec on June 14, 1610, to reconnoiter with Wendat, Montagnais, and Algonquin warriors at the mouth of the Richelieu River for another attack on the Mohawks. Five days later, an advance scout reported an "Iroquois" force of 100 men "who had barricaded themselves well" on the banks of the Richelieu near present-day Sorel, Quebec. The Algonquins and Montagnais chose to attack the "Iroquois barricade" without waiting for Champlain and were beaten back with losses. Champlain and his French companions then fired into the enclosure, but the Mohawks retaliated in spirited fashion, sending "arrows flying on all sides as thick as hail," one of which lodged in Champlain's neck. They also dodged volleys of gunshot by "throw[ing] themselves upon the ground." The Mohawks held out long enough for Champlain's ammunition to run low, but the arrival of a relief force of French gunmen permitted the allied Natives to open a breach in the Mohawk fort, through which "some twenty or thirty, both Indians and whites, went in, sword in hand." The Montagnais captured fifteen Mohawks while the French dispatched the rest with "arquebuses, arrows, and swords." The Montagnais carried off their prisoners (the Algonquins and Wendats had arrived too late to participate) and a "small" booty of "some beaver-skins" from the Mohawks, giving the French "much praise" for their assistance.[42]

In addition to these early Franco-Mohawk engagements, contacts with the English and Dutch during the first decade of the seventeenth century further complicated the geopolitical circumstances of the Iroquois. After learning from Susquehannocks of their "mortall" enmity with a group of Indians they called "Massawomekes" in 1607, Captain John Smith encountered "7 [or 8] Canowes of the Massawomeks" in July 1608 near the head of Chesapeake Bay. After bluffing his way through a threatened attack, Smith invited the Massawomecks aboard his vessel, "had conference by signes," and traded some bells for their venison. These Massawomecks, who came from a "great" and "very populous" country to the northwest of Chesapeake Bay, were then on an offensive expedition against the local Algonquian populations and had the "greene wounds" to show for it. Nevertheless, Smith remarked on the superior quality of Massawomecks' "Targets [shields], Baskets, Swords, Tobacco pipes, Platters, Bowes, and Arrowes," and noted especially their "dexteritie in their small boats, made of the barkes of trees, sowed with barke and well luted with gumme." The "Massawomeks" described their homeland as near the "river of Cannida" (the St. Lawrence), where they traded with the French. Although recent scholarship has characterized the Massawomecks as a distinct Iroquoian group, more convincing evidence indicates that the term represented a local Algonquian reference to the western four nations of the Iroquois League.[43]

John Smith's *Map of Virginia*, 1612 (note the location of the "Massawomecks" in the upper right section)

Following the contact between members of western League nations and Captain John Smith, another Englishman appeared on the Mohawks' doorstep. In September 1609, Henry Hudson's voyage on behalf of the Netherlands took him as far as Norman's Kill, south of modern-day Albany, New York, just fifty miles from Mohawk villages. Although direct Mohawk contact with the Dutch is not documented in written sources until five years later, archaeological evidence suggests extensive Mohawk involvement in the Hudson River valley trade by 1611, and the rapid movement thereafter of what one archaeologist has described as a "tidal wave" of those goods as far west as Seneca country.[44] Ongoing interactions with Dutch traders in the Hudson River valley over the next two years appear to have resulted in the formal negotiation of a trading agreement between the Dutch and the Mohawks in 1613. The so-called Tawagonshi Treaty of 1613 has been dismissed by many scholars on the basis of the disputed authenticity of the original document. Leaving aside the question of the document's physical properties, since it may well be a twentieth-century copy of another text, its contents, when analyzed in tandem with other documentary evidence and Iroquois oral tradition, sheds light on a crucial moment in precolonial Iroquois history.[45]

Negotiated by Jacques Eelckens prior to the formal establishment of Dutch Fort

Indigenous Exchange Routes in Eastern North America, ca. 1614–1634

Nassau at Norman's Kill in 1614, the agreement established formal guidelines for the Dutch-Iroquois trade relationship. Abundant seventeenth-century documentary evidence exists to substantiate the existence of this covenant, which also played a crucial role in completing the process of League formation. On June 27, 1689, a delegation of Seneca, Cayuga, Onondaga, and Oneida headman told the magistrates of Albany that the Mohawks, Oneidas, and Onondagas "did carry the Ankor of the ship that Jaques [Eelckens] came in to onnondage, that being the meeting place of the Five Nations," and that they had then come "to renew the old Covenant made with

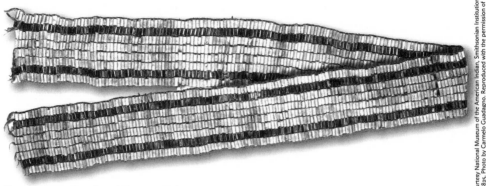

Kaswentha, or Two-Row Wampum Belt

Jaques many years ago who came with a ship into their waters and rec[eive]d them as Bretheren, & then the maquase [Mohawks], oneydes, and onnondages desired him to establish himself in this country and the Sinnekes & Cayouges they drew into that General Covenant, & that they had with one accord Planted the Tree of Good Understanding."[46]

Contemporary Iroquois oral tradition associated with this early agreement with Dutch traders establishes it as the original elaboration of *kaswentha* relationships between Iroquois nations and Europeans. This pattern of diplomacy, also referred to as "Two Row," is represented visually in wampum belts by two parallel rows of purple wampum on a white wampum background (or vice versa), signifying a separate but equal relationship between the two entities based on mutual benefit and noninterference. The spatial metaphor bound up in *kaswentha* asserts the right of each entity to free movement in its own "canoe" along the paths represented in white wampum. Neither side in a *kaswentha* relationship may attempt to "steer" that of the other. Put another way, we may understand *kaswentha* to involve mutual recognition of the patterns of spatial mobility that brought the two entities into contact, and a subsequent mutual commitment to recognizing and preserving those patterns of mobility.[47]

Relationships patterned on the principles articulated in postcontact *kaswentha* ideology doubtless existed among indigenous nations prior to the intrusion of Europeans. Yet an awareness of the significant role of spatiality in Iroquois external relations permits a fuller appreciation of how the nations of the emerging League endeavored to establish relations of mutual assistance and noninterference with the European nations on the periphery of their homelands after 1613 as an extension and a refinement of similar processes they had initiated with neighboring indigenous populations during the late sixteenth century.

To the north of Iroquoia, Champlain's second victory over the Mohawks had convinced his Native allies to grant some limited, supervised French movement west of Quebec. Étienne Brûlé, a young French settler, spent the winter of 1610–11 learning the skills of a *truchement* (interpreter/intermediary) with the Iroquets and Ahrendahronon Wendats. Between 1611 and 1613, Iroquets escorted Algonquins, Nipissings, Ahrendahronon Wendats, and Neutrals to the Lachine Rapids to trade with the French, and in 1613 Champlain made an escorted journey to the Ottawa River valley. These movements did not go unnoticed by the Iroquois, who appeared regularly in canoes in the vicinity of the Lachine Rapids to intercept Native groups seeking to trade with the French. By 1613, the frequency of these Iroquois incursions generated fears that invaded the dreams of Algonquian and Wendat traders, leading some to make propitiatory offerings of tobacco in hopes of obtaining supernatural assistance against the Iroquois, and others, more prosaically, to seek alternate routes to the French.[48]

To the south of Iroquoia, the Mohawks, in an early test of their *kaswentha* relationship with the Dutch, persuaded three sailors left at Fort Nassau over the winter of 1614–15 to accompany them on an expedition against the Susquehannocks. Captured by the Susquehannocks at some time during April or May 1615, these sailors were recovered later in 1615 near Delaware Bay by another Dutch trader, Cornelis Hendricksen, who ransomed them from the Susquehannocks for "kettles, beads, and merchandise." News of this event, which reached Champlain via Susquehannock visitors to the Ahrendahronon Wendat village of Cahiagué, confirmed the competitive Dutch presence on the Hudson River. This knowledge, combined with Wendat complaints of their "ancient" Iroquois enemies' interference with their journeys from Wendake to the St. Lawrence valley, obliged Champlain to honor his earlier pledge of military assistance by undertaking a third anti-Iroquois expedition in 1615.[49]

The Susquehannocks offered 500 men (perhaps one-fourth of their total military strength) for this expedition against the "Antouhonorons," reflecting their desire to maintain contact with the French and Wendats despite increasing hostility from Iroquoia. Direct Susquehannock-Wendat communications required "a very wide detour" around "thickly populated" Seneca country by 1615, and hinged on guarantees of secure passage through the Neutral communities in the Niagara peninsula. Iroquois efforts to interdict Wendat-Susquehannock relations derived from the Senecas' recent, near-complete reorientation of their exchange patterns toward the Dutch on the Hudson River. Archaeological evidence of a distinct population of individuals with trading ties to groups south and west of Iroquoia at the Seneca Fugle site (a small satellite community occupied approximately 1605–25) suggests a possible hedge by the westernmost prospective members of the League against uncertainties in the dramatic rearrangement of their exchange patterns mandated by affiliation with Iroquois nations to the east. Nevertheless, these newly altered economic and political arrangements facilitated an escalation in the Five Nations' military activity against former indigenous trading partners in the Susquehanna River valley.[50]

On September 1, 1615, Champlain departed Cahiagué with allied Ahrendahronon Wendats, Iroquet Algonquins, and a number of Montagnais warriors. The French

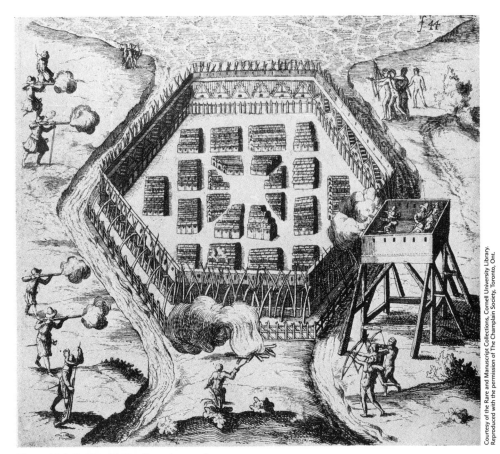

Champlain's Battle with the Onondagas, 1615

and Wendats dispatched advance canoes to the Susquehannocks to make arrangements for a reconnaissance near the intended target of the expedition: Kaneenda, a palisaded Onondaga installation (possibly a fishing station or a small satellite community of adoptees) located at the head of Onondaga Lake.[51] After crossing Lake Ontario, Wendat scouts captured eleven Onondagas (four women, three men, three boys, and a girl) at a fishing camp on the Oswego River on October 9, 1615. One day later, an unplanned Wendat-Onondaga skirmish thwarted Champlain's plan for a surprise attack on Kaneenda.

Confronted by a thirty-foot-high palisade and defenders abundantly "stocked" with provisions and stones to hurl, Champlain decided to attack the occupants of Kaneenda with musket fire from an elevated platform (or *cavalier*). On October 11, 1615, Champlain advanced the *cavalier* to "within a pike's length" of the palisade. Three or four French musketeers then launched volleys into the fort, but the Onondagas responded with a shower of arrows and thrown stones, and used their "waterspouts" to douse Wendat-set fires along the palisade's walls. After a three-hour siege, several Wendat leaders had incurred serious arrow wounds, and the allied force withdrew. Although severely wounded himself, Champlain opposed this withdrawal, and he later remarked bitterly on the lack of military valor demonstrated by his allies. But considered in light of the identity of the particular Wendats and Algonquins on the campaign, and the likely presence of Laurentian Iroquois people or their first-generation descendants among them, their conduct appears much more understandable. Banking on the arrival of the Susquehannocks to assist their efforts to flush the Onondagas from the fort for hand-to-hand combat, which increased the likelihood of enemy captures, the Ahrendahronons and Iroquets had no interest in Champlain's demands for an all-out assault. Champlain remained encamped in proximity to the Onondaga fort until October 16, 1615, long enough to hear Onondagas berate him for interfering in their battles, while also mocking their Wendat and Iroquet enemies for their lack of courage in employing French assistance in the attack.[52]

The 1615 expedition represented a near-complete failure for Champlain and his allies. Iroquet Algonquin warriors recaptured one Algonquin woman adoptee among the Onondagas, but they and the Wendats fought bitterly over the fate of the few prisoners (an Onondaga man and one or possibly two women) known to have reached Wendake. Champlain, in addition to being forced to retire "with loss and shame," had unwittingly killed a Neutral man visiting Onondaga during the siege. This unresolved murder compromised French-Neutral relations for the next twenty-five years, and likely also amplified anti-French sentiment among the Iroquois, who in 1627 were described as having "friends and relatives" in the easternmost Neutral town of Ouaroronon.[53]

Étienne Brûlé, who had accompanied the advance Wendat embassy to Susquehannock country in 1615 to assist in retrieving their promised warriors for the campaign against the Onondagas, fared little better than Champlain in his objectives. He later claimed to have arrived with promised Susquehannock reinforcements at Onondaga two days after Champlain's allied force had departed for Wendake, but after realizing they had missed their planned reconnaissance with Champlain, the Susquehannocks elected to return home. Brûlé's narrative offers important further insight into the Iroquois perspective on French "interference" in their affairs after the 1615 Champlain expedition.[54]

Wandering into a Seneca town early in 1616 after becoming separated from Susquehannocks escorting him back to Wendake, Brûlé was taken to "the lodge of one of the principal chiefs" for questioning. The Seneca headman demanded to know "who he was, whence he came, what cause had driven and led him to this place and how he had got lost, and further whether he were not one of the French nation which was making war" on the Iroquois. Brûlé tried to pass himself off as a person "desirous only of their acquaintance and friendship," but the Senecas refused to believe him, "and rushed upon him, tore out his nails with their teeth, burned him with red-hot firebrands, [and] plucked out his beard hair by hair." After a rainstorm interrupted these preliminary tortures, the Seneca leader released Brûlé and arranged for the latter's wounds to be "cleaned and doctored." Brûlé spent an unknown period of time among the Senecas, attending many "dances and feasts or rejoicings," before expressing his desire to leave. The liberated captive promised the Senecas that he would "make them friends with the French and their enemies." The Senecas escorted Brûlé "four days' journey from their village" to Lake Ontario, by which route he reached Wendake.[55]

Étienne Brûlé's promise, fulfilled in part by a 1620 peace embassy of some 400 Iroquet Algonquins escorted to Iroquoia by French interpreter Jean Nicollet de Belleborne, may have opened the Iroquois to the possibility of negotiations with the French and their Algonquian and Wendat allies in 1622. The timing of these overtures corresponded with the Dutch presence on the Hudson assuming a more intermittent and unreliable character after Fort Nassau's destruction in a 1618 flood. In 1622, a Dutch trader named Hans Jorisz Hontom, a longtime associate of Jacob Eelckens who possessed extensive North American experience, for reasons unknown took an unnamed Mohawk "sachem" hostage and demanded a ransom. After the Mohawks paid the ransom, Hontom reportedly "cut out the male organs of the aforesaid chief, and [hung] them on the mast stay with rope, and thus killed the sachem." This act, as overt a rejection of *kaswentha* principles as exists in the documentary record, could well have encouraged Iroquois diplomatic overtures to the north, or validated such efforts already under way.[56]

On June 6, 1622, two unidentified "Iroquois" (likely Mohawks) appeared at the mixed Montagnais and Algonquin settlement near the Recollét mission station/ French trading outpost at Trois-Rivières. These Iroquois visitors wanted "to see their relatives and friends who had been kept prisoners amongst them a long time," and offered to discuss peace. Upon learning of their presence, Champlain encouraged the Montagnais and Algonquins to enter into negotiations with the Mohawks. French authorities hoped that such a peace would yield an "increase in traffic, greater facility for discovery, safety for our savages who go in quest of beavers, but do not [now] dare go into certain parts where these abound, because they are afraid of their [Iroquois] enemies."[57]

French-dispatched canoes escorted the two Iroquois delegates to Quebec, where they offered condolence presents of 100 beaver skins to the French and Algonquins prior to a formal meeting with Champlain and the Algonquin headman Mahigan Aticq, the son of Algonquin headman Anadabijou. Champlain first met Mahigan Aticq while Anadabijou was celebrating victory over the Iroquois at Tadoussac in 1603. Mahigan Aticq now claimed to be "sick and tired of the wars they had had [with the Iroquois], which had lasted over fifty years." After reaching a preliminary mutual agreement involving free hunting in the St. Lawrence River valley, the Algonquin headman urged the Iroquois delegates to report this "good understanding" back to their people. The two Iroquois delegates then engaged in a dance with three Algonquins, after which

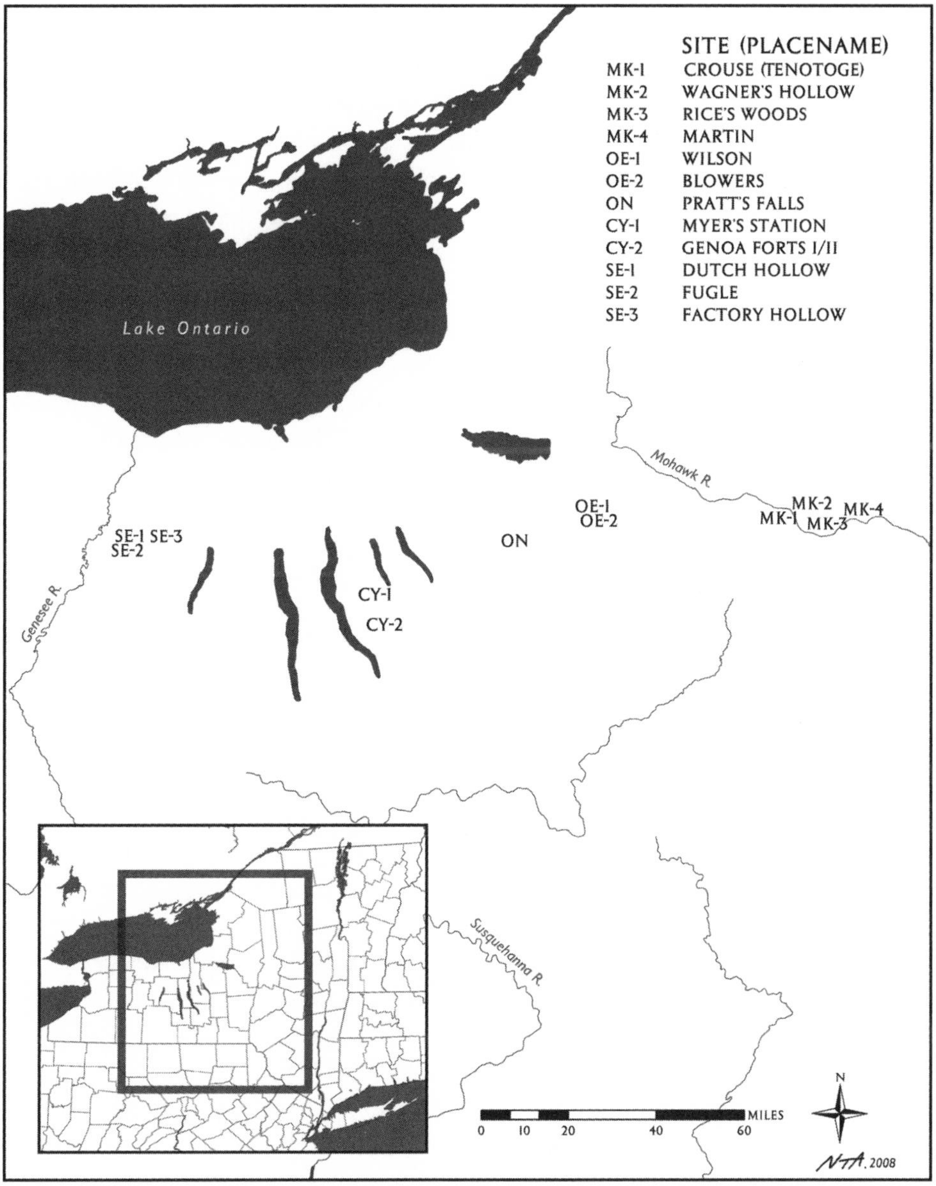

SITE (PLACENAME)

MK-1	CROUSE (TENOTOGE)
MK-2	WAGNER'S HOLLOW
MK-3	RICE'S WOODS
MK-4	MARTIN
OE-1	WILSON
OE-2	BLOWERS
ON	PRATT'S FALLS
CY-1	MYER'S STATION
CY-2	GENOA FORTS I/II
SE-1	DUTCH HOLLOW
SE-2	FUGLE
SE-3	FACTORY HOLLOW

Lake Ontario

Mohawk R.

OE-1
OE-2

MK-2 MK-4
MK-1 MK-3

Genesee R.

SE-1 SE-3
SE-2

ON

CY-1

CY-2

Susquehanna R.

N

MILES
0   10   20   40   60

NTA. 2008

Map by Nij T. Anantsuksomsri

Iroquoia, ca. 1620

each dancer "kissed his [Anadabijou's] hand and came and placed it in [Champlain's], in token of peace and goodwill." These symbolic acts served to integrate the French into the Iroquois-Algonquin pact, which emphasized mutual freedom of movement as the primary condition of peace.[58]

Four Algonquins bearing thirty-eight beaver skins sent as a peace offering by Champlain departed from Quebec with the two Iroquois men in June 1622. Yet the murder of an Iroquois man by a member of the Algonquin embassy during the party's subsequent return journey from successful peace negotiations in Mohawk country rendered the effort moot. On July 25, 1622, Champlain noted the arrival of six more Iroquois delegates at Quebec seeking to "confirm peace with all the savages," notwithstanding the murder, which they viewed as an individually motivated act. This Iroquois delegation appeared to be offering Champlain the opportunity to mediate relations in the aftermath of their comrade's death, but Champlain failed to recognize the cues underlying this overture. Evidence of Iroquois discontent with the lack of French action following the treacherous behavior of the Algonquins represented the origin of Iroquois opposition to the French presence in the St. Lawrence valley.[59]

During the summer of 1622, the Iroquois, according to the Jesuit historian Pierre F. X. de Charlevoix, "raised three large parties to attack us separately." The first of the two Iroquois parties whose activities Charlevoix described targeted a group of Frenchmen "guarding the passage" at the Lachine Rapids. The Iroquois captured a Récollet priest named Guillaume Poulain in this attack, but several of their own men were killed or captured in the effort. Unable to overtake the retreating Iroquois war party, the French released a captive Iroquois "chief" in exchange for Poulain, and notwithstanding the arrival of this man among his compatriots "at the moment when all preparations were made to burn" Poulain, the Iroquois honored the exchange and released him. The second Iroquois party "embarked in thirty canoes" toward Quebec. Upon arrival, they used a small fort on the St. Charles River to "invest" the nearby Récollet convent. The Iroquois warriors then "ravaged the neighborhood of the country and retired."[60]

These attacks, which represented the first incident of direct Iroquois hostilities against the French settler presence in the St. Lawrence valley, demonstrated to French eyes the Iroquois capacity for long-range, coordinated offensive actions against high-profile targets. Wendats and Algonquians, who of course had longer familiarity with such attacks, also experienced escalated Iroquois aggression at the same time. Recollét lay brother Gabriel Sagard noted in 1623 the ease with which Iroquois raiders penetrated eastern Wendake and the portage at Rideau Falls on the Ottawa River for surprise attacks on Wendat personnel. Sagard also described similar retaliatory expeditions by "five or six hundred young Huron men, or more, [who] go and scatter themselves over some Iroquois territory, five or six in one place, five or six in another," in search of victims "whether man, woman, or child," to attack by surprise, and either kill and scalp them on the spot or "carry them off to their own country to put them to death over a slow fire." Sagard's eyewitness accounts document changing patterns in Iroquoian warfare during the second and third decades of the seventeenth century; earlier, mass battles in open country yielded increasingly to stealth attacks by small groups. This innovative technique facilitated the success of captive taking in Iroquois warfare, for Native access to iron, copper, and brass for arrowheads had increasingly rendered wooden body armor obsolete, thus reducing the likelihood of obtaining unwounded prisoners in large-scale combat.[61]

In 1623, Wendat warriors seeking revenge for the murder of two of their men near Quebec the previous year captured sixty Iroquois south of Lake Ontario. The Wendats killed most of the prisoners at the battle site, but brought a number of Iroquois prisoners back for distribution among the Wendat towns that had contributed warriors for the expedition. This offensive may have been responsible for a reported 1624 Iroquois-Wendat truce, likely negotiated in nonaligned Neutral territory, where neither the Five Nations nor the Wendats "dare[d] to utter or do anything displeasing to one another," and "often would even sit together as if they had been friends."[62]

Following the negotiated détente with the Wendats, an embassy of six Mohawk headman, accompanied by a flotilla of twenty-five canoes "loaded with furs," arrived at Trois-Rivières in July 1624. The Mohawks planned to participate in the annual French trade fair and to resume the abortive peace conversations of 1622 with the Algonquins, the Montagnais, and French colonial authorities. Champlain, having learned from his prior neglect of Iroquois condolence protocol, now seized the opportunity to mediate an indigenous peace accord. The governor ensured full French participation in the attendant ceremonies, including "the kettle of peace, presents, feasts, dances." Following the successful negotiations, a number of Iroquois reportedly took up temporary residency in Montagnais settlements in the St. Lawrence valley. Having thus secured the northern and western flanks of Iroquoia, the Iroquois embarked on a campaign to displace their Mahican rivals from Dutch traders at newly established Dutch Fort Orange, then located on Castle Island in the Hudson River.[63]

COLLABORATION

The decade after 1624 witnessed the first substantial collaborative initiatives undertaken by the constituent nations of the Iroquois League. Although existing interpretations of Iroquois history have emphasized the temporary or situational character of the League as a functioning entity during the seventeenth century, attention to the spatial context of League actions after 1624 indicates Iroquois peoples' capacity for coherent planning and achievement of broader goals benefiting all five member nations of the Iroquois polity. While international interactions were rarely without a degree of friction, mutual assistance in trade, war, and peace enabled the League nations to optimize the benefits of local or regional spatial initiatives and to establish a comprehensive system of balanced internal and external relations in a much more cosmopolitan context than hitherto appreciated.[64]

Documentary evidence, considered in tandem with the Iroquois oral history related at Albany in 1689 and the archaeological record, suggests that wider Iroquois objectives (such as securing continued direct access to Fort Orange for all League nations and the concomitant power to broker such access for Native peoples of the *pays d'en haut*) operated in what scholars have usually described in more parochial terms as the "Mohawk-Mahican War." As a Dutch settler testified many years later, shortly after her arrival in the Hudson River valley in 1623 the "Mahikanders or River Indians, [the] Maquase: Oneydes: Onnondages Cayougas & Sinnekes, [with the] Mahawawa [Mississauga] or Ottawaes Indians came & made Covenants of friendship" with the Dutch at Fort Orange. The Native nations offered "great Presents of Bever" and requested "free Trade" with Dutch settlers.[65]

The woman's testimony implied separate "Covenants" negotiated by the Mahicans and the Five Nations with the Dutch, and the events that followed the establishment of Fort Orange clearly reflect divergent objectives on the part of these two indigenous entities. The Algonquian-speaking Mahicans established a village on the eastern shore of the Hudson River directly opposite Fort Orange in 1624 and invited their northern Algonquin and Montagnais neighbors to trade there. The opening of this new exchange outlet may have motivated subsequent efforts by Algonquin hunters to extend their ranges to the peripheries of Iroquoia. Iroquet and twenty of his men, for example, visited Neutralia during the autumn of 1626, where they reportedly were "well-known" and took a reported 500 beavers.[66]

Iroquois observers quickly realized that the Mahicans, if successful, would connect rich northern pelts from the St. Lawrence valley with Dutch trade goods, notably the highly desired shell wampum that was chronically scarce in New France. Given the crucial role that east-west exchange routes linking Iroquoia and the Hudson River valley had played in completing the process of League formation after approximately 1613, we can better appreciate the collective interest of the Five Nations in challenging the Mahicans' effort to reorient regional trade patterns. After an initial 1624 Mohawk offensive, the Mahicans, possibly with some Algonquin and/or Montagnais assistance, destroyed the easternmost village of the Mohawks in either 1625 or 1626.[67]

Following that defeat, the Mohawks relocated their three villages from the north to the south side of the Mohawk River, moving closer still to Fort Orange and increasing pressure on the Mahicans and the Dutch. Daniel van Krieckenbeeck, the fort's commander, and six men from his garrison joined a Mahican party "going to war with the Maquaes" in the early months of 1626. Less than three miles from the fort they ran into a Mohawk ambush, which killed twenty-four Mahicans and four of their Dutch allies, including Krieckenbeeck. Angered over Krieckenbeeck's violation of *kaswentha* and possibly recalling Hontom's murder of the Mohawk leader in 1622, the Mohawks "devoured" one of the Dutch corpses, burned the others, and "carried a leg and an arm home to be divided among their families, as a sign that they had conquered their enemies." Several days later, a Dutch trader approached the Mohawks, "who wished to excuse their act," but, echoing the Onondagas' criticism of Champlain in 1615 and the Senecas' interrogation of Brûlé in 1616, they "asked the reason why [the Dutch] had meddled" in their conflict with the Mahicans.[68]

Dutch meddling, notwithstanding official West India Company recommendations to the contrary, continued after Krieckenbeeck's death. Officials in Manhattan received a Susquehannock embassy requesting an alliance in 1626. Unidentified Dutchmen at Fort Orange offered wampum belts to Montagnais leaders visiting Fort Orange over the winter of 1626–27 in hopes of encouraging attacks on the Mohawks. At least one Montagnais headman, known as Cherououny, or "The Reconciled," accepted the Dutch invitation. News of this event prompted Champlain to intervene in an attempt to preserve the peace negotiated in 1624. In May 1627, Champlain reminded Algonquin and Montagnais leaders that peace with the Iroquois had enabled them to "travel freely up the Great River [the St. Lawrence], and to other places, instead of being in terror from day to day of being massacred and taken prisoners, they and their wives and children, as had been the case in the past." But Champlain's words did not prevent a small party of Montagnais "hot-heads" from departing Trois-Rivières with hostile intent. On June 9, 1627, "under pretence of still being friends," the Montagnais captured three Mohawks on Lake Champlain. One escaped, but the Montagnais brought the other two (reportedly brothers aged seventeen and twenty-eight) to Trois-Rivières, where they underwent preliminary torture before the arrival of Champlain and Mahigan Aticq at Trois-Rivières put a stop to those proceedings.[69]

Hoping to defuse a volatile situation, Champlain reiterated his argument before Montagnais and Algonquin listeners that "once war [with the Iroquois] was begun, the whole river would be closed to them, and they would neither be able to hunt nor to fish without incurring great danger, and being in constant fear and anxiety." He urged his Native audience at Trois-Rivières to preserve their freedom of movement (which, of course, also benefited French fur traders) by sending "presents" to the "chiefs" of the Mohawk towns "to compensate, according to custom, for the wrong done in the capture of the two men—which, they should declare, had not been sanctioned by their Captains or Head-men, but was entirely the work of some rash young fools, and had caused them all great indignation." The conversation resulted in Cherououny agreeing to escort one of the two Mohawk prisoners back to his home settlement with condolence presents. Champlain detailed a French settler, Pierre Magnan, to join the embassy, and the group departed for Mohawk country on July 24, 1627.[70]

Champlain received two accounts of the fate of this expedition. The first, via an Algonquin escapee from Mohawk captivity who appeared at Quebec on August 25, 1627, indicated that Magnan and Cherououny had been killed in Mohawk country by visiting Senecas, who had come there "in all haste to avenge themselves on the allies of the [Mahican] aggressors," the Mahicans having recently killed five Mohawks. These Senecas, while reportedly slaying Cherououny and Magnan with ax blows, lambasted the two men for the audacity of attempting peace negotiations while their Mahican "companions" continued hostilities.[71] This report, if accurate, strongly suggests mutual assistance between the Senecas and their Mohawk allies (one of the "Fundamental Rules" of the League), and further evidence of pan-Iroquois interest in the so-called Mohawk-Mahican War.[72]

The second account, which did not reach Champlain until April 1629, attributed the murder of the ambassadors directly to the Mohawks. The report originated with two Mohawk captives among the Mahicans, who related the account to a Montagnais chief named Erouachy prior to their torture and execution. A Kichesipirini Algonquin man, learning of Cherououny's embassy, "went off to the Iroquois amongst whom he had some relatives" in advance of the embassy and advised the Mohawks that Cherououny's intent was "only to spy out their land" and to "carefully reconnoit[er] their forces" under the cover of a peace embassy. The Mohawks did not relish the prospect of such surveillance. After making an initial show of hospitality to Cherououny's party with an offer of food, the Mohawks reportedly began to cut pieces of flesh from his arms, "ordered him to sing," and "then gave him some of his own flesh, half raw, which he ate; they asked him if he wanted more, and he said he had not had enough, so they cut pieces off his thighs and other parts of his body until he said that he had had enough." The Mohawks then burned Magnan "with lighted brands" and "made him endure intolerable agonies, before he died." Another member of the embassy attempted escape and was killed by a blow from an ax. The fourth member of the party turned out to be "an Iroquois by birth, who had been captured when a little boy" by the Montagnais and raised among them. Although initially "tied" and prepared for ritual torture and execution, owing to concern over his potential to return to the Montagnais, the Mohawks eventually "resolved to keep him, hoping that time would cause him to lose the memory of our Quebec savages, and the affection he had for them, they holding him meantime as a prisoner."[73]

The initial report of the failure of Cherououny's embassy resulted in the immediate torture and execution of the remaining Mohawk prisoner by the Montagnais and Algonquins at Trois-Rivières. Dutch plans to have the Mohawks "come to an agreement with the French Indians whereby they [the Algonquins and Montagnais] may obtain forever a free passage throughout their country" to trade at Fort Orange were now effectively scuttled. The Dutch settler population in the vicinity of the fort evacuated in 1626, and did not return in significant numbers for five years. By 1628, the Mohawks had driven the Mahicans away from Fort Orange, reducing some to tributary status and causing others to relocate as far away as the Connecticut River valley.[74]

Whether Mohawks or Senecas killed Cherououny and Magnan in 1627, the clear message the Iroquois sent via these murders convinced Champlain of the futility of diplomacy with the Five Nations. This news came at a time when the French governor also faced increasing pressure from English privateers in the St. Lawrence estuary, who were using the pretext of the English-French war of 1626–29 to attempt to expel the French and seize control of the region's fur trade. The inability of the French to get reinforcements and supplies through to Quebec ultimately forced Champlain to surrender the town to an English naval force under Admiral David Kirke on July 19, 1629.[75]

The Iroquois took immediate advantage of the unwillingness of the English occupiers of Quebec to follow Champlain's practice of providing military assistance to the Algonquins and Montagnais of the St. Lawrence River valley. Iroquois warriors burned the palisaded Native settlement opposite Trois-Rivières in the autumn of 1629. This act, along with the efforts by Jean Nicollet to discourage the Wendats from trading with the English at Quebec, permitted the Iroquois to further diversify their exchange and communications linkages. As many as 200 English traders reportedly penetrated over 1,200 miles into the interior from their base at Quebec from 1629 to 1632, adding to ongoing Iroquois exchange with the Dutch in the Hudson valley, and possibly also with refugee French traders in Wendake via Neutralia.[76]

Still another opportunity for the diversification of Iroquois external relations developed after October 1631, when Virginian trader Henry Fleet considered the prospect of a run "up the [Susquehanna] river to the heads, there to trade with a strange populous nation called Mowhaks, man-eaters." Although Fleet, a former captive of the Anacostanks (an Iroquoian-speaking people then residing on the Potomac River who had economic ties to the League nations), decided against the autumn 1631 journey, he returned to the Susquehanna valley the following summer eager to pursue trade with northern Native nations.[77]

Fleet established preliminary contacts with representatives from the four western nations of the League (whom he referred to as "Massomacks") as well as the Mohawks (whom he referred to as "Hereckeenes") in July 1632. According to Fleet, both Iroquois constituencies were seeking to supplement their regular trade with English traders in "Cannida." Fleet and his competitors, William Claiborne and other Virginia-based traders at Kent Island (150 miles north of Jamestown in Chesapeake Bay), did brisk business exchanging "Dutch cloth" and "Spanish axes" for Native-procured peltry between 1631 and 1638. In May 1634, Maryland governor Leonard Calvert reported that the "Massawomeckes" regularly undertook seven- to ten-day journeys to exchange as many as 3,000 "skins" at a time with his colony's traders. Seven months later, Dutch records documented an encounter between a Mohawk headman and an English trader in the Susquehanna River valley.[78]

This expanded Iroquois outreach to English traders south of Iroquoia corresponded with ongoing Iroquois military offensives against the Susquehannocks. Continuing to make inroads into the Susquehannocks' extensive network of trade and communications, which then spanned from the Delaware River basin to Wendake, the Senecas led a dispersal of the Monongahelas (aka "Black Minquas" or Eries) from southwest Pennsylvania by 1635. The Senecas relocated a number of Monongahela adoptees to a satellite community, while other Monongahelas sought refuge among the Susquehannocks and other Native populations in the upper Ohio River valley.[79]

To the north of Iroquoia, the Mohawks directed cooperative Iroquois campaigns against the Montagnais and Algonquins, sending numerous parties to the St. Lawrence valley during the early 1630s. Members of one multigenerational men's clan Mohawk war party met a violent end after being captured by Montagnais warriors in June 1632. Carried to different Montagnais villages near Quebec and Tadoussac, the Mohawk prisoners suffered excruciating torture. Montagnais women and girls applied fire to "the most sensitive and private parts" of the captives' bodies, slashed them with awls, bit them, threw burning coals and hot ash at them, and poured heated sand into gashes sliced in their foreheads. In the midst of the ordeal one of the Mohawk captives managed to taunt his Montagnais tormentors by describing his extensive network of personal allies and trading partners, one of whom was a "Flemish [Dutch] Captain." Thus, the doomed Mohawk exacerbated the rage of the Montagnais, already aggrieved as a result of the recent Mohawk offensives, Iroquois domination of the trade with the English on the St. Lawrence between 1629 and 1632, and the ongoing refusal of the Iroquois to allow "the French savages who now trade on the river of Canada [the St. Lawrence]" to "pass through" their territory to trade with the Dutch at Fort Orange.[80]

The return of the French to Quebec in July 1632 after the conclusion of peace with England in the 1632 Treaty of St. Germain-en-Laye enmeshed renewed Franco-Iroquois hostilities into the ongoing Five Nations' offensives against the Native peoples of the St. Lawrence valley. On June 2, 1633, eighteen Iroquois warriors ambushed a group of Frenchmen landing a ship on the shore of the St. Lawrence River near Trois-Rivières. This ship had been sent down to provide security for the approaching Wendat fur convoy. Hatchet blows and a "storm of arrows" killed two Frenchmen immediately, and a third died later of his wounds. The Iroquois raiding party dispersed after a French sailor aimed an "arquebus" in their direction.[81]

An infuriated Champlain advised metropolitan officials in July 1633 of the urgent need to eliminate the ability of the Iroquois to "give trouble" to the "free movement" of Native populations allied with New France. Amazed, frustrated, and humiliated that the Iroquois could "hold more than four hundred leagues" of territory in "subjection" and thereby attack New France with impunity, his 1633 request for 100 armed men to march against the Iroquois restored the fundamental French posture of hostility toward the Five Nations that persisted (with intermittent periods of peace) for the remainder of the seventeenth century.[82]

Jesuit missionaries had accompanied Champlain to Canada in 1632, and their annual *Relations* provide an extraordinarily rich window into contemporary Iroquois affairs, given the presence of the missionaries among many of the Algonquian and Wendat peoples increasingly forced to contend with Iroquois aggression. In May 1633, for example, an Algonquin speaker named Kepinat described his people's strategy of sending gifts of "Moose skins" to "foreign" nations on the borders of Iroquoia in order to shorten the "long arms" of the Five Nations by preventing those nations from affiliating with the League.[83]

The Wendats, like the Algonquins, had also evolved strategies for coping with Iroquois offensives. Jesuit Jean de Brébeuf noted in 1634 the presence among the Wendats of a "female soothsayer" who employed "pyromancy" to predict the success of war parties sent from Wendake across Lake Ontario, then referred to as the "lake of the Hiroquois." Aware of their status as guests on the route from Wendake to the St. Lawrence valley, the Wendats observed "great caution" in their relations with the Algonquins of the Ottawa River valley in order to "pass by in security." Wendat trade convoys traveled in scattered groups of seven to ten canoes so as to reduce the potential for catastrophic losses, and also concealed "supplies of Indian corn in certain places about two days' journey apart" on their outbound journeys to the St. Lawrence valley for use when returning home. The Wendat fur convoy that arrived in New France in July 1633 consisted of 140 canoes bearing an estimated 500 to 700 Wendat traders.[84]

Though sizable, the Wendat convoy had initially been larger still. A number of Wendat traders had turned back in 1633 after hearing Algonquin reports of French plans to avenge the Wendats' murder of Étienne Brûlé earlier that year. Yet the French were eager for renewed trade and did not want to jeopardize relations with the Wendats. Champlain did not even press them for an explanation of the circumstances surrounding Brûlé's death. Not until the winter of 1640–41 would French authorities learn that Brûlé had met his end at the hands of Wendats opposed to his efforts to broker peace with the Senecas.[85]

The Senecas' interest in rapprochement with the Wendats in 1633 originated in part from the demonstrated capacity of the Iroquois by 1633 to project military force over great distances and also from declining relations between the League nations and the Dutch. When Saggodryochta, the Mohawks' "head chief," discovered that Hontom, who had murdered one of his nation's leaders in 1622, had been appointed commissary at Fort Orange in 1633, 900 Iroquois warriors appeared before the fort and demanded his surrender. Hontom refused to leave, and the assembled Iroquois army demonstrated its anger by burning a West India Company sloop anchored in the Hudson River and slaughtering all the livestock on Kiliaen van Rensselaer's patroonship of Rensselaerswyck. The potential loss of Iroquois business (an April 1633 report suggested that the Mohawks alone had "four thousand beaver skinnes" ready to trade) worried Dutch officials at Fort Orange and indicated that the latter's economic well-being depended to a far greater degree on ties to the Mohawks than vice versa. Trade links to the English in the Susquehanna River valley and, after 1633, in the Connecticut River valley, along with the potential for the "Sinnekens" to broker access to French Canada via their former captive Brûlé and the Wendats, enabled the Iroquois to divert substantial traffic from the Dutch after 1633.[86]

Peace negotiations between the Five Nations and the Wendats accelerated further following a July 1634 assault by a reported 1,500 "Hiroquois" warriors, mostly Senecas, on a party of 500 Wendats encamped at Trois-Rivières, which resulted in 200 Wendats killed and 100 more taken captive. Subsequent reports of Wendat peace embassies in Iroquoia, likely arranged via contacts between Senecas and Wendats in Neutralia, soon reached French missionaries in Wendake. Jesuit Paul Le Jeune noted in 1634 that all five nations of the League, named individually for the first time by a European writer, "wish[ed] to become parties" to negotiations with the Wendats.[87]

The Seneca-brokered Iroquois-Wendat peace of 1633–34 may therefore represent the final act that dissolved lingering differences between the Mohawks and the Senecas, the westernmost of the four western Iroquois nations (recall the Senecas' satellite community at the Fugle site; Henry Fleet had also witnessed friction between the "Massawomecks" and "Hereckeenes" as late as 1632), and brought the Iroquois League into being. Archaeological, documentary, and oral evidence supports an interpretation of League formation as a dynamic process rooted in the precontact era but completed several decades after direct contact with French, English, and Dutch colonizers in northeastern North America. Although traditionally considered to have occupied the lifetimes of its fifty founding leaders, the negotiations that resulted in the historically known Iroquois League more likely required the efforts of multiple generations of founding lineages, who, as Tuscarora scholar John Napoleon Brinton Hewitt has noted, "looked beyond the constrained limits of tribal boundaries to a vast sisterhood of all the tribes of men, dwelling in harmony and happiness."[88]

The first documented reference to the existence of the Iroquois League reflected the completion, by 1634, of crucial Iroquois movements, assimilations, and formations deriving from multiple journeys undertaken during the first century of their encounter with European goods and peoples. New patterns of Iroquois movement had established an extensive network of connections between Iroquois people and others on the periphery of their homelands, and stimulated the completion of the process of founding the historically known League. More than simply a mutual non-aggression pact, the League's geography of solidarity also provided a means for its constituent nations to achieve consensual unity on initiatives designed to promote the good of all members.[89]

The League, as it existed in 1634, was the product of four related historical developments formed during the previous century's journeys: first, the diverse, direct contacts that members of Iroquois nations had sought and maintained with other indigenous peoples as well as with the English, French, and Dutch colonizers on the periphery of Iroquoia; second, the increasing volume and rate of the circulation of information and economic commodities among the five constituent nations after approximately 1610; third, the sophisticated, collaborative planning of offensive and defensive operations by national leaders; and fourth, a shared consciousness of Iroquoia as a vital central space vis-à-vis Native nations and non-Native intruders on the peripheries of League nations' homelands. The lengthy process of League formation reflected active efforts by the Iroquois to convert a number of spatial innovations into a desired social order. Lessons learned during the century after Stadaconans encountered Jacques Cartier also proved vital to Iroquois peoples' engagement with changed circumstances brought about by their first sustained encounter with population loss from introduced European diseases after 1634. Prior experience with assimilating new peoples and with articulating and resolving common concerns among communities distributed throughout a substantial range of territory facilitated the League nations' subsequent spatial initiatives.

2.

THE EDGE OF THE WOODS
1635–1649

There is nothing in the world as cruel as an Iroquois war.
—FRENCH HISTORIAN CLAUDE-CHARLES LE ROY DE LA POTHERIE,
WRITING IN 1722 OF SEVENTEENTH-CENTURY IROQUOIS WARFARE

On the morning of December 30, 1634, a Mohawk guide led Harmen Meyn-dertsz Van den Bogaert, the Dutch West India Company's surgeon at Fort Orange, to the periphery of the Oneida town of Oneyuttehage. After firing a musket shot to announce their arrival, Van den Bogaert and his companions, Je-ronimus de la Croix and Willem Thomassen, "confidently went to the castle where the Indians divided into two rows and let us pass in between them through their entrance." The Oneidas provided food "immediately" for their "cold, wet, and tired" visitors, and lodged them in the home of their then-absent "chief." That afternoon one of the local Oneida "councilors" called on Van den Bogaert's party, asking "what we were doing in his country and what we brought him for gifts."[1]

From 1634 to 1650, the Iroquois redefined the "edge" of their "woods," undertaking an extraordinary geographic and scalar expansion of their military campaigns in search of adoptees to replenish their numbers and to facilitate access to new spaces of resource procurement. Patterns of Iroquois movement, formed "on the journey" during the prior century of contact, provided the basis for the newly formed League's innovative engagement with changes brought about by unprecedented number of deaths in their communities following their first extensive exposure to European epidemic diseases in 1634. Over the next fifteen years, the spatial history of Iroquoia underwent dramatic change as the League nations enacted principles associated with the Edge of the Woods phase of the Condolence ceremony, which at once enjoined participants to rejoice in their survival while undertaking a realistic assessment of contemporary problems and reminding leaders of their responsibility to address those problems by effecting constructive change.[2] Van den Bogaert's journal of his tour into Mohawk and Oneida country during the early winter of 1634–35 offers rich

Iroquois Places of Interest, 1634–1650

insights into the nature and extent of Iroquois movements, along with glimpses of the League's internal operations and evidence of negotiations related to external trade and diplomacy.[3]

Van den Bogaert, de la Croix, and Thomassen departed Fort Orange with an escort of five Mohawk men on December 11, 1634. Two days later, they arrived at the easternmost Mohawk settlement under the leadership of "Adriochten" (Saggodryochta), who, due to a recent outbreak of smallpox, was then living a quarter mile from the village in a small cabin. Prevented from holding any substantial negotiations by the alleged absence of most of the community's members on a hunting expedition, the Dutch ambassadors moved on to the town of "Canagere" (Canajoharie). There, they found "three women of the Sinnekens" trading dried and fresh salmon and convinced a Mohawk man to guide them to the "Sinnekens'" town in exchange for "half a yard of cloth, two axes, two knives, and two awls."[4]

En route to Oneida country, the Dutch passed through the third Mohawk "castle," inhabited by people who demonstrated great curiosity at their presence, even pushing "one another into the fire" in order to catch a glimpse of the visitors from Fort Orange. Van den Bogaert's party arrived at the "fourth [Mohawk] castle" on December 21, 1634, and conversed with the local headman, who had recently returned from thirty days' travel overland. This headman, named "Oquoho," claimed that on his journey he had met an English settler in the Susquehanna valley who was there to "learn the language of the Minquase [Susquehannocks]" and to trade for peltry. Oquoho also reported that "French savages," most likely Wendats, were then visiting the "Sinnekens."[5]

The latter bit of news gave Van den Bogaert some hope that he would be able to determine the extent of western League nations' trade with the French. Escorted by Mohawk guides, the Dutch embarked on a four-day journey through heavy snowfall from Mohawk to Oneida country on December 26, sleeping each night in "huts" along the route, as the travelers had done during their journey from Fort Orange to Mohawk country. After arriving at Oneyuttehage, Van den Bogaert learned of a recent visit by seven French traders to the town. These traders had reportedly walked overland from Oneida Lake (approximately eighteen miles northwest of the village), which they had reached from Lake Ontario via the Oswego and Oneida rivers. Once the Oneidas realized that Van den Bogaert's party, unlike their French predecessors, had no presents to offer, several Oneidas offered bitter criticisms of Dutch parsimony. Oneida headman Arenias returned to Oneyutehage on December 31, fresh from conversations with "French Indians" elsewhere in Iroquoia. In a demonstration of his extensive spatial knowledge, Arenias "put down kernels of corn and stones" and arranged them to map "the locations of all their [League] castles" for Van den Bogaert. Arenias also reported that the Iroquois desire for access to beaver-hunting grounds motivated their recent peace negotiations with the Wendats.[6]

Throughout their conversations with the Dutch emissaries, the Oneidas took care to demonstrate their ties to the Wendats (and, by extension, to the French). Van den Bogaert's conversations with Oneida headmen occurred in a longhouse where Arenias had hung wampum strings and belts that documented his negotiations with the Wendats. Van den Bogaert reported that the wampum represented "a token of peace that the French Indians were free" to trade and travel in Iroquoia. On January 3, 1635, the Oneidas got down to business with the Dutch, stating their desire for premium pricing on their peltry at Fort Orange owing to the distance they had to travel to reach Dutch traders. The Oneidas assured Van den Bogaert that if they received "four hands of sewant and four hands of long cloth for each large beaver" (a potentially significant increase in their buying power at Fort Orange), they would trade their peltry "with no one else." They then offered Van den Bogaert a present of five beaver pelts and sang a song that authorized Van den Bogaert's (and, by extension, all Dutch) free movement among all the "castles" of the constituent League

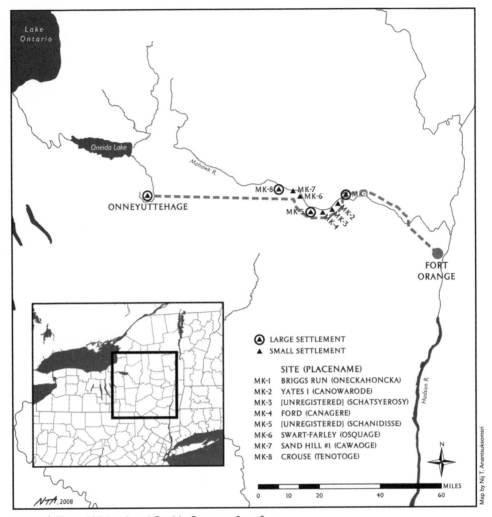

Bogaert's Tour of Mohawk and Oneida Country, 1634–1635

nations, pledging that all future Dutch traders and emissaries would have "house and fire, wood and anything else" throughout Iroquoia.[7]

The Oneidas punctuated their statement by offering to escort Van den Bogaert to trade with the French if he so desired, which indicated their own sense of the *kaswentha* relationship they were proposing: the Oneidas sought ties to the Dutch, but not at the expense of their own independent relations with the French and French-allied Native nations. Van den Bogaert, claiming to lack authority to confirm a price increase, promised to report the Oneidas' request to his superiors. The Dutch remained at Oneyuttehage for nine more days, during which time they received a visit from an Onondaga embassy of "six old men and four women," who gave the Dutch a present of beaver pelts. The senior male leader of the Onondaga party invited Van den Bogaert to visit his country that summer and offered to show the Dutch "that lake [Ontario] where the French came to trade in their sloops." Departing Oneida country on January 12, Van den Bogaert's men returned home on a nine-day trek through Mohawk country, passing by numerous Iroquois people "returning home from the hunt to their castles" and, at the Mohawk town of "Schanadisse," nine Onondagas carrying pelts for trade.[8]

Van den Bogaert's tour documented the presence of not only Iroquois economic and political ties to Wendake and the French but also, to a limited degree, smallpox in Iroquoia during the latter months of 1634. This epidemic, believed to have spread to the Wendats, Algonquins, and Montagnais via French traders at Trois-Rivières during the summer of 1634, also reached "virgin soil" in Iroquoia (possibly via contact with Wendat emissaries and/or an Iroquois captive returned from Trois-Rivières in the autumn of 1634). Although we might expect the surgeon Van den Bogaert to have noted widespread suffering from disease if he witnessed it, he described only the easternmost Mohawk village as afflicted with smallpox (but possibly coping by apparent quarantine methods), and mentioned just three other incidents in which Mohawks and Oneidas asked him to heal "very sick" individuals (whose ailments he did not identify as smallpox-related). While smallpox evidently killed significant (yet uncertain) numbers of Iroquois people in 1634, the demise of the nascent Wendat-Iroquois rapprochement represented the most immediate consequence of the disease. By early 1635, all groups in the St. Lawrence valley and lower Great Lakes experienced substantial population losses, which in turn rekindled widespread mourning wars to assuage grieving families with captives for adoption or ritual torture.[9]

MOURNING WARS

Contemporary European accounts of indigenous conflict in northeastern North America from 1635 to 1641 documented seemingly chaotic scenes of carnage. In reality, these conflicts represented deliberate responses from within the cycle of retribution and ritual violence that fueled Iroquois mourning wars. New patterns of Iroquois movement emerged during this period that had crucial implications for Native and non-Native neighbors of the League. Mourning wars undertaken by Iroquois warriors increasingly entangled the French in the St. Lawrence valley, as allies and supporters of local indigenous peoples, as well as the Dutch and English, as suppliers of a growing Iroquois military arsenal, into what had previously been exclusively indigenous affairs. In this new context of foreign relations, the League nations developed innovative practices that facilitated long-distance offensives against indigenous targets deemed most likely to represent useful adoptees.

Although we can only imagine today the traumatic impact of the unprecedented 1634 smallpox epidemic in Iroquoia, we must resist the facile conclusion that this initial disease outbreak left the "socialization process" of the Iroquois irretrievably "hobbled given the loss of people who had carried cultural information and passed it on to others." Though smallpox and other diseases exerted disproportionate lethal impact on the very young and the very old in Iroquois society, the notion that core cultural values and knowledge vanished with elderly deceased individuals is at odds with the large-scale, public nature of Iroquois sociopolitical and ritual practice, especially the Condolence ceremony. Presumptions of permanent and severe truncations of Iroquois culture in the postepidemic era also neglect the documented success of matrilineal Iroquois kinship systems in "repackaging" families that incorporated children without parents and adults without spouses, many of whom, after 1634, were adoptees originating from an increasingly diverse range of Native nations. Additionally, documentary evidence indicates the growing significance of a cohort of younger, "self-made" Iroquois leaders (also including a number of adoptees) who collaborated with hereditary League titleholders to implement key innovations that engaged the novel constellation of circumstances in Iroquoia after 1634.[10]

While the Jesuits attributed post-1635 Iroquois aggression against other Native peoples to Dutch intrigues, indigenous mourning-war patterns provide a better explanation for such activity. Iroquois relations with the Dutch remained chilly in the aftermath of Van den Bogaert's sojourn. The surgeon never fulfilled his promise to bring the League nations an answer to their proposed terms of alliance in the spring of 1635. In October 1636, patroon Kilian van Rensselaer described persistent Mohawk antagonism toward Fort Orange and the settlers of Rensselaerswyck (van Rensselaer's proprietary manor near Fort Orange), but he failed to draw the connection between Mohawk sentiments and his dogged efforts to collect an indemnity from that nation for the property destroyed at Rensselaerswyck in 1633.[11]

The Iroquois spent most of the time from 1635 to 1637 pursuing offensive campaigns in Wendake and Algonquin country. The Wendats and Algonquins responded in kind with their own attacks on Iroquoia, increasingly launched from Trois-Rivières or Quebec, where French officials offered departing warriors traditional feasts and where they witnessed the occasional torture of Iroquois prisoners by returning war parties. Shocked but fascinated by the sheer intensity of the physical abuse inflicted on one Iroquois captive by the Algonquins at Quebec in August 1636, Jesuit Jean de Quen sought an explanation from the man's tormentors. He learned that "the men or women who indulge most fiercely in these acts of cruelty are those whose fathers or husbands or nearest relatives have been treated with equal fury in the country of their [Iroquois] enemies; it is the recollection of the death of their kindred that fills their hearts with this madness." Given such an explanation, one might comprehend how mourning wars could quickly escalate in intensity and cruelty.[12]

In September 1636, Jesuits witnessed another incident of ritual torture and execution of an Iroquois prisoner in the Tahontaenrat Wendat town of Scanonaenrat, then "one of the largest towns" in Wendake. Saouandanoncoua, the fifty-year-old

Scaffold Torture, Detail from Bressani's Map, ca. 1657

Seneca captive in question, had been given to one of the "chief men of the country, in consideration of one of his nephews who had been captured by the Iroquois." Saouandanoncoua had reportedly been so opposed to the 1634 Seneca-Wendat peace negotiations that he had married into an Onondaga family in order to preserve his freedom to "carry arms" against the Wendats. Although the Jesuits were stunned by the violence inflicted on the captive's body, they were even more perplexed by the manner in which the Tahontaenrats vented their rage on the Seneca prisoner by means of clear, sequential, and carefully paced procedures. The Jesuits marked especially the "raillery" between the Wendats and their captive "uncle" during his torture, describing how the Wendats reminded Saouandanoncoua of his former pleasures in burning Wendat prisoners, and how they asked him (mockingly) if he thought he had killed all the Wendats. Once he had finally expired, the Tahontaenrats dismembered and consumed Saouandanoncoua's corpse.[13]

The Jesuits and the scant French settler population in the St. Lawrence valley (which numbered less than 200 people in 1641), though eager to see the Iroquois "exterminated," tried nevertheless to remain officially aloof from what they regarded as the "madness" of intertribal conflict during the mid-1630s. Yet by sponsoring feasts for Algonquian and Wendat war parties heading toward Iroquoia, by tolerating the public torture and execution of Iroquois captives in French settlements, and by providing refuge for Wendats, Algonquins, and Montagnais from Iroquois offensives, the French permitted their Native allies to entangle them in the intensifying regional cycle of blood revenge after 1635. In August 1636, Théodore Bochard du Plessis, an official of the colony's governing Compagnie des Cent-Associés, rather naively accepted a captive Iroquois woman from the Algonquins at Trois-Rivières, whom the Algonquins offered in condolence for the Frenchmen killed by the Iroquois in 1633. Shipped to France, this woman ended up in the Carmelite convent in Paris. Baptized "Anne-Thérèse," she sought respite from constant ridicule for her mispronunciation of French words in long walks through the city's streets. By 1640, she died after a "long sickness," like so many of her Iroquois predecessors taken involuntarily to France. Such actions—in addition to persistent French statements of a desire to make "all one people" with the "daughters" of the Wendats, Algonquins, and Montagnais—posed a direct challenge to Iroquois social, political, and economic objectives in northeastern North America after 1634.[14]

Successful pursuit of mourning wars and long-distance exchange by indigenous people required a capacity for rapid movement, which in turn depended on comprehensive spatial knowledge. In these qualities the Iroquois possessed no significant advantage over their Native rivals in the St. Lawrence valley and upper Great Lakes. The Wendats, for example, counted among their number an "Admiral," whom Jesuit observers identified as the recipient of "all the news of the nations to which these Hurons go by water on their fresh-water sea." In April 1637, the leader of an Algonquin and Montagnais war party originating near Tadoussac produced a pencil sketch of his party's route to the "country of the Hiroquois." Field communications among these combatant nations appear also to have been mutually intelligible, given a 1637 Algonquin report of Iroquois warriors' presence in the vicinity of Trois-Rivières, which they learned "from the little sticks which [the Iroquois] fasten to a tree to make known to those who shall pass that way how many of them there were."[15]

After 1634, the factor that ultimately distinguished the Five Nations from their Wendat, Algonquin, and Montagnais rivals was the kinship-based alliance structures of the Iroquois League. While other nations struggled in the postepidemic era to form cooperative military efforts, the Iroquois benefited from already-established cultural patterns that obliged young men to join war parties composed of relatives from either their maternal or paternal clans. In so doing, the League nations were able to assemble large, occasionally multinational war parties that undertook coordinated and effective movements over long distances. Additionally, by 1637 Iroquois warriors had added increasing numbers of firearms to their military repertoire. Wendats, Algonquins, and Montagnais armed only with "javelins," hatchets, "iron arrow-heads," and knives increasingly confronted musket-bearing Iroquois opponents.[16]

Official French policy banned the sale of firearms to Native people until 1641 and even afterward limited access to firearms to Christian converts among allied indigenous nations. Dutch traders at Fort Orange and English traders like William Pynchon on the Connecticut River at Springfield did not share the reluctance of their French counterparts toward trading firearms to Native customers. The Mohawks, given their proximity to these two markets, became the first League nation to

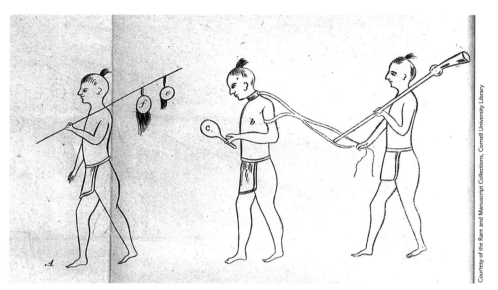

French Sketch of Iroquois Warriors with Gun and Captive, ca. 1666

acquire them in quantity. By 1641, the Mohawks, who as the League's eastern door-keepers bore responsibility for protecting the Five Nations from threats originating in the east, could field "four hundred armed men." Archaeological evidence indicates that firearms, like shell wampum and brass kettles before them, soon spread rapidly throughout Iroquoia via internal exchange and direct procurement by members of the four western League nations.[17]

The first reports of Mohawk muskets reached French ears in August 1637. Fresh from their plunder and execution of Pequot sachem Sassacus, the Mohawks had sent an armed party estimated at 200 men to ambush a small flotilla of Wendats returning homeward from Trois-Rivières on Lake St. Pierre. Shortly thereafter, the French realized that there were actually more than 500 canoe-borne Mohawks on the lake who had also attacked another convoy of Wendats approaching Trois-Rivières with cargoes of peltry. Outraged by the Mohawks' offensive and no doubt interested in retrieving the "quantity of skins" that the Mohawk raiders had taken from the Wendats, Governor Charles Hualt de Montmagny sent two armed "shallops" in pursuit of the retreating aggressors. On August 11, 1637, the pursuers discovered "upon the banks of the [Richelieu] river a plank which had served as the crossbar of a cross, which Monsieur the Commandant du Plessis had erected the year before. These [Mohawk] barbarians had torn it down and upon this plank had painted the heads of thirty Hurons whom they had captured," delineating by specific colors and sizes the "quality and age" of the prisoners, and their intended fates. The French pursuit party managed only to retrieve and interpret this symbolic message; they never caught up to the retreating Mohawks.[18]

In addition to Mohawk-led offensives in the St. Lawrence valley, other Iroquois nations launched direct attacks westward into Wendake after 1637. These campaigns had commenced after the breakdown of the 1634–35 Iroquois-Wendat peace. But they also involved an extension of concurrent Iroquois operations in the Niagara Peninsula, where the Wenros, an Iroquoian-speaking population (formerly affiliated with the Neutrals and possibly former trading partners of the Senecas and Cayugas), resided in the midst of still-abundant beaver populations. A glimpse into the origin and composition of one Iroquois expeditionary party that reached the periphery of Wendake appears in the record of a Jesuit interview with a Mohawk captive in December 1638. This unfortunate young man, baptized "François" prior to his ritual torture and execution, had "left his own country to come to the Hiroquois nations nearer to us, intending to trade some porcelain [that is, wampum] that he had brought for some beavers." But shortly after his arrival in Oneida country he reportedly gambled away his resources. Unwilling to return home empty-handed, François joined an Oneida war party in hopes of securing plunder, a prisoner, or a scalp. This decision led to his capture and ultimately to his conversation with the Jesuits in Wendake.[19]

The story of François demonstrates the ongoing significance of spatial mobility among League nations during the mourning wars of the 1630s. This Mohawk trader had combined business with pleasure, carrying surplus wampum from Mohawk country westward into Oneida territory in hopes of acquiring peltry in trade. His decision to make such a journey instead of hunting on his own may have held three potential boons: a goodwill opportunity to distribute the wampum then abundant in Mohawk country to other League nations, an economic opportunity to obtain a higher rate of exchange for his wampum among the Oneidas (insofar as he had absorbed the carrying costs of which the latter had complained to Van den Bogaert in 1635), and possibly the chance to visit (or make) friends and relatives and to share news.[20]

Unfortunately for the Mohawk François, a mixed Wendat-Algonquin force of 300 men defeated and captured eighty members of the Oneida party that he had joined in November 1638, causing a blow to Oneida demography serious enough to lead many Oneida women to marry Mohawk men "so that their tribe might not become extinct." The substantial loss of young Oneida men in this campaign inspired references to the Oneidas as the Mohawks' "children" or "daughters" for decades thereafter. The Wendats distributed François and his captive colleagues throughout Wendake for torture and ritual cannibalization. Twelve more Senecas captured in May 1639 were similarly dispersed and consumed as part of the Wendats' own mourning-war complex. While the Wendats held their own against Iroquois offensives into Wendake during the late 1630s, they and the Algonquins of the Ottawa River valley confronted a sharp increase in Iroquois raiding on the water routes linking their respective homelands to the St. Lawrence River valley after 1639.[21]

Post-1639 Iroquois military campaigns—occasionally launched from temporary field "forts" or bivouacs erected as base camps for the aggregation of disparate war parties and for collective planning of actions—increasingly drove their peltry-carrying Native targets to seek refuge at Jesuit missions in Trois-Rivières, Quebec, and Wendake. Fifteen families of Iroquet Algonquins, for example, spent the winter of 1640–41 among their longtime Ahrendahronon Wendat allies at Contarea, home to the mission of St. Jean-Baptiste. But instead of undertaking preparations for offensives against the Iroquois, as they had done between at least 1603 and 1638, these Wendats and Algonquins found themselves increasingly on the defensive. By retreating to Jesuit mission stations, these people further entangled their nations and French settlers alike in an intensifying conflict with the Iroquois League.[22]

On August 2, 1640, Joseph Chihouatenhoua, a prominent Wendat Christian who evangelized on behalf of the Jesuits throughout Wendake, set out to clear wood from his family's field in the town of Ossossané. Two Senecas emerged from the brush and murdered Chihouatenhoua with a "long javelin," leaving his scalped corpse amid trampled cornstalks. The high-profile nature of their victim, whom the Jesuits lamented as "our first and our good Christian," and his role in preaching to the immigrant Wenro population at Ossossané suggest deep planning on the part of the Seneca perpetrators. Their victim was not only a Wendat, but by dint of his prominent Christian status, he may have been regarded as part of the French Jesuit community as well.[23]

Increasingly after 1640, Native communities experimenting with Christianity faced concerted Iroquois aggression. For the League nations, this strategy made sense at numerous levels. These so-called Native converts had already shown evidence of their own willingness and capacity to change allegiances, which may have rendered them optimal candidates for assimilation in Iroquois eyes. Additionally, these people resided in relatively fixed and readily identifiable positions, not only in Wendake but also at the Algonquin-dominated missions of La Conception at Trois-Rivières and Sillery opposite Quebec, as well as at the mission in the Tionnontaté (Petun) village of Ehwae. The Native residents of such communities also possessed firsthand, intimate knowledge of the French, which the Iroquois sought to obtain through interrogation of captives taken from the mission settlements.[24]

Finally, by attacking settled communities of Native people at mission stations in New France, as well as Native villages hosting missions, the Iroquois made a dramatic statement of their opposition to the French colonial project of making "all one people" with their Native allies. Iroquois mourning wars had evolved by 1640 into an effort that endeavored to take from the French the human resources that these "Christian" Algonquians and Wendats represented: military strength, trade contacts, and spatial knowledge of (and access to) hunting territory. These wars also made clear to would-be French-allied or "Christian" Indians the ability of the Iroquois to act with relative impunity toward the French, and demonstrated, often with visceral impact (as in the case of Joseph Chihouatenhoua), that French Jesuit missions offered no secure refuge from League warriors.

ONLY ONE PEOPLE

Mohawks took the lead after 1641 in articulating a new, more comprehensive approach to the League's spatial, demographic, and political circumstances. Bargaining from a position of relative demographic and military strength vis-à-vis their Native and non-Native neighbors, the League's eastern doorkeepers initiated efforts to integrate the French and the Dutch into the Five Nations' network of alliances. Captives of European origin, who represented at once testimony to prior Iroquois freedom of movement and facilitators of future mobility, played a key role in the Mohawks' creative, albeit tentative, diplomacy.

Writing in June 1641, Father Paul Le Jeune opined that the Iroquois had "reached such a degree of insolence, that we must see the country [New France] lost, or bring it to a prompt and efficacious remedy." Citing the ability of the Iroquois to move freely through a range of territory extending from Acadia to Virginia, their tendency to "lend a hand to one another in their wars," their murders of French citizens in 1627 and 1633, and their recent assaults on the Wendats and Algonquins, Le Jeune worried that the dispersed character of French settlements in the St. Lawrence valley would soon become prey to Iroquois warriors "who hunt men as we do wild beasts." Le Jeune had sounded this alarm in his *Relation* as prefatory material to his recounting of the story of the Mohawks' capture of two French settlers, François Marguerie de la Haye and Thomas Godefroy de Normanville, while the latter hunted near Trois-Rivières during the autumn of 1640. Beneath Le Jeune's sensationalist rhetoric we can detect more complex developments under way in Iroquoia at this time.[25]

Following their capture, neither Marguerie nor Godefroy suffered the common preliminary tortures of having their fingernails torn out or being beaten and burned. Instead, the Mohawks permitted their captives to leave "a wretched paper, scribbled upon with a coal," attached to a tree branch fixed in the snow, and another charcoal-written note on a debarked tree. Both documents described the events that had befallen them and identified their captors. Upon their arrival in Mohawk country, the French captives learned that a delegation from the "upper Nations" of the Iroquois had arrived in Mohawk country, offering "presents that these two captives might be set free." After this formal opening gesture, the League nations held a "council" and resolved to use the two captives to facilitate a Mohawk embassy to Trois-Rivières during the following spring to negotiate, in their role as eastern doorkeepers, peace on behalf of the League with New France. The captives were "given in keeping to two heads of [Mohawk] families, who treated them like their own children" over the winter of 1640–41. Marguerie's adoptive family even permitted him to write to the Dutch at Fort Orange (in English, using rust from a brass kettle scratched onto a beaver skin) seeking clothing, blankets, pens, and paper. The recipients of this improvised correspondence, "touched with compassion," sent the French prisoners the goods they requested.[26]

In late April 1641, 500 Mohawks assembled to escort Marguerie and Godefroy to Trois-Rivières, marking the first of many subsequent Iroquois diplomatic embassies carrying such human "passports." Aware of the relative strength of their bargaining position, a large number of Mohawk warriors "broke from the ranks" of the escort en route in order to intercept Wendat and Algonquin hunters approaching the St. Lawrence valley with their peltry, reportedly "with the design of pillaging, killing, and massacring all those whom they could surprise."[27]

On June 5, 1641, twenty canoes paddled by 150 Mohawks arrived opposite the French settlement at Trois-Rivières. The Mohawks sent Marguerie across the St. Lawrence, alone, in a canoe bearing a flag of peace. Marguerie advised François de Champflour, the town's governor, that his Mohawk escort included thirty-six "arque-busiers" (men bearing muskets), and that they were demanding thirty more "good arquebuses" as a condition of his release. Marguerie also conveyed intelligence he had obtained from an Algonquin woman prior to his departure. A longtime Mohawk captive, she told him that the Mohawks intended to use the pretext of his return with Godefroy for a surprise attack on French-allied Natives near Trois-Rivières.[28]

The Mohawks, for their part, claimed in preliminary discussions with the Jesuit Paul Ragueneau and interpreter Jean Nicollet that they wanted to invite the French to make a settlement near their country, "where all the Hiroquois nations could come for their trade." On June 6, 1641, an elderly member of the Mohawk "squadron" stated his desire for peace with the Montagnais, Algonquins, and Wendats, in hopes that "the river shall have no more waves, [and] one may go everywhere without fear." But an Algonquin captain responded scornfully to these Mohawk claims, pointing out the Mohawks' failure to repatriate any of the prisoners they held from those nations. This argument provoked a subsequent Mohawk attack on an Algonquin canoe at Trois-Rivières just prior to the arrival of Governor Montmagny.[29]

The Mohawks made a point of "saluting" Montmagny's arrival with a loud volley of musket fire, after which they escorted Ragueneau and Nicollet to a palisaded bivouac they had erected on the south shore of the St. Lawrence River, across from Trois-Rivières. There the French found the Mohawks "seated in a circle, in very good order, without tumult, and without noise." A Mohawk speaker named Onagan opened the proceedings by describing Marguerie and Godefroy as adopted "Hiroquois, they are no longer Frenchmen, the right of war has made them ours." Onagan claimed that while the Iroquois had once feared the French, both the Mohawks and the "more distant" League nations had since "learned to change Frenchmen into Hiroquois." Onagan asserted that Marguerie and Godefroy, even after being repatriated, "will be French and Hiroquois at the same time, for we shall be only one people." The Mohawk speaker then took the hands of Ragueneau and Nicollet, applied them to his face and chin, and stated that "not only shall our customs be your customs, but we shall be so closely united that our chins shall be reclothed with hair, and with beards like yours." After releasing the French prisoners with formal presents of several strings of wampum and two packages of beaver skins, Onagan asked the French to nail up a beaver pelt as a standard for "the house we shall have at Three Rivers," remarking that all the League nations would come there to trade and "smoke therein without fear" now that they had "Onontio [Montmagny] for a brother."[30]

The decision of the French and their Native allies to continue peace talks even as Mohawk warriors assaulted, plundered, and captured Algonquin and Wendat people near Trois-Rivières reflected the comparative political advantages of the Iroquois vis-à-vis the French and their Native allies. An Algonquin who escaped from the Mohawks' bivouac warned that his captors planned to kill Montmagny during the negotiations. Montmagny eventually made his reply to the Mohawks (per their insistence) in the middle of the St. Lawrence River (he in his shallop and they in their canoes). The governor offered the Mohawks a ransom of blankets, hatchets, and knives for Godefroy and Marguerie, but refused to satisfy their demand for firearms. In Mohawk eyes, Montmagny's denial of muskets meant that their gesture of returning the two prisoners had not been properly recognized. The Mohawks requested firearms once more, sweetening their demand with an invitation to the French to live in their country, where they promised to "call a general assembly of the most distinguished persons of all the Hiroquois Nations in order to publish everywhere the generosity and liberality of the French," pledging also to "give a kick to the Dutch, with whom they no longer wished to have any intercourse."[31]

Montmagny responded to this last Mohawk offer by insisting that the Mohawks release one Algonquin captive as a show of good faith. The Mohawks rejected this demand, bringing an end to diplomatic proceedings. Montmagny then decided "to give them arquebuses to eat, but not in the way they asked." French troops opened fire on the Mohawks' field fort with muskets and cannon, and the Mohawks fled. Or at least the French believed they had fled. When Montmagny's party approached the deserted Mohawk bivouac, they got another taste of the Mohawks' "cunning and ability." The Mohawks had erected another field fort, "hidden further within the woods" and sufficiently "well constructed and well supplied" to withstand French muskets and light artillery. From this second bivouac, Mohawk "arquebusiers" opened fire on the French and forced their retreat back across the St. Lawrence before they departed for home.[32]

In the eyes of the French, the June 1641 negotiations at Trois-Rivières were merely a sham, a way for the Mohawks to obtain a "patched-up peace" with the French, along with French firearms to "massacre our confederates." But given the evolution of League objectives in northeastern North America by 1641, the verbal exchange at Trois-Rivières indicates a more complex and sincere approach on the part of the Mohawks. The words of the elderly Mohawk who spoke of smoothing the St. Lawrence River's waves to permit free movement for all parties to the peace undoubtedly resonated with some Wendats and Algonquins at Trois-Rivières, as did the Mohawks' decision to bring along a number of Wendats "who had been naturalized among them, and had become Hiroquois." Onagan's statements about the collective character and strength of the League, his claim to have turned Marguerie and Godefroy into "Hiroquois," and his pledge that the Mohawks would even grow beards when they became "all one people" with the French provided further evidence of the new scope of the League's initiative. The ensuing midriver, watercraft-borne exchange between the Mohawks and Montmagny represented a literal enactment of *kaswentha* principles characteristic of their relations with the Dutch (initiated circa 1613 and restated to Van den Bogaert by the Oneidas in 1635), which a sizable constituency of Mohawks, on behalf of the League, now sought to extend to the French.[33]

The Mohawk-led initiative to open negotiations with the French at Trois-Rivières between 1640 and 1641 via hostage diplomacy failed due to the inability of any of the parties involved in the negotiations to diminish the prevailing atmosphere of mutual distrust. The Mohawks, ironically, came closest to establishing a basis for peace, returning two French prisoners and extending the offer of a *kaswentha* relationship to the French and their Native allies. The Mohawks were bargaining from a dominant position, and their demands for firearms, their refusal to formally repatriate Wendat and Algonquin captives (though a number accompanied the expedition and either took the opportunity to escape or were deliberately released by their Mohawk captors), and their hostile actions during the negotiations are not surprising, however alarming these actions seemed to the French, Wendats, Algonquins, and Montagnais. The Mohawk headmen who favored extending this olive branch to the peoples of the St. Lawrence valley after two years of intense raiding needed the security of such an extensive warrior escort. But these young men did not take orders, and their decision to attack Native enemies during the negotiations played a role in scuttling the proceedings. A nonassimilated Wendat captive who escaped from the retreating Mohawk party claimed that "the whole country of the Hiroquois breathed only war," an indication that support for the Mohawks' effort to extend peace to Native and non-Native populations in the St. Lawrence valley was not yet widespread among the League nations.[34]

In the aftermath of the failed Trois-Rivières negotiations, Iroquois warriors returned in force to the St. Lawrence and Ottawa river valleys after the autumn of 1641. Contemporary French observers estimated that the following winter's campaigns involved more than 600 Iroquois men. An Algonquin who escaped from his Mohawk captors in the autumn of 1641 advised the French at Trois-Rivières that the Mohawks now bragged that "the Dutch, with whom [they] traffic," had promised to assist them against New France. Two captive Christian Algonquin women, who escaped while carrying provisions for a Mohawk war party traveling near Trois-Rivières early in 1642, reported the horrific carnage inflicted by Mohawks on the men and elderly women in their village during the autumn 1641 attack that had resulted in their capture, along with twenty-eight other young women, whom the Mohawks spared "in order that they might dwell in their country, and marry as if they had been born there." Evidence from French parish records dating from 1639 to 1646 indicates that some of these Algonquin adoptees may have returned with their Iroquois spouses to Sillery, Trois-Rivières, and Montreal to have children of these unions baptized, suggesting an interest on the part of some Iroquois people in perpetuating ties to their captives' birth families and homelands.[35]

By August 1642, French officials, in an effort to form a "dyke" against the "fury" of the Iroquois, had established Ville-Marie, a fortified village on Montreal Island, and had begun construction on another fort on the Richelieu River. Jesuit Barthélemy Vimont doubted that such establishments would do the trick. He argued that the Iroquois, who prosecuted "war in the fashion of the Scythians and Parthians," would have to be "either won over or exterminated." Two hundred Iroquois warriors attacked Fort Richelieu on August 20, 1642, using iron hatchets to breach the newly erected palisade and then firing their muskets through holes in the wall. Ursuline Mother Marie de l'Incarnation interpreted the attack as an effort by the Iroquois to "keep the way free" to the St. Lawrence valley. After a fierce exchange of musket fire, the French drove off the Iroquois, but by now it was clear to all informed persons in New France that the Iroquois used guns "as well as our Europeans."[36]

The attack on Fort Richelieu had followed an August 2, 1642, waterborne assault by seventy musket-toting Mohawks in a dozen canoes on a convoy of twelve Wendat canoes on their return voyage from Quebec to Wendake. This raid netted the Mohawks not only the trade goods the Wendats were carrying home but also some significant captives, including Jesuits Isaac Jogues and René Goupil, their *donné* Guillaume Couture, and at least twenty-one Wendat prisoners, three of whom were prominent military leaders. News of the fate of the Wendat captives reached the French via four Algonquin women escapees from Mohawk country and a bark message affixed to a tree branch along the Richelieu River. This Mohawk communiqué, echoing the painted note left behind five years earlier, depicted "twelve heads painted red, which is a sign that those represented are to be burned, six others painted black, which is a sign that those are not yet condemned." French authorities were also aware of the presence of two other Christian Wendats accompanying this convoy, Joseph Chiouatenhoua's fourteen-year-old niece Thérèse Kionhreha (aka Oionhaton), who had spent the previous two years with Ursuline nuns at Quebec and who was returning with the trade convoy to "marry one of her own people" in Wendake, and her fifteen-year-old male cousin. Neither of the teenagers appeared on the Mohawks' bark message, which the French interpreted as a signal that their lives would be spared.[37]

These two major August 1642 Iroquois offensives marked the beginning of a change in the League's strategy toward the St. Lawrence valley. Pressing their comparative advantage in firearms over French-allied Native nations, the Mohawks altered previous patterns of seasonal summer raiding by large parties, maintaining after August 1642 a near-constant presence of smaller parties of 20 to 100 men along the St. Lawrence and Ottawa rivers. This strategy reduced the likelihood of substantial casualties from the defeat of a single large body of men, rendered enemy tracking and pursuit more difficult, and enhanced the psychological impact of these offensives on the French and their allied Native nations, who began to fear the presence of Iroquois warriors behind every tree. Vimont opined that the "skill and boldness" with which the Iroquois used firearms would permit them to assault French-allied tribes with impunity, then to sell the plundered peltry to the Dutch for more powder and lead "in order to ravage everything and become masters everywhere." By 1643, Iroquois offensives had "scattered" much of the Algonquin population from the St. Lawrence and Ottawa river valleys.[38]

The Iroquois, however, did not achieve success from firearms alone. Their other key weapon in their quest to become "masters everywhere" was much less dramatic but perhaps even more effective: the integration of captives as Iroquois adoptees. Documentary evidence indicates an increased tendency among mobile Iroquois parties (whether military or diplomatic in character) at this time to carry such captives with them, often people taken from regions where the party in question was headed. This practice, which likely existed long before the arrival of Europeans, served not only as a solvent of ethnic differences between adoptees and their Iroquois hosts, but it also permitted the Iroquois to profit from the geographic knowledge these captives possessed, from the linguistic assistance these captives may have provided in negotiations with their birth nations or in interrogations of newly taken captives from their homelands, and finally from the potential insurance these individuals offered as human shields against the prospect of total defeat.

Attaching captives to war parties might seem a rather drastic test of the degree to which would-be adoptees had been assimilated into host Iroquois families, communities, and nations, insofar as these journeys brought captives to places of former affiliation and pitted them against their birth nations. Yet the high-risk nature of military action often forged the mutual trust and cooperation that contributed to a sense of common identity. One seventeenth-century French observer remarked with surprise that adoptees were often among "the first to go to war against their own tribe," and how such behavior reflected these individuals' greater affiliation with the "second life" their captors had given them as opposed to "the life they received from their fathers and mothers." Although these traveling captives occasionally escaped, many others were deliberately released by their Iroquois captors in order to convey information to their opponents, as apparently occurred at Trois-Rivières in 1641. Another such instance occurred in June 1643, when several Wendats who had been captured with Jogues were liberated from a Mohawk war party and appeared at Fort Richelieu to hand deliver a timely letter from the captive Jesuit to French officials.[39]

The letter described how the Mohawks had taken Jogues, Goupil, and Couture to their Turtle clan village of Ossernenon in August 1642. There, Jogues's captors subjected him to six days of scaffold torture before giving him to an "old woman, who was a leader among the Indians," to "take the place of a son who had died." Reports of Mohawk casualties incurred during the August 1642 attack on Fort Richelieu led some Mohawks to murder Goupil on September 29, 1642. Jogues escaped this fate after his adoptive "aunt" (suggesting that the individual he replaced may actually have been one of her sisters' sons) hid him in her cornfield. After locating and burying Goupil's corpse with the aid of an Algonquin "formerly captured and now a true Iroquois," Jogues (known by his Wendat name "Ondessonk," or "Bird of Prey," the name of an Ataronchronon Wendat war leader) was put to work carrying dried corn to Mohawk hunting parties some ninety miles distant from their home village.[40]

Over the winter of 1642–43, Jogues accompanied his "aunt" on fishing expeditions and helped her to gather firewood. Along the way he acquired some linguistic facility in Mohawk. He and Couture subsequently traveled in relative freedom between Mohawk villages, ministering to Christian Wendat and Algonquin captives but taking care not to "speak of God" to their uniformly disinterested Mohawk hosts. Jogues escaped death once more in April 1643, when news of the loss of a young leader of a military expedition led "one or two wretched women and a feeble old man" to demand the sacrifice of Jogues to alleviate their grief. Only the subsequent arrival of another Mohawk war party with twenty-two Sokoki prisoners spared his life. Jogues noted the Mohawks' intention "to destroy all the [Sokoki] men and to enslave the women and children," but also claimed that the Mohawks sacrificed at least one Sokoki woman to their god "Areskoui," in place of the normal offering of two bears.[41]

In late April 1643, a "Sokokiois" captain, possibly seeking to negotiate the return of some of his own recently captured people, appeared in Mohawk country with presents to offer for Jogues's ransom and letters to the Jesuit prisoner from Montmagny. The Mohawks refused the Sokoki-brokered offer from the French, but permitted Jogues to send his own letter of reply (which was delivered to Fort Richelieu in June by the released Wendat captives). News of Jogues's precarious circumstances may also have motivated Dutch officials at Fort Orange to send a delegation headed by Arent van Curler (then the *commies,* or chief representative, of patroon Kiliaen van Rensselaer in the manor of Rensselaerswyck) to Mohawk country in late May 1643 to attempt to ransom the Jesuit prisoner.[42]

Dutch efforts to mend fences with the Mohawks had been under way since 1638. The Mohawks were able to drive increasingly hard bargains for their peltry in the hypercompetitive economic atmosphere in New Netherland as the Dutch grew more and more aware (following the West India Company's termination of its monopoly on the fur trade in 1639) that the Mohawks were crucial allies in the fur trade. After seven years of failing to collect the indemnity he believed the Mohawks owed him for the property they had destroyed in 1633, van Rensselaer finally abandoned the effort in July 1640, ordering Van Curler to deliver "three very fine blankets" to "*Sader Juchta*" (Saggodryochta) and two other Mohawk headmen as a sign of the patroon of Rensselaerswyck's "great friendship." Willem Kieft, governor of New Netherland, had ordered Bastiaen Jansz Crol to ransom Jogues, Goupil, and Couture in September 1642, hoping that such an action would assuage the French and contribute to ending "the cruel war which the savages wage against one another, [which] is the reason no skins arrive." Crol either failed to accomplish his objective or ignored the order, which left the task to Van Curler.[43]

Van Curler set out with unspecified "presents" to Mohawk country on horseback in late May 1643. In a dramatic reversal of circumstances from Van den Bogaert's journey of 1634–35, when curious Mohawks and Oneidas importuned the Dutch to offer ceremonial displays of musket fire, the Mohawks "obliged" Van Curler's party "to halt fully a quarter of an hour before each [Mohawk] castle, in order that the Indians might salute us by the firing of muskets." The *commies* made an initial speech proposing that "we should keep on good terms as neighbors and that they should do no injury either to the colonists or to their cattle," which headmen from all three Mohawk "Castles thankfully accepted." Yet when Van Curler proposed the idea of ransoming the French captives, the Mohawk headmen refused to discuss the matter and turned down "about 600 guilders in goods" offered by the Dutch in exchange for the prisoners. Realizing that there was "no chance" of redeeming Jogues and his compatriots, Van Curler's party departed with an escort of ten Mohawks, who accompanied them all the way back to Fort Orange.[44]

Following Van Curler's failed ransom attempt, the Mohawks brought Jogues to Fort Orange with an embassy of "Hiroquois captains" en route "to visit some small nations which are, as it were, tributary to them, in order to get some presents." In this endeavor, apparently folded into a planned fishing and trading expedition, the Mohawks intended to use Jogues as evidence of "the triumphs of the Hiroquois over even the nations which are in Europe." This initiative may have represented a Mohawk-led effort to secure tribute payments from the lower Hudson River nations to ensure continuing Iroquois noninvolvement in Kieft's War, then raging between those nations and the Dutch settler population of New Netherland.[45]

After completing this mission, Jogues's Mohawk escorts stopped on their return journey to fish on a river twenty miles distant from Fort Orange. There, the Mohawks received news that warriors from Ossernenon had defeated a party of Wendats, killing five or six and returning with four prisoners, two of whom had already been burned. Jogues asked permission of his adoptive aunt to return to go and baptize the Wendat prisoners. She consented, but en route to Ossernenon, Jogues learned that the Mohawks planned to burn him alive as well, to avenge the loss of a Mohawk warrior recently killed by French settlers during a raid on Montreal.[46]

Jogues subsequently headed for Fort Orange, where he learned from local authorities of a ship at Manhattan fitting out for La Rochelle. This news convinced

Jogues to take flight. The fugitive Jesuit hid for two days in the bottom of a ship's hold in the Hudson River opposite Fort Orange, during which time his Mohawk captors undertook a vigorous search of the Dutch outpost, threatening "to burn the houses and kill the cattle and herds" if Jogues was not found. The Dutch finally effected Jogues's ransom by giving the Mohawks "presents to the value of three hundred livres." Jogues received new clothes and a letter of safe conduct from Kieft in Manhattan. He arrived at Brittany (via Falmouth) on December 24, 1643.[47]

During his time at Fort Orange in late June 1643, Jogues had written another letter, which reached the French at Fort Richelieu via another captive Wendat, reportedly now "an Iroquois by affection," who accompanied a Mohawk war party of 100 men. In that letter, written "partly in French, partly in Latin, and partly in the Savage tongue so that if it fell into the hands of someone else than the one to whom it was addressed [Montmagny], he could not easily discover the good counsel which the Father gives us," Jogues provided one of the clearest assessments of contemporary Iroquois objectives to appear in documentary sources. Reflecting on the League's conflict with the Wendats, he stated his belief that the former intended "to take, if they can, all the Hurons, and having put to death the most considerable ones and a good part of the others, to make of them both but one people and only one land."[48]

Much of the evidence concerning Iroquois offensive campaigns during the 1640s derives from Jesuit-authored accounts of the experience of Native groups on the receiving end of League aggression, and as a result the complexities surrounding specific events are often obscured by voluminous missionary rhetoric detailing the impact of Iroquois assaults on nations the Jesuits themselves had targeted for conversion. The Jesuits clearly understood the threat posed to their entire project, then centered in Wendake, by "the fury of a Hiroquois enemy who closes the way [to Wendake] to us, who deprives us of the necessities of life," and "who depopulates the country, and makes our Hurons think of giving up the trade with the French, because they find it costs them too dear, and they prefer to do without European goods rather than expose themselves every year" to the prospect of capture and torture by League nations. Yet despite Jesuit Jerôme Lalemant's 1644 description of the "pitiless" character of the Wendat-Iroquois conflict, one that in his view spared no "age, sex, or condition of persons," there were those who managed to survive and even to thrive in the wake of captive experiences. One of Thérèse Kionhreha's uncles, who escaped from Mohawk captivity in June 1643, reported that she still had all her fingers and could thus recite her rosary (fashioned from pebbles) and pray to the Christian God. A significant number of captive Wendat adult men, as we have seen, also became "Iroquois by affection."[49]

What Jogues had described in 1643 as the Mohawks' desire to make "but one people and only one land" with the Wendats represented a mere glimpse of the League's broader spatial objectives at this time. A French priest, writing in September 1644, noted that the Iroquois continued to employ their Dutch- and English-procured firearms advantage to wage "constant warfare" against New France. For example, Iroquois movements into the St. Lawrence River valley certainly targeted the French settler presence on Montreal Island. An unidentified French prisoner who escaped from the Mohawks in 1643 reported not only that he had been treated well but also that the Mohawks had told him that other French prisoners elsewhere in Iroquoia were "tilling the soil" in their adoptive communities, a clear allusion to Mohawk efforts to assimilate certain captives of European origin. Others, like Jesuit François-Joseph Bressani, who was captured by Mohawks on April 30, 1644, were tortured and then ransomed for "quite dear" sums to the Dutch at Fort Orange. The "edge of the woods," in the eyes of French settlers, represented by 1644 literally a space of terror, where Iroquois war parties "lurked," awaiting the opportunity to emerge from a dark and foreboding landscape to wreak havoc on fledgling settlements. Assaults on New France by Iroquois warriors, whom fearful French settlers came to refer to as "Goblins," continued for the remainder of the year.[50]

Iroquois movements reduced the flow of Native-procured peltry to New France to a trickle by 1644 and pushed the fur trading Compagnie des Cents-Associés toward bankruptcy. In the meantime, the Montreal hospital filled with victims of Iroquois "butcherings," and Iroquois war parties "boasted aloud that they would soon force the French to return across the sea." One Iroquois warrior recalled in 1688 how League war parties had formerly "plyed" New France with such frequency that its settlers were "unable to go over a door to pisse." Montmagny realized that he could no longer sustain a posture of hostility against the Iroquois. An opportunity to open peace negotiations presented itself in late July 1644, when a Wendat captive escaped from a Mohawk war party near Trois-Rivières and, to regain the trust of the Wendats there, offered to lead them to another Mohawk party staking out an ambush near Fort Richelieu. On July 26, 1644, a mixed Wendat and Algonquin war party, using the intelligence supplied by the Wendat escapee, surprised Mohawks "lurking in the woods" near Fort Richelieu, took three prisoners, and brought them back to Trois-Rivières.[51]

Hoping to capitalize on the diplomatic potential these captives represented, Montmagny dispatched Christian Algonquin messengers from Quebec to Trois-Rivières to request a halt to the preliminary torture of the Mohawk prisoners. Echoing Champlain's words of 1622, Montmagny warned the Algonquins and Wendats "that if they went any further it would be the worse for them" since "the whole tranquility of the country" depended on making peace with the League. Upon his arrival at Trois-Rivières, Montmagny endeavored to ransom the Mohawk prisoners from the Algonquins and Wendats with "three huge piles of axes, blankets, kettles, iron arrow-points and other similar articles." This offer convinced the Algonquins to surrender their prisoner to Montmagny. The Wendats proved less compliant, insisting that such a serious matter as the repatriation of the final two Mohawk captives had to be decided by their leaders back in Wendake. Montmagny conceded the Wendats' demand to return home with their two Mohawk captives, but he detailed "more than a score" of soldiers, freshly arrived in New France, to escort the party. Montmagny's decision to expend scarce military resources in this fashion revealed the significance he attached to this endeavor.[52]

PARALLEL MOHAWK INITIATIVES

While the French, Wendats, and Algonquins struggled to find means to conclude peace with the Iroquois League, Mohawk headmen devised a comprehensive plan to introduce elements of the Condolence ceremony into diplomacy with the two settler colonies bordering on Iroquoia. The rhetorical forms employed by Mohawk speaker Kiotsaeton in his 1645 speech at Trois-Rivières have long attracted the interest of anthropologists and literary scholars.[53] Less attention has been paid to the historical context in which this important speech occurred, or to the ways in which Kiotsae-ton's address demonstrated the vitality of Iroquois cultural practices in the wake of epidemic disease-induced population losses after 1634. Far from representing a loss of cultural integrity, the pattern of Mohawk-led League relations with the French and Dutch in 1645 reflected bold, innovative initiatives that applied lessons from the previous century's experience with the assimilation and incorporation of peoples into Iroquois nations (and of those nations into the League itself), and established a comprehensive pattern of outreach to New France and New Netherland after 1645.

On July 12, 1645, Kiotsaeton opened peace negotiations with assembled French, Wendat, and Algonquin delegates in the courtyard of the French fort at Trois-Rivières. Under "large sails . . . spread to keep off the heat of the Sun," Kiotsaeton, on behalf of "all the Iroquois," stated through his interpreter (the adoptee Guillaume Couture), that the League nations sung no longer of war, but only of the prospects of peace. On cue, his accompanying Mohawk delegates began to sing while he "walked about that great space as if on the stage of a theatre; he made a thousand gestures, he looked up to Heaven; he gazed at the Sun, he rubbed his arms as if he wished to draw from them the strength that moved them in war." By a series of "presents," or belts of wampum, Kiotsaeton symbolically cleared the St. Lawrence River, effecting "calm, from Québec to the Iroquois country. . . . With his hands and arms he smoothed and arrested the torrents." Once he had "by his gestures rendered the route easy, he tied a collar of porcelain beads [wampum] on the arm of a Frenchman, and pulled him straight across the square, to show that our canoes could go to their country without any difficulty." Kiotsaeton then "performed the whole journey that [one] had to make on land" in order to reach Trois-Rivières. Armed with an invisible hatchet, he "felled trees . . . lopped off branches . . . pushed back the bushes . . . [and] put earth in the deepest holes" before pronouncing the "road quite smooth and quite straight." Kiotsaeton then informed his audience that there were no more thorns, bushes, "or mounds over which one might stumble in walking," and that now "we can see the

SITE (PLACENAME)

MK-1 OAK HILL #1 (THEONTOUGEN)
MK-2 ALLEN II
MK-3 VAN EVERA-MCKINNEY
MK-4 RUMRILL-NAYLOR
MK-5 YATES II (ONEUGIORÉ)
OE   STONE QUARRY
ON   CARLEY
CY-1 CULLEY'S
CY-2 CRANE BROOK
SE-1 POWER HOUSE
SE-2 MENZIS
SE-3 WARREN
SE-4 CORNISH

Iroquoia, ca. 1645

smoke of our villages from Québec to the extremity of our country. All obstacles are removed." With a clear path for travel and communications established, he invited the French, Wendats, and Algonquins to visit Iroquoia in peace, where they would find hospitable fires lit for them in Iroquois houses, and "good meat" to hunt and eat. Kiotsaeton concluded his address by expressing hope that "we would be but one Nation, and I would be one of you."[54]

Kiotsaeton's July 1645 embassy came about as a result of the French repatriating the Mohawk captive surrendered to Montmagny by the Algonquins in late 1644. This dramatic enactment of Iroquois efforts to forge an alliance with the French has heretofore been interpreted as an isolated event. However, a similar scene was unfolding in Manhattan between Mohawk and Dutch interlocutors. Prior to his arrival at Trois-Rivières, Kiotsaeton had allocated a share of the advance peace presents sent by the French not only to each of the Mohawks' "allies" in the League but also to the Dutch of New Netherland. While Kiotsaeton negotiated with officials in New France, another Mohawk headman named Agheroense (reportedly fluent in Dutch) offered similar terms of peace and alliance to Dutch officials during an August 1645 embassy to Manhattan. Agheroense, with "glittering yellow paint" streaked across his face, brokered with Governor Willem Kieft and the Munsees of the Hudson River valley an end to the bloody war the latter two parties had waged for the previous two years.[55]

Departing from prior patterns of hostility toward New France and its Native allies, Kiotsaeton attempted in his conference at Trois-Rivières to achieve significant objectives on behalf of the League via negotiation and an extension of condolence-based alliance to the French, Wendats, and Algonquins. Yet the degree to which Kiotsaeton emphasized the questioning of his plan even among fellow Mohawks during his address at Trois-Rivières indicated that his efforts were provisional and contingent in character. Nevertheless, by claiming to represent all five nations, Kiotsaeton established a context for future collective League ratification of his preliminary negotiations.[56]

The dual Mohawk diplomatic initiatives of 1645 reflected a clear enactment of ideas embedded in the Iroquois Condolence ceremony. Two clear-minded Mohawk orators undertook journeys to settlements of prospective alliance partners on the periphery of their homelands and articulated for their grieving French, Wendat, Algonquin, Munsee, Mahican, and Dutch listeners the pattern of spatial arrangements upon which they sought to establish peaceful relations. Kiotsaeton's address at Trois-Rivières ordered the space of northeastern North America in terms of Iroquois relational patterns and established the League nations as arbiters of human movement within that space. By locating Iroquoia as central (geographically and metaphorically) and by asserting mutual visibility under a cloudless sky, "so that all might see quite plainly that our hearts and theirs were not hidden, that the Sun and the truth might light up everything," Kiotsaeton's address demonstrated newly articulated Mohawk ideas about how to craft *kaswentha* relations of mutual assistance and noninterference in an increasingly complex context of interactions with Native and settler communities adjoining Iroquois territory.[57]

Kiotsaeton's proposal for an Iroquois peace with New France did not, however, extend to French-allied Native nations. During secret negotiations with Montmagny and the Jesuit Barthelmy Vimont, the Mohawk leader had elicited from the French the right to continue Iroquois offensives against non-Christian Algonquins. Iroquois raids on Wendake also continued unabated through the summer of 1645. Despite sustaining these attacks, a Wendat convoy of sixty canoes arrived at Trois-Rivières after Kiotsae-ton's July 15, 1645, departure. After surrendering one of the two Iroquois prisoners they had taken to Wendake during the previous autumn to Montmagny, the Wendats informed the governor that they had "orders from the whole of their country to enter into full negotiations for peace, and to follow the judgment of Onontio."[58]

The French sent immediate word of the Wendats' statement to Mohawk country, but heard nothing in response until five Mohawk messengers appeared at Trois-Rivières on September 15, 1645. These messengers advised the assembled Wendats, Algonquins, and Montagnais, estimated at 400 in number and then on the verge of "dispers[ing] and scatter[ing]," of Kiotsaeton's return. Two days later, Kiotsaeton, accompanied by three Mohawk "ambassadors" and also by three Wendats placed conspicuously amid the party, announced their presence with a "harangue on the bank of the river, according to their custom." They were then escorted by French troops to the fort. French soldiers, approximating an Edge of the Woods welcome, "formed in two lines and the Iroquois passed through them without being impeded by a large number of persons who gazed at them on all sides."[59]

The ensuing discussions at Trois-Rivières between September 18 and 23, 1645, reflected the prominent and intensely personal role of hostage diplomacy in intercul-tural peace negotiations. Speaking once again through Couture, Kiotsaeton, whose delayed return possibly resulted from his desire to learn the outcome of Agheroense's August 1645 proceedings at Manhattan, promised lavish hospitality in Iroquoia to any French, Wendat, or Algonquin visitors, even assuring his audience that they as "friends and allies" would find "wives" among the Iroquois nations. Kiotsaeton of-fered a mass repatriation of nonadopted Wendat and Algonquin prisoners, whom he claimed were then "seated on logs or stumps of trees" outside of their host villages, "ready to return to their country like the dried trees on which they sat, which have no roots and can be easily removed." Kiotsaeton even offered to exchange Thérèse Kionhreha for the Iroquois woman known to the Jesuits as Anne-Thérèse, whom the Algonquins had captured and "given to the French" in 1636. The Mohawk orator concluded his opening speech by linking one arm with an unidentified Frenchman and the other with an Algonquin and a Wendat, and then dancing while singing in "a loud voice a song of peace."[60]

Responding to Kiotsaeton, a Christian Wendat "Captain" proclaimed that "now we are all relatives, Hiroquois, Hurons, Algonquins, and French; we are now but one and the same people." To demonstrate their commitment to the peace, the Wendats released the second Mohawk captive they had taken in 1644. An unnamed Algonquin speaker then expressed his nation's commitment to the peace, modifying Iroquois *kaswentha* rhetoric in his statement that all parties would thereafter "sail in the same ship or in the same canoe, so that we shall be but one people, but one village, one house, one Calumet, and one canoe will be needed." Finally, Montmagny offered the Mohawks condolence presents for Anne-Thérèse, admitting that she had long since died in France. The governor assured Kiotsaeton, however, that there would be "a road from your villages to ours," before he proceeded to remove (symbolically) all hatchets from the hands of Iroquois warriors, to silence "the reports of their arque-buses," to wash the paint from the faces of their warriors, and to break the "kettle they used to boil Huron and Algonquin captives."[61]

Although dismissed by one contemporary French chronicler as another "patched-up," meaningless set of peace negotiations, evidence suggests that Kiotsaeton took the preliminary agreements seriously. Kiotsaeton's party departed on September 23, 1645, with two Frenchmen, two Algonquins, and two Wendats, while leaving three Mohawks behind among their new Native allies at Trois-Rivières "as pledges of their friendship." Five more Mohawks reportedly spent the winter of 1645–46 with Montagnais and Algonquin hosts, and the fur trade of New France recovered once the Iroquois lifted their effective blockade of indigenous traffic to and from the St. Lawrence valley. Upon arriving in Mohawk country in October 1645, a national council of Mohawk "principal persons having assembled from various places" ratified Kiotsaeton's preliminary negotiations, stating that the Mohawks "had no more arms except for the chase."[62]

Although the Mohawks had come to terms with the Wendats and Algonquins in 1645 as a result of Kiotsaeton's efforts, the other League nations had not yet agreed to this initiative, and thus they did not consider themselves bound by Mohawk-nego-tiated terms in lieu of broader League discussion and ratification. "Upper Iroquois" (Oneida, Onondaga, Cayuga, and Seneca) incursions into Wendake continued over the winter of 1645–46, and the Wendats responded in kind with direct attacks on Seneca towns. The Oneidas also sent warriors to raid in the vicinity of Montreal dur-ing the autumn of 1645. Sokoki efforts to incite the Mohawks against the Algonquins and Montagnais also threatened the nascent peace agreement, yet the Mohawks held firm throughout the winter of 1645–46. Jesuits described Montreal as literally a Mo-hawk "frontier" at that time. Their writings documented many Mohawks traveling to the island to participate in Algonquin-hosted hunts of locally abundant game animals, in a possible reflection of mutually recognized ancestral ties among descendants of the sixteenth-century residents of Hochelaga.[63]

Kiotsaeton returned to Trois-Rivières on May 7, 1646, with the two Wendat emis-saries who had accompanied him to Mohawk country in September 1645 to renew and confirm the previous year's peace. Forced to acknowledge the lack of consensus among the League nations toward his peace initiative, the Mohawk leader warned the Wendats and Algonquins "to be on their guard in the roads, until the upper Iroquois—the Onontagueronons, the Sonontweronons, and some others, should have their ears pierced—that is to say, [they were not yet] open to the benignity of peace." In the meantime, Kiotsaeton pressed on with his effort to secure peaceful Iroquois ac-cess to Trois-Rivières, an important node of trade and indigenous communications.[64]

Kiotsaeton offered local French officials a gift of wampum to kindle a council fire at Trois-Rivières, followed by "a great necklace of three thousand beads to serve as wood, or fuel for this fire." This burning fire, he claimed, would light tobacco for councils, and transform Trois-Rivières into a place "suitable for assembling . . . as do relatives and friends." The French, for their part, pledged to keep the council fire lit at Trois-Rivières and stated that the Mohawks "would always be welcome, and that hearing would be given to Captains who come to treat of affairs." Kiotsaeton concluded by informing the Wendats and Algonquins that they could still come to Iroquoia "to ask after their daughters and kinswomen who were held captive," but he advised these nations to repatriate all of their Iroquois prisoners to their nations of origin, which would facilitate the conclusion of a "universal peace."[65]

French officials hoping to advance League ratification of Kiotsaeton's preliminary accord sent former Mohawk captive Isaac Jogues to Mohawk country on May 18, 1646. In canoes "laden with gifts . . . for the confirmation of the peace," and paddled by a four-man Mohawk escort, Jogues and Jean Bourdon, the "engineer of New France," reached Fort Orange on June 4 and spent the next two days seeking assistance in carrying their baggage to Mohawk country. With Mohawk porters carrying their load of French gifts, Jogues and Bourdon reached the "first small village," known as "Oneugiouré, formerly Osserrion" (the easternmost, Mohawk Turtle clan town), on June 7, 1646.[66]

Despite the positive overtones of the unprecedented French embassy to Iroquoia, Jogues and Bourdon's visit to Oneugiouré proved a disaster. Jogues opened his June 10, 1646, public address in promising fashion by formalizing arrangements with the Mohawk Wolf clan, "one of the great families of the Annieronon [the Mohawk Wolf clan, a possible indication of Kiotsaeton's affiliation] scattered through their three villages, in order to keep a fire always lighted when the French should come to visit them." Yet Jogues then proceeded to make three significant breaches of protocol. First, he requested the repatriation of captive Wendat Thérèse Kionhreha, despite having learned in a serendipitous conversation with her at a fishing camp a few days previously that she had been "given in marriage" by her Mohawk captors to an Onondaga family. Next, he offered 2,000 "Porcelain beads" to some Onondagas attending, in hope that the gift would purchase direct French access to Onondaga country. Finally, Jogues announced to an audience of the League's eastern doorkeepers that the French knew of two additional routes to Iroquoia in addition to the "road through the Annieronons" (Mohawks): one "by the great lake which they name Ontario" and another through Wendake.[67]

A number of senior Mohawk headmen "were not too well pleased that Jogues should exhibit such knowledge of the country, or with the intention of the French to visit" the Onondagas, and they reminded Jogues that the terms of Kiotsaeton's preliminary peace agreement limited the French to "the road which Onontio has opened" to Mohawk country. All other means of access, they continued, were "too dangerous; one meets in them only people of war, men with painted and figured

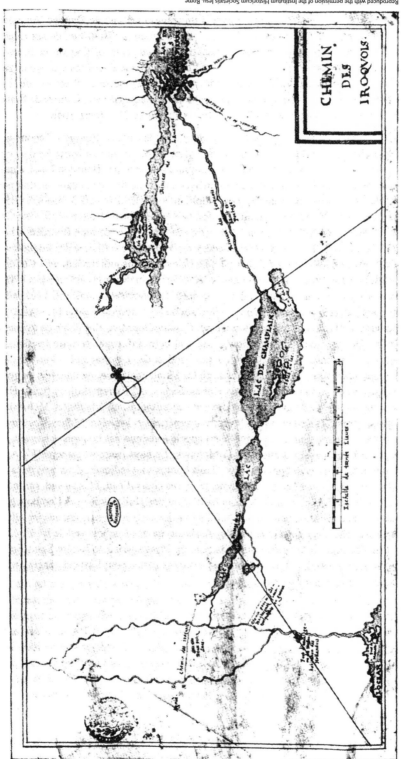

Jogues, "Chemin des Iroquois," 1646

faces, with clubs and war hatchets, who seek only to kill." French travel through the League's eastern door, on the other hand, "was now excellent, entirely cleared, and very secure." Oblivious to these clear recommendations to observe League spatial protocols, which at that time assigned the Mohawks primary responsibility for Iroquois relations with New France, Jogues averred that French authorities did not want to depend on the Mohawks "in order to go up to the nations above." He then berated his former captors for the "shame and disgrace" of letting other Iroquois nations "pass through [their] territory to murder at will anyone they meet," and he pointed out that they would be "blamed for all the thefts and murders" committed by their League allies on French settlers and French-allied Native nations. The offended Mohawks "pressed" Jogues and Bourdon to "hasten their departure" following the Jesuit's outburst, and offered an ominous warning for the French to avoid on their return journey an "upper Iroquois" war party then returning from a raid in the St. Lawrence valley.[68]

Jogues returned to Quebec on July 3, 1646, with Bourdon and, significantly, "a tolerably accurate [sketch] map" of the route from Trois-Rivières to Mohawk country. The two maps Bourdon later produced from this sketch represented a substantial improvement in French reconnaissance of Iroquoia over a 1641 map that had been drawn with the assistance of returned Mohawk captives Godefroy and Marguerie. Considered in tandem with the first accurate spatial delineations of the five League nations recorded in 1640 by Jesuit Jerôme Lalemant and by French medical doctor François Gendron during the winter of 1644–45 (the latter likely obtained from a Neutral visitor to the Jesuit hospital at the Ste. Marie mission in Wendake), the French, after four decades of direct contact with the Mohawks, had acquired a reasonably accurate sense of the nature and geographic extent of the Iroquois polity. Canadian officials would later employ Bourdon's 1646 maps in efforts to assert French suzerainty over Iroquoia.[69]

Jogues's open disregard for Iroquois spatial protocol, however, destroyed the fragile peace of 1645. Historian Benjamin Schmidt has identified early modern mapping as an intellectual weapon: "lands could be sketched, sovereignty staked, and ambitions articulated." Mohawks certainly shared such an understanding of spatial knowledge, and their perception of Jogues's underlying motives in reconnoitering Iroquoia, like those attributed to Cherououony in 1627, ultimately cost him his life.[70]

Jogues, despite claimed premonitions of his own death, set out for Mohawk country once more in late September 1646, accompanied by the *donné* Jean La Lande, one *"Otrih8re, huron yroquoisé"* (i.e., Otreouti, a Wendat adoptee who would later become an influential Onondaga leader), and two or three other Wendats "who were going to see their captive relatives." Abandoned by all their Wendat escorts but Otreouti en route, Jogues and Lalande reached Oneugiouré on October 17, 1646. The local Mohawks formed a gauntlet, beating and stripping the two Frenchmen upon their arrival. The next day a member of the Mohawk Bear clan plunged a hatchet into the back of Jogues's head. Other Bear clan Mohawks killed Lalande in similar fashion on October 19. The Mohawks then impaled the two men's severed heads on Oneugiouré's palisade "as a warning to the French" that war had resumed.[71]

ROBBERS MORE CRUEL THAN
ALL THE PIRATES OF THE SEA

After five years of struggling to reach consensus on Mohawk-proposed terms of peace with New France, the League nations encountered little difficulty in agreeing to resume hostilities in the aftermath of Jogues's two embassies to Mohawk country. In addition to targeting New France directly, however, the Iroquois also launched an unprecedented wave of offensives against the Wendats. In doing so, they demonstrated not only the dramatic range of free movement they enjoyed but also their determination to deny the French all access to the trade and human capital of the Native nations residing in the upper Great Lakes. The League's attempt to assimilate Wendake after 1648 inaugurated patterns of conflict that would reverberate for the remainder of the century.

As reports of Jogues's death trickled back to New France, the French learned that the Mohawks had "sent presents to the Hiroquois of the upper country in order to strongly confirm their alliances" just prior to murdering the Jesuit and his assistant. Immediately after the killings, the Mohawks resumed hostile movements along "their former routes," blockading the "approaches" used by the Wendats and Algonquins to reach New France and spreading "themselves about in various places, in order to capture, kill, and massacre as many French, Algonquins, and Wendats as they could." From November 1646 through November 1647, Algonquins and Wendats in the St. Lawrence valley faced unrelenting assaults from Iroquois war parties seeking captives and peltry. After burning the abandoned Fort Richelieu to the ground early in 1647, Iroquois war parties also moved unhindered into New France, where they terrorized the colony's 300 French settlers by firing musket volleys from concealed positions, robbing their homes, and "perpetrat[ing] such tricks [as] acting [as] escaped prisoners" near French settlements "in order to attract and massacre those who should go to seek them."[72]

Mohawks who had spent the winter of 1645–46 hunting with the Algonquins in the St. Lawrence valley accompanied these war parties, "and knowing every turn and byway, came to surprise [the latter] in their hunting." One group of Mohawks employed this newly acquired geographic knowledge to locate and kill Pieskaret, a longtime Algonquin nemesis, in March 1647. In another incident, Pierre Achkameg, a Mohawk captured by the Algonquins as a young boy with his brother (and later retaken by the Mohawks), led a March 5, 1647, attack on an Algonquin hunting camp, inadvertently killing his brother (who was still living with the Algonquins) in the process. Still other Iroquois war parties employed interrogations of freshly taken captives to locate Algonquin women and children (encamped in the bush while the men hunted), enabling them to "seize persons and baggage" en masse. According to an Algonquin woman escapee, Iroquois captors "soon married" their young Algonquin women captives, reflecting apparent Iroquois concern for their adoptees' reproductive potential in the postepidemic era.[73]

Captives proved useful to the Iroquois in other military contexts as well. In early June 1647, Jesuits learned of a Wendat man "taken some years ago by the Hiroquois" and now a "captain of these robbers," leading Iroquois war parties to Wendat points of reconnaissance on their canoe route to New France, where they collected together to form convoys. This "he did the more easily, because he had a thorough knowledge of all those regions." In this particular instance, the appearance of the Iroquois led the Wendats to abandon their peltry and flee. The Iroquois, "dazzled by the great number of beavers" left behind by the Wendats, consequently elected to load their canoes with plunder rather than to offer pursuit.[74]

Although this group of Wendat traders escaped with their lives, the Iroquois managed to prevent any more Wendat fur convoys from reaching New France in 1647. Described by the Jesuit Paul Ragueneau as "robbers more cruel than all the Pirates of the sea," all five League nations participated in ambushes of Wendats en route to New France. The Iroquois also launched direct assaults into Wendake and Neutralia in 1647, employing as guides individuals like Soionés, "a Huron by birth, but who had become so naturalized among the [Iroquois] enemies for many years that no Hiroquois had committed more massacres in [Wendake], nor struck more evil blows than he."[75]

Confronting escalated Iroquois hostilities, a Wendat embassy under Christian leader Charles Ondaaiondiont tried to recruit defensive assistance from their long-time Susquehannock allies, and in June 1647 employed Susquehannock brokerage to forge economic ties to Fort Christina, the Swedish trading post on the Delaware River. The Ahrendahronon Wendats, however, attempted to initiate separate peace negotiations with the Onondagas, "one of the five Hiroquois nations that hitherto has most harassed this country," by releasing a captive Onondaga headman named Annenraes. Annenraes had convinced the Ahrendahronons that his influence in Onondaga country could bring about not only the repatriation of numerous Ahrendahronons in Onondaga country but also the extension of peace to the Cayugas and Oneidas, leaving the Wendats to contend with only the Mohawks and Senecas. Unfortunately for the Ahrendahronons, the subsequent Wendat peace embassy fell victim to a Mohawk ambush in April 1648 and never reached Onondaga country.[76]

Three years after Kiotsaeton's peace negotiations, the posture of the League nations toward the Wendats had undergone a near-complete reversal. In 1648, three of the formerly hostile upper nations (excluding the Senecas) sought peace, while the Mohawks, who in 1647 had suffered through "a great malady" that caused significant reported losses, were the most "averse" of all to the idea. From July 1648 to December 1649, the Mohawks and Senecas led a series of massive Iroquois assaults on Wendake. Distraught Jesuit observers, witnessing the elimination of their showpiece missionary project in North America, routinely depicted these Iroquois attacks as causing the destruction of the Wendat nation. Subsequent historians have generally followed the Jesuits' interpretation, while debating the relative primacy of economic or demographic motivations on the part of Iroquois aggressors. But closer examination of the documentary evidence reveals that the campaign against Wendake actually resembled the final phases of a "civil war," insofar as the two combatants were by no means completely distinct ethnic groups ante bellum. Contemporary French observers found the nature and scale of these attacks unprecedented, but they certainly originated in and may not have differed greatly in character from the sixteenth-century campaigns that resulted in the large-scale integration of peoples from the St. Lawrence River valley into the Iroquois polity.[77]

The campaigns of 1648 and 1649 demonstrated, however, the most dramatic representation to date of the enhanced spatial range of Iroquois war parties carrying an ever-growing number of firearms. A contemporary Dutch observer described the Iroquois as "exceedingly fond" of guns, "sparing no expense for them, and are so skilful in the use of them that they surpass many Christians." Documentary and archaeological evidence attests to the extensive integration of firearms into the Iroquois military complex by the mid-seventeenth century. Dutch traders ignored official restrictions on trading firearms and carried large cargoes of arms and ammunition directly into Mohawk country to exchange for Iroquois-procured beaver pelts. The Mohawks, who had 400 warriors to equip in 1647, also obtained firearms, ammunition, and teams of horses to haul timber for reinforcement of their towns' palisades in exchange for permitting the Dutch to reside at Rensselaerswyck, land they claimed to have recently "gained from the Mahikanders with the sword." To reinforce their point, Mohawk parties commandeered the "patroon's house" on a regular basis from 1648 to 1650 in order to collect gifts of Dutch military stores and tribute payments from "subsidiary" Native peoples. These military supplies facilitated Iroquois campaigns that targeted Christian Wendat communities in much the same manner and for the same reasons underlying Iroquois offensives against Christian Native enclaves in the St. Lawrence valley during the previous decade.[78]

At dawn on July 4, 1648, the air surrounding the Attigneenongnahac Wendat village of Teanaustayé "resounded" with "the noise of muskets." Following this deafening initial volley, Iroquois warriors "scaled the rampart" of the town, one of the five Wendat communities then hosting a Jesuit mission, and fired its palisade and structures with burning torches. During the assault, Iroquois warriors also shot Jesuit Antoine Daniel and hurled his corpse into the burning village chapel. The Iroquois attack resulted in an estimated 700 of the 2,000 residents of Teanaustayé "killed or captured," with women and children constituting the bulk of the captives.[79]

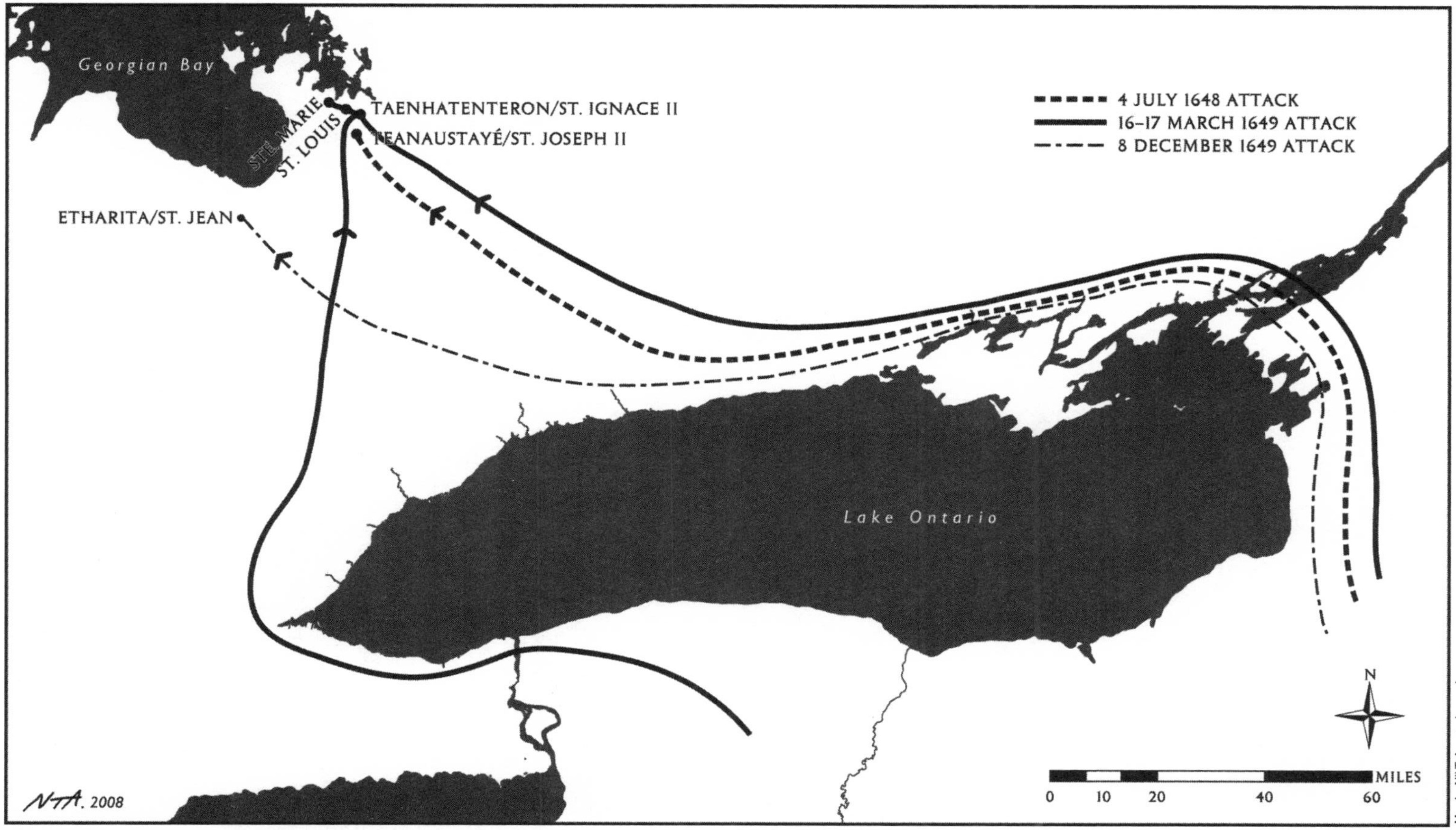

Georgian Bay
STE. MARIE
ST. LOUIS
TAENHATENTERON/ST. IGNACE II
TEANAUSTAYÉ/ST. JOSEPH II
ETHARITA/ST. JEAN
4 JULY 1648 ATTACK
16–17 MARCH 1649 ATTACK
8 DECEMBER 1649 ATTACK
Lake Ontario
N
0 10 20 40 60 MILES
NTA. 2008
Map by Nij T. Anantsuksomsri

Iroquois Campaigns Against Wendake, 1648–1650

The Iroquois followed up this initial mass assault by assembling an army of 1,200 men, including numerous "wretched Huron renegade[s]." Departing Iroquoia in the autumn of 1648, members of this force ("most" of whom carried firearms) proceeded deliberately to Wendake, hunting en route for several months until they reached the Attignawantan Wendat village of Taenhatenteron, home of the St. Ignace II Jesuit mission. At dawn on March 16, 1649, the Iroquois used iron hatchets to hack holes in Taenhatenteron's palisade, into which they slid their musket barrels and opened fire. The attackers carried the village, killing or capturing an estimated 400 Wendats. The Iroquois army then marched approximately four miles to the Ataronchonon Wendat community hosting the mission of St. Louis, where they once again employed their hatchets to create "considerable breaches" in the palisade prior to overcoming the eighty Wendat defenders who remained in the town.[80]

Jesuit eyewitnesses of these attacks described the prominent roles played by "Huron Infidels, former captives of the Iroquois, naturalized among them, and former enemies of the faith" in the ensuing dramatic torture and execution of their colleagues Jean de Brébeuf and Gabriel Lalemant at Taenhatenteron. Smoke arising from burning bodies and longhouses at St. Louis alerted a number of Wendat warriors assembled at the Ataronchronon mission village of Ste. Marie to the approaching Iroquois army. On March 17, 1649, the Iroquois attacked and dispersed the Wendats from Ste. Marie, sustaining nearly 100 of their own casualties in the process. Two days later, the entire Iroquois force began its withdrawal, "driving forth in haste a part of their captives, who were burdened above their strength, like packhorses, with the spoils the victorious were carrying off." The Iroquois bound Wendats deemed unfit for the return journey to stakes in longhouses, then set the structures ablaze before departing. Surviving Wendats fled en masse to Christian Island in Georgian Bay on March 21, 1649, and the remaining Jesuit and French population joined them there after burning the ruins of Ste. Marie on May 15, 1649.[81]

The final large-scale Iroquois incursion into Wendake occurred on December 7–8, 1649, when a force of 300 Iroquois warriors attacked Etharita, the Tionnontaté town hosting the Jesuit mission of St. Jean. This settlement housed an estimated 500 to 600 Tionnontaté families while also providing refuge for an unknown (but substantial) number of recently displaced Wendats. Jesuits Charles Garnier and Noel Chabanel died in this attack, although the Tionnontatés may have killed Chabanel. Once more, the Iroquois force took numerous captives, but to facilitate their retreat they "put to death" all individuals "they deemed unable to keep up with them in their flight." It was perhaps the memory of Iroquois campaigns against the Wendats that prompted an Onondaga leader named Teganissorens to distinguish League military practices from those of neighboring "Christians," who repatriated prisoners at the conclusion of wars and thus forfeited their capacity to "rout" their opponents. When the Iroquois declared war against an enemy nation, according to Teganissorens, they endeavored "to destroy them utterly."[82]

By moving outward in multiple directions, constantly expanding the "Edge" of Iroquoia's "Woods," or the League's horizons of interaction with Native and non-Native peoples, from 1634 to 1649, the five Iroquois nations not only engineered the beginnings of a demographic recovery following their initial exposure to epidemic disease, but they also strengthened the collective identity of the Iroquois polity. Effective League function derived from the symbiotic relationship between centrifugal everyday movements and centripetal cosmological consciousness, which facilitated the establishment and maintenance of a dynamic, expanding Iroquoia. In lieu of the formal, joint establishment of *kaswentha* relations with the Dutch and French (despite renewed attempts by Oneidas in 1635 and a complex, jointly negotiated effort by Mohawks a decade later), the Iroquois opted, beginning with the Wendats in 1648–49, to "requicken" themselves by means of a dramatic extension of mourning-war practices.

3.

REQUICKENING
1650–1666

> The lands of which they are masters stretch out as far as they
> want. . . . They are always in extensive communication with one
> another. When it is a question of carrying some news from one
> village to another, they have only to make a command and im-
> mediately they are obeyed.
>
> —RÉNÉ CUILLERIER, A FRENCH CAPTIVE OF THE ONEIDAS,
> WRITING CIRCA 1662

On November 5, 1655, Onondaga headman Gonaterezon greeted Jesuits
Pierre-Joseph-Marie Chaumonot and Claude Dablon three miles distant
from the newly established principal Onondaga town. Gonaterezon escorted the missionaries to the edge of the town's cleared fields, where the "Elders
of the country awaited" their arrival. After a meal of "some Squashes cooked in the
embers," an Onondaga "Captain" named Okonchiarennen arose, imposed silence, and
delivered a fifteen-minute "harangue" that welcomed the Jesuits and expressed the
Onondagas' desire for peace with New France. Then the Onondaga leaders "arose,
gave the signal, and led us through a great crowd of people, some of whom were
drawn up in rows to see us pass through their midst, while others ran after us."
Passing through the symbolic Edge of the Woods into Onondaga, Dablon noted the
"carefully-cleaned" streets and the children "crowded" on longhouse rooftops to witness their procession to a "large cabin which had been prepared for us."[1]

Chaumonot and Dablon had undertaken their unusual autumn journey to Onondaga country to discuss the founding of a Jesuit mission in Iroquoia. While the
Jesuits viewed this conversation as evidence of their growing influence among the
Iroquois, the Onondagas had other ideas in mind: namely the role such a "mission"
would play in effecting the relocation of several hundred refugee Wendats to Onondaga country from the French-sponsored refugee settlement established on the
Isle d'Orléans opposite Quebec in August 1650. Reintegrating Wendat populations

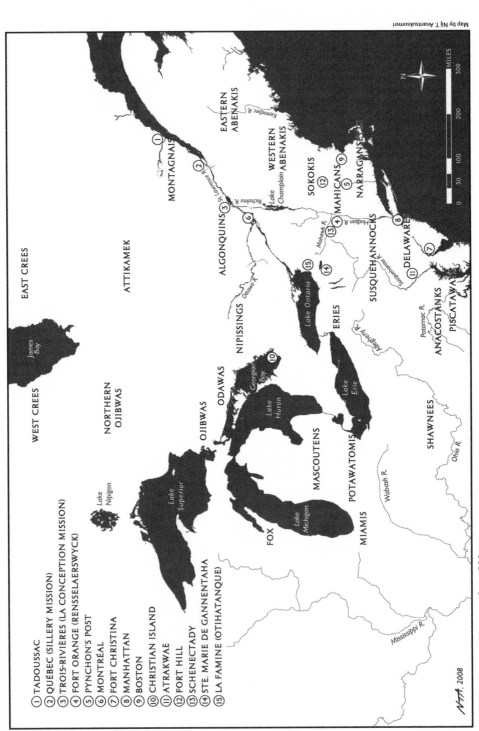

① TADOUSSAC
② QUÉBEC (SILLERY MISSION)
③ TROIS-RIVIÈRES (LA CONCEPTION MISSION)
④ FORT ORANGE (RENSSELAERSWYCK)
⑤ PYNCHON'S POST
⑥ MONTRÉAL
⑦ FORT CHRISTINA
⑧ MANHATTAN
⑨ BOSTON
⑩ CHRISTIAN ISLAND
⑪ ATRAKWAE
⑫ FORT HILL
⑬ SCHENECTADY
⑭ STE. MARIE DE GANNENTAHA
⑮ LA FAMINE (OTIHATANQUE)

N̄ṯṯ·A 2008

Iroquois Places of Interest, 1650–1666

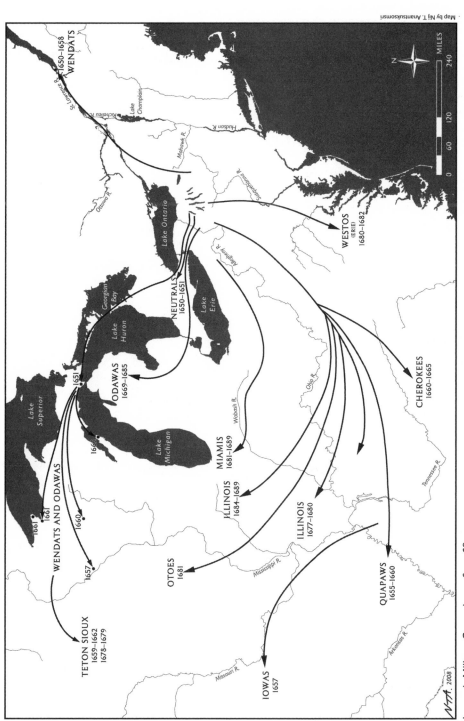

Iroquois Military Campaigns, 1650–1689

Map by Nij T. Anantsuksomsri

into their own nation embodied the Onondagas' novel approach to "requickening" the League in the aftermath of population losses stemming from epidemic disease outbreaks after 1634.[2]

Iroquois military campaigns in the wake of the League's large-scale assault on Wendake had far-reaching implications in northeastern North America during the middle decades of the seventeenth century. At a time when all indigenous nations and settler colonies in this region were seeking to build effective alliances to ensure reliable trading relationships and mutual defense against potential rivals, Iroquois nations played pivotal roles in shaping the evolving patterns of international diplomacy. Put another way, the Iroquois might best be regarded as one of the key "straws that stirred the drink" at this time. The French struggled to retain their ties to the Wendats and Algonquian peoples of the St. Lawrence valley and encountered even more opposition from the Iroquois as the Jesuits and Canadian traders began to turn their attention to the Algonquians of the upper Great Lakes. Anglo-American officials up and down the Atlantic seaboard found themselves dealing with the reverberations of a variety of Iroquois initiatives and labored to find common cause transcending the boundaries of their individual colonies. The Dutch clung to their ties to the Mohawks and the Algonquians of the Lower Hudson valley while confronting increasing aggression from their English neighbors. Of all the nations actively engaged in the contest for survival in the Northeast from 1650 to 1666, the Iroquois proved most adept at mobilizing their human and spatial resources to that end.

An Engine of Destruction?

From 1649 until the last decade of the seventeenth century, focused Iroquois military and diplomatic operations brought at least 1,600 and possibly as many as 2,800 Wendat adoptees into Iroquoia.[3] The League nations' pursuit of Wendat refugees throughout Neutral homelands, the St. Lawrence valley, and the upper Great Lakes and Ohio valley, and even in Susquehannock country, spawned successive Iroquois movements that dramatically enhanced the Five Nations' access to diverse new peoples and places over a vast extent of eastern North America. Standard accounts of these events depict the League as undertaking a "rampage" against "virtually every Indian people in the Northeast." The Five Nations, in the view of many historians, represented a malevolent force that wantonly "shattered" other indigenous nations in the interests of access to beaver-hunting grounds and of securing captives for ritual torture and execution.[4]

While these motives were not absent from Iroquois movements after 1650, such a limited view of Iroquois objectives overlooks the roots of these conflicts, which dated back to the sixteenth-century wars involving the Wendats in northeastern North America; as a result, it fails to comprehend the significance and complexity underlying Iroquois movements. Seeking to recover from substantial population losses, the Five Nations embarked on innovative efforts to "requicken" the League, to create it anew in an increasingly multifaceted and complex landscape of settler colonies and other indigenous peoples. One way to requicken the League was to adopt Wendats (a significant number of whom descended from Laurentian Iroquois people dispersed from the St. Lawrence valley during the sixteenth century). Incorporating Wendats had the potential to swell Iroquois numbers. Wendat women adopted into League nations were especially valued for their role in repopulating Iroquois clan segments and communities; Wendat men represented potential warriors.[5]

The adoption of the Wendat people also carried special significance to the various members of the protean Iroquois League. While the five League nations were certainly tied together by alliances on many cultural levels, there was still room for constituent nations to shape the patterns of association in the "extended lodge." To be able to claim the honor of requickening one's nation by integrating an ancestral people into the Iroquois fold held a strong symbolic power—beyond the mere demographic potential the Wendat people held. Intense competition arose between the Mohawks and Onondagas to requicken the League in the spirit of the Condolence ceremony after 1650, and this rivalry accounts for much of the evident determination of the Iroquois to complete the assimilation of Wendake during the seventeenth century.

The situation was further complicated by the interest of the French in the Wendats. As the indigenous people among whom the Jesuits had found the most receptive audience to date, the French felt strongly about protecting the Wendats and even perhaps using them as a springboard to gain access to other indigenous nations. The Wendats were seen as crucial to the future of the Jesuit mission in New France. The post-1650 conflicts surrounding the Wendats were thus not simply a matter of one people brutally "shattering" another; the battle for the Wendats held crucial symbolic meaning for members of the Five Nations and the French alike.

Iroquois pursuit of the Wendats after 1649 focused on the St. Lawrence valley and witnessed increasingly diverse, often highly personal interactions among the indigenous people caught up in these events. During the spring of 1650, for example, one Wendat warrior abandoned an Algonquin war party, exposed the party's position to an approaching Iroquois war party, and joined in the latter's successful ambush. This "Uncoverer" hoped to earn a return trip to Iroquoia, where his "relatives and compatriots" were becoming "one people" with their Five Nations hosts. On November 22, 1650, seventeen Mohawks in three canoes captured seven Wendats in sight of French settlers at Montreal. One of these captives was Otreouti, the Wendat adoptee who had escorted Jogues to his death in Mohawk country in September 1646.[6]

Iroquois campaigns in the St. Lawrence valley during the winter of 1650–51 brought captives and material rewards to Iroquoia. Peltry plundered by the Iroquois in these raids offered an unprecedented impetus for Dutch traders to go "roaming through the Mohawk country," where Mohawks reportedly paid premium prices in beaver in exchange for Dutch goods carried to their towns. Additionally, ransoming French captives at Fort Orange continued to provide a valuable economic sideline for some Iroquois warriors.[7]

In addition to these campaigns to the north, the Iroquois also commenced attacks on Neutral settlements straddling the Niagara River during the winter of 1650–51. These offensives netted "exceedingly large" numbers of captives, among whom were members (or descendants) of sixteen other Native nations then reportedly living as adoptees in Neutral towns.[8] Prominent among these Neutral adoptees were a number of individuals from the so-called Fire Nation (likely Mascoutens or Potawatomis) who had recently been captured by Neutral warriors during their own mourning wars in the upper Great Lakes from 1641 to 1643.[9]

The most significant demographic result of the League's war against the Neutrals followed the destruction of the principal Neutral settlement near modern-day Hamilton, Ontario by a 1,200-man Iroquois army early in 1651. This event convinced at least 600 Tahontaenrat Wendats, who had been living as refugees among the Neutrals since 1649, to negotiate a mass relocation to Seneca country. Many of these Wendat refugees took up residency in a newly founded Seneca satellite town known as Gandougourae, where they soon achieved renown throughout Iroquoia for their effective curing rituals. Saouandanoncoua, the Seneca warrior so avidly tortured and consumed by the Tahontaenrats in 1636, had been requickened with interest.[10]

Following the dispersal of the Wendats and Neutrals, the Mohawks, seeking, as one French observer phrased it, "other bones to gnaw," led a 1,000-man multinational Iroquois army against the heavily fortified hilltop Susquehannock settlement of Atrakwae during the winter of 1651–52. Undeterred by the size and defenses of the Susquehannocks' fort, which one archaeologist has described as "one of the largest and most densely populated Indian communities yet found" in northeastern North America, the Iroquois raiders secured a reported 500 or 600 Susquehannock captives (among whom were likely some refugee Wendats) at the expense of 130 Iroquois casualties. Significant numbers of Mohawk and Seneca warriors cooperated in further attacks on the Susquehannocks during the following three years.[11]

The escalation of League militancy after 1650 made the residents of the three settler colonies bordering Iroquoia nervous enough to pursue unprecedented transnational diplomacy. Officials in New France, whose settler population was then less than half that of New Netherland, continued to court a number of Algonquian tribes residing between New France and New England (specifically the Sokokis, Pocumtucks, Pennacooks, Mahicans, and Abenakis) as allies against the Iroquois, whom they described as "the plague of the country, the scourge of the human race and of the Christian faith." Yet the French also appealed to the United Colonies of New England, sending Jesuit Gabriel Druillettes to Boston in December 1650 to request English aid against the Iroquois in exchange for free trade arrangements first proposed by the

United Colonies in 1649. The Anglo-American commissioners, who recalled the Mohawks' behavior during the Pequot war, ultimately refused Druillettes's offer. Dutch authorities had also approached the United Colonies regarding a defensive alliance in November 1650 in hopes of reducing what the former regarded as "the insolence of the Mohawks." Although the commissioners of the United Colonies shared Dutch apprehensions of the potential threat posed by the well-armed Five Nations, no agreement could be reached.[12]

In the wake of these failed settler diplomatic initiatives, Iroquois assaults on Wendat refugees, French settlers, and Algonquian nations in the St. Lawrence valley continued from April 1651 to June 1653. Despite reported efforts of the newly arrived Tahontaenrats in autumn 1651 to encourage their Seneca hosts to abandon Mohawk-inspired aggression and make peace with the French and restore trading relations, Iroquois war parties "lurked in the woods" near Trois-Rivières throughout the winter of 1651–52, cycling parties of men back and forth to their home towns for supplies and returning with reinforcements in order to maintain constant pressure on their intended targets.[13]

Jesuit François Le Mercier described in 1652 the terror inspired by the Iroquois "continually laying ambuscades, and holding our French so closely besieged that no one ventured on a ramble, to even the least distance, without manifest danger of losing his life." One female Montreal resident managed to survive an early 1651 Iroquois attack by grabbing hold of her assailant's genitalia, which permitted her to escape, albeit with a severe clubbing sustained while her compromised would-be captor sought his own release. Other settlers, however, were neither as resourceful nor fortunate. Iroquois raids on Montreal and Trois-Rivières from March to October 1652 left behind so many "fragments of human bodies" that the remains became food for the town's dogs. French fears of "wanton [Iroquois] rascals abound[ing] everywhere, and at all times" were well-founded. Although the French retaliated against Iroquois attackers, Sulpician historian François Dollier de Casson understood that the demographic superiority of the League nations meant that the League "always had men to replace those they lost in fighting."[14]

Was Iroquois behavior as "wanton" as the French believed? The League continued efforts to assimilate French captives deemed suitable for adoption. The experience of Pierre Esprit Radisson in Mohawk country represents a noteworthy example of this phenomenon. Captured in April 1651, Radisson became the adopted "brother" of his Mohawk captor. His adoptive "mother" (herself a Wendat adoptee who had borne nine children to her Mohawk husband) encouraged Radisson to make himself "more familiar with her daughters," an offer he claimed to have declined. Radisson's Mohawk family lavished considerable attention and mercy on him (even forgiving an early escape attempt), and for at least a brief time before his departure from Mohawk country in 1653, the prisoner thought of himself as no longer "Asserony, a French," but "Ganugaga [Kanienkehaka], that is, of their nation."[15]

While Radisson's case demonstrated the willingness of certain Iroquois communities to incorporate select non-Native prisoners, securing Wendat refugees remained the top priority for League offensives into the St. Lawrence River valley during the early 1650s. French commentators remarked on how Iroquois "wretches" would "hide in the woods, behind tree trunks, or in holes which they make in the ground, where they pass two and three days sometimes without eating, in order to lie in wait and surprise their [Wendat] prey," as one group did in May 1652 before capturing two Wendat women and a young boy. Other Iroquois, after ambushing a "Squad of Hurons" near Trois-Rivières and burning its leader alive in May 1652, offered the surviving Wendat captives their lives, employing this means to "swell their troops."[16]

Although each of the Five Nations pursued Wendat and other adoptees during the early 1650s, League authorities had yet to engage in any collaborative planning of appropriate means to this mutually desired end. Individual nations were therefore free to attempt independent initiatives, and, given the high desirability of Wendat adoptees, internal Iroquois conflicts developed. An Onondaga party approached Montreal in June 1653 with the intent of procuring refugee Wendats through peaceful means. Employing an Attignawantan Wendat adoptee as an interpreter, the Onondagas urged the French to make "careful distinction" between their behavior and that of the Mohawks, who, they claimed, kept "deep in their breast, their rancor and bitterness of heart, while their tongues are uttering fair words." Following this brief exchange at Montreal, the Onondaga embassy traveled downriver to the Isle d'Orléans, where they held an "assembly" with the French and Wendats at the refugee Wendat village, offering condolence presents and expressing their ardent desire for peace.[17]

Two months later, the implications of the Onondagas' subtle warning became clear when a Mohawk-led army of 500 Iroquois warriors advanced on Trois-Rivières, seeking to avenge a French-sanctioned Wendat execution of a Mohawk headman at that town in 1652. The Iroquois commenced their siege of Trois-Rivières on August 23, 1653. After one day of destroying French crops, killing settlers' livestock, and burning carts and plows abandoned in fields, the attackers were approached by a group of Wendats then residing nearby and "eager to learn news of their relatives and friends who had formerly been taken in war, and had become Iroquois." One "Huron who had turned Iroquois" used the lull in fighting to retrieve one of his daughters from Trois-Rivières. This Wendat girl informed her Mohawk-affiliated father of more Mohawk captives among a group of Wendats near Montreal, and this intelligence led the Iroquois attackers to approach the French with a proposal for a prisoner exchange. In return for the captive Mohawks, the Iroquois would return the Jesuit Joseph-Antoine Poncet and Mathurin Franchetot, both of whom had been captured on August 20 at Cap Rouge, roughly ten miles from the French fort at Quebec, by a party of four Mohawks and "[s]ix Hurons, turned Iroquois."[18]

Shortly after the prisoner exchange at Trois-Rivières, the Mohawks moved to assert control over reshaping the League's relationship with New France. An Onondaga embassy en route to Montreal to resume their nation's peace talks encountered a Mohawk party carrying a Wendat captive in early September 1653. Concerned that the actions of the Mohawks would compromise their agenda, the Onondagas argued for the release of the Wendat prisoner. The captive used the opportunity provided by this dispute to make a bold speech criticizing the Mohawks' post-1649 campaign against his nation as a violation of "the exchange of promises that took place between our Ancestors," which obligated victors in a war to show mercy to the vanquished "if a mere woman should undertake to uncover the Sweat-house (where decisions of war are adopted) and take away the stakes supporting it." Though they denied the charge of having "trampled under foot the orders and the promise of [their] Ancestors," the Mohawk warriors released their prisoner.[19]

The Onondagas' victory was short-lived, however. Mohawk Turtle clan headman Teharihogen, who had broken off the siege of Trois-Rivières and accepted presents from local authorities "in behalf of the life of Father Poncet," encountered the Onondaga embassy at Trois-Rivières while the Onondagas were en route to Quebec. Teharihogen, in an apparent exercise of his authority as a hereditary titleholder of the League's eastern doorkeepers, "plundered" the Onondagas' "presents," and then detailed six or seven members of his Mohawk party to accompany the peace embassy to Quebec.[20]

Teharihogen's actions led to Mohawk domination of the preliminary peace terms negotiated at Quebec, with local Wendat brokerage, on September 8, 1653. Mohawk headman Andioura offered a condolence speech to Canadian governor Jean de Lauson in which he modified Kiotsaeton's 1645 address, inviting the French to form a "fine Colony" in Mohawk country. Emphasizing the benefits of free movement in times of peace, Andioura expressed his hope that among all the "confederated nations" (Iroquois, Wendat, Algonquin, and French) "there might be no more war except on the Beavers, Bear, and Deer." Lauson, in his response, symbolically straightened and cleared the road between Mohawk country and New France "in order that visits might be exchanged with greater ease." But instead of establishing a French colony in Mohawk country, Lauson returned to Kiotsaeton's proposed arrangements of 1645, spreading a "carpet or mat" at Trois-Rivières "on which might be held the councils and assemblies of all the nations." Lauson's final present to the six Mohawk ambassadors urged them to return the captive Jesuit Poncet unharmed.[21]

While these negotiations occurred at Quebec, Poncet had indeed been adopted by a Mohawk woman to replace her deceased brother. The captive Jesuit joined two adult women (one a Wendat and the other an Algonquin) as adopted members of this particular Mohawk family. But Poncet's time spent in Mohawk country would be brief. After Teharihogen returned from Trois-Rivières, Poncet learned that he would be returned to New France. Accompanied by several Iroquois men "who were going to hunt the beaver about Lake Ontario" and a number of Iroquois "Anciens" (elders), including Teharihogen, Poncet returned to New France via Onondaga country and the St. Lawrence River. The Mohawks chose this route instead of the more direct Lake Champlain–Richelieu River passage because they wanted to recruit Onondagas to accompany their embassy. Jesuits would later recover Poncet's cassock in Onondaga country, possibly indicating its status as a gift from Teharihogen intended to resolve any ill will remaining from the Mohawk leader's earlier disruption of the Onondaga embassy.[22]

Poncet and his Mohawk and Onondaga escort reached Quebec on November 5, 1653. The Mohawks offered preliminary terms of peace to French officials on November 6, 1653. Three days later, the French responded with gifts and a feast prepared by Ursuline nuns. After the conclusion of official proceedings, a number of Onondagas and "others of the upper Iroquois" attending the Mohawk embassy spent the winter of 1653–54 hunting with the Algonquins, a gesture that convinced the Algonquins to permit some "widows and girls of their Nation to marry some Iroquois men." Yet the expedited return of a Jesuit captive in a relatively unharmed state and the readiness of the Iroquois embassy to offer terms of reconciliation led some French authorities to suspect that the Iroquois had only repatriated Poncet in order to "treat more freely with the Hurons and [to] be able to handle these important matters more quietly and effectively."[23]

Beneath the polite rhetoric manifested in the November 1653 peace talks, officials in New France also plotted an independent agenda. Poncet's description of his "very easy route" from Onondaga country to New France, previously unknown to the French, attracted the attention of his fellow Jesuits. Le Mercier, in particular, now hoped to establish a Jesuit mission among the Onondagas, noting, on the strength of Poncet's report, only two portages between Onondaga homelands and Quebec. With just a "small redout" at Onondaga, Le Mercier argued that the French could establish a launch point for the eventual reestablishment of the Jesuit missionary project in the continental interior.[24]

EASTERN DOOR OR SMOKEHOLE?

These initial disputes between the Onondagas and the Mohawks regarding the destination of Wendat refugees in the St. Lawrence River valley soon developed into a crucial debate between competing constructions of the League's spatial relations with Native and non-Native neighbors. While the Mohawks asserted their own nation's primacy, as keepers of the eastern door of the League's metaphorical longhouse, in determining the fate of the Wendats, the Onondagas embarked on experimental diplomacy aimed at reorienting League relations with New France and its neighboring indigenous nations through their homelands, in the center, or "smokehole," of the League's longhouse. Though often viewed as evidence of dysfunctional levels of factionalism within the League, this dispute was actually representative of one of the key hallmarks of the League polity: openness to innovative attempts to build consensus around a particular initiative. Such flexibility ensured occasional controversies, but ultimately facilitated a far greater degree of cohesion among the members of the Five Nations than historians have hitherto recognized.[25]

French and Jesuit observers became aware in November 1653 of opposing Iroquois plans for the Wendats' future. Marie de l'Incarnation reported that the Mohawks who had repatriated Poncet had later invited the family of one of her ten-year-old female Wendat "seminarists" to relocate to that "wretched [Mohawk] country." Still more alarmingly for the French, on November 18, 1653, a group of Wendat elders described how Teharihogen had secretly delivered three "large Porcelain collars of rare beauty" urging the approximately 500 Wendat refugees residing on the Isle d'Orléans to relocate to Mohawk country, "where were already their kinsfolk who had been formerly carried away captive, and who bore their absence only with regret and inconsolable sadness." Preliminary reports suggested that at least some Wendats favored accepting the Mohawk Turtle clan headman's invitation.[26]

Refusing to be outmaneuvered by Teharihogen's assertion of Mohawk control over efforts to assimilate the Wendat refugees near Quebec, four Onondagas arrived at Quebec on January 30, 1654, carrying their own clandestine offer to the Wendat refugees residing on the Isle d'Orléans. Six days later, an Onondaga headman held a formal council with the Wendats and French authorities at Quebec, during which he planted the League's "May-tree" in "the middle of the great River St. Lawrence, opposite the fort of Québec, the house of Onontio, the great Captain of the French." This "May-tree," explained the Onondaga speaker, "should rear its summit above the clouds, in order that all the nations of the earth might be able to see it, and that it might mark a rendezvous where all the world could rest in peace under the shade of its leaves." In addition to offering a comprehensive peace with New France, the Onondagas hoped to persuade the Wendats to "go in a body, men, women, and children, into their country."[27]

Many Wendats feared hostile intent underlying these Iroquois invitations, especially that of the Onondagas, since the Wendats claimed to have murdered thirty-four Onondaga "men of high rank and importance" by deception merely "three years ago in our former country when they themselves tried to beguile us." They also cited the inability of the Mohawks to forgive the Wendats' execution of a Mohawk leader at Trois-Rivières in 1652, and claimed that the League as a whole viewed the Wendats as "criminals for having escaped death at their hands when they had planned it."[28]

The Wendats' subsequent request for advice from French civil and ecclesiastical authorities on how to respond to the Onondagas' offer opened the door to the implementation of Le Mercier's nascent plan to establish a Jesuit mission in Iroquoia. The French advised the Wendats to ask for a one-year deferral of the Onondaga-planned relocation, during which time the Onondagas would be asked to construct a "dwell-ing for the Black Robes" as a gesture of respect toward the Wendats' so-called teach-ers. Le Mercier hoped that this offer to the Onondagas would allow the French (at least) to escape the looming threat of conflict over the fate of the Wendat refugees by manifesting friendliness to the League as a whole, while leaving "each of the Iro-quois Nations hopeful of winning to its own side the Wendats, whom they so eagerly desired."[29]

In February 1654, the Onondagas returned home with the French-inspired Wen-dat request for a deferral of their planned relocation to Iroquoia. Two months later, the capture of a French "surgeon" on Montreal Island by an Oneida war party inspired Sagochiendagehté, the Onondagas' "grand chief," to offer himself as a hostage to the French at Montreal until the Oneidas returned the French prisoner. This dramatic gesture demonstrated the Onondagas' commitment to their proposed peace with New France, which made sense in light of increasingly frequent attacks on Iroquois hunters in the upper Great Lakes by refugee Wendats, Neutrals, and Algonquins (who had negotiated a military alliance with their Potawatomi, Ojibwa, Odawa, Missis-sauga, and Winnebago hosts at Sault Ste. Marie during the early months of 1653). The Oneidas quickly restored the captive surgeon.[30]

Sagochiendagehté, having completed the initial phase of his hostage diplomacy, held a formal conference at Montreal, during which he rooted more firmly the Onondaga-planted "treaty-tree" there. To assuage Governor Paul Chomedey de Mai-sonneuve's lingering anger over the Oneidas' behavior, Sagochiendagehté offered "an emetic . . . to cause him to vomit whatever resentment still remained in his heart."[31] The Onondaga leader then extended an invitation for the "Black Robes" to settle in Onondaga country, promising them a hospitable reception. Sagochiendagehté also promised that his young men would direct their energies away from New France and toward the Eries, an Iroquoian-speaking group then residing in what is now southwestern New York and northwestern Pennsylvania, with whom the League had previously enjoyed a relatively peaceful trading relationship. The Onondaga leader concluded his address by proclaiming his nation's unity with the French, "our arms being linked together in a bond of love."[32]

Concluding peace with the French in this manner allowed Sagochiendagehté to redeem a dozen Seneca and Mohawk hunters who had been captured by Wendats and Odawas in the upper Great Lakes and brought to Montreal in their captors' joint summer trade convoy. The Onondaga headman's diplomacy also kept alive prospects of a mass refugee Wendat emigration to Onondaga country, albeit now with some "Black Robes" in tow. Onondaga concerns over their intensifying conflict with the Eries might have influenced Sagochiendagehté's willingness to accept the idea of a Jesuit mission in Iroquoia. The French surgeon returned from Oneida captivity re-ported in June 1654 that the Eries had recently burned a Seneca village and "cut to pieces" an Onondaga party of eighty men returning from a campaign in the upper

Great Lakes. This event, in the surgeon's view, had "compelled them to seek for Peace with us."[33]

Sagochiendagehté left behind some Onondagas at Quebec to escort Jesuit Simon Le Moyne to Onondaga country. Several days after Le Moyne's July 3, 1654, departure, the dilemma the Wendats and the French believed they had resolved reappeared at Quebec in the person of Canaqueese, a man known to the Jesuits as "an execrable issue of sin, the monstrous offspring of a Dutch Heretic Father and a Pagan [Mohawk] Woman," and also referred to by European contemporaries as Smits Jan, John Smith, or Flemish Bastard.[34]

Upon learning of Le Moyne's embassy to Onondaga, which the French justified on the idea that the Onondagas "first brought the news of Peace," Canaqueese argued in reply that Le Moyne should visit Mohawk country first, "because they are nearest to us, being situated, as it were, on the frontier." Faced with the apparent failure of the French to observe what the Mohawks, as keepers of the League's eastern door, considered proper spatial protocol for French diplomatic initiatives (a failure even more significant than Jogues's rhetorical missteps in Mohawk country eight years earlier, given the potential impact of Le Moyne's embassy on the fate of the Wendats), Canaqueese "made his complaints on the subject with cleverness and intelligence." "Ought not one," said he, "to enter a house by the door, and not by the chimney or roof of the cabin, unless he be a thief, and wish to take the inmates by surprise? We, the Five Iroquois Nations, compose but one cabin; we maintain but one fire; and we have, from time immemorial, dwelt under one and the same roof." In fact, from the earliest times, these five Iroquois Nations have been called in their own language, which is Huron, *Hotinnonchiendi,* that is, "the completed Cabin," as if to express that they constituted but one family. "Well then," he continued, "will you not enter the cabin by the door, which is at the ground floor of the house? It is with us, the Anniehronons [Mohawks], that you should begin; whereas you, by beginning with the Onnontaehronnons [Onondagas], try to enter the roof and through the chimney. Have you no fear that the smoke may blind you, our fire not being extinguished, and that you may fall from the top to the bottom, having nothing solid on which to plant your feet?"

This critical Mohawk assessment of the Onondagas' revision of what Canaqueese characterized as normative spatial orientation of League foreign relations prompted Governor Lauson to draft letters ordering Le Moyne to alter his course for Mohawk country, "provided" Canaqueese "overt[ook] him on the road."[35]

Although Canaqueese, or some Mohawks with him, caught up to Le Moyne's traveling party, murdered several Wendats and Algonquins accompanying the Jesuit, and bound Le Moyne briefly as a captive, the Onondagas convinced the Mohawks to allow them to complete their journey in safety. As the party approached the principal Onondaga town on August 5, 1654, the Jesuit, drawing on his past experience in Wendake as well as a "written list" of notes, became the first European known to have offered an Edge of the Woods greeting to a host Iroquois community. In his "harangue," Le Moyne "called by name all the Captains, families, and persons of importance, speaking slowly, and in the tone of a Captain." The Jesuit advised his reportedly intrigued Onondaga audience "that peace was attending [his] course."[36]

Le Moyne spent the next four days offering Christian ministry to the local population of Wendat adoptees, including Thérèse Kionhreha, who was then living in an "outlying cabin" with a teenage Neutral girl whom she "loved as her own daughter." In the meantime, a number of Seneca, Cayuga, and Oneida envoys arrived at Onondaga for a conference in "Ondessonk's [Le Moyne's] cabin." On August 10, 1654, Le Moyne claimed to have "astonished" the assembled listeners by performing a roll call of League chiefs, naming all the "Nations, bands, and families, and each person individually who was of some little consequence." Le Moyne followed up his impressive opening act with a two-hour-long discourse that emphasized themes of condolence and peace between the French, the League, and the Wendats. The assembled League headmen (among whom was one Mohawk leader "who by good luck happened to be present") responded to Le Moyne's speech through an Onondaga "captain . . . who is the tongue of the country, and acts as its orator." The Onondaga speaker, who claimed that "Five whole Nations" spoke through his mouth, uprooted the "May-tree" symbolizing Franco-Iroquois peace from Montreal and replanted it at Onondaga, indicating that the latter "would be henceforth the scene of the assemblies and the parleys relating to the Peace." He then invited the French to settle "in the heart of" Iroquoia, at Onondaga.[37]

The Onondagas elicited de facto French sanction for the Iroquois war against the Eries by having Le Moyne baptize the Onondaga leader of a multinational Iroquois army undertaking a campaign to Erie country on August 14, 1654. The Jesuit returned with an Onondaga escort to Quebec on September 11, 1654, raving about not only the size of the "captive church" of "old-time Hurons" of "both sexes" among the Onondagas but also about Otihatangué, the site the Onondagas initially allotted for the prospective French settlement at the mouth of the Salmon River (later known to the French as "La Famine"). Le Moyne believed that the Jesuits would be situated in a place rich in game animals, "beautiful prairies and good fishing." He described the future mission site as "a resort for all [Iroquois] Nations."[38]

The Jesuits intended to use their mission in Iroquoia for two key objectives: first, as a lever to facilitate the wholesale conversion of the League nations to Catholic Christianity, and second, to divide the unity of the Iroquois League on economic lines by offering direct French trade in Onondaga country. Le Mercier expected that the Mohawks would not "suffer lightly" any such initiative by the "upper [Iroquois] Nations" to redirect their trade away from Fort Orange, since that would mean those nations "would no longer be compelled to pass through [Mohawk] villages, which their route obliges them to do when they carry their merchandise to the Dutch."

Le Mercier's prediction proved accurate, as traders from the four western League nations reported increasingly "uncivil" treatment from the Mohawks after 1654.[39]

Rather than accept Jesuit intentions as the sole explanation of the August 1654 League negotiations with Le Moyne at Onondaga, we need to consider what those discussions may have meant to the Iroquois participants. In late 1654, a sufficient number of League delegates from the four "upper nations" (and at least one Mohawk headman) considered a carefully restricted and supervised French presence on the periphery of Onondaga country a worthwhile risk. Rather than simply an expedient measure to bring a new supplier of trade goods into upper Iroquoia, these negotiations are better understood as the continuation of an innovative effort, spearheaded by the Onondagas' "women chiefs" (*oianders,* or clan matrons), to reorient League relations with New France. This approach reflected the intense competition among League nations for the remaining Wendat population and also the Onondagas' desire to attract French personnel to Onondaga country. Once established there, the Jesuit and French population could serve as hostages and/or human shields whose presence would permit the League nations to extend their own range of spatial movement in greater security.[40]

The Onondaga-led Iroquois war of 1654–57 with the Eries offers a striking example of the League's expanding spatial initiatives in the aftermath of the previous decade's campaign against Wendake. The Iroquois conflict with the Eries arose from a tangle of competing influences among refugee Wendats in the respective combatant nations. Jesuit accounts indicated that Wenro adoptees among the Wendat refugees with the Eries "stirred up" an Erie attack on the Senecas in 1654. In response, Wendat adoptees in Onondaga country reportedly pressured their hosts into assuming leadership of a retaliatory attack on the Eries.[41]

The Iroquois war with the Eries began with an autumn 1654 offensive to avenge four Onondaga hunters killed by the Eries during the previous summer. An after-action report of the late 1654 campaign described an Onondaga-led 1,200-man Iroquois army burning several Erie towns, including Gentaienton and the capital town of Rigué, and then pursuing any Eries who took flight rather than surrender. In one notable instance, two Onondaga headmen, one of whom was the individual baptized by Le Moyne, approached an Erie field fort dressed "in French costume" (possibly the cassock of former Mohawk captive Joseph Poncet) "in order to frighten their opponents by the novelty of this attire." The Onondagas urged the Eries to surrender, but they refused, and the Iroquois attackers subsequently "wrought such carnage" that "the blood was knee-deep in certain places." An estimated 600 Erie captives (among whom were an unspecified number of Wendat refugees) eventually returned to Iroquoia in the aftermath of the battle, while the surviving remnants of the Eries moved to the Chesapeake Bay region, where they were known as Westos, and became active in the burgeoning trade of Native American slaves to plantation owners.[42]

In the midst of the Onondaga-led offensive against the Eries, a party of Mohawk leaders appeared at Fort Orange on January 6, 1655, to request that "some Dutchmen" go to the "Sinekens to compose the difficulties between them and the Mohawks," since the latter had reportedly killed "the chief of the Sinekens of Onnedaego." Although the circumstances of the killing are not known, the Dutch claimed to be unable to find anyone to undertake this critical errand owing to inclement weather. In a subsequent report on these proceedings to Governor Petrus Stuyvesant, authorities at Fort Orange concluded that it would be "a dangerous thing to interfere with this exciting quarrel."[43]

Failing to secure Dutch mediation of their conflict with the Onondagas, the Mohawks resumed hostilities against New France in May 1655, sending parties led by Wendat and Algonquin "renegades" throughout the St. Lawrence valley from Montreal to Quebec. Although these raids netted a number of French prisoners, the French captured a party of Mohawks whose canoes were forced aground at the Lachine Rapids on June 1, 1655. Four Mohawks, seeking an exchange for their captive countrymen, arrived at Trois-Rivières on July 31, 1655, with six French prisoners.[44]

Once notified of the Mohawks' arrival, Lauson "hastened" to Trois-Rivières. Throughout the proceedings, which echoed themes of earlier discussions, the Mohawks insisted on a separate peace between their nation and New France, refusing to agree to French attempts to include the Algonquins and Wendats in a peace agreement. The Mohawks also demanded the return of nine Mohawk prisoners held in custody at Montreal, and, in a conciliatory gesture, they requested that one priest be sent to their country to ensure a lasting peace. Following an exchange of prisoners, Lauson agreed to a separate peace with the Mohawks, but requested that future Mohawk warfare against the Wendats and Algonquins take place "at a distance from our territories." Lauson and the Mohawks agreed that the latter's indigenous campaigns would be confined to lands west of Trois-Rivières. This significant jurisdictional concession circumscribed the French security perimeter for the colony's Native allies.[45]

Simon Le Moyne embarked for Mohawk country on August 17, 1655, with a twelve-man Mohawk escort. The Mohawks initially received Le Moyne with "extraordinary cordiality," and in a brief council they gave him a "large image of the sun, made of six thousand porcelain beads," in order "to dispel all the darkness from our councils." But Le Moyne began receiving death threats shortly thereafter, and upon witnessing a Mohawk's murder of a Wendat captive upon suspicion that he had revealed sensitive information to Le Moyne, the Jesuit ended his sojourn in Mohawk country. Escorted by three Mohawks, he reached Montreal on November 13, 1655.[46]

Le Moyne's 1655 journey to Mohawk country had not only failed to address the substantive issues raised by Canaqueese in 1654, it also coincided exactly with a September 1655 Onondaga embassy to Quebec. Attended by at least one Onondaga "Chieftainess" (likely a clan mother), the Onondagas offered the French a comprehensive peace, including the Wendats and Algonquins, in the name of all League nations except the Mohawks. Formal proceedings between the Iroquois, Wendats, Algonquins, and French at Quebec commenced on September 12, 1655, before a large crowd of French observers. The unnamed "chief Ambassador" of the Iroquois invited the French to send "a company of Frenchmen to their country in order to make but one people of us." He offered the French space in the "center of all their Nations," to "build a new Sainte Marie." In exchange, the French would send some soldiers to Onondaga to assist in the defense of their villages against the Eries. The "May-tree" metaphorically planted before this "new house of Sainte Marie" would be "so lofty that it could be seen from all directions, and all the Nations, even those most distant, could come to it."[47]

The conference's dramatic concluding address outlined the associative adoption offered by the Onondagas to the Wendats of the Isle d'Orléans. The speech came from an unidentified Wendat "Captain, formerly a captive of the Iroquois, and now a Captain among them." This unnamed adoptee assured his Wendat "brothers" of the benevolent motives underlying the Onondagas' invitation for them to relocate to Iroquoia. "I have not changed my soul," he claimed, "despite my change of country; nor has my blood become Iroquois, although I dwell among them. My heart is all Huron, as well as my tongue. I would keep silence, were there any deceit in these negotiations of peace. Our proposals are honest; embrace them without distrust."[48]

French authorities made no formal response to the Onondaga's speech at Quebec, electing instead to send Jesuits Chaumonot and Dablon to Onondaga country for that purpose. The Jesuits left Quebec on September 19, 1655, with an escort of thirty Onondagas and as many as eighteen Wendat "Ambassadors." On the evening of November 5, 1655, following the formal welcome at the Edge of the Woods described at the beginning of this chapter, several Onondaga senior leaders came to the Jesuits' longhouse and offered 1,000 beads of wampum to wipe away the Jesuits' tears and "to strengthen our lungs, to remove the phlegm from our throats, and to make our voices clear, free, and strong." During conversations over the next five days at Onondaga, leaders from the host nation granted formal permission for the establishment of a Jesuit mission in Onondaga country, conditional on French acknowledgment of the "equal power" of Onondaga headman Sagochiendagehté and the king of France, and the Wendats' promise to relocate their remaining population from the Isle d'Orléans to Onondaga country.[49]

On November 11, 1655, the Jesuits visited the "the salt spring, four leagues distant and near the Lake called Gannentaa" (Onondaga Lake), the site allotted for their mission settlement (evidently revised from the more distant location identified in 1654). Four days later, in a formal session with Cayugas and Oneidas present, Chaumonot, speaking for effect "in the Italian style, having sufficient space for walking about," communicated a series of requests to his audience. He asked the Onondagas to build a chapel for the Jesuits, in exchange for which a party of Frenchmen would come in the spring and construct "a palisade for the public defense." He asked the Onondagas and Cayugas to "stay" the Mohawks' anti-French "hatchet," and urged them to "unite their minds" with the keepers of the League's eastern door. He invited the Oneidas and Cayugas to "move their Villages nearer [to Onondaga], in order the better to share the advantage of the vicinity of the French." Chaumonot concluded his speech by symbolically clearing his own "path for walking, with head erect, through all the Iroquois villages." In return, Iroquois nations agreeing to peace would have "liberty to traverse the entire country of the French."[50]

The Onondagas, Cayugas, and Oneidas replied formally to Chaumonot the next day in a council held at the home of the Onondaga "Chieftainess" who had attended the September 1655 council at Quebec. Proceedings commenced with an Onondaga elder singing "six airs, or chants" (possibly a performance of the Six Songs of the Condolence ceremony). After the ceremonial opening, Sagochiendagehté thanked Chaumonot for his role in making comprehensive peace between the French, Iroquois, Wendats, and Algonquins, and then used a wampum belt to grasp Chaumonot in a "close embrace." After the Cayugas and Oneidas endorsed these terms, Sagochiendagehté announced that "the kettle of war against the Cat nation [Eries] was over the fire," and that hostilities would resume in the spring.[51]

While Chaumonot brokered peace with the three westernmost nations of the League, 300 Mohawks appeared at Fort Orange on November 19, 1655 (just six days after Le Moyne's departure), seeking "a renewal of harmony and peace" with New Netherland. Unhappy about the "not altogether brotherly" requests of the Dutch blacksmiths for payment for the repair of Mohawk firearms, the Mohawks requested assurances of Dutch "neutrality" prior to commencing a campaign against the Wendats and Algonquins. The Dutch, then embroiled in the so-called Peach Tree War with Algonquian peoples residing in the lower Hudson River valley and Long Island, were only too happy to promise nonintervention in Mohawk conflicts they considered "external to" New Netherland's concerns. To encourage the Mohawks' efforts in the St. Lawrence valley, the Dutch presented the Mohawks with fifteen bars of lead and twenty-five pounds of gunpowder. Apparently dissatisfied with this insubstantial gesture, the Mohawks plundered Dutch traders near Fort Orange, "taking away by force guns, powder, shot, [and] coats."[52]

Following this effort to replenish their military stores, Mohawk warriors returned to the St. Lawrence valley in force. Subsequent events revealed the potential for tragedy created by conflicting objectives among the highly mobile League nations. Two of three Seneca "hostages" who had pledged in September 1655 to winter at Quebec changed their minds and set out to hunt en route homeward to Seneca country early in November. Late in December 1655, they were shot and killed after passing Montreal. The murderers were never identified, but the Jesuits suspected Mohawk culpability. One month later, an embassy of ten Senecas, "the chief of whom was one of the leading Captains of their entire country, from fifty to sixty years of age," appeared at Quebec to state their peaceful intentions and to request a visit from the

Jesuits. One of the Seneca headmen undertook a hunting trip between Quebec and Trois-Rivières, when he also was shot from a distance. A group of Mohawk hunters came upon the scene and upon realizing what had happened claimed that they had opened fire at too great a distance to "recognize" the man they had killed.[53]

The deaths of these three Senecas did not bring an end to the Mohawks' pursuit of a resolution of the Wendat question on their own terms. On April 25, 1656, while one Mohawk war party attacked the Wendats at the Isle d'Orléans, another group of 300 Mohawks approached Pierre Boucher, the governor of Trois-Rivières, request-ing peace talks. The next day an unidentified Mohawk speaker reprised the 1645 terms of peace offered by Kiotsaeton. Presenting "a great collar of Porcelain beads" to Boucher, which the Mohawk orator described as an "iron chain, larger around than the trees that grow in our forests, which shall bind the Dutch, the French, and the Agnieronnons [Mohawks] together," the Mohawks offered the French a comprehen-sive peace (which included New Netherland), but the eastern doorkeepers insisted on French recognition of the Mohawks' interpretation of appropriate spatial protocols in League diplomacy. The Mohawk speaker informed the French that they would have to renounce the peace they had concluded with the Onondagas in September 1655.[54]

Following their parley with Boucher at Trois-Rivières, the 300-man Mohawk party moved toward Quebec and the nearby Isle d'Orléans. French authorities, confronting yet another dilemma with this latest Mohawk proposal, sent Simon Le Moyne to intercept them. On April 27, 1656, Le Moyne reported having successfully diverted the Mohawks from their intended journey. But the Mohawks' efforts over the winter of 1655–56 had complicated both the internal relations among League nations and the planned relocation of the Wendats to Onondaga country. After a February 1656 council that concerned the "general affairs of the country" and involved all League nations but the Mohawks, the Onondagas warned Chaumonont and Dablon that unless the Wendats and French arrived in Onondaga country as promised, they (and presumably the Senecas, Cayugas, and Oneidas as well) would "break entirely" with the French.[55]

Upon considering their options, the French opted to take what Canaqueese had referred to as the "smokehole" route in their relations with the League, persuaded by fears that notwithstanding recent friction, the western League nations might reunite with the Mohawks and "wage endless war against" New France. The prospect of a pan-Iroquois "revolt" led authorities in New France to conclude that "exposing a handful of French" to an uncertain fate in Onondaga country was preferable to risk-ing the colony's annihilation. On April 12, 1656, Governor Lauson drafted a document that authorized a Jesuit-owned seigneury throughout a thirty-mile perimeter from the site of the prospective French settlement on Onondaga Lake.[56]

While preparations for the establishment of the Jesuit mission in Onondaga country began, a Wendat escapee from captivity in Iroquoia reached Quebec and reported that the Onondagas' "sole design was to attract to their country as many of the French and Hurons as possible and then to kill them in a general massacre." This intelligence led many of the Wendat refugees on the Isle d'Orléans, who had pledged to accompany Jesuits to Onondaga, to reconsider their decision. They did not realize that warriors from elsewhere in Iroquoia were then on the move toward their community.[57]

The Mohawk army that Le Moyne believed he had convinced to return home in April 1656 had not abandoned their objective. At dawn on May 20, 1656, forty Mohawk canoes landed undetected on the Isle d'Orléans. The Mohawks then "scattered in all directions, stationing themselves at the approaches to the fields that were then being sown with Indian corn," and launched separate ambushes that killed or captured as many as eighty-five Wendats. Notably, the Jesuits counted among the Wendat prisoners "a large number of young women who were the flower of that Colony." To further demonstrate to French authorities how their freedom of movement translated into power, the Mohawks passed by Quebec in broad daylight, forcing their Wendat captives to sing, "in order to humiliate them still more."[58]

The Mohawks' well-timed, large-scale surprise attack persuaded the Isle d'Orléans Wendats to send a three-man embassy to Mohawk country to sue for peace. The Wendats agreed to relocate en masse to Mohawk country during the spring of 1657. Thereafter, they would "inhabit but one land, and be but one people" with their Mohawk hosts. Demonstrating their commitment to integrating the Wendats, the Mohawks pressed some of the surviving male Wendat captives taken in May 1656 into immediate military service on a long-distance campaign targeting refugee Tionnontaté Wendats residing among Ojibwas and Odawas near modern-day Green Bay, Wisconsin.[59]

Endgame on the Isle d'Orléans

Rival efforts by the Mohawks and Onondagas to secure the Wendat refugees on the Isle d'Orléans came to a head in 1657. These endeavors, summarized by one scholar as the "rape" of the "Québec" Wendats, actually proceeded in a largely peaceful manner.[60] Subtle diplomacy by Onondaga and Mohawk leaders achieved what brute force alone had failed to accomplish: the evacuation of nearly all the remaining Wendat refugees to Iroquoia. Determined Iroquois negotiations on this matter also forced the French to abandon their claimed status as protectors of allied indigenous nations, which sent a crucial message to indigenous peoples throughout much of northeastern North America.

The Jesuits, unaware of the complex and deeply rooted motivations of the Mohawks and Onondagas (to repopulate their nations with an ancestral people and to define their respective role in the League), continued to interpret the two nations' competition for Wendat adoptees solely in economic terms. Jesuit writers attributed

the Mohawks' aggressive movement against Wendat refugees in the St. Lawrence valley to "jealousy almost verging on fury" at the prospect of the Onondagas obtaining
French trade goods directly instead of being "compelled to pass through" Mohawk
country to access the Dutch market at Fort Orange. Although the potential trade opportunities afforded by such a mission station factored into the Onondagas' decision
to invite the Jesuits to reside in their homelands, the missionaries failed to recognize
the manner in which that decision served larger Onondaga objectives of reincorpo-
rating ancestral peoples into the League and, in turn, expanding the League's capacity for effective movement through an increasing extent of geographic space.[61]

An Onondaga-Wendat-Jesuit convoy that departed from the Isle d'Orléans just
days before the late May 1656 Mohawk attack arrived in Onondaga country on July 11,
1656. Six days later, French troops began building "a good Redout" for the new mission of Ste. Marie de Gannentaha on "an eminence commanding [Onondaga] Lake and
all the surrounding places." On July 24, 1656, the newly arrived Jesuits participated
in a council of "all the Allied Nations" at Onondaga. The League meeting's primary
purpose was to reconcile the Senecas and the Mohawks, who were reportedly "on the
point of going to war" as a result of the Mohawks' killing of the Seneca leader near
Trois-Rivières earlier in the year.[62]

In an early test of the resident Jesuits' viability as allies, the Onondagas placed the
resolution of this potentially explosive issue in the "hands" of the Jesuits. Chaumonot
initially "delighted" his audience by taking up the challenge. Speaking in Onondaga,
he distributed "porcelain collars, beads, arquebuses, powder, lead, coats, hatchets,
kettles, and other similar articles" to the assembled Iroquois headmen. Chaumonot
then expressed his wish that the Wendats and Algonquins "might but form one heart
and one people with all those [Iroquois] Nations." Yet in a rhetorical miscalcula-
tion reminiscent of that of Jogues in Mohawk country a decade earlier, Chaumonot
not only ignored what he had been asked to do regarding the reconciliation of the
Mohawks and Senecas, he also openly disavowed trade as a motive for the French
presence in Iroquoia. The Iroquois could "keep [their] beaver-skins, if [they chose],
for the Dutch," he announced, since the Jesuits did not seek "perishable things" but
rather aimed "much higher," intending to expose all of Iroquoia to "the word of
God." The "vehemence" of Chaumonot's words thrilled his fellow Jesuits, but caused
general "astonishment" among the assembled League headmen.[63]

Several Onondaga "chief men" visited the French at Ste. Marie de Gannentaha on
August 30, 1656. Unwilling to abandon their experiment of hosting the French, they
reasserted their status as "but one people" with the French. At least one Onondaga
leader relocated to the mission to oversee deliveries of food to the mission's French
residents, thereby "cultivat[ing] a brotherly relationship." Yet most of the Onondagas
took Chaumonot at his word and assembled a sizable delegation that set out for
Manhattan carrying a reported "4000 beavers" to trade. Given the uncertain nature
of internal relations among the League nations, the Onondagas asked Dutch officials

to build a trading house opposite Manhattan on the Hudson River. This post would allow traders from the western League nations to bypass Mohawk country and Fort Orange.[64]

As the Jesuits settled into their mission in Onondaga country, Wendats, Algonquins, and colonists in New France contended with warriors from the eastern League nations in the St. Lawrence River valley. In late October 1656, forty Oneidas landed in seven canoes at Trois-Rivières, announcing that they had come on behalf of the Mohawks to "take away with them the Hurons of Quebec." Shortly thereafter, Le Moyne confirmed that the Mohawks and Oneidas had resumed independent peace negotiations with the Wendats.[65]

On November 3, 1656, an Oneida delegation met at Trois-Rivières with Wendat leader Étienne Annaotaha, who had formerly engineered a daring escape from would-be Iroquois captors on Christian Island during the autumn of 1650. In the presence of Algonquin, French, and Wendat observers, the unidentified Oneida speaker advised Annaotaha that he had come to "take thee by the arm to lead thee away." He reminded the Wendat headman that "formerly we comprised but one Cabin and one country. I know not by what accident we had became separated. It is time to unite again. I have twice before come to seek thee, once at Montréal, speaking to the French in thy absence, the second time at Québec. It is for the third time I now come." The significance of the Oneida speaker's statement would not have been lost on contemporary listeners familiar with League tradition, which mandated three offers of peace prior to undertaking war on a nation. After placing a symbolic "mat" in his "cabin" for the Wendats, the Oneida speaker offered them "land for raising Indian corn" to encourage their voluntary relocation to Iroquoia.[66]

The Oneida speech at Trois-Rivières masked simultaneous direct Mohawk negotiations with the Wendats in Mohawk country during the autumn months of 1656. French authorities learned of the conclusion of the Mohawk-Wendat peace on December 26, 1656. At least two Mohawk leaders spent the winter of 1656–57 on the Isle d'Orléans to help plan the promised Wendat relocation, residing in a Wendat leader's "cabin" as a means of ratifying the agreement, demonstrating the Mohawks' good intentions.[67]

As the Mohawks upped the ante in the competition for the Wendat refugee population, the Onondagas, outraged by the Wendats' conclusion of peace with the Mohawks, prepared their own movement against the remaining Wendats on the Isle d'Orléans. Citing their long-standing effort to induce the Wendats to "form but one people with [them]," the Onondagas sent 100 warriors toward Quebec in April 1657 to "outbid" their League rivals and to secure Wendat refugees "either with their consent or by force."[68]

On May 6, 1657, eight Onondagas arrived at Sillery and demanded an audience with the French and the Wendats. The Jesuits hosted a conference between Onondaga and Wendat delegates at their Quebec seminary the next day, which the two

Mohawk leaders wintering on the Isle d'Orléans also attended. After the Ononda-gas and Mohawks committed to peaceful cooperation, the Onondagas agreed to limit their Wendat relocation efforts to the Ahrendahronons, or the "Tribe of the Rock," leaving the other two Wendat nations present among the Isle d'Orléans refugee population (the Attigneenongnahacs, known as the "Cord nation," and the Attignawantans, or "Bear nation") to determine their own fate. An Attignawantan Wendat headman "called Le Plat" (the dish), who had personally hosted Mohawks over the preceding winter, agreed to send three Ahrendahronons with the Ononda-gas back to Montreal, where they would await a formal escort of "peace canoes" to Onondaga country in order to verify their would-be hosts' promises of a hospitable reception.[69]

The Mohawks, however, were not far behind the Onondagas. One hundred "young and very resolute" Mohawk warriors escorted a formal embassy of two head-men (one of whom was Teharihogen) to Quebec in the spring of 1657 to oversee the promised relocation of Wendat refugees. On May 29, 1657, Teharihogen arrived at the Jesuits' seminary at Quebec and informed the Wendats that it was "time for [them] to come" home with him. Teharihogen promised the Attignawantan Wendats that his nation would regard them as cherished "relatives," and that Mohawk country would "also be thine." Given the Onondagas' prior concession of the Gannentaha mission, Teharihogen invited "Father Ondessonk" (Le Moyne) to reside in Mohawk country. Teharihogen balanced this offer with a demand for French "shallops" to assist in the Mohawks' evacuation of the Isle d'Orléans.[70]

The French, confronted by such determination on the part of the Mohawks and Onondagas, realized that they could no longer resist the Wendats' relocation to Iro-quoia. Only the Attigneenongnahac Wendats had refused to leave the Isle d'Orléans, convinced that the Onondagas and the Mohawks alike harbored hostile intent. The Ahrendahronons had agreed to relocate to Onondaga country, and the Attignawa-ntans had resolved to accept the Mohawks' invitation. Denied French shallops, the Mohawks began building bark canoes, and in six days they had an impromptu flotilla ready to carry away all the Attignawantan (Wendats) who had "given themselves up." Departures from the Isle d'Orléans began on June 2, 1657, when fourteen Wendat women and several "little children" embarked in seven Mohawk-paddled canoes, in order to "form but one people" with their host nation.[71]

The Mohawks' intense struggle with the Onondagas for Wendat adoptees neces-sitated efforts on their part to gauge the degree to which their Dutch allies would support their eastern door initiatives. Mohawk headman Sasiadego traveled to Fort Orange and requested a hearing before the court in the name of "the sachems of the three castles of the Mohawks" on June 16, 1657. Noting the urgency of needed repairs to the Mohawks' "castles," Sasiadego asked the officials at Fort Orange to provide horses and draftsmen to haul logs out of the woods, as the Dutch had done eight years previously. He also requested cannons for each of the Mohawks' towns (for use as a distress signal) and asked the Dutch if they would provide shelter for Mohawk women and children in the event of an attack by the "Sinnekens."[72]

The Dutch response likely disappointed Sasiadego. Fort Orange authorities offered merely to help Mohawks find people from whom to rent horses, refused their request for cannons, and agreed only grudgingly to offer shelter for Mohawk women and children "in the event of an emergency with the Sinnekens." Mohawk country never sustained the rumored attack from the western League nations, and the remaining months of 1657 witnessed separate Mohawk and Onondaga canoe fleets shuttling back and forth from their respective homelands to transport Wendats from the Isle d'Orléans to new homes in Iroquoia.[73]

These movements were not without occasional friction. At least one joint Seneca-Onondaga escort convoy opted to kill the adult male Wendats among their passengers and plunder the remaining Wendats' baggage. Ongoing conflicts sparked by Wendats refusing to accompany prospective Iroquois escorts forced French officials in October 1657 to advise any Wendats resisting relocation to Iroquoia that they would only provide defensive assistance against Iroquois incursions "in sight of the French houses" throughout New France, and warned that the French would not undertake any offensive against the Iroquois which might "break the peace."[74]

The success of the Iroquois efforts to relocate the Wendats from the St. Lawrence valley to League homelands, notwithstanding divisions between the Onondagas and Mohawks, had the immediate effect of greatly reducing the effective security perimeter that the French could offer to current (or prospective) indigenous allies. Iroquois military and diplomatic initiatives had forced the French to abandon their pretense of sheltering Wendat refugees, a clear indicator of the relative power dynamics at the time. But rather than simply acknowledging the extent of the League's achievement with regard to the assimilation of Wendake by the end of 1657, we must assess what that achievement meant to the subsequent history of the League.

Requickened with Adoptees

Wendats and other adoptees played a vital role, as we have seen, in the League nations' postepidemic demographic recovery. Archaeological evidence indicates that the Onondagas and Senecas, evidently hosting the greatest number of adoptees during the middle decades of the seventeenth century, built towns in dimensions not seen since the sixteenth century to house them. Jesuit writings, read against the grain of their authors' assumptions concerning ethnic purity, provide the best documentary evidence of the adoptees' value to the Iroquois.[75]

The character of all the nations of the Iroquois League, opined Jesuit Paul Le Jeune in 1657, was "warlike and cruel; and, as they have no neighbors to fight, because they have subjugated all of them, they go [now] to seek enemies in other countries."

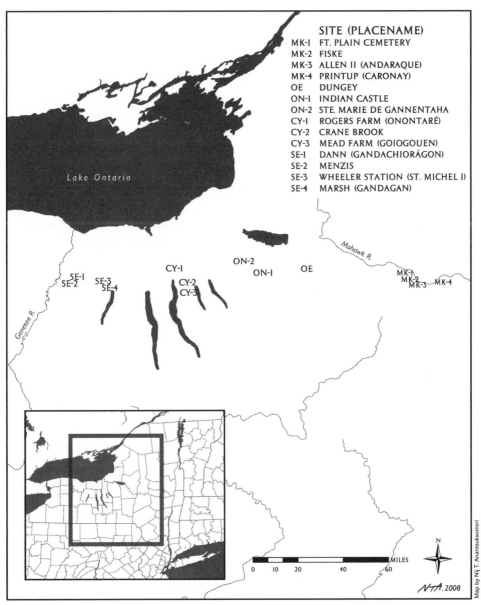

Iroquoia, ca. 1657

Le Jeune claimed that Iroquois war parties then had a range of 200 or 300 leagues (600 to 900 miles) from their home settlements, and that some remained in the field for more than a year at a time. Condemning what he viewed as the excessive militarism of Iroquois society, Le Jeune argued further that the "continual raids" of the young men not only delayed the "conversion" of the Iroquois to Christianity, but their "warlike and impetuous nature" had led to the "depopulation" and cultural "Ruin" of Iroquoia. To support his claim, Le Jeune noted that there were then "more Foreigners than natives of the country" in Iroquois villages, identifying specifically members of seven different alien nations among the Onondagas and as many as eleven among the Senecas. Yet Le Jeune failed to fully consider the potential advantages that these so-called "Foreigners" provided to their Iroquois host communities, nations, and the League itself.[76]

Le Jeune documented "three classes of captives" among the Iroquois in 1657. The first were those who had willingly submitted to "the yoke of the conquerors and elected to remain among them." These individuals were eligible to marry into Iroquois households and led what Le Jeune described as "tolerably easy lives," despite being "looked upon as slaves" and denied a "voice, either active or passive, in the public councils." The second class of prisoners, according to Le Jeune, included those who had "fallen into slavery after having been the richest and most esteemed in their own villages, and who receive no reward from their Masters, in exchange for their ceaseless labor and sweat, than food and shelter." The final, most numerous category (and the one that most troubled Jesuit sensibilities) included the young, unmarried women and girls, who were "constantly exposed to the danger of losing their honors or their lives through the brutal lechery or cruelty of their Masters or Mistresses," and reportedly punished by death for the "slightest faults."[77]

Uncritical reading of Le Jeune's statement has led some scholars to the erroneous conclusion that the Iroquois forced alien captive populations into a form of chattel "slavery" during the middle decades of the seventeenth century.[78] While the Iroquois subjected each of their captives to a preliminary probationary period (during which time they were most likely to be tortured and/or executed), actual killings of captives destined for adoption occurred infrequently, and almost never for reasons that contemporary Iroquois people would have regarded as capricious. Male and female adoptees moved freely throughout Iroquoia and performed the same labor as their Iroquois hosts. Adoptees integrated into Iroquois communities and nations contributed not only personnel but also elements of their own diverse cultural backgrounds to their hosts. The Tahontaenrats, as we have seen, offered new curing rituals, and Jesuit Simon Le Moyne described unspecified "captives" of "another nation" among the Onondagas performing ritual healings with plants from their own homelands while masked as "counterfeit Bears" during the winter of 1661–62. At least two male adoptees became holders of hereditary titles among the Iroquois during the seventeenth century, while several others achieved merit-based leadership positions. Female adoptees occasionally assumed prominent roles of authority over the hereditary male titleholders in their adoptive lineages.[79]

While we have only rare glimpses of how the integration of captives into Iroquois clans, towns, and nations operated at the ideological level, evidence of adoptees' identification with their Iroquois hosts apparently superseded the spiritual affiliations of supposed Christians in their ranks. Jesuits who possessed the most direct experience with Iroquois populations during the middle decades of the seventeenth century admitted that many of the League nations' adoptees who had previously been exposed to Jesuit proselytization, especially former residents of Wendake, offered the most strenuous opposition to their missionary efforts throughout Iroquoia. The weight of this evidence supports the view of anthropologist Bruce Trigger, who argues that far from becoming slaves, "within one or two generations, thousands of prisoners had come to regard themselves as Iroquois."[80]

The Iroquois managed large populations of ethnically diverse captives during the middle decades of the seventeenth century by practicing assimilative adoption (bringing individuals or small groups directly into host clan segments) when possible and associative adoption (whereby adoptees retained their former ethnic affiliation alongside their identity as an adoptive member of an Iroquois nation) when necessary. While Jesuits regarded captive "husbands separated from [their] wives, and the children from their parents" as evidence of the Iroquois treating their prisoners "as slaves," this process of distributing captives throughout clan segments represented a long-standing means of integrating individuals into larger cultural units. Le Jeune's 1657 claim that the "Iroquois language" was intelligible to members of seventeen different indigenous nations in a perimeter extending 1,200 miles from the center of Iroquoia doubtless also proved of great value in accelerating assimilative adoptions in individual households.[81]

Various techniques of associative adoption enabled Iroquois nations to relocate substantial populations (especially the constituent nations of the Wendat Confederacy) to their homelands, and to establish separate settlements for them, thereby permitting the process of assimilation by intermarriage to occur over one or two generations. Evidence for spatially separate, clan- or tribal-based satellite settlements of Wendats among the Mohawks, Onondagas, and Senecas, which peaks in the archaeological and documentary record during the 1650s, dwindles after 1680, but the people, and their descendants, did not. Jesuit Jerôme Lalemant reported that "pureblooded" Iroquois accounted for less than 20 percent of the population of the League nations in 1660, which he characterized as "aggregates of different tribes they have conquered."[82]

Conscious of their need to compete with the Iroquois for the hearts and minds of these adoptees, the Jesuits staked considerable hopes on the Gannentaha mission. They regarded its location "in the center of these [Iroquois] nations" as most advantageous to their spiritual objectives, since it granted them access to "a great number of travelers" who made Onondaga country "very populous," especially during the well-attended annual meetings of the League. Access to these gatherings, which Le Jeune described in 1657 as "the custom observed by these nations, of giving one another each year friendly presents in the Councils and public assemblies," was all-important in Jesuit eyes, since it represented a crucial opportunity to offer Jesuit explanations of their own "mysteries" to counter public Iroquois recitations of "stories of olden times" during League meetings.[83]

After making preliminary contact with the four upper nations of the League by the end of 1657, the Jesuits identified the Mohawks as "the stumbling-block which might hinder our design." The Oneidas, however, proved the Jesuits wrong. Three Oneidas, described as then living peacefully near Montreal, killed three French settlers in late October 1657. In response, authorities in New France ordered a blanket arrest of all Iroquois in New France, which netted eleven Mohawks and one Onondaga then present at Trois-Rivières and another Onondaga man discovered near Montreal. Keeping six of the Mohawks detained at Trois-Rivières, Governor Louis d'Ailleboust ordered Guillaume Couture to escort the five other Mohawks to Quebec, "shackled together two by two [*sic*]." On November 7, 1657, d'Ailleboust released two of the Mohawk detainees to advise their nation of the recent murders and of French officials' demand for redress. The French also sent letters intended for the Jesuits at Gannentaha with the released Mohawk captives, but the correspondence never arrived.[84]

Having cut off communications between the Gannentaha mission and New France, the Mohawks sent three headmen to Montreal to treat with d'Ailleboust on February 4, 1658. Demonstrating their ongoing effort to coordinate League external relations through the "eastern door," these Mohawks informed French officials that the members of the Five Nations were "united" with the Dutch "by a chain of iron," and that they wanted to "make Onontio enter that union." D'Ailleboust declined the Mohawks' offer of peace in his reply, demanding instead the surrender of the Oneida murderers as a precondition to any discussion of returning the Iroquois prisoners. Until then, the only chains that mattered to the governor were those that confined the Iroquois hostages in a Quebec prison.[85]

In the meantime, a "very secret" League council was under way in Mohawk country. This gathering of "a small number of the chiefs and Elders of all the Nations" endeavored to formulate potential responses to the Oneidas' decision in November 1657 to publicly display the scalps of the three murdered French settlers in their town, which represented an independent Oneida "declaration of war" on New France. Given d'Ailleboust's imposition of blanket retributive justice on Iroquois individuals who happened to be in New France at the time of the Oneidas' attack, and the subsequent failure of the Mohawk peace embassy, the League delegates resolved to expel the French from Gannentaha once all Iroquois prisoners had returned from New France.[86]

This League council ended the Onondagas' experiment of "smokehole" diplomacy with New France. By late February 1658, the French at Gannentaha reported increasingly hostile attitudes demonstrated by their Onondaga hosts. News of an army of 200 Mohawks and forty Oneidas departing to attack New France convinced the Jesuits that they were no longer secure at Gannentaha (notwithstanding the small cannon mounted on the mission's palisade). At 11:00 P.M. on March 20, 1658, the entire French population of the mission, consisting of some fifty or sixty men, took flight in canoes built in secret behind the locked doors of the mission's chapel (an unwitting admission, perhaps, of the limited number of Onondaga visits to that structure). The French convoy reached Montreal in two weeks, and put in at Quebec on April 23, 1658.[87]

By February 1658, with the League's assimilation of Wendat refugees in the St. Lawrence valley nearing completion, Iroquois headmen had come to regard the risks associated with a Jesuit mission in the center of Iroquoia as too high to sustain. The French and Jesuits, unlike other adoptees, not only refused to accommodate to Iroquois norms and values but also represented a source of potential information leakage to New France. The French had built a palisaded structure in Onondaga country as a refuge for Onondaga women and children in the event of attack (a considerable homeland security benefit during a time of intense intertribal conflict), in addition to providing the services of a blacksmith to repair Iroquois firearms. Yet Gannentaha's Jesuits had ensured that the mission station never became a significant enough trade entrepôt to compete with direct (or Mohawk-brokered) procurement of goods by the so-called upper four Iroquois nations at Fort Orange. The Mohawks' "eastern door" approach—keeping both the French and Dutch at arm's length on the periphery of Iroquoia while asserting control over the continental interior through the gradual assimilation of neighboring indigenous populations—regained ascendancy in League foreign relations in 1658.[88]

Hostages and Hostilities

Following the flight of the French mission from Gannentaha, the five League nations renewed efforts to resolve their relations with neighboring settler colonies via Mohawk-led parallel negotiations with Dutch and French officials. These efforts proved difficult, and the other League nations' independent raiding of French settlers soon undermined the eastern doorkeepers' diplomacy. Escalating hostilities with New France occurred alongside expanding League military campaigns beyond the immediate periphery of Iroquoia, and by 1658 Iroquois people found themselves vulnerable to enemy offensives into the Five Nations' homelands. French settlers realized by this time that they were involved in a potential death struggle with the League, and they sought new ways and means to combat their most powerful rivals.

On April 19, 1658, Mohawk delegates brought Jesuit Simon Le Moyne to Fort Orange, where, in the presence of New Netherland authorities, they expressed their desire for brotherly relations with New France. Restating the principles of their *kaswentha* relationship with the Dutch, the Mohawks planned to have Le Moyne ask officials in New France to "do like the Dutchman, who interferes not in the wars of" allied native nations. Finally, in an unprecedented move reflecting the ascendant idea of a Mohawk-forged iron chain linking the League, New France, and New Netherland, several "Manhattan Dutch" accompanied an embassy representing each of the three

Mohawk clans and Le Moyne to Quebec, where on May 21, 1658, the Mohawks asked d'Ailleboust once more for the return of their hostages.[89]

D'Ailleboust, who manifested a more conciliatory attitude following the evacuation of the Gannentaha mission, released all the Mohawk detainees but retained the lone Onondaga hostage. The governor then pledged to maintain a "fire" at Quebec for future Mohawk visitors, indicating his receptiveness to future diplomacy. Yet the conference concluded with the elevated "gallery" of the fort at Quebec collapsing under the combined weight of the Mohawk, Dutch, Jesuit, Wendat, Algonquin, and French delegates, who all tumbled to the ground in an accidental but telling omen of future conflicts.[90]

Three weeks after the Mohawks' late May 1658 departure from Quebec, Iroquois war parties returned to the St. Lawrence valley, attacking French settlers, Montagnais, and Algonquins residing between Montreal and Quebec. In the meantime, the Mohawks, continuing their efforts to build on their preliminary achievements with d'Ailleboust, sent fifteen of their "eldest sachems" to Fort Orange. After reminding Dutch officials of earlier Mohawk assistance in bringing an end to hostilities in the Peach Tree War in 1657 and the subsequent "duty" of the Dutch "to do the same in such circumstances for them," the Mohawks obtained a soldier fluent in French to accompany a planned embassy to repatriate a French prisoner, along with a cover letter attesting to the sincerity of Mohawk intentions for peace.[91]

Confronted by renewed Iroquois attacks on the Native and settler population of New France, officials at Trois-Rivières captured seven Mohawks on September 4, 1658, and shipped them off to Quebec. D'Ailleboust's successor, Pierre de Voyer, the Vicomte d'Argenson, conferred with the seven Mohawk prisoners, whose leader was an adoptee known as "Atogwatkann, called La Grande cueilliere ['The Large Spoon']." D'Argenson released two of the Mohawks to carry word home of the joint resolve of the French, Wendats, and Algonquins to have peace with "all or none" of the League nations, albeit on certain terms: the Iroquois would have to agree to a mass repatriation of all French, Wendat, and Algonquin captives residing throughout Iroquoia.[92]

French authorities at Montreal, in the meantime, ordered an attack on an Onondaga party (who claimed to be traveling as a diplomatic embassy) on September 16, 1658. The French killed two members of the group (who were later identified as Wendat adoptees) and incarcerated eleven more. One of these captured ambassadors was Otreouti, the Onondagas' well-traveled Wendat adoptee. Nine days later, a French shallop reached Quebec with five Oneidas captured during a skirmish at Trois-Rivières that also left three Oneidas dead.[93]

In the midst of this escalating violence, a second delegation of Onondagas under Garacontié (a nephew of Sagochiendagehté and his successor) appeared at Montreal to exchange the two French prisoners taken by the Oneidas in July for the Onondagas remaining in French custody. Garacontié, speaking on behalf of all League nations but the Mohawks, delivered an extensive condolence speech in which he offered to forget the French assault on the preceding Onondaga party if the French would agree to peace and permit the Iroquois free passage to attack the Algonquins. Montreal governor Charles Le Moyne responded by insisting on a discussion of the Jesuits' return to Gannentaha as a precursor to peace talks. If the Onondagas agreed to receive the Jesuits in their country, "matters shall be thoroughly settled on all sides." Garacontié declined these terms, and Otreouti and his Onondaga colleagues remained behind "iron bars" in a Montreal prison.[94]

While civil authorities in New France continued to round up and detain Iroquois people indiscriminately, the Jesuits extended an olive branch to Iroquoia. On September 28, 1658, Chaumonot sent a "Huron Oneida" messenger to Mohawk country to report that the five remaining Mohawk hostages were still alive at Quebec. The Jesuits also sent condolence presents for the two slain Wendat adoptees back to Onondaga country. The message accompanying these gifts offered peace but included conditions that would not only authorize the return of the Jesuits to Onondaga country but also obligate the Onondagas to deliver a number of "little girls to be placed with the Ursuline Mothers" at Quebec. This effort to secure Iroquois children (ideally those "of the chief men of the country") as hostages for the security of Jesuit missionaries in Iroquoia had first been proposed by Ursuline Marie de l'Incarnation in 1655.[95]

The Jesuits recognized the high stakes of these negotiations for their North American missionary enterprise. Iroquois warriors harassed Native residents of Jesuit missions at Tadoussac, at Quebec, and in Abenaki country. Other Iroquois war parties, motivated in part by their ongoing pursuit of refugees from Wendake, traveled as far as Lake Superior and launched attacks on Potawatomi, Mascouten, and Odawa communities hosting Tionnontatés. The expansion of Iroquois warfare into the upper Great Lakes region by 1658 meant that "nearly everywhere the door is closed to the Gospel."[96]

While mobile Iroquois parties blocked Jesuit access to the indigenous nations of the upper Great Lakes, the Mohawks continued efforts to make a comprehensive peace for the League at its eastern door. An embassy of six Mohawk headmen accompanied by a "Dutchman" and the Jesuit Le Moyne (whose presence ensured their secure travel) arrived at Quebec on November 22, 1658. Teharihogen, speaking for the Mohawk delegation, made a formal offer of peace to Governor d'Argenson. Making specific reference to "Otsindiakhon, namely, the captain of New Holland," as his "companion in this embassy" (the individual in question was actually a French-speaking soldier from Fort Orange named Jacob Begyn), Teharihogen advised French authorities of the Mohawks' ties to seven allied nations, whom he delineated from west to east as the Senecas, Cayugas, Onondagas, "the Frenchmen of Ganentaa," the Oneidas, the Mahicans, and the Dutch. Urging d'Argenson to join this alliance and to abandon his offensive practice of "chain[ing] men," Teharihogen employed *kaswentha* rhetoric to smooth the troubled waters of the "river" between New France and Iroquoia so that it could be navigated in peace by all parties.[97]

D'Argenson acknowledged the desire of the French, Wendats, and Algonquins for a comprehensive peace with all Iroquois nations, so that the "Preachers of the gospel might have free access to them." He offered to send Le Moyne to an upcoming meeting of League delegates in Mohawk country to assist in negotiations that would yield an "eternal peace," one that would "unite our country with yours." In an effort to render more formal the de facto conditions of peace, he invited the Mohawks to come and "dwell among" the French, or at least to "bring us girls," promising that he would send some Frenchmen to live in their country. D'Argenson then released an Oneida prisoner from custody at Quebec, and the next day most of Tehariho-gen's party departed for Mohawk country. The Mohawk titleholder remained in New France to await an Oneida embassy for negotiations on the release of the remaining hostages.[98]

Three Oneidas arrived at Quebec on April 3, 1659, to offer "satisfaction" for the French settler they had killed and to request the release of the Oneidas in French custody. The Oneidas justified their aggressive acts against the French settler popula-tion on the grounds of the abrupt French abandonment of Gannentaha, which in their view had broken "the Bond" of linked arms between the French and the League. Infuriated French authorities made no response for nearly two weeks.[99]

D'Argenson rebuked the Oneidas in open council on April 28, 1659, dismissing their rationalization for aggression against New France and remarking on their "bad grace" in requesting the repatriation of all their prisoners when they themselves had brought none of their own French captives. D'Argenson informed the Oneidas that "collars of porcelain beads" would no longer suffice as evidence of "the voice of their Elders" in the eyes of the French. A stable peace could only result from an exchange of "men whom each side should give to reside with the Other." The French governor concluded the conference by releasing four Oneidas to accompany Jesuits Le Moyne, Jerôme Lalemant, and Gabriel Druillettes to Mohawk country for further peace negotiations.[100]

Iroquois patience with d'Argenson's efforts to micromanage hostage diplomacy by insisting on precise, tit-for-tat exchanges ended during the summer of 1659. Far from diminishing hostilities, d'Argenson's tactics actually provoked a fresh cycle of violence as Iroquois parties began, after June 1659, to take significant numbers of French captives. One Wendat defector from Iroquoia reported that the Five Nations even planned to target French "children to repeople their country."[101]

Following the renewal of open hostilities against New France in August 1659, the Mohawks endeavored to shore up their ties to the Dutch. On September 6, 1659, a Mohawk delegation appeared at Fort Orange and complained that "the Dutch say we are brothers and that we are joined together with chains, but that lasts only as long as we have beavers. After that we are no longer thought of." The Mohawks com-municated a lengthy list of grievances that suggested many reasons for the recent decline in the volume of Iroquois-procured peltry arriving in New Netherland. The

Mohawks asked Dutch traders to "cease their viciousness and not beat them as they have done in the past." They requested free repair of their firearms by Dutch smiths, and pressed for a commitment on the part of Dutch authorities to provide fifty to sixty men to assist the Mohawks in the event of "enemy" attack. They also demanded the immediate assistance of thirty men with horses to haul logs for the repair of their towns' palisades ("through which," reported a former French captive, one could then "easily pass"). Finally, the Mohawks also reminded Fort Orange authorities that Dutch spouses of deceased Mohawks were obligated to supply their mourning in-laws with "one or two suits of cloth," a subtle but significant indicator of increasing interpersonal bonds between the Mohawks and New Netherland settlers.[102]

Alarmed by this Mohawk speech, Dutch authorities at Fort Orange assembled a seventeen-man delegation (including Jeremias van Rensselaer, Arent van Curler, and Philip Pietersen Schuyler) to issue a direct reply in Mohawk country. On September 24, 1659, at the Mohawks' easternmost "Castle called Kaghnuwage," the Dutch announced their intention to "renew our old friendship and brotherhood." Referring to Van Curler's 1643 embassy, the Dutch renewed the "iron chain" that had linked them with the Mohawks "sixteen years ago" and stated that "henceforth you will have no reason to doubt that we shall be and remain brothers." The Dutch failed to answer the Mohawks' specific grievances, but concluded their speech with a substantial present (consisting of 75 pounds of powder, 100 pounds of lead, fifteen axes, and "two beavers' worth of knives"), in hopes that their words and gifts would suffice.[103]

Unfortunately for the Mohawks, the weak gesture offered by their Dutch allies did little to resolve their ongoing conflict with the French, who during the autumn of 1659 had begun to employ mixed "squads" of settlers and allied Wendats and Algonquins to intercept invading Iroquois parties. The escalation of war with the Iroquois led some Jesuits to criticize d'Argenson's strategy of detaining Iroquois prisoners for diminishing the likelihood of the Jesuits' return to Iroquoia and for doing nothing to counteract long-distance Iroquois movements into the upper Great Lakes as far as Sioux country, estimated to be 1,800 miles from League homelands. Yet a speech offered by the Isle d'Orléans Wendats to newly arrived Bishop François de Laval during the summer of 1659 had planted the seed of a potential solution to the Iroquois problem in the minds of the Jesuits. The unidentified Wendat speaker, possibly after some prior Jesuit coaching, advised Laval that if an army from France could achieve the mere "destruction of two or three of these enemies' villages thou wilt make for [the French] a great highway to vast lands and to many nations" in the upper Great Lakes.[104]

The Wendats of the Isle d'Orléans supported their anti-Iroquois proposal by offering their defensive assistance to the French settler population. Forty Wendat warriors under Étienne Annaotaha accompanied seventeen Frenchmen under the leadership of Adam Dollard des Ormeaux in April 1660 to the Long Sault of the Ottawa River to ambush Iroquois parties returning to their homelands from military and hunting journeys in the upper Great Lakes via this former Wendat route. Yet on May 3, 1660, the sight of canoes carrying 200 Onondagas convinced the badly outnumbered French and Wendats to take refuge "in a wretched remnant of a fort" (located on the south side of the Ottawa River, less than a mile east of the outlet of the Little Rideau River).[105]

After surrounding the French and Wendats' position, the Onondagas, in a stunning demonstration of the efficiency of Iroquois field communications, dispatched messengers who summoned 500 Mohawk reinforcements from a planned point of rendezvous in the islands of the Richelieu River, over 125 miles distant. Upon the arrival of the Mohawks, the 700-man Iroquois army commenced a ten-day siege of the French and Wendats. Twenty-four of the Wendats abandoned the French and surrendered themselves to the Iroquois attackers, among whom were "a great number" of Wendat adoptees. Failing to convince Dollard des Ormeaux and Annaotaha to give up the fight, the Iroquois launched a final assault between May 9 and 12, 1660, which killed all but five of the Frenchmen and four of the remaining fourteen Wendats. The Iroquois, who had lost fourteen killed and nineteen wounded in the siege, subsequently tortured and killed all of the French and Wendats captured at Long Sault (even those Wendats who had voluntarily surrendered), save for four Wendat men known to have escaped at later dates.[106]

The Onondaga and Mohawk army elected not to undertake a subsequent assault on St. Lawrence valley settlements, and as a result the French would later come to identify the heroic efforts of Dollard des Ormeaux at Long Sault as achieving the salvation of New France. Yet other Iroquois war parties assaulted the settler population of New France continually from May to July 1660. At least one such instance involved an attack by a multigenerational men's clan party of "Iroquoised Hurons" (Wendat adoptees). In the meantime, the Mohawks and Onondagas discussed forming "an army corps once more, by a junction of their forces," to destroy New France, and rumors persisted into November 1660 that the Mohawks planned to employ Wendat adoptees to guide an army "by night into the very heart of Québec, in order to steal away from us the rest of the Huron Colony."[107]

Despite the League's war with New France, Iroquois headmen also warned officials at Fort Orange that ongoing physical assaults and verbal insults by Dutch traders threatened an end to the peace and friendship they had "enjoyed for more than thirty years." In late July 1660, an Onondaga delegation echoed the Mohawks' complaints of abuses committed by Dutch traders outside the boundaries of Fort Orange and Beverwijck and demanded guaranteed, secure freedom of movement for Iroquois traders at Albany as a means of eliminating these problems. Finally, the Onondagas cited their pressing need for gunpowder, given newly reopened hostilities with the Susquehannocks, who employed firearms obtained from Dutch traders on the Delaware River to intercept Onondagas and Senecas carrying beaver pelts from interior hunting grounds (or raids) to Fort Orange.[108]

In 1660, the Jesuits' annual *Relation* concluded with an extensive lamentation decrying "the Iroquois, who, like an obtrusive phantom, besets us in all places." Then commanding a perimeter of "five or six hundred leagues" around their homeland settlements, the Iroquois, according to the author of the *Relation,* had the power "to subject all our settlements to fire and massacre whenever they choose." In the opinion of the Jesuits, only a commitment from France on par with that of the Church during the Crusades could bring about the rescue of the "Holy land [New France] from the possession of the [Iroquois] infidels."[109]

A "late winter" 1661 assault by 160 Iroquois warriors on Montreal inaugurated the deadliest season of raiding yet witnessed in New France. From that time until the following October, Iroquois attacks on French settlers, Algonquins, and Wendats occurred over a 300-mile extent of territory, "from Tadoussac to Montréal," and resulted in an estimated 114 deaths (French settlers accounted for at least 70 of this total) and dozens of captives. Residents of Montreal confronted once more the gruesome task of recovering the dismembered trunks, legs, and arms of French victims strewn about the island by Iroquois warriors. Terrified habitants offered accounts of Iroquois parties appearing "at the edge of the woods," like "importunate harpies or birds of prey," who "pounce[d] upon us whenever they found us off our guard, without fear of being captured themselves."[110]

While the Iroquois pushed New France to the brink of elimination, they continued to optimize their access to rivers leading to the upper Great Lakes to pursue large-scale, long-distance campaigns in search of captives and new sources of peltry. In late May 1661, the Iroquois attacked a group of Tionnontaté Wendats at Keewenaw Bay (on the modern-day Upper Peninsula of Michigan), and in July 1661 another party of 180 Iroquois journeyed to the vicinity of James Bay, where they attacked and dispersed the so-called Squirrel nation. According to the Jesuits, there were "no Pirates on the China Sea so dangerous" as the Five Nations, who then represented nothing less than "the great scourge of Christianity" in North America.[111]

While the French related accounts of Iroquois military exploits with alternating expressions of shock and awe, evidence suggests that the dramatic increase in the duration and spatial range of Iroquois warfare after 1658 had left Iroquois homeland settlements increasingly susceptible to attacks by indigenous enemies. Following a 1660 Oneida attack on the Piscataways, Maryland colonial officials supported Susquehannock retaliatory offensives that penetrated Cayuga country in 1661. By October 1661, the Mohawks and Oneidas were reportedly defending their settlements against Mahican, Abenaki, and Pocumtuck attacks. Ongoing Susquehannock ambuscades of Seneca traders heading east to New Netherland (following a pattern identical to that the Iroquois had themselves pursued previously against the Wendats) forced the Senecas to form caravans of 600 people in order to travel to Fort Orange in security. Offensive expeditions against the Susquehannocks and Lenapes of the Delaware River valley occupied the elements of the four western League nations from at least

June 1661 to November 1662. As the military situation intensified, the Onondagas, Cayugas, and Senecas renewed peace negotiations with New France.[112]

On June 29, 1661, a delegation of Cayuga and Onondaga ambassadors bearing a white flag and four French captives landed their canoes on Montreal Island. The captives served this peace embassy as "a passport that relieved them of all fear" of French or French-allied Native interference with their diplomacy. Saonchiogwa, "one of the principal captains" of the Cayugas and a former host of Jesuit visitors to Cayuga country, offered the French prisoners in exchange for eight Cayugas then detained at Montreal. He promised the future repatriation of a reputed twenty more French prisoners then held by the Onondagas. Saonchiogwa also delivered a condolence speech to the French, which "made smooth the course of the river, clearing away all its rocks, and leveling out all its rapids, in order to establish a ready inter-communication." Skeptical Montreal officials accepted the repatriated French prisoners but released no Cayugas. Jesuit Simon Le Moyne was detailed to return with the embassy to Onondaga country to restate to League authorities that the French would make peace with all Iroquois nations or none.[113]

Almost immediately after Le Moyne's July 21 departure, French settlers on Montreal Island reported taunts (apparently in French) from Mohawks "prowling about our fields." These warriors scorned the Cayuga and Onondaga embassy, promising to continue their attacks until the French released all the "captives of their nation that were in custody at Montréal." Mohawk and Oneida warriors harassed Le Moyne and his Onondaga and Cayuga escorts intermittently as the party made their way to Onondaga country. En route to Onondaga, Le Moyne also encountered a "Canoe-full" of eight or ten Onondagas following a larger party of thirty more under the leadership of Wendat adoptee Otreouti, who, in spite of his nation's recent peace overtures, was going to Montreal to "avenge the insult he believed he had received in having been detained there in prison."[114]

Two "leagues'" distance from the principal Onondaga town, Le Moyne received a formal Edge of the Woods welcome ceremony from Garacontié and four or five "other [Onondaga] elders," which the Jesuit viewed as a distinct honor, "never, as a rule, paid to other Ambassadors" since Onondaga headmen typically greeted all visitors "scarcely an eighth of a league outside their village." Yet the lack of Onondaga consensus concerning peace with New France extended beyond the obvious personal motivations of Otreouti. Le Moyne noted that Garacontié, in order to "conciliate the men of his Nation, who might have felt jealous at having no share in procuring this new peace," led the Jesuit guest to his rivals' longhouse "in order to give them first the honor of lodging me, and to remove all cause for envy on their part of the happiness which he was to enjoy in being my host." Le Moyne addressed a League council at Onondaga on August 12, 1661, asking the assembled headmen of "the five Iroquois nations" to confirm the Cayugas' speech at Montreal. After several days' deliberation, League authorities offered to release seven French prisoners from Onondaga custody and two from Cayuga custody, while retaining their remaining French prisoners in "fetters" at Onondaga "for reasons of State." Garacontié would head up a Seneca, Cayuga, and Onondaga delegation to Montreal to repatriate the French prisoners, while Le Moyne would remain at Onondaga to await his return.[115]

While League officials deliberated at Onondaga, Otreouti entered Montreal on August 29, 1661, "crying 'Hay, hay,' which is a sign of peace." After receiving a cordial reception and presents from local authorities, Otreouti's party killed two men roofing a house on their way out of town. Otreouti also murdered and decapitated the Jesuit Jacques Le Maistre, stripped off his cassock, and "[c]lothed in this precious spoil, he paraded pompously in sight of Montréal, braving the town with an insolence truly barbaric." In late September 1661, Otreouti, still wearing Le Maistre's cassock during his return journey to Onondaga country, came upon Garacontié's peace embassy en route to New France. This "surprise" encounter led to "council upon council" between the two Onondaga headmen. Despite concerns that Otreouti's recent actions had ruined any chance of peace, Garacontié pledged to continue, "fully convinced that the French who were left at Onondaga with Father le Moyne were a sufficient surety for the safety of his own life," along with the French captives he planned to repatriate. The Onondaga peace embassy arrived at Montreal on October 5, 1661.[116]

After exchanging nine French prisoners for the Cayugas detained at Montreal, Garacontié invited the French "to come and dwell" in Iroquoia "in order to form but one people." Newly arrived governor Pierre Dubois d'Avaugour, abandoning his predecessor's insistence on a comprehensive peace with all League nations, authorized a provisional peace with Garacontié's Onondaga-led embassy on the strength of intelligence from the repatriated French prisoners pertaining to the demography of the League nations. If the Mohawks truly were, as the repatriated prisoners reported, "absolutely determined on war, and resolved to conquer or perish," it made sense to conclude terms with the Onondagas, Senecas, and Cayugas, three nations believed to account for at least 75 percent of the League's reputed 2,000 warriors. In the view of d'Avaugour, this would isolate the Mohawks and Oneidas, two nations considered the "smaller part" of the Iroquois League, then estimated at a combined strength of only 400 to 500 men.[117]

The Mohawks, for their part, had spent the summer months of 1661 crafting a new approach to the Dutch alliance. On July 27, 1661, three Mohawk headmen representing the nation's constituent Bear, Turtle, and Wolf clans signed a deed at Fort Orange granting Van Curler a tract of land in the vicinity of modern-day Schenectady, New York. In doing so, the Mohawks alienated then-unoccupied territory they claimed after their 1628 dispersal of the Mahicans. The 1661 Schenectady deed added an important new twist, however. The Mohawks hoped to leverage their gift of cleared land to Van Curler into a new Dutch trading post twenty-four miles closer to their easternmost town. Mohawk-brokered trade and diplomacy at this new locale would spare Iroquois traders a tedious overland passage to the increasingly rough-and-tumble trading scene at Fort Orange. The Mohawks' plans were grounded on their growing kinship ties to the Dutch settler population, personified by Van Curler, who then had a nine-year-old daughter living with her mother's family in Mohawk country. Additionally, Van Curler had a long-established track record in selling firearms to Iroquois customers. Despite delays in surveying that deferred settlement of the Schenectady patent until 1664, and official bans by Dutch and, later, English colonial authorities, the Mohawks' innovative sale of Schenectady lands demonstrated Iroquois peoples' capacity to think creatively about the potential uses of their abundant territorial holdings in the context of engaging settler colonialism.[118]

RECONNAISSANCE AND INVASION

As Iroquois military campaigns spread outward from Iroquoia in a web of multiple directions, after 1661 the French obtained (from escaped captives and other, unidentified sources) long-sought detailed reconnaissance of Iroquois homelands. This spatial knowledge, combined with the resolve of King Louis XIV after 1663 to stabilize New France and thereby to render it a productive component of the emerging French overseas empire, soon yielded plans for an armed French invasion of Iroquoia. French officials now understood clearly how reducing the League nations' freedom of movement represented a necessary first step toward enhancing their own exploitation of New France and its hinterlands.

Despite the conclusion of preliminary terms with Garacontié during the autumn of 1661, a sense of desperation prevailed among the 3,000 settlers of New France. Colonial authorities dispatched Pierre Boucher, who had served as governor of Trois-Rivières since 1654, to France in 1661 to make the case for an invasion of Iroquoia. Significantly, Boucher based his argument on Jesuit Paul Ragueneau's opinion that any planned French invasion of Iroquoia would best proceed up the Hudson River, "through New Holland," as the "most effective means" of accessing Mohawk country. Yet after Governor d'Avaugour interrogated one of the French prisoners repatriated by Garacontié in October 1661 about the rivers and portages employed by Mohawk war parties, he recommended an alteration of French military plans. Instead of relying on the unlikely prospect of securing Dutch permission to move a French army up the Hudson River, the French, in d'Avaugour's view, could reach Iroquoia using the Mohawks' own route through the Lake Champlain–Richelieu River corridor.[119]

As rumors of the pending arrival of French "vessels laden with soldiers" began to circulate, Iroquois offensives into the St. Lawrence valley diminished in number and intensity. Following Garacontié's 1661 negotiations, the Iroquois directed their efforts away from French settlers, focusing instead on the Algonquins and Wendats residing on the Isle d'Orléans for nearly two years. Otreouti participated in a peaceful, four-day Onondaga visit to Quebec in March 1662, and on August 31, 1662, Le Moyne returned to Montreal with eighteen other repatriated French prisoners after nearly a year of residency in Onondaga country under unofficial house arrest.[120]

While French settlers enjoyed temporary respite from Iroquois offensives, long-distance Iroquois military campaigning reached its farthest documented spatial range in 1662. Jesuit Simon Le Moyne, during his sojourn in Onondaga country, recorded a stunning array of destinations for Iroquois war parties assembled that year. A number of Onondaga warriors (possibly motivated to replace 120 members of their nation lost to an outbreak of smallpox in their homelands over the winter of 1661–62) journeyed southward to attack Susquehannocks and unnamed nations residing on the "Virginia coast." Other Iroquois war parties targeted the "Ontôagannhas" (Shawnees) in 1662, some 400 "leagues" to the southwest of their homelands; these attacks were likely undertaken in retaliation for losses sustained by the Onondagas in that quarter over the winter of 1653–54, and these war parties may have employed some Shawnee adoptees then residing at Onondaga to guide their journey. These campaigns appear also to have engaged the Quapaws and other peoples residing in the lower Ohio valley prior to the Quapaws westward relocation to modern-day southern Illinois, where Europeans first encountered them in 1673. Still other Iroquois war parties set out in 1662 for a planned two-year expedition against the Sioux, while Mohawks attacked Abenakis on the Kennebec River and took captives among Cree peoples residing north of Tadoussac. Le Moyne also noted that at least two Iroquois war parties of undocumented strength also attacked Tionnontaté Wendats residing near modern-day Green Bay, Wisconsin, in 1662.[121]

Although they possessed more European firearms than any of their Native rivals and could project force over vast distances, Iroquois war parties were not invincible. From 1662 to 1663, they suffered several serious defeats on their campaigns beyond Iroquoia. In one of the most famous of these incidents, a Mohawk and Oneida war party consisting of 100 people sustained a near-total defeat at the hands of the Ojibwas on the southern shore of Lake Superior during the spring of 1662. The victorious Ojibwas documented their victory by painting pictographic images on nearby rocks. In April 1662, Abenakis on the Kennebec River responded to an effort by thirty Mohawks to collect a tribute payment by murdering the entire party, save for one man whom they sent back to Mohawk country with part of his scalp and entire upper lip cut off as a sign of their opposition to such "molestation."[122]

One year later, an 800-person army of Onondagas, Senecas, and Cayugas traveled down the Susquehanna River for an attack on "the Village of Andastogué" (Atrakwae). Members of the Iroquois expeditionary force, which included an unknown number of women, were surprised to find the Susquehannocks' town "flanked by two bastions erected in the European manner, and even supplied with some pieces of Artillery." Deciding to request a parley, the Iroquois sent a delegation of men into the "Barken City," but the Susquehannocks immediately seized the Iroquois ambassadors and burned them on scaffolds atop their palisade "in sight of their own army." The

Iroquois army subsequently fled homeward, sustaining additional casualties at the hands of pursuing Susquehannocks. Once back in Iroquoia, the Onondagas, Senecas, and Cayugas appealed to the Mohawks for assistance against a threatened Susquehannock invasion.[123]

In late May 1663, a party of Algonquins returned from Lake Champlain with ten Iroquois scalps, including that of Mohawk war leader Garistatsi, known to the French as "Le Fer" (The Iron), supposedly "the most renowned" of all Iroquois military leaders. Following the Mohawks' autumn 1663 execution of all members of a Susquehannock peace embassy (which included two Lenape women), a Mohawk, Onondaga, and Seneca force attacked the fortified Squakheag town known as "Fort Hill" on December 11, 1663. Warriors retreating homeward after this attack admitted losses of 100 men while passing by Fort Orange. In May 1664, a 600-man Iroquois army (composed mostly of Mohawks) attacked a Mahican village, but sustained numerous casualties in the attempt. Operating in tandem with Algonquins and Abenakis, the Mahicans subsequently "infest[ed] the Maquas trail and [kept] it unsafe," much to the chagrin of beaver-deprived merchants in Albany. The Mohawks sent a peace embassy to the Abenakis, but the latter murdered the would-be Mohawk diplomats. The outbreak of another smallpox epidemic in Iroquoia in 1663 compounded the impact of all these military setbacks.[124]

The Algonquians' effective blockade of Fort Orange rendered the "roads very dangerous" for all would-be Iroquois traders. The reduced capacity of the Senecas to procure arms and ammunition from the Dutch led them to ask the Jesuit Le Moyne, who spent the winter of 1663–64 in Seneca country, for French assistance in "surround[ing] their villages with flanked palisades (possibly an allusion to those they had seen at Atrakwae and Fort Hill), and furnish them with munitions of war," which they needed for defense against ongoing, Maryland-supported Susquehannock and Piscataway aggression.[125]

While the Iroquois struggled with battlefield defeats and disease, newly enthroned King Louis XIV sent royal emissaries to Canada in May 1663 to take formal possession of the country for France and to set up new systems of governance. The resulting French report noted the natural beauty and abundance of the St. Lawrence valley and its potential value to France. The Iroquois, however, represented the primary obstacle to French control over this "great treasure." A steady flow of correspondence from civil authorities in New France now joined the frequent appeals of the Jesuits for the Sun King to send an expedition against the Iroquois. Montreal governor Paul Chomedey, Sieur de Maisonneuve, endeavored to show the colonists' commitment to the project by organizing a 139-man settler militia. One cartographer even provided a visual argument for armed French intervention against the League: the "Map of New France" published in Du Creux's *History of Canada* (1664) distorted the location of the Five Nations in order to emphasize the menace they posed the colony.[126]

Yet despite French perceptions of the League as a unified threat to the existence of New France, the Onondagas sent "advance couriers" to Montreal in August 1663 who reported that all League nations but the Oneidas now sought peace with New France. The messengers carried a letter drafted by "one of the prominent men of New Holland" that attested to the sincerity of their words. French authorities sent the messengers back with "friendly words" that inspired Garacontié to spend the winter of 1663–64 assembling "a prodigious collection of porcelain" (wampum) in order to prepare "the most beautiful presents which had ever been given" to the French. Garacontié's embassy of thirty Onondaga and Seneca delegates set out in May 1664, notwithstanding opposition from at least some Onondaga "families" to the idea of a general League peace with New France. En route to Montreal, however, the Iroquois diplomats were ambushed by Montagnais and Algonquin warriors. Garacontié's project subsequently "vanished in smoke."[127]

Five months after the dispersal of Garacontié's embassy, a Cayuga delegation headed by Saonchiogwa, the "old friend" of the French and Jesuits, arrived at Montreal. Saonchiogwa offered peace on behalf of all League nations except the Oneidas, but French officials took little interest in his proposal. Citing their impatience with such visits, which had in the past "concealed deadly treasons," colonial authorities dismissed the Cayuga headman's message as a mere deception from "faithless Barbarians." Even the Jesuits abandoned their usual practice of recording at least a summary of such proceedings. Instead, the annual *Relation* contained a detailed description of the "five different Cantons" of the Iroquois League, updating secondhand reconnaissance obtained by Ragueneau in 1648 from Wendat sources. The 1664 document listed the nations from east to west, and noted the number of days' travel between each nation's settlements. It represented a key piece of military intelligence.[128]

While Saonchiogwa's delegation failed to obtain its objectives at Quebec, another Iroquois embassy attended to important new business on the League's eastern door. Following the September 7, 1664, surrender of New Netherland to English forces, a party of headmen from all the League's constituent nations arrived at the former site of Fort Orange (now "Fort Albany") for a conference with English officials on September 24–25, 1664. George Cartwright and Richard Nicolls, treating on behalf of the Duke of York, offered the Iroquois favorable terms. They would have "wares and comodityes" from the English in quantities and at the prices equivalent to those of the former Dutch regime. Additionally, English authorities pledged to punish any offense committed by the settler population against "Indyan princes or their subjects," throughout "all other English Plantations," provided Iroquois "sachems" agreed to undertake investigation, punishment, and compensation for any crimes committed by their people throughout Anglo-America.[129]

In their reply, the Iroquois delegates (one of whom was Canaqueese) accepted these terms and even provided an overview sketch of their homelands for their new allies. Yet the agreement by no means represented a submission of the League, as

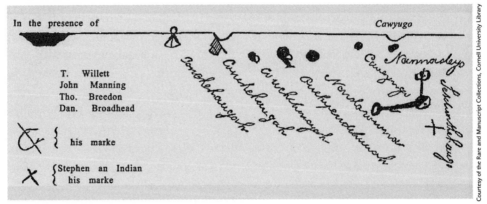

Iroquois Sketch Map Representing the League, 1664

the negotiators added *kaswentha* demands for the Iroquois right of free trade and for English noninterference in their war with the Pocumtucks and Abenakis. Despite the regime change, most of the Dutch population remained in New York after 1664, and the Iroquois resumed a brisk trade with their former business contacts at Fort Albany after agreeing to terms with English officials.[130]

Arms and ammunition from the Dutch in New York enabled the Five Nations to send joint war parties on distant campaigns during the winters of 1664–65 and 1665–66, despite continuing League conflicts with the Abenakis, Algonquins, Montagnais, and Susquehannocks. One Iroquois party traveled to within three days' journey of Hudson's Bay in 1665, where they captured or killed eighty Crees near Lake Nemiskau. Iroquois warriors also blockaded the approaches to the St. Lawrence valley and employed their superior quantity of firearms to secure cargoes of peltry abandoned by fleeing Odawa and Ojibwa traders. Still other war parties returned once more to the upper Great Lakes during the summer of 1665, motivated in large part by their ongoing search for Tionnontatés, who were still in the process of brokering residency agreements and military alliances with the region's Algonquian nations.[131]

In the meantime, French metropolitan authorities announced in March 1665 the first significant policy statements by King Louis XIV regarding the Native population of New France. The French committed themselves to a program of protecting the homelands of allied Native populations while also continuing *francisation* efforts that would transform friendly indigenous nations into "subjects" of France. Such benevolent rhetoric did not extend to the Iroquois, however. In 1665, the French Crown announced that one regiment of regular troops would be sent to New France to "carry war" to the Five Nations' "firesides in order totally to exterminate them, having no guarantee in their words, for they violate their faith as often as they find the inhabitants of the colony at their mercy."[132]

Civil and ecclesiastical authorities in New France, then "groaning under the Iroquois's cruelty," could barely contain their joy when 1,200 men of the French

Carignan-Salières Regiment arrived at Quebec during the summer of 1665. The regimental officer corps spent the month of June 1665 analyzing a document entitled "Of the Iroquois Country, and the Routes Leading Thither," which offered two detailed maps, even more specific measures of distance between League settlements than the intelligence obtained in 1664, and estimates of each constituent nation's military strength (with the sum of all League warriors reported as 2,240 men). French troops began rebuilding Fort Richelieu (which had been destroyed by the Iroquois in 1646) in July 1665; they built four more forts proceeding upriver toward Lake Champlain over the next two months. In the eyes of the Jesuits, these unprecedented military measures would ensure the "destruction of the Iroquois" and thereby "open a door" for the Jesuit penetration of the continental interior. No longer would the missionaries be obliged "to seek a passage through the fires and hatchets of the Iroquois, and to choose the most difficult routes, in order to avoid the most dangerous."[133]

Notwithstanding the French military buildup, the Iroquois resumed their "customary marauding expeditions" in July 1665, ambushing an Odawa trading caravan near Trois-Rivières. Later that month an Iroquois party captured Charles Le Moyne near Montreal. Despite widespread reports of the longstanding Iroquois desire to torture and execute Le Moyne, the Onondagas chose to adopt him given his potential utility as a human shield and diplomatic bargaining chip.[134]

On December 4, 1665, Garacontié, accompanied by six other Onondaga headmen (including Otreouti), arrived at Quebec with the captive Charles Le Moyne. After receiving a welcome speech of condolence from Lieutenant-General Alexander de Prouville, the Marquis de Tracy, Garacontié repatriated Le Moyne "without even one of his nails being torn off or any part of his body burnt." The Onondaga leader then asked for a restoration of the Franco-Iroquois alliance, and he offered to host two Jesuits in Onondaga country, provided they were accompanied by an "Armorer" to repair their weapons and a "surgeon" experienced in dressing gunshot wounds. Pledging to have abandoned his former practice of holding the French "only by the fringe of the coat," Garacontié now grasped them "around the waist" and urged the cancellation of the planned French military expedition. Tracy responded to Garacontié's speech by releasing three Onondaga prisoners from French custody and by promising vaguely that all Iroquois nations could enjoy peace with the French if they manifested a "respectful attitude" toward New France. Members of the League unwilling to adopt that position would be "constrained by arms."[135]

Garacontié's embassy departed Quebec on December 8, 1665. En route homeward, Otreouti earned the nickname by which he was known thereafter to the French ("La grande geule," or "Big Mouth") by advising Garacontié that Tracy had decided to attack the "fickle and perfidious" Mohawks regardless of any statements to the contrary. Upon learning this news, Garacontié returned immediately to Quebec. He insisted on another meeting with Tracy, and on December 13, 1665, the French officer agreed to a formal treaty with the Iroquois. The terms of the agreement, which

Chaumonot read aloud "in the Iroquois tongue," pledged mutual forgetting of past hostilities by both the French and all League nations but the Mohawks (who neither sent delegates to Quebec nor authorized the representatives there to speak on their behalf), and "mutual friendship" between the French, Iroquois, Wendats, and Algonquins. Emulating indigenous practices, the agreement obligated several "principal" Iroquois families to relocate to Montreal, Trois-Rivières, and Quebec, where they would enjoy farmland as well as rights to hunt and fish "in common" with their hosts. At the same time, a number of French families would take up residency in Onondaga, Seneca, and Cayuga homelands and enjoy similar privileges. This spatial integration of the Iroquois and French settler populations would "render the desired union of the Iroquois and French nations the stronger and more stable."[136]

Despite Garacontié's substantial diplomatic efforts, authorities in New France had no intention of honoring such terms in lieu of formal concessions from the Mohawks, whom they considered the greatest threat to the colony's security. Intendant Jean Talon hoped that the conquest of "interven[ing]" Iroquois homelands would open the way to French territorial claims "as far as Florida, New Sweden, New Holland, and New England," and perhaps even "Mexico." Governor Daniel de Rémy de Courcelles, anxious to put the Carignan-Salières Regiment to good use, departed on an ill-advised midwinter expedition with 300 of the French regulars and 200 settler militiamen toward Mohawk country on January 9, 1666. Despite marching on snowshoes with provisions drawn on dogsleds, the French expedition lost so many men to frostbite that they were forced, after their Algonquin guides failed to arrive in timely fashion, to "try unknown routes" in hopes of reaching Mohawk country with adequate numbers.[137]

Staggering into the new Dutch settlement at Schenectady on February 19, 1666, Courcelles learned from Van Curler that most of the Mohawks' and Oneidas' warriors had recently left their homelands on a military expedition. Only women, children, and the elderly remained in these nations' towns. Courcelles, satisfied that his effort had at least persuaded the Mohawks and Oneidas that they were not "inaccessible" to French offensives, elected to return to New France. He purchased provisions for his return journey from local Dutch settlers, left seven wounded French soldiers at Schenectady for medical treatment, and wrote to English officials at Fort Albany, assuring the latter that the French targeted the Mohawks, not any English subjects.[138]

Courcelles did not enjoy a secure return journey. On February 20, 1666, a small party of Mohawks drew sixty of Courcelles's "fuzileers" into an ambush, where they encountered "neare 200 Mohaukes planted behind trees" who killed eleven French soldiers with "one volley" at the cost of three Mohawk warriors' lives. The Mohawks then pursued Courcelles's "dishonorable retreat" all the way to Lake Champlain. The remnants of his expeditionary force limped into Quebec on March 17, 1666, having lost over sixty men to the Mohawks, the weather, and starvation.[139]

Notwithstanding Courcelles's failed winter expedition, French authorities continued to reject subsequent offers of peace by Iroquois delegations visiting the colony. Tracy initially dismissed a group of Seneca headmen who arrived at Quebec on May 22, 1666, to ratify the December 13, 1665, agreement. Yet after learning how greatly his refusal of the Senecas' peace overtures, embodied in their gift of "porcelain" (wampum belts), had offended them, he consented to their ratification of Garacontié's treaty. Raiding by unspecified Iroquois war parties continued at Montreal and at the Richelieu River posts in May and June 1666, which may have influenced Tracy's decision to detain the members of an Oneida delegation (which included at least one woman) who arrived at Quebec on July 7, 1666. Five days later, on condition of the Oneidas returning all French, Wendat, and Algonquin prisoners in their homelands, Tracy agreed to the Oneidas' ratification of the December 1665 peace agreement.[140]

The French continued preparations for an expedition against the Mohawks, who, as late as July 1666, had sent no delegates to Canada to ratify Garacontié's treaty. Instead, the Mohawks approached their new English "Brethren" in Albany. On July 18, 1666, a group of visiting Mohawks reported the pending French invasion of their homelands and requested arms and ammunition. The Albany "Commissaries" cobbled together a token gift of powder and shot, and then hustled the Mohawks out of town. The conduct of the Albany officials reflected official attitudes among English authorities in New York and Massachusetts. Once informed of French invasion plans, Governors Nicolls and Winthrop had agreed to avoid involvement and let "the French and Mowhawks try it out a while." For Nicolls, then unaware of the official French declaration of war (as an ally of the Netherlands) against England in January 1666, "the Interest of Europe" in North America took precedence over that of "the barbarous Indyans."[141]

On July 19, 1666, Mohawk warriors surprised a group of French officers hunting on Isle La Motte (in Lake Champlain near Fort Ste.-Anne, the closest French outpost to Iroquoia). The attackers killed seven of the officers and took four prisoners (one of whom was Tracy's nephew). News of this incident led Tracy to incarcerate all but one of the remaining Oneida delegates at Quebec, whom he dispatched with Guillaume Couture to Albany to make a formal complaint of this attack. Couture conferred with the Mohawks in the presence of English officials at Fort Albany from August 13 to 15, 1666, and ultimately elicited from his former Mohawk captors a promise to send "as many of their male prisoners as want to go" with a delegation to ratify Garacontié's peace terms of December 1665. Canaqueese and three other Mohawk headmen (French sources identified one as the leader of the raid on Isle La Motte, a Neutral adoptee named Agariata), departed Albany for Canada shortly thereafter, escorting the four French officers taken at Fort Ste.-Anne. The presence of the officers with Canaqueese's party caused a retaliatory French expedition of 200 men under Pierre Sorel (dispatched after Couture's departure) to turn back before reaching Mohawk homelands.[142]

Arriving at Quebec on August 28, 1666, Canaqueese's embassy stopped outside the town and, adhering to Edge of the Woods protocol, "cried out in a loud voice, 'Onontio, Onontio, ho, ho, Squenon, Squenon.'" Following this formal appeal for peace, the Mohawk diplomats found over 100 members of the four other nations of the League in town, a clear reflection of widespread Iroquois knowledge of and concern regarding the potential French invasion of Mohawk country. Yet Iroquois negotiations with French authorities had reached a stalemate by September 6, 1666, notwithstanding a last-ditch effort by the Seneca Snipe clan hereditary title-holder "Onnonkenritiwi" (who was, significantly, one of the two Seneca leaders charged with keeping the League's western door) to "stay Onontio's arm raised against" his allies at the League's eastern door. Tracy, convinced that only a show of force would render the Mohawks "more tractable," confined twenty-two Iroquois diplomats at Quebec. In a pointed gesture that reflected his frustration with the havoc previously wreaked by mobile Iroquois war parties on the settler population of New France, Tracy forced the detainees to make snowshoes for the expeditionary force.[143]

During September 1666, Tracy and Talon assembled a European army of unprecedented size in northeastern North America to attack the Mohawks. It consisted of 600 men of the Carignan-Salières Regiment and 600 settler militiamen, along with 100 allied Wendat and Algonquin warriors. Tracy had apparently also invited the participation of "many hundreds" of Algonquian warriors from nations bordering the New England colonies, but Connecticut Governor John Winthrop, Jr. claimed to have persuaded the "chief sachems" of these nations to recall their men prior to reconnoitering with Tracy on "Lake Hieracoies" (i.e., Lake Champlain). The bulk of the expeditionary force departed from Fort Ste.-Anne on October 3, 1666, with an Algonquin woman, a former Mohawk captive, serving as a guide. Mohawk scouts perched on "mountain tops" some sixty miles north of their homelands easily perceived the 300 light French boats floating down Lake George and sent word homeward of the French approach. Although many Mohawks were reportedly "out a hunting" at the time of Tracy's invasion, all remaining Mohawk women and children were subsequently evacuated to "Sunnuck," the homelands of the four western League nations.[144]

As the French army approached Iroquoia's eastern door in mid-October 1666, the Mohawks initiated a planned, orderly, westward retreat from their settlements in order to deny the French any opportunity for a direct engagement with a critical mass of Mohawk people. One Mohawk man "prevented by [his] great age" from fleeing his hometown prior to the arrival of the French invaders, two elderly Mohawk women (who committed suicide after seeing the French enter their town), and a young boy (whom the French took prisoner) were the only Mohawks the French expedition encountered face-to-face.[145]

Possibly discouraged from pursuing the Mohawks by the sight of "the mutilated

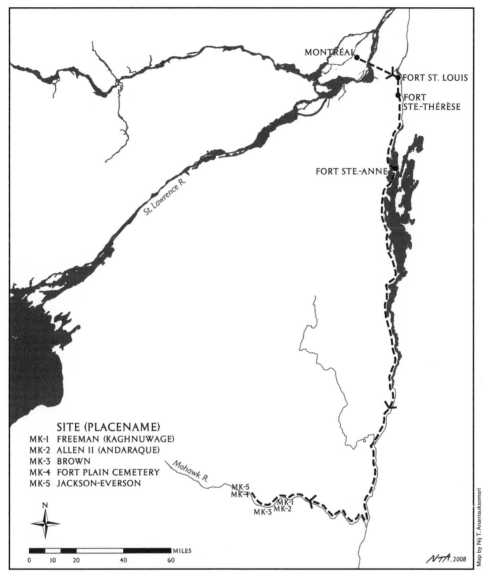

SITE (PLACENAME)
MK-1   FREEMAN (KAGHNUWAGE)
MK-2   ALLEN II (ANDARAQUE)
MK-3   BROWN
MK-4   FORT PLAIN CEMETERY
MK-5   JACKSON-EVERSON

The French Invasion of Mohawk Country, 1666

bodies of two or three savages of another nation, whom these people had, with their wonted rage, half burned over a slow fire" in one abandoned Mohawk town, the French contented themselves with erecting a cross in the Mohawk town of "Andaraque" on October 17, 1666. Officers of the expeditionary force drafted a document taking "possession" of the Mohawks' "forts," and chanted *Te Deum* prior to burning the town's remaining structures. French reports enumerated 100 "large cabins" destroyed throughout Mohawk country. The soldiers reportedly looted 400 copper kettles and other portable elements of the Mohawks' property and plundered some of the Mohawks' stored food on their homebound journey. Yet in their haste they neither destroyed food that they could not carry nor burned the Mohawks' outlying fields.[146]

Tracy's army returned to Quebec on November 5, 1666. Reports of the expedition disappointed Talon, who realized that Tracy and Courcelles had accomplished nothing more than the destruction of the Mohawks' towns. Anticipating Mohawk retaliation, colonial officials authorized diplomatic outreach to the Mohawks. On November 8, 1666, Tracy released Canaqueese, along with an unnamed Mohawk "elder" and two Oneida detainees, from French custody at Quebec. The liberated Iroquois were to communicate an official French offer of peace to Mohawk country. Tracy granted the Mohawks "four moons" (months) to "give satisfaction to Onnontio on the propositions made by him for the good of their people" via an embassy to New France. If the Mohawks failed to respond, Tracy threatened to hang all the remaining Iroquois detainees. The manner in which the Mohawks and their allies in the League responded to this French edict after 1666 would profoundly alter the course of North American history.[147]

Jesuit Jerôme Lalemant's 1660 claim that the "pure-blooded" composed less than 20 percent of the Iroquois population, even if only an impressionistic indication of Iroquois demography at that time, represents a compelling testimony to the integrative capacity of League tradition and social structure in the aftermath of their first three decades of experience at the Edge of the Woods with European epidemic diseases. Far from representing a "dilution" of Iroquois "ethnic identity," these mass adoptions derived from the very assumptions constituting the core of Iroquois ethnic identity over at least the preceding century. As we have seen, the power of Iroquois social organization rested not with static forms of supposedly "authentic" governance subject only to erosion over time, but rather in the "dynamic ideals" underlying Iroquois social organization, which provided not only "moral force" to various social, political, and spatial innovations but also a critical yet flexible frame of reference for ensuing internal conversations about different choices and options in an increasingly complex world.[148]

From 1650 to 1666, all of the five League nations had "requickened" themselves at the level of the household by repackaging adoptees into clan segments residing in multifamily longhouses, employing traditional architectural patterns in order to socialize newcomers efficiently.[149] At the level of the League, the Iroquois mobilized and deployed the crucial human and spatial resources represented by their adoptees to broaden and intensify their range of contacts with other peoples at the Edge of the Woods, diversifying their economic and diplomatic contacts in the process. In the aftermath of the French military expedition into Mohawk country in 1666, Iroquois people acknowledged the likelihood of a continued European presence on the periphery of their homelands, but they offered no submission. Instead, they reoriented their spatial engagement with settler colonialism. In a series of movements demonstrating the requickened state of the ethnically diverse, increasingly multi-valent League, the Iroquois established new settler communities after 1666 on the north shore of Lake Ontario and in the vicinity of Montreal. Bringing the "songs" of these new communities into harmony with those in League homelands constituted a key challenge of the next phase of late precolonial Iroquois history.

4.

SIX SONGS
1667–1684

We have a power to go where we please, to conduct who we will
to the places we resort to, and to buy and sell where we think fit.
—WENDAT-ONONDAGA HEADMAN OTREOUTI, IN A SPEECH
TO THE GOVERNOR OF NEW FRANCE IN 1684

On September 13, 1667, Jesuits Jacques Frémin, Jean Pierron, and Jacques Bruyas approached "the Capital of this whole [Mohawk] country, called Tionnontogouen, which the Iroquois have rebuilt, at a quarter of a league from that which the French burned down last year." Escorted by "two hundred men, who marched in good order," the Jesuits "went last, immediately in front of the hoary Heads and the most considerable men of the country. This march was executed with an admirable gravity until, when we had arrived quite near the Village, every one halted, and we were complimented by the most eloquent man of the Nation, who was awaiting us with the other Deputies. After this, he conducted us into the Village, where we were received with the discharge of all the artillery, each one firing from his Cabin, and two swivel-guns being discharged at the two ends of the village."[1]

The massive display of firepower accompanying the Edge of the Woods welcome for the Jesuits at the Mohawks' westernmost Wolf clan village in 1667 demonstrated the rejuvenation in less than one year's time of an Iroquois community destroyed by the largest European army assembled to date in North America. Tionnontogouen in 1667 was an imposing hilltop settlement consisting of thirty longhouses surrounded by a double palisade that served as home for an estimated 700 to 900 Mohawks. The deafening salute offered to the newly arrived "*Atsientatsi*," or "Black Gowns," whose presence the Mohawks and Oneidas had consented to in July 1667 peace negotiations at Quebec, reflected the degree to which the League's eastern doorkeepers welcomed the Jesuits from a position of strength.[2]

FOR WHOM DOES ONNONTIO TAKE US?

Conceding a limited Jesuit presence in Iroquoia after 1667 represented a small part of a much broader strategy in which the Five Nations undertook a dramatic expansion of their homelands. Unlike the Onondagas' earlier experiment with the Gannentaha mission, which attempted to domesticate a French diplomatic and economic entrepôt in the center of Iroquoia, the second wave of Jesuit "Envoys" admitted to a limited number of Iroquois towns served as French hostages facilitating Iroquois freedom of movement. As Récollet missionary Louis Hennepin recognized, the Jesuits' primary role in Iroquoia after 1667, from the perspective of their Iroquois hosts, amounted to "Security for their Lives and Goods" while the League nations embarked on an innovative series of spatial movements to reoccupy the north shore of Lake Ontario and the St. Lawrence River valley.[3]

Movements to these spaces were deeply rooted in prior affiliations of ancestral Iroquois populations as well as adoptees from as many as "sixteen nations" who had become, in the eyes of Jesuit observers, "Iroquois in temper and Inclination." Post-1667 Iroquois population movements represented planned returns to former areas of residency rather than a haphazard, "uncoordinated drift" of "a breakaway group of Iroquois," or "dissident Mohawks," or "christened Iroquois" who, as many historians claim, "eschewed kinship with their pagan relatives" and "fled" from "ostracism" in their so-called traditional homelands.[4] Enacting principles embodied in the "Six Songs" stage of the Condolence ceremony, which invokes and offers thanksgiving for the social institutions and movements constitutive of the ceremony while admonishing participants to "keep listening to the grandfathers" (to remain mindful of core cultural values while adapting to contemporary circumstances and conditions), Iroquois people employed the mobility sanctioned by the Condolence ceremony to effect permanent changes in the spatial composition of the League.[5]

Nine new Iroquois settlements established after 1667 in the St. Lawrence River valley and on the north shore of Lake Ontario (three of which persist to this day) represented the "most precious fruits reaped" from the League's peace with New France: a northward projection of satellite communities peopled by families and clan segments from all constituent League nations. Extending from the Seneca-dominated community of Quinaouataoua (in proximity to a former Neutral town near modern-day Hamilton, Ontario) in the west to the Mohawk-dominated Laurentian valley settlements (near Montreal and Quebec) in the east, these newly established Iroquois towns represented an expansion of the League's preexisting spatial organization. Residents of these communities practiced matrilocal residency, maintained matrilineal forms of social organization, built longhouses, planted traditional crops, attended League meetings at Onondaga, and enjoyed many other linkages with existing League national towns based on ties of kinship and economic reciprocity. Patterns of movement to and from these reoccupied Iroquois homelands contributed

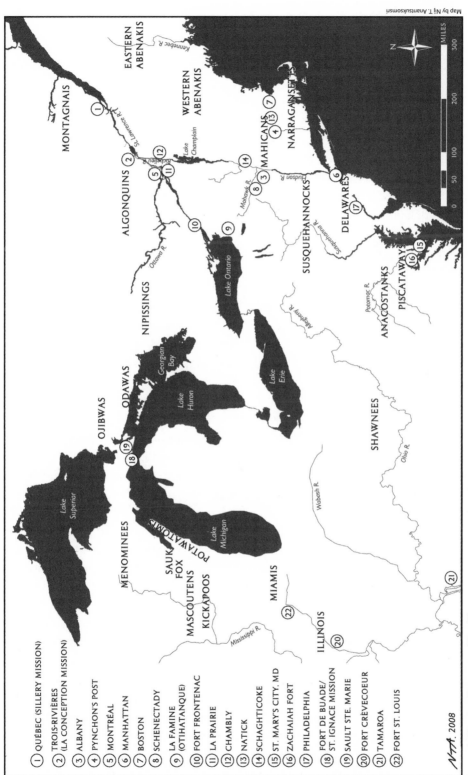

MILES

0   50   100   200   300

MONTAGNAIS

EASTERN
ABENAKIS

Kennebec R.

WESTERN
ABENAKIS

ALGONQUINS

St. Lawrence R.

Richelieu R.

Lake
Champlain

NARRAGANSETTS

MAHICANS

Hudson R.

Mohawk R.

SUSQUEHANNOCKS

DELAWARES

Susquehanna R.

Ottawa R.

Lake Ontario

NIPISSINGS

ANACOSTANKS

PISCATAWAYS

Potomac R.

Alleghney R.

Georgian
Bay

ODAWAS

OJIBWAS

Lake
Superior

Lake
Huron

Lake
Erie

SHAWNEES

Ohio R.

MENOMINEES

SAUK
FOX

POTAWATOMIS

MASCOUTENS
KICKAPOOS

Lake
Michigan

MIAMIS

Wabash R.

ILLINOIS

Mississippi R.

N

① QUÉBEC (SILLERY MISSION)
② TROIS-RIVIÈRES
   (LA CONCEPTION MISSION)
③ ALBANY
④ PYNCHON'S POST
⑤ MONTRÉAL
⑥ MANHATTAN
⑦ BOSTON
⑧ SCHENECTADY
⑨ LA FAMINE
   (OTIHATANQUE)
⑩ FORT FRONTENAC
⑪ LA PRAIRIE
⑫ CHAMBLY
⑬ NATICK
⑭ SCHAGHTICOKE
⑮ ST. MARY'S CITY, MD
⑯ ZACHAIAH FORT
⑰ PHILADELPHIA
⑱ FORT DE BUADE/
   ST. IGNACE MISSION
⑲ SAULT STE. MARIE
⑳ FORT CRÈVECOEUR
㉑ TAMAROA
㉒ FORT ST. LOUIS

NTA. 2008

Iroquois Places of Interest, 1667–1684

not only to a redefined League polity, they also informed a growing League consensus from 1667 to 1684 on the importance of asserting rights of free movement, vis-à-vis neighboring settler colonies, throughout a vast swath of territory encompassing the modern-day Upper Peninsula of Michigan as well as Illinois, Virginia, and Maine.[6]

Uncertainty abounded among officials in New France and the Anglo-American colonies in the aftermath of the October 1666 Tracy expedition into Mohawk country. Intendant Jean Talon worried in November 1666 that the Mohawks' efficient strategic withdrawal had blunted the potential impact of the invasion. By December 1666, the Mohawks had torn down the "French scutchion" nailed up at Andaraque on October 17, 1666, and delivered it to New York governor Richard Nicolls via Albany authorities. They also purchased from Albany traders "two iron guns which will carry three pounds of bullets apiece" (likely the "swivel-guns" that would later greet the Jesuits at Tionnontogouen), yet they withheld information on the extent of destruction caused by Tracy's army. Not until February 1667 did the normally well-informed John Pynchon report that the French had "only burnt their houses." After assessing the reports of the Tracy expedition from Canadian authorities, French metropolitan officials could only concur with this view. Communicating Louis XIV's April 1667 order for another assault on Iroquoia, French Minister of Finance Jean-Baptiste Colbert noted that the previous year's expeditions had not been sufficient to secure the colony against future Iroquois offensives.[7]

The Mohawks' diplomacy with New France began in late April 1667, when Canaqueese, who had been liberated by Tracy in November 1666, arrived at Quebec. Yet Canaqueese had failed to repatriate any of the Wendat or Algonquin adoptees from Mohawk country per French demands. Tracy sent Canaqueese back with all but two of the male Iroquois prisoners held at Quebec (he continued to detain an unspecified number of Iroquois women) and another time-sensitive ultimatum to accept his dictated peace terms or face another invasion of Mohawk country. Tracy also attempted to enlist the assistance of Schenectady resident Arent van Curler in brokering terms of peace with the Mohawks. To render this prospect more palatable to Nicolls, Tracy pledged to observe "allwayes the Interest of Europe, against the barbarous Indyans of America."[8]

Nicolls consented to Van Curler's brokerage of a Franco-Mohawk peace, but the latter's desire to supplement his diplomatic efforts in New France with private trading caused a delay sufficient to allow the Jesuits to insert themselves into the peace negotiations. Jesuit Jacques Frémin arrived at Quebec on July 5, 1667, with several Mohawk and Oneida representatives. During the next five days, these delegates, who chose to ignore Nicolls's advice that they identify themselves as "subordinate" to the king of England, requested peace. To ratify the agreement, they invited Jesuits to their homelands and left several of their own "families as hostages" at Quebec. Some time later, in July 1667, Van Curler's overloaded canoe took on water during a storm on Lake Champlain, and two of his Mohawk traveling companions reported that he drowned after refusing to throw his goods out of the sinking craft. On July 14, 1667, Frémin, Pierron, and Bruyas set out for Mohawk and Oneida country with the remaining Iroquois hostages released from Tracy's custody.[9]

Detained for a month at Fort Ste.-Anne on the Richelieu River by reports of a threatened Mahican attack, the self-described Jesuit "Angels of peace" did not reach the reconstructed eastern Mohawk Turtle clan town of Gandaouagué (the successor of the town that Jogues had formerly "watered with his blood") until September 9, 1667. Upon arriving, Frémin noted that Wendat and Algonquin adoptees constituted "two-thirds" of Gandaouagué's population. After three days of ministering to a few "old Christians" among this substantial adoptee community, the Jesuits departed for Tionnontogouen, pausing only briefly at another (unnamed) Mohawk village en route.[10]

Following the Mohawks' military reception for the Jesuits at Tionnontogouen described at the beginning of this chapter, Frémin reprised an all-too-familiar pattern for Jesuit speakers in Iroquoia, squandering the Mohawks' initial goodwill and hospitality with a stunning act of rhetorical aggression. After raising in the midst of an assembled Mohawk audience a pole reportedly "forty or fifty feet in length, from the top of which hung a Porcelain necklace," Frémin announced that "in like manner should be hanged the first of the Iroquois who should come to kill a Frenchman or any one of our [Native] Allies." With Tracy's 1666 hanging of Agariata still a fresh memory, the "astounded" Mohawks remained silent "for a long time with their heads down, without daring either to look at this spectacle or to talk about it, until the most prominent and most eloquent of their Orators—having recovered his spirits—arose" and "seized himself by the throat with both his hands, in a horrible manner—squeezing it tightly to represent, and at the same time to inspire a horror of, this kind of death, in the multitude of people who surrounded us!"[11]

No Mohawks watered the ground at Tionnontogouen with Frémin's blood in 1667, but their restraint in the aftermath of his theatrics did not reflect wholesale Mohawk capitulation to New France. Indeed, for all Frémin knew, the "Orator" may have been mocking him or issuing a warning of his own to the Jesuits. The Mohawks allowed the matter to blow over, focusing instead on fulfilling their end of the agreement with French authorities. The Jesuits received a site in Tionnontogouen for a chapel, as well as construction assistance, and the Mohawks also released a number of French and upper Great Lakes Algonquian prisoners. The Mohawks regarded the Jesuits' presence as a necessary "assurance of peace" with New France that enabled them to focus their attention on more pressing matters, especially their ongoing conflict with the Mahicans.[12]

In similar fashion, the Oneidas welcomed Bruyas to their town in late September 1667 and immediately resumed long-standing hostilities against the Susquehannocks. Afterward, Oneida headmen helped to broker similar arrangements for the remaining League nations. On December 13, 1667, a delegation of Onondaga and Oneida

Chauchetière's Drawing of the First Oneida Arrivals at La Prairie, ca. 1686

Courtesy Archives Départementales de la Gironde. Ref. H, Jésuites, "La Narration annuelle de la mission du Sault, par le père Claude Chauchetière."

headmen that included Garacontié and Otreouti renewed peace with the French at Quebec on behalf of the remaining League nations. The Onondaga and Oneida delegates invited "two Black Robes" to reside at Onondaga and repeated previous requests for a "gunsmith to repair their broken arms for use against their enemies and a surgeon to dress their sick and wounded."[13]

The post-1667 Iroquois program of hosting French personnel in Iroquois towns, spearheaded by the Mohawks and Oneidas, yielded low-cost security for new Iroquois spatial initiatives under way in the St. Lawrence River valley and the Lake Ontario basin. The Jesuits soon recognized that grudging toleration of their "prayers" by even the "most superstitious" Iroquois people did not mean that they would "suffer any opposition to their ceremonies." Pierron complained in 1668 that whenever he tried to speak of religious matters to the Mohawks of Gandaouagué, they plugged "their ears with their fingers" and said "'I do not hear.'" Writing from Seneca country two years later, Jesuit Julien Garnier felt certain that his hosts would "brain" him in the event of any French military offensive against Iroquoia.[14]

Immediately after the conclusion of peace with New France in July 1667, a significant number of Iroquois hunters "dispersed" into the St. Lawrence valley to hunt beaver, otter, elk, and moose. While hunting opportunities represented a primary factor motivating the post-1667 Iroquois movements into these lands (of which they considered themselves the "original Owners"), contemporary evidence indicates that the region could support the entire Iroquois seasonal subsistence cycle. Fertile soils for maize-based agriculture, abundant fishing, annual runs of passenger pigeons, plentiful firewood, as well as medicinal and berry plants awaited those willing to relocate there. The annual trade fair at Montreal provided a nearby outlet for peltry, supplementing the market at Albany and offering ample opportunities for contact with a diverse range of Native nations from the upper Great Lakes region. Also, by moving toward the western limits of the French settler population at Montreal, the Iroquois enhanced their capacity for collecting information about French affairs, which later proved vital for asserting and maintaining their own freedom of movement.[15]

Missionary writings represent our primary window into the history of post-1667 Iroquois movements, and the emphasis in these sources on religious motivations for Iroquois relocations to the St. Lawrence valley/Lake Ontario basin has led many subsequent historians to depict this crucial development in Iroquois history as a Jesuit-managed exodus of religious zealots that ultimately had a corrosive effect on the integrity of the League. Although some individuals among the early Iroquois resettlers of the St. Lawrence valley manifested interest in Catholicism, and although these movements lacked universal popularity among the Iroquois, a closer look at the evidence reveals that missionaries were responding to, rather than directing, Iroquois movements. Iroquois decisions to relocate to the St. Lawrence valley did not involve their surrender of independent political status to French authorities, and the intense disputes over these movements did not leave hopelessly "faction-ridden" villages in their wake. Rather, these disputes occurred, and were often resolved, almost exclusively at the level of individual Iroquois families after 1667. The development over time of widespread consensus on the overall benefit these movements provided to the Iroquois polity meant that any related controversies did not disrupt traditional patterns of League governance.[16]

A 1668 Jesuit description of Onondaga identified it as the place "where every year the States-general" of the League was held, "to settle the differences that may have arisen among them in the course of the year." The Iroquois, recognizing that "their preservation depends upon their union," held these annual general assemblies to allow "Deputies" from the constituent nations to "make their complaints and receive the necessary satisfaction in mutual gifts, by means of which they maintain a good understanding with one another." Integration of satellite communities in the St. Lawrence valley and on the north shore of Lake Ontario into the wider League polity represented a crucial innovation for Iroquois people after 1667.[17]

Writing in 1686, Jesuit Claude Chauchetière traced the origins of the "Mission of the Sault," later the Jesuit seigneury of La Prairie de la Magdelaine, to the winter 1667–68 relocation of an Oneida named Tonsahoten; his Erie adoptee wife, Gandeak-teua; and ten others, including five other Oneidas and at least one Wendat and two Susquehannock adoptees. This group erected a "simple shed of boards" on lands being cleared under the supervision of Jesuit Pierre Raffeix and entertained visits from the numerous Iroquois who came to hunt in the St. Lawrence valley. By the early spring of 1668, a number of the relatives of the Oneida pioneers had "built a fine village" they named Kentaké.[18]

In June 1668, an embassy of Cayugas traveled from their recently established settlement at Quinté on the north shore of Lake Ontario to Montreal, where they requested missionaries for their community. On September 15, 1668, Bishop François de Laval authorized two Sulpician priests, Claude Trouvé and François de Salignac de Fénelon, to establish a mission among the Iroquois residing on the north shore of Lake Ontario. Referred to by French authorities as the "Iroquois du Nord," these Iroquois had begun moving, likely relying on guidance from Wendat and Neutral adoptees, into these nations' former settlement areas and hunting grounds on the north shore of Lake Ontario as early as 1665. Seven different north shore communities were established during the next five years, from which hundreds of Iroquois hunters "dispersed" over distances estimated at 450 miles. While French authorities assumed simple economic motives for these movements, believing that the "Iroquois du Nord" planned merely to hunt beavers and then carry the pelts to Albany, the opportunity for Iroquois people and their adoptees to return to ancestral spaces of residency and use outweighed any defensive concerns or the supposed widespread depletion of beaver populations in existing areas of Iroquois residency (for which no convincing faunal evidence exists).[19]

These rapidly developing, large-scale, and widespread Iroquois movements after 1667 caught both Anglo-American and French colonial authorities off-guard. New England settlers found particularly unnerving the sudden visits of well-armed groups of Iroquois men, each toting "a firelock gun, a pistol, an helved hatchet, a long knife hanging about [his] neck," and carrying packs "well furnished with powder and bullets" en route to hunt, trade, or fight. Three years after wresting control of the colony from the Dutch, English officials in New York had only begun to establish protocols for conducting Indian trade and diplomacy at Albany. Local authorities in Albany struggled with declining Iroquois trade volumes during the late 1660s stemming from the Iroquois-Mahican war and from economic competition with traders at Schenectady as well as the French at Montreal and even French traders in Albany itself. Nicolls also failed to comprehend, much less fulfill, an innovative 1668 Iroquois request for New York's assistance in brokering a peace with English settlers in Maryland by which the Iroquois likely intended to secure free passage for campaigns against the Piscataways and Susquehannocks.[20]

In New France, secular and ecclesiastical authorities alike attempted after 1667 to use threats of another invasion of Iroquoia as punishment for any Iroquois behavior that ran counter to French interests. Yet officials' bluster did not match their actions on the ground, where the French acknowledged Iroquois power in a variety of different everyday contexts. In October 1667, Marie de l'Incarnation described how her Ursuline colleagues had been obliged, "for the sake of the peace" with the Iroquois, to release "an Algonquin girl to an Iroquois" from their seminary, since this woman was "his wife, as well as his captive." For the same reasons, the Ursulines returned other Iroquois girls to their parents the moment they became "sad," since they realized that any attempts to retain them would backfire.[21]

Meanwhile, Jesuits in Iroquoia wrote in great detail of their frequent experience of physical violence, including firebrands thrown at their heads, burned papers, chapels demolished by metal hatchets, death threats, attempts on their lives, and a "thousand [other] acts of insolence." Missionaries in Iroquois towns peppered their reports with descriptions of strenuous Iroquois resistance both to their teachings (which evidently contained harsh criticisms of Iroquois cultural practices and past behavior) and to their efforts to baptize Native prisoners from enemy nations undergoing ritual torture in Iroquois villages. In 1668, Pierron had appealed to Governor Nicolls for official protection from New York for the Jesuits in Mohawk country, an act that exposed the fallacy of the French-claimed conquest of the Mohawks two years earlier. In October 1669, Sulpician René de Bréhant de Galinée had to say Mass at Quinaouataoua behind an impromptu curtain constructed of paddles and sails from his party's canoes, so as to avoid the prospect of the local population making "a mockery of our holy ceremony." Finally, in a dramatic July 1669 episode, Courcelles ordered the public execution at Montreal of at least three, and possibly as many as five, French regular troops accused of murdering "one of the most prominent" Seneca leaders and stealing the moose skins he had obtained in his winter 1668–69 hunting expedition in the St. Lawrence valley. Courcelles had the murderers shot in the presence of a large number of Odawa and Seneca delegates to persuade them of the official French disavowal of the crime, fully aware of the potential, in the aftermath of the Odawas' repatriation of three Iroquois prisoners captured in Odawa country in the early months of 1669, that these two nations might "join together to exact revenge" on the French.[22]

French fears of an independent rapprochement between the League and the Odawas and other indigenous peoples of the upper Great Lakes in 1669 stemmed from colonial officials' suspicion that the Iroquois sought peace with these nations in order to "induce" them "to bring their peltries to them, that they might sell the furs to the English in New York." If French officials were correct, these negotiations represented the beginning of a more complex relationship, one that involved the brokerage of Tionnontatés affiliated with the Algonquians of the *pays d'en haut* and Wendat adoptees among the Iroquois. Since the upper Great Lakes nations were beginning to move back eastward from their places of refuge in the far western reaches of Lake Michigan and Lake Superior (due to the recent Franco-Iroquois peace and to pressure from the Sioux), any agreement would need to include provisions for free Iroquois hunting in the upper Great Lakes (for which the "Iroquois du Nord" villages served as a springboard) in exchange for offers to escort upper Great Lakes Algonquians to Albany traders.[23]

In September 1669, Bruyas reported that Onondaga headman Sagochiendagehté had returned from the Montreal conference in high spirits, carrying an important symbolic gift from the Odawas: "ten wild-cows' skins, well adorned with their paintings, as assurance to the Elders that they would repair to Montréal in the Spring, to plant the tree of peace there, in order to put a stop to all these acts of hostility." Despite the incipient and incomplete nature of these negotiations (the Iroquois still were engaged in wars with several upper Great Lakes nations after 1669, and Odawas residing on Mackinac Island claimed in 1671 to have raided as far east as Mohawk country), the French panicked at the prospect of losing a single Iroquois- or Algonquian-trapped beaver pelt from the *pays d'en haut* to an English trader.[24]

These concerns led authorities in New France to wink at the increasing numbers of French traders who, after 1669, conducted direct business with Iroquois and other Native hunters in the forests of the St. Lawrence valley as well as in the "Iroquois du Nord" villages, a practice that ran counter to metropolitan desires to concentrate the colony's fur trade at Montreal. One ambitious French settler named René-Robert Cavelier de la Salle, while hosting members of a Seneca hunting party at his home near Montreal during the winter of 1668–69, heard "many marvels of the river Ohio," with which the Senecas claimed to be "thoroughly acquainted." La Salle came away believing that he could make his own journey to the Ohio valley by ransoming captives of the Senecas from that region to serve as his guides. Courcelles granted La Salle permission to assemble an eclectic group of French *coureurs de bois,* two Sulpician missionaries (Galinée and Dollier de Casson), and a "Dutchman" for an interpreter. The motley expedition departed Montreal on July 6, 1669, with two Seneca guides.[25]

After a journey down the St. Lawrence River and the south shore of Lake Ontario, the French party reached Irondequoit Bay on August 11, 1669. The next day, La Salle's party received an Edge of the Woods welcome at the large eastern Seneca town of Gandagan. During the ensuing discussions between the French and the Senecas, facilitated by the Jesuit Frémin's *donné* (all Jesuits in Iroquoia were then holding their own general meeting at Onondaga), La Salle and the Sulpicians attempted to use their knowledge of the Senecas' ongoing conflicts with the Mahicans and Susquehannocks to ingratiate themselves as friendly allies, offering a gift of "a double barreled pistol worth sixty *livres*," from which they claimed a single shot could kill both of the Senecas' enemies.[26]

At the time, however, the Iroquois held the upper hand in both conflicts. The Mahicans, attributing an early 1669 murder of six "Loups" in the St. Lawrence valley to the Iroquois (the actual perpetrators were three French peltry thieves), organized a large expeditionary force that included five men from one of the Reverend John Eliot's Massachusetts "praying Indian" towns seeking revenge for prior Mohawk attacks. The Mahicans laid siege to the eastern Mohawk town of Gandaouagué on August 18, 1669. After male and female Mohawk defenders broke up the siege, warriors from Gandaouagué, reinforced by a detachment sent from Tionnontogouen under Mohawk military leader Kryn, pursued, ambushed, and defeated decisively the retreating Algonquian army at a place known as "Kinaquariones" in the Mohawk River valley west of Schenectady. This battle, followed by a subsequent multinational Iroquois attack on a Mahican settlement, marked the last major engagements of their six-year conflict with the Mohawks.[27]

As for the Susquehannocks, Galinée reported a 1669 Susquehannock incursion near his host Seneca village in which the Senecas lost ten men killed, but witnessed no evident distress over this matter during his sojourn in the region. Elsewhere throughout Iroquoia, Jesuits reported numerous war parties departing to attack the Susquehannocks in 1669, and returning with Susquehannock captives, some "destined for the flames," while others, after adoption, "considerably augmented" Iroquois numbers. By March 1670, the Cayugas felt secure enough to execute a Susquehannock "Ambassador" whom they had detained for the previous six months in their towns.[28]

The gift of the double-barreled pistol, while clever, failed to elicit what La Salle and the Sulpicians desired. The Senecas, then on the verge of sending nearly 1,000 men, women, and children on military and hunting campaigns near Lake Huron, declined to offer a single person to guide the French party to the Ohio River. In their public reply to La Salle, the Senecas claimed to have sent all their "slaves" with a trade caravan to Albany, although they promised to provide La Salle with one porter when the party returned. In the interim, the French spent eight increasingly uneasy days in the Seneca town consuming a steady diet of dog meat (oblivious to the apparent threat or insult this represented) and witnessing the ritual torture and execution of a Great Lakes Algonquian captive, a symbolic denial of Galinée's effort to redeem this individual for potential service as a guide. The French spent sleep-deprived nights in Ganadagan, keeping alternating watches owing to death threats from relatives of the murdered Seneca headman, who "did not consider themselves satisfied" by

Courcelles's execution of the French perpetrators. When a "tumult" ensued after the return of the Seneca trade caravan with barrels of liquor, the French fled to Irondequoit. A Seneca man from the north shore settlement of Quinaouataoua, en route home from trading at Albany, informed the French that they could find a guide to the Ohio country in his village, where a number of adoptees "from the nations to which we desired to go" then resided.[29]

Arriving at Quinaouataoua on September 24, 1669, the French party met Louis Jolliet, then on his return to Montreal from a voyage of exploration in the upper Great Lakes with a former Iroquois captive of the Odawas, whose repatriation Jolliet claimed to have procured. Conversations with the liberated Iroquois prisoner persuaded the Sulpicians to alter their destination to the upper Great Lakes, via a new route their informant described from Lake Erie through the Detroit River and Lake St. Clair to Lake Huron. La Salle returned to New France at this point, but the Sulpicians set out from Quinaouataoua in late October 1669, only to be forced by the weather to winter on the north shore of Lake Erie. In late March 1670 they entered the Detroit River, where they discovered a painted rock "idol" erected by the Iroquois, to which passing Iroquois travelers made offerings of peltry and provisions to ensure secure movement through the region. Rejecting earlier Iroquois advice to "honor" the rock, the Sulpicians spent the better part of a day tearing it down and sinking the largest pieces to the bottom of the Detroit River. Despite their evident disregard for Iroquois travel protocols, the Sulpicians, relying on Iroquois directions, arrived at the Jesuit mission of Sault Ste. Marie on May 25, 1670.[30]

The Senecas' denial of direct assistance to La Salle's effort to reconnoiter the Ohio valley allowed the League nations to pursue their own objectives in the upper Great Lakes. While the Onondagas promoted peace with French-allied upper Great Lakes nations over the winter of 1669–70, the Cayugas and Senecas sent out a 600-man army to attack the Odawas. In March 1670, a segment of this Seneca/Cayuga force, "under the guidance of two fugitive Iroquois Slaves of the Pouteouatamis," attacked "six large cabins" of Fox on the Fox River and carried off thirty Fox women captives.[31]

When reports of the Iroquois attack on the Fox reached Quebec, Courcelles sent word (via Jesuit correspondents) to the Senecas informing them of his displeasure with the news that they had "taken in war some people adjacent to the Outaouak Algonquins, our allies." Courcelles warned the Senecas "that unless they wished to see him with his Army in their Country, they must restore those captives to him with the utmost dispatch, being further expressly forbidden to mutilate them, or exercise toward them a single one of their customary acts of cruelty." The audacity of the governor's "order" elicited a sharp response from Seneca leaders. "For whom," they asked, "does Onnontio take us?" Dismissing the notion that "all the peoples discovered by the bearers of God's word" (missionaries) automatically earned the French governor's "protection," the Senecas reminded the French that Fox warriors (whom the Senecas evidently knew had no formal allegiance to New France) had also committed hostilities in Iroquoia. "Let Onnontio check their hatchet," the Senecas replied, "if he wishes to stay our own." In conclusion, the Senecas responded to Courcelles's threatened invasion with a threat of their own, stating their eagerness to learn whether the French governor's "arms will be long enough to remove the scalps from our heads, as we have done in past times with those of the French."[32]

This Franco-Seneca exchange made manifest the refusal of the Iroquois to concede French power to dictate their freedom of movement, especially when they had carefully selected (with the assistance of two Iroquois captives who had recently escaped from the Potawatomis) the non-French allied Fox as a target for their attack. In the aftermath of the exchange of heated words, however, Seneca "Elders," with the approval of the warriors and all the other "young men," arranged to send eight Fox prisoners back to Courcelles with an embassy headed by Cayuga headman Saonchiogwa and Onondaga leader Garacontié.[33]

This decision reflected the persistence of traditional Iroquois leadership patterns among the Senecas, in which senior civil leaders governed in consultative, consensual fashion with military leaders, who were often younger men. The decision also marked the beginnings of a pattern by which the League nations, after 1667, maintained their freedom of movement by conceding occasional, fractional repatriations of captives in order to quell the complaints of French (and later Anglo-American) authorities regarding Iroquois threats to the security of their ostensibly allied Native nations. Garacontié, whom the Jesuits considered very friendly to French interests (although he was also "very well-known" at Albany), defended the Senecas' actions during his late July 1670 meeting with Courcelles at Quebec. Pointing out "in the name of all the Iroquois" that the Senecas had attacked people "whom Onontio had never taken under his protection," Garacontié argued that the Senecas could not be accused of having violated the League's peace with New France. After accepting the returned Fox prisoners from Saonchiogwa, Courcelles dropped the matter.[34]

Iroquois leaders refused to recognize Courcelles's self-appointed status as "umpire in their quarrels" with other Native nations. Instead, they sought their own solutions to these conflicts. An unspecified number of Iroquois people spent the winter of 1670–71 in "the Outawac's country, to carry some presents there to confirm their union, as they said." During the winter, their conversations reportedly turned to "the prices of merchandise among the Dutch," which the Iroquois reported (accurately) as "much lower than among the French," and claimed that one beaver in Albany would bring the equivalent of four beavers' worth of goods in Montreal. A party of twenty-five Odawa traders reportedly visited Iroquoia (but not Albany) during the spring of 1671 but came away dissatisfied with the poor quality of weapons the Iroquois were willing to trade. Nevertheless, the Odawas promised to return the following year with peltry if the Iroquois would escort them to Albany.[35]

Compounding the threatening economic impact of these Iroquois diplomatic initiatives in the upper Great Lakes, Intendant Jean Talon complained in November 1670 that the Iroquois hunters had themselves taken an estimated 1.2 million livres' worth of beaver pelts from indigenous territories he regarded as "subject" to France during the previous four years. Citing the demonstrated proclivity of the Iroquois for "pull[ing] down all the arms and written placards attached to trees in the places of which [French] possession is taken," Talon argued in the autumn of 1670 for the establishment of a French fort on Lake Ontario, garrisoned with 100 men and aided by a "small vessel" to patrol canoe traffic on the lake and thereby keep the Iroquois "in duty, respect, and fear."[36]

Once news of the winter 1670–71 Iroquois-Odawa negotiations reached New France, Courcelles, arguing that such "familiar intercourse" between these two nations might produce an indigenous military alliance that threatened the colony's ruin, pulled out all the stops in an effort to "prevent this commerce." He wrote letters to all the missionaries in the upper Great Lakes, urging them to remind the Algonquian nations of past Iroquois treachery. Courcelles also encouraged the Jesuits in Iroquoia to suggest to their Iroquois hosts the security risks of permitting Algonquian peoples to enter their territory on the pretext of trade in order to conduct reconnaissance of their villages and hunting grounds. Courcelles then embarked on a whirlwind fifteen-day journey to Lake Ontario, in order to prove to the "insolent" League nations that he could "ruin them at his pleasure" by ferrying "a large plank Bateau" up the numerous rapids of the St. Lawrence River to Lake Ontario as quickly as Iroquois canoes moved down that river to New France.[37]

Expanding League Homelands

In retrospect, Courcelles's demonstration of the reach of his "arms" laid the foundation of Iroquois disputes with New France regarding freedom of movement and trade for the next three decades. During the early 1670s, however, Iroquois leaders were more concerned with containing internal disputes that arose from the increasing numbers of people relocating to the St. Lawrence valley and building consensus on the useful role these communities might play in the League's broader engagements with settler colonialism on Iroquoia's periphery. These innovative movements occurred alongside renewed long-distance Iroquois military campaigns against Native nations bordering Anglo-American colonies from Maine to Virginia. Free movement by members of all League nations now extended outward from Iroquoia in the four principal directions, and manifested a growing awareness among Iroquois people of the importance of defining their homelands as a crucial central space vis-à-vis neighboring Native and settler communities.

Courcelles's 1671 voyage proved most alarming not to the League nations but to authorities in New York. On June 18, 1671, an extraordinary session of the Albany

Court exchanged "propositions" with the "Canadian chief of the Iroquois," one "Canadasse," who had come to Albany from the St. Lawrence valley. Canadasse informed the Albany Court of Courcelles's recent expedition to Lake Ontario, and this news prompted the court to summon "Robertus Renatus de la Salle," who was then visiting Mohawk country. La Salle denied any aggressive motivations on the part of Courcelles, noting that he never would have obtained the governor's permission to "go hunting 150 [men] strong" if the French had planned to attack New York. Following La Salle's testimony, a Mohawk leader named Sagoestesi urged the Albany Court to "give no further credence to Canadasse," referring to him as a "great liar" and denying his status as a Mohawk "sachem."[38]

The magistrates likely found Sagoestesi's contestation of Canadasse's status confusing. In their eyes, the latter represented a legitimate Iroquois leader, one whom they obviously knew well enough (likely via trade contacts and/or his prior residence in the Mohawk valley) to appeal for his aid in brokering an Iroquois-Mahican peace agreement. By 1671, Iroquois residency in the St. Lawrence valley ranged from the Wendat mission of Notre-Dame-de-Foy, which reportedly included individuals from all constituent League nations as well as Neutral and Susquehannock adoptees among its estimated 150 residents, to Kentaké on the south shore of the St. Lawrence River, which had grown from five "cabins" in 1669 to a settlement of eighteen to twenty families two years later. The residents of Kentaké fished, tended clearly delineated fields producing "very fine" yields of corn, and hosted regular "throng[s] of Savages resorting thither from all directions" to hunt. Canadasse may have been one of the two "Chiefs" appointed by the people of Kentaké in 1671 to speak "the word[s] from the elders of the village."[39]

Although not all Iroquois people agreed at this time that these movements represented positive change (as Sagoestesi's denial of Canadasse's legitimacy clearly suggests), Iroquois social conventions contained potentially serious disputes to the level of individual families or clan segments. When the family of a Mohawk woman named Skaouendes learned of her decision to relocate with her husband and two young children from Gandaouagué to the St. Lawrence valley in 1671, they "degraded her from her noble rank, in an assembly of the Village notables; and deprived her of the name and title of *Oiander*." But rather than permit Skaoundes's decision to leave a gap in her clan's matrilineal organization, her kinfolk simply "installed another woman in her place." Skaouendes then departed with her family, unopposed and "entirely undisturbed by her relatives' action." After her arrival at Notre-Dame-de-Foy, Skaouendes kept in touch with her kinfolk at Gandaouagué by letters she dictated to Jesuit priests, who sent them to her former Mohawk hometown, where other Jesuits read them aloud. By 1672, as many as fifty Mohawks had their canoes "all in readiness" to join Skaouendes at Notre-Dame-de-Foy.[40]

Jesuit writings emphasized the devotional piety of the Iroquois pioneers in the St. Lawrence valley. While not discounting the presence of these individuals or even the legitimacy of their spiritual commitment to Catholicism, the larger story of Iroquois movements to the St. Lawrence valley settlements may only be discerned by reading between the lines of missionary sources. On the one hand, the Laurentian communities represented secure spaces for Iroquois individuals pursuing conversion to Catholicism as a response to changing conditions in their homelands. On the other hand, the majority of Iroquois people came to view relocation to these settlements not as flights to spiritual refuge from their pagan kinfolk, but rather as an effort to expand League homelands. The Laurentian communities developed from seasonal bases incorporated into Iroquois peoples' annual subsistence cycle into centers of trade and strategic nodes of League diplomacy and communications.

One of the Laurentian communities' most crucial functions was to facilitate the assimilation of adoptees into the larger Iroquois polity. Jesuits described the residents of Kentaké in 1671 as "people gathered from different countries—Wendats, members of the Neutral nation, Iroquois, people from Andastogué" (Susquehannocks), all originating from "different Iroquois Nations, and either natives of that country, or dwellers there as prisoners of war." Once collected at La Prairie, they "made but one" community with the League nations through "sociability, visits, hospitality, feasts, and mutual gifts."[41]

Although the Jesuits took some satisfaction in reporting Iroquois "elders" complaints that relocations of their people to the Laurentian settlements threatened to "destroy their land," the missionaries also noted that as these complaints increased, more Iroquois people traveled, particularly to Kentaké, "to see what was going on." As early as 1672 the Jesuits found themselves dealing with ever-larger numbers of unbaptized Iroquois people in these so-called mission villages. Movement occurred in both directions, as some individuals chose to leave Kentaké and return to their former homes, occasionally persuaded by delegations sent to retrieve them. Therefore we need not accept at face value Jesuit claims that the Laurentian settlements constituted merely an "asylum" for Iroquois Christians. Within the structure of the League, notwithstanding some initial internal debate, they represented crucial spaces employed for far more diverse and significant Iroquois purposes.[42]

Reports from Sulpician and Jesuit missionaries of widespread Iroquois hunting on the north shore of Lake Ontario, combined with declining peltry volumes at Montreal, convinced French colonial authorities to bolster their claim to lands drained by Lakes Huron and Superior (and, by extension, the fur-bearing animals inhabiting them) with a June 14, 1671, ceremony of possession at Sault Ste. Marie. In his public address to the assembled Algonquians, Allouez, who claimed that Louis XIV held sovereign authority over "all the countries commonly included under the designation of Outaouac" (Odawa), also tried to persuade the assembled Native audience that Onontio was "the terror of the Iroquois, and that his very name makes them tremble, now that he has laid waste to their villages," a belated attempt to capitalize on the 1666 Tracy expedition. Realistic officials in New France, however, including

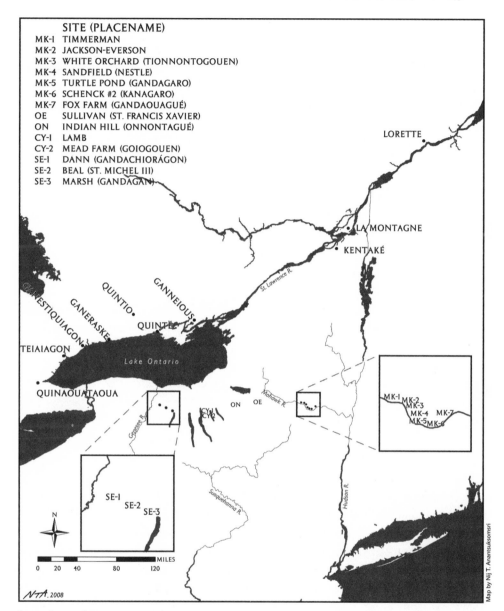

SITE (PLACENAME)
MK-1　TIMMERMAN
MK-2　JACKSON-EVERSON
MK-3　WHITE ORCHARD (TIONNONTOGOUEN)
MK-4　SANDFIELD (NESTLE)
MK-5　TURTLE POND (GANDAGARO)
MK-6　SCHENCK #2 (KANAGARO)
MK-7　FOX FARM (GANDAOUAGUÉ)
OE　　SULLIVAN (ST. FRANCIS XAVIER)
ON　　INDIAN HILL (ONNONTAGUÉ)
CY-1　LAMB
CY-2　MEAD FARM (GOIOGOUEN)
SE-1　DANN (GANDACHIORÁGON)
SE-2　BEAL (ST. MICHEL III)
SE-3　MARSH (GANDAGAN)

Iroquoia, ca. 1673

newly arrived Governor Louis de Buade, Comte de Frontenac, began to contemplate seriously Sulpician recommendations for French posts at both the mouth of Lake Ontario and near the Niagara River portage, manned by French traders if possible, or soldiers if necessary, as a means of intercepting Iroquois hunters.[43]

The Iroquois, for their part, returned in large numbers to the upper Great Lakes over the winter of 1672–73. These movements followed the successful resolution of their war with the Mahicans and other New England Algonquians via a treaty at Albany in November 1671. Jesuit Henri Nouvel reported from Sault Ste. Marie a joint Iroquois-Mississauga hunting expedition as well as a flood of "very considerable presents" to all the nations of the upper Great Lakes in order to "get their peltries." Senecas carried gifts and messages of peace to the Fox during the winter of 1672–73 and secured the release of two Seneca women, reportedly longtime prisoners among the Fox. Several Fox delegates also visited Seneca country in late 1672 or early 1673, likely returning with these repatriated captives. By 1673, Jesuits in the upper Great Lakes commented on the growing rapprochement between the Iroquois and the region's Algonquians. These reports convinced French authorities that the Iroquois concrete plans to redirect the western fur trade to Albany via their settlements on the north shore of Lake Ontario.[44]

Frontenac departed Montreal on June 29, 1673, reportedly for a tour of "the whole extent of his government," but in reality he intended to scout a potential location for a French fort on Lake Ontario. He sent La Salle ahead to Iroquoia in the early months of 1673 with an invitation for deputies from each nation to rendezvous with the new governor at the Sulpician mission near Quinté. While traveling up the St. Lawrence River on July 9, 1673, Frontenac received an Iroquois-delivered letter from La Salle advising that while over 200 of the League's "most ancient and influential leaders" had agreed to meet with Frontenac, they objected to Frontenac's proposed venue, claiming that a meeting there would manifest undue preference for the local Cayugas. They recommended a neutral meeting site instead. Alarmed by the reported size of the Iroquois delegation, Frontenac, aided by directions from some Iroquois guides who had approached his convoy, stopped some sixty miles short of Quinté at the mouth of the "Katarakoüi" River, a place he described as "one of the most beautiful and agreeable harbors in the world."[45]

The Iroquois knew better, however. Swampy terrain, and rocky, poor-quality soils surrounded the future site of Fort Frontenac. "Cataraqui," the Iroquois name for this installation, has been translated to mean "fort in the water." The League delegates, during their preliminary July 17–18, 1673, conference with Frontenac, granted the governor permission to establish what he described as a trading post with fixed, cheap prices. On July 21–23, 1673, Garacontié mediated talks between Frontenac and more than 100 delegates from the "Iroquois du Nord" villages of Ganestiquiagon, Ganeraské, Quinté, and Ganneious that confirmed the League delegates' earlier arrangements. Frontenac later claimed to have elicited a promise from the leaders of these communities to abandon their practice of carrying peltry obtained by their own hunters and in exchange with Odawas and other Algonquian nations of the *pays d'en haut*. A map dating to the early 1680s, however, indicates that the "Iroquois du Nord" simply shifted their primary center of exchange with the upper Great Lakes nations from Ganestiquiagon to Teiaiagon after 1673, further distancing themselves from potential French interference with their economic and diplomatic initiatives.[46]

Raffeix's Map of Lake Ontario, ca. 1688

Meanwhile, the pace of Iroquois movements to and from the St. Lawrence valley increased significantly. In June 1673, "nearly fifty" individuals relocated from Tionnontogouen to Notre-Dame-de-Foy, and Bruyas suggested that still more Mohawks would follow if they heard that their "compatriots" received a "good reception." By late 1673, Jesuits reported that the amount of firewood consumed by the growing number of "recruits" from Iroquoia at Notre-Dame-de-Foy necessitated plans for its relocation to a new site at Lorette, roughly eight miles distant.[47]

Kentaké also experienced burgeoning numbers in 1673, after hosting an estimated 800 of their fellow Iroquois "countrymen" over the previous winter's hunting season. Such hospitality on the part of the Laurentians was facilitated by two years' worth of stored corn in the community, a testimony to the innovative agricultural practices of Kentaké women, who developed techniques of starting plant seedlings "between sheets of bark" in their longhouses during the late spring as a means of coping with their community's comparatively short growing season. The Laurentians' hospitality also coincided with the reported outbreak of a "malignant fever" in Iroquoia during the summer of 1673, and with increasingly scarce trade goods in New York stemming from interruptions in shipping during the Third Anglo-Dutch War (1672–74). High prices in Albany convinced large numbers of Mohawks, and possibly some Senecas, "to provide themselves" with "stuffs" at Montreal during the summer 1673 trading season.[48]

Favorable assessments of the Laurentian communities from individuals who returned from visits and trading journeys to the St. Lawrence valley in 1673—such as the Mohawk military leader Kryn and a Mohawk "elder" named "Assendassé," who was "head of one of the leading [Mohawk] families"—encouraged further relocations. Still, not all Iroquois people favored the idea of moving to the St. Lawrence valley. Some Tionnontogouen residents "who are not yet fully inclined toward the faith" complained in 1673 "of the black gowns, who seemed intent upon making a desert of their country and completely ruining their villages." This Jesuit-recorded statement assigned the missionaries a prominent role in encouraging movements of Mohawks to the Laurentian communities, but it may actually have reflected the Mohawks' attribution of blame for the 1673 disease outbreak.[49]

While not all relocations occurred without strain, Iroquois social conventions prevented the development of widespread factionalism. Prior to his departure from Mohawk country, one of Assendassé's relatives, who deliberately made himself "half-intoxicated," tore the rosary and crucifix from his kinsman's neck and threatened to kill him. But the aggressor backed down after Assendassé claimed he would be "happy to die for so good a cause" as relocating to Kentaké. An Onondaga man brought his family back to Onondaga country in 1673 following two years' residency at Kentaké, having yielded to "solicitations" of a delegation of his countrymen charged with effecting his return. When this unnamed man tried to "compel his wife to renounce Christianity" upon their return, she refused. He then abandoned her (and his young son) and took up with another woman. Yet when he returned to his first wife's longhouse and beat her in a drunken rage, her relatives "made themselves drunk also," inflicted a retaliatory beating on the abuser, and permitted their kinswoman to return to Kentaké with her son. Freedom of movement, in this instance, defused a volatile family situation.[50]

Despite optimistic Jesuit assessments of the Laurentian settlements as potentially fertile spiritual ground, Chauchetière reported that the arrival of 200 new residents at Kentaké in 1673 had actually provided "the occasion for greater evils." Increasing numbers of "infidels" from the Five Nations threatened to corrupt (in Jesuit eyes) the "Christians" in these communities. The influx of new Iroquois arrivals drew the attention of Montreal traders and prospective tavernkeepers. By the end of 1673, Jesuits claimed that the number of Mohawk warriors in the St. Lawrence River valley exceeded that of the Mohawk River valley. Yet despite Jesuit Jean de Lamberville's report of efforts by the Dutch (during their brief interregnum in New York that followed their recapture of the colony from the English) to have the Five Nations expel the Jesuits from Iroquoia during the summer of 1673, Iroquois leaders made no significant effort to do so. The Iroquois still valued their Jesuit hostages as human shields and guarantors of their freedom of movement.[51]

By 1674, Jesuit observers' writings attested to the prevalence of Iroquois cultural norms in the Laurentian valley settlements. At the funeral of Laurentian pioneer Gandeakteua in the early months of 1674, her surviving kin distributed her personal effects (goods valued at 300 livres, which the Jesuits considered "a good deal for a savage") to the "recipients of charity" among the Iroquois population at Kentaké. A Lorette Wendat leader, despite having formerly been tortured while a prisoner among the Iroquois, "nevertheless adopted one of that nation, with his wife and two children, all these he lodged and fed [at Lorette] for five or six months" in 1674. Hundreds of other Iroquois people continued to pass through Kentaké, the "lake of the Two Mountains," and Lorette during their military expeditions and winter hunts, taking advantage of the increasing numbers of French traders drawn to these Iroquois-dominated settlements. By November 1674, the growth of the Native population at Kentaké led the Jesuits to petition for an augmentation of their seigneury.[52]

Despite the combined impact of epidemic disease, isolated family disputes arising from the movement of people to the Laurentian missions, and increasing debate over the merits of the Jesuits' presence in Iroquois communities, Iroquois society did not disintegrate during the latter decades of the seventeenth century. Raffeix complained in 1674 of the powerful influence of diverse "superstitions" imparted to the Senecas by their adoptees, which in his view constituted "a considerable impediment to the propagation of the Gospel" in Iroquoia. Later in 1674, Jesuit Pierre Millet witnessed the condolence of an unspecified Oneida leader by "several embassies from the other Iroquois" nations. Millet's description of the event represents the most elaborate seventeenth-century description of the ceremony and reflects the persistent integrity of League tradition, as does Lamberville's account of the supposed Christian convert Garacontié being "deputed with all the most notable men of the village as an ambassador of the Onnontagués, to bear their gifts to the four other Iroquois nations" during the winter of 1673–74, and the statement of a delegation of Mohawks in New York on June 1, 1674, of their plan to "renew their peace" with the four other League nations after renewing their preliminary covenant with Dutch authorities.[53]

In addition to documenting the League's functional integrity, Jesuit and other contemporary observers noted the continuing effectiveness of long-distance Iroquois military campaigns in the mid-1670s. Jesuit Jacques Marquette described a sizable Shawnee presence on the Wabash River in modern-day western Kentucky in July 1673. He identified these Shawnees as "the nations whom the Iroquois go so far to seek, and war against without any reason; and because these poor people cannot defend themselves, they allow themselves to be captured and taken like flocks of sheep." Maryland authorities began in June 1674 to discuss the issue of making peace with the "Cynicoes Indians" (a collective ethnonym for the Iroquois akin to the term "Sinnekens" employed by the Dutch and English of New York), whose routes to

Piscataway and Susquehannock settlements brought them into increasingly frequent contact with colonial settlers. Authorities in Massachusetts possessed by 1674 nearly a decade of sporadic experience with similar movements by Iroquois warriors as far as the outskirts of Boston against Native peoples allied to their colony and residing within its jurisdiction.[54]

Both Anglo-American and French colonial authorities recognized the ways in which the capacity of the Iroquois for extensive spatial mobility posed a challenge to their respective colonial projects. Anglo-American officials, for their part, attempted after 1675 to strike a difficult balance in their relations with the League. They sought to harness Iroquois military power for use against hostile Native nations, while also endeavoring to preserve the integrity of allied Native groups in their respective colonies from unhindered Iroquois aggression. French colonial authorities already understood how Iroquois mobility posed a challenge to their desire to engross the fur trade of the upper Great Lakes, and they worked to retain the claimed possession of that territory through the Native alliances that trade sustained.

King Louis XIV granted La Salle a seigneury on the north shore of Lake Ontario on May 13, 1675. This development reflected metropolitan authorities' acceptance of Frontenac's arguments asserting the fundamental significance of a French fort in this area for preserving the fur trade of the upper Great Lakes for New France against Iroquois competition. Yet La Salle proved more interested in the post as a base for further interior exploration rather than a means to interdict Iroquois movement to and from the upper Great Lakes. Many Iroquois hunters and traders moving through the area simply stayed out of the range of Fort Frontenac's guns. Others, however, manifested opposition to the French installation. Raffeix reported from Seneca country in 1675 that since his hosts had "utterly defeated" the Susquehannocks, they had resolved to destroy "Fort Catarakoui" (Frontenac) and to resume campaigns against the nations of the *pays d'en haut*.[55]

Raffeix exaggerated when he reported the total defeat of the Susquehannocks by the Iroquois in 1675, but that year did witness key turning points in the conflict. In early March, the Maryland Assembly received a delegation of Susquehannock headmen who asked for land in the province. Suspecting "Private Correspondence" between these Susquehannocks and the "Senecas," the assembly authorized the Susquehannocks to settle "above the falls of [the] Potomack" River, distant from the Piscataways and other "friend Indian nations" of the colony. Seven months later, after the outbreak of King Philip's War in New England, New York governor Sir Edmund Andros questioned Albany authorities on the status of the Iroquois war against the Susquehannocks. He learned that the Mohawks considered the Susquehannocks their "Off-Spring" and therefore might be willing to "Concorporate again." Aware of the potential for Susquehannock adoptees to produce a substantial increase in Mohawk military power, and hoping to affirm his status as the primary Anglo-American contact with the League, Andros asked Maryland authorities to send Susquehannock delegates to New York in October 1675 so that he might "Order Matters accordingly" in a joint meeting with Iroquois leaders.[56]

As Iroquois-Susquehannock relations assumed a more peaceful character, the first news of King Philip's War arrived in Mohawk country in June 1675 via a "head (or heads) of the Qunnihticut Indians" sent by Mohegan sachem Uncas in an effort to secure access to supplies of military stores from Mohawk traders. By September 1675, New York's acting governor Captain Anthony Brockholls and the Albany Court were attempting to curtail the flow of Mohawk-traded ammunition from Albany to potentially hostile New England Native nations. One month later, the extent of damage inflicted by those hostile nations on New England settlements (including the destruction of John Pynchon's trading post at Springfield) led to increasing calls by colonial officials for Iroquois assistance against King Philip and his allies. Uncas, speaking from long-standing personal experience, affirmed that the Iroquois represented "the only persons likely to put an end to the war," since they could force King Philip and his allies from their winter refuge in northwestern New England and drive them back toward waiting settler military forces to the south and east.[57]

In December 1675, Andros received news that the indigenous foes of New England, flush with their "great Successes" of the previous summer, had approached Mohawks residing in both the Mohawk and Laurentian valley settlements about joining their war against New England. With the concurrent outbreak of Susquehannock hostilities against Virginia settlers in September 1675, much of Anglo-America now faced serious conflicts with Native peoples. For the moment, Andros believed that the Mohawks, "and by their means the Sinnekes," would "remain firme." Yet he knew that losing the friendship (or at least the neutrality) of the League nations, whom he estimated at "3000 or more good fitting [fighting] men," posed a significant threat to the English settler presence in eastern North America. Convinced of the League's ability to "do good or harme," and confronting increasingly damning evidence that King Philip and his allies obtained military supplies from Albany by trading plunder from English settlers (either directly or with possible Iroquois brokerage), Andros, upon learning in January 1676 of King Philip's encampment near Hoosick, just "40 or 50 miles" northeast of Albany, seized the opportunity to enlist the Mohawks to "destroy these bloody upland Indians."[58]

In early February 1676, Andros sailed up to Albany with a body of English regular troops. He arrived to find nearly 300 Mohawk "Souldiers in towne," who returned the previous evening from their "pursuite of Phillip and a party of five hundred with him, whom they had beaten, having some prisoners and the crowns, or hayre and skinne of the head, of others they had killed." Per Andros's prior request, New York's commander in chief Captain Anthony Brockholls had provided the Mohawk warriors with "all sorts of arms and necessarys [sic] they wanted, and received their Old Sachems, wives, and children into the towne" of Albany, while the warriors had dispersed King Philip's encampment from Hoosick. Although the refusal of Connecticut authorities to permit independent Iroquois movement into their colony prevented Andros from offering official encouragement of any Mohawk pursuit of the eastward-retreating Algonquians, a number of Mohawk and Onondaga warriors elected to do so anyway, inaugurating a new round of Iroquois attacks on New England Native communities during the early months of 1676.[59]

In the meantime, renewed Seneca aggression against the Susquehannocks and other Native peoples in Maryland in May 1676 had prompted at least one Susquehannock ambassador to approach Lenapes residing in what is now eastern Pennsylvania for discussions of possible refuge in their homelands. Andros traveled in June 1676 to the head of Delaware Bay, where he informed Susquehannock headmen of the Mohawks' regard for their people as "brother[s] and Children" and offered the Susquehannocks not only secure residency in New York but also his brokerage of a comprehensive peace on their behalf with the Iroquois League, Maryland, and Virginia. The Susquehannocks declined the offer, however, stating that they had "no mind to go up to Albany."[60]

By August 1676, a number of Susquehannocks had regrouped in the vicinity of their "Old Fort about sixty miles above Palmer's Island" on the Susquehanna River, having concluded "peace with their Old Enemy the Senecas." Andros feared that the movement of Susquehannocks toward Iroquoia's periphery might enable the Susquehannocks to secure the assistance of their Iroquois neighbors in undertaking retaliatory attacks on "Christians" in Virginia and Maryland, "wholly out of [the] reach" of Anglo-American military forces. Maryland governor Thomas Notley shared Andros's apprehension of a "confederat[ion]" between the "Sennico and Susquehannoh Indians," since together they constituted, in his view, "the bloodiest people in all these parts of America."[61]

As Iroquois campaigns against Native peoples in New England and Maryland intensified during the winter of 1676–77, Anglo-American colonists groped for solutions to the problems posed by Iroquois freedom of movement. An anonymous writer blasted Lord Baltimore in late 1676 for failing to prevent the "Mischief done by the Sinnico Indian[s]," whose annual expeditions against the Piscataways now included "robb[ing] divers plantations" in both Maryland and Virginia. Officials in New England colonies welcomed Iroquois attacks on the "common [Algonquian] enemie," but settlers in this region also experienced occasional friction from passing Iroquois war parties. In April 1677, Andros advised the Mohawks to recall their warriors from the "Eastward" until he could ensure that they would be received "as friends" by New England's "Christians."[62]

These developments enabled Andros to advocate the centralization of Anglo-American relations with the Iroquois League at Albany. League headmen initially cooperated with Andros, since he had tacitly acknowledged Iroquois protocol by meeting near the League's eastern door in Mohawk country. League delegates had only to travel as far as Albany to undertake discussions with, and often to receive cash payments and/or presents of material goods from, an increasing number of would-be Anglo-American allies.[63]

John Pynchon led one such delegation from Massachusetts to Albany in April 1677, and distributed gifts valued at £128 to several Mohawk headmen, partly as a gesture of thanks for their role in King Philip's War and partly to encourage continued Mohawk aggression against troublesome Algonquians like the Abenaki headman "Blind Will," whom the Mohawks reportedly killed not long after their meeting with Pynchon. Despite apparent compliance with Anglo-American initiatives, the Iroquois placed their own objectives at the forefront of these campaigns. When Andros demanded the release of all Native prisoners taken in a June 1677 Mohawk attack on the "Mahicanders and North Indians," Mohawk leaders from all the principal towns, echoing the behavior of the Senecas seven years previously, agreed only to a partial return of the prisoners. They advised the Albany Court that most of the prisoners would remain with their captors, explaining that "while we are indeed sachems, we cannot simply turn our backs on our soldiers, for they are our protectors, and have to fight for us since we are old people." Iroquois war parties, one of which consisted of thirty Algonquian adoptees and "but one" Mohawk, continued to conduct raids as far east as the outskirts of Boston.[64]

While the Mohawks interpreted Pynchon's gifts and encouragement as sanction for their ongoing, independent offensives in New England, Maryland authorities charged Colonel Henry Coursey in late April 1677 with the task of ending Iroquois attacks on the Piscataways and other tributary Native populations (who had exchanged their political independence for bounded reservations and promises of protection from colonial governments) in both Maryland and Virginia. Worse still, in the eyes of the Anglo-American colonists, such campaigns increasingly witnessed "divers murders and other outrages" perpetrated on the settler population of these two colonies by the "Cinnigos and divers other Nations of Indians residing to the northward of this Province." The New York Council sent wampum strings inviting delegates from "each of the five Respective [Iroquois] castles" to meet with Coursey at Albany in early June 1677. Coursey spent the months of July and August 1677 meeting with delegates from all five League nations.[65]

Coursey hoped that liberal presents would bring an end to Iroquois and Susquehannock attacks on the Piscataways. He received in return for those presents a comprehensive lesson from all League nations regarding the value the Iroquois attached to their freedom of movement. Garacontié, making his final public appearance in a July 21, 1677, speech to Coursey (the Onondaga leader died of a "bloody flux" in Onondaga country six weeks later), acknowledged past incidents of Iroquois killing "Christians and Indians" but attributed responsibility for these deaths to a Maryland trader named Jacob Young, whom Garacontié claimed had even participated as a "Capt[ain]" with his Susquehannock friends and trading partners in some of these expeditions. An Oneida speaker followed Garacontié, and while he admitted that warriors from his nation had in the past killed "som[e] hoggs and beasts" when hungry, he claimed that they had never plundered settlers unless they had been directly provoked. On August 6, 1677, a delegation of Mohawk headmen agreed to Maryland's inclusion in their "Covenant Chain" alliance with New York. In keeping with previous patterns of *kaswentha* diplomacy, the Mohawks defined the relationship in Iroquoian terms as a forum for resolving future differences rather than committing to an absolute, immediate cessation of military campaigns to the south of Iroquoia. Finally, on August 22, 1677, a party of Seneca and Cayuga leaders arrived in Albany. They promised merely to provide advance notice if they took "up the axe" against Native peoples in Virginia and Maryland, but informed Coursey that settlers would be unmolested if they did not "Intertein" Indians they targeted for attacks.[66]

As had been the case in New England, Iroquois campaigns on the frontiers of Maryland and Virginia persisted during and after League negotiations with Coursey. Paralleling the Mohawks' earlier effort to smooth relations with New Englanders, the Oneidas in late December 1677 ransomed in Albany several Susquehannock prisoners taken "behind Virginia" during the summer of 1677, but asserted their right to retain selected Susquehannock adoptees. A "Senneke" delegation in Albany during March 1678 stated their understanding of the "Covenant" with Maryland as recognizing their freedom of movement, including "Liberty to come among the Xtians [Christians] in Peace and Quietness."[67]

CONTESTING THE *PAYS D'EN HAUT*

While Anglo-American officials argued about the respective extent of their territorial jurisdiction in North America, the Iroquois acted to shape their own theater of spatial influence. Intensified Iroquois military campaigns against Native peoples residing in or near Anglo-American colonies during the mid-1670s represented significant assertions of the League's freedom of movement in one theater that relied to no small extent on similar demonstrations of independent Iroquois mobility into the upper Great Lakes. New York officials, who bore primary responsibility for brokering Anglo-American relations with the League, possessed significant economic interest in the peltry of the *pays d'en haut* and realized that the Iroquois represented their best hope of acquiring those furs. League leaders, cognizant of the value of maintaining New Yorkers' allegiance in the broader context of their foreign relations, moved quickly to confront increasing French interference with their freedom of movement (as hunters, traders, and warriors) into the upper Great Lakes after 1676.

Jesuits in Seneca and Cayuga towns suffered ongoing harassment from local residents who in 1676 reportedly ran "after the missionaries with hatchets in their hands," pelted them with stones, tore down "their chapels and their little cabins, and in a thousand other ways subject[ed] them to the most infamous treatment."

Archaeological evidence attests to the very limited degree of the Jesuits' spiritual influence—just one of sixty-three graves excavated during the early twentieth century at the Seneca Bunce site (a burial ground associated with the Ganondagan community) revealed decisive indications of an individual's conversion to Christianity. Yet no Iroquois nation expelled the Jesuits, as they continued to provide essential cover for Iroquois initiatives in the *pays d'en haut.* A delegation of Senecas traveled to the St. Ignace mission near the straits of Lakes Huron and Michigan early in 1676 and "gave valuable presents" to the local Tionnontatés, who then numbered between 300 and 600 people. Jesuit Philippe Pierson noted that the Senecas publicly claimed to recruit Tionnontaté assistance for a joint expedition against the "Nadoussiens" (Sioux), but feared that the Senecas actually intended to "lure all our savages to their country." This report, along with persistent threats of renewed Iroquois attacks on New France, motivated the Canadian governor to make a personal trip to Fort Frontenac during the summer of 1676 to "reconcile the minds of the Five Iroquois Nations." In fact, Frontenac's effort represented an attempt to purchase security both for the fort (where he conducted substantial private trading) and for the Jesuits in Iroquoia with an outlay of presents valued at 2,435 livres for the Oneidas, Onondagas, and Cayugas who accepted his invitation.[68]

Frontenac's view of the Jesuits, notwithstanding his personal exertions on their behalf in 1676, grew increasingly dim one year later. The governor made extensive complaints about the Jesuits' conduct in a lengthy 1677 letter to Colbert. Few Iroquois residing with Jesuits, Frontenac argued, would be qualified for baptism if objective observers assessed the extent of their spiritual knowledge. Additionally, the governor charged the Jesuits with failing to teach the residents of Kentaké and Lorette the French language, and with permitting Iroquois individuals with no demonstrated interest in Christianity to live in these towns alongside potential converts. Finally, Frontenac excoriated the Jesuits' hypocrisy in engineering the relocation of the Kentaké mission upriver to a place the French called Sault St. Louis in 1676 (via concessions of land they obtained from Intendant Jacques Duchesneau, which interfered with earlier concessions made by Frontenac to La Salle at the latter site) on the claimed pretext of settler proximity to Kentaké while simultaneously renting out lands cleared by Iroquois residents of Kentaké to French settlers.[69]

Frontenac had learned of the Jesuits' rental of Iroquois-cleared lands from an Iroquois woman of Kentaké named "Marie-Félix," who possessed a traditional Iroquois perspective on territoriality. The relocation of Kentaké "a league and a quarter higher up" to Kahnawake in July 1675 matched normative distances and rationales for village relocations elsewhere in Iroquoia. Jesuits claimed that the land at Kentaké, "being low in ground," was not suitable for raising crops sufficient to support by the growing settlement, but otherwise failed to acknowledge Iroquois initiative underlying the move. By clearing the lands west of Kentaké and naming their new settlement Kahnawake (an echo of the Mohawk valley settlement of Gandaouagué that illustrated the strength of the relocated Mohawks' ties to their families and their nation), Marie-Félix argued that the land had become Iroquois property. She also advised Frontenac in no uncertain terms of her community's intense dissatisfaction with the Jesuits treating them "like slaves."[70]

The majority of Iroquois people by this time had come to regard the St. Lawrence valley towns, particularly Kentaké and its successor Kahnawake, as integral components of the League polity. When Bishop François de Laval visited Kentaké in May 1675, he received an elaborate Edge of the Woods welcome from "a captain of the onontagués and an elder from onneiout," who spoke, as Garacontié had when he brokered the 1673 meeting between Frontenac and the delegates from the north shore Iroquois communities, "in the name of all the 5 Iroquois nations." As a result of recruiting missions to Iroquoia undertaken by residents of Kentaké, and ongoing extended visits by Iroquois families during winter hunts, the population of Kahnawake in 1676 numbered some 300 people from all five League nations. Both the Jesuits and French civil authorities continued to interpret in providential terms the actions of individuals like Kahnawake headman "Hot Powder," whose public speeches about the St. Lawrence valley in Mohawk and Oneida settlements evoked "all the noise which hell made by the mouths of the [Iroquois] elders, who perpetually declaimed in their councils against" relocation to the St. Lawrence valley. More prosaically, these competing speeches persuaded their audiences to "see for themselves" what was happening in the Laurentian communities.[71]

Individuals from all walks of Iroquois life continued to move to the St. Lawrence valley during the mid-1670s. In May 1675, Jesuits reported the "captain of the Agniés" (Mohawks) participating in a joint hunting expedition with associates from Kahnawake. If this was indeed "Canondondarwe," a Tionnontogouen headman whom Albany authorities considered the "chief sachem of the Maquase" in 1677, at least one of his sons was living at Kahnawake in 1684. Beneath the Jesuits' rhetorical conception of a supernatural contest between good and evil reflected in these movements we can detect rational decision making on the part of Iroquois actors, who considered both sides of the issue and made independent decisions to relocate, to stay put, or to move back and forth. In February 1675, Mohawk headman Assendassé, an early advocate of relocation to the St. Lawrence valley, returned to spend his final days in the Mohawk valley. By the time of his death six months later, his Mohawk colleagues mourned the loss of "the best mind among them."[72]

By January 1677, Kahnawake consisted of twenty-two longhouses organized on matrilineal residency patterns. Jesuit Pierre Cholenec described a typical Kahnawake household as consisting of "a good old woman and three of her daughters, all married and living in the same cabin as her," a clear indication of continued adherence to matrilocal residency and the bonds of matrilineal kinship. Leadership patterns from Kentaké persisted in the new Laurentian community. Cholenec identified the town's four "captains" in January 1677 as a Mohawk named "Tiwates'kon," an unnamed

Onondaga, and two unnamed Wendat adoptees. The residents of Kahnawake were also expecting in January 1677 the imminent arrival of "4 captains of the principal Iroquois nations" to take up residency in their community, reflecting increasing linkages between this multinational settlement, another at La Montagne (host community for a Sulpician mission), and the League.[73]

Concrete proof of these ties appeared in the late spring of 1677, when 300 or 400 Iroquois "transient dwellers" appeared at Kahnawake after their winter hunt and profited from local residents' contacts with Montreal traders as well as the generous hospitality offered by their Iroquois kinfolk. After "having eaten much [of the stored] corn" at Kahnawake, the Iroquois visitors "also carried off a great deal for their provision" on their return journey to their home settlements. Though Jesuits interpreted this visit as an Iroquois effort to "starve out the village of the Sault," no corroborating complaints from local Iroquois hosts appear in the record. Iroquois ethics of hospitality mandated such generosity.[74]

Missionaries continued to stress the "lofty sentiments of piety" they considered prevalent among the Iroquois residents of Kahnawake, La Montagne, and Lorette. But historians must not assume that the Jesuits' lengthy descriptions of the extreme Christian devotions of a few individuals like Catherine Tekakwitha necessarily represented mainstream Iroquois behavior at these settlements. Tekakwitha's life narrative reveals the degree to which adoptees in the Laurentian communities experienced pressure to shed ties to their birth nations and to behave with loyalty toward the "Iroquois nation." Although the Jesuits cited evidence of the growing annual number of adult baptisms at Kahnawake after 1675 to support their claimed influence over the Laurentian Iroquois population, they also admitted that most of the Iroquois arriving in the St. Lawrence valley possessed not only little "inclination" for Christian teachings, many manifested "quite contrary dispositions" and stated that they were "fully determined not to believe and not to listen on this point to the Fathers who instruct them." Of course, the Jesuits regarded engaging such opposition as their raison d'être: of what spiritual value would their mission be without such crosses to bear? Yet the weight of evidence indicates that opportunities to reconstitute families, to hunt, to trade, and to establish a functional, persistent, League-sanctioned Iroquois presence in the St. Lawrence valley prevailed over exclusively religious motives underlying Iroquois movements to nominal mission villages even during the late 1670s and early 1680s, a time the Jesuits identified as the pinnacle of these towns' Christian spiritual intensity.[75]

Sulpicians reported even less interest in religion among the "Iroquois du Nord." Resident missionary Louis Tronson lamented in 1675 the negative effects of the "very great wanderings" of the Cayugas of Quinté on his efforts to provide religious instruction to the community. The Senecas of Teieaiagon preferred the company of French traders from Fort Frontenac to that of the Sulpicians. Hennepin persuaded a number of the Cayugas at Ganneious to relocate to the vicinity of Fort Frontenac in 1676. The Cayugas turned this move to their advantage, establishing a small town of about "Forty cottages," where they planted corn and traded freshly killed game to their fifty French neighbors (soldiers, laborers, and settlers attached to the garrison). Hennepin hoped that the proximity of this settlement would also facilitate the conversion of the Cayugas' children, but soon found his efforts frustrated by the Cayugas' five- to six-month hunting expeditions "through their vast huge forests" at distances of "two hundred leagues from their ordinary abode." Since entire Cayuga families participated in these long-range expeditions, the children quickly forgot Hennepin's teachings. By 1677, the "frequent journeys" and "instability" of the Iroquois residing on the north shore of Lake Ontario persuaded the Sulpicians to withdraw from Quinté and concentrate their efforts at La Montagne on Montreal Island. But the missionaries could not escape the mobile "Iroquois du Nord." An influx of Senecas, Onondagas, and Cayugas from the north shore communities made members of Iroquois nations the dominant population at La Montagne (previously home to Algonquins and Wendats) by 1680.[76]

Missionary-documented Iroquois mobility north of Lake Ontario indicated the failure of La Salle's plans in 1677 to employ Fort Frontenac and a newly constructed "barque" vessel as a means of holding the League nations in "bridle." Jesuits noted the presence of "a goodly number of Iroquois" among the flotilla of thirty Kiskakon Odawa canoes escorting Jacques Marquette's remains from the Illinois country (where the mixed Odawa-Iroquois party had spent the previous winter hunting) to St. Ignace on June 8, 1677. In the aftermath of this visit to the *pays d'en haut,* the Iroquois commenced a long-distance military campaign against the indigenous residents of the Illinois country, which represented the League's ongoing pursuit of groups previously displaced from the upper Ohio River valley during the 1650s. Iroquois diplomats also resumed efforts to broker trading relations with Albany for the upper Great Lakes nations.[77]

On October 3, 1678, an Onondaga "Deputation" arrived at the Albany courthouse to "confirm the Ancient Brotherhood," the origins of which they traced back to the original *kaswentha* agreement to Jacques Eelckens, then to Arent van Curler ("Old Corlaer"), and finally to Andros, the current bearer of Van Curler's ceremonial name. In return for an unspecified "present" issued by Andros, the Onondagas offered one that recalled the recognition of free Iroquois movement underlying the League nations' peaceful coexistence with their "Bretheren" at Albany. The Onondagas' token gift came from the "Indians having Holes thro' their noses" and the Tionnontatés, whom the former sought "to bring to trade here." All that remained to be worked out, according to the Onondagas, was "whether the passage near the Sinnondowanes [the Niagara River portage] be too wide or too narrow, for that is the passage [for the nations of the upper Great Lakes] to come to Albany." In other words, the Onondagas would gauge by the New York authorities' response how much of the upper Great Lakes Algonquians' peltry would reach Albany.[78]

No specific record of the Albany Court's response to this Onondaga offer survives, but it likely represented music to the ears of many Anglo-American officials who wanted to eliminate French economic competition for the affiliation of the League. The Onondagas' offer seemed to represent a crucial opportunity to turn Iroquois mobility to Anglo-Americans' advantage. In August 1678, a "Mohawk from Canada" visiting Schenectady reported French plans to erect a new fort "up the lake neere to the Sinnickes" that threatened to "hinder" all Iroquois-conducted traffic from the *pays d'en haut* to Albany.[79]

A French expeditionary force of sixteen men under Dominique de la Motte de Lussière departed Fort Frontenac in a ten-ton "brigantine" on November 18, 1678. Arriving at the mouth of the Niagara River on December 6, 1678, the French were surprised to find a "little village" of Senecas nearby. The Senecas drew 300 whitefish from the river with one pass of their nets and offered them to the French as a symbolic gesture of hospitality, which also communicated their control, as keepers of the League's western door, over this vital and increasingly contested "strait of communication" between the Atlantic Ocean and the upper Great Lakes. Hennepin, a member of the French party, described the six-mile overland portage at Niagara as "a very fine road," indicating extensive Iroquois usage. When La Salle announced French plans to build a fort and a vessel to sail the "Fresh Seas" to Lake Superior, the Senecas reportedly took "umbrage." La Salle tried to assuage Seneca concerns by promising that the French merely planned to build "a house defended by palisades." He claimed that the post (which he named Fort de Conty), would serve as "a great Hanger or Store-house" to facilitate French trade with the Senecas.[80]

Concerned with securing official Seneca sanction for his project at Niagara, La Salle dispatched Hennepin and La Motte to the large western Seneca town of "Tegarondies" to offer presents and promises to the Senecas of blacksmith and gunsmith services at the new post on the Niagara River. La Motte spoke on behalf of the French to forty-two Seneca leaders assembled at Tegarondies on New Year's Day 1679. A Seneca speaker offered public thanks for La Motte's speech, but the Senecas' subsequent actions spoke louder than their words. Replicating their response to the intrusion of La Salle and the Sulpicians a decade earlier, the Senecas invited Hennepin and La Motte to witness a public ceremony on January 3, 1679, during which two Native prisoners (one Shawnee and one Piscataway) were subjected to excruciating scaffold torture and cannibalization. Grasping the Senecas' message, Hennepin and La Motte retreated to the Niagara River post and spent an uneasy winter overseeing construction of La Salle's *Griffon*. Persistent Seneca attempts to burn the vessel and physical attacks on the workmen forced the French to keep a "strict watch" until they could sleep on the partially completed forty-five-ton vessel while it was anchored in the Niagara River about three miles above Lake Erie.[81]

La Salle returned to the Niagara River in late July 1679 to launch the *Griffon* on its maiden voyage. Prior to departing, he and his crew spent several days in Seneca country "very busie in bartering their Commodities with the Natives, who flock'd about in great numbers about us to see our Brigantine, which they admir'd, and to exchange their Skins for Knives, Guns, Powder, and Shot." After a strenuous effort to tow the vessel against the Niagara River's current, the *Griffon* entered Lake Erie on August 7, 1679. A "great many Iroquese," returning home from a "Warlike Expedition against the Savages of Tintoha" (the Teton, or Prairie, Sioux, who then resided several months of the year in what is now southwestern Minnesota), witnessed the launch.[82]

Although Hennepin claimed that the Senecas immediately reported La Salle's movements to New York officials, no mention of the *Griffon* appears in Anglo-American documents. Albany officials had learned from visiting Senecas in late March 1679 of the recent conclusion of peace between their nation and the Tionontatés. La Salle's waterborne trading venture offered not only a direct challenge to Iroquois diplomatic and economic initiatives in the *pays d'en haut,* it also represented a potential means of access to military stores for the comparatively poorly armed Illinois and other nations in the continental interior. Witness the effort by the Senecas to preempt this possibility through their active trade for La Salle's "knives, guns, powder, and shot." Unswayed by La Salle's efforts to "remove the Jealousie they had conceiv'd of [his] undertaking" with words and presents, the Senecas considered the *Griffon* a threat to their freedom of movement in the upper Great Lakes.[83]

While the Senecas of the large eastern town of Ganondagan had endeavored to buy out La Salle's military stores in July 1679, those of "Sanchioragon" (likely the predecessor of Tegarondies, indicating that the western Seneca community was then in the process of relocating their town) were negotiating an anti-Illinois alliance with a delegation of six Miamis (five men and one woman). These talks were conducted in the Wendat language and employed the mediation of a Seneca woman who had formerly been a captive of the Miamis. The willingness of the Senecas to overlook recent Miami hostilities reflected the significance they attached to these proceedings in light of La Salle's aggressive move into the *pays d'en haut.*[84]

The Senecas' outreach to the Miamis proved successful. When La Salle encountered a party of Fox in Wisconsin in late October 1679, they reported learning from the Illinois (via the death song of an Iroquois prisoner) that "the war the Iroquese made against them [the Illinois] had been fomented by the inhabitants of Canada, who hated them." This news made La Salle's companion Hennepin "very melancholy, for all the savages we had already met [in the upper Great Lakes after leaving Seneca country in the *Griffon*] had told us almost the same thing." Throughout his first winter (1679–80) in Illinois country, La Salle confronted widespread Native suspicion of his status as the vanguard of a combined Franco-Iroquois invasion force.[85]

On August 10, 1679, three days after the launch of the *Griffon,* Virginia colonels William Kendall and Southey Littleton arrived in New York. The Virginians had been sent by their governor, Sir Henry Chicheley, to persuade the Oneidas, "or others in confederacy with them," to end their military campaigns against the Piscataways and other Native groups residing in Maryland and Virginia. During the two years that had passed since Coursey's negotiations in Albany, increasing numbers of Susquehannock adoptees had provided both instigation and assistance to their respective Iroquois hosts in these campaigns. Maryland governor Notley learned from an Anacostank adoptee of the Senecas in March 1679 that the Susquehannocks residing among the Cayugas and Onondagas "will never cease doing mischief to both the English and Pascattoway Indians so long as a man of them is left alive." These adopted Susquehannocks believed that their residency in Iroquoia protected them from retaliation by their Maryland and Virginia enemies. The efficiency with which mixed Susquehannock and Iroquois war parties "scour[ed] the heads of rivers" in Maryland and Virginia now threatened to remove these colonies' tributary— and nominally allied—Native populations wholesale to Iroquoia. In addition to the obvious challenge the League nations' campaigns posed to settler colonies' military power and claims of jurisdictional authority over their colonial boundaries and indigenous populations, the outrages committed by these "foreign Indians" from the north increasingly embroiled frontier settlers who could (or would) not "easily distinguish one Indian from another." Southern colonial officials had no choice but to send Kendall and Littleton to Albany, the very place where the Iroquois and their Susquehannock adoptees traded their "Skinns and receive in truck Powder, Shot, Guns, and Matchcoats."[86]

After a brief meeting with the Mohawks at Albany on October 5, 1679 (Littleton had died unexpectedly shortly after his arrival in New York), Kendall waited for more than a month for delegates from any of the other League nations. A delegation of Oneidas and Onondagas arrived on November 9 after learning of Kendall's promise to repatriate an Oneida woman who had been captured while accompanying warriors from her nation to the Virginia frontier early in 1679. The Oneidas contended that their earlier agreement with Coursey permitted them to "freely come towards your Plantations when we went out fighting our Indian Enemys to refresh ourselves if we wer[e] hungry." The Oneidas further explained that the recent friction with Maryland and Virginia settlers stemmed from the failure of the latter to observe Coursey's terms. Disputes had arisen only after colonial settlers had denied food to Oneida warriors, and then shot at Oneidas who helped themselves to modest amounts of "Indian Corn and tobacco."[87]

Confronted by the Oneidas' evident resolve, Kendall backed down from his initial threat to "Engage all our Confederatt [sic] English neighbours" in a "violent war" against League aggressors. He offered instead to forgive all the damages inflicted by the Iroquois on settler lives and property in exchange for a return of all remaining Native and settler prisoners in Iroquoia and a promise of no further such incidents. But, like Coursey before him, Kendall came to realize the degree to which the Iroquois insisted on retaining their freedom of movement. After advising Kendall that they could not compel their Susquehannock adoptees to repatriate captives, the Oneidas made limited concessions, promising only to "forebear" approaching Virginia planta-tions "when we go to war against our Indian Enemys not in friendship with you."[88]

Poor Iroquois attendance at Kendall's Albany conference might be explained by evidence of concurrent independent Piscataway-Iroquois peace talks during the win-ter of 1679–80. After the latter negotiations failed, Susquehannock adoptees among the Iroquois (and possibly some still residing at the "Susquahannough Fort" on the upper Potomac River) played a prominent role in an ensuing wave of "Senniquo" attacks on Piscataways and settlers in Maryland and Virginia from May to July 1680. In the meantime, another Seneca-led Iroquois expeditionary force of "eight hundred men armed with guns" set out on a journey of "four hundred Leagues" to the Illinois country to take up unfinished business with the Illinois nation as well as with the French.[89]

Multiple French accounts of the September 1680 Iroquois attack on the Illinois town of Tamaroa attested to the careful advance planning undertaken by the Senecas for this campaign. The Senecas had secured the assistance of several hundred Miami and Shawnee warriors en route, partly to augment their own strength and partly to demonstrate the diplomatic isolation of their Illinois and French targets. Seneca headman Tekanoet, the leader of the expedition, wore a black robe, hat, and leggings in order to emulate "a Jesuit" and thereby maintain the appearance of French com-plicity in the Iroquois offensive. Following an open-field battle between the advanc-ing Iroquois force and the Illinois on the periphery of Tamaroa in which both sides sustained casualties, the Iroquois pulled back. A French officer named Henri de Tonty emerged from Tamaroa to attempt to broker a peace for the Illinois, but his claim that the Illinois were allied to France and thus enjoyed the "protection" of Louis XIV "greatly irritated" many of his Iroquois listeners. Although Tekanoet wanted to burn Tonty alive, he eventually decided to send Tonty back to Tamaroa to communicate the Iroquois army's demand for the town's surrender.[90]

The entire Iroquois and allied Miami and Shawnee expeditionary force followed Tonty to Tamaroa, where they destroyed scaffold burials and trampled cornfields during several more days of fruitless negotiations. Finally, the Iroquois dismissed Tonty, Hennepin, and several other Récollets then present in Illinois country with a present of "six packets of beaver-skins" for Frontenac to testify that they had not "eaten [his] French children." The Iroquois and their allies then attacked the hapless Illinois "who had only bows and arrows to defend themselves," and took an estimated 400 to 1,200 prisoners.[91]

An unknown number of Iroquois warriors remained in the Illinois country for several months after the attack. Some pursued Tamaroa residents as far as "Ozage" country west of the Mississippi River, while as many as 400 others appear to have mounted an unsuccessful expedition against the Otoes residing west of the Missouri River. Iroquois warriors escorting the initial contingent of Illinois captives to Iro-quoia reportedly attacked several parties of Miami hunters on the Ohio River during their return journey, suggesting that at least some Iroquois no longer considered the Miamis' alliance necessary or desirable. When the Miamis offered "three thousand beavers" to ransom their prisoners from the Iroquois, the latter took the pelts but refused, "contrary to the custom of all Indian nations," to restore any Miami captives.[92]

As Tekanoet's army marched homeward, having "embarrassed Sieur de La Salle's discoveries" in the *pays d'en haut,* the Massachusetts General Court made arrangements with John Pynchon in October 1680 to travel to Albany to negotiate another treaty with the Mohawks that would convince the latter to cease any further "invasions, depredation, and insolencys towards our neighbours, Indians and friends, that live within this jurisdiction." Activity in this third principal theater of Iroquois warfare had extended by 1680 as far east as Casco Bay in Maine. Following a July 1678 Mohawk attack on Natick (whose residents, like the tributary groups residing in Maryland and Virginia, were entitled to protection from Massachusetts), at least one group of fifty New England Algonquians had elected to seek refuge among Potawatomis residing west of Lake Michigan rather than surrender to Iroquois aggression. These Mohawk-led campaigns struck New England authorities as clear violations of the treaty negotiated by Pynchon with the League at Albany in 1677. New York governor Anthony Brockholls also wondered why the peace between New York, Massachusetts, and the League "should be held on such unequal and ticklish Termes, that notwithstanding we deal with them in all Friendship yet that they shall presume to break it when they please without controule."[93]

The Mohawks, in their address to Pynchon at Albany on November 19, 1680, proved as resolute and assertive as the Oneidas and Onondagas had been with Kendall one year previously. The Mohawks reminded their Anglo-American audience that they had been "set on" King Philip and his allies by Andros in 1676. Why should they now be criticized for having come to "the defense of our brother Pynchon"? While the Mohawks admitted that some "Christian Indians" from Massachusetts were then residing in their towns, they claimed that the former were not prisoners, but adoptees, "free and given over to them that receive them as their children." Pynchon pressed the Mohawks for their release nevertheless, but the Mohawks made no promises to do so, pointing out how hard it would be for adoptive Mohawk families to part with individuals they regarded as their "flesh and blood." Following this response, Pynchon reported that "many hard things were spoken," but claimed that after presenting the Mohawks with goods he valued at "near £90," they promised a temporary cessation of hostilities. The Mohawks warned Pynchon that they would retaliate against any offensive by Natives from "the eastward side of Hudson's River" in Mohawk country.[94]

The Mohawks made another significant comment in their November 1680 reply to Pynchon. They advised the New York and New England authorities that in addition to their "covenant" with New York, they also had made one with the "Governor of Cannida, [both of] which we shall continually keep whole." Andros, significantly, acknowledged the Mohawks' freedom "to go to Canada or where you think proper."[95]

The Mohawks' assertion of Iroquois rights of free movement up and down the Lake Champlain and Richelieu River corridor came at a time when both French and Anglo-American authorities had grown increasingly concerned about the potential impact of these Iroquois journeys on their respective colonies' economies. In late June 1679, the Albany Court had ordered a ban on the trade of "seawan [wampum], pipes, and other Indian jewelry" to French traders in Albany. The court reasoned that such trade ultimately attracted Iroquois and upper Great Lakes Native traders to Canadian markets, "to the great prejudice and detriment of the colony and particularly of this place."[96]

French authorities expressed similar concerns. Intendant Duchesneau called for a renewed effort to encourage Iroquois relocation to the St. Lawrence valley. Duchesneau recognized that the hunting these Iroquois people engaged in "constitutes their wealth and ours." He believed that more Iroquois people in the Laurentian communities would ultimately result in a greater proportion of Iroquois trade flowing to the French, and he was willing to defer or abandon plans for the *francisation* of these communities to achieve this end. Frontenac was less optimistic. He hoped that a reported outbreak of smallpox reported at Albany in the summer of 1679 would deter the Laurentian Iroquois from "carry[ing] their peltries thither as they ordinarily do."[97]

Evidence suggests that Iroquois traders, whose freedom to travel and trade was guaranteed by League "covenants" with New France and New York, had acquired intimate knowledge of both the Albany and Montreal markets by the late 1670s. After obtaining high-quality pelts from the north shore of Lake Ontario and the St. Lawrence valley, Iroquois hunters exchanged some locally to French traders, either in Montreal or "in the bush." Some of the Iroquois hunters would then travel to Albany in small groups of no more than four or five persons, "for whom all the inhabitants lie in wait." By avoiding simultaneous arrivals of "large numbers" of pelts, Iroquois traders elicited "great promises of gifts and presents" from their ruthlessly competitive Dutch and Anglo-American counterparts, maintained price levels for peltry that yielded at least "double" that which they could obtain in New France, and paddled off "with the profits." Such behavior so aggrieved Albany traders that they petitioned for the reform of local trading regulations in July 1681, complaining that "the Indians make no effort at all to catch any beavers, as 4 or 5 beavers sufficiently supply their needs because the goods are given to them scandalously cheap."[98]

Frontenac estimated in November 1681 that the unlicensed Iroquois trade of peltry to Albany represented an annual loss of 25 percent of the colony's fur revenues. But he claimed to be powerless to combat this growing problem with "anything but remonstrances" because he feared that any forcible seizure of contraband pelts or Iroquois individuals carrying them would provoke a "rupture" with the "Five Nations, who have pursued this trade for a long time by means of those of their tribe who have settled at Sault St. Louis, near Montreal, which is, as it were, their entrepôt for this traffic." Frontenac admitted in 1681 that New France could not withstand renewed hostilities with the League, especially with Iroquois people constituting the majority of the 1,100 Natives then residing in St. Lawrence valley settlements. Frontenac also worried that the recent success of the Seneca-led army in the Illinois country might persuade the Iroquois to "push their insolence farther, and on perceiving that we do not afford any succour to our allies, attribute this to a want of power that may create in them a desire to come and attack us."[99]

After waiting over a year for an official Iroquois delegation to offer formal "satisfaction" for the 1680 attack on Tamaroa, Frontenac resolved in November 1681 to invite League headmen to "explain their conduct" in Canada. Although he claimed past success in keeping the Iroquois in line with only "a little address and management," Frontenac interpreted the ominous silence from Iroquoia as an indication of League leaders' disregard for French claims of authority in the *pays d'em haut.* Evidence supporting Frontenac's apprehension may be found in Hennepin's report of an exchange with Tekanoet in the eastern Seneca town of Ganondagan in May 1681. When Hennepin complained about a recent Seneca attack on the Odawas, the Seneca leader, who "spoke for his whole nation in all the councils," offered merely a token gift of peltry in response. He made no effort to repatriate the dozen Odawa captives then in Seneca custody.[100]

Intendant Duchesneau hoped that "influential" Iroquois leaders in the Laurentian communities could help to patch up French relations with the League, but Franco-Iroquois relations became even more unstable after September 1681, when a Seneca headman named "Hannonsache," then trading at French Fort de Buade (Michilimackinac), was murdered by an Illinois warrior in the neighboring Kiskakon Odawa village during a "Feast of the Dead" celebration. Subsequent rumors of an Iroquois attack on New France, according to the Jesuit Chauchetière, "kept all Canada in suspense."[101]

On March 20, 1682, Seneca "Speaker" Tekanoet advised Albany officials that a Tionnontaté delegation had traveled to Seneca country to offer condolences for Hannonsache, apparently concerned about the potential impact of the murder on upper Great Lakes nations' trade with Albany. Three days later, the Jesuits, after assessing field reports from members of their order during a conference at their Quebec seminary, concluded that Frontenac would also need to offer formal French condolences for the death of the Seneca headman at Michilimackinac. Convinced that the League nations would continue their attacks on the French-allied Illinois, Miamis, and Odawas unless the governor made such a gesture, the Jesuits advised Frontenac to reach out to the Iroquois "at the fort which bears his name" rather than wait any longer for Iroquois delegates to come to him. To forestall the possibility of large-scale Iroquois retaliation against the nations of the *pays d'en haut,* the missionaries offered Frontenac very specific advice. The governor could expect at least fifty Iroquois deputies to attend such a conference, "men [as well] as women." The governor would have to offer liberal presents not only to Iroquois civil leaders but also to the warriors if he hoped to persuade them to abandon plans for an expedition against the upper Great Lakes nations.[102]

The fate of the French colonial economy, grounded on its alliance network with peltry-producing Native peoples in the upper Great Lakes, depended on effective deterrence of Iroquois offensives into that region and disruption of Iroquois brokerage of trade relations between the peoples of the *pays d'en haut* and Albany. Crown instructions for Joseph-Antoine Le Febvre de la Barre, designated to replace Frontenac as governor of Canada in May 1682, acknowledged the urgency of this situation. Upon his arrival in Canada, La Barre was to march at least 500 troops to Fort Frontenac in hopes that a fresh demonstration of the French capacity to project military force into Iroquoia would quiet the "restless and warlike" nations of the League.[103]

As La Barre prepared to sail for Canada, Frontenac temporized with the Iroquois. League leaders offered to meet with the governor to discuss their recent movements into the upper Great Lakes, but they would only travel as far as "Téchoueguen, or la Famine," an Onondaga fishing station on the south shore of Lake Ontario. Frontenac, in his official correspondence, refused to concede pride of place to Iroquois demands. He may also have been loath to risk his personal safety among people who in 1682 reportedly discussed how best to "put Onontio into the kettle" during their feasts, dances, and sweats.[104]

The Iroquois began to make good on such threats during the summer of 1682 by assaulting several French traders at the north shore village of Teiaiagon, robbing 1,300 livres worth of merchandise from one of Fort Frontenac's vessels as it lay at anchor in the Niagara River, and extorting still more goods from the intimidated garrison of Fort Frontenac itself. When the commanding officer at Fort Frontenac traveled to Seneca country to complain about these actions, he failed to "obtain any satisfaction." He also reported direct Seneca threats against both La Salle and Frontenac, an expression of the League's western doorkeepers' ongoing resentment of the explorer's "discoveries."[105]

In an effort to reclaim his status as the "common father" of the upper Great Lakes nations and the Iroquois, Frontenac attempted in August 1682 to persuade Odawa and Tionnontaté delegates trading at Montreal to offer condolence presents to the Senecas commensurate to their loss of Hannonsache. Placed on the rhetorical defensive, Frontenac consented to war between his "Outaois and Iroquois children" if the former would confine "operations to their own country, to repelling those [Iroquois] who come thither as enemies to attack them." He refused to approve offensive raids by the *pays d'en haut* nations into Iroquoia, but by abandoning peaceful means of mediating grievances between these indigenous rivals, Frontenac had exposed New France to the prospect of Iroquois vengeance.[106]

That possibility greatly alarmed Jesuit Jean de Lamberville, who wrote two lengthy reports on Iroquois affairs during August and September 1682 while posted at the newly built Onondaga principal town, which he described as the "largest in the Iroquois country." Lamberville reported a staggering number of captives in Iroquoia during the first eight months of 1682. He claimed that 700 Illinois captives taken in 1680 remained "alive" for integration into Iroquois towns. Another 600 "men, women, and children" of the Eries, then residing on the Virginia frontier, where they were known as Westos, had surrendered voluntarily to the Senecas in 1681. In making this decision, the Westos obtained refuge from conflicts with unnamed "Southern Indians" and reunited with kinfolk adopted into Iroquois nations during the 1650s. Lamberville also noted that the League nations "have never had a larger store of weapons and munitions of war than they have this year." This lethal combination of adoptees and weapons would enable the Iroquois, in Lamberville's view, to continue to "annihilate" French-allied Native nations in order to "make Iroquois" of them. The Jesuit predicted ominously that after "strengthening themselves with those who might have aided us to make war against them, that they will all together fall upon Canada, to overcome it in a single Campaign."[107]

An Onondaga headman named Teganissorens, however, carried a different message to Montreal in September 1682. In a meeting with Frontenac, accompanied by Iroquois delegates from Kahnawake and La Montagne, Teganissorens, who claimed to have been "deputed by the whole House, that is, the Five Iroquois Nations," invited the governor once more to bring his "big canoe" to the south shore of Lake Ontario for a conference. By characterizing himself as a "man with two arms, and two hands, one for peace, and another for war, [who] had run through the Whole House to persuade them not to undertake any thing without first having heard Onontio's word," Teganissorens indicated that Frontenac had little time left if he wanted to deter the Iroquois from offensive operations in the upper Great Lakes. Frontenac refused once more to travel to Iroquoia, but he attempted to stay the "arms" of the League's warriors by offering Teganissorens a belt of wampum and liberal personal gifts. Teganissorens departed, promising to transmit Frontenac's words to the "whole house" of the League.[108]

PARALLEL PREDICAMENTS

Authorities in Anglo-America, like their counterparts in New France, believed they had reached a crisis point in 1682. Colonial officials from Massachusetts to Virginia were desperately seeking a means to curtail independent Iroquois military campaigns against English-allied Native nations without fatally antagonizing the League. At the same time as large Iroquois parties were venturing into the upper Great Lakes and Illinois country, armed groups of "Sinniquos" numbering in the hundreds and employing Mattawoman, Susquehannock, Doeg, and Piscataway adoptees as guides ranged the backcountry of Maryland and Virginia in search of Piscataways, Nanticokes,

Pamunkeys, and Choptanks. Two Iroquois leaders escorted by Jacob Young to a meeting of the Maryland Council in mid-August 1681 had returned seven English settlers captured during one of these raids but also stated their determination to "make an end" of the Piscataways.[109]

On September 6, 1681, Coursey approached an Iroquois force consisting of over 200 warriors and "great men" from all League nations except the Senecas surrounding the Piscataways' "Zachaiah fort." Instead of firing muskets, this Iroquois army conducted its siege with Piscataway adoptees, whom they sent "into the fort to fetch out their Relations." When Coursey protested, the Iroquois informed him that their grievances stemmed from a former time when "the Pascattoway Indians had joined with the Susquehannohs" in a war against the Onondagas, and that such matters "could not be wiped away" by treaties arranged by settler colonies.[110]

After months of wrangling with a reluctant Governor Brockholls, who did not share Lord Baltimore's opinion that it was "well within the power" of New York officials to restrict Iroquois movements, Coursey and Colonel Philemon Lloyd returned to Albany in August 1682. The Maryland officials intended to secure full monetary satisfaction for Iroquois-inflicted damages (estimated at 500 beaver pelts' value) to settlers' property during the League nations' recent incursions into the colony. Coursey and Lloyd came away from these proceedings with a grand total of eighteen beaver pelts offered by the Cayugas, Onondagas, and Oneidas as compensatory payment for their claimed damages. Brockholls managed to secure fourteen Piscataway prisoners from Mohawk country for repatriation to Maryland in exchange for the governor's agreement that any Indians from nations bordering Maryland and Virginia who remained in Iroquoia were "not detained but stay[ed] on their own accounts." Further proof that Anglo-American authorities could not "wipe away" these deeply rooted indigenous conflicts came in December 1682, when nine of the fourteen Mohawk delegates who had escorted these Piscataways to Maryland "suddenly died" on their return journey, reportedly victims of poisoning by the "Maryland Indians."[111]

While Anglo-American authorities tried to assert control over Iroquois military campaigns east of the Appalachians, newly arrived Governor La Barre convened an unprecedented assembly of colonial officials, military officers, Jesuits, and other dignitaries at Quebec on October 10, 1682. After concluding from a review of Frontenac's papers that the Iroquois attacks on French-allied nations in the upper Great Lakes and Illinois country constituted the preliminaries of an Iroquois plan to "ruin" New France, La Barre pressed local experts for their opinion on how a war with the Iroquois could be best avoided or won. Since the Canadians viewed Iroquois aggression as a function of Anglo-American-inspired efforts to redirect interior peltry to Albany, they advised La Barre to amplify Frontenac's earlier efforts to block Iroquois passage over Lake Ontario with a larger garrison and more ship-borne patrols. Contemporary French estimates of the League's ability to put 2,500 musket-bearing warriors into the field (compared to less than 2,300 spottily armed adult male French settlers) underscored their desire to avoid direct conflict with the Five Nations.[112]

Unfortunately for La Barre, La Salle abandoned Fort Frontenac shortly after the formation of official plans to intimidate the Iroquois with a show of French force on Lake Ontario. Worse still for the governor, the men he sent up to the abandoned fort to prevent it from falling into the hands of unnamed "Montreal rascals" soon arranged with nearby Iroquois leaders to begin carrying "beaver" to Albany, which the French entrepreneurs exchanged for cash and "goods adapted to the [Indian] trade."[113]

The ability of the Iroquois to blunt the impact of potential French economic and territorial aggression on the north shore of Lake Ontario extended into Iroquoia as well. Jesuit Thierry Beschefer reported in October 1683 that the success of Iroquois military campaigns after the late 1670s left the Iroquois "so haughty that they consider themselves masters of the earth." Far from asserting French authority among their hosts, Jesuits in Iroquoia endured "only Crosses, rebuffs, contumelies, [and] Threats" from Iroquois people who "regarded them as slaves who are at their mercy."[114]

The French were powerless to deter the Iroquois from continuing offensives into the upper Great Lakes. The Senecas, Cayugas, and Onondagas sent out 500 warriors in May 1683 to attack the Odawas. After reconnoitering with two additional Iroquois parties (each consisting of 150 men) already in the upper Great Lakes pursuing Miamis, the combined Iroquois army was to attempt an assault on the French at Michilimackinac. French authorities, as usual, attributed this campaign to Anglo-American economic incitement. While the attack on the French post never materialized, officials in New France now recognized that the Iroquois wanted to achieve "sole mastery" of the upper Great Lakes, a goal that implied broader spatial objectives than merely attaining a middleman position to divert the region's furs to Albany.[115]

French assumptions of Anglo-American economic advantages notwithstanding, authorities in New York expressed contemporaneous concern over declining Iroquois peltry volumes. In an October 1683 meeting with newly arrived New York governor Thomas Dongan, a Mohawk speaker assured the governor that the Iroquois were not trading peltry to "some other Government." He explained that increasing conflicts between Iroquois hunters and Native groups who formerly "would not dare to come on their hunting places" in the upper Great Lakes represented the reason for "so little Beaver" reaching New York. Dongan, who lacked awareness of recent Iroquois efforts to limit the flow of peltry to Albany in order to sustain favorable prices, continued to suspect the Iroquois of diverting peltry to the French. This misgiving, coupled with his orders to assert a greater degree of English hegemony over Iroquois land and people south of Lake Ontario, led the governor to press the assembled Mohawk headmen to repatriate their kinfolk who had "gone to Canada." The Mohawks offered to consider the matter, but would only undertake the effort if Dongan provided material "assistance" so "that they may go hand in hand to promote" the idea of an

English-sponsored return movement to their relatives and friends residing at Kahnawake, La Montagne, and Lorette.[116]

Had Dongan been able to visit the Laurentian Iroquois towns in 1683, he might have realized the futility of his request. Kahnawake, the most populous of these settlements, was by then an established Iroquois town of sixty multifamily longhouses situated "in a very high and beautiful location, with a fine view." The community was home to as many as 150 families, predominantly Mohawks but including people from all five nations of the League. Contemporary observers estimated that Kahnawake could put 200 "good Iroquois soldiers" into the field, indicating a population of 800 to 1,000 people. Kahnawake residents held to a traditional Iroquois subsistence cycle, rejecting Jesuit efforts to encourage more labor-intensive wheat cultivation in favor of a more familiar, seasonal routine of hunting and planting "Indian corn." By 1682, the extent of planted fields around Kahnawake reached "180 *arpents*" (approximately 150 acres), forcing the Jesuits to procure a new, larger bell to reach the ears of women tending distant crops or gathering firewood. Although isolated pockets of individuals practicing intense Catholic spirituality persisted at Kahnawake, and Anglo-Americans referred to them regularly as "Praying Indians," Chauchetière pronounced the majority of Kahnawake's people "very fickle" in their Catholicism. He even admitted that by 1682 the "savage women" at Kahnawake who manifested the most interest in Catholic teachings "sometimes propound to us doubts in spiritual matters, as difficult as those that might be advanced by the most cultured persons in France."[117]

Close reading of Jesuit-authored accounts of the Iroquois people living in the rapidly growing Laurentian towns indicates the continued primacy of larger Iroquois social, economic, and political concerns over any widespread Iroquois interest in employing these communities as retreats to facilitate a "truly Christian" existence. When Jesuits witnessed Iroquois people assisting new arrivals with food, construction of shelter, planting of crops, and material goods, they interpreted these activities as divinely inspired charity. In fact, such behavior aligned with long-standing Iroquois patterns of hospitality for kinfolk and equitable distribution of resources. When Jesuits celebrated the successes of Laurentian Iroquois in religious "disputes" with the Dutch at Albany as a spiritual victory over heresy, they also unwittingly acknowledged the ongoing significance of free movement for purposes of trade for Iroquois people in the Lake Champlain–Richelieu River corridor. When Jesuits described the Dongan-funded 1683 visit to Kahnawake by a party of Iroquois bearing "presents given them by the dutch" to "induce them to return to their own country," they noted that some of these emissaries were actually "won over by those they wished to pervert," and remained in the St. Lawrence valley. Finally, when Jesuits confessed that some Laurentian Iroquois people returned "from time to time to their own country," they documented the ongoing pattern of rational, individual Iroquois decision making in selecting sites of residency, which generated substantial two-way traffic between these new communities and towns elsewhere in Iroquois homelands.[118]

The deep-rooted connections between the Laurentian communities and the Five Nations were tested by the efforts of French colonial officials to secure allied indigenous warriors prior to an anticipated war with the League. During the summer of 1683, the Laurentian Iroquois offered La Barre the assistance of 150 warriors from their communities in a war, "even against their own Nation, if the latter undertook to break the peace with the French." In making this pledge, they did not commit an act of treason against their nations of origin; instead, the offer reflected the Laurentians' confidence that such a break would never occur. They believed that their status as the "nephews and children" of the League nations provided critical security against the prospect of an all-out Iroquois war against New France.[119]

Far from seeking conflict with their kinfolk, the Laurentian Iroquois had been working to mediate the root cause of the escalating conflict between La Barre and the League. After Five Nations delegates failed to appear for a promised conference with the Canadian governor in December 1682, four of the "principal chiefs" from Kahnawake and the "Captain" of La Montagne escorted former Iroquois captive Charles Le Moyne to Seneca country in the late spring of 1683, carrying "private presents" and an invitation to speak with La Barre. Thirteen Senecas accompanied the Laurentian headmen back to Montreal, and during the course of the summer thirty deputies from the other four League nations, including "men and some women," had assembled to receive La Barre's formal offer of condolence for the 1681 death of Seneca headman Hannonsache at Michilimackinac. The Laurentian Iroquois of both Kahnawake and La Montagne assumed key roles as brokers of this meeting, attending "all the Councils."[120]

A Sulpician account of La Barre's August 1683 conference reveals not only extensive French awareness of Iroquois Condolence ceremony protocol but also persistent French interest in restricting Iroquois movement in the upper Great Lakes. La Barre wiped away the attending Seneca elders' tears with "eight white hats and as many shirts," offered four guns to the Seneca warriors, and then (having ignored the thirteenth Seneca delegate, who may have been a woman) endeavored to bury the memory of Hannonsache's murder under "four coats decorated with gold braid," one for each of the Senecas' four "cabins" (towns). La Barre then asked the Iroquois to desist from further retaliatory actions, promising in return to punish La Salle for "arming the Illinois." Teganissorens, responding on behalf of the League, remained resolute on that issue. Notwithstanding the belated condolence for Hannonsache, he insisted that the Illinois "deserved to die" for their killings of Iroquois people. "No one," reported François Vachon de Belmont, superior of the La Montagne mission, "dared to answer him."[121]

Despite evident tension between La Barre and Teganissorens, Jesuit Jean de Lamberville reported from Onondaga country in February 1684 that at least two other Iroquois leaders had come away from the conference with a favorable impression of the Canadian governor. "Sieur de la grand Geule" (Otreouti), whom Lamberville described in 1683 as a leading "man of business" among the Onondagas (who often worked in tandem with Garacontié II, brother and successor of the individual carrying that name who had died six years previously), claimed that La Barre not only promised an "armorer" for Onondaga country in August 1683 but also began paying Otreouti a personal "pension." A Cayuga headman named Ourehouare, who had personally driven Jesuit Étienne de Carheil out of his home village in 1682, and who had led a recent raid near Michilimackinac that netted six Tionnontaté adoptees, also expressed an interest in visiting La Barre.[122]

Ourehouare had missed the August 1683 meeting at Montreal to attend a conference at Albany with Dongan instead. There, the Cayuga headman blocked an attempt by William Penn to purchase Susquehannock lands. In July 1682, Penn had issued a formal offer of friendship and trade to the Iroquois League, but soon became interested in acquiring title to land in the Susquehanna River valley from the "Sachems of the Mohwak and Synacher Indians and their Alleys" (Allies). Lord Baltimore of Maryland bitterly opposed Penn's plans, claiming (disingenuously) that Susquehannock hunting grounds conveyed to his colony after its people had purportedly incurred "great expence of Blood and money" in dispersing that nation. Dongan, retaining the assertiveness of his predecessors with regard to New York's dominant role in Anglo-American relations with the League, had also balked at Penn's proposal. In mid-September 1683, all League nations but the Senecas (whom, according to the Mohawks, "had nothing to do with the River and Land of Susquehanne" in any event) met with Dongan to discuss a potential sale to Penn.[123]

On September 17, 1683, two Cayugas and a Susquehannock adoptee of the Onondagas appeared at the Albany courthouse. Local magistrates questioned the Indians about the location of their settlements relative to the Susquehanna River. The Albany officials wanted these Indians' opinion on whether "folks should settle" on the Susquehanna River. The Cayugas and the adopted Onondaga stated that they would be "very glad" to see a trade-oriented settlement on the Susquehanna, citing its favorable location compared to Albany: all League nations could transport their peltry by water to the Susquehanna, whereas the journey to Albany required the western League nations to travel at least part of the way overland, carrying pelts on "their backs." The enthusiasm of the Cayugas led them to draft, in collaboration with Court Secretary Robert Livingston, a map of the Susquehanna River depicting "how near their Castles lie to it."[124]

Alarmed by the potential of a Susquehanna trading post to cause the "utter ruine" of Albany's already-diminished Iroquois trade, Dongan endeavored to "put a stop to" Penn's negotiations with the League. On October 6, 1683, Ourehouare and two other Cayuga headmen appeared before the Albany Court. They stated that lands in the Susquehanna valley were under Cayuga and Onondaga jurisdiction and asked to speak with "Corlaer" (Dongan) about formalizing an earlier, unauthorized transfer of that region to New York. Albany magistrates drew up a "conveyance" for the

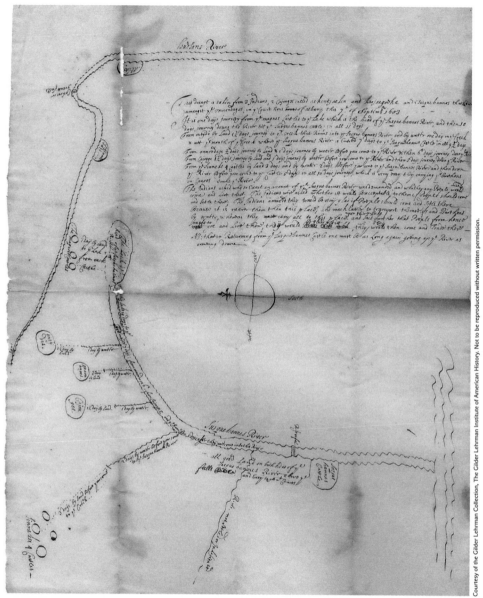

"Draught of ye Susquehannes River," ca. 1683. GLC 03107.01923. [Settlements along the Susquehanna River, 7 September 1683].

Cayuga headmen that attested to the "gift" of Susquehanna lands to New York and sent off the Cayuga delegates with "a half piece of Duffels, Two Blankets, Two guns, Three kettles, Four Coats, Fifty lbs. of Lead and Five and Twenty lbs. of Powder."[125]

Despite the enthusiasm expressed by some Cayugas for access to traders on the Susquehanna River, Cayuga leaders evidently wanted to retain control over the Susquehanna valley for themselves. Ourehouare and his colleagues had signed

Dongan's conveyance in order to prevent any settler presence on Susquehanna lands. One disappointed Pennsylvanian recognized that Dongan would do everything in his power to "hinder" Penn's purchase of Susquehanna lands for the foreseeable future.[126]

By forestalling an influx of traders and settlers into the Susquehanna valley, the Cayuga leaders had ensured continued free movement for Iroquois war parties against the Native populations bordering Maryland and Virginia. Despite the frequent "censure" they received from these colonies' officials at Albany, the League nations elected to continue such activities, since the benefits they derived outweighed any "apprehension of losing the trade" at Albany. During the autumn of 1683, Seneca, Onondaga, and Oneida warriors had captured the "Mattapony Indian town," laid siege to the "Chickahominy fort," and also "riffed" several settlers' houses. To appease aggrieved Anglo-American authorities, the Oneidas repatriated fourteen Choptanks (of approximately fifty individuals captured in 1683 from Maryland's "Eastern Shore") in March 1684.[127]

Although League warriors enjoyed considerable success in their southern campaigns during the early 1680s, meetings of League headmen over the winter of 1683–84 focused on the French challenge in the *pays d'en haut.* "The most influential Captains here," reported Lamberville from Onondaga country in February 1684, "who decide affairs of war with the Ancients," had changed their minds about formal negotiations with La Barre concerning "the boundaries of the territory" of French-allied tribes in the upper Great Lakes region. Iroquois civil and military authorities agreed that ongoing French activities in Illinois country posed a threat to the League nations' objectives in the North and West, and had opted to contest the French with force.[128]

In March 1684, fourteen French traders in seven canoes loaded with "fifteen or sixteen thousand pounds of merchandize" (reportedly intended for the Illinois and possibly the "Scious" [Sioux]) departed Fort St. Louis. They immediately encountered a force of 200 Senecas and Cayugas on the Illinois River who plundered their vessels, dumped all the military stores into the water, and detained them for nine days prior to mounting three assaults on the fort itself from March 21 to 27, 1684. Fort St. Louis's commander, Sieur Chevalier de Baugy, managed to drive off the besieging Iroquois with the assistance of Henri de Tonty and a number of Illinois, Miami, and Shawnee warriors residing in proximity to the garrison. Yet the Senecas and Cayugas had made clear that they would not tolerate the French supplying the League's Native enemies with "powder Lead and Gunns by way of Trade." Though they did not know it, Iroquois leaders had already convinced Governor La Barre of this point. Tonty received La Barre's orders to abandon Fort St. Louis on May 23, 1684.[129]

While La Barre preferred to appease Iroquois demands, his superiors in France advocated force. Metropolitan authorities drafted orders for a one-year campaign against the Iroquois in April 1684, but news of the Iroquois attack on Fort St. Louis had forced La Barre's hand. Treating with Seneca "ambassador" Tekanoet and his "suite" at the very moment news of the Illinois incident reached Quebec, La Barre reverted to the policies of his predecessors. He placed the Seneca headman and his entourage under house arrest in hopes of employing them as bargaining chips to broker the secure withdrawal of the remaining Jesuits from Iroquoia. He then wrote to Dongan to advise of him of French plans to invade Seneca country, and asked his counterpart in New York to "forbid those at Albany selling any Arms, Powder, or Lead to the Iroquois who attacked us and to the other tribes who may dispose of these articles to them." La Barre simultaneously dispatched Kryn and two other Kahnawake headmen to Mohawk country to invite any Iroquois people who were willing to relocate to Canada for their own safety prior to his planned campaign.[130]

La Barre's behavior signaled his strong preference for achieving a negotiated settlement with the Iroquois rather than engaging them in battle. He also faced substantial domestic hostility to the idea of reopening hostilities with the Five Nations. Intendant Jacques de Meulles predicted in early July 1684 that La Barre would "paddle" the fleet of twenty-five foot "pine bateaux" then being built in New France no farther than Fort Frontenac.[131]

In La Barre's defense, all intelligence flowing into the colony from Iroquoia warned of the potential disaster facing New France in the event of war with the League. Lamberville reported on July 10, 1684, that a "general assembly of all the Iroquois" at Onondaga reached a consensus to "unite against" the French. Shocked by La Barre's belief that he could isolate the Senecas diplomatically, the longtime Jesuit observer of the Iroquois reminded the governor that "all these villages were confederated, and that one could not be attacked without becoming embroiled with the others." Lamberville urged La Barre to await the outcome of efforts by some Onondaga headmen to discuss a potential offer of "satisfaction" from the Senecas for their attack on Fort St. Louis. In a comment that would prove prophetic, Lamberville warned that while a French invasion might cut down the Senecas' "Indian corn," it would "cost much blood and many men." The Senecas' ability to "conceal themselves in the grass and prepare embuscades everywhere," their "vast hunting ground in their rear, towards Merilande and Virginia," their abundant stored corn and newly built "retreat in the woods for the children, women, and old men," all argued against the wisdom of a French invasion.[132]

Aware by July 1684 of La Barre's planned attack, some Senecas expressed "joy" at the prospect of determining whether French "flesh" was "as good as that of their other enemies whom they devour." Other Senecas approached officials at Albany to learn how their Anglo-American allies planned to respond to La Barre's threats. Dongan, apprehensive that the Five Nations might "weaken themselves" by accepting Kryn's invitation to relocate to the St. Lawrence valley, seized the opportunity presented by the Senecas' visit to ratchet up tensions between New York and New France. He ordered a dramatic reduction in the prices of military stores at Albany for Iroquois customers and then, in proceedings that built on the precedent of the October 1683 agreement with the Cayugas, arranged for the Senecas to place their homelands under official English protection. In a July 15, 1684, letter to La Barre, Dongan reported that the Senecas had "voluntarily given up both themselves and their lands" to New York, and posted "the coates of armes of His Royal Highness the Duke of York" on the gates of their "Indyan Castles." In Dongan's view, La Barre now risked an international incident if he proceeded with plans to invade Iroquoia.[133]

Dongan's claims merit careful assessment. Had the Senecas (and subsequently, the other League nations) actually surrendered control over their homelands to New York? Recent history would have taught the Iroquois to expect little from Anglo-Americans' claims to "protect" Native peoples, as their own campaigns against nations in New England, Maryland, and Virginia revealed only too clearly. When Dongan sent the Mohawks a "ragged ship's flag" over the winter of 1683–84, they demonstrated their regard for the "armorial bearings of England" by placing the colors in their "public chest" out of "the light." Although members of some Iroquois nations appear in English sources to have expressed desire for the "Duke of York's armes to put on their Castles" (the Mohawks supposedly "catched at [them] very greedily"), French sources present a more complex picture. La Barre reported in October 1684 that not all of the Iroquois towns had accepted the English coats of arms. Just days after the arrival of Dongan's "proclamations" from Albany in August 1684, Lamberville noted that a "drunken man" at Onondaga tore them down, leaving nothing behind but the post to which the "Duke of York's escutcheon was attached." Intendant de Meulles also scoffed at Dongan's "rhodomontade" in attempting to raise the Duke of York's arms in Iroquoia. The Iroquois themselves recognized that the wooden shields "cannot defend us against the Arms of La Barre." Three years after their distribution, the Chevalier de Baugy discovered "the arms of England" still posted at the small western Seneca village of Keinthé, the current hometown of the Seneca doorkeeper "Ganon-kentahaoui" (Onnonkenritaoui), who was reputedly a "great friend of the English." Baugy also reported that Dongan had fraudulently backdated the English-claimed protectorate in Iroquoia to 1683.[134]

The mixed Iroquois response to Dongan's last-minute, purely symbolic offer of protection indicates that very little should be read into the claimed "surrender" of Iroquoia to England in 1684. Iroquois leaders understood the difference between an outright surrender of territory to European settler jurisdiction and the placement of indigenous homelands under European protection. Baugy's 1687 discovery spoke volumes about Dongan's true intent, which was to establish an English paper claim to Iroquois territory. By 1687, even those Iroquois disposed to accept an English protectorate would have recognized Dongan's gesture as a dead letter, since "the great Sachim Charles that lives over the great lake" had not bothered to confirm the proposed arrangements of 1684 by returning "Two White Drest Dear Skins" with his "great Red Seal" affixed to his erstwhile Iroquois subjects.[135]

Crucial Iroquois decisions centered not on coats of arms from Dongan but rather occurred at a League meeting on July 16–17, 1684, during which Laurentian Iroquois delegates played a vital advisory role. These negotiations resulted in the Seneca "Chiefs and warriors" agreeing to "place their affairs" in the hands of Onondaga headman "La Grand Geule [Otreouti] and his triumvirate" (which likely included Teganissorens and Garacontié II). Though born a Wendat, Otreouti was a respected Onondaga leader by 1684, and reportedly possessed the "strongest head and loudest voice among the Iroquois." Armed with intelligence from Iroquois kin residing near Montreal, he would represent the League's interests against La Barre's threatened invasion.[136]

HUMILIATION

La Barre's expeditionary force departed Quebec on July 9, 1684. Thirteen days later, he wrote to Dongan from Lachine, announcing that he would attack the Senecas "towards the 20th of August, New Stile" and needling his New York counterpart with the suggestion that the Duke of York would doubtless appreciate French "chastisement of those who insult you and take prisoners from you every day, as they have done this winter in Merilande." By August 17, La Barre had reached Fort Frontenac, where neighboring Iroquois from Ganneious and Quinté exchanged freshly caught game with the expeditionary force for "Needles, Knives, Powder and Ball." A muster of the assembled men at Fort Frontenac noted some 900 French soldiers (mostly Canadian militiamen) and 378 allied Indian warriors (161 of whom were "Iroquois chrestiens" from Kahnawake and La Montagne).[137]

These allied warriors had traveled separately up the St. Lawrence River (though occasionally assisting French troops at portages for payments of "Brandy and Tobacco"). Although Jesuits marveled at the apparent fidelity of the Laurentian Iroquois in taking up arms against "their own nation," their decision to join the French had been reached in open council after public consideration of alternative options (including a mass emigration back to their former hometowns). Ultimately, it was the opportunity to continue their role as "ambassadors among the Iroquois" that led them to participate in such large numbers. Several Laurentian warriors carried advance news of La Barre's approach to Onondaga country, where Father Jean de Lamberville (the last Jesuit in Iroquoia) reported their arrival with released hostage Tekanoet, Charles Le Moyne, and a wampum belt "underhand" from La Barre for his "pensioner" Otreouti.[138]

On August 28, 1684, Albany interpreter Arnout Viele arrived on horseback at Onondaga with a message for League leaders from Dongan. Viele reported that Dongan "absolutely forbade" the Iroquois from negotiations with La Barre on the grounds that the governor of New York was "complete master of their country and of their conduct" toward the French. In Dongan's view, the Five Nations "belonged to the King of England and the Duke of York." These imperious orders elicited "furi-ous rage" from the assembled Iroquois leaders, who asserted that their creator "had granted them their country without subjecting them to any person." Otreouti and Tekanoet calmed the assembled "warriors and chiefs" by recommending that they ignore such commands from an individual who must be "drunk, so opposed to all reason was what he uttered." League headmen dismissed Viele from Onondaga with two "wretched belts," which affirmed their resolve to "settle matters" independently with La Barre. Tekanoet returned to Fort Frontenac to invite La Barre to "conclude affairs" at La Famine.[139]

En route to La Famine during the last days of August 1684, La Barre sent orders to Daniel Greysolon du Lhut to "dismiss" a second army of 400 allied Native Americans and 200 French soldiers and *coureurs de bois* collected in the upper Great Lakes and then marching toward Niagara for the planned attack on the Senecas. Upon learning of La Barre's orders, the "dissatisfied" allied Native warriors "threw out all manner of Invectives against the French nation" for bringing them so great a distance from their families only to be denied an opportunity to fight. In addition to eliminating crucial reinforcements, La Barre had also "uselessly consume[d] all his provisions" during extensive delays after leaving Montreal. While traveling to La Famine, La Barre even "aggravated the sickness in his army" by ordering nightly camps near swamps. Intendant de Meulles concluded that La Barre "had not the least desire to make war" on the Iroquois.[140]

Two detailed accounts of the September 5, 1684, meeting between La Barre and Otreouti at La Famine exist. An official French account, likely penned by La Barre, depicts the French governor granting conditional terms of peace to the Senecas in a polite exchange with the "Orator" of the Onondaga nation. Another eyewitness version of the events, written by the Baron de Lahontan, a French soldier on the expedition, offers much deeper insights into the tenor of the proceedings.[141]

According to Lahontan, La Barre arrived at La Famine in late August 1684 and waited several days for Onondaga delegates to appear. On September 3, 1684, "one of their most considerable Grandees, who had a Train of thirty young warriors, and was distinguished by the title of Grangula" (Lahontan's slurred rendering of La Grand Geule, or Otreouti), appeared at La Famine. La Barre greeted the Onondaga headman solicitously, offering gifts of bread, wine, and fish and announcing that he had left the bulk of his force behind at Fort Frontenac as a symbolic gesture of his desire for peace. In fact, La Barre had sent back a large number of sick men from La Famine in hopes of preventing the Onondagas from learning the weakness of his forces. But one of the Laurentian Iroquois allies encamped with La Barre, who possessed a "smattering of the French Tongue, having stroul'd in the Night-time toward our Tents," overheard French officers discussing the extent of sickness among their troops and exposed La Barre's lie to Otreouti. Armed with this intelligence, Otreouti announced his readiness to speak with La Barre on September 5.[142]

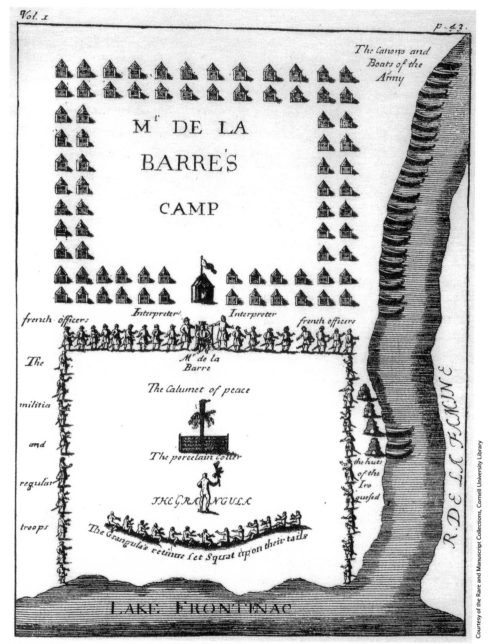

Lahontan's Drawing of La Barre's Conference with Otreouti, 1684

The conference opened with Otreouti sitting on the ground at the head of the Iroquois delegation with "the great Calumet of peace before him." The symbolic message conveyed by Otreouti's innovative use of the calumet was significant and unmistakable. French observers had long noted the use of such pipes for ensuring freedom of movement among Native nations in the upper Great Lakes and Mississippi valley.

La Barre spoke first, stating his desire for peace with the Iroquois once they made "reparation" for the March 1684 Seneca actions in the Illinois country and promising to stop escorting Anglo-American traders into French-claimed territory in the upper Great Lakes. Failing to acknowledge wrongdoing in these actions would earn the Senecas a visit from not only French forces but also from the "Governor of New-York," whom La Barre claimed (falsely) had "orders from the King his Master, to assist me to burn the five [Iroquois] Villages." Once La Barre finished, Otreouti rose and (echoing Kiotsaeton's performance at Trois-Rivières nearly forty years earlier) "took five or six turns in the Ring that the French and the Savages made," and then "return'd to his place, and standing upright," to commence his reply to La Barre, who was "seated in his Chair of State."[143]

Otreouti characterized La Barre's speech as that of a man who mistakenly regarded Iroquoia as a "burnt or drown'd country," a place either exposed to invasion or one where people lived "confin'd as Prisoners." Speaking as the "Voice of the five Iroquois Cantons," Otreouti mocked La Barre for issuing such "rav[ings]" from "a camp of sick people" and then addressed La Barre's complaints about the actions of the Senecas and Cayugas in Illinois country. Otreouti attributed the origins of the League's conflict with the Illinois and Miamis to these two nations' reckless hunting practices. "They came to hunt Beavers upon our Lands," he reported, and "contrary to the custom of all the Savages, have carried off whole stocks, both male and female." These acts, along with their offer of refuge to Iroquois-targeted "Chaouanons" (Shawnees), amounted to the Miamis and Illinois "cut[ting] down the trees of Peace that serv'd for limits or boundaries to our Frontiers." Otreouti responded in equally resolute terms to La Barre's complaints of Iroquois conduct in escorting Anglo-American traders into the upper Great Lakes. "We are born Freemen," he asserted, "and have no dependence either upon the Onontio or the Corlar. We have a power to go where we please, to conduct who we will to the places we resort to, and to buy and sell where we think fit." La Barre should not regard the Iroquois as his "Slaves or [his] Children." At the conclusion of Otreouti's speech, which Jesuits Jacques Bruyas and Charles Le Moyne translated for La Barre, the governor "retir'd to his tent and storm'd and bluster'd" while Otreouti and his entourage "danc'd after the Iroquese manner." So much for the governor's notion of keeping that ostensibly "venal being" (Otreouti) in French pay.[144]

La Barre departed La Famine with nothing more than Iroquois promises of an unspecified future surrender of three Tionnontaté captives among the Senecas and Cayugas (as "satisfaction" for the March 1684 losses in Illinois country) and to avoid molesting any French they might encounter in future campaigns against the Illinois. French reactions to La Barre's campaign varied considerably. Jean de Lamberville breathed a sigh of relief, asserting that La Barre had spared New France from a mass Iroquois attack. Lahontan, while disappointed in the result, opined that La Barre could have accomplished "no more than he did," given the circumstances.

De Meulles, however, blasted La Barre for deferring to Otreouti (whom he ridiculed as a "sycophant who seeks merely a good dinner, and a real buffoon") instead of confronting the Senecas directly, and for permitting himself to have been "fooled" in a "most shameful manner" into abandoning the Illinois country to the Iroquois, thereby reducing French prestige among allied Native nations (in de Meulles's opinion) to an all-time low. The most telling response to La Barre's campaign, however, came from Louis-Hector de Callières, the newly arrived governor of Montreal, who in November 1684 put more than 500 local men to work cutting down and bringing in "great Stakes, of fifteen Foot in length," to fortify the town.[145]

Two related patterns of seventeenth-century Iroquois movement thus combined to stop a French military invasion of Iroquoia dead in its tracks. A Wendat adoptee had outmaneuvered a European colonial governor with crucial intelligence supplied by Iroquois warriors who lived in the St. Lawrence River valley and who were nominally attached to the French expeditionary force. Otreouti's humiliation of La Barre at La Famine illustrated the extent to which the constituent nations of the League profited, by 1684, from the human capital represented by "all [the] Indians of other Nations living amongst" them as adoptees, and from the opportunities for trade and intelligence gathering that derived from their resettlement of the St. Lawrence valley and along the north shore of Lake Ontario. Officials in New France realized that Otreouti had successfully asserted the right of "the entire Iroquois nation" to pursue "war on the Illinois as long as a single one of them would remain on earth." As if to underscore the point, a party of forty Onondaga warriors set out in mid-October 1684 on a campaign against the Illinois and the Shawnees. New patterns of Iroquois movement after 1667 had established a spatially redefined League and sustained its multiple, complex engagements with other indigenous people and colonial settlements on the periphery of Iroquoia.[146]

5.

OVER THE FOREST, PART 1
1685–1693

Hail Grandfathers
Now hear us
While your grandchildren
Cry mournfully to you
For now it has grown old
What you established
Namely the Great Law [League]
We hope that they may hear us
Hail Grandfathers
You said that
It would be tough on those
Who came in later times . . .

—EXCERPT FROM TRANSLATED ONONDAGA TEXT
OF THE "OVER THE FOREST" COMPONENT
OF THE CONDOLENCE CEREMONY

On January 16, 1694, Major Peter Schuyler of Albany headed an embassy of Albany officials to the westernmost Mohawk "Castle" of Canajoharie. Schuyler reported that upon his party's arrival, "all the Sachims and young Indians" gathered to offer an Edge of the Woods welcome, "making a long speech of what had passed in former times." Yet the Mohawks sounded forlorn about their contemporary circumstances. "We lye amazed and discomfited upon our knees," they told Schuyler, "and know not what we shall do."[1]

Enactments of "Over the Forest," the fifth stage of the Condolence ceremony, occur in two distinct phases. The first involves lamentation of the loss of ritual knowledge and calls on the League's founders for guidance. The notion of the temporary abandonment of core cultural values and the need to reclaim them through renewed dedication to ritual practice represents a common trope in Iroquois traditional thought.[2] Otreouti's accomplishment at La Famine in 1684 had brought a constellation of Iroquois political, economic, military, and spatial objectives to the verge of successful resolution, yet they remained unrealized a decade later due to an unprecedented six years of violence in Iroquoia from 1687 to 1693. This relatively brief but undeniably painful era of the seventeenth century represented a time of conflict, challenge, and crisis for the League as its member communities sought unity in their collective struggle to contain aggressions engendered by European colonial rivals on the periphery of Iroquoia.

Humiliated by Otreouti's deflection of La Barre's expedition in 1684, the French undertook to exact revenge on the League with an assault on Seneca country in 1687, and then both they and the Anglo-American colonies exploited the opportunity provided by the export of a European dynastic conflict (King William's War) to North America after 1689 to further embroil Iroquois communities in an escalating cycle of conflict that witnessed unique levels of internecine bloodshed. Schuyler expressed surprise at the Mohawks' uncharacteristic lack of confidence in 1694, but he and his colleagues had arrived in Mohawk country less than a year after a French military invasion had burned three of their five settlements. Schuyler and his colleagues did not realize at the time the ways in which the Iroquois, notwithstanding their publicly-expressed sentiments of the Mohawks, were drawing on the cultural tradition of the Condolence ceremony to rebuild their approach to foreign relations in order to meet the new and complex challenges of their post-1684 world.

REVENGE

The scale and stakes of conflict escalated rapidly in North America after La Barre retreated from La Famine in 1684. King Louis XIV, in his March 10, 1685, instructions to La Barre's replacement, Jacques-René Brisay de Denonville, ordered the new governor to reclaim the allegiance of the nations of the upper Great Lakes, whom La Barre had abandoned to the League's mercy. Although New York governor Thomas Dongan had promised military assistance to the Iroquois against any French invasion, officials at Versailles decided that they could wait no longer to act. If the Senecas (whom French authorities identified as the primary Iroquois aggressors in the *pays d'en haut*) refused to renegotiate the terms of peace concluded with La Barre, Denonville must "attack [them] as soon as it will be thought convenient."[3]

Word of Denonville's threatened invasion of Iroquoia spread rapidly through New France and the *pays d'en haut*. The news reached Seneca country by June 1685, communicated by several Fox traders who passed through en route to the Montreal trade fair. Four Seneca representatives traveled to Albany early the next month to remind local authorities that the League's Anglo-American allies must "take care that no mischief befall us." Another group of Seneca headmen visited Albany in early

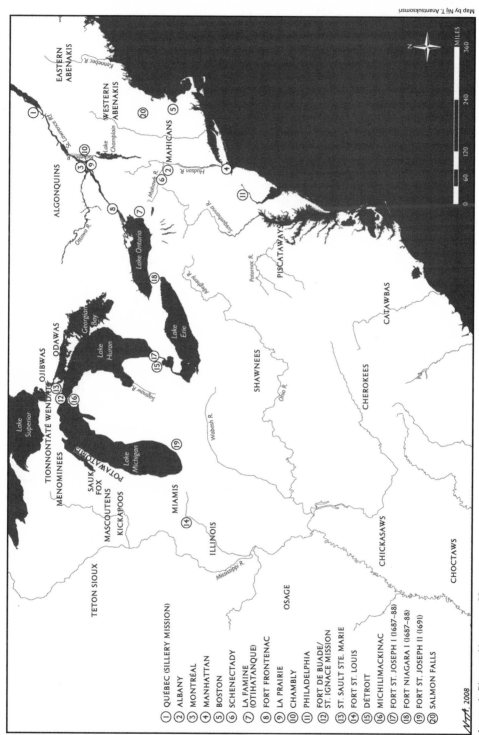

1 QUÉBEC (SILLERY MISSION)
2 ALBANY
3 MONTRÉAL
4 MANHATTAN
5 BOSTON
6 SCHENECTADY
7 LA FAMINE (OTIHATANQUE)
8 FORT FRONTENAC
9 LA PRAIRIE
10 CHAMBLY
11 PHILADELPHIA
12 FORT DE BUADE/ ST. IGNACE MISSION
13 ST. SAULT STE. MARIE
14 FORT ST. LOUIS
15 DÉTROIT
16 MICHILIMACKINAC
17 FORT ST. JOSEPH I (1687–88)
18 FORT NIAGARA I (1687–88)
19 FORT ST. JOSEPH II (1691)
20 SALMON FALLS

Iroquois Places of Interest, 1685–1701

August 1685 and planted a "Tree of welfare so Hey [high] that it may be seen in our Cuntrey," with roots growing underground "as far as our Nation." This metaphorical tree planting represented another effort to refresh New York officials' awareness of their obligations as allies in the context of increased French saber rattling.[4]

The "Tree of welfare" in Albany did nothing to restrain Iroquois military campaigns on the frontiers of southern Anglo-American colonies, which continued notwithstanding the agreements negotiated with Lord Howard of Effingham in 1684. Aware that the Virginia backcountry remained a favorite Iroquois target, Colonel William Byrd headed an official, multicultural embassy from that colony to Albany in September 1685 in hopes of ratifying the agreement made the previous year. Accompanying Byrd were "two Indians from Appomattocks, two Indians from Nanzatico, two from Chickahominy, and two from Pomunkey," all nations in a tributary relationship with Virginia who had experienced recent Iroquois attacks. League representatives renewed a preliminary peace with Byrd and his Native entourage, but since there were, as usual, Iroquois "troops" in that region who had yet to return home, the Virginians and their Native tributaries could expect no final resolution of the issue at that time.[5]

While Iroquois leaders maintained an active diplomatic schedule, Iroquois hunters contributed significantly to the successful fur trade season reported in both New France and New York in 1685. Buoyed by this economic surge, Dongan sought to further extend not only New York's beaver revenues but also the "King's Dominions" by means of an Iroquois-brokered trade alliance with the Native nations of the upper Great Lakes. After discussing this proposal with a group of Senecas visiting New York in late August 1685, Dongan reported Iroquois plans to send two "sachems" from each nation with an English-escorted trade convoy to the Tionnontaté Wendat and Odawa settlements at Michilimackinac. There they would undertake the joint task of opening formal economic and political relations between Albany and the upper Great Lakes nations while also negotiating "a durable peace and covenant" between the League and the peoples of the *pays d'en haut*. Once accomplished, these "faraway Indians" would "also be protected by the branches of the great tree of welfare" planted at Albany, and the League nations would enjoy the security and economic benefits that would flow from these "new brethren" traveling annually to Albany to trade and renew their "covenant as the [Iroquois] brethren do now."[6]

When the Senecas reported their conversation with Dongan at Albany on September 18, 1685, local officials attempted to incorporate into the plan a mass repatriation of captives from the upper Great Lakes nations then held in Iroquoia. Seneca representatives refused to agree to this request, noting that such an important matter would have to be resolved by senior "sachems in the country." Ongoing hostilities between the Senecas and Odawas stemming from the 1681 murder of Seneca headman Hannonsache at Michilimackinac meant that any large-scale return of Iroquois-held captives would require official sanction. Yet one Seneca leader suggested that a fresh start on peace negotiations could be made if the convoy of Albany traders fitting out under Johannes Roseboom managed to ransom and return with his "sister's child," then held captive among the Tionnontaté Wendats.[7]

While on a tour of Fort Frontenac several weeks after his August 1, 1685, arrival in Canada, Denonville learned that Roseboom's trade convoy had just passed nearby en route to Michilimackinac. French reports described the convoy as consisting of "eleven English canoes, loaded with goods for the Seneca trade, conducted by French deserters." Though Denonville emphasized the presence of French deserters in the convoy, the implicit message in his description was clear: not only were the Iroquois attacking French-allied Native nations in the upper Great Lakes, but they were now also facilitating an Anglo-American incursion into the fur trade of the region through the Seneca-controlled Niagara River portage. This news, compounded by Denonville's personal observation of the inability of the sparsely garrisoned French post at Chambly to prevent Iroquois and Anglo-American traders from "smuggling" peltry obtained from unscrupulous Montreal merchants down the Lake Champlain–Richelieu River corridor to Albany, made for an alarming situation. Nothing, it seemed to Denonville, stood in the way of the Iroquois capitalizing on their freedom of movement to acquire even more cheap English gunpowder, and thus further augmenting their political and military power via the "number of prisoners they daily make among their [Native] neighbors, whose children they carry off at an early age and adopt."[8]

Disabused of any notion of a possible quick strike against the Senecas in autumn 1685, Denonville realized that he would have to repair French relations with the allied nations of the upper Great Lakes in order to recruit a sufficient number of warriors to ensure that the Senecas would not be "chastise[d] by halves" but "annihilated." Aware that the Senecas could retreat southward "into the distant forests" to escape an invading French army, these allied warriors would be necessary to mount the pursuit required to accomplish French campaign objectives. In order to avoid arousing Iroquois suspicion, Denonville kept diplomatic channels to Iroquoia open by sending Jesuit Pierre Millet to Fort Frontenac to communicate the governor's offer to meet with Otreouti.[9]

Denonville's hopes of deceiving the Iroquois were in vain. Jesuit Jean Enjalran, writing from Michilimackinac, reported that the Iroquois maintained awareness of French objectives through networks of Native contacts and by means of their ties to the English, "who have free access to the ocean during the entire winter, [and who] take care that the Iroquois be informed of whatever concerns them." Acting on their knowledge of French aggressive intent, the Iroquois stepped up their offensive raids over the winter of 1685–86 against Odawa and Tionnontaté Wendat hunters in the Saginaw River valley. These campaigns netted a reported seventy Wendat and thirty-six Odawa prisoners. Enjalran informed Denonville that the Iroquois had only managed this sizable coup with the compliance of a "Native Huron" from Michilimackinac, who orchestrated the mass surrender of these prisoners to the Senecas in hopes of effecting a Wendat-mediated Iroquois peace with the upper Great Lakes Algonquians. Clearly, a growing number of *pays d'en haut* nations were anxious to build on the nascent Seneca-mediated trade initiatives with Albany.[10]

This news forced Denonville to take steps in the early summer of 1686 to restrict English and Iroquois access to the upper Great Lakes by posting small French parties at the Toronto portage, and the "Détroit de lac Érie" (Fort St. Joseph, located at the head of the St. Clair River). Denonville also ordered Captain Rémy Guilloust d'Orvilliers, then in command of Fort Frontenac, to take post with twenty men at Niagara after shipping a load of trade goods in the "Sieur de la Salle's bark" for exchange with Seneca hunters returning from the *pays d'en haut.* By November 1686, only Detroit and Toronto had been occupied by small French garrisons (under Daniel Greysolon du Lhut and Olivier Morel de la Durantaye, respectively). D'Orvilliers had returned to Fort Frontenac, which led Denonville to conclude that nothing less than a fort large enough to hold 200 to 400 men at Niagara would suffice to make the French "masters of the passage by which the Senecas go after peltries."[11]

News of independent Iroquois negotiations involving trade and peace with the upper Great Lakes nations also troubled Dongan. In late May 1686, he voiced his disapproval of the unregulated European trading among the "farr Nations of Indians," and warned the Iroquois that once these traders "found the way to hunt and trade as the [Iroquois] Brethren do, [it] will contribute much to [their] Losse." Attempting to assuage the economic concerns of Albany traders grumbling about French Jesuits "debauching" their Iroquois suppliers and customers "away to Canada," Dongan granted them a monopoly on New York's fur trade and also resumed efforts to encourage the Iroquois to repatriate residents of the Laurentian communities. He asked Iroquois delegates in Albany to permit free passage for any of "our Indians" seeking to relocate from Canada. By August 1686, with intensifying rumors of a French invasion of Iroquoia "when the corn would be nearly ripe," Dongan sent a Mohawk messenger to the "Christian Indians in Canada," offering them land at Saratoga and even "a priest there to instruct them in religion." The Laurentians declined the invitation. They retained the freedom to come and go as they pleased "on the route to the English by Lake Champlain," and had no interest in a mass return to what New Yorkers considered their proper homeland.[12]

In an increasingly charged political atmosphere, Iroquois leaders and warriors continued to work to identify common interests across the constituent League nations and to advance the process of achieving consensus on those objectives through balanced forms of outreach to their Native and non-Native neighbors. While a delegation of Onondagas and Oneidas traveled to Fort Frontenac in August 1686 to participate in a French-mediated repatriation of ten Tionnontaté Wendat prisoners, the Senecas had reoriented their military offensives during the summer of 1686, undertaking large-scale, southwesterly oriented campaigns against the Miamis and Shawnees so as not to jeopardize the potential for rapprochement with the Wendats

SITE (PLACENAME)

MK-1   WHITE ORCHARD (TIONNONTOGOUEN)
MK-2   ALLEN III
MK-3   FOX FARM (GANDAOUAGUÉ)
OE   MARCH
ON   WESTON
CY   YOUNG FARM (ST. JOSEPH II)
SE-1   ROCHESTER JUNCTION (TOTIAKTON)
SE-2   KIRKWOOD (KEINT:HE)
SE-3   GANONDAGAN
SE-4   BEAL (GANNOGARAE)
SE-5   DAMASKY
SE-6   NIAGARA

Iroquoia, ca. 1687

and Odawas near Michilimackinac. In the meantime, the Senecas also hoped to employ their Wendat and Odawa captives as hostages for trade and peace negotiations. "Antoine L'Epinart, an old resident among the Dutch" at Albany, advised French authorities at Montreal during the autumn of 1686 that a number of Seneca-held Odawa and Wendat captives would be carried home with another Iroquois-escorted convoy of fifty traders from Albany (headed by Johannes Roseboom) then wintering in Seneca country in preparation for a spring 1687 trip to Michilimackinac.[13]

The capacity of such far-ranging and calculated Iroquois mobility to cause significant problems for New France constituted the thesis of Denonville's lengthy November 8, 1686, letter to Minister Seignelay. The "colony must be put down as lost," Denonville argued, "if war [against the Iroquois] be not waged next year." Enjalran had reported that the Wendats and Odawas of Michilimackinac were on the verge of traveling to Seneca country to "submit themselves" to that nation during the spring of 1687. Worse, the Iroquois plundered French traders' canoes wherever they found them, "unwilling that we should carry ammunition to the Savages, their enemies and our allies." The only hope, according to Denonville, lay in a coordinated, simultaneous attack on the "corn fields at both ends of the [Iroquois] cantons."[14]

A coordinated French invasion of Mohawk and Seneca territories would also, in Denonville's view, silence Dongan's increasingly antagonistic assertions of English claims to the upper Great Lakes region. Denonville argued that by turning back at La Famine in 1684, La Barre had failed doubly, since he caved in to Iroquois resistance and also failed to test New Yorkers' promises to protect the Senecas from French aggression. Dongan's willingness to assert not only direct English jurisdiction over Iroquoia proper but also proxy entitlement to extensive Iroquois hunting territories in the upper Great Lakes threatened French claims to the continental interior. French metropolitan authorities took Dongan's assertions seriously enough to order a search of their archives for documents to support an official "Memoir in Proof of the Right of the French to the Iroquois Country and to Hudson's Bay." But such jousting on paper only went so far: the real contest, for all concerned parties, would take place on the ground in Iroquoia and beyond.[15]

On February 28, 1687, a group of Mohawk leaders, claiming to speak on behalf of "all the tribes [clans] of the Maquase," appeared in Albany to meet with local officials. The Mohawks reported that the Oneidas, Onondagas, and Cayugas had accepted an invitation from the Wendats to meet at Fort Frontenac for French-mediated peace negotiations in the upcoming spring, "when the bark is being peeled from the trees." The Mohawks and Senecas had declined to attend, however, owing to their joint involvement in Major Patrick Macgregory's trading expedition (scheduled to depart Albany in April 1687 for Michilimackinac with "messages to the Indians of the west"). That initiative required substantial cooperation between the League's eastern and western doorkeepers, and Macgregory's escort included at least one prominent leader from the Senecas (Tekanoet) and Mohawks (Garistatsi) alike. The Mohawks' ties to Albany traders facilitated the expedition's initial planning and organization. The Senecas, who continued to avoid military offensives in the vicinity of Michili- mackinac, had preserved the prospects of an interindigenous peace and also supplied crucial human capital, in the form of Wendat and Odawa captives, to enable ongoing League efforts to broker an independent peace with upper Great Lakes nations.[16]

Though optimistic about Macgregory's Iroquois-escorted expedition, Albany authorities' ears had pricked up at the mention of the planned embassy of the three interior League nations to Fort Frontenac. Efforts to persuade the Iroquois to ignore Denonville's invitations (unless they had become "his subjects and have taken back [their] land from the great King of England") occupied New York officials for the next five months. Despite ambitious Anglo-American claims of sovereign authority over Iroquoia, unfettered movement by the Iroquois and their allies posed as many problems for English colonial authorities as it did for the French. Even if Dongan had actually managed to have "the arms of his Royal Highness" nailed up in each Iroquois "castle," that gesture in no way translated into effective control.[17]

While New Yorkers argued about the terms of their allegiance with the Iroquois League during the spring of 1687, Louis XIV approved plans for an invasion of Iroquoia. Denonville received his official orders from France on June 2, 1687, although preparations for the campaign, including efforts to secure allied warriors from the upper Great Lakes nations, had been under way in New France since November 1686.[18]

Once again, news of French intentions reached the Iroquois quickly. Intelligence of the French military buildup at Fort Frontenac over the winter of 1686–87 reported by a longtime Onondaga resident of Ganneious proved the value of communications links with the north shore communities for collective League planning. In early June 1687, Iroquois leaders recalled a 600–man army from a planned campaign against the Miamis and convened "a generall meeting of the sachems of the five Nations" at Kaneenda, the site of the former palisaded Onondaga fishing station that their parents and grandparents had defended against Champlain's 1615 attack. Gathered in a place that evoked positive and relevant memories of resisting French aggression, League delegates considered their options in light of the pending French invasion. Attending Denonville's conference at Fort Frontenac, while risky, offered an opportunity to repeat Otreouti's diplomatic victory of 1684, and also to retrieve some Oneida prisoners reportedly en route from Odawa country. Sending a League embassy to Fort Frontenac would also defy Albany officials' attempts to restrict Iroquois freedom of movement. At the same time, Albany authorities were offering liberal presents of ammunition (for purposes of self-defense) to any Iroquois parties willing to retrieve them. Those supplies could be useful in the event of a French invasion, or they could be employed against the Miamis.[19] Why not pursue both opportunities?

After the conclusion of the League meeting at Kaneenda, the Onondagas informed Jesuit Jean de Lamberville (who had returned to Iroquoia) that they would dispatch a multinational League delegation to meet with Denonville at Fort Frontenac. Confident in their kinsmen's ability to thwart Denonville's advance with diplomacy, the Senecas dispatched a 300-man war party to go south into Virginia. Both the Onondagas and Senecas would come to regret these decisions. A French and allied Indian army under Henri de Tonty captured Macgregory somewhere on the Niagara peninsula (in modern-day Ontario) in late June 1687 and freed the Wendats and Odawas whom the Senecas had intended to repatriate at Michilimackinac. The departure of the Seneca army for the Virginia frontier reduced the domestic manpower available to confront

Denonville, who had no intention of succumbing to artful Iroquois rhetoric en route to his objective in Seneca country (plans for a concurrent attack on the Mohawks had been abandoned). "All my hope," the governor wrote on June 8, 1687, "is to spoil and lay waste [to the Senecas'] fields, and to this end we shall apply ourselves; perhaps we may be able to catch their women and children."[20]

Denonville's pending invasion afforded Iroquois an opportunity to assess the commitment of their New York–based allies. A party of Mohawk and Oneida leaders picking up free supplies of ammunition in Albany on June 27, 1687, expressed surprise and frustration when they were not given firearms, wondering aloud if they were supposed to throw powder and lead at the French with their "hands." Stating their knowledge of Dongan's recent "exchange of letters with the Governor of Canada," they also questioned the New York governor's honesty: would the "tree of peace" planted in Albany remain "steady and straight" and not "grow sideways"? Local officials responded with a token gift of six muskets and assurances of "fatherly" protection from "Corlaer." Eleven days later, the New York Council resolved that the Iroquois, "as subjects of the Crown, ought to be protected and defended" from any French effort to "molest or disturb or invade" their homelands.[21]

The paltry gift of firearms given at Albany and the empty rhetoric from the provincial council would prove to be accurate measures of New Yorkers' willingness to defend Iroquoia from Denonville. Dongan's plan for assisting the Crown's so-called Iroquois subjects amounted to sending the League nations four more copies of the royal arms of England "in case any of the[ir] Castles should be without them," and advising the Iroquois to abandon their towns and fields to Denonville without resistance, after which they were to retreat to Albany, where he would provide them with them shelter and food as refugees (and also prevent them from negotiating an independent peace treaty with Denonville). Additionally, Dongan's announcement that he would deal "very severely" with any "of our Indians that are turned Catholiques and live in Canada" who attempted to "debauch others after them" reflected a significant escalation of New York efforts to restrict Iroquois freedom of movement.[22]

The pusillanimous nature of Dongan's conduct became increasingly clear after news of the arrival of Denonville's expeditionary force at Irondequoit Bay on July 11, 1687, reached Schenectady just one day later via a series of Iroquois "messengers who have traveled by foot from castle to castle" in relay. Denonville had departed Montreal on June 11, 1687. His army consisted of 832 French regular troops, 930 Canadian militia (headed by "old Carignan Officers"), and between 300 and 400 "domiciled" Indians from "various missions." Among these allied warriors were an estimated 120 to 140 Iroquois from the Laurentian communities, under the leadership of Mohawk headman Togouroui (aka "Krynne the Maquase") and accompanied by the aging Canaqueese. French authorities believed that by enlisting these "Christian Iroquois," they would obtain the military services performed by "dragoons in France": scouting, assisting at portages, and covering the flanks of the moving army. By the end of the

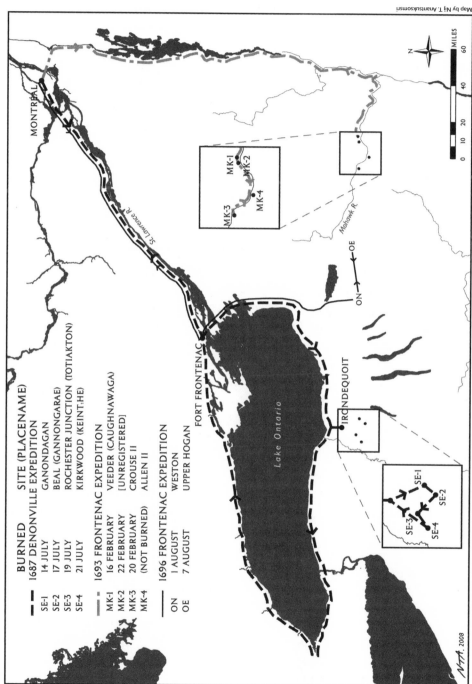

BURNED   SITE (PLACENAME)
1687 DENONVILLE EXPEDITION
SE-1   14 JULY   GANONDAGAN
SE-2   17 JULY   BEAL (GANNONGARAE)
SE-3   19 JULY   ROCHESTER JUNCTION (TOTIAKTON)
SE-4   21 JULY   KIRKWOOD (KEINT:HE)

1693 FRONTENAC EXPEDITION
MK-1   16 FEBRUARY   VEEDER (CAUGHNAWAGA)
MK-2   22 FEBRUARY   [UNREGISTERED]
MK-3   20 FEBRUARY   CROUSE II
MK-4   (NOT BURNED)   ALLEN II

1696 FRONTENAC EXPEDITION
ON   1 AUGUST   WESTON
OE   7 AUGUST   UPPER HOGAN

MONTREAL

St. Lawrence R.

Mohawk R.

MK-3
MK-1
MK-2
MK-4

FORT FRONTENAC

Lake Ontario

IRONDEQUOIT

ON
OE

SE-3
SE-1
SE-4
SE-2

N

0   10   20   40   60
MILES

NTA. 2008

French Invasions of Iroquoia, 1687–1696

campaign, many French observers realized that these particular allies were actually more Iroquois than Christian.[23]

French conduct on the march toward Seneca country appalled accompanying Laurentian Iroquois warriors. Nine days out from Montreal on Lake St. Francis, the French commenced an aggressive campaign of arresting and incarcerating any and all Iroquois people (including women and children) they encountered. An early French prize was Cayuga headman Ourehouare, reputed not only to have "cruelly maltreated and prosecuted" Jesuit Étienne de Carheil in years past but also to be "strongly attached to the Senecas" and deeply involved in recent negotiations with the Tionnontaté Wendats of Michilimackinac. The discovery of cords employed to bind prisoners in Ourehouare's "baggage" earned his entire party of "spies" a trip to prison in Montreal. The women and children with Ourehouare's party were later distributed among the multi-family households of the Laurentian communities, but the "most disorderly" of the men were deported across the Atlantic to row in Louis XIV's Mediterranean galleys. Denonville's force also seized Iroquois people fishing at Otondiata (an Iroquois-named island in the St. Lawrence River) en route to Fort Frontenac, where Intendant Champigny had arranged for the capture of not only the forty-man League embassy escorted by Lamberville for the purpose of peace negotiations but also all residents of the two nearby north shore Iroquois communities to "prevent their carrying news of our march to the enemy." By July 3, 1687, more than 200 Iroquois prisoners were in French custody at Fort Frontenac (at least 150 of whom were women and children).[24]

Upon their arrival at Fort Frontenac, the Laurentian warriors (who by that time accounted for 220 of the 353 French-allied warriors) witnessed a distressing spectacle of fellow Iroquois people "tied to Posts with Cords round their Necks, Hands, and Feet," being whipped by French soldiers while they sang death songs lamenting French cruelty and contrasting it to their former services in supplying the garrison of Fort Frontenac with "Fish and Venison" and in "procuring to the French a Commerce in the Skins of Beavers and other Animals." All "five villages," assured one bound captive from Ganneious (referring to the League nations), would surely avenge such "tyrannical Usage" of their common "Blood." [25] What could the Laurentian Iroquois do in the meantime?

Unable to stop Denonville's advance, Laurentian warriors nevertheless took steps that greatly affected the remainder of the campaign. On July 4, 1687, the Chevalier de Baugy reported that 100 allied Laurentians, "enraged because their people were seized by us at the fort," had abandoned the expedition. At least two of these warriors, identified as "Garistatsi and Gannagenroguen, Agniers [Mohawks]," "slip[ped] into the woods" to provide fresh intelligence to the Senecas of French numbers and plans. Those Laurentians who remained with the French manifested their discontent through several fruitless pursuits of Onondagas spotted scouting the French army during its advance from Fort Frontenac to Irondequoit Bay over the next six days.

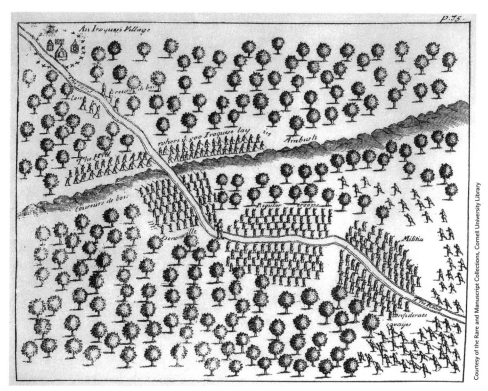

Lahontan's Drawing of Denonville's Battle with the Senecas, 1687

Another critical information leak occurred when an "Iroquois slave" belonging to the "Hurons at Missilimaki" escaped while traveling between Niagara and Irondequoit Bay on July 10, 1687. This fugitive "boatman" also informed the Senecas "of the marks which our [French-allied] savages bore to recognize each other." When Denonville's army landed at Irondequoit Bay on that same day, several Seneca parties hailed them, demanding to know their intentions. One Seneca leader later recalled that an allied Laurentian Mohawk confirmed that they had come to invade Seneca country, and then fired at, but missed, the Seneca scouts. These final pieces of news convinced the Senecas to remove their wives, children, and elderly people to Cayuga country on July 11, while hundreds of young Seneca men, along with five women who "were resolved not to leave their husbands but [to] live and dye with them," moved to the palisaded enclosure they had constructed in 1684 on a high hill near the large eastern Seneca town of Ganondagan and prepared to defend their homelands.[26]

Despite the existence of a path wide enough to march "three columns" of men and covering a distance Lahontan estimated at just twenty-one miles from the landing site at Irondequoit Bay to Ganondagan, Denonville elected to spend nearly three days constructing a palisaded retreat at Irondequoit. On the July 13, 1687, journey from Irondequoit, the French and allied Indian force marched into a Seneca ambush three miles from Ganondagan. The Senecas' "hoop and hollow" (battle cries) terrified many of the regular troops newly arrived from France, and also caused a number of the allied Odawas to flee. Experienced French Canadian officers later admitted that the Senecas "fought very well" and nearly succeeded in repelling the French advance. Reports of immediate Seneca casualties ranged from 14 to 28 men out of an estimated force of 800 (an undetermined number left the battlefield wounded), while the French reported eleven to twenty-six killed (among whom at least five and possibly as many as fifteen were allied Laurentians). "The reason why we killed so few of the Iroquois," grumbled Baugy, was "because they wore the same badge as our savages." Laurentian intelligence, confirmed by the Mohawk escapee, had dramatically limited the French capacity to kill Senecas. Laurentian warriors also refused to pursue the Senecas from the battlefield, enabling the Senecas to retrieve all but one of their wounded men. Upon realizing that Denonville would not order a pursuit of the Senecas, many of the allied Native warriors painstakingly recruited from as far away as Illinois left in disgust for "their own country."[27]

On July 14, 1687, Denonville's army marched in full battle array to Ganondagan, the "famous Babylon" of the Senecas, only to find it burned and abandoned. Rather than "follow a flying enemy to a distance, and excite our troops only to catch some straggling fugitives," Denonville ordered the systematic destruction of the Senecas' abundant agricultural resources in fields and storage facilities at all four Seneca towns over the next ten days. But problems dogged the execution of Denonville's plans. Allied Laurentian Iroquois warriors refused to assist French crop destruction, by which means a number of Seneca "out-fields" remained undiscovered by the French and were thus spared. Allied warriors from the *pays d'en haut* also showed little interest in either the "fruitless Adventure" of cutting corn or mounting an organized pursuit of the retreating Senecas, preferring instead to plunder valuables the Senecas had left behind.[28]

The French took formal possession of Seneca country in a ceremony at Totiakton, "the largest of the Seneca villages," on July 19, 1687. Sifting through the burned remains of the town, the French discovered a "board written upon in the Iroquois manner." According to some Laurentian Iroquois asked to interpret the pictographs, the text indicated that only the small, westernmost Seneca community of "Gannounata," whose leader was reportedly "a great friend of the English," had accepted an anti-French English "hatchet" delivered by Arnout Viele, the Albany authorities' official interpreter, earlier in 1687 while en route to Michilimackinac with Macgregory's ill-fated expedition. The news conveyed by this Seneca-authored document, which also depicted Onondaga efforts to broker peace with the French, seriously weakened Denonville's rationale for the invasion of Seneca country in the eyes of his Laurentian Iroquois allies.[29]

Although the Denonville expedition forced the Senecas to abandon their towns and much of their personal property (including an estimated 1.2 million bushels of corn destroyed by Denonville), their human losses were astonishingly few. A dozen Seneca-adopted Miami and Illinois women repatriated themselves to kinsmen accompanying Denonville's army. A Wendat warrior from Lorette, possibly seeking to settle an old score, mounted an independent pursuit of retreating Senecas and returned with two scalps. Unspecified French-allied Indians executed at least one of the five or six elderly Senecas physically unable to flee their home villages by a hatchet blow to the head (without prior ritual torture) and rounded up a handful of other Seneca prisoners. These few unfortunates, along with those killed and wounded in the battle of July 13, 1687, represented the extent of Seneca casualties.[30]

Denonville returned to Irondequoit on July 23, 1687. Although many of his Native allies had begun to melt away, he ordered the expeditionary force to move west. Arriving at Niagara one week later, the French army spent four days overseeing the construction of a palisaded fort on the east, or "Iroquois," side of the Niagara River. Reminded by the few remaining allied warriors from the *pays d'en haut* of earlier French promises that the war against the Iroquois would continue until the latter were "either destroy'd or dispossess'd of their country," Denonville offered his personal assurances to Kondiaronk (aka Adario and "The Rat"), the "General Chief Counselor" of the Tionnontaté Wendats at Michilimackinac, that the Iroquois would eventually be "totally routed." For the time being, however, the governor recommended the fort at Niagara to the nations of the upper Great Lakes as "a secure asylum" from which to launch autumn and winter raiding parties into Seneca country.[31]

After leaving a garrison of 100 men at Niagara under the command of Philippe de Rigaud, Marquis de Vaudreuil, captain of the French regiments sent to Canada in 1687, and detaching two more parties of French troops to reinforce Michilimackinac and Fort St. Joseph, Denonville departed Niagara on August 3, 1687. His retreating army coasted down the north shore of Lake Ontario toward Fort Frontenac, where on August 9, four days prior to his arrival at Montreal, Denonville received a visit from Kahnawake headman Louis Atériata. The Laurentian leader warned the governor that his expedition had stirred up a "wasp's nest" and that he could expect retaliatory "stinging" from Iroquoia in short order.[32]

ESCALATION AND INNOVATION

Contrary to the boasting of Denonville and other French officers in the aftermath of the expedition, the 1687 invasion of Seneca country neither destroyed the capacity of the League for unilateral military action nor reflected their inability to defend their homelands.[33] Consciousness of common Iroquois identity across European colonial boundaries not only limited the impact of Denonville's expedition, it also represented the basis of the League's innovative response to French aggression after 1687. Otreouti reappeared on the scene four years after his performance at La Famine and articulated principles of Iroquois neutrality vis-à-vis the settler colonies on the periphery of League homelands. In the meantime, warriors from all five League nations amplified the stakes of diplomacy by rededicating themselves to large-scale, coordinated attacks on New France.

Many contemporary French observers expressed doubts about the efficacy of Denonville's war on the Senecas' "corn and bark houses" in the aftermath of the campaign. Lahontan, in a letter of August 2, 1687, identified the aroused antagonism of the League as the single most "unfavorable issue of the Campaign." Writing in 1690, a French officer opined that the Denonville expedition had made only a "trifling impression" on the Senecas. "Not one of them perished of hunger," despite the extensive destruction of Seneca crops, this writer continued, "as two arrows are sufficient to enable a savage to procure meat enough for a year's support, and as [their] fishing never fails." Perhaps most tellingly, officials in Versailles, after reading reports of Denonville's expedition and its unhappy aftermath, began drafting new plans for the "Termination of the Iroquois War" in March 1688.[34]

The League's collective response to Denonville's invasion was swift and decisive. While Seneca noncombatants found secure refuge in towns throughout Iroquoia, leaders from all the constituent nations convened for a general council at Onondaga in late July 1687. Though no record of that meeting's proceedings has survived, the tenor of the discussions may be inferred from the rapidly organized, large-scale, cooperative, and far-ranging retaliatory actions undertaken by warriors from all League nations against New France over the next five months. Lahontan reported pursuit by "a thousand Iroquese" during his passage through the Niagara River portage to Lake Erie in early August 1687. This Iroquois force, "composed of all the 5 nations," then turned their attention to Denonville's retreating army, snatching up and torturing several straggling French soldiers they encountered along the north shore of Lake Ontario en route to Fort Frontenac. There, after capturing three more soldiers and a female civilian, the Iroquois commenced a six-month siege of the fort on August 20, 1687. Lamberville described in harrowing detail how hundreds of canoe-borne Iroquois warriors on Lake Ontario unleashed furious volleys of musket fire on the fort and its vessels and burned the garrison's winter supply of firewood, "inspired by the desire to revenge [both] their [Seneca] comrades" and those "who had been treacherously put into irons and taken to the galleys in France."[35]

The Iroquois warriors present in the St. Lawrence River valley during the winter of 1687–88 intercepted supplies intended for Forts Frontenac and Niagara and disrupted French communications with Michilimackinac and the other upper Great Lakes posts. Tionnontaté Wendat warriors advised Lahontan (at Fort St. Joseph) in January 1688 that Niagara was "block'd up by 800 Iroquese." Only in February 1688 could a thirty-man rescue mission (fifteen of whom were Laurentian Iroquois) get through to Fort Frontenac to drag Lamberville and thirty-nine other members of the garrison back to Montreal on dogsleds. At least forty and possibly as many as eighty members of the 140-man garrison at Fort Frontenac had died of scurvy from their Iroquois-imposed diet of salt meat by that time. A mere dozen French soldiers remained there when the Iroquois lifted their siege in April 1688.[36]

The aftermath of the Denonville campaign also witnessed immediate efforts by Laurentian warriors accompanying the French invasion force to reach out to their Iroquois kinfolk. Kryn, the Laurentian "Captain" whom French authorities held in great "esteem," elected not to follow Denonville west from Seneca territory to Niagara in late July 1687. Instead, he and four other Mohawks had traveled east to determine whether the Onondagas, Oneidas, and Mohawks "would have peace or war, or if they were united with the Sinnekes." Anglo-American authorities incarcerated and interrogated two members of Kryn's party who had accompanied some Mohawks to Albany on September 10–11, 1687, but in their haste to secure prisoners, they ignored Iroquois sensibilities and overstepped the limits of their jurisdictional authority, as the Mohawks' "General" Tahaiadoris explained in Albany eight days later. The Iroquois, according to this Mohawk headman, were at war with the French, not with "Cryn and his company." Mohawk leaders secured the release of their two kinsmen from the Albany jail and sent an escort to accompany them back to the Laurentian settlements, demonstrating their persistent disregard for Dongan's repeated demands that they repatriate the so-called "Christian Indians at Canada" to what Anglo-Americans considered their "Native Country."[37]

Kryn's outreach to his "Brethren, sisters, uncles, [and] a[u]nts" among the Mohawks, Oneidas, and Onondagas played a significant role in helping the Iroquois clarify and prioritize their objectives in the wake of the Denonville campaign. Three Albany traders who had been captured near Michilimackinac and who later escaped from Canada reported a mid-September 1687 encounter with Kryn near Lake Champlain, where the Laurentian headman informed them that he was en route home from Mohawk country. Accompanying Kryn were three Mohawks of the "first Castle" (where Kryn's nephew resided), sent to continue the discussion initiated in the Mohawk valley towns, which reportedly included the prospects of large-scale Iroquois population movements either to or from the St. Lawrence valley. The latter option likely gained some momentum after Kryn and his colleagues returned to Kahnawake in late September 1687 to discover not only 300 members of their community sick with measles communicated by the troops sent from France but also 200 of those French soldiers stationed in a newly built fort within their town.[38]

Despite French and English efforts to divide Iroquois communities against one another, Kryn's efforts to repair relations in the aftermath of the Denonville expedition facilitated retaliatory Iroquois strikes against French settlers, crops, and livestock in the St. Lawrence valley. On September 7, 1687, sixty Iroquois warriors burned several settlers' houses and barns on Montreal Island. On October 4, a Mohawk army "besieged" the French outpost at Chambly and captured a soldier of the garrison, along with his wife and child. Eighteen days later, Jesuit Thierry Beschefer noted that

Iroquois raiding in the aftermath of the Denonville campaign had already claimed the lives of at least twenty-three French settlers in the St. Lawrence valley. Another Mohawk force returned to New France in December 1687 and burned the seigneury of Verchères, killing a French officer and eighty head of cattle. Laurentian Iroquois warriors offered no documented opposition to any of these offensives.[39]

While the Iroquois mounted rapid, effective retaliation against the French settler population and Forts Niagara and Frontenac in the aftermath of the Denonville expedition, the French invasion derailed Seneca and Tionnontaté Wendat–led trade and peace negotiations between the League and the upper Great Lakes nations. The disruption of these indigenous diplomatic and economic initiatives in 1687 exerted substantial influence over the next fourteen years of North American history. Dongan had hoped that these negotiations would allow him to leverage a proxy English claim to the continental interior, a plan no less far-fetched than discovery- and missionary-based French claims to the same region that the New York governor ridiculed as akin to the French claiming "Jappan" on the grounds "that some [French] Priests had resided" there. By defining Denonville's expedition as an illegitimate French trespass into "the Kings Territoryes" in North America that sought to engross both the fur trade and the allegiance of the Five Nations, Dongan escalated the stakes of a brewing Anglo-French imperial controversy. The French attack on the Senecas, in Dongan's view, placed "all his Majesty's subjects in these parts of America in danger." Peace, in Dongan's opinion, would require the French to abandon the newly built forts at Niagara and Detroit, to pay restitution for all the goods plundered from the Anglo-Iroquois trade convoys, and to repatriate all English-allied Iroquois prisoners detained in Canada and France.[40]

Denonville, replying to Dongan's criticism, justified his 1687 invasion of Seneca country on the grounds that New York authorities had supplied the Iroquois with arms and ammunition to make war on New France. That action, according to Denonville and other French officials, represented a clear violation of the 1686 Anglo-French Treaty of Neutrality. In reality, Denonville's expedition, and the affiliated establishment of interior posts on the Niagara and Detroit rivers, represented a desperate French attempt to stem the Iroquois-mediated flow of peltry from the *pays d'en haut* to Albany, an annual loss contemporary French estimates placed at 400,000 livres, representing tens of thousands of pelts or about half of the annual value of the French trade at Michilimackinac. Denonville advised Dongan of his willingness to make peace with the Iroquois, but only if the French-allied nations of the upper Great Lakes nations were included. Denonville warned that true peace would only be possible when the English and French could ensure that their respective Native allies would attack neither each other nor any Europeans.[41]

On August 16, 1687, Mohawk headman Sindacksegie discussed with Albany officials why the hostilities provoked by Denonville's expedition had destroyed prospects for what both Dongan and Denonville wanted to see happen: a European-dominated comprehensive peace. Evoking the terms of *kaswentha* relations, he explained that the League nations warred with "the Far Nations of Indians because they kill our people and take them prisoners when we go a Bever hunting and it is custome amongst Indians to war with one another; but what hath the Christians to do to join with either one side or the other?" Denonville had no more right, in the opinion of this Mohawk leader, to interfere with Iroquois freedom of movement to Odawa country than he did to object to Iroquois trade in Albany, where at that time Native people enjoyed significantly greater buying power than at Montreal.[42]

Despite obvious economic incentives, the Iroquois were in no mood to "bury the hatchet" with their former Tionnontaté Wendat and Odawa negotiating partners who had taken part in Denonville's campaign. A Tionnontaté Wendat embassy sent to "make their excuses" for accompanying the French invasion received a frosty reception from leaders at a reoccupied Seneca town (possibly located near one of the Laurentian-preserved Seneca out-fields) during the late summer of 1687. In response to this rebuff, the Michilimackinac-based nations resolved to continue hostilities against the League nations. In November 1687, a Wendat party departed Michili-mackinac in search of "Iroquese Beaver-hunters." The Wendats surprised a camp of sixty-two Iroquois hunters somewhere in the Niagara peninsula of modern-day Ontario during December 1687, killing forty-four and taking eighteen prisoners (four of whom were Iroquois women) before retreating hastily to Fort St. Joseph.[43]

These unfortunate hunters were among the majority of Iroquois people who had chosen not to accept Dongan's September 1687 invitation to take up temporary winter quarters at Albany. Hints of cooperative Anglo-Iroquois military retaliation against the French likely motivated the 800 Iroquois who eventually came to Albany to hear Dongan out. Yet once again the New York governor shied away from direct confrontation with New France. Instead, he urged the Iroquois to preserve (rather than torture and kill) their ever-growing numbers of French prisoners "to exchange for their own Prisoners" held by the French. Dongan had such hope that his brokerage of a comprehensive Franco-Iroquois prisoner swap would achieve de facto recognition of the League's dependency on the English Crown and restitution of the trade goods confiscated from the two Anglo-Iroquois convoys in 1687 that he was willing to rack up a stunning £6,400 in expenses feeding his Iroquois guests and over 500 royal and provincial troops who accompanied him to Albany.[44]

Dongan found the Iroquois unwilling, however, to comply with his agenda. Widespread Iroquois involvement in retaliation against New France and the subsequent distribution of at least forty French captives "among [all] the 5 Nations" by returning war parties gave all member nations of the League a stake in the war and precluded any English-mediated mass repatriation effort. League headmen had their own terms for peace with New France, which they itemized in a late February 1688 meeting with Dongan. Iroquois demands included the return of all prisoners in French custody (especially Ourehouare and eight other prominent Oneidas, Onondagas, and Cayugas

listed by name); destruction of the French forts at Niagara, Fort Frontenac, and Detroit; restitution for "the goods taken from [their] people" on the 1687 convoys; and
the withdrawal of the new French garrison from Kahnawake. The League nations
would no longer tolerate any French trespass on Iroquois-"possessed" lands on the
north shore of Lake Ontario, in the St. Lawrence valley, or in territories gained from
their 1649 conquest of Wendake. They explicitly rejected French-claimed rights deriving from military invasions of Mohawk and Seneca territories, which, in the opinion
of the Iroquois, merely "burnt some bark houses and cut down our corne." If those
fleeting, indecisive actions yielded "good title" to territory, the Iroquois contended,
then they could "claim all Canada" on the basis of their former offensives that "sub-
dued whole nations of Indians that lived there" and reduced the French to a point
where they "were not able to go over a door to pisse."[45]

As they demonstrated in the aftermath of the Denonville campaign, the Iroquois
continued to confront European colonizers on the periphery of their homelands
from a position of strength. Dongan acknowledged as much in his March 1688 assessment of the League's capacity to "ruine all the Kings Collonyes" in North America
notwithstanding the previous year's French invasion. French efforts to leverage the
Denonville campaign into an opening for offensives by warriors from the *pays d'en
haut* into Iroquoia achieved only mixed success, owing in no small part to the Iroquois severing French communications to the scurvy-ridden garrisons of Forts Frontenac and Niagara. A Seneca ambush killed nearly all members of a sixty-five-man
Miami war party who attempted to surprise a Seneca town during the spring of 1688.
Another Miami party managed to kill three Onondagas later that summer, but 300
Onondaga warriors chased them all the way back to Niagara, killing four Miamis in
the process. Expeditions of Illinois warriors sponsored by Henri de Tonty reportedly
brought sixty Iroquois captives back to French Fort St. Louis over the summer of
1688, but a force of 300 or 400 Iroquois repulsed a joint French–Odawa and Ojibwa
party (recruited and accompanied by Lahontan from Sault Ste. Marie) in late July
1688, before the invaders could reach Seneca country.[46]

The Iroquois also engaged in their own offensives in 1688. An Iroquois party composed partly of Senecas attacked Abenakis on the Kennebec River during the spring
of 1688 as a preliminary to renewed peace negotiations with these so-called Relations
of the League (an appellation suggesting Iroquois consciousness of ties of common
ancestry dating from the dispersals of the sixteenth century). The Ojibwas and Odawas forced to retreat from Seneca country in July 1688 redeemed themselves early
in the next month by ambushing an Iroquois party returning along the south shore
of Lake Erie with thirty-four Miami prisoners (among whom were seven pregnant
women who rode in Iroquois-paddled canoes). The Odawas and Ojibwas killed and
beheaded a dozen Iroquois, captured a dozen more, and repatriated the Miami prisoners. Although the newly freed Miamis, both alive and unborn, had escaped Iroquois
captivity, the incident demonstrated Iroquois efforts to preserve the human capital

these particular prisoners represented, in sharp contrast to frequently cited Miami oral tradition alleging genocidal Iroquois behavior on their military campaigns.[47]

In addition to pursuing wide-ranging mourning-war offensives, some Iroquois people also made efforts in early 1688 to convince their Laurentian kinfolk to relocate to the Mohawk River valley in advance of a potential mass Iroquois invasion of New France. In March 1688, Sulpician missionary Vachon de Belmont reported the relocation of thirty men and fifty women from Kahnawake to the Mohawk valley. In June 1688, Iroquois leaders demanded the return of "ninety-one slaves" then residing at Kahnawake and La Montagne. Four months later, Albany interpreter Akus Cornelisse confirmed the arrival of an unknown number of returnees into several Mohawk towns and reported that "many more will come this winter with their families." This movement to Mohawk country may have resulted in the reoccupation of the Schoharie valley, a long-standing place of national use and occupancy that had begun to attract the interest of Anglo-American speculators. Nineteenth-century oral tradition identified the "founder" of the Schoharie Mohawk community as Karighondontee, a "French Indian prisoner" (or adoptee) who relocated from Kahnawake to lands associated with his Mohawk wife's family "within about twenty years of the first German settlement in Schoharie," or circa 1688–90.[48]

After retaliating against New France and many of the Native nations involved in Denonville's invasion of Seneca country, the Iroquois extended diplomatic overtures to their northern European neighbors. A formidable embassy of 900 warriors headed by Otreouti approached Montreal in June 1688, ready to offer peace or to fight, if necessary. Defying Denonville to repeat his capture of Iroquois delegates at Fort Frontenac in 1687, they requested a parley with French authorities, brokered once again by Lamberville. When Denonville asked whether Dongan's claims of their subjection to the English Crown were true, Otreouti, reprising elements of his 1684 speech at La Famine, assured Denonville and Callières that they were not, and that they had consistently rejected such Anglo-American pretensions. After reminding Denonville of the recently demonstrated ease with which the Iroquois could "exterminate" New France by assaults on settlers' houses, livestock, and crops, he assured the governor that the League nations "wished only to be friends of the French and English, equally, without either the one or the other being their masters, because they held their country directly of God, and had never been conquered in war, neither by the French nor the English." To emphasize this point, Otreouti and twenty-one other Onondaga, Oneida, and Cayuga headmen placed their totemic signatures on a June 15, 1688, document signifying their intention "to observe a perfect neutrality" between England and France in North America.

Otreouti departed Montreal with a preliminary truce. Denonville agreed to refer the League leaders' assertion of their neutral status for approval by metropolitan authorities, to cease sponsoring offensives by French-allied nations into Iroquoia, and to retrieve the Iroquois prisoners sent to France. In his final recorded public appearance, Otreouti had used his "Big Mouth" to inaugurate a new era of relations between the League and its colonial neighbors.[49]

Otreouti's June 1688 assertion of the League's neutral status represented another clear expression of the evolving Iroquois consciousness of their own spatial centrality vis-à-vis the European colonies on the periphery of Iroquoia, and the advantages the League nations derived from freedom of movement. Iroquois speakers in Albany had reminded Dongan just five months earlier of their stance toward the French and English in terms at once literal and figurative. Facing east, a Mohawk speaker had extended the League's (symbolic) left hand to New France, and its right hand to Albany.[50] Metaphorically, and literally with the resettlement of the St. Lawrence River valley and the perimeter of Lakes Erie and Ontario, the Iroquois had placed themselves athwart European intruders' means of access to the continental interior. Otreouti, building on early-seventeenth-century ideals of *kaswentha* in 1688, established a framework for Iroquois diplomacy with European colonies that would endure for nearly another century.

Otreouti's innovative neutrality proposal brought a number of Iroquois political and diplomatic initiatives to the point of resolution during the summer of 1688. Small-scale Iroquois raiding of French settlements in the St. Lawrence River valley continued, and this pressure, combined with effective Iroquois blockades of French supply convoys, forced Lahontan to abandon Fort St. Joseph in April 1688 and convinced Denonville to order in mid-September 1688 the evacuation and destruction of the Niagara post. The relief expedition sent from Fort Frontenac to Niagara found just seven starving soldiers remaining from the original garrison of 120 men established in 1687, evidence of the failed French encroachment on this "advantageous pass" at the League's western door. But by October 1688, the delegates promised by Otreouti had not arrived in Montreal to ratify the preliminary agreement of June. Denonville's concern over his inability to get word of the pending peace to the *pays d'en haut* in time to "prevent some blow being struck" by the nations of the upper Great Lakes proved prophetic.[51]

Wendat headman Kondiaronk, born into the turbulent context of Wendake in 1649, initiated a decade of conflict in eastern North America in October 1688 when he intercepted a four-man Iroquois diplomatic embassy en route to ratify Otreouti's preliminary peace terms with Denonville. Invited by Lahontan to accompany the Ojibwas and Odawas against the Iroquois in May 1688, Kondiaronk had elected instead to lead a war party of 100 Tionnontaté Wendats toward Fort Frontenac. After learning of Otreouti's preliminary truce, Kondiaronk took a small party to the falls near La Famine, where he predicted that the Iroquois embassy would pass. There Kondiaronk's men ambushed the Iroquois party, killing one of the Iroquois "ambassadors" and a number of the young men escorting them, and taking three other headmen prisoners. One captured Iroquois leader, despite having his arm broken by a musket shot, escaped to Fort Frontenac. Kondiaronk released Teganissorens, identified as the "chief Embassadour," before leaving La Famine, claiming that Denonville had put him up to such a "black Action." Kondiaronk returned to Michilimackinac with the fourth Iroquois leader and surrendered him to French authorities. Unaware of the June 1688 truce, local French officers promptly executed the unfortunate prisoner.[52]

Officials in Canada felt certain that the Iroquois would interpret Kondiaronk's act as "a snare laid for them by the French," but Lahontan and Nicolas Perrot reported from the *pays d'en haut* that Kondiaronk had actually hoped to employ his disruption of the Franco-Iroquois truce to revive independent Wendat-Iroquois peace and trade agreements. Lahontan claimed that Kondiaronk even freed an "old Iroquese Slave that had serv'd him a long while" at Michilimackinac, believing that such a gesture would signal his desire to resume independent indigenous negotiations and ultimately yield a more comprehensive and lasting peace than the preliminary terms Denonville had concluded with the Iroquois in June 1688. But Kondiaronk's plans went awry when a convoy of Odawa canoes carrying nine Iroquois captives (each standing upright and singing death songs) floated up to Michilimackinac in the autumn of 1688. French authorities, though willing to execute an individual Iroquois diplomat, realized that they could not permit a replay on a larger scale of the 1681 murder of Seneca chief Hannonsache. Perrot himself clambered up onto an Odawa-built scaffold to interrupt the torture of five Iroquois prisoners condemned to death (the other four had been spared and assigned to adoptive "masters"). Perrot managed to persuade the Odawas not to execute any of the Iroquois captives. An Odawa headman named "La Petite Racine" agreed to escort two of the five liberated Iroquois prisoners to Montreal the following spring so that Denonville could make a formal repatriation to League delegates.[53]

Despite the preliminary indigenous and French-mediated peace efforts under way at Michilimackinac, officials in New France realized that Kondiaronk's interception of the Iroquois peace embassy portended serious problems for colonial security. Callières noted in January 1689 that Canada's survival of Iroquois offensives to date owed more to simultaneous Iroquois involvement in wars with other Native nations than anything else. Now that the Iroquois had "added considerably to their numbers by the quantity of the prisoners they had made," they posed a potentially lethal threat to the French enterprise in North America. "The uncertainty we always confront concerning the movements of the Iroquois," penned one French official, made for gloomy prospects indeed.[54]

French apprehensions proved well-founded. In early October 1688, League leaders received a visit from two Onondaga residents of the Laurentian communities. These two men had traveled to Onondaga country to offer condolences for the members of Teganissorens's embassy killed and captured at La Famine as a preliminary to collective discussions of League priorities for the coming year. One result of these conversations was a mutual decision to confine long-distance Iroquois military campaigns to territories south of Michilimackinac. Documentary evidence indicates the presence of Iroquois war parties during the first six months of 1689 in Illinois and Miami homelands and on the frontiers of Virginia. Evidence of another result of the autumn 1688 League congress appears in the winter 1688–89 departure of 100 Iroquois hunters to the northern *pays d'en haut,* who may have represented the escort for two Seneca deputies charged with reopening independent League talks with the Tionnontaté Wendats, Odawas, and other Native nations in the vicinity of Michilimackinac.[55]

Once the Iroquois made these plans, in evident collaboration with kinfolk in the Laurentian settlements, the intricacies of England's Glorious Revolution and France's subsequent declaration of war on King William and Queen Mary in June 1689 mattered little to the League. Renewed Iroquois attempts to provide advance warning to Laurentian towns of planned offensives against New France, employing the brokerage of an Onondaga whose wife resided at La Montagne, represented yet another outcome of the autumn 1688 discussions. Other Iroquois people, however, continued to encourage adoptees and family members residing in the Laurentian towns to get out of harm's way. In June 1689, the Mohawks advised Albany officials that "any of the Praying Indians *who are their Tributaries*" had the liberty to return to Mohawk country unmolested, a crucial assertion of freedom of Iroquois movement in what was by then a wartime context in North America.[56]

Anglo-American authorities respected these Iroquois demands because they feared the potential loss of the Five Nations' allegiance. English concerns about Iroquois loyalties in early 1689 approached the paranoia manifested by French authorities. The depth and reality of these fears expressed by both French and English contemporaries reveal the relative political and military power of the Iroquois vis-à-vis neighboring settler colonies during the final decade of the seventeenth century. Any rumors of a potential Iroquois defection to the French evoked dire Anglo-American predictions of the "utter Ruin of all the English settlements on this Continent." Interest in "how matters stand between them of Albany and the Indiens Macques & Ciniques &c." extended throughout Anglo-America. War with France prompted royal officials in England to begin overseeing and funding "Presents to be made in His Majesty's name, to the five Indian Nations" in order to "engage them to adhere to the Crowne of England" (see table 2). This practice had hitherto been delegated to provincially appointed officials in Albany, whose accounting suggests that as late as 1687 they received a higher value of Iroquois-gifted peltry than that of the goods they issued in return. The balance would shift decidedly in favor of the Iroquois after 1689.[57]

Anxious Anglo-American observers breathed a sigh of relief when Mohawk headmen replanted the "tree of love and unity, unity and commerce" with New York, New England, Maryland, and Virginia in Albany on June 4, 1689. Delegates from the other four League nations arrived in Albany on July 7, 1689, and stated their intent to "Renew the old Covenant made with Jaques [Eelckens] many years ago." Recounting the paired Tawagonshi traditions of the "General Covenant" and the planting of

TABLE 2. OFFICIAL ENGLISH PRESENTS TO THE IROQUOIS, 1689–1701

DATE	VALUE (IN STERLING) OR CONTENTS
1689	£100
1691–92	£965
1693	£600
1694	(unspecified, possibly included 200 light muskets requested in 1693)
1696	£508
1698	£200
1699	"two hundred pounds of powder and lead"
1700	£800
1701	£800

SOURCES: For 1689, see CSPC 13:139; APC 2:141; NYCD 3:619, 690, 772, 774. For 1691–92, see CSPC 13:643, Item 2243; NYCD 3:836–37, 842; LIR, 163–64, 167. For 1693, see Van Cortlandt to Blathwayt, August 18, 1693 (O.S.), BP-CW, vol. 9; NYCD 4:37, 39, 41–42. For 1694, see Account of the Treaty, 31; NYCD 4:56–57. For 1696, see APC 2:287; NYCD 4:118, 126–27, 149, 183, 186, 197, 236; DHNY 1:324. For 1698, see NYCD 4:265–66, 342, 363, 9:686; Propositions Made by the Five Nations, 7–8, 12. For 1699, see NYCD 4:568. For 1700, see ibid., 4:640, 666, 740, 876. For 1701, see ibid., 4:881, 900, 9:904; APC 2:485; Redington and Shaw, Calendar, 2:389; Stock, Proceedings and Debates, 2: 388–89; Labaree, Royal Instructions, 2:466.

"the Tree of Good Understanding," the Oneidas, Onondagas, Senecas, and Cayugas reminded Albany officials that this had been affirmed after the Mohawks, Oneidas, and Onondagas carried "the Ankor of the Ship that Jaques came in" to Onondaga. They also pointed out the shared obligation of partners in a *kaswentha* relationship to share military intelligence with one another. The Iroquois demanded that the English share any news of French "Plots," and they also stated their expectation of defensive assistance in the event of a French attack on any of the five League nations. They concluded by announcing their own planned offensive against Fort Frontenac.[58]

A 300-to-400-man army composed of warriors from all League nations arrived outside Fort Frontenac during the last days of June 1689. A failed attempt to capture a French soldier on their approach to the fort cost the Iroquois the element of surprise for a planned assault on the fort, but they managed by a ruse to persuade Jesuit Pierre Millet (who had evacuated Niagara in 1688) and a surgeon to visit their camp, and then hustled off with these two high-profile French captives. Though stripped and assaulted, intervention by "Chief Manchot of Onneiuot" spared the lives of these captives. Manchot, reportedly the "second chief" of the Oneidas, delivered Millet to his wife, the matron of the Oneida Bear clan and reportedly a "good Christian woman." She later arranged for Millet's adoption, in which he received the hereditary title of Odatshedeh, which the Jesuit identified as "an ancient name of the first founders of the Iroquois republic." The Oneidas thus "resurrected" a recently deceased headman in the person of a captive French Jesuit.[59]

En route to Oneida country, Millet reported passing by another Iroquois army of 1,400 men (among whom were a significant number of "women in men's dress") heading down the St. Lawrence River toward New France. Advance parties from this second Iroquois force reached Laurentian towns in July 1689 and informed local Iroquois residents of their planned attack on Lachine. Louis Atériata, who had just returned to Kahnawake from Onondaga country that month, failed to inform French authorities of this news, evidently confident that the Laurentian villages would not be harmed.[60]

Early in the morning of August 5, 1689, nearly 1,500 Iroquois warriors landed their canoes at Lachine, the "Lands-end" of Montreal Island less than ten miles from the French town. Evading notice by the garrisons of two French defensive posts on the island, the Iroquois army launched a devastating wave of attacks that "burnt and sacked all the Plantations" over an extent of territory French accounts estimated at between ten and twenty miles. Eyewitness reports documented as many as 200 settler men, women, and children killed, and another 120 captured.[61]

The next day thirty Laurentian Iroquois warriors accompanied a French relief force sent from Montreal to organize a counterattack against Iroquois invaders in the vicinity of Lachine. En route they came under fire from a party of Iroquois warriors. Sulpician Vachon de Belmont reported that the Iroquois initially left the Laurentians unharmed and trained their muskets instead on the French soldiers. But the decision of seven warriors from La Montagne to take refuge in a church may have caused their Iroquois counterparts' sympathy to evaporate. After shooting the seven Laurentians and dispersing the French relief force, the Iroquois took more twenty Laurentian prisoners and burned the majority of them. By the end of the day, after engaging in public burnings and ritual cannibalization of dozens of French settlers, the Iroquois left Montreal Island "covered with corpses." Having sustained fewer than twenty casualties, the victorious Iroquois "shouted ninety times to indicate the number of prisoners or scalps they had taken" while crossing Lake St. Louis. One French-speaking Iroquois warrior punctuated these cries by calling out Denonville personally for his conduct at Fort Frontenac in 1687: "You deceived us, Onontio, now we have tricked you!"[62]

Despite the large-scale nature of the Iroquois attack on Lachine, Iroquois warriors went to great lengths to preserve the lives of their kinfolk in the St. Lawrence valley. They made no direct move against either Laurentian community, and only Laurentian warriors who took up arms against the invading Iroquois warriors were killed. Two Iroquois men captured by the French were surrendered to La Montagne, but the Iroquois residents left the torture and execution of these prisoners to the Algonquin members of the community. Frustrated by the conduct of the Laurentians during the attack on Lachine, Denonville withdrew the French garrison from Kahnawake and burned the town's "Fort, Church," and some of its houses. Yet the loss of these structures and the departure of French troops may actually have been welcome developments for many people at Kahnawake. At most, these were very minor penalties for communities that did next to nothing to interfere with the Iroquois avenging the Denonville campaign and causing "general Consternation" among the French settler population.[63]

While the impact of the attack on Lachine reverberated throughout the upper Great Lakes and beyond, the assault also brought about substantial alterations to the western frontiers of Iroquoia. Recognizing Fort Frontenac's now-perilous condition, Denonville ordered the withdrawal of its fifty-one-man garrison. Prior to their departure, the troops destroyed the fort and all its military stores, including three vessels formerly employed to ship trade goods to Iroquoia. Yet by abandoning Fort Frontenac, Denonville eliminated the last site of secure retreat on the borders of Iroquoia for allied Native war parties, a development that "caused much grief" for the fort's namesake, who had returned to New France for his second term as governor in October 1689.[64]

Unraveling Relationships

In the aftermath of the attack on Lachine, League leaders had avenged Denonville's invasion and restored what in their view would have represented a favorable climate for negotiations with New France. They had demonstrated their military strength once more to their European and indigenous rivals alike without jeopardizing the security of their kinfolk residing in the St. Lawrence valley. Yet League leaders had no way to anticipate how the dynastic conflict in western Europe after 1689 would alter the nature of warfare in North America. For the first time since 1666, French metropolitan authorities committed significant military and political resources to Canada, not least of which was a decision to return the experienced Frontenac to office.[65] Rather than sue for peace with the League after Lachine, the French retaliated with an attack on Schenectady in early 1690, triggering a series of campaigns on Iroquoia's eastern door that enmeshed Iroquois communities in a cycle of internecine violence that might well have reminded Iroquois people of traditional accounts of life prior to the League's existence.

One of the most significant, yet often overlooked, results of the League's assault on Lachine was the deep and enduring impression of Iroquois power it left on several hundred members of an upper Great Lakes Native trade convoy present at Montreal in early August 1689. These Indians, accompanied by some of the Iroquois hunters who had come to the *pays d'en haut* during the previous winter, had brought over 800,000 livres' worth of beaver and other peltry down to the annual French trade fair. This massive cargo may explain the "very slender trade" reported at Albany that year, and certainly suggests that contemporary French assumptions of the "incomparably more advantageous" commercial circumstances of New York were not universally true. Yet the Iroquois attack on Lachine eliminated any political capital the French may have hoped to realize in the aftermath of this bonanza of upper Great Lakes beaver. Among the witnesses of the Iroquois attack on Lachine and the supine French response were Kondiaronk (who had come in defiance of Denonville's threat to have him "hang'd") and La Petite Racine (who had failed to bring down the two Iroquois prisoners he had promised to deliver to Denonville). Members of the Wendat and Odawa trade convoy departed hastily for home, "their minds full of terror and distrust."[66]

Upon his return to Michilimackinac in the autumn of 1689, La Petite Racine wasted little time in responding to the "universal alarm" caused by the Lachine attack. He collected the two Iroquois prisoners taken in 1688 and departed immediately for Iroquoia, escorted by the two Seneca deputies who had come to Michilimackinac that spring and who would attest to the Odawas' and Wendats' desire for a "close alliance" with the League. French officials at Michilimackinac attempted damage control in the aftermath of Lachine, downplaying the impact of the attack and attempting to revive the spirits of the region's Native population. When a relief expedition under Louis de la Porte Louvigny arrived at Michilimackinac with an Iroquois prisoner captured en route in October 1689, Perrot offered the captive to the Michilimackinac Native community for ritual torture and execution. After the Wendats refused to torture the prisoner, angry French officials burned him themselves.[67]

This execution earned the French no credit, however. The diplomatic foundation laid by the Iroquois hunting and peace embassy of early 1689, who had sent many "fine collars" (belts) of wampum accompanied by "artful words" to the Fox, Mascoutens, Sauks, and Potawatomis, amplified by Odawa and Tionnontaté Wendat traders' eyewitness testimony of Denonville "not dar[ing] to go outside" Montreal's palisade while the Iroquois destroyed outlying settlements in August 1689, created broad support throughout the *pays d'en haut* for La Petite Racine's embassy to Iroquoia. Warriors whom Perrot hoped to employ in retaliatory strikes against League settlements now turned their attention to westward-oriented campaigns against the distant Osages and Sioux. Even the Miamis, who were recent targets of Iroquois aggression, elected to go buffalo hunting in 1689 rather than undertake French-sponsored attacks on Iroquois nations. Assessing the circumstances at Michilimackinac in November 1689, the distraught Jesuit Étienne de Carheil feared that Iroquois warriors would soon arrive en masse and make themselves "master[s] of everything."[68]

Frontenac had found "all things in Confusion and Distress" upon his autumn 1689 arrival in New France, but hoped to employ the mediation of Cayuga leader Ourehouare (who, with twelve other Iroquois survivors of the Mediterranean galleys, had returned to New France with the governor) in peace negotiations with the League. Prospects for reconciliation dimmed, however, after another Iroquois offensive struck Montreal Island in November 1689. An army of 150 warriors killed twenty French settlers, "spilling their members and entrails" on freshly fallen snow, and carried off thirty others into captivity. Frontenac dispatched a mixed French and Algonquin pursuit party that managed to sink (with volleys of musket fire) two large canoes carrying an estimated twenty-two or twenty-seven retreating Senecas on Lac des Deux Montagnes. All but two Senecas drowned, and the French and Algonquins burned the survivors (one at La Montagne).[69]

Although Laurentian Iroquois warriors continued to avoid involvement in pursuits of retreating Iroquois attackers, French authorities from King Louis XIV down continued to try and encourage these "Iroquois allies" to fight against the Iroquois "enemy." Yet ties of common Iroquois identity sustained an ethos of mutual nonaggression among Iroquois communities that would continue to prove strong enough to withstand directive pressure from neighboring Europeans. In October 1689, Iroquois leaders treated in Albany with New York and Massachusetts representatives. Despite the distribution of valuable presents from these two members of the Covenant Chain alliance, the Iroquois ultimately refused the colonists' requests for military assistance against French and northeastern Algonquian attacks on their frontier settlements, fully aware (though the English were not) that many Laurentian warriors participated in those campaigns.[70]

While Iroquois warriors and diplomats parried French and English efforts to persuade them to kill one another, Ourehouare and three other Iroquois prisoners who had returned to Canada with Frontenac made their way to Onondaga. Escorted by a "Praying Onnondaga Indian" from one of the Laurentian communities, Ourehouare's party carried belts and speeches from Frontenac to the League's headmen. Mohawk reports of Ourehouare's embassy in January 1690 indicated that the returnees had deferred their formal report until a League meeting could be convened. Albany officials, eager to eavesdrop on this conversation and hoping to elicit an Iroquois declaration of war against New France, sent Arnout Viele and local trader Robert Sanders to attend the League council.[71]

By February 1, 1690, eighty Iroquois "Sachims" had assembled at Onondaga, revealing once again the importance of collaboration between the fifty hereditary titleholders and leaders of achieved status at the highest level of the Iroquois polity. Ourehouare delivered an invitation from Frontenac to meet at the ruins of the fort bearing his name during the upcoming spring. There, Frontenac planned to "kindle his fire again," and he wanted Iroquois delegates (naming Teganissorens specifically) to come and "Treat about the old [Franco-Iroquois] Covenant Chain." A Laurentian Mohawk headman also urged his kinfolk to come and "give Ear to Onondio."[72]

After considering Frontenac's invitation, the League headmen communicated their consensual negative response. Fully aware of recent French behavior at Michili-mackinac, which included anti-Iroquois speeches, at least two executions of Iroquois prisoners, and assertions of French hegemony over the *pays d'en haut*, Onondaga headman Aqueendara advised Ourehouare's Laurentian escort to inform Frontenac that the governor's fire at Fort Frontenac had been "Extinguished with Blood" as a result of Denonville's treacherous seizure of Iroquois diplomats in 1687. Furthermore, Aqueendara continued, the League had already concluded an independent peace with the upper Great Lakes nations, likely via La Petite Racine's autumn 1689 embassy. League headmen had distributed wampum belts from the Wendats and Odawas throughout Iroquoia and had sent three leaders and a number of hunters back to Michilimackinac with La Petite Racine's party. With the prospect of a formal ratification of these indigenous arrangements via an Odawa pledge to repatriate twenty-six Iroquois prisoners remaining at Michilimackinac in five months' time, League leaders had no interest in further talks with Frontenac until he repatriated all Iroquois prisoners held in Canada.[73]

Although Iroquois negotiations with the nations of the *pays d'en haut* were not yet comprehensive (Mascouten, Kickapoo, and Nipissing warriors brought Iroquois scalps into Michilimackinac over the winter of 1689–90), they represented a striking example of the capacity of the League to pursue independent foreign relations in the context of an intensifying Anglo-French contest for empire in eastern North America.[74] Far from having their conduct directed by hostilities between New York and New France, Iroquois leaders subordinated resolution of peace with Frontenac to their own objectives in the upper Great Lakes. In the meantime, Iroquois warriors in the field exerted crucial influence over the course of colonizers' military campaigns.

On February 1, 1690, the same day that the League nations had announced their disinterest in peace negotiations with Frontenac, the governor dispatched an army of 210 men, including eighty warriors from Kahnawake and La Montagne under the leadership of Kryn, from Montreal. The French officers accompanying the expeditionary party carried orders for an attack on Albany, the source of Iroquois arms and ammunition. But when the allied Laurentians learned of French intentions, they rejected such a "rash" plan. "Since when," asked one warrior recalling French conduct at Lachine, had they "become so bold?" The Laurentians insisted on diverting the French expeditionary force to Schenectady.[75]

Late in the afternoon of February 18, 1690, the snowshoe-clad French and allied Native force glided up to the outskirts of Schenectady. Locating a Mohawk-built structure outside the town's palisade (possibly a menstrual hut), Kryn obtained fresh intelligence of the town's circumstances from four Mohawk women. The attack began just before midnight on February 18. Slipping through an open gate at the west end of the unguarded town, the French and Laurentians fired houses and "slaughtered" the local inhabitants. French officers managed to save a few prominent local residents (including Jacob Sanders Glen, whose family had tended to Courcelles's wounded men in 1666). The Laurentians, who lost one Mohawk in the battle, ensured that all of the thirty Mohawks found in their "houses" at Schenectady got out alive. By dawn the next day, 54 of the approximately 250 residents of Schenectady were dead, and only a handful of the community's eighty houses remained standing. Significantly, only two Schenectady residents with documented ties of marriage or ancestry to the neighboring Mohawk communities were among the casualties. The French and Laurentians collected twenty-seven prisoners (all male, including five identified as

"Negroes") and considerable plunder, which included fifty horses (all but sixteen of which were consumed on their return journey), and a number of ice spurs and skates that they used to speed their return over frozen Lake Champlain.[76]

A party of eighty Mohawks and Mahicans under a Mohawk military leader named Laurence, a recent returnee from one of the Laurentian communities, mounted a pursuit of the retreating French and Laurentian force. Laurence pledged to chase the French invaders "quite to Canida," but killed fewer than twenty laggards (no more than four of whom were Native people) while losing four of his own men in the process. Laurence's party did bring back one "French Indian prisoner" to Albany, but this man promptly escaped. Albany officials complained about the Mohawks' and Mahicans' "backwardness" in pursuing the retreating Laurentians, but recognized their allies' reluctance to kill their "kindred" and "Relations" among the Laurentians.[77]

The Schenectady attack and its aftermath demonstrated the degree to which allied Iroquois warriors exerted control over European-planned military actions in the field. It also highlighted the bitter political controversy dividing New York in the midst of Jacob Leisler's 1689 rebellion, in which Dutch settlers resentful of the colony's English authorities deposed Lieutenant Governor Francis Nicholson and attempted to seize political control over the colony. Schenectady authorities, who supported Leisler, had ignored advice from anti-Leislerian Albany officials to take precautionary measures for just such an attack, but the latter had also refused to accept men and ammunition sent up by Leisler several months earlier. In the wake of the attack on Schenectady, Anglo-Americans refocused their attention even more sharply on their alliance with the League. If "rent from the English Crowne" by the French, the Five Nations would tip the balance of power in North America away from England.[78]

Albany represented "the principal land Bulwark in America against the French," its officials contended, and the Iroquois (not the town's puny sixty-man garrison) controlled its fate. Frontenac's recent peace overtures to the League and the long-standing presumed success of the Jesuits in removing both Iroquois personnel and peltry to Canada convinced Albany authorities in early 1690 that the Iroquois might soon abandon their Albany-based alliance with Anglo-America. Appealing to neighboring Massachusetts and Connecticut for military and financial assistance, Albany representatives claimed that only by supplying Iroquois material needs, no matter the cost, could they hope to retain the League's allegiance. Even Robert Livingston, who with other prominent Albany officials had long benefited from the illicit Iroquois-brokered trade with New France, had resigned himself to the changed military and political landscape by April 1690. "We must turn our trading into warring," he noted in a telling letter to Connecticut officials, "and instead of loading our Canoes with goods for Canida for Beaver as formerly we must load the Canoes with provisions and ammunition to be revenged of our cruel and perfidious enemies."[79]

New England authorities, who had sustained French and allied Native American attacks on their frontiers since September 1688, agreed that joint offensive operations with the Iroquois might reduce some of the pressure on their settler populations. Yet the Anglo-Americans remained unaware of the extent of Laurentian Iroquois involvement in campaigns on the New England frontier. Kryn and other warriors, for example, had returned from the attack on Schenectady and joined French, Algonquin, and Abenaki fighters to achieve the June 4, 1690, capture of Fort Loyal in Maine. Mohawks visiting Albany in May 1690 refused invitations to assist in the defense of New England's outlying settlements in order to eliminate the risk of encountering their kinfolk in battle. The Mohawks wanted their "powder bags" filled for use in independent campaigns against New France.[80]

While Albany officials armed Iroquois warriors, French officials, notwithstanding Laurentian reports of the February 1690 League meeting, attempted to reopen direct talks with the Five Nations. As soon as the ice melted on the St. Lawrence in the spring of 1690, Ourehouare and four more of the former Iroquois *galériens* paddled a canoe carrying Chevalier Pierre d'Aux, Sieur de Jolliet, "an Interpreter of the Iroquese Language" who had attended the Iroquois galley slaves on their return voyage to New France) and two Canadian officers to Onondaga. Upon Ourehouare's arrival, the Onondagas not only offered no Edge of the Woods welcome, they demonstrated their posture of hostility toward New France by assaulting the French emissaries and taking them into custody. After a discussion between the "ancient Men" and the "young Barbarians," the Onondagas tortured and killed the French interpreter, sent one French officer to Seneca country (where he met the same fate), delivered d'Aux to Arnout Viele (who was then present in Onondaga), to replace the latter's son (also named Arnout, who had been captured in the Schenectady raid), and gave the remaining French officer to the Oneidas, where he joined the Jesuit (and Oneida Bear clan titleholder) Millet in captivity.[81]

While the Onondagas manifested the League's widespread antipathy to New France through their attack on d'Aux's embassy, the Oneidas' rationale for preserving Millet alive became clear in early 1690. Despite the expressed fears of Albany authorities, the Oneidas did not take marching orders from Millet. Even though he was an adopted "Sachim" and therefore "had a vote with the rest of the Sachems of Oneyde," Millet later admitted that he attended national councils only occasionally, and almost never spoke. The Oneidas arranged for Albany Dutch Reformed Minister Godfredius Dellius to vet Millet's correspondence and record-keeping to ensure he acted "faithfully." The Jesuit's adoption into the position of Odatshedeh likely provided a measure of security against threats to his life from hostile Oneidas. Millet's Bear clan protectors clearly considered him worth saving as not only a key diplomatic bargaining chip but also as another means of acquiring useful information. Familiar with Jesuit practices, the Oneidas knew that once reports of Millet alive in Oneida country reached New France, his fellow Jesuits would attempt to communicate with him.[82]

By January 1690, Mohawks reported the pending arrival of letters from Canada for "the Priest at Oneyde." Another such letter recovered from d'Aux at Onondaga led New York officials to incarcerate Reverend Dellius for a brief time after it became apparent that he had supplied Millet with paper and ink. Millet, for his part, professed to welcome the opportunity his captivity offered to sacrifice himself "in Imitation of Jesus Christ" for the Oneidas' "temporal and eternal welfare," and shared with his Oneida hosts the news he obtained in his correspondence with clergymen in Albany and Montreal.[83]

The Oneidas' initiative with Millet notwithstanding, overwhelming League sentiment at this time remained hostile to New France. News of ambitious Anglo-American plans to send "600 Christians and 1500 Indians" from Albany to attack Montreal during the summer of 1690 represented an opportunity for the Iroquois to use allied military service to accomplish their own objectives. Anglo-American authorities hoped that this expedition, the first of numerous subsequent joint Anglo-American efforts to coordinate a land-based attack on Montreal with a naval siege of Quebec, would at last "firmly settle the disposition of the 5 [Iroquois] Castles" in support of England. Ultimately, neither the Iroquois nor the English would be satisfied with the results of the 1690 campaign.[84]

The Albany-based expedition against Montreal suffered numerous logistical and organizational shortcomings from the very outset. General Fitz-John Winthrop of Massachusetts arrived at Albany on July 31, 1690, to find "all things confused and in no readiness or posture for marching." Worse, a "very mortall" outbreak of smallpox plagued the town and its soldiers. Winthrop marched out of Albany on August 8, reconnoitering with New York provincials in garrison at Saratoga with Peter Schuyler (elder brother of Arent and then mayor of Albany) and Dirck Wessells (Albany's recorder) four days later. On August 18, Winthrop and Schuyler conferred with Mohawk civil and military leaders, seeking their advice for the planned campaign. The Mohawk headmen, insulted by the Anglo-Americans' refusal to use the elm-bark canoes that Mohawks and Oneidas had spent the previous month constructing, remained closedmouthed. Upon learning that the smallpox outbreak had reached Onondaga country, the Mohawks informed Winthrop that no warriors from a promised contingent of 1,400 Onondagas, Cayugas, and Senecas would participate in the expedition. Stuck at Wood Creek (just 100 miles north of Albany) for six more days awaiting canoes and provisions, Winthrop attempted to salvage something from the campaign by detaching Johannes Schuyler (younger brother of Peter and Arent) with a force of forty settler militiamen and 100 Mohawks, Oneidas, Mahicans, and Schaghticokes to attack La Prairie de la Madelaine, the French settlement nearest to Kahnawake.[85]

Unbeknownst to Winthrop or Schuyler, however, Laurentian Iroquois scouts had already detected their movements. On August 19, 1690, a Kahnawake warrior named La Plaque, nephew of the late Kryn (who had been killed by Abenakis while returning from the Maine frontier earlier that year), informed Frontenac in Montreal of the advancing Anglo-Native party and reported that he had "suspended three toma-hawks within sight" of the Mohawk and Oneida encampment, on which he "carve[d] figures" that "defied them to come to Montréal." Five days later, in a war council attended by 500 Wendat and Odawa members of a trade convoy, Frontenac took up a hatchet and began singing and dancing, enjoining the Laurentians and upper Great Lakes nations alike to wage war "unremittingly" against the Iroquois.[86]

Frontenac's invitation threatened nascent League peace talks with the *pays d'en haut* nations and compounded the prospect of damage to internal League relations raised by Winthrop's selection of Schuyler's target. Such a high-stakes scenario demanded careful Iroquois management, and fragmentary documentary sources reveal evidence of successful, collaborative Iroquois efforts to reduce the potential for a large-scale battle at Kahnawake's doorstep. Laurentian scouting parties sent out in late August 1690 returned with several Iroquois men found hunting near Lake Champlain. These "Prisoners" reported that the bulk of the Anglo-American army had abandoned plans for the attack. Once the Laurentian Iroquois corroborated this intelligence, the French withdrew a large body of troops and allied Native warriors from La Prairie prior to the approach of Schuyler's party.[87]

Two days after the September 2, 1690, decision of Laurentian warriors and scouts to return home from La Prairie, Johannes Schuyler's expeditionary force commenced widely scattered attacks on French settlers in the fields of La Prairie. French ac-counts reported eleven farmers, ten soldiers, three women, and one girl captured or killed, and six Iroquois warriors dying in the attack. Upon his return to Albany with nineteen French prisoners (fifteen men and four women), Schuyler claimed to have killed twelve French settlers at La Prairie. Before retreating, the attackers had also destroyed a number of houses, haystacks, and draft animals.[88]

All parties involved in the attack on La Prairie felt victimized in its aftermath. French authorities lamented the "negligence" of the Laurentian scouts, whose with-drawal from La Prairie facilitated the surprise attack. Fitz-John Winthrop attributed the expedition's relative failure to the "want of the 5 Nations performance." The League's deceitful conduct, in Winthrop's opinion, had fooled "the most skillful of the [Albany] Burgers, and those of the most ancient and intimate friendship with them." Millet, writing from Oneida country, opined that the abortive attack on Montreal indicated that the Iroquois were "more Masters of the English, than the English were of the Iroquois." Yet the Iroquois, who lost six Mohawks in the attack on La Prairie and between thirty and sixty more warriors in an unrelated mid-August 1690 engagement near Lake St. Francis, had their own reasons to feel betrayed. After returning to Albany, English observers noted that the Mohawks and Oneidas refused to consider proposals for "another adventure." The lack of regard for Iroquois wel-fare demonstrated by the English exposing them to smallpox had "incensed" the Iroquois. Aggrieved Mohawks and Oneidas "destroyed all the grain around Orange [Albany] and killed most of their Cattle" before returning home in September 1690.

Contemporary French estimates of collective Iroquois deaths from the autumn 1690 smallpox outbreak ranged from 100 to 500 people.[89]

The Iroquois- and smallpox-induced failure of the Montreal campaign preceded Frontenac's successful repulse of Sir William Phips's ill-fated siege of Quebec in October 1690. The conclusion of the 1690 campaign left Anglo-Americans throughout eastern North America demoralized and wracked with debt. New France had survived, but its officials could not rest easily. Despite significant losses from smallpox, the Iroquois still managed to send independent raiding parties into the Montreal area in autumn 1690. Frontenac also remained apprehensive about the prospect of a separate Odawa-Iroquois peace after an attack involving Iroquois warriors in the vicinity of Montreal had interrupted the annual trade fair with upper Great Lakes Algonquians for the second consecutive year. Some Mahicans and Esopuses who had been residing in Odawa country for a decade repatriated one Seneca captive and discussed ties of trade and peace with their kinfolk in the Hudson River valley during the summer of 1690, indicating that indigenous peace negotiations between the League and the nations of the *pays d'en haut*, notwithstanding ongoing small-scale raids into Iroquoia by Odawa and Illinois war parties, remained alive.[90]

After blunting the potential impact of the September 1690 attack on La Prairie on their Laurentian kinfolk, Mohawks took the lead in reopening communications. In March 1691, a party of forty Mohawks (including Laurence) encountered six former residents of the recently abandoned north shore town of Ganneious hunting near Chambly. The Mohawks disarmed and escorted their six "prisoners" back to their new hometown of Kahnawake, where they advised the Laurentians of their interest in restoring peace and security to the Lake Champlain–Richelieu River corridor. If the Laurentians would continue to withhold active military assistance from New France and smoke instead "in peace on their mats," Onnonouagaren, the Mohawks' speaker, promised that his nation would do the same to their "Dutch" allies. Although French authorities worried that this Mohawk initiative portended a large-scale Laurentian return to the Mohawk valley, the "most reasonable men" at Kahnawake agreed to the preliminary terms and dispatched the Mohawks with two prisoners taken at Schenectady to use as a means for obtaining an audience with the English at Albany. Prior to leaving Kahnawake, the Mohawks informed the Laurentians of an 800-man Iroquois army approaching Montreal Island. Roughly half of this expeditionary force attacked French settlements directly in May 1691, burning twenty-five houses and a mill, while the other half "scattered themselves in divers[e] bands, through different places without anyone being aware where they will strike as they [remained] in the woods."[91]

This Mohawk-organized diplomatic and military offensive amounted to a one-two punch that left French authorities "more confused than ever" about Iroquois movements. Younger Mohawk leaders of achieved status had spearheaded this effort to reach out to their Laurentian kin in the aftermath of the 1690 smallpox epidemic, which cost the lives of many elder Mohawk statesmen. Other Iroquois efforts to build on the Mohawk warriors' peace initiative became apparent in May 1691, when a detachment of seventy Iroquois warriors approached La Montagne. French observers interpreted the warriors' advance as an attack, but contemporary descriptions noted the initial efforts of the Iroquois to detain several "Squaws busy at their Indian corn" outside the town before any shots were fired. The Iroquois dispatched two of the captured La Montagne women with wampum belts inviting leaders from Kahnawake and La Montagne to Iroquoia. Before the Laurentian headmen could answer, a skirmish broke out between the Iroquois warriors and a party of French troops coming to the "assistance" of La Montagne. The brief battle claimed the lives of seven Iroquois "attackers" and two or three La Montagne warriors.[92]

The French organized several pursuit parties immediately after this engagement. One detachment led by Vaudreuil and accompanied by Ourehouare (the sole Iroquois member of the party and then reportedly receiving "the pay of a [French] Captain") surrounded forty Oneidas in an abandoned house on the north shore of the St. Lawrence River near Repentigny. Ignoring the Oneidas' cries of "*Osquenon,* by which they asked for peace," Vaudreuil's party surrounded the house, firing into the doors and windows until those inside shouted "*Sadreyo,* by which they surrendered." All but six of the Oneidas died in the firefight. Mimicking Iroquois practices of prisoner distribution, the French gave one of the five captured Oneidas to a Kahnawake family, retained another to give to the Odawas at a later date, and delivered at least three more "into the hands of [French] farmers who [had] lost their relatives" in earlier Iroquois attacks. French settlers tortured and burned alive three of the Oneida captives. Another pursuit party, composed mostly of Kahnawake warriors, chased an eighty-man Mohawk or Oneida army all the way to the "Long Sault" of the St. Lawrence River. From that point, however, the Kahnawake warriors permitted their retreating Iroquois kin to "pass unharmed," citing the recent Mohawk-initiated peace negotiations as the reason for calling off the pursuit.[93]

The Iroquois initiatives of spring 1691 convinced Intendant Champigny to propose a tacit acknowledgment of Iroquois solidarity by employing Laurentian warriors exclusively on campaigns against New England and encouraging only allied warriors from the upper Great Lakes to undertake offensives into Iroquoia. Despite heartening reports of successful Wendat, Odawa, Illinois, and Miami offensives over the winter of 1690–91 against Iroquois towns as well as their "fishing and hunting grounds" over the winter of 1690–91, Frontenac was by then convinced that upper Great Lakes raiding parties could no longer be relied upon as an exclusive means of bringing the Iroquois to terms. In a departure from his reported efforts the previous year to feed, clothe, and liberate "Enemy" Iroquois prisoners, Frontenac established a bounty of "*dix écus*" (thirty-three livres) for Iroquois scalps in June 1691. He hoped that the financial incentive would bolster Laurentian support for New France and disrupt their recent peace talks with the Mohawk warriors.[94]

In the meantime, Onnonouagaren's Mohawk party headed directly for Albany to confer with League headmen and Henry Sloughter, New York's new royal governor. Sloughter opened formal proceedings with more than thirty League headmen on July 11, 1691. Reminding the Iroquois to attend to their "fidelity and duty as good subjects to the Crowne of England," Sloughter repeated Dongan's demand that they make no separate treaty with the French and then distributed the Crown's "presents." The next day an unidentified speaker representing the Oneidas, Onondagas, Cayugas, and Senecas related the *kaswentha* tradition to Sloughter, in an attempt to educate another newly arrived European official about the significance they attached to the "Tree of peace and tranquility" planted in "former times" at Albany. Acknowledging that this "Tree hath shaked and quaked much of late" (a reference to the recent political "troubles" in the colony), the League speaker expressed hope that it would revert to its intended "immoveable" condition. For that to happen, Sloughter would need to ensure cheaper prices for ammunition and other supplies in Albany. He would also have to send blacksmiths to Onondaga and support the Iroquois war against New France. Significantly, the League speaker stated the resolve of all League nations but the Mohawks to suspend hostilities with the nations of the upper Great Lakes.[95]

On June 14, Onnonouagaren reached Albany and informed League representatives (in Sloughter's presence) of his preliminary negotiations with Laurentian Iroquois leaders. Then, after repatriating one of the Schenectady captives in their custody, the Mohawk warriors offered to parlay these negotiations into a broader, Iroquois-brokered peace between Frontenac and their new brother "Corlaer" (Sloughter). Unfortunately for the Mohawks, the other "Four Nations" rejected the proposal for peace with New France, in light of fresh reports of a pending French invasion of Onondaga country. Oneida headman Ohede, emphasizing his disregard for the Mohawk effort, dropped the latter's wampum belts unceremoniously "upon the ground" in the yard of the Albany courthouse. Sloughter also rejected the proposal, arguing that the Schenectady invasion had revealed the Laurentian Iroquois "as much Enemies to the Brethren as the French." He asked for, and received, a promise of League assistance for another collaborative attack on La Prairie to preempt the rumored invasion of Iroquoia.[96]

Plans for the summer 1691 Anglo-Iroquois offensive repeated the pincer movement attempted in 1690. Three hundred Mohawks and Mahicans and 130 New York provincials under Peter Schuyler would head up the Lake Champlain–Richelieu River corridor and rendezvous with a separate body of 500 warriors from the four upper League nations for an attack on Montreal. As Schuyler undertook late June preparations in Albany, however, Laurentian warriors commenced raids throughout Iroquoia. Ourehouare, with Oneida blood already on his hands, led a party of fifteen La Montagne and Lorette Wendat warriors on a raid into Onondaga country that netted two Onondaga prisoners and three scalps, suggesting that Frontenac's promised bounty may have influenced some Laurentians' behavior. The Laurentian attacks, which also targeted Anglo-American settlers north of Albany, threatened to force widespread abandonment of New York farms prior to the harvest, adding a greater sense of urgency to Schuyler's expedition.[97]

Schuyler departed Albany on July 1, 1691, and two weeks later reported that only fifteen Mohawk warriors and sixty Mahicans had arrived in his camp at Wood Creek. Worried Albany authorities sent Dirck Wessells to Mohawk country, where he reported the two easternmost towns ready to provide seventy-four warriors. The third "Castle," however, was then mourning the death of their "cheife Sachem," and its residents refused to release any warriors for the expedition. Upon learning this news, Robert Livingston vented his frustrations in a letter to Sloughter. "I wish to God we had such a force that we needed not to court such heathens for any assistance," he wrote, "for they are a broken reed to depend upon."[98]

One month to the day after leaving Albany, Schuyler received "a bundle of ninety-two sticks" from a Mohawk military leader on the shore of Lake Champlain near the mouth of the Richelieu River. The sticks indicated the number of Mohawk warriors from the two easternmost towns who had joined the expedition. Five "principal" Mohawk field leaders (including Laurence and Onnonouagaren, two of the Mohawk military leaders involved in the previous spring's negotiations at Kahnawake) were also named. While the participation of these two individuals might suggest a change of attitude on their part, the Mohawks' conduct on the campaign proved otherwise. Unbeknownst to Schuyler, one of the Mohawk warriors slipped away from the advancing expeditionary force to alert the Laurentian towns, confirming intelligence that the Laurentians had already obtained from their own recently taken Anglo-American prisoners.[99]

On August 10, 1691, a Mahican party from Schuyler's expeditionary force launched a preliminary attack on La Prairie, reportedly killing thirty-four French men and six members of an Odawa trade convoy encamped nearby. At dawn the next day, Schuyler and the Mohawks attacked the town, encountering stiff resistance from 420 French troops and militiamen. French observers described the ensuing battle as "the most obstinate" fought in Canada "since the foundation of the Colony." After fending off three sallies from the French fort, Schuyler and the Mohawks had to fight their way back to the Richelieu River through a "halfe moon" of 300 more French and forty allied Native warriors.[100]

Despite the scale and intensity of the engagement, advance Iroquois intelligence sharing and behavior in the field once again ensured that Europeans sustained the vast majority of casualties incurred in the attack on La Prairie. The French reported losses at La Prairie of approximately fifty soldiers and habitants. Schuyler's provincials suffered fewer than twenty men killed. The Mohawks lost seventeen men, including Onnonouagaren. The Laurentians suffered the death of one leader in the 1691 battle of La Prairie, but had detained the bulk of their warriors at Kahnawake so as to reduce the likelihood of killing members of their "own nation." One hour after the end of the battle, 120 Laurentian warriors mounted a sufficiently slow pursuit of the retreating Mohawks to enable all of the survivors to return safely to Albany ten days later. The promised 500-warrior Iroquois army never arrived from the west to assist the Albany-based offensive. Many of these warriors had gone in the opposite direction to the Illinois country, while others scattered throughout the St. Lawrence valley to mount independent attacks on French settlements during the autumn of 1691.[101]

The battle of La Prairie once again demonstrated the willingness of the Iroquois to act as allies to both New France and New York while limiting dramatically the potential for losses of Iroquois lives. Neither the French nor the English were satisfied with Iroquois conduct, however. Frontenac, in an effort to improve French surveillance of the Laurentians, attempted (unsuccessfully) in September 1691 to relocate the entire community of Kahnawake within Montreal's palisade. Albany authorities, having just witnessed another example of Iroquois behavior that exposed the fallacy of their claimed status as English "subjects," castigated an Iroquois delegation visiting Albany in mid-September 1691 for the League's failure to send the promised army of 500 warriors down the St. Lawrence to Montreal. The New Yorkers expressed their hope that in the future their Iroquois "Brethren" would "take better care in matters of so great consequence." Despite their public indictment of Iroquois conduct, Albany officials privately begged for Crown funding for a Protestant missionary for the easternmost Mohawk town of Tionnonderoge, arguing that such a gesture would effectively counter the long-standing efforts of the French to "draw away many of our Indians into Canada." By September 1691, New York authorities opined that these movements had "so weakened the Maquase nation that they are not capable to do Your Majesty the service as formerly."[102]

FRATRICIDE AVERTED

The Mohawks and other League nations had indeed been weakened by the autumn of 1691, although not, as Anglo-American contemporaries believed, by the mere fact of population movement to the St. Lawrence River valley. Rather, their weakness was a consequence of increasing breakdowns in the relationships that sustained ties of common Iroquois identity over geographical distance. Unprecedented levels of European-sponsored violence, demographic losses to the 1690 smallpox epidemic, and the recent failure of the Mohawk warriors' peace initiative resulted in a very fragile atmosphere for intercommunity relations within Iroquoia at that time. In this charged context, minor, family-level disputes found new outlets for expression, and the League nations approached the brink of fratricidal warfare for several months in 1691 and 1692 until they found the means and motivation to avoid a descent into mutual destruction.

While few among the English and the French appreciated the determination of the Iroquois people to use mobility to advance their own interests, increasing numbers of colonial observers began to recognize how Iroquois freedom of movement posed a threat to European objectives in North America during King William's War. In the aftermath of the August 1691 battle of La Prairie, Intendant Champigny reflected on the French military situation vis-à-vis the Iroquois League. While Frenchmen struggled to travel through the "Rapids and other inaccessible places" required to reach Iroquoia, the intendant noted that such obstacles offered "no impediment" to Iroquois warriors traveling overland with speed and efficiency that European troops could not match. Champigny acknowledged that official French presents distributed at interior posts (the French established Fort St. Joseph II for this express purpose in 1691) might prevent the upper Great Lakes nations from allying with the League to destroy New France, but that practice did not represent a long-term solution to the colony's Iroquois problem. Since the French were unlikely to achieve the "utter annihilation" of the colony's most dangerous indigenous foes, the intendant advocated a comprehensive peace with the Five Nations.[103]

Although Champigny assumed that Anglo-American officers could direct Iroquois military actions, New York's commander in chief Richard Ingoldsby (who served as New York's de facto executive officer after the August 2, 1691, death of Henry Sloughter) worried in May 1692 about the degree to which the Iroquois had become "debauched" and "indifferent" in the aftermath of New York's late political upheavals. Precarious relations with the League had forced New York authorities to shoulder "an expense of great presents" (reporting outlays of £700 in 1691 and another £500 in June 1692) to supplement those sent by the Crown. Yet despite this largesse, and despite the degree to which Iroquois warriors relied on Albany traders for "Guns, powder, lead, duffels, and other Indian Merchandize from Europe," the League's affiliation was by no means assured. Ingoldsby noted especially the threat posed by Iroquois mastery over an extent of territory spanning from Albany to Virginia. If permitted to become enemies, the Iroquois could threaten the lives and livelihoods of English settlers throughout much of Anglo-America. Similar apprehensions occupied the minds of New York Council members, who remarked in June 1692 that French Jesuits had "seduced" more than "400 of our best Indians, now call'd the praying Indians of Canada." Worse still, the Laurentian Iroquois had recently "killed several of our Mohawks their own Brethren."[104]

The New York councillors were referring to the December 1691 deaths of two prominent Mohawk military leaders, Gaxari and Garistatsi, the latter of whom, also known to the French as "Le Fer" (The Iron), had informed the Senecas of Denonville's advance four years previously. French accounts reported these two Mohawks leading thirty others in an attack on seventeen Laurentian men and women near Kahnawake (nine of whom were killed). A pursuit party sent from Kahnawake caught up with the Mohawks, killed fifteen, and then captured and reportedly "slaughtered" the two above-named Mohawk captains.[105]

English reports of the incident, obtained from Mohawk survivors, differed substantially from French accounts. According to the Mohawks, Garistatsi, the "chief Sacham" of Tionnonderoge, was escorting four French boys and "an Indian Squae" captured near La Prairie down the Richelieu River when he encountered twenty-nine Mohawks and Oneidas, among whom were his son and his brother Gaxari. After Gaxari stated his desire to avenge "blood shed by the French" in the August 1691 attack on La Prairie, Garistatsi, following "men's clan" obligations, joined the Mohawk-Oneida party. En route to Montreal, the aggressors encountered thirteen Laurentians hunting near Chambly with two "Christian boys that were taken at Schenectady." The last detail is crucial for understanding the hostile encounter, which may have resulted from Mohawks or Oneidas with ties to Schenectady families attempting to repatriate these individuals. In the ensuing engagement, warriors with Garistatsi and Gaxari killed four Laurentian men, captured six men and ten women, and liberated the two Schenectady captives. But five days later, a much larger force composed of "all sorts French North Indians and Praying Indians" pursued, surrounded, and killed all the Mohawk and Oneida attackers, save for four Mohawks who escaped to report the story. Among the dead were "all the principall Captains" of the Mohawks and Oneidas, bringing total manpower losses in these two nations to ninety men during the two previous years and reportedly leaving them "quite out of heart."[106]

Iroquois efforts to limit internecine violence had proven remarkably successful ever since the La Barre campaign of 1684. Yet the December 1691 incident revealed the extent to which escalating Anglo-French hostilities on the periphery of Iroquoia had strained this ethic of mutual nonaggression. For the next eleven months Iroquois people killed and captured one another with an intensity that was both unprecedented in the postcontact era and never since replicated. Jesuits claimed that cannon mounted on the palisade of Kahnawakon burst over the winter of 1691-1692 from overuse in efforts to repel Iroquois attackers. Despite the undeniable suffering experienced by Iroquois people during this painful moment in their history, the events still represent something other than unrestrained fratricidal conflict within the League. Though precise figures are elusive given the nature of the sources, the trend of increasing internecine conflict is unmistakable. At least eight instances of inter-Iroquois violence occurred between December 1691 and November 1692. During this time, Laurentian Iroquois were involved in the killing of up to sixty-six people from other Iroquois communities and the capture of an additional forty-six. Non-Laurentian Iroquois people killed twelve Laurentians and captured sixteen others.[107]

The figures alone, though startling, do not tell the whole tale. Large-scale incidents of Iroquois-on-Iroquois violence such as the one described above were few, and originated most commonly when Laurentian warriors with French reconnaissance and pursuit parties encountered Iroquois people in the field. Frontenac had posted a detachment of 200 men in Kahnawake's "Indian fort" for these purposes early in 1692. A February 1692 allied French and Laurentian attack on fifty Iroquois fishing at

Toniata Island in the St. Lawrence River left twenty-nine Iroquois people dead. Five months later, a French and Laurentian force dispersed a large Iroquois party from a field fort on the Ottawa River, incurring further Iroquois casualties.[108]

Analysis of the evidence, however, reveals that much of the violence in Iroquoia during 1691 and 1692 remained at the level of family disputes, as had been the case in previous decades. Four Laurentian Iroquois people are known to have been captured, publicly tortured, and executed by "the hands of their own kindred" (specifically their Mohawk and Onondaga relatives), between 1690 and 1693. Similarly, one prominent Iroquois woman captive was executed by her relatives at Kahnawake in 1692. These incidents, though dramatic, ultimately reflected family- and clan-level conflicts related to the post-1688 efforts by individual Iroquois families to retrieve adoptees and relatives in the Laurentian towns. Evidence of Frontenac revising his bounty policy in November 1692 (offering payments of thirty-three livres per Iroquois scalp or prisoner, but doubling the reward for each Iroquois prisoner surrendered to French authorities) suggests that the Laurentians had to date employed the bounties primarily as funding for personnel recruiting rather than a license to undertake indiscriminate killings of Iroquois people on behalf of New France.[109]

Despite an atmosphere of turmoil, arguments for peace with New France began to surface in Iroquoia as early as March 1692. According to Ourehouare, who retained connections to Onondaga notwithstanding his own role in provoking intra-Iroquois hostilities, Otreouti's "family" was interested in opening negotiations with Frontenac, but Teganissorens's kin were not, and the latter, reportedly "much superior" in either their arguments or their numbers, continued to prevail in national Onondaga councils.[110]

Iroquois opponents of peace with New France received a boost on June 16, 1692, when League headmen met with Ingoldsby in Albany. After communicating New York's formal condolence for Iroquois warriors killed since December 1691 with a "present of 1000 or 1200 gilders in white strung wampum," the commander in chief delivered an "Animating Speech upon carrying on the war against the French." Fresh reports of the Tionnontaté Wendats' desire to "keep Neuter [neutral] in the Present war" from a repatriated Seneca prisoner further encouraged Ingoldsby, and he urged League headmen to seek rapprochement with the upper Great Lakes nations as a means of weakening the French.[111]

Despite Ingoldsby's innovative distribution of private gifts for Iroquois leaders at the Albany conference, he did not sway League headmen from advancing collective League interests. Oneida headman Ohede noted the discrepancy between Ingoldsby's effort to encourage the Iroquois to fight New France and the short supplies and high prices of military stores in Albany. Presents of powder and lead were appreciated, but Oheda pointed out that in lieu of guns, they could not "kill the Enemy by throwing [bullets] at them with our hands." Rode, the "Cheife Sachem of the Maquaes," wondered aloud about the failure of other Anglo-American partners in the Covenant

Chain alliance to provide a "helping hand" in the war. The Iroquois had kept warriors in the field despite recent personnel losses. How could the other Anglo-American colonies "and we be subjects to our great King and Queen," asked Rode, "and not [be] engaged in the same war"?[112]

Rode's question assumed pressing significance for the remainder of the 1692 campaign. French minister Louis Phélypeaux de Pontchartrain rejected Champigny's proposal for a separate peace with the Iroquois and ordered Frontenac instead to undertake an expedition against Albany and Mohawk country. Officials at Michili-mackinac claimed to have fitted out over 800 upper Great Lakes warriors for attacks on the Iroquois during the spring and summer of 1692, and reported nearly fifty Iroquois scalps redeemed by those parties. Yet to the east, the impact of mounting casualties from Iroquois-on-Iroquois conflicts had begun to sink in by the end of the summer of 1692. French officials found the Laurentian communities disinclined to participate in a direct French invasion of Iroquoia.[113]

Efforts to resolve the crisis of internecine violence were also under way among the Five Nations. Upon learning that a force of 350 Iroquois warriors were encamped at Schenectady en route to Canada on August 22, 1692, Peter Schuyler hustled up-river from Albany to deliver an encouraging speech and supplies of ammunition and food. Significantly, no provincial troops accompanied this Iroquois-planned expedition. Mohawk headman Rode advised Schuyler of the army's intent to "put the Praying Indians [Laurentians] out of a Capacety of ever doing you or us any more harm." Schuyler soon realized, however, that his assumptions about the means the Iroquois planned to employ to achieve that end were incorrect. The Iroquois leaders had no plans for a direct assault on the Laurentian towns. Rather, the assembled army would escort an adopted Mohawk "Captain" to the outskirts of Kahnawake. The adoptee would then enter "the Plantacion of his father as he calls the Indian that was [formerly] his master," and deliver League wampum belts in order to open peace negotiations.[114]

Reports of the advancing Iroquois army reached the Laurentian communities in September 1692 via a woman from La Montagne who had recently escaped (or had been released from) two years' captivity in Mohawk country. This woman corrobo-rated Rode's description of the Iroquois army's plan to camp near Kahnawake and "draw out the greatest number of the Indians possible under plea of negotiation." She claimed, however, that this represented a ruse, and that the Iroquois planned either to capture any Laurentians who came out to parley or to "knock them on the head." Whether or not this woman's report was true, it alarmed Laurentian lead-ers and effectively thwarted Iroquois plans. Montreal governor Callières sent up a number of French troops to reinforce the garrison already present at Kahnawake. The appearance of the Iroquois party on Lake St. Louis at midday (the precise date is not reported in French accounts) would have signaled their peaceful intent to the Laurentians, but the French troops at Kahnawake had no interest in permitting such negotiations. They drove off the would-be Iroquois diplomats with "several volleys" of musket fire.[115]

The Iroquois army, estimated by French observers at 500 to 800 men, retreated and scattered in small parties throughout the St. Lawrence valley to attack French settlers. Youthful members of one French family managed a famous defense against the Iroquois at the Verchères seigneury in October 1692, but many other Canadian settlers were not so fortunate. The French, who had enjoyed significant Laurentian assistance against Iroquois attackers for much of the previous year, now had to face these aggressors almost completely on their own. Only a handful of Laurentians participated in pursuit parties against their kinfolk in September and October 1692.[116]

Now it was French authorities' turn to fret about the lukewarm loyalty of their Iroquois allies. Writing in November 1692, Intendant Champigny explained recent Laurentian behavior as a reflection of war weariness. He argued for the need to divert a significant proportion of the annual French presents sent to the *pays d'en haut* nations to the Iroquois and Algonquian settlements in the St. Lawrence valley. Doing so would, in his opinion, demonstrate commensurate levels of French regard for the Laurentians' contribution to the war effort and provide charitable support to families who had lost warriors. Exaggerating for dramatic effect, Champigny claimed that the Laurentian Iroquois in particular had lost "nearly half" of their fighting men in campaigns against the English and the "Iroquois, their relatives," since 1684. Champigny echoed the rhetoric of his rivals in New York by casting the Anglo-French contest for Iroquois allegiances as a zero-sum game. If recent "caresses, presents, and threats" from the Iroquois encouraged the Laurentians to return to their "Compatriots," the intendant warned that the days of the French in North America were numbered.[117]

Frontenac agreed that the Iroquois could not be permitted to build on their autumn 1692 effort to persuade the Laurentians to withhold military assistance from the French. In November 1692, he began preparations for an expedition into Mohawk country in consultation with Iroquois leaders he identified as the "oldest and best heads" of Kahnawake and La Montagne. Though the Mohawks were not the most populous of the Five Nations, French officials believed that an invasion of Mohawk country would bring an end to the "frequent negotiations, secret communications, [and exchanges of] messages" between that nation and their "brethren and relatives" in the Laurentian communities. On January 20, 1693, 350 French troops marched out of Montreal, accompanied by 200 Native allies (at least 60 to 80 of whom were Lorette Wendats and Odanak Abenakis). Once again, the Laurentians had chosen to participate in a French military campaign. Once again, these warriors would place Iroquois interests ahead of those of their European allies and sponsors.[118]

The snowshoe-clad invasion force arrived at the easternmost "little Mohawk fort" of Caughnawaga on February 16, 1693, only to find it abandoned by all but five men and several women and children. Detaching a party to the nearby, larger "second fort" (Gandagaro), the French found "still fewer people" there. After burning

Caughnawaga and posting a guard detail at Gandagaro to secure their few Mohawk captives (none of whom were killed), the French departed for the westernmost, "principal" Mohawk settlement of Tionnonderoge, located over twenty miles up the Mohawk River. On February 18, the French and their Native allies forced open Tionnonderoge's gate and carried the town, losing only one French soldier in the assault. Some thirty Tionnonderoge men and women lost their lives in the attack, but the majority of the town's residents survived. After the French burned Tionnonderoge two days later, they retreated to Gandagaro with over 300 Mohawk prisoners (men, women, and children).[119]

French historian Claude Charles Le Roy de la Potherie recalled the invasion of Mohawk country as "a great victory in which the allies of Kahnawake had executed their promises." But French officers on the expedition reported their experience differently, singling out the "obstinacy" and "caprice" of the Laurentians as the primary reasons why "this expedition was not accompanied by all the success that was anticipated." The Laurentian Iroquois had refused to harm any of the Mohawk prisoners. They also refused, despite two days of arguments, to launch a follow-up attack on Albany. Worse, from the French viewpoint, on the night of February 16 the Laurentians liberated "two young Dutchmen" taken at Schenectady (Arnout Viele and Jan Baptist Van Eps), and this intelligence leak forced the French to factor into their planning the prospect of English involvement in a potential Mohawk pursuit. Two days of negotiations passed at Gandagaro before the increasingly desperate French officers finally managed to get their retreat moving by offering a public invitation to captive Mohawk senior leaders to relocate their people to the Laurentian settlements, and even promising land for a new town.[120]

On February 22, 1693, the French burned Gandagaro and departed with 150 Mohawk prisoners. Word of the invasion had reached Albany on February 18, and within five days reports of a large Mohawk pursuit party led the retreating Laurentians to insist on the construction of a defensive field fort. When the Mohawks caught up to the French on February 27, the majority of the French-allied Native warriors "remained in the fort, doing nothing," forcing the French to drive off the Mohawk attackers alone. After decamping the next morning in "extreme bad cold snowy weather," the French and Laurentians released several Mohawk prisoners, who advised pursuing kinfolk of the presence of their "wives and children" with the Laurentians. Upon learning this news, Peter Schuyler (who accompanied the pursuit party) reported that the Mohawks could "not be perswaded to march." On March 2, the retreating Laurentians parted company with the French at Lake George, citing their desire to hunt. Since the Laurentians "alone were masters of the [Mohawk] prisoners whom they did not guard very strictly," reported one French observer, "many of [the latter] escaped." Vachon de Belmont claimed that at least 100 Mohawk prisoners liberated themselves from French captivity on the return journey. Although the Laurentians collected a significant number of bounty payments for Mohawks captured in 1693, subsequent reports indicated that no more than five Mohawk men and a handful of women and children ended up as prisoners in the Laurentian settlements. Two weeks after being abandoned by their Laurentian allies, exhausted, starving French soldiers straggled into Montreal, cursing what they viewed as the "false pity of the [allied Laurentian] Indians for their prisoners." As many as 80 French soldiers were reported to have perished during the expedition.[121]

Frontenac's hopes of realizing a significant political victory with the invasion of Mohawk country were not realized. French observers noted further decline in the reported efficacy of allied military service on the part of the Laurentian Iroquois during the spring of 1693. Officials at Versailles, reviewing Frontenac's 1693 reports and expenditures, flagged the Laurentians' manipulation of the governor's bounty-payment plan in the aftermath of the invasion of Mohawk country as evidence that the expedition had not only been useless but "damaging" to French interests and resources.[122]

The 1693 French invasion of Mohawk country provided another example of the ability of Laurentian Iroquois people to limit dramatically the potential military impact of European offensives. Their actions during the French expedition also made a crucial contribution to ending the cycle of inter-Iroquois violence that had arisen after December 1691. Iroquois observers recognized the life-saving actions of their Laurentian kinfolk in Mohawk country, and this manifestation of League solidarity promoted a spirit of rapprochement and rededication to the pursuit of mutual interests among all League communities after 1693.

REBUILDING CONNECTIONS

The evident concern of the Laurentian Iroquois for the lives of their kinfolk in the Mohawk valley in 1693 stood in stark contrast to the empty bluster offered by the League's nearest Anglo-American ally, New York governor Benjamin Fletcher (who had arrived in September 1692). Upon learning of the French invasion of Mohawk country, Fletcher had traveled to Albany to provide men and matériel to support the Mohawks. Though he later claimed in a self-congratulatory published pamphlet to have marched 300 men as far as Schenectady in pursuit of the French, subsequent eyewitness testimony stated that Fletcher had in fact taken only 18 men, and had marched only after he had definite intelligence of the French retreat. Iroquois observers soon recognized that Fletcher, like his predecessors, was more worried about the potential impact of the invasion on English claims to suzerainty over the Iroquois than protecting League communities.[123]

In a conference with League headmen at Albany on March 7, 1693, Fletcher blasted the Mohawks for their "supine and careless" behavior in suffering the "French and their Indians to enter their Castles without the least resistance." In his reply,

Onondaga headman Aqueendara reminded Fletcher of the League nations' need, as "all one heart, one blood, [and] one soul," to condole the deaths of those Mohawks killed and then consider their options. Aqueendara also conferred the name "Cajenquiragoe" on the governor, which meant "Lord of the Great Swift Arrow," which Fletcher reputedly earned because of his "speedy arrival" from New York. In fact, as one later critic of Fletcher recalled, the name was a "sarcasticall pun" employed by the "very discerning" Iroquois leaders as a "droll upon the man and his vainglory."[124]

The Mohawks, far from being left "scatter-brained" (as Frontenac claimed) or "mostly destroyed" by the French invasion (as Fletcher claimed), had regrouped, conducting retaliatory raids on French settlements during the month of June 1693, and by mid-August they had rebuilt their towns. In doing so, they followed the example of their parents and grandparents, who had bounced back from Tracy's 1666 expedition, as well as the recent example of the Senecas, who had resettled in two towns in the aftermath of the 1687 Denonville expedition. While a few Mohawks relocated to the Laurentian communities in the months immediately following the 1693 French expedition, most used the opportunity to reorganize their Mohawk River valley settlements. The Turtle clan residents of Caughnawaga and the Bear clan residents of Gandagaro moved upriver from their preinvasion locations and formed the new Mohawk "upper castle" at Canajoharie. Residents of the westernmost (circa 1689–93) Wolf clan town of Tionnondoroge relocated to an eastern site overlooking Schoharie Creek, a decision partially influenced by Wolf clan "Protestants" who sought access to clergymen in Schenectady.[125]

While the Mohawks rebuilt and reoriented their towns, warriors from the other League nations journeyed to the Ottawa River valley above Montreal in May 1693 to await French and Native fur convoys from the *pays d'en haut*. In keeping with recent efforts to balance aggressive actions and peace overtures, an Oneida embassy headed by Tareha, a member of Millet's adoptive Bear clan family, approached Montreal in late June 1693. To ensure secure travel and to signify their sincerity, the Oneidas brought back fourteen French prisoners (one of whom, former Seneca captive Louis-Thomas Chabert de Joncaire, would later become a prominent broker of Franco-Iroquois diplomacy) and a packet of letters from Millet. In an audience with Frontenac, Tareha claimed that "the most influential cabins of the Oneidas" sought peace with New France, and he offered his mediation services to Frontenac. Frontenac agreed to a future discussion of terms, but only if the League sent a representative delegation to New France consisting of "two of the principal and most influential Chiefs of each Nation," one of whom was to be Teganissorens, "his oldest acquaintance." Departing with presents from Frontenac and also his nephew (who had been captured by the French in 1691 and held to date at one of the Laurentian settlements), Tareha promised to return with a fully constituted embassy by mid-September 1693.[126]

Rumors of Tareha's initiative and a pending League meeting to discuss peace with New France soon reached the ears of Albany authorities. They attributed these developments to Millet's "Secret Intrigues," but noted also the virtually nonexistent Iroquois trade at Albany and the recent failure of already deeply indebted provincial authorities to issue the "usual Supplies and presents" to the League nations. The decision of authorities in Springfield, Massachusetts, to incarcerate a Mohawk and a Schaghticoke in June 1693 on suspicion of their role in the murder of several settlers near Deerfield also threatened Anglo-Mohawk relations. Anxious Albany officials urged John Pynchon to exonerate and release the prisoners, even going so far as to have a recent escapee from Laurentian Iroquois captivity swear out an affidavit that attributed the "marks and figures" on war clubs left at the scene to anonymous "French Indians."[127]

These developments prompted Fletcher's return to Albany in July 1693, where he opened formal proceedings on July 13 by warning the League nations not to repeat the "Supine watchless humour" demonstrated by the Mohawks five months previously. He then condoled the Mohawks' losses, renewed the Covenant Chain, and distributed Crown presents (including some set aside for individual headmen). The unidentified League spokesman returned formal thanks the next day, but expressed disappointment in the lack of concrete English plans for an invasion of Canada. Fletcher then shifted to a series of private conferences with small groups of League leaders, whom he pressed to surrender Millet. Though League headmen deferred the question of the Jesuit's release, they reported a crucial, consensual decision "by all the five Nations" to reopen peace negotiations with the Tionnontaté Wendats via a Seneca embassy then en route to the *pays d'en haut* bearing "presents of Wampum from the rest of the Nations to confirm the Peace."[128]

The announcement of the Seneca embassy revealed the ability and willingness of League leaders to resuscitate dormant negotiations with the nations of the *pays d'en haut* at a time when the latter were still launching small-scale attacks on Iroquois towns and occasionally torturing Iroquois prisoners to death at French interior posts. The Iroquois had undertaken advance groundwork for the 1693 Seneca embassy by repatriating the son of an Ojibwa leader from captivity in Iroquoia during the winter of 1692–93. This ex-Iroquois captive circulated League wampum belts "under-ground" as far as the Sauk and Fox communities at modern-day Green Bay, Wisconsin. The message in these belts recalled the preliminary peace concluded with La Petite Racine in 1690, condoled the *pays d'en haut* nations for their losses to Iroquois war parties, and "hung up a sun at the strait between Lake Herier [Erie] and Huron" (modern-day Detroit) to "mark the boundaries between the two peoples" and to shed "light on their hunting." The Iroquois amplified the message of peaceful, shared hunting by sending a bowl with their belts, "so that they [all] might have but one dish from which to eat and drink." The Iroquois also invited the northern *pays d'en haut* nations to join in their planned attacks on the Miamis, Illinois, and other nations in southern areas of the Great Lakes region and to eat "the white meat, meaning the flesh of the French," who subsidized Native attacks on Iroquoia.[129]

While the Seneca delegation made their way to the Wendat community at Michilimackinac, they may have crossed paths with Odawa diplomats carrying wampum
"collars, redstone calumets, and bales of beaver-skins" to Iroquoia. These intensifying
indigenous negotiations led the Iroquois to call off a rumored large-scale attack on
New France during the summer of 1693 (though isolated raiding continued), thereby
permitting the safe arrival of the upper Great Lakes trade convoy at Montreal. By August 17, more than 200 canoes carrying 700 Wendats, Odawas, French trappers, and
a "prodigious heap of beaver" (estimated at 800,000 livres' value) from the *pays d'en
haut* arrived in New France. Not a word of these nations' independent negotiations
with the Iroquois reached French ears during the ensuing trade fair's festivities and
diplomacy. In the meantime, League authorities journeyed to Onondaga to discuss
the prospect of Tareha's return to Montreal.[130]

Once New York authorities learned of the Oneida-initiated negotiations with
Frontenac, they pulled out all the stops to try and influence League headmen meeting at Onondaga to oppose the Oneidas' initiative. In late August 1693, an embassy
consisting of Dirck Wessells, Robert Sanders, and the interpreter Hilletie van Olinda
traveled to Onondaga to deliver Fletcher's "orders" for the League to abandon talks
with New France. Aqueendara, the Onondagas' "chief Sachim," criticized Fletcher's
egregious presumption to issue orders to the Iroquois League and promptly barred
the Albany emissaries from attending the council. Eighty League headmen assembled
on August 28, 1693, to discuss Fronentac's proposals, which had likely been woven
into wampum belts by their kinswomen at Kahnawake.[131]

League leaders resolved to send Tareha back to New France in October 1693
to inform Frontenac that New York representatives would have to be included in
any Franco-Iroquois peace. Tareha also invited Frontenac to send "two Frenchmen
capable [of] regulating affairs" to Albany, the site of the League's "Tree of Peace and
War," to expedite these negotiations. Frontenac, who believed (on the basis of intelligence from a French prisoner who had escaped from a year's captivity in Onondaga
country in July 1693) that Tareha lacked significant support, initially refused to accept
Tareha's belt. Yet after consultation with Jesuits anxious to secure Millet's return,
Frontenac, while refusing to treat at Albany, repeated his earlier invitation to negotiate peace with a representative League delegation at Quebec. He also promised to
exempt the Oneidas from future French military expeditions into Iroquoia and sent
Tareha off once more with "considerable presents."[132]

By the end of 1693, the League had established the outlines of the spatial
relationships that they would pursue with Native and non-Native nations on the
periphery of Iroquoia for the next eight years. Independent negotiations with the
peoples of the *pays d'en haut* promised an end to military stalemate beyond the
League's western door, secure access to still-bountiful hunting grounds for League
nations, and an opportunity for the Iroquois to broker the trade of the upper Great
Lakes nations in Albany. Tareha's embassy to Quebec laid the groundwork for a

comprehensive, Iroquois-brokered Anglo-French peace on the League's eastern door. The uncertainty voiced by the Mohawks of Canajoharie in their January 1694 conversation with Schuyler led Governor Fletcher to conclude that the Five Nations could "not long continue neutral," and would soon align with New France. In reality, the complex constellation of Iroquois spatial initiatives that European observers would later define as neutrality was moving closer to realization in 1693 than at any previous time in the precolonial era.[133]

6.

Over the Forest, Part 2
1694–1701

> You think these of the Cannossoene [*kanonsionni*] to be the Eldest
> in the Country and the greatest in possession. O noe. Yea all the
> Asseroenis [English of New York] doe think the same, Cayenquira-
> goe [New York governor Benjamin Fletcher] also. . . . Noe, o, noe,
> wee Onqwes are the first and we are the eldest and the greatest.
> These parts and countries were Inhabited and trede upon by the
> Onqwes before there was any Asseroenie.
>
> —Onondaga headman Aqueendara, addressing Frontenac
> in a speech at Onondaga, February 15, 1695

On July 28, 1701, a group of Oneida, Onondaga, and Cayuga "ambassadors," accompanied by some other members of their nations "who had
come to trade their peltry," arrived in the Laurentian Iroquois town of
Kanatakwente (successor to Kahnawake) prior to their scheduled appearance at a
multinational peace treaty hosted by Governor Callières at Montreal. Escorted to
the longhouse of Laurentian Oneida headman Tatacouiceré, the visitors smoked tobacco offered by their hosts for "a good quarter of an hour" before a Kanatakwente
Mohawk speaker named Ontonnionk (aka "The Eagle") rose up and offered a formal
welcome to the ambassadors. Ontonnionk reminded his audience that the ambassadors had the advantage of traveling on a road originally "cleared" by their mutual
ancestors; the Iroquois delegation's use of it represented the maintenance of a long-
established route employed for the purpose of "speaking of Peace." Ontonnionk then
offered formal condolence presents of "three strings of wampum" to "unblock" the
ambassadors' throats, and they replied with "three cries" and with a reciprocal gift of
wampum strings. All sat down thereafter to a meal of kettle-cooked "*sagamité.*" The
next day the assembled Iroquois party traveled to Montreal, where they received a
formal salute from French cannons and commenced peace negotiations with more
than 1,000 other Native delegates from the upper Great Lakes region.[1]

The Edge of the Woods welcome enacted in Tatacouiceré's longhouse represented a crucial preliminary step to the well-documented 1701 Iroquois treaty with New France and Native nations throughout northeastern North America. Although the League's "Grand Settlement of 1701" has attracted substantial scholarly attention, historians have yet to fully grasp the relationship of these arrangements to prior patterns of Iroquois mobility. While the story of the League's jointly negotiated diplomatic neutrality between New France and the Anglo-American colonies is relatively familiar, the interindigenous conversations initiated long before 1701 and ratified by treaties that year at Montreal and Albany actually exerted much more influence on the course of events than hitherto recognized. The French and the English represented mere hosts in 1701, as we shall see, for the resolution of a much broader and more deeply rooted set of Iroquois initiatives that extended beyond their relations with the two competing colonial empires.

The history of Iroquois movements from 1694 to 1701 embodied themes prevalent in the final phase of the Condolence ceremony. During the conclusion of "Over the Forest," Iroquois ritualists recall the core principles of the Condolence ceremony and entreat their audience to remain conscious of the imperative of creating the League anew through the act of replacing its fallen leaders. In so doing, they define a means of confronting current and future challenges. The closing years of the seventeenth century, an era that the Seneca chief Red Jacket would later recall as one when "Indians were hired to fight Indians, and many of our people were destroyed," posed significant challenges to the social and spatial integrity of Iroquoia.[2] Iroquois leaders accomplished a far-ranging renewal of the League after 1694 through the resolution of complex negotiations with Native and non-Native neighbors that established Iroquoia as a crucial, central space through which Iroquois people moved freely to engage the challenges and opportunities posed by the presence of competing European settler and indigenous populations on the periphery of their extensive homelands.

REJUVENATION

Mohawk leaders' expressions of doubt in their early 1694 Edge of the Woods welcome to Albany visitors masked complex initiatives under way throughout Iroquoia that aimed at rejuvenating the League in the aftermath of the previous decade's conflicts. Rapprochement between Five Nations and Laurentian communities following a brief period of internecine bloodshed facilitated outreach by League nations to those of the *pays d'en haut*. The new possibilities raised by these indigenous connections allowed Iroquois leaders to articulate a comprehensive new agenda for peace in eastern North America by the autumn of 1694.

French reports from the *pays d'en haut* indicated that Iroquois diplomacy had made considerable inroads among the ostensibly French-allied, League-hating nations of the upper Great Lakes by the autumn of 1693. These peace overtures followed long-standing patterns of individual-, local-, or national-level initiatives aimed at consensus building and the establishment of lasting, reciprocal human relationships. Such ties could not be achieved overnight; they could only be created and maintained through careful attention to the long-standing processes and protocols of indigenous intergroup relations, then manifested in the increasingly enmeshed Iroquois and Algonquian ceremonies of condolence and the calumet. Although low-intensity conflict continued between Iroquois warriors and the Native nations of the *pays d'en haut*, Tionnontaté Wendats from Michilimackinac had carried "a calumet ornamented with plumes, and several collars" of wampum to Iroquoia at some time over the winter of 1693–94, reportedly to request a "full union" with the League.[3]

In the meantime, Iroquois leaders worked to maintain the dialogue with New France that Tareha had opened in 1693. Two Iroquois messengers came to Montreal in late March 1694 to advise French officials that a delegation of "Chiefs of the Five Nations" planned to visit New France and sought assurances of secure travel for their desired meeting with Frontenac. Callières identified the messengers as "Torskim, the nephew of the Big Mouth [Otreouti] and one of the principal chiefs of the Onondaga Council," and the "son of Garioye," a resident of Kahnawake.[4]

The identity of the messengers revealed three crucial pieces of information underlying the League's outreach to New France. First, hereditary patterns of leadership in Iroquois society extended to descendants of leaders of achieved status. Second, the political landscape of Onondaga had changed substantially in two years. Clearly, advocacy of peace with New France by Tareha and by Otreouti's "family" had produced sufficient consensus to make such an embassy possible. Third, League leaders had resolved the recent crisis of relations with the Laurentian communities and had now taken formal steps to secure their crucial brokerage assistance in making peace with Frontenac and the Native nations of the *pays d'en haut*. Half a century later Onondaga leaders would recall how the "Warr between the French and English" during the late 1680s and early 1690s had "Eat[en] up all their People that had too rashly engaged in it." The experience reminded them of circumstances surrounding the League's founding era, and after 1693 they would "be more careful before they destroy'd one another again."[5]

Ultimately, the reported League delegation (to whom Callières had promised safe passage to Quebec) traveled no farther than Kahnawake, where Torskim delivered speeches and three "belts from all the Iroquois Nations" to residents of the Laurentian towns. The first wampum belt reopened lines of communication between the Laurentian communities and Five Nations towns, as well as to Albany and Schenectady, a vital signal of diplomatic and economic stability in the aftermath of recent conflicts. Underscoring this invitation, Teganissorens had informed Albany officials in February 1694 that the so-called Praying Indians would have "a free pass" to travel between the Laurentian communities, Albany, and elsewhere in Iroquois country.

Torskim's second belt declared a suspension of hostilities with the French, and the third asked that Iroquois peace proposals be conveyed "even to the Kings of France and England," indicating the League's desire to arrange a comprehensive resolution of international affairs in eastern North America. The "Agoiandres Iroquois" (the League's clan matrons) had played a key role in the composition of Torskim's message. Tareha's initiative had now become the consensual approach of "the whole house, or all the Indians [of the League] together."[6]

The League's new consensus on a comprehensive peace revealed that the Iroquois were far from "the brink of total ruin" in 1694 as some contemporary observers believed. The traditional workings of the Iroquois polity were alive and well, not descending into dysfunction, as demonstrated by the rare behind-the-scenes glimpse of the origins of Torskim's embassy provided by documentary sources. Not surprisingly, evidence of a rejuvenated League proved extremely discomfiting to officials in both New York and New France. Frontenac, upon receiving news of the League's 1694 overtures to the Laurentian communities, angrily refused to consider any further peace talks with the League. Marveling at what he perceived as the contemptuous attitude of the Iroquois, whom he termed "the proudest nation throughout this New World," the governor promised to execute any Iroquois delegation rash enough to propose arranging peace between New France and the Anglo-American settler colonies.[7]

Albany authorities, informed of Torskim's embassy in February 1694, also responded negatively. They redoubled their efforts to prevent independent Iroquois travel to New France, arguing that such "truckl[ing] to the French" dishonored the memory of the League nations' deceased ancestors. Yet Teganissorens and other Iroquois leaders had their own sense of how best to honor their ancestors. Although Albany officials ultimately elicited from Teganissorens a promise to delay the League's planned visit to Frontenac, they could not shake their suspicion that "the Indians were playing a double and deceitful part."[8]

By April 1694, New York governor Benjamin Fletcher reported that Albany officials, suspicions notwithstanding, advocated yielding to the League's "humour of making peace with Canada," as long as that peace included assurances of New York's security. Yet Fletcher could not openly support an Iroquois-brokered security agreement between New York and New France, since such arrangements portended "fresh troubles" for frontier settlements of the New England colonies. The governor dismissed the Albany authorities' suggestion as mere war weariness, which he believed would disappear once the Anglo-American colonies resumed vigorous cooperative offensives against the hated French. Yet as Fletcher made his way to Albany to meet with League headmen in late April 1694, he had no idea of just how far the Iroquois had already carried their plans.[9]

During a two-day meeting with Fletcher in Albany (May 14–15, 1694), a delegation of League headmen recited the *kaswentha* tradition to Fletcher, reminding the governor of the kind reception that the Iroquois had provided at the time of the Europeans' first arrival on the periphery of their homelands. Citing the relative weakness of the Dutch at that time, the unidentified Iroquois speaker recalled how his ancestors had formed an alliance with the newcomers in order to "protect them from all Enemies whatosoever." The speaker then advised his stunned Anglo-American audience that the League's leadership had resolved to continue this long-standing policy of "protection" for their New York–based allies in the Covenant Chain by sending "Agents to Canada to negotiate a Peace." No longer content to wait for promised assistance in their war with New France from New York or "the Neighbouring Colonies who are in the Covenant Chain," the League would make peace with New France on Anglo-America's behalf.[10]

On May 23, 1694, Teganissorens and an embassy consisting of two headmen from each constituent nation of the League commenced formal peace negotiations with Frontenac at Quebec. Claiming to speak on behalf of not only the League but also their "Brethren" of New York, Teganissorens rehearsed the origins of Iroquois hostilities with La Barre and Denonville and stated the desire of the League and the Anglo-American colonies for a lasting peace with New France. Significantly, Teganissorens also reported that "all subjects of contention" between the residents of the two Laurentian communities and other League towns had been resolved, a statement lent additional weight by his own marriage to a Kahnawake woman and his repatriation of a La Montagne woman to her family. Echoing Kiotsaeton's rhetoric of 1645, Teganissorens noted that in order "to preserve the living," both the Iroquois and the French must "think no more of the dead" and cease "butcher[ing] each other." Teganissorens then employed a metaphorical "hoe" to break up the blood-encrusted and "polluted" soil at Fort Frontenac, thereby restoring the "path of peace" from New France to Onondaga. That gesture did not, however, amount to Iroquois permission for French reoccupation of the post. After concluding his address, Teganissorens repatriated two French prisoners (one of whom, the "Sieur de la Chauvignerie," had been captured with the Chevalier d'Aux in 1690 and who, like Joncaire, would go on to a career as an interpreter and agent in Franco-Iroquois diplomacy). A French officer who witnessed Teganissorens's speech described it as "enunciated with as perfect grace as is vouchsafed to an unpolished and uncivilized people."[11]

In his reply the following day, Frontenac agreed to a preliminary cessation of hostilities and offered Teganissorens eighty days to return with all French and French-allied Native prisoners in Iroquoia for comprehensive peace negotiations. Reciprocating the League's preliminary surrender of two prisoners, he repatriated four Iroquois captives taken by unspecified French-allied Native war parties. Though willing to conclude peace with the League on these terms, Frontenac, like his counterpart in New York, continued to reject outright the idea of Iroquois mediation of peace between New France and the Anglo-American colonies.[12]

Laurentian delegates responded even more favorably to Teganissorens's speech, and the Onondaga headman later seized an opportunity to communicate news of these preliminary terms of peace to an embassy of Tionnontaté Wendat and Odawa leaders who had come down to Quebec in early June 1694. Teganissorens and his party invited the Wendats and Odawas to participate in future Franco-League negotiations and then departed for their journey home.[13]

The spatial impact of the preliminary peace talks between the League and New France became apparent over the summer of 1694, when Iroquois nations resumed their military campaigns. Jesuits in the *pays d'en haut* reported resumed Iroquois offensives "in the direction of the Illinois and the Miamis." French and allied Laurentian war parties that had attacked the Albany frontier as recently as October 1693 now turned their attention toward New England. Settlers at Oyster River, New Hampshire, and Groton, Massachusetts, sustained heavy assaults during July and August 1694. Alarmed officials from Massachusetts, Connecticut, and East and West Jersey proceeded to Albany with Fletcher for a meeting with League headmen in late August 1694.[14]

The Reverend Benjamin Wadsworth, a Massachusetts minister who accompanied his colony's commissioners to the Albany treaty, described the opening of formal proceedings on August 25, 1694. Mohawk headman Rode marched at the head of twenty-five of his colleagues (including Teganissorens and Carachquinno, a Seneca "Queen"). The Iroquois delegation processed "two in rank" down Albany streets to the town "Meeting-house," singing "all the way songs of joy and peace."[15]

Onondaga speaker Aqueendara opened the conference with a relation of the *kaswentha* tradition that emphasized the sentient character of the League's metaphorical "Tree of Peace and Wellfare" long planted at Albany. To Iroquois minds, the "Tree of Peace" provided a "protective aura," or a "space of internal peace." All parties encompassed by its "Roots and Branches" were, in Aqueendara's view, to "feel and resent" any "breach" in its integrity. Reminding his audience of the agreement's mandate of mutual noninterference, Aqueendara made a crucial assertion of the League nations' right to freedom of movement, which in his view upheld their right to conduct independent foreign relations. Anglo-American authorities had no grounds for complaint when League headmen traveled to Canada to pursue their own political agenda.[16]

Teganissorens, reflecting the League's newly articulated consciousness of its role as the spatial center of international relations in eastern North America, then described how Iroquois leaders, in their conversations at Quebec during the previous May, had denied the French permission to reoccupy Fort Frontenac. Rather, they had merely arranged a cessation of hostilities and authorized French diplomatic embassies to pass by that place en route to Onondaga, where, with Fletcher's representatives, League leaders planned to broker a comprehensive peace. Fletcher promptly rejected the wampum belt accompanying Teganissorens's speech, ending the day's proceedings.[17]

The League's comprehensive agenda for peace left Fletcher completely flummoxed. He attempted to save face with his Anglo-American audience by criticizing Iroquois disobedience, challenging their bravado, and refusing to accept a League-brokered peace with Frontenac. But Teganissorens had backed the governor into a corner. No longer would Iroquoia serve as "the Barrier between the English and the French."[18] Instead, the Onondaga headman articulated a vision of Iroquoia as an extensive geography of solidarity in which the League sanctioned access and movement by Iroquois and other peoples for the purposes of establishing reciprocal relations of trade and peace. Such relationships would now extend from the Mohawks' European neighbors at the League's eastern door to the Native nations of the upper Great Lakes at its western door. Unlike European officials, who viewed international relations as a zero-sum game across contested spatial boundaries, League leaders now proposed to extend the principles of indigenous intergroup relations embedded in the original *kaswentha* agreement concluded with the Dutch during the second decade of the seventeenth century to a broader spatial scale. In the century's final decade, the Iroquois sought the expansion of the roots of the League's sentient "Tree of Peace" in multiple directions from its center at Onondaga to a diverse range of Native and non-Native nations on the edges of Iroquoia's metaphorical woods. Full realization of this objective would not be achieved until 1701.

FINAL HOSTILITIES

The League's vision of comprehensive peace built on themes expressed in prior Iroquois initiatives of the seventeenth century, such as Kiotsaeton's effort to conclude peace with New France in 1645 and Otreouti's 1684 negotiations with La Barre. Like these earlier projects, the proposed extension of the League's "Tree of Peace" in 1694 over a vast geographic area would need to overcome external indigenous and settler opposition in order to build internal consensus among Iroquois communities. Resistance to Iroquois ideas remained high in New France and the *pays d'en haut,* and Frontenac led the final French invasion of Iroquoia in 1696.

While Mohawk, Onondaga, and Oneida headmen dominated the League embassy to Albany in September 1694, a small party of Seneca and Cayuga leaders traveled to Montreal. On September 22, with Ourehouare's mediation, the Seneca and Cayuga delegation repatriated thirteen French prisoners and requested an audience with Frontenac. But after learning of Teganissorens's presence in Albany, Frontenac refused to discuss peace unless the League nations agreed to "make war against the English colonies." He also pledged to place "the ax" once more in the hands of his Native allies and to offer bounties for Iroquois scalps in defiance of appeals from metropolitan authorities to cease that costly and, in their view, inhumane and useless practice. Scalps, unlike captives, "told no news."[19]

Yet Frontenac found few takers for his "ax," according to a Mohawk woman who had returned to Tionnondoroge in October 1694 after three years of purported captivity in the Laurentian settlements. This woman reported that the few Laurentian Iroquois who accepted the governor of Canada's "hatchet" planned to use it to "kill Cayenquiragoe" (Fletcher). Frontenac, realizing the extent to which the Five Nations had achieved rapprochement with the Laurentian towns, moved to undermine Iroquois diplomatic efforts in the *pays d'en haut.* He dispatched Antoine de La Mothe de Cadillac to Michilimackinac with orders to purchase the anti-Iroquois allegiance of the "Upper Nations" with liberal supplies of trade goods.[20]

Severe cold forced Cadillac's party to spend the winter of 1694–95 in the Ottawa River valley in the midst of numerous Iroquois hunters. Though beavers were reportedly "very scarce" in Michilimackinac following roughly two decades of intense Iroquois commercial activity, the animal's populations in the triangular region between the St. Lawrence and Ottawa rivers, former homelands of the Weskarini and Kichesipirini Algonquins, had recovered to what French observers described as abundant levels. This development offered Laurentian and other Iroquois people opportunities to reaffirm ties of family and friendship through peaceful shared hunting, visiting, and exchanges of information.[21]

On March 24, 1695, two men from La Montagne (a Mohawk military leader named Thioratarion and an Oneida named Ononsista) arrived at Montreal and reported their winter's activities to the town's governor, Callières. With them was a resident of Mohawk country who planned to visit his sister at Kahnawake. The two Laurentian representatives had accompanied Oneida headman Tareha back to Onondaga after his autumn 1694 meeting with Frontenac, carrying a message from the governor to League authorities. Thioratarion recalled the warm reception he had received from League leaders at Onondaga, with whom he remained until February 1695, promoting discussions of a conclusive Iroquois peace with New France. Additionally, he reported learning from either Johannes or Arent Schuyler that the people of Albany "were so strongly in favor of peace" with New France that they planned to send three delegates with an Iroquois embassy to Frontenac "in the spring." Thioratarion then advised Callières that the Iroquois would demand the repatriation of all Iroquois prisoners among the French and French-allied Native nations as well as Frontenac's commitment to "stay the hatchet of his nephews, the Lorette and Abenakis Indians" (which Callières interpreted as an Iroquois attempt to pacify the New England frontier in addition to that of New York). Thioratarion did not tell Callières about the two belts he had carried back "underground" from Onondaga to the Laurentian towns, however. These belts conveyed League authorities' endorsement of the "union that ought to exist" between the Five Nations and Laurentian communities and urged their northern kinfolk to be mindful of their "ancient country," advising League leaders "of the designs of Onontio without letting him know it." "Fear not visiting us," the League headmen reportedly urged the Laurentians, "you will always be welcome."[22]

Arnout Viele's eyewitness report of the Laurentian representatives' participation in a February 1695 League council at Onondaga added further details that Thioratarion had elected not to share with French authorities. According to Viele, the Laurentians reported that Tareha's repatriation of Millet in October 1694 had convinced Frontenac to agree to a meeting with League delegates during the spring of 1695, to be cemented by an exchange of all captives held by each side. Upon hearing this news, the League headmen signified their approval with four collective shouts of "Jo: Hue: Hue: Hogh!" Thioratarion and Ononsista, addressing their "Brethren and Countrymen" at Onondaga, then pledged the assistance and brokerage of their home community in the pending peace negotiations. They offered to meet the League embassy "half way in good canoes" to convey them securely to a meeting with Frontenac.[23]

Yet not all the news the Laurentians offered pleased League authorities. Frontenac had sent the French-allied Abenakis, Sokokis, Pennacooks, and Algonquins of Odanak to collect "scalps" on the New England frontier during the autumn months of 1694, and he had also sent a party of 300 men to reconnoiter the site of Fort Frontenac in July 1694 with a view toward its reestablishment in the aftermath of Teganissorens's ritual cleansing. The latter news evoked an impassioned response from Onondaga headman Aqueendara, speaking on behalf of the League Council. Recalling significant Iroquois efforts to "bury in oblivion" their memories of recent French invasions of Mohawk and Seneca country, as well as the late attack on Schenectady, Aqueendara pointed out how Denonville's treacherous capture of Iroquois prisoners at Fort Frontenac in 1687 "smart[ed] still." According to Viele, the League headmen had resolved that Frontenac's "fyre shall burn no more at Cadaracqui" because its flames had been "quenched" by the Iroquois blood spilled there eight years previously. Recalling the "stolen" character of the land on which Fort Frontenac had been built, Aqueendara thrust his finger into Viele's chest and described the ancestral, pre-League indigenous ties to the extensive space of Iroquoia (see the epigraph to this chapter).[24]

Two months after Thioratarion's informative conversation with Callières, Ourehouare came into Montreal from a winter hunt in the St. Lawrence valley accompanied by three Mohawks who had reportedly come to live in the Laurentian communities, "having, as they said, no nearer relatives than those residing there." The Mohawks informed Callières of a 200-man Seneca and Cayuga party that had set out in late 1694 for Miami country. The Senecas and Cayugas had extended their initial attack on the Miamis into a full-scale assault of Courtemanche's garrison at Fort St. Joseph during the spring of 1695. Though the Iroquois did not carry the fort, they accomplished their primary objective in making the attack: two Tionnontaté Wendat prisoners taken by the Seneca and Cayuga army witnessed the direct Iroquois assault on Fort St. Joseph, another example of the League's continued ability to project military force over considerable distances. The Seneca and Cayuga party then returned with their Wendat prisoners to Onondaga, where they reported their actions and dispatched one of the captives to Michilimackinac and the other to Montreal to spread the news.[25]

When intelligence of ongoing Iroquois "tampering with the Upper Nations" reached French officials at Michilimackinac during the spring of 1695, Cadillac at once attempted to encourage the local Wendats and Odawas to reject Iroquois offers of peace and invitations to attack the French-allied Miamis and Illinois. A Tionnontaté Wendat headman whom the French called "the Baron" responded to Cadillac, urging him not to interfere with indigenous diplomatic initiatives. The Baron claimed that the League had resolved over the winter of 1695 not to attack "any of the Lake Tribes," and, recalling their 1693 proposal of shared hunting, had invited the nations of the *pays d'en haut* to the "neighborhood of Detroit" for a "rendezvous" during the autumn of 1695.[26]

The Baron's speech stimulated a heated debate among the nations residing at Michilimackinac. Kondiaronk, in Cadillac's presence, rejected the idea of a separate peace with the Iroquois, arguing that the Wendats and Odawas could not make peace without Frontenac's involvement. This prompted the Baron to call a separate, exclusively Native-attended council at Michilimackinac on June 1, 1695, "for the purpose of considering some dreams, and drawing important conclusions from them." There, the Wendat leader summarized a dream reported by an elderly man of his nation, who had resided with his wife in the Saginaw River valley since 1649. In the Wendat man's dream, the "Master of Life" had discouraged the upper Great Lakes nations from being the "first to strike the Iroquois, as he who should begin [such a war] would be infallibly destroyed, and the Iroquois himself would be annihilated were he so bold as to [attack] them with his hatchet." Capitalizing on the resonance such a story would have had with the Native residents of Michilimackinac (the Tionnontaté Wendats and at least two of the four constituent Odawa bands then residing there had relocated as a result of post-1649 displacement by the Iroquois), the Baron's speech represented far more than a "ridiculous tale" that the French dismissed out of hand. By recalling the "ancient" conflict with the Iroquois and adding the symbolic authority of supernatural advice communicated in a dream, the Baron struck a significant blow in favor of rapprochement with the League.[27]

The appeal of the League's message, amplified at Michilimackinac by the Baron, extended far into the *pays d'en haut* by the summer of 1695. Perrot reported that the Fox, whom Cadillac believed to have a long-standing arrangement to protect Iroquois hunters and warriors in the upper Great Lakes, had received two Iroquois captives from the Ouiatanons and were keeping them for potential use as human passports to facilitate relocation to Iroquoia if the pressure of Sioux offensives necessitated such a move. The Mascoutens had also reportedly expressed interest in joining a future Iroquois campaign against the Miamis and Illinois. The "Miamis of the river St. Joseph" had spared several Iroquois prisoners from ritual torture and execution with an eye toward their potential repatriation in peace negotiations. Finally, Cadillac reported the departure of a Tionnontaté Wendat embassy headed by the Baron's son for Seneca country. The Wendats escorted three Seneca captives for repatriation and fourteen wampum belts signifying the Wendats' offer to "join arms" and make peace with the League without French participation. All this took place, Perrot later noted, while the Baron visited Montreal and feigned "submission to the voice of Onontio."[28]

As close as these indigenous negotiations came to fruition during the first half of 1695, not all members of the upper Great Lakes nations supported reconciliation with their Iroquois enemies. Six unidentified "Dawaganhaes or far Indians" who confronted Frontenac directly about his plans for peace early in 1695 learned that the governor's "heart was for war" and received six barrels of gunpowder to support their anti-Iroquois offensives. Yet Kondiaronk, not French colonial authorities, deserves the lion's share of credit for scuttling the peacemaking efforts that his fellow Wendat headman the Baron had initiated with the League. While the Baron's son traveled to the League's western door, Kondiaronk ensured that several Wendat warriors accompanied a large multinational war party from the upper Great Lakes heading toward Iroquoia.[29]

The Algonquian and Wendat warriors eventually came upon Iroquois scouts covering 300 men making canoes on the Lake Erie shore. Despite having finished only a few craft, the Iroquois piled thirty, twenty-five, and sixteen men (respectively) into three canoes and paddle out to meet the invaders in open water. An initial volley from canoe-borne Iroquois musketeers inflicted considerable casualties on the *pays d'en haut* contingent, but the latter maneuvered themselves into position to fire a retaliatory round that shattered and sunk the thirty-man Iroquois canoe and enabled the Algonquians to finish off nearly all of the impromptu Iroquois naval force, "some by the war-club, some by arrows." The Iroquois lost at least forty men killed at the scene and fifteen captured (most of whom were later tortured and executed). One of the Iroquois mortally wounded in the battle was "the great chief of the Tsonnontouans" (possibly Onnonkenritaoui, engaged in a final defensive act of western doorkeeping), whom the attackers also "tomahawked" and scalped.[30]

As these developments on the periphery of Seneca country derailed the latest effort to achieve rapprochement between the League and the Native peoples of the upper Great Lakes, the Iroquois resumed attacks on French settlers in the vicinity of Montreal in late June 1695. Members of these Iroquois war parties avoided the Laurentian communities (except to visit their relatives for fresh intelligence of French affairs), and pursuit parties consisting of Laurentian Iroquois warriors reciprocated by rendering ineffective service to their ostensible French masters. Still other Iroquois war parties returned to the Ottawa River valley, where they commenced carefully targeted ambushes of approaching French and Native traders. The first-ever "Sioux Indian" to visit New France arrived in mid-July 1695, having barely survived an Iroquois attack en route. Yet a number of Ojibwas and Odawas passed through the Ottawa River valley without incident shortly thereafter.[31]

Upon their arrival at Montreal, the Odawas and Ojibwas witnessed the departure of a convoy of 700 men, "including Regulars, Militia, and Indians" sent by Frontenac to repair and reoccupy the fort bearing his name. The French convoy carried one year's worth of supplies for allied Indian warriors and the forty-eight-man garrison that would be left behind at the fort. Frontenac had spent an estimated 12,000 livres on the expedition, notwithstanding the objections of Intendant Champigny, who had opposed such outlays of scarce men and money for what he viewed as a "useless" structure. Members of the French convoy spent just eight days at Fort Frontenac before racing back to Montreal on August 14, 1695, a mere twenty-six days after their departure. Relieved French officers congratulated themselves on having accomplished their mission without having been "discovered" (as they believed) by the Iroquois, a revealing insight into how they viewed the military context of the *pays d'en haut* at that time.[32]

"Ching8abé," the Ojibwa headman who observed the departing convoy, perceived Frontenac's aggressive intent, but he and his party did not rally immediately to Frontenac's calls for renewed war on the Iroquois. The Ojibwas reminded Frontenac that war was "not the same with us as with you." While Frontenac could "command" the French, neither he nor Native leaders exerted similar authority over young Native warriors. Ching8abé, noting that his authority was limited to his near relations and family allies. promised only to communicate Frontenac's request to the Ojibwas of Sault Ste. Marie.[33]

The hesitation demonstrated by the Ojibwas and Odawas in July 1695 revealed the extent to which ongoing Iroquois diplomatic efforts in the *pays d'en haut* had reduced the likelihood of significant participation by warriors from the upper Great Lakes in French-sponsored campaigns against Iroquoia. Cadillac reported the arrival of three Iroquois delegates at Michilimackinac during the midsummer of 1695 who came in response to earlier Wendat messages and embassies in order to continue peace negotiations. Cadillac noted that not all the nations residing near Michilimackinac were "disposed for peace" with the League, but lamented that each manifested at least "some leaning for it, in the hope of English trade, and of obtaining goods at a cheaper rate." Excluded from the indigenous negotiations by the local Wendats, whom Cadillac increasingly mistrusted as an "intriguing" and "evil-disposed" people, the post commander later gleaned some intelligence of the proceedings from an Odawa headman named Onaské. The Iroquois delegates had departed Michilimackinac in early October 1695 with a "Calumet of red stone, of extraordinary beauty and size." The calumet carried an invitation to the Five Nations from the Tionnontaté Wendats and their "allies" at Michilimackinac to continue negotiations leading to a lasting, comprehensive peace.[34]

The Wendats sent the calumet to Iroquoia in defiance of blustery rhetoric from Cadillac, who touted newly reoccupied Fort Frontenac as "the Great Kettle" from which allied Native warriors could obtain supplies to "keep alive the war [against the Iroquois] to the end." Frontenac, drawing on Lahontan's earlier advocacy of establishing forts in Iroquois territory, claimed that Fort Frontenac would allow New France to reap the security benefits of having their allies of the *pays d'en haut* nations "harass the Iroquois in their hunting, and right up to the doors of their villages." Additionally, Frontenac argued that the fort could provide "sure depots for provisions" that would sustain future French military invasions of Iroquoia.[35]

News of the French reoccupation of Fort Frontenac reached Albany in early September 1695. An unspecified Iroquois scouting party had observed the French reoccupation and vented their frustration by capturing ten upper Great Lakes Algonquians they found in the vicinity of Fort Frontenac and burning all but one of these captives upon their return home. On September 7, 1695, ten Mohawk leaders came to Albany and demanded that local authorities assemble 500 men with cannons for an expedition against Fort Frontenac. Now was the time, the Mohawks argued, for Fletcher and governors from neighboring Anglo-American colonies to make good on their past promises of military assistance. In addition to this example of eastern doorkeeping by the Mohawks, the Oneidas had sent messengers to Conestoga to request warrior support, and Teganissorens asked Fletcher to send a thirty-man garrison to protect the Onondagas' principal town.[36]

Three weeks after the Mohawks' visit, Fletcher surfaced in Albany to respond to their demands. But instead of offering support for an attack on Fort Frontenac, he castigated Iroquois leaders for their "Drunken, supine, Negligent, and Careless" character, which, in his view, had allowed the French to reoccupy Fort Frontenac without opposition. After claiming that the lateness of the season precluded sending a "proper body of men" against the French fort, Fletcher departed as hastily as he had arrived. "Disgusted" Iroquois observers witnessed once more the New York governor's lack of commitment to defending the interests of his allies in the Covenant Chain.[37]

As much as the Iroquois complained about Fort Frontenac, the post was, as Champigny recognized, incapable of protecting New France from Iroquois offensives. Iroquois attacks on French settlers continued into late August and early September 1695. As usual, these incursions not only disrupted the harvest of crops in New France, they also signaled ongoing Iroquois military capacities to Native peoples from the *pays d'en haut* visiting the colony to trade and confer with French officials. A party of Mohawks and Oneidas claimed responsibility for one late August attack by leaving their nationally inscribed "tomahawks sticking in the ground, according to their custom." French officials managed to enlist some Odawas to pursue the Iroquois attackers, but for the most part both the Laurentian Iroquois and the upper Great Lakes nations declined to participate in these French-sponsored sorties.[38]

As the summer of 1695 yielded to autumn, the Iroquois shifted their attention to winter hunts in several directions. Nearly 100 Senecas, enabled by the previous summer's diplomacy at Michilimackinac, spent the winter of 1695–96 hunting with Tionnontaté Wendats and Odawas in the vicinity of Detroit and the Saginaw River valley. To ease their movement into this formerly contested region, the Seneca hunters carried a quantity of goods consigned to them by Anglo-American traders for exchange with their hosts. French traders wintering in the Saginaw River valley sent word of these developments back to Michilimackinac, initiating another serious debate among the local Native population about the propriety and wisdom of attacking the Seneca hunting party. Onaské resolved to oppose what he and at least one Potawatomi leader viewed as an Iroquois intrusion, notwithstanding efforts by members of their own nations (some of whom were already "trad[ing] with New York via the Iroquois") to discourage their plan. Emotions ran so high that Onaské's canoes were cut during the night before his planned departure, but even this act of sabotage failed to deter the Odawa-Potawatomi expedition. Tionnontaté Wendat hunters advised the Senecas of the approaching war party from Michilimackinac, which convinced the Senecas to "bundle up their packs" and head for home. Onaské's party overtook the Senecas while they paddled their canoes homeward, and a "rough fight" ensued, which the Odawa and Potawatomi aggressors won. Returning to Michilimackinac with thirty Seneca scalps and thirty-two Seneca prisoners (men, women, and children) in the spring of 1696, Onaské reported that another forty Senecas had drowned in the canoe battle. The Odawas and Potawatomis had also plundered nearly 500 beavers (valued at 15,000 francs) from their Iroquois victims, along with the remainder of the Anglo-American trade goods.[39]

At about the same time as Onaské's attack on the Seneca hunters near Detroit, reports of Iroquois hunters present in the "triangular tract of country" between the St. Lawrence and Ottawa rivers prompted French authorities to send "300 picked French" troops and an unspecified number of allied Indians to the area. Over a span of two days in February 1696, this French-dominated force assaulted three different Iroquois hunting camps. Significantly, only three Iroquois men who offered resistance were killed on the spot. The party returned to Montreal with eight Iroquois prisoners (six men, a boy, and a woman). Frontenac had four of the prisoners (all Onondaga men) burned alive "on their arrival." But Laurentian intervention revealed the identity and spared the lives of the other Iroquois captives. The two remaining men, both Senecas, were presented to La Montagne headman Thioratarion, "who happened to be the uncle of one of them." The boy turned out to be a grandson of Garacontié, and he was surrendered to the custody of Kahnawake leaders. The Wendats of Lorette, near Quebec, who had participated in the expedition, received the Iroquois woman in recognition of their service.[40]

On the surface, reports of the Iroquois 1695–96 winter hunt would appear to support the impression of consistent Iroquois defeat during the 1690s, which many historians, relying uncritically on Algonquian and Wendat oral tradition, have emphasized as a means of explaining the League's ostensible seventeenth-century demise.[41] In reality, the fighting between the Iroquois and the *pays d'en haut* nations during the 1690s was not only much more balanced than oral tradition alone would indicate, it was also punctuated by repeated efforts to negotiate a peaceful conclusion prior to 1701. Iroquois rapprochement with their Laurentian kinfolk after

1692 had blunted the potential impact of French interference with Iroquois winter hunting in the St. Lawrence valley, and similar outreach to the Tionnontaté Wendats and Odawas of Michilimackinac had nearly managed to achieve the same outcome in the upper Great Lakes. French authorities realized by March 1696 that they were waging an uphill public relations battle against the Iroquois for the allegiance of Native nations from the St. Lawrence valley all the way to the *pays d'en haut.* Frontenac's response was to pursue ongoing offensives against the League in hopes of encouraging the colony's erstwhile Native allies to abandon plans for a separate peace with the League.

Yet "frequent deputations" sent by the Five Nations to kinfolk in the St. Lawrence valley and potential trading partners in the *pays d'en haut* from 1694 to 1696 had, in the view of French officials, yielded sufficient opportunities for the Iroquois to procure, via relatively unimpeded hunting in peltry-rich regions, the means "to obtain ammunition and arms" for an assault on New France. French colonial authorities also reported that Iroquois "intrigues" had come perilously close by 1696 to convincing the upper Great Lakes nations to "league themselves" with the Iroquois.[42]

While French authorities voiced apprehensions of a large-scale indigenous assault on New France, the inevitable consequence of Iroquois rapprochement with the peoples of the *pays d'en haut,* in their view, Anglo-American observers fretted over the prospect of a separate Iroquois peace with New France facilitated by the Laurentian Iroquois. If the French, who in the eyes of New Yorkers had already secured the relocation of many Iroquois people to the St. Lawrence valley, managed to win over the rest of the League through lavish presents distributed by Jesuit priests and ex-captives who were "perfect masters of [Iroquois] Languages and Customs," then the settlers of all the "northern colonies must abandon their dwellings or be destroyed." Some Anglo-Americans believed that they could stave off this catastrophe only by exceeding French largesse. Even Governor Fletcher was moved to dispatch agents to England during the autumn of 1695 to make the case for more attentive policies aimed at winning the League's exclusive allegiance. All talk of the Iroquois as living in "subjection" to the king of England had disappeared by 1696. The Iroquois, opined Fletcher in a June 1696 letter to William Blathwayt, "tho[ugh] monsters want not sense." They understood how fecklessly their Anglo-American allies (especially Fletcher) had behaved in recent years. When news of Frontenac's preparations for another expedition into Iroquoia reached New York in July 1696, residents of the colony faced another crucial moment in their relations with the League.[43]

Unable and unwilling to oppose the French reoccupation of Fort Frontenac in 1695, Fletcher hoped to redeem himself in the eyes of the League by sending 400 men (both English regulars from the independent companies posted in New York and provincial levies) to Onondaga country in advance of Frontenac's pending invasion. The provincial assembly balked at the plan, however, citing the failure of neighboring colonies to contribute to the colony's defense expenditures and declining revenues from New York's peltry trade. Not even a "belt from Onondage" communicating the nation's request for immediate defensive aid against the approaching French invasion force moved the provincial council from the position staked out by their colleagues in the assembly. During their August 6, 1696, meeting in New York, the councillors resolved merely "that a letter be wrote to the Indians to give them encouragement and to acquaint them that the king of England has sent them some presents and [to] desire them to be watchful."[44]

Frontenac's plan to "decapitate" the League via an attack on Onondaga had been in the works ever since the August 1695 reoccupation of Fort Frontenac. Convinced that only another military strike would bring the Iroquois to terms, Frontenac spent from late June to early July 1696 assembling an army of 2,200 men at Montreal, which included roughly 500 allied Native Americans. Laurentian Iroquois warriors were once again well represented on the expedition.[45]

Departing Montreal on July 8, 1696, the French and allied Native army moved at a deliberate pace up the St. Lawrence River, arriving at Fort Frontenac in eleven days. After a week at the fort, Frontenac moved the expeditionary force toward Onondaga country on July 26, 1696. Approaching Onondaga Lake, a scouting party led by Vaudreuil discovered on August 1 the first sign of Onondaga resistance the expedition had encountered: "a descriptive drawing of our army on bark, after the manner of the Indians, and two bundles of cut rushes," a symbolic tally indicating that a total of 1,434 Onondaga, Cayuga, and Oneida warriors had assembled to oppose the French invasion. The next evening, however, scouts with the French expeditionary force noticed a bright light coming from the direction of the Onondaga town. Advised by two Senecas who had abandoned the invading army of the size of Frontenac's force, the Onondagas had elected to follow the recent example of the Senecas and Mohawks. They had burned their town and retreated seventy-five miles south "to the head of the Siskehanna River," where they built a temporary settlement amid already-planted cornfields at a location later described as "within three or four leagues of their ancient village."[46]

As had been the case during Denonville's expedition against Seneca country nine years previously, reports of the Onondagas' retreat did not stimulate a rapid French advance. Frontenac spent two more days at Onondaga Lake constructing a field fort to serve as a secure retreat. Not until August 4, 1696, did the French march in "order of battle" to the smoldering ruins of the Onondaga town. The Onondagas had sacrificed their town and their crops, but limited their casualties to two elderly people: a woman captured in the woods by French soldiers, who subsequently "broke her skull," and a man whom Frontenac insisted on "burn[ing] at a slow fire," in sight of his relatives who had accompanied the French expeditionary force.[47]

As Frontenac's army sifted through the ashes of Onondaga for plunder, an Oneida man escorting a French captive as a human shield approached the town to remind the governor to honor his earlier promise to leave Oneida settlements unharmed.

Frontenac promised not to attack the Oneidas if they agreed to relocate en masse to the St. Lawrence valley and provided "five of their most influential chiefs as hostages." To oversee the evacuation, he dispatched Vaudreuil with 700 men, guided by Millet, to the Oneida town on August 6. The next day, while Frontenac's men commenced the destruction of the Onondagas' fields, Vaudreuil parleyed with the Oneida Bear clan matron, Millet's adoptive mother, outside the Oneida town's palisade. Endeavoring to spare the nation's home settlement, she and eighty other Oneidas agreed to remove to the St. Lawrence valley and reside with their Laurentian kinfolk. Vaudreuil accepted these terms, but before matters could be resolved some French troops broke rank and "tumultuously entered" the Oneida town, which caused many of its residents to flee. Vaudreuil eventually secured only thirty to thirty-five Oneida prisoners, including the "principal chiefs of the tribe," before he ordered his men to burn the Oneidas' town and crops. Vaudreuil's detachment then returned to Onondaga and departed with Frontenac on August 9. Eleven days later, the army reached Montreal. Frontenac represented the expedition as a "considerable" victory over the Onondagas and Oneidas, whom he believed were now "reduced to the necessity of perishing of hunger, or of accepting peace" on French terms.[48]

At the precise time of Frontenac's expedition, however, Mohawk war parties had killed or captured as many as thirty French settlers between Trois-Rivières and Lake St. Pierre, burned their barns, and slaughtered their cattle. The Senecas and Cayugas remained "undisturbed in their own country"; the vast majority of the Onondagas were secure in their refuge near the headwaters of the Susquehanna River; and the temporarily homeless Oneidas quickly found relief in Mohawk towns and at Albany, where the New York Council authorized the distribution of subsidized provisions to displaced Iroquois people. Neither widespread Iroquois starvation nor a French-dictated peace would result from the last French invasion of Iroquoia.[49]

In late September 1696, League headmen arrived in Albany for a meeting with New York authorities. Fletcher hoped to patch up matters with the Five Nations via "presents sent from His Majesty and an addition from this province." On October 9, 1696, Fletcher condoled the Onondagas and Oneidas for the recent loss of their towns and distributed goods valued at over £660 (in provincial currency) to the Iroquois delegates present. But the Iroquois were not to be bought off so easily. A Mohawk headman named Sanonguirese responded to Fletcher's offering with "a bundle of six Bever skins" marked on the outside with a draft "map of the river of Canida with the chief places" indicated to "show the smallness of the enemy." The Mohawk leader then demanded that this message-bearing gift be delivered to the king of England to elicit a response concerning his plans to "destroy Canida." If the League nations received no positive reply by "the next time the trees grow green," they would make their own peace with Frontenac. The impressive collective shout with which the League headmen concluded the public proceedings left no doubt about the consensual nature of the sentiment expressed by Sanonguirese.[50]

INDIGENOUS INITIATIVES

As had been the case in 1666, 1687, and 1693, the French military invasion of 1696 caused few human casualties and evoked creative responses by League leaders. The three years following Frontenac's last anti-Iroquois expedition witnessed the formal end of the Anglo-French conflict in Europe, but while the 1697 Treaty of Ryswick resolved matters for the residents of New France and the Anglo-American colonies, the peace concluded in Europe had no effect on indigenous international relations in northeastern North America. Iroquois leaders of hereditary and achieved status undertook extensive collaborative efforts after 1696 with the aim of securing peace in spaces beyond the reach of European diplomacy.

In the aftermath of the French burning of the Onondagas' and Oneidas' towns and crops, Iroquois leaders, rather than relying on empty English promises or waiting passively for an answer from King William, took matters into their own hands. League headmen made several visits to Fort Frontenac during the early winter of 1696–97, where Ourehouare brokered their discussions with local French authorities and also hosted his distinguished guests on hunts in the region. The commander of Fort Frontenac, Louis de la Porte, Sieur de Louvigny, encouraged all of his Iroquois visitors to send an embassy to Canada to appeal to Frontenac's mercy.[51]

On February 5, 1697, a delegation of thirty Oneidas arrived at Montreal. Kahnawake Oneida headman Tatacouiceré brokered their conversation with Callières. The Oneida delegation "did not say much" to French officials, but the record of their speech indicated that more significant proceedings had already occurred behind the scenes. The Oneidas had convinced Odatsedeh, one of their hereditary titleholders taken hostage by Vaudreuil in 1696 and then residing at Kahnawake, to return with them. This Oneida leader was likely Tareha, evidently raised up to the position in the aftermath of Millet's repatriation. The recently condoled Odatsedeh departed for home with his kinsmen, promising to report the "cordial reception" he had received during his sojourn in the Laurentian community.[52]

The Oneidas' diplomatic outreach represented one political option then under serious consideration throughout Iroquoia. A Kahnawake warrior who had gone to Mohawk country "for the purpose of learning some news" in the spring of 1697 advised Frontenac that he had spoken there with Teganissorens. The Onondaga headman was reportedly also considering the assembly of "a general deputation of the Five Nations" to treat with Frontenac. Yet in late June 1697, an Iroquois woman captured near Schenectady informed Frontenac that thirty Tionnontaté Wendats belonging to the Baron's "family" had recently visited Iroquoia. These Wendats, accompanied by an Odawa headman, had revived negotiations with League leaders and Albany officials to extend Five Nations–brokered English trade into the *pays d'en haut*. These indigenous initiatives assumed new levels of urgency at that time, owing to official French orders in 1696 to close all posts in the *pays d'en haut* and to ban travel to the region by French traders in hopes of alleviating a glutted beaver market in France, and also because of escalating Iroquois conflict with the upper Great Lakes nations. French authorities claimed that 102 Seneca warriors alone had been killed or captured from 1695 to 1697, but also noted effective retaliation by Senecas and "Huron deserters" against Native peoples in the vicinity of Michilimackinac.[53]

On June 19, 1697, Teganissorens headed a delegation of Onondaga leaders to a meeting with Albany Indian affairs commissioners (officers appointed by Fletcher to manage relations with the League). Teganissorens reported Odatsedeh's delivery of a belt from Frontenac signifying the governor's desire to make peace with the League. In response, the Onondagas had sent two headmen, Aredsion and Sontragtowane, to escort Odatsedeh back to Canada, where all three leaders planned to secure the assistance of their Laurentian kinfolk in arranging a long-sought general peace treaty. Albany authorities tried to argue that by conducting independent diplomacy, the League had effectively broken its "many repeated promises" not to negotiate directly with Frontenac, but in the aftermath of Frontenac's invasion Teganissorens and his colleagues no longer had faith in New Yorkers' willingness or ability to intercede on their behalf. The "Kanack Konje" (kanonsionni, or League council) had made its consensual decision, and had sent the delegation to New France without regard for Anglo-American objections.[54]

The identity of the two Onondaga leaders sent with Odatsedeh to New France in 1697 reflected crucial ongoing collaboration between senior civil leaders and younger military leaders in forming collective League decisions. French sources identified Aredsion as one of the "Anciens" of the Onondaga Council, whereas his partner, Sontragtowane, was a "young War chief whose family possesses some influence among his nation." Arriving at Quebec (via Montreal and the Laurentian communities) in early November 1697, Aredsion spoke first for the Oneida-Onondaga party. He announced their visit as a manifestation of the League exercising its freedom of travel by land and water to make peace. Pledging to follow the example of his "Ancestors who always maintained peace with Onontio," he offered Frontenac a "cordial" to remove any sorrow from his heart, and then disavowed vengeance for any of his people killed by the French or their Native allies. Acknowledging that the League had not yet reached consensus on concluding peace with the French, Aredsion assured Frontenac of his commitment to building that consensus among "all the Iroquois Nations."[55]

Yet the Onondaga ambassadors had brought no French prisoners to buttress their words, and as a result Frontenac not only dismissed their offer of peace but also issued some "sharp reproofs" accusing Aredsion and Sontragtowane of espionage. Odatsedeh offered his personal attestation of the sincerity of the Onondagas' message, but to no avail. Convinced that the desire of the Iroquois for peace did not extend beyond a few "Oneida cabins," Frontenac dismissed Odatsedeh and Sontragtowane, who returned to Kahnawake with a few token presents, and detained

Aredsion as a hostage at Quebec. Once more, despite significant Iroquois efforts, there was "no conclusion of peace" with Frontenac.[56]

Frontenac resisted peace with the League in 1697 because of his belief that free Iroquois access to the *pays d'en haut* posed a potential threat to the colony at the precise moment he had received orders to withdraw all the French garrisons from the interior posts. With only a recalcitrant cohort of several hundred *coureurs de bois* remaining in the upper Great Lakes, and mounting evidence of disdain on the part of the region's indigenous population for obligatory travel to Montreal to secure their supplies, Frontenac could ill afford the prospect of any peace that might permit the Iroquois to move in and drain off what remained of New France's peltry trade in the *pays d'en haut* (via their standing offer of brokered access to English traders), not to mention the potential impact such developments would portend for the colony's alliances with Native nations residing in the upper Great Lakes.[57]

While matters in North America had reached a military and diplomatic stalemate, the September 1697 Treaty of Ryswick marked the end of Anglo-French hostilities in Europe. Official news of the peace reached the Iroquois via Anglo-American sources at least seven months before French authorities in Quebec had formal notification from Versailles, and the intervening period presented the Iroquois with a new opportunity to implement plans for a comprehensive resolution of affairs in eastern North America. One Mohawk accompanied a New York embassy headed by Abraham Schuyler and Rev. Godfredius Dellius of Albany to communicate news of the Treaty of Ryswick to Callières in Montreal during late January 1698. But Governor Fletcher, who neither spoke nor wrote French, failed to send an official letter with the embassy. In lieu of proper official correspondence, neither Callières nor Frontenac considered themselves obligated to cease hostilities against either the Anglo-American colonies or the Iroquois.[58]

Fletcher's diplomatic gaffe played a key role in perpetuating interindigenous violence between the Iroquois and the Native peoples of the *pays d'en haut*. New York councillor Stephen van Cortlandt noted that after being advised of peace in Europe by Fletcher during the autumn of 1697, the Iroquois went hunting in large numbers, confident that the peace would "prevent mischief on both sides." Some of these Iroquois remained in the field for a considerable period of time, venturing as far as Detroit and the Ohio River, where they encountered opposition from Odawas and Miamis (respectively).[59]

One group of thirty Onondaga hunters headed by a leader named Black Kettle arrived at still-occupied Fort Frontenac early in 1698. They informed the French commander that, notwithstanding Frontenac's earlier abusive treatment of Aredsion, a delegation of League headmen would meet with the governor during the upcoming spring. In the meantime, they announced their plan to hunt in the vicinity of the former Iroquois town of Quinté while some of their young men set out on a campaign toward the upper Great Lakes to avenge the previous year's losses to the Odawas and

Ojibwas. The Onondagas were clearly relying on an expectation of secure hunting on the north shore of Lake Ontario, given League claims to the area, their hunts during the previous four years, and the Anglo-French peace in Europe. But Algonquin hunters captured a woman of the Onondaga party shortly after the latter departed Fort Frontenac, and a "pretty obstinate fight" ensued in which the Onondagas suffered twenty people killed, including Black Kettle, his wife, and "four other chiefs." The Algonquins captured eight more Onondagas (six men and two women). Callières accepted the Onondaga scalps and ransomed the Onondaga captives at Montreal, but rather than liberate the Onondagas, he sent them to the town's prison. This incident reportedly "spread consternation through the whole of the Iroquois Cantons," owing to the "quality, rather than the quantity," of those killed and captured. It also served as a painful reminder of the inability of exclusively European-brokered arrangements to secure peace between indigenous nations in North America.[60] Once more, the League nations would have to pick up the pieces, condole the Onondagas' losses, and resume independent efforts to form a lasting, satisfactory peace.

At first glance, reports of the attack on Black Kettle's hunting party and a late April 1698 Anglo-American census claiming a 50 percent decline in the League nations' warrior population (from 2,550 men in 1689 to a mere 1,230 men in 1698) might suggest that the Iroquois undertook peace efforts after this time from a position of relative weakness vis-à-vis their Native and non-Native neighbors. Yet contemporary Anglo-American claims that the League had been "half destroyed" by 1698 as a result of the previous decade of warfare overlooked the extended winter 1697–98 hunting season undertaken by Iroquois communities, which casts considerable doubt on the extent of Iroquois population decline claimed in these particular census figures. Far from teetering on the edge of oblivion, the Iroquois were actively engaged in rebuilding ties to the upper Great Lakes nations during the early months of 1698, aided once more by their brokerage of Anglo-American trade goods. This initiative, and other manifestations of Iroquois freedom of movement, enabled the League to assert a distinct role in post-Ryswick international diplomacy between New York and New France.[61]

On June 5, 1698, Abraham Schuyler and Dellius arrived at Quebec with twenty French prisoners ransomed from captivity in Iroquoia and an official letter from Richard Coote, the Earl of Bellomont (who had replaced Fletcher as New York governor earlier in the year), to Frontenac. Although Bellomont attempted by this gesture to undo Fletcher's previous faux-pas, the governor, like his predecessors, hoped that by assuming control over peace negotiations and captive exchanges with Frontenac, he could resuscitate dormant English claims of suzerainty over the Iroquois nations. Schuyler and Dellius learned from Laurentian Iroquois informants of the six Onondagas detained at Montreal by Callières, but French colonial authorities refused to entertain the New York messengers' appeal for the Onondagas' release on grounds of their ostensible status as English subjects. Although frustrated in their attempt to free the incarcerated Onondagas, Schuyler and Dellius reported that forty Laurentian Iroquois had elected to travel back with them, bringing at least 500 beaver pelts to ease their transition to new homes in Mohawk country.[62]

The possible rationale underlying this latest Laurentian relocation became apparent after two reputed Protestant Mohawk "Converts" delivered sworn testimony before Bellomont in New York during early June 1698. The Mohawks' concerns related to a pair of troubling land deeds. The first originated in a circa 1695 sale by "six idle drunken" Mohawks of "a vast tract of land" at Schoharie to Arent Schuyler, who had acted on behalf of Colonel Nicholas Bayard of New York. The second involved a July 1697 deed to literally the entire Mohawk country (valued at £25,000) to several prominent Albany officials (including Peter Schuyler, Dirck Wessells, Evert Bancker, and Dellius). Though the latter deed had been explained to the Mohawks as a wartime effort to place the deed holders in the position of "Guardians or Trustees," the Mohawk deponents now claimed that they had been deceived into alienating the land. They demanded that Bellomont void and destroy both documents. On the strength of advice from provincial authorities who suggested that the antagonism engendered by these two deeds, as well as other extravagant land patents issued by Fletcher, might persuade the remaining Mohawks "to desert this Province and fly to the French," Bellomont requested official power to "vacate" Fletcher's grants prior to his July 1698 meeting with League delegates in Albany. The well-timed, public nature of the Mohawks' complaint alerted the other nations of the League to the value of independent political status as they embarked on a new round of parallel diplomatic initiatives.[63]

On July 20, 1698, after concluding discussions with an Odawa embassy at Montreal, Frontenac received a visit from Tegayesté, a young Onondaga man who had resided "for some years" at Kahnawake. After traveling back to Onondaga country with Odatsedeh after the latter's dismissal from Quebec in the autumn of 1697, Tegayesté had returned to present Frontenac with a wampum belt from the Onondagas' national council proposing an exchange of prisoners: if Frontenac sent Aredsion back with Paul Le Moyne de Maricourt (another former Iroquois captive who had leveraged linguistic and cultural knowledge into a role as a broker of Franco-Iroquois relations), the Onondagas would repatriate all their remaining French captives. Frontenac, unwilling to accept the Onondagas' proposal in the presence of Odawa witnesses, "flung this proposal and Belt in the face of him who brought it." But this brusque dismissal opened the door for Egredere, an Onondaga resident of La Montagne, to give Tegayesté a formal condolence present of "three strings of wampum" that dried the eyes, cleared the throats, and cleaned the bloodstained mats of his grieving Onondaga kin. Egredere pledged the assistance of the Laurentian communities in brokering peace with Frontenac, and urged Tegayesté to recommend full repatriation of French prisoners remaining in Iroquoia as a first step in this process.[64]

Egredere was not the only Laurentian Iroquois individual actively assisting his kinfolk in the League nations with complex negotiations aimed at securing a comprehensive peace in eastern North America. In late May 1698, Schuyler and Dellius had crossed paths on Lake Champlain with a canoe paddled by Laurentian Iroquois, who claimed that they planned to trade their impressive load of beaver pelts in Albany. Three of these paddlers, however, were later identified by Albany authorities as "praying Indian sachems of Canada" who attended Bellomont's late July 1698 Albany conference with the Five Nations. Albany officials extended a particular welcome to these Laurentian delegates, noting the delegates' evident love for their "Native country," assuring them of continued freedom to visit Mohawk country and trade in Albany, while also encouraging them to relocate permanently among their "kindred." The Laurentian leaders, identifying themselves as "young men," excused themselves from a formal reply to the invitation but promised to inform the "Elders of their Nation in Canada" upon their return.[65]

The Iroquois raised a number of concerns in their discussions with Bellomont during August 1698. Mohawk headman Sanonguirese repeated his nation's earlier demands for the destruction of Fletcher's fraudulent deeds. Onondaga speaker Aque-endara informed Bellomont that the League nations had suffered ninety-four people killed in engagements with French-allied nations of the *pays d'en haut* since receiving notification of the 1697 Treaty of Ryswick. He then recounted the *kaswentha* tradition for Bellomont, employing the associated rhetoric of the "Tree of Welfare and Peace" as a means of critiquing English failures as alliance partners: the lack of "protection" they offered, their failure to dislodge the French from Fort Frontenac, and the "unreasonable" prices of trade goods and essential services (especially blacksmithing) in Albany. Most pressing, however, in the eyes of Iroquois leaders, was the need to recover the seventy Iroquois prisoners (identified as twenty-five men, forty-two women, and three children from all constituent League nations except the Mohawks) then detained in Canada. For this purpose, Teganissorens informed Bellomont that the League had undertaken its own efforts. The "Praying Indians of Canada" would intercede on the prisoners' behalf with Frontenac.[66]

Bellomont, afflicted by gout throughout the proceedings, found his Iroquois interlocutors "so sullen and cold in their carriage" that he believed they had transferred their "affections" wholesale to New France. Miffed by the League's tepid response to the respectable official present he had procured locally at exorbitant prices in Albany, the governor attributed the evident Iroquois antipathy to the actions of his predecessor Fletcher and his appointed Albany Indian Affairs managers (Dellius, Wessells, Bancker, and Peter Schuyler). In response to the League's expressed grievances, Bellomont promptly relieved the latter officers of their duties, citing their implication in the Mohawk deed scandal, and returned responsibilities for managing Indian affairs to the town's magistrates. After the conference concluded, the governor sent Johannes Schuyler to Canada with letters warning Frontenac to terminate anti-Iroquois campaigns by French-allied Native nations, posted Lieutenant Governor John Nanfan at Albany with a detachment of regulars from New York as a show of defensive commitment to the League, and ordered Wessells to attend an upcoming meeting of League headmen at Onondaga and to discourage separate League negotiations with Frontenac.[67]

The three young Laurentian headmen who had attended the League's conference with Bellomont in Albany discussed the proceedings with Frontenac in Montreal on August 21, 1698, possibly while wearing the "red Jackets" they had each received as personal gifts from the New York governor. The Laurentians confirmed Bellomont's effort to deter the League from parlaying an exchange of the remaining French prisoners in Iroquois custody into independent peace negotiations with New France. On September 14, 1698, Wessells argued that very point with League headmen at Onondaga. The next day, Iroquois leaders informed Wessells they would bring to Albany all the French prisoners in Five Nations' settlements who desired to return to Canada. They also stated that an official League embassy would travel at the same time to Canada in order to speak "face to face" with Frontenac. Bellomont had no right, in their view, to "hinder [them] from going to Canada" for such vital negotiations.[68]

In October 1698, Aqueendara arrived in Albany and delivered five French prisoners from all League nations but the Mohawks to be held in the garrison at Albany until the League requested them at a later date for delivery via a formal embassy to Canada. Despite the token nature of the gesture, it satisfied Nanfan of the League's ongoing fidelity to the Covenant Chain alliance. In the meantime, individual Iroquois nations that retained, for the most part, the "little [French] children who [had] become almost Iroquois since their captivity" began independent repatriations of adult French prisoners in private negotiations with French emissaries in Iroquoia and via their relatives in the Laurentian communities. The resulting trickle of French returnees convinced Frontenac to avoid any further hostilities, and this lull enabled League delegates, employing the brokerage of Laurentian kinfolk, to negotiate a renewed ceasefire with the nations of the *pays d'en haut*. These arrangements facilitated secure Iroquois hunting in the vicinity of Detroit during the winter of 1698–99, a region with newly abundant game populations owing to its relative abandonment by Native people for much of the previous decade.[69]

The pace of independent Iroquois negotiations with New France quickened over the winter of 1698–99. Onondaga headman Teganissorens, accompanied by an Oneida leader, described to Albany officials in February 1699 the results of an autumn 1698 visit by an Onondaga man named "Cohensiowanne" (i.e., Ohensiowanne) and his brother to their father, who resided in Kanesatake, the successor town of La Montagne. Ohensiowanne reported considerable consternation in the Laurentian communities regarding the delay in the arrival of a formal League embassy to negotiate peace with Frontenac. After Ohensiowanne delivered this news on his return to Onondaga in late December 1698, League authorities resolved to send a formal

League embassy to New France by the next "time of the strawberries." This embassy would repatriate four French prisoners (whom the Iroquois had not surrendered to English custody in Albany so as to retain opportunities for free movement to New France) to exchange for the five Onondagas incarcerated at Montreal.[70]

Teganissorens's report of Ohensiowanne's proceedings upset Albany officials but confirmed what French prisoners repatriated from Iroquoia had told Canadian authorities throughout the autumn of 1698. The Five Nations were ready to negotiate peace, the ex-prisoners claimed, and they planned to do so "by themselves, independent of the English." Additionally, the Iroquois had also resolved to continue trading with both the English and French, as they had done prior to and even after the outbreak of Franco-Iroquois hostilities in 1687. This intelligence, and the death of Frontenac in late November 1698, caused a critical shift in French thinking with regard to their relations with the League over the winter of 1698–99. More than a decade of brutal conflict had finally convinced a critical mass of French colonial officials that attempting to "take sides with the Barbarians" threatened perpetual "hostilities, misunderstanding, and division." Persuaded by recent experience that the "Savage Mastiffs" of Iroquoia posed a greater threat to New France than the Anglo-American colonies, French authorities saw new value in making a peace that recognized the League's independent, neutral status vis-à-vis the French and English settler colonies, the idea first articulated by Otreouti in his 1684 conference with La Barre at La Famine.[71]

Despite efforts by Albany's commissioners for Indian Affairs to discourage direct Iroquois communications with New France, the League sent a delegation of three "considerable" headmen (which included Odatsedeh and Ohensiowanne) to Montreal in March 1699 to offer condolences for Frontenac's death. The next month, Callières released four of the six Onondagas detained in Montreal prisons, adding further momentum to Franco-Iroquois rapprochement. Odatsedeh and Ohensiowanne shuttled back and forth between Onondaga and Montreal in their "birch Canoe" during the first half of 1699 with the blessing of League authorities, who ignored repeated demands from Albany authorities to cease their "correspondence with the French in Canada."[72]

Independent League negotiations with New France had at last borne fruit in the form of liberated Iroquois prisoners, something "Brother Corlaer" had not accomplished. Yet New York officials continued to oppose these activities, which posed a grave threat to their cherished vision of English sovereignty over the League in the Covenant Chain alliance. Bellomont assumed that the League's talks with Callières stemmed from the weakness of the Iroquois resulting from what he believed to be massive demographic losses during the previous decade, as well as from Iroquois apprehensions of ongoing French-sponsored raids from the *pays d'en haut* and of a potential invasion from Fort Frontenac. In fact, Frontenac had reduced the garrison of that post to a mere twenty men prior to the winter of 1698, and succeeding authorities in New France hoped that the Iroquois would reestablish their "ancient towns" on the north shore of Lake Ontario as a means of improving French communications with the League. The Iroquois bargained from a position of relative strength with New France, and as a result they would soon elicit concessions from New York as well. The "most knowing people" in New York advised Bellomont in May 1699 that "we shall entirely loose [*sic*] the Five Nations of Indians unless an effectual and speedy course be taken to retrieve their affection."[73]

Bellomont believed that "vacating" Fletcher's land grants via an act of the provincial assembly (which he accomplished on May 26, 1699) and constructing a fort at Onondaga represented the best means of retrieving the League's affection. Robert Livingston recommended building an English trade post in the European-contested region of Detroit to assert direct Anglo-American influence in concluding peace between the League and the nations of the *pays d'en haut* and thereby staking a claim to the region's promising peltry trade. In the meantime, debate in the League's "proposition house" at Onondaga intensified as League headmen considered a growing number of peace belts sent from Canadian officials and "strung wampum" accompanying rival messages from Albany emissaries. Teganissorens advised Bellomont in late May 1699 that Bellomont could best demonstrate his affection for the League by stepping aside and recognizing Iroquois freedom to travel to Canada to retrieve "our friends detained by the French" and also by ensuring that "the goods be cheap" when Iroquois traders and delegates visited Albany.[74]

In June 1699, Callières freed the last two Onondagas taken at Black Kettle's defeat from prison in Montreal. Once news of the Onondagas' liberation reached Albany officials, they tried to reassert a ban on Iroquois travel to New France, claiming that the League no longer had any reason to undertake such journeys. Yet Onondaga headmen among a delegation of over forty Iroquois leaders visiting Albany in late June 1699 rejected this effort to interfere with their free communications with the French, remarking on the irony of Albany efforts to impose such restrictions at a time when they themselves had established "a beaten path knee deep" from their own business and political travels to Canada. Aqueendara pointed out that the release of the Iroquois prisoners was merely a preliminary step and did not amount to full reconciliation of the League and New France.[75]

Although Laurentian brokerage had led to substantial progress in peace talks between the Five Nations and the French, more remained to be done regarding peace between the League and the upper Great Lakes nations. Aqueendara reported that League headmen had received news that the son of a Seneca headman, who had been taken prisoner during the summer of 1698 by the Tionnontaté Wendats, had been returned to New France. The Seneca leader planned to visit his son, demonstrating that Iroquois people, not Albany authorities, would decide whether the League's path to Canada would be open or closed. Iroquois leaders further emphasized their freedom of movement by advising Albany officials of the presence of Pennsylvania traders at the Iroquois community of "Conestoga a Place upon the Susquahanna River" just three days' journey "southward" from their country, where they could obtain "goods very cheap."[76]

A five-man Seneca and Onondaga embassy arrived at Montreal in late July 1699. Invited to confer with Callières and the "principal chiefs" of Kanesatake and Kanatakwente at the Sulpician residence on Montreal Island, the Iroquois delegates proceeded to the negotiations in a formal line, with a Seneca headman singing a condolence song (which French observers described as dominated by the phrase "*Hai, Hai*") for all French killed in the late war. Maricourt and Joncaire, "adopted sons" of the Onondagas and Senecas (respectively), served as interpreters. The Iroquois complained that fifty-five of their people had been killed by French-allied nations since they had been notified of the 1697 Anglo-French peace. They asked Callières to "overturn" his war kettle so that they might enjoy free hunting in the *pays d'en haut*. In exchange, the Iroquois offered to repatriate (via Maricourt and Joncaire) all remaining French and Native prisoners in Iroquoia. They concluded by evoking the *kaswentha* relationship, planting a "tree of peace" at Montreal and clearing metaphorical "rocks" from the rivers between Iroquoia and New France to facilitate free movement for subsequent League peace delegations. Callières accepted these provisional terms on the condition that the League nations returned with a representative delegation from all five constituent nations to ratify the terms of peace with both New France and the upper Great Lakes nations. Callières concluded by offering the Onondaga and Seneca headmen a gift of a kettle with one spoon inside to symbolize their access to all the "hunting and fishing places" of the *pays d'en haut,* and by joining his Iroquois counterparts in the shared smoking of a single "calumet."[77]

PRELIMINARIES

By persuading the French to agree to peace in late July 1699, League diplomats converted a long-standing adversary into a powerful advocate. Canadian authorities, influenced by daily interactions with the Laurentian communities on their very doorstep, reached a better understanding of Iroquois spatial objectives by the turn of the eighteenth century than their Anglo-American counterparts ever enjoyed. French support of Iroquois initiatives after 1699 helped League leaders parry attempts by New York officials to derail crucial consensus building among Five Nations communities and to complete preliminary negotiations with the nations of the upper Great Lakes.

Despite the Five Nations' achievement of reconciliation with New France, Iroquois conflicts with the nations of the *pays d'en haut* continued. In late September 1699, a party of unidentified "far Indians" attacked and killed five Senecas "hard by" one of the latter's towns. Iroquois headmen remarked once more how "the General peace made by the two great Kings over the great water" had not resolved ongoing indigenous clashes between the Five Nations, the *pays d'en haut* nations, and the "Rondax," an appellation for French-allied Algonquian nations residing in the St. Lawrence valley.[78]

Low-intensity raiding did not deter the Iroquois from a planned winter hunt on the north shore of Lake Ontario, however. Louvigny reported over 600 Iroquois hunters, primarily Onondagas and Senecas, in the vicinity of Fort Frontenac during the winter of 1699–1700. Concerned that the Iroquois were "meditating" a revenge attack on Algonquins hunting nearby, Louvigny embarked on an ambitious, impromptu program of local diplomacy, offering feasts and generous presents (including some of his own shirts) to calm the "turbulent spirits" among the Iroquois. Louvigny even permitted his garrison to trade for the meat and skins of "elk and deer," which the Iroquois hunters had taken locally in great numbers. Although Callières later charged Louvigny with illegal trading, the colony's Sovereign Council declined to convict Louvigny due to the sheer volume of peltry he had diverted from Albany (valued at 60,000 livres) and because of Iroquois testimony supporting his own arguments of having "conciliated" the minds of the Iroquois, which kept alive the prospect of a formal peace treaty with the French-allied Native nations.[79]

While Onondagas and Senecas hunted and treated on the north shore of Lake Ontario, eastern League nations worked with their Laurentian kinfolk, particularly the members of two or three Mohawk families who had recently relocated to Kanatakwente or Kanesatake, to address the problems of "Rondax" aggression as well as a rumored Anglo-French plan for a joint attack on Iroquoia. The rumored European plot stimulated widespread indigenous rapprochement north and east of Iroquoia. Though negotiations between Iroquois and Algonquian peoples centered on shared hunting and fishing agreements and the extension of the League's "tree of welfare" eastward to Abenaki country, they proved greatly unnerving to Anglo-American officials. By March 1700, Bellomont feared a "General Insurrection of all the Indians" (meaning both the Five Nations and the so-called Eastern Indians, or the Algonquian residents of areas bordering on northern New England and New France). The threat, in Bellomont's opinion, was grave. Such a "conjunction" of indigenous strength could "in a short time drive [the English] quite out of the continent." The security of the Anglo-American colonies from "South Carolina to the Easternmost part of" Maine was now, according to Bellomont, "bound up in the preservation of the 5 Nations of Indians in Amity with us."[80]

Bellomont's assessment of circumstances in northeastern North America reflected apprehension in Anglo-American circles regarding the increasing range of Iroquois-brokered security arrangements with New France and neighboring Algonquian peoples by early 1700. Yet not all Anglo-Americans agreed with the governor's acknowledgment of the League's power. New York provincial authorities clung to their view that the League nations were "much dejected and in a staggering condition."

Robert Livingston wrote that statement about the League following his April 20 to May 13, 1700, journey from Albany to Onondaga. Echoing the zero-sum thinking of his predecessors, Livingston claimed that the Mohawk nation's purported wartime population losses had been exacerbated by further relocations to Laurentian valley settlements after the conclusion of peace in Europe in 1697. Livingston claimed that "near two-thirds" of the Mohawk nation lived in "Canada with their families" as of May 1700. Three months later, David Schuyler heard an unnamed Jesuit in Montreal reading off Native names from a manuscript census of "all the Praying Indians" in New France and was shocked to learn that Kanatakwente now boasted "three hundred and fifty fighting men," or quadruple the number previously assumed by Anglo-American officials.[81]

Such increases in "Canada's Store" of Native allies made for "thin Castles" on New York's frontier. Livingston proposed an extensive chain of fortifications throughout Iroquoia to bolster provincial defenses and (he argued) League spirits. Yet League nations did not share the perspective reflected in Livingston's assessment of Mohawk residency percentages. All Iroquois people benefited from having so many Mohawks (and members of other League nations) living in the St. Lawrence River valley.[82]

Information sharing represented the key advantage conveyed by the League's extended geography of solidarity. Laurentian Iroquois people communicated up-to-date news of their communities' proceedings with French officials to Oneida, Onondaga, Cayuga, and Seneca hunters on the north shore of Lake Ontario during the winter of 1699–1700. Such reports reached Onondaga shortly thereafter, providing League leaders with an expanded base of intelligence to consider in determining their next moves. Onondaga and Oneida hunters trading moose skins in Montreal early in 1700 visited friends at Kanatakwente and returned home with a wampum belt that documented the peace concluded by the Laurentian communities with the "Rondax Indians." Ohensiowanne, who continued to travel regularly between Montreal and Onondaga over the winter of 1699–1700, conveyed news of Callières's reported willingness to "take the hatchet out of the hands" of the upper Great Lakes Algonquians, a crucial aspect of League plans for a comprehensive peace agreement.[83]

By July 1700, the scale and complexity of Iroquois diplomatic efforts were registered in the increasingly voluminous records of French and Anglo-American colonial officials. Seneca and Onondaga leaders conferred with Callières at Montreal on July 18, 1700. Rehearsing the *kaswentha* principles articulated in 1699, the Seneca headmen affirmed the status of their "son Joncaire" as "Plenipotentiary" of their affairs with New France, charged with "communicat[ing] Onontio's opinions to us, and convey[ing] ours to him." The Onondagas assigned the same responsibilities to Maricourt. The Seneca and Onondaga delegates, who employed their own nations' wampum (in lieu of officially sanctioned belts from the League's "publick treasury"), explained the incomplete nature of their party's composition by noting that leaders from the other three League nations had gone to Albany to determine why Bellomont "opposed our coming to our father Onontio to conclude business completely." Callières repatriated an Iroquois captive held by the Algonquins and invited the Senecas and Onondagas to return with a fully representative delegation of League headmen to treat with "Deputies" from the nations of the upper Great Lakes scheduled to arrive in Montreal in August. At that time, Callières claimed, "we shall fasten all together [to] the great Tree of Peace," and "all the rivers shall be cleared," and "all the War kettles be overturned."[84]

While the Senecas and Onondagas were treating with Callières in Montreal, four headmen from Kanatakwente (two civil leaders and two military captains) arrived in Albany to meet with local officials. Sagronwadie, identified as the "Chief Sachim" and speaker of this delegation, had come to reassert the right of the Laurentian Iroquois to free communications with Albany. The efficacy of Laurentian brokerage for League negotiations in Canada depended on social, political, and economic arrangements that supported a thriving Iroquois presence in the St. Lawrence valley. The right of unimpeded travel and trade to an alternate market represented a key aspect of such arrangements, and Sagronwadie's embassy elicited from Albany authorities a promise that all Iroquois traders could participate in the city's fur trade, even so-called deserters from their "native country." This promise came at a critical juncture, since French authorities had increased efforts during the spring of 1700 to interdict the flow of peltry from Montreal to Albany by sending patrol canoes into Lake Champlain.[85]

Sagronwadie's exchange with Albany officials occurred two days before an official League embassy led by Teganissorens's delegation opened discussions with the commissioners of Indian Affairs in Albany on July 11, 1700. Teganissorens likely spoke with a heavy heart, as Bellomont reported that the Onondaga leader's wife, a so-called Praying Indian from Canada who had accompanied Sagronwadie's embassy, had just been murdered in Albany by a Protestant Mohawk who claimed that she was a Jesuit-educated poisoner of Anglophile Mohawks. Albany authorities interpreted this event and the flight of Aqueendara with his reportedly "bewitch'd" son and twenty-five other Onondagas to Peter Schuyler's property near Albany as evidence that the League nations were "full of faction" as a result of "very subtile [sic] and vigilant" efforts by the French. Yet Teganissorens did not permit any grief he may have felt over the loss of his spouse to deter him from communicating the League's utter contempt for Bellomont's efforts to restrict their freedom to travel to New France to conclude peace with Callières and the nations of the *pays d'en haut*.[86]

In his public address, Teganissorens related how conversations between Iroquois and Algonquian hunters in the *pays d'en haut* over the winter of 1699–1700, which had been facilitated by Iroquois adoptees among the latter nations, had advanced indigenous peace efforts. These preliminary talks had resulted in the visit of five upper Great Lakes Algonquians to Onondaga in late June 1700. These emissaries came to finalize a preliminary agreement that involved the League nations inviting members of three (unnamed) *pays d'en haut* nations (possibly an early reference to the "Three

Fires" confederacy of the Odawas, Ojibwas, and Potawatomis) to reside on Seneca territory on the north shore of Lake Ontario in exchange for Iroquois-brokered access to "Corlaer's house" (Anglo-American traders) in Albany. Teganissorens then pressed Albany officials to ensure favorable pricing at Albany to enhance the persuasive appeal of a comprehensive alliance between these upper Great Lakes nations and the League. Although low-intensity hostilities between the Five Nations and peoples of the *pays d'en haut* continued, Teganissorens claimed that the nascent peace terms concluded at Onondaga would result in the League and upper Great Lakes nations sharing hunting territories, boiling their meat "in one kettle, eat[ing] out of one dish, and one spoon, and so be one." Rather than permit ongoing warfare to "devour us both," League negotiators had managed to persuade sixteen towns of these three upper Great Lakes Algonquian nations to "grow old and grey-headed together" with their longtime Iroquois adversaries.[87]

New York authorities, stunned by Teganissorens's speech, hoped to recover some diplomatic influence with the Iroquois at a conference in late August 1700, where Bellomont would distribute Crown presents valued at £800 to the League. The royal gift to the Five Nations in 1700 included "400 light fuzils" that the Lords of Trade had shipped in hopes that such a large proportion of military stores from England would "remove the jealousy that has been raised amongst them of a design to disarm them." Yet official English communications across the Atlantic could not keep pace with fast-moving independent Iroquois diplomacy, and Bellomont feared that English imperial "mismanagement" had enabled the League to conduct independent, wide-ranging preliminary peace agreements with New France and its allied Native nations. These developments, Bellomont predicted, would result in the loss not only of the Iroquois League's allegiance but possibly also all the English "Plantations on this Continent."[88]

Bellomont opened formal proceedings in Albany on September 6, 1700, with fifty Iroquois "Sachems" accompanied by fifty more "young Indians" from all five League nations. In a clumsy attempt to redefine the League's geography of solidarity, the governor urged his Iroquois audience to retrieve individuals who had been seduced and deceived by the "artifices of the French" to relocate to the Laurentian settlements. The return of those "debauched" Iroquois would, in Bellomont's view, strengthen the League and allow all its constituent nations to live in "obedience to the great King our Master."[89]

In his reply the next day, Aqueendara addressed Bellomont's demand that the League repatriate residents of the Laurentian communities by pointing out how generous French gifts of food and clothing had represented a considerable "inducement" for many of the Iroquois people who chose to relocate to the St. Lawrence valley. Aqueendara contrasted French "charity and caresses" to what he described as extortionate pricing then prevalent at Albany. Prices were so high in Albany that some Laurentian Mohawks who had recently carried beaver pelts from Montreal to trade for English stroud blankets had returned home with their furs, claiming that they could procure English woolens more cheaply in New France. "You must certainly conclude," Aqueendara argued before Bellomont on September 8, 1700, "that when our people come here with four or five Beavers and they get but one coat for it, it must trouble us much." Reminding Bellomont once more of the *kaswentha* tradition, Aqueendara stated that mutually beneficial trade was what "induced us at first to make the Covenant Chain together." Only "good pennyworths" at Albany would enable the Iroquois to continue to live as "Brethren" with the English. Aqueendara underscored his point by reporting the planned relocation of more than 3,000 members of unnamed *pays d'en haut* nations to the north shore of Lake Ontario. Did the English want to lose League-brokered access to this long-sought-after indigenous market?[90]

Confronted by Aqueendara's formidable arguments and attempting to escape the stench of bear's grease and tobacco smoke that permeated Albany's crowded city hall, Bellomont held a private conference on September 9, 1700, with two principal leaders from each of the Five Nations. The governor attempted to insert himself into the League-initiated trade and peace arrangements with the nations of the upper Great Lakes, arguing that only by formally incorporating these nations into the Covenant Chain alliance could the League nations expect to hunt in the *pays d'en haut* "without any sort of hazard." The Iroquois headmen replied that New York's formal involvement was unnecessary, since these negotiations were already complete. The League had extended its geography of solidarity by means of "friendly correspondence" between the Five Nations and the "Praying Indians" in the St. Lawrence valley.[91]

At the precise moment the large League delegation was engaged with Bellomont in Albany, nineteen Onondaga, Seneca, and Cayuga headmen opened formal discussions with Callières at Montreal. On September 3, 1700, Teganissorens added metaphorical roots to the "tree of peace" planted at Montreal in July 1699. These roots signified the newly extended reach of the "tree of peace" to the allied "Far Nations" of the *pays d'en haut.* He then surrendered thirteen French prisoners, emphasizing the "considerable pain" he and his colleagues experienced in "witnessing their separation from us, having long since adopted them as our nephews." Teganissorens requested in return the delivery of all remaining Iroquois prisoners among the French and upper Great Lakes Native nations party to the agreement, Iroquois access to a smith at Fort Frontenac, and the restoration of trade there "at Montreal prices" to ensure that "Corlard" (New York authorities) could not treat the Iroquois as "Slaves" and "Vassals." He concluded by offering a wampum belt to the upper Great Lakes nations' delegates that expressed the League's pleasure at the prospect of "eat[ing] together when we should meet" from "one joint kettle."[92]

Callières and a group of headmen from the *pays d'en haut,* which included Kondiaronk, responded to Teganissorens's speech later the same day. The French governor metaphorically placed all his "weapons of war" into a deep hole, covered the hole with a rock, and then underscored French commitment to the peace by throwing down "a [wampum] Belt six foot long." Callières invited Iroquois hunters to exchange their beaver, moose, or elk skins for "all necessary merchandize" at Fort Frontenac at subsidized Montreal prices. He also pledged to send a smith to the fort and, crucially, promised not to "hinder" direct trade between the "remote Indians" and the Five Nations. The upper Great Lakes delegation, along with some attending Abenaki and Mahican leaders, assented to these terms and assured the Iroquois that they would not cut the "roots" of the "Tree of Peace."[93]

All present at Montreal agreed on a date of August 1701 for a formal ratification of the peace and a general exchange of prisoners, sealing the agreement in a document "signed" with the totemic clan signatures of the Native "Deputies" present. Callières dispatched Jesuit Jean Enjalran and the Sieur de Courtemanche to Michilimackinac with a copy of the preliminary treaty in order to advertise the planned August 1701 summit at Montreal to the *pays d'en haut* nations. A Kanatakwente headman delivered the final words of the conference, and his expression of support for the peace, echoed by headmen from Kanesatake, signaled the vital role of the Laurentian Iroquois communities as key hosts and brokers of the September 1700 proceedings at Montreal.[94]

When the League delegates returned from Albany and Montreal to Onondaga on October 16, 1700, they found a party of Albany officials (which included Mayor Peter van Brugh, Aldermen Hendrick Hansen and Lawrence Claessen, and a royal engineer, Colonel Willem Wolfgang Römer) waiting for them. Teganissorens, although exhausted by his travels over the previous three months and ready to grieve the loss of his wife, communicated a full report of the September 1700 negotiations at Montreal to the New Yorkers. He stressed how important a role the Laurentian Iroquois had played in brokering the preliminary peace treaty.[95]

Teganissorens recognized no discrepancy between his activities in New France and the League's Covenant Chain alliance with New York. He still professed to share "one heart and soul" with "Brother Corlaer." Yet Teganissorens's sense of allegiance did not extend to any willingness on his part to tolerate Römer's plans to undertake extensive reconnaissance of League homelands, a preliminary step toward construction of an English fort in Onondaga country. Having seen a sketch map Bellomont produced in Albany that indicated "an isthmus or neck of land on a vast lake lying northward of the Onondages" (Oswego) as the planned site of the English post, Onondaga leaders "quickly comprehended" its underlying intent as an English attempt to leapfrog some of the League nations in order to gain direct access to the trade of the upper Great Lakes nations.[96]

This New York initiative threatened the League's preliminary negotiations with the upper Great Lakes nations, which entailed shared hunting on the north shore of Lake Ontario and League-brokered access to Albany for the peoples of the *pays d'en haut*. Teganissorens demonstrated his regard for Römer's plans by escorting

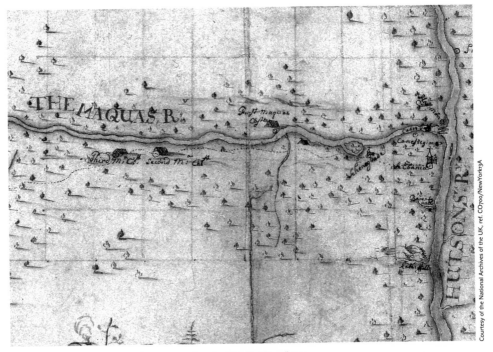

"A Mappe of Coll. Römer his Journey to the 5 Indian Nations," 1700

him on a cursory canoe tour of Onondaga and Oneida lakes that came nowhere near the engineer's desired site of Oswego. When another party of Albany men arrived at Onondaga on October 18, 1700, with a "pass" from Bellomont for a planned hunting and diplomatic expedition to the upper Great Lakes, Teganissorens and his colleagues turned them back. The Onondaga leaders would tolerate no unauthorized Anglo-American travel through Iroquoia to the upper Great Lakes. They also explicitly prohibited any further surveying or construction work on a fort, and the extent of their "prejudice" on this matter caused engineer Römer to "abscond into the bushes" the next day, initiating his entourage's hasty departure from Onondaga country.[97]

In the aftermath of Römer's failed expedition, Bellomont attempted to account for what he perceived as a point of low ebb in Anglo-American relations with the League. "Enemies of Government" in the assembly had failed to vote adequate taxes to support the governor's diplomacy with the League. Bureaucrats in England had thrown up repeated "obstacles" that delayed Bellomont's effort to vacate Fletcher's extravagant land grants. Corrupt officials in Albany had undermined Bellomont's authority with Iroquois leaders and run up huge public expenses to further ingratiate themselves with particular headmen. The "scandalously weak" condition of forts at Albany and Schenectady had made a mockery of Anglo-American claims to "power and greatness." Neighboring Anglo-American colonial governors had refused to cooperate with Bellomont's efforts to centralize in New York all trade and diplomatic

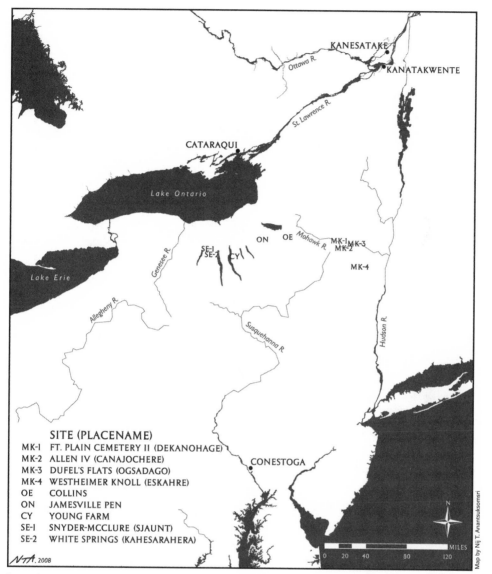

SITE (PLACENAME)
MK-1   FT. PLAIN CEMETERY II (DEKANOHAGE)
MK-2   ALLEN IV (CANAJOCHERE)
MK-3   DUFEL'S FLATS (OGSADAGO)
MK-4   WESTHEIMER KNOLL (ESKAHRE)
OE   COLLINS
ON   JAMESVILLE PEN
CY   YOUNG FARM
SE-1   SNYDER-MCCLURE (SJAUNT)
SE-2   WHITE SPRINGS (KAHESARAHERA)

Iroquoia, ca. 1701

relations between the Anglo-American colonies, the League, and other Native nations. The New York governor was "almost at [his] wit's end" by the autumn of 1700, after learning how Teganissorens had thwarted his efforts to engage in direct trade with the "remote nations" and thereby revive New York's diminishing fur trade.[98]

Meanwhile, authorities in New France had responded eagerly to the League's request for a "store of goods" at Fort Frontenac to serve Iroquois hunters on the north shore of Lake Ontario during the winter of 1700–1701. Callières and Champigny had also agreed to Cadillac's request to establish a trading post at Detroit, provided that trade would be open to both the Iroquois and the nations of the *pays d'en haut* Native "allies" of New France, and that Cadillac's expeditionary party took "possession of that post from the Lake Huron side, by that means avoiding the Niagara passage so as not to give umbrage to the Iroquois." French officials had also begun as early as June 1700 to encourage offensive campaigns by the *pays d'en haut* nations toward the "Flat Heads," a collective appellation used to describe the Choctaws, Catawbas, Chickasaws, and other Native nations residing between the Carolina backcountry and the lower Mississippi River valley. The League nations had also reoriented their military efforts toward the southeast, facilitated by decades of familiarity with the frontiers of Maryland and Virginia. Jesuit François de Montigny noted the commonplace appearance of Iroquois canoes on the Mississippi River between what is now southern Illinois and "Biloxi Bay" in August 1699, which they accessed via the Wabash and Allegheny rivers, the latter of which extended into Seneca homelands. Similarly, Albany officials reported the October 4, 1700, departure of an Oneida military leader named Kanaghquaindi with a party of warriors "to the Southward, where the Flatheads live."[99]

Although the French made substantial concessions to the League during the negotiations of 1700, colonial observers still credited Callières for having "concluded the peace with the Iroquois with great glory" to King Louis XIV. By acting as "arbiter" and host for peace negotiations between the Iroquois and the nations of the upper Great Lakes, Callières had achieved an important diplomatic victory over English claims to suzerainty over the League and had also reduced the "heavy expenses" incurred by French-sponsored warfare between the League and the peoples of the *pays d'en haut.* Callières, unlike his Anglo-American counterparts, accepted that recognition of the League's "neutrality" (which he understood to mean that "neither we nor the English would be allowed to settle on their lands") was the necessary price of peace in eastern North America by 1701.[100]

Parallel Conclusion

The League's conclusion of parallel treaties with New France and New York in 1701 reflected the crucial significance of freedom of movement to the Iroquois polity. Bonds of kinship extended across an extensive geographic space that transcended European efforts to impose colonial boundaries facilitated flows of information that allowed Iroquois leaders to maintain delicate balance in their foreign relations. Consecutive treaties hosted by officials of settler colonies in Albany and Montreal in 1701 facilitated the peaceful resolution of a complex indigenous diplomatic agenda.

New York authorities worried about the extent to which the French had "prevailed" with the Iroquois over the winter of 1700–1701. Robert Livingston noted the difficulty of distinguishing between the so-called French Iroquois and those he described as "ours," given that both groups employed their common "kindred and language" to advance their own interests at the expense (in Livingston's view) of their ties to New York. Livingston even went so far as to admit the fallacy of both French and English claims to the Iroquois as "subjects" of their respective kings. The Iroquois "do not so understand it," he wrote in late May 1701, but with good reason "look upon themselves in the state of freedom."[101]

The Iroquois continued to exercise their freedom in 1701. A report in Albany of Maricourt's arrival at Onondaga in May 1701 to invite League headmen to a "grand Dyet" at Montreal led the Albany Indian "Commissioners" to dispatch Johannes Bleecker Jr. and David Schuyler to Onondaga to discourage direct League negotiations with New France. Upon their arrival at Onondaga three weeks later, Bleecker and Schuyler learned of Teganissorens's recent return from Montreal. Callières had reportedly showered the Onondaga leader with presents (including "a gun with two barrels, a laced coat, a hat, a shirt, Tobacco, and sundry other things"). The Albany emissaries pressed for a meeting with League leaders but were refused on the grounds that those present at Onondaga did not constitute "a full house and so could not give a positive answer." This assertion effectively muted Bleecker and Schuyler while a number of League headmen met separately with Maricourt at Kaneenda, the fishing station eight miles distant from the Onondaga town.[102]

On June 30, 1701, in a "publick meeting of all the Indians" at Onondaga, Teganissorens notified his colleagues of Callières's decision to establish a French post at Detroit. In the view of French officials, the Iroquois could trade their peltry and obtain their supplies wherever they pleased; Cadillac's post at Detroit would merely offer Iroquois hunters and traders another commercial venue in proximity to productive hunting grounds. Although the governor had taken this step without consulting League authorities, he assured Teganissorens that Detroit would not become a haven for raiding parties of the upper Great Lakes nations. Callières, while unwilling to concede the entire trade of the *pays d'en haut* to Albany traders via League hunters and commercial brokers, nevertheless restated his official French recognition of the League's "strict neutrality." This final concession had persuaded Teganissorens to propose assembling a delegation of League headmen to travel with Maricourt to the planned formal ratification of a comprehensive peace in August 1701.[103]

Bleecker and Schuyler tried to prevent League headmen from traveling to New France, reminding them of their long-standing conflicts with Canada and urging them not to squander the League's renowned military reputation by agreeing to peace with Callières. Yet the Albany emissaries did not realize how far matters had already progressed. Iroquois hunters had confirmed the preliminary peace negotiated in August 1700 with four more nations of the *pays d'en haut* during the previous winter, returning with gifts of "skins" as a sign of these upper Great Lakes nations' commitment to attending the 1701 peace conference at Montreal. League leaders underscored this announcement by giving Bleecker and Schuyler a painted elk skin that mapped the names and locations of all "seven nations" of "Farr Indians" with whom the League had made preliminary peace terms. Iroquois leaders planned to conclude matters in 1701 through parallel diplomacy, sending one group of headmen to Montreal and another to Albany.[104]

Thirty-two League headmen from all Five Nations arrived in Albany on July 23, 1701, where they met with Nanfan, who had ascended to the governor's office after Bellomont's death during the previous March. Nanfan, who like his predecessor believed that he could confirm the League's "obedience to his Majesty" with official presents, emphasized predictable themes in his formal welcome to the Iroquois headmen. He assured his audience of the king's esteem for his "Brethren of the Five Nations," and he urged them to repatriate Iroquois people who had "deserted" to Canada and to oppose the French establishment at Detroit, the "principal pass" to the League's best "beaver hunting country." Nanfan argued that the terms of the Covenant Chain agreement precluded independent Iroquois negotiations with New France, and claimed that he would issue directives about how the allied League nations were to behave in the event of a future Anglo-French conflict. He concluded by delivering a substantial present from the Crown, valued at £800 sterling, to the Iroquois delegation on July 29, 1701.[105]

A senior Mohawk headman named Onucheranorum offered the League's response to Nanfan the next day. In a gesture designed to check the potential for Callières's post at Detroit to upset the fragile balance achieved by the League's painstaking diplomacy with the indigenous nations of the upper Great Lakes, the speaker offered to donate to the English Crown all the League's "Beaver hunting" lands between Iroquoia and Detroit that the Five Nations had won "with the sword eighty years ago." Onucheranorum made clear that the arrangements obligated King William to "protect and defend" the League's continued unimpeded access to the donated territory, and asked that Albany Indian Affairs Secretary Robert Livingston draft an appropriate "instrument" and deliver it personally to the king, so that the agreement would not be "laid aside and forgot."[106]

The "Deed from the Five Nations to the King of their Beaver Hunting Ground," drawn up by Livingston and signed by twenty different headmen from all five League nations on July 30, 1701, conveyed crucial information about Iroquois leaders' sense of seventeenth-century spatial history and the legacy of that history for contemporary circumstances in eastern North America. The text of the deed, analyzed carefully, reveals remarkable insight into the organization and integrity of the League polity at this time. At least 3 of the signatories appear to have been hereditary titleholders (one each from the Mohawks, Senecas, and Onondagas, the so-called "elder brothers" of the Five Nations). Fourteen of the 20 League signatories were affiliated with the "elder brothers," and 9 of the 20 signatories were either Mohawks or Senecas, the two nations charged in League tradition with guarding, or "keeping" the metaphorical "doors" of the League's longhouse (an allegorical reference to the geographical extent of League homelands at any given time).[107] In this carefully-articulated state-ment, the Iroquois signers asserted their claim to an extensive portion of the eastern Great Lakes region (estimated by Nanfan at "800 miles long and 400 miles broad") on the basis of their military victory over the Wendats. The document attested that the Iroquois had enjoyed "peaceable hunting" in the region for the previous six decades, and their claim to exclusive jurisdiction over the region as its "true owners" had been further strengthened by the incorporation of the majority of the Wendats into League nations. The relocation of the Tionnontatés, a "remnant" of the Wendats, to the vicinity of Michilimackinac and subsequent French sponsorship of Tionnontaté Wendat and Algonquian opposition to Iroquois hunting in the *pays d'en haut* had caused the recent conflicts in the region. Far from an outright surrender of territory to the "Crown of England," the deed signed at Albany represented a supplemental, parallel effort by League headmen to commit their Anglo-American allies to protect-ing what they had already achieved in separate, preliminary negotiations with the upper Great Lakes nations and New France in 1700: "free hunting for us and the heirs and descendants from us the Five Nations forever."[108]

Nanfan and other Anglo-American officials, not surprisingly, interpreted the deed in a less nuanced manner, believing that it represented a permanent Iroquois surren-der of claimed territory to the English Crown, and Nanfan credited himself with hav-ing "fix'd our Indians in their obedience to his Majesty and in their friendship to this and his Majesty's neighbouring Provinces." Many subsequent historians have accepted Nanfan's assessment; yet such an interpretation overlooks how "Five of the Principal Sachims of the Five Nations" reiterated the conditional character of the arrangements in an August 1, 1701, discussion with Nanfan. Everything related to the deed hinged, in their view, on Livingston delivering the document personally to the king and return-ing with an official response. When Nanfan denied Livingston permission to travel to England in early September 1701 (the secretary was seeking substantial compensa-tion for claimed arrears in Crown payments of his salary and other nonreimbursed expenses), the governor effectively nullified any legitimate English claim to the region identified in the deed as the Crown's protectorate, despite subsequent English asser-tions to that effect, which persisted until the eve of the American Revolution. In the meantime, events revealed the emptiness of any purported "obedience" of the League nations to New York. On September 7, 1701, reports of French officers in Iroquoia led Nanfan to order Bleecker and Schuyler back to Onondaga once more to "hinder" any Franco-Iroquois negotiations they might discover.[109]

The Albany emissaries arrived at Onondaga eight days later and found a buoyant group of League leaders who welcomed the Albany visitors with "great Joy" and in-formed them that Frenchmen were also then present at Onondaga with "a great deal of Goods." Exasperated by this news, Bleecker and Schuyler belittled recent League diplomatic efforts with New France as "needless, for our King had made peace for you and all his subjects in his Dominions." Teganissorens interjected, advising Bleecker and Schuyler that they were "misinformed." The trade goods delivered by the French represented ransom payments for Iroquois families still holding French and upper Great Lakes Native captives. On September 23, 1701, Onondaga leaders "obliged" Joncaire to "repeat before" Bleecker and Schuyler "all the propositions which the Governour of Canada had made to the five nations in Canada," so that Albany officials could be made fully aware of what had happened during the League leaders' recent embassy to Canada. Joncaire's speech represented the first intelligence obtained by Anglo-Americans of the unprecedented August 1701 Montreal conference in which over 1,200 Native delegates from more than forty different nations had assembled to ratify the preliminary agreement concluded in September 1700.[110]

Joncaire delivered a largely accurate account of the Montreal treaty at Onondaga in late September 1701 for the Albany emissaries. The adopted Seneca diplomat explained how Callières had permanently buried the French "hatchet" formerly used to incite Natives of the upper Great Lakes against the Iroquois. The nations of the *pays d'en haut* and the League nations would henceforth "live in Peace together" as "Brethren," sharing hunting grounds throughout the upper Great Lakes. The new French post at Detroit would serve as both an entrepôt of subsidized French trade and a site for the resolution of any conflicts that might arise between the newly allied Native nations. Finally, Callières had communicated formal French recognition of the League's assertion of neutral political status. If any future war between England and France materialized (the War of Spanish Succession then loomed on the horizon), the Iroquois were "by no means to intermeddle," but rather to stand aside and let the Europeans "fight alone" while continuing to enjoy freedom of movement between Iroquoia, New France, and the *pays d'en haut*. On August 4, 1701, Callières announced the successful conclusion of the proceedings and proclaimed "Peace over all the world."[111]

Eyewitness French accounts of the August 1701 Montreal treaty reveal additional evidence of the extent of the League's diplomatic achievement. Upper Great Lakes headmen had repatriated twenty-four Iroquois prisoners in exchange for four surrendered by Teganissorens (and promises of future repatriation of those remaining in Iroquoia). Iroquois leaders from Kanesatake expressed their delight with the formal reconciliation with the *pays d'en haut* nations that they had brokered for their brethren, and a speaker from Kanatakwente reminded Teganissorens of how long the Laurentian communities had worked to "procure peace for" the League with both New France and "all Indians." Although the Mohawks absented themselves from the formal proceedings at Montreal in August 1701 (due in large part to the number of their headmen occupied at the Albany negotiations and to their substantial representation by Laurentian kinfolk), several Mohawk leaders concluded a preliminary ratification of the Montreal treaty later in the month of August 1701. A separate delegation of the League's eastern doorkeepers visited Callières in 1702 to confirm their acceptance of the previous year's "Neutrality" treaty.[112]

The Iroquois treaties of 1701 with New France and New York arose not from a context of Iroquois defeat, crisis, or weakness after the mid-1690s, but rather from more than half a century of League efforts to establish Iroquoia as a crucial, central space between French and Anglo-American settler populations on the periphery of their homelands. More than simply an "accident" or a "partial victory snatched from the jaws of defeat," these two treaties resolved a number of social, political, economic, and spatial issues generated by patterns of Iroquois mobility after 1534.[113]

The Edge of the Woods welcome offered to the Iroquois delegates at Kahnawake in July 1701, described at the beginning of this chapter, occurred within sight and earshot of the Lachine Rapids, where the Hochelagans had stopped Cartier's progress in 1535 and reasserted ancestral Iroquois ties to the St. Lawrence River valley. The Laurentian communities of Kanatakwente and Kanesatake, as crucial yet largely forgotten mediators and local hosts of the Montreal treaty, reaffirmed their places in the League as key sites from which the Iroquois polity could engage Native and settler populations throughout much of eastern North America. Thousands of adoptees and their descendants within Iroquois nations facilitated diverse contacts with an array of Native peoples over a vast geographic area and enabled those professing identity as a member of the Iroquois League (*kanonsionni*) to assert simultaneously a precontact affiliation to an extensive indigenous homeland vis-à-vis the claims of would-be imperial expansionists. Finally, the 1701 peace between the League and the Native peoples of the upper Great Lakes, strengthened by exchanges of prisoners and by a shared hunting agreement (which built on the precedents of early-seventeenth-century interindigenous agreements involving shared access to the St. Lawrence valley), represented a mutually agreed upon resolution of postcontact Iroquois expansion into the *pays d'en haut.*

NEUTRALITY

What European observers identified as Iroquois neutrality in 1701 might better be understood as the League's achievement of balance in its spatial relations with neighboring Native nations and settler colonies. What is particularly striking about the two treaties of 1701 is the degree to which they foregrounded the resolution of indigenous issues via exchanges of captives, shared hunting agreements, and diversified trade relationships. Officials from settler colonies participated in but did not direct the proceedings at Albany and Montreal: that task fell largely to Iroquois leaders, whose commitment to cultural ideas of *kaswentha,* the "tree of peace," and the "bowl with one spoon" enabled them to shape a comprehensive vision of Iroquoia as a crucial, central space in eastern North America in 1701. Understanding this fact helps us to challenge persistent historical constructions that privilege colonial settlements as core areas and represent precolonial indigenous homelands as peripheral and marginal. If we read the sources with an awareness of how Iroquois people constructed their spatial relations, we may better appreciate the nature of Iroquoia as a distinct, dynamic historical space that played a unique and formative role in North American history from 1534 to 1701 and beyond.[114]

In 1701, the Iroquois achieved peace with a diverse array of indigenous nations as well as recognition of the League's long-asserted freedom of movement throughout a vast extent of eastern North America. Notwithstanding their conditional deed to Nanfan, League negotiators had agreed in Montreal to the establishment of Detroit in the midst of territory their colleagues had supposedly donated to the king of England. Though English imperial officials fretted about the potential of this new French fort to "overawe" Iroquois hunters and thereby further diminish New York's peltry revenues, knowledgeable French observers held no illusions about the extent to which Detroit was militarily "useless" against the Iroquois, who remained potential enemies worthy of "dread." The extent of French economic and territorial concessions to the Iroquois in 1701, at both Detroit and Fort Frontenac, caught the attention of some upper Great Lakes Algonquian observers who remarked on how rapidly the French had shifted, in their view, from seeking to destroy the Iroquois to cultivating the League's favor. Relations with demanding Iroquois consumers and interior French posts remained "ticklish" after 1701, and officials in New France realized that if their new League allies became "discouraged," they might "break the neutrality they have promised." Far from opposing Iroquois neutrality, Canadian officials attempted during the early eighteenth century to employ that neutrality as a basis for a regional non-aggression agreement with the Anglo-American colonies.[115]

Authorities in New York also adopted a solicitous attitude toward the League after 1701. The terms of the League's 1701 conditional deed of their hunting grounds to England, which committed the Crown to protecting free Iroquois movement in the continental interior, had exposed the fallacy of English claims to the subaltern political status of the Five Nations. New York officials informed their counterparts in England that the health of the Covenant Chain alliance now depended on "yearly presents (or rather bribes)" issued to the League, without which it would be "impossible to secure them to the English interest." Although they accepted annual presents from the king of England, League leaders continued to exercise their right to independent negotiations with New France, thereby underscoring their hard-won diplomatic neutrality between competing European empires in North America.[116]

Broadening the focus of analysis of Iroquois activities in 1701 beyond the formal treaties hosted in Montreal and Albany reveals even more clearly how the year's events represented at once the culmination of long-standing Iroquois social, political, and spatial objectives and a significant turning point in the League's spatial history. Iroquois movements, while maintaining patterns established during the sixteenth and seventeenth centuries, would extend in new directions over an increasingly larger extent of eastern North America during the eighteenth century. Jean Louis de la Corne, the commanding officer of Fort Frontenac in 1701, granted the request of a "number of Iroquois families" who wanted to establish a town on the periphery of the French installation, thereby reestablishing a formal, settled presence on the north shore of Lake Ontario that persisted through the end of the French regime. Free travel and trade by Iroquois people also continued in the Lake Champlain–Richelieu River corridor. On August 28, 1701, Albany fur trader Evert Wendell noted in his account book a pending journey by two Mohawk women (one "Rapecke" and her daughter "Rotsie") from Albany to Montreal, where they planned to trade. In September 1701, Albany emissaries described the return of Kanaghquaindi, the Oneida military leader, from his year-long southern campaign during which he reported conversing with "some Indians who live behind Carolina and Maryland who told him all was in peace and quietness and that there should be no differences between them as there had been formerly." Finally, on December 7, 1701, Seneca leaders conferred with Cadillac at Detroit. The League's western doorkeepers repatriated three Miami women in a formal ceremony that at once served as an expression of Seneca commitment to the indigenous principles of the previous August's Montreal treaty and also as a means to domesticate the French installation at Detroit as an "end" of the League's "house," or a site of League trade and mediation for interindigenous disputes.[117]

The geography of solidarity created by Iroquois people from 1534 to 1701 was an evolving network of social, political, and ethical relations among individuals, communities, and nations. It relied on transversal patterns of alliance that minimized potential social conflicts by encouraging frequent human movement between communities spread out over a significant extent of space, instead of constructing hierarchical relations of power that concentrated authority at particular locales.[118] The increasing spatial range of Iroquois mobility from 1534 to 1701 facilitated the ongoing assessment and recalibration of not only internal relations between Iroquois nations but also the terms of their connections to Native and non-Native peoples on the periphery of their homelands. Sixteenth- and seventeenth-century Iroquois movements to the north shore of Lake Ontario, the St. Lawrence River valley, the Virginia and Maryland backcountry, and the upper Great Lakes region had provided Iroquois people with access to still more distant regions for diverse social, economic, and political purposes. Each of these four theaters of Iroquois mobility linked the previous seven generations of Iroquois connections to distant spaces to the post-1701 world of Iroquois entanglement with their colonial neighbors.

EPILOGUE

The territory once exhibited on the map as the "Country of the Iroquois," comprising almost the entire state of New York, is now the seat of a highly intelligent, Christian civilization, teeming with populous cities, beautiful villages, highly cultivated farms, mills, manufactories, schools, churches, and everything that denotes enterprise, intelligence, and universal prosperity. When it is considered that this change in western New York has been wrought within the space of less than one hundred years—yes, within the life-time of many now living—it will be admitted that the change is most extraordinary, wonderful.

—HISTORIAN WILLIAM KETCHUM, WRITING IN 1864

This account of the geography of solidarity constructed in Iroquoia during the sixteenth and seventeenth centuries has been written in the midst of numerous postcolonial struggles between contemporary Iroquois people and the settler governments of the United States and Canada—all of which stem from starkly contrasting ideas of Iroquois people's relation to spatial mobility. Over the past decade, increasing public calls for cash-strapped New York State to collect taxes on the sale of cigarettes and gasoline to non-Native customers at Iroquois-owned reservation establishments have elicited retaliatory threats of Iroquois tolls and blockades on several of the state's major highways. The Supreme Court of Canada, in its landmark 2001 ruling in *Mitchell v. Minister of National Revenue*, placed severe restrictions on the rights of Iroquois people to transfer goods across the U.S.–Canada border for purposes of trade. Most recently, in January 2008 the U.S. Department of the Interior rejected the St. Regis Mohawk tribe's petition for an off-reservation casino in the Catskills region of New York State on the grounds that the distance of the proposed casino from the reservation would result in "negative impacts on tribal life."[1] The cultural impasse on the relationship between spatial mobility and Iroquois identity has changed little since the early nineteenth century, when Iroquois people were first confined to reservations.

Much of the history of early America written since the nineteenth century has reflected a particular view of space as a surface: mere territory to be traversed, mapped, conquered, and integrated by Europeans into various systems of imperial governance. Yet such a passive conception of space is not, as geographer Doreen Massey has argued, an "innocent manoeuvre." It promotes an understanding of non-European peoples, places, or cultures "simply as phenomena 'on' this surface" and thereby deprives them of their deep and distinctive histories. Previous treatments of precolonial Iroquois history have held their indigenous subjects largely immobile, "on space, in place," awaiting the arrival of European colonizers and succeeding generations of ethnographers and historians to tell the story of Iroquois decline. In contrast, this study has attempted to reconstruct the histories lived and created by Iroquois people from within their own conceptions of space from 1534 to 1701. In doing so, it calls attention to the ways in which persistent conceptions of early American space as a surface upon which Europeans acted and Native peoples reacted have yielded narratives that obscure the contemporaneous temporalities and heterogeneities of space for non-European actors. Such accounts fail to acknowledge the coeval yet vastly different experience of the Iroquois (and other indigenous) peoples. Subordinated to the self-producing narrative of the emergence of the United States, the Iroquois have been denied their own historical trajectories and effectively (though artificially) held still while others have done the moving.[2]

From its origins as an inquiry into the spatial correlates of precolonial Iroquois social organization, this study has mapped the extensive terrain of Iroquois activity throughout eastern North America from 1534 to 1701. By focusing on the thematic structure of the Condolence ceremony, it has demonstrated the degree to which mobility was imperative to Iroquois cultural integrity insofar as it facilitated a broadening sense of Iroquois identity construction during the sixteenth and seventeenth centuries. Multiple lines of documentary, archaeological, and oral evidence—ranging from the first glimpses of spatial consciousness and protocols during the earliest-documented Iroquois engagements with European colonizers to the comprehensive diplomacy of 1701—reveal the significance of active mobility to precolonial Iroquois culture and militate against notions of its ostensibly locally minded and sedentary character.

Freedom of movement on the part of precolonial Iroquois people bore a direct relationship to the degree of economic and political independence from European colonizers they enjoyed before and after 1701. The map dictated by Onondaga leaders to Robert Livingston in 1697 offers a fleeting, but critical glimpse of the extensive Iroquois spatial domain at the end of the seventeenth century and the effort of those leaders to communicate their own spatial narratives through an indigenous cartography. Although their European contemporaries appear to have been unable to reconcile the Onondagas' map with their emerging sense of cartography as a discipline that mapped territory on fixed grids for ease of visual and political appropriation, we must recognize that Iroquois people had the ability to store and retrieve information about vast geographic areas for their own purposes. Enhanced awareness of the ways in which League leaders pursued and accomplished independent spatial objectives nearly two centuries after their initial encounter with Europeans changes our perception of late precolonial Iroquois history, which is so often portrayed as a story of swift and steady Iroquois decline into economic dependency and ultimately to marginalized status on fixed, bounded reservations. Proponents of rapid post-contact Iroquois decline have relied on artificial, "upstreamed" constructions of Iroquois cultural authenticity to exaggerate the impact of post-contact population decline, acceptance of alien technology, participation in an exchange economy, political factionalism, and changes in housing and residency patterns, and to minimize contravening indications of the ongoing enterprise, intelligence, and prosperity of Iroquois people.[3]

My hope is that this book has laid a foundation for a new understanding of the role of spatial mobility in the historical construction of Iroquois cultural identity. Far from being confined to isolated localities, that identity has long been grounded upon the ability of Iroquois people to communicate, associate, and interact with one another at the Edge of the Woods. From 1534 to 1701, Iroquois people undertook profound changes in the spatial organization of their polity, yet those adaptations occurred in a context that attended to long-standing traditional values and thus kept both the past and the future in mind.

The processes that resulted in the colonization of Iroquois people after 1783 were not apparent to contemporary European observers in 1701. The key factor in the post-Revolutionary colonization of Iroquoia was the unprecedented ability of the new American nation and British Upper Canada to gradually confine Iroquois nations to fixed, bounded reservations, thereby enabling citizens of these settler societies to construct a definition of indigeneity as "first-order connections (usually at a small scale) between group and locality," and subsequently to appropriate the freedom of movement formerly enjoyed by indigenous peoples for their own economic and political benefit. Seneca leader Red Jacket made this point in his September 3, 1797, speech at the Treaty of Big Tree, drawing an explicit connection between Iroquois nations "having land of our own" (beyond mere reservations to "raise corn on") and Iroquois status as "a free people." Understanding the timing of Euro-American colonization of Iroquoia is essential for coming to terms with postcolonial Iroquois assertions of free movement and nationhood in their extensive ancestral homelands.[4] Additionally, it is crucial to recognize that Iroquois movements continued under constrained circumstances during the postcolonial era and were rooted in precolonial patterns of Iroquois spatial mobility. These movements include the involvement of Iroquois traders in the fur trade of the Far West, innovative relocations by small groups to Wisconsin and Oklahoma, and the reoccupation of ancestral spaces of use and residency on the Grand River (Six Nations), the Bay of Quinte (Tyendinaga), the Thames River (Oneida

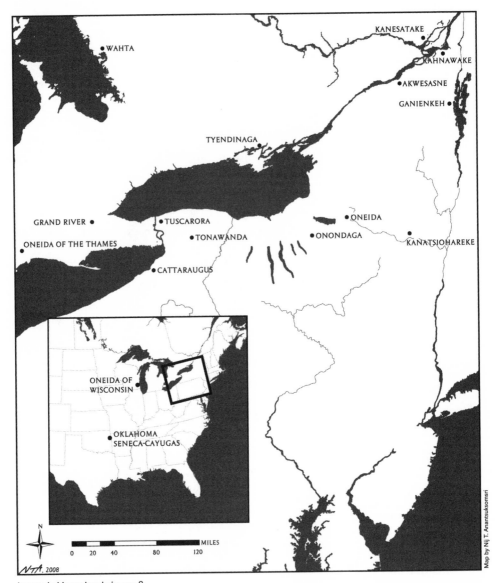

Iroquois Homelands in 2008

of the Thames) and north of Georgian Bay (Wahta) in present-day Ontario, and at the Tuscarora Reservation, Ganienkeh, and Kanatsiohareke in New York.[5]

Interrogation of the constructions of "authentic" Iroquois culture history as it pertains to spatial mobility and the use and occupancy of land in the context of power relations spun by settler colonialism allows us to more fully grasp the immense political and spatial implications of the process of rendering precolonial Iroquois mobility "inauthentic" for the nation-building projects of the United States and Canada. Representations of Iroquois cultural authenticity as a frozen precontact essence in existing historiography have provided an efficient means for North American settler governments to disqualify many Iroquois people and communities from effective claims to indigenous citizenship and nationhood.[6]

Recognizing that contemporary North American settler colonialism has imposed severe restrictions on Iroquois mobility need not translate into the assumption that such was the case from the moment Europeans arrived or that a sedentary lifestyle is somehow essential to Iroquois cultural identity. The colonial thinking that has rendered spatial fixity normative for the Iroquois (and other North American indigenous peoples) took a long time to develop, and self-reproducing historical narratives have played no small role in sustaining such beliefs (not to mention the substantial material interests arrayed against contemporary recognition of prior indigenous use and proprietorship of settler-occupied spaces). The choice before us now is whether to continue to trudge along the worn path of deeply entrenched mindsets that continue to confine Iroquois people to a colonized past or whether we will venture to the Edge of the Woods and rethink our approach to the dynamic history of Iroquoia on its own terms.

Iroquois Settlements 1600–1701

Τhis appendix provides a comprehensive summary of existing knowledge concerning 124 distinct locations of Iroquois residency during the seventeenth century in two tables: the first provides an overview of the Iroquois settlement sequence (broken down by nation), and the second documents the geographic area (in square miles) contained by all known Iroquois sites during each year. The first table lists documented historical place-names (if known) in the rightmost column for association with named archaeological sites (listed in the leftmost column). Use-affiliated locations such as fortified defensive structures (for example, the Fort Hill site abutting the Seneca town of Ganondagan circa 1684–87) or fishing stations (such as Kaneenda in Onondaga country) have been excluded from this analysis. In lieu of documented evidence of concurrently occupied sites in a particular sequence, dates of site occupancy begin at the first known (or estimated) full year of Iroquois residency at a given settlement in order to avoid overlap in calculating the number of extant Iroquois settlements in a given year.

This approach to dating site occupancies admittedly depicts transitions between Iroquois settlements as "events" rather than "processes." Movements of Iroquois people from one settlement to another likely took considerable time, and may have resulted in concurrent occupations of old and new settlements. Additionally, it is possible that not all settlements have been identified archaeologically, that confusion in documentary sources might exist as a result of place-names reused for successor settlements, and that variations occur in the naming of places in different sources. These caveats aside, the occupation dates offered below represent the author's interpretation of extant documentary and archaeological evidence, and should be considered as provisional findings inviting future refinement.

SEVENTEENTH-CENTURY IROQUOIS SETTLEMENT SEQUENCE

SENECA SEQUENCE

WESTERN SITE	DATES	PLACE-NAME
Dutch Hollow[1]	1605–1625	
Fugle[2]	1605–1625	
Lima[3]	1626–1640	Skahasegao
Bosley Mills[4]	1626–1640	
Power House[5]	1641–1655	
Menzis[6]	1641–1670	
Dann[7]	1656–1675	Gandachiorágon/La Conception
Kirkwood[8]	1676–1687	Keint:he/Gannounata
Rochester Junction[9]	1676–1687	Tiottohatton/Tegarondies/Totiakton
Niagara[10]	1678–1687	Onjagara
Snyder-McClure[11]	1688–1701	Sjaunt

EASTERN SITE	DATES	PLACE-NAME
Cameron[12]	1600–1610	
Factory Hollow[13]	1611–1625	
Warren[14]	1626–1645	
Cornish[15]	1626–1645	
Steele[16]	1646–1654	Sononteeonon
Wheeler Station[17]	1651–1669	Gandougaraé/St. Michel I
Marsh[18]	1655–1675	Gandagan/St. Jacques
Cherry Street[19]	1670–1671	Gandagarae/St. Michel II
Beal[20]	1672–1687	St. Michel III
Ganondagan[21]	1676–1687	Gannagaro/Kohoseraghe
Damasky[22]	1687–1688	
White Springs[23]	1688–1701	Kahesarahera

CAYUGA SEQUENCE

SITE	DATES	PLACE-NAME
Genoa Forts I/II[24]	1600–1624	
Myer's Station[25]	1620–1640	
Culley's[26]	1641–1653	
Crane Brook[27]	1641–1665	
Mead Farm[28]	1653–1677	Goiogouen/St. Joseph I
Rogers Farm[29]	1655–1671	Onontaré/St. René
René Ménard Bridge Hilltop[30]	1666–1671	Thiohero/St. Stephen
Lamb[31]	1672–1677	
Young Farm[32]	1677–1701	Oiogouen/St. Joseph II

ONONDAGA SEQUENCE

SITE	DATES	PLACE-NAME
Pompey Center[33]	1600–1620	
Pratt's Falls[34]	1621–1630	
Shurtleff[35]	1631–1640	
Carley[36]	1641–1650	
Lot 18[37]	1651–1655	Nontageya
Indian Castle[38]	1656–1663	
Gannentaha[39]	1656–1658	
Indian Hill[40]	1664–1682	St. Jean Baptiste/Onnontagué
Weston[41]	1683–1696	
Jamesville Pen[42]	1697–1701	

ONEIDA SEQUENCE

SITE	DATES	PLACE-NAME
Cameron[43]	1600–1615	
Wilson[44]	1600–1625	
Blowers[45]	1600–1625	
Thurston[46]	1626–1640	Oneyuttehage
Marshall[47]	1637–1640	
Stone Quarry[48]	1641–1650	
Dungey[49]	1651–1660	
Sullivan[50]	1661–1676	St. Francis Xavier
March[51]	1677–1693	
Upper Hogan[52]	1691–1696	
Collins[53]	1697–1701	Kanadagerea

MOHAWK SEQUENCE [54]

WESTERN SITE	DATES	PLACE-NAME
Mother Creek[55]	1600–1614	
Wagner's Hollow[56]	1615–1624	
Crouse[57]	1625–1634	
Failing[58]	1635–1645	Tenotoge/Theontougen
Sand Hill #1[59]	1625–1634	Cawaoge
Oak Hill #1[60]	1635–1645	
Lipe #2[61]	1646–1655	
Fort Plain Cemetery[62]	1656–1666	
Jackson-Everson[63]	1658–1676	
White Orchard[64]	1667–1688	Tionnontogouen/Tionondogue
Timmerman[65]	1669–1680	
Crouse II[66]	1689–1693	Tionnondagé

[unknown site][67]	1693–1700	
Fort Plain Cemetery II[68]	1700–1701	Dekanohage
CENTRAL SITE	**DATES**	**PLACE-NAME**
England's Woods[69]	1600–1610	
Rice's Woods[70]	1611–1620	
Coleman–Van Deusen[71]	1621–1630	
Swart-Farley[72]	1625–1635	Osquage
Ford[73]	1631–1635	Canagere
Kittle[74]	1631–1640	Schanidisse
Rumrill-Naylor[75]	1636–1645	
Van Evera–McKinney[76]	1636–1645	Andagaron/Banagiro
Prospect Hill North[77]	1646–1655	
Allen II[78]	1641–1666	Andaraque
Mitchell[79]	1646–1655	
Janie[80]	1646–1655	
Fiske[81]	1650–1657	
Brown[82]	1658–1666	
Sandfield/Nestle[83]	1667–1680	
Schenck #2[84]	1667–1685	Kanagaro/Canajorha
Allen III[85]	1685–1693	
Horatio Nellis[86]	1693–1700	Iuchnawrede
Allen IV[87]	1700–1701	Canajochere/Canaedsishore
EASTERN SITE	**DATES**	**PLACE-NAME**
Barker[88]	1600–1610	
Cromwell[89]	1605–1614	
Martin[90]	1615–1624	
Briggs Run[91]	1625–1634	Oneckegoncka
Yates I[92]	1625–1634	Canowarode
[unregistered site][93]	1635–1642	Schatsyerosy
Bauder[94]	1635–1643	Ossernenon/Asserué
Yates II[95]	1644–1650	Oneugioré
Printup[96]	1651–1658	Caronay/Agniequé
Freeman[97]	1658–1666	Kaghnuwage
Fox Farm[98]	1667–1688	Gandaouagué/St. Pierre/Cahaniaga
Turtle Pond[99]	1667–1679	Ganadagaro/Canagora
Westheimer Knoll[100]	1688–1701	Eskahre
Veeder[101]	1688–1693	Caughnawaga
[unregistered site][102]	1688–1693	
Empire Lock[103]	1691–1701	Tionnonderoge
Milton Smith[104]	1693–1700	Ornechte/Orachkie
Dufel's Flats[105]	1700–1701	Ogsadago/Ochniondage

MULTINATIONAL SETTLEMENT SEQUENCE

SETTLEMENT/SITE	DATES	PLACE-NAME
Quintio[106]	1665–1680	
Quinaouatoua[107]	1667–1687	
Ganeraské[108]	1667–1687	
Quinté[109]	1667–1687	
Ganneious[110]	1667–1687	
Ganneious II[111]	1676–1687	
Kentaké[112]	1667–1676	St. Francis Xavier de la Prairie
Bead Hill[113]	1669–1687	Ganestiquiagon
Notre-Dame-de-Foy[114]	1669–1674	
La Montagne[115]	1671–1698	
Teiaiagon[116]	1673–1687	
Ancienne Lorette[117]	1673–1683	
Kahnawake[118]	1677–1689	St. Francis Xavier du Sault
Conestoga[119]	1687–1701	
Ville-Marie[120]	1689–1690	
Kahnawakon[121]	1690–1696	
Ville-Marie II[122]	1691–1692	
Kanatakwente[123]	1697–1701	
Sault-au-Récollet[124]	1696–1701	Kanesatake
Cataraqui[125]	1701	

The second table provides estimates of change over time in the spatial area encompassed by Iroquois settlements from 1600 to 1701. Each Iroquois settlement's geographic coordinates (in latitude and longitude) were defined in decimal degrees. Using ArcGIS software, Nij Tontisirin projected all sites into the NAD 1983 State Plan Central New York and exported them as point shapefiles (each assigned to the specific years of its occupancy). To calculate the estimated area contained by all the sites in a given year, Tontisirin used "Hawth's analysis tool" (an extension tool for ArcGIS created by Hawthorne Beyer) to draw a polygon encompassing all the sites (see the four examples in figure 2). The square-mile area of each polygon was then calculated with a geometry tool in an attribute table.

THE SPATIAL DIMENSIONS OF IROQUOIA, 1600–1701

YEAR	NUMBER OF SETTLEMENTS	AREA (SQ. MILES)	YEAR	NUMBER OF SETTLEMENTS	AREA (SQ. MILES)
1600	10	2,012	1602	10	2,012
1601	10	2,012	1603	10	2,012

YEAR	NUMBER OF SETTLEMENTS	AREA (SQ. MILES)	YEAR	NUMBER OF SETTLEMENTS	AREA (SQ. MILES)
1604	10	2,012	1643	13	1,577
1605	13	2,281	1644	13	1,581
1606	13	2,281	1645	13	1,581
1607	13	2,281	1646	13	1,543
1608	13	2,281	1647	13	1,543
1609	13	2,281	1648	13	1,543
1610	14	2,281	1649	13	1,543
1611	13	2,291	1650	14	1,543
1612	13	2,291	1651	15	1,678
1613	13	2,291	1652	15	1,678
1614	13	2,291	1653	16	1,678
1615	12	2,245	1654	15	995
1616	11	2,094	1655	16	1,471
1617	11	2,094	1656	14	1,637
1618	11	2,094	1657	14	1,637
1619	11	2,094	1658	16	1,716
1620	12	2,094	1659	14	1,506
1621	12	2,067	1660	14	1,506
1622	12	2,067	1661	14	1,515
1623	12	2,067	1662	14	1,515
1624	12	2,067	1663	13	1,495
1625	14	1,935	1664	14	1,515
1626	14	1,848	1665	15	7,385
1627	14	1,848	1666	15	7,385
1628	14	1,848	1667	21	30,493
1629	14	1,848	1668	19	30,493
1630	14	1,848	1669	22	44,668
1631	15	1,879	1670	24	44,870
1632	15	1,879	1671	24	44,760
1633	15	1,879	1672	23	44,760
1634	15	1,879	1673	25	45,387
1635	15	1,888	1674	25	45,387
1636	13	1,816	1675	24	44,967
1637	13	1,715	1676	26	44,979
1638	14	1,816	1677	26	45,356
1639	14	1,816	1678	24	45,709
1640	14	1,816	1679	24	45,709
1641	14	1,577	1680	24	45,709
1642	14	1,577	1681	21	45,709

YEAR	NUMBER OF SETTLEMENTS	AREA (SQ. MILES)	YEAR	NUMBER OF SETTLEMENTS	AREA (SQ. MILES)
1682	21	45,709	1692	15	29,557
1683	21	45,709	1693	15	29,496
1684	20	31,769	1694	12	29,496
1685	21	31,769	1695	11	28,738
1686	20	31,734	1696	12	30,173
1687	22	58,015	1697	12	29,887
1688	14	31,430	1698	12	29,887
1689	13	29,632	1699	12	29,887
1690	13	29,557	1700	14	29,887
1691	15	29,557	1701	14	34,953

POSTEPIDEMIC IROQUOIS DEMOGRAPHY, 1634–1701

This appendix summarizes extant documentation concerning Iroquois population change following their initial exposure to introduced European diseases in 1634. While acknowledging the limitations imposed by the current state of research on precontact Iroquois demography, the evidence presented below suggests the need for revision of existing scholarly assumptions of dramatic, unidirectional Iroquois population decline during the postcontact era.[1] The history of seventeenth-century Iroquois demography reveals a comparatively striking success story of population recovery and maintenance in the wake of substantial losses sustained during the first "virgin soil" epidemic of 1634. Unlike other estimates of Iroquois population, this table does not treat Iroquois people who relocated after 1666 to multinational communities on the north shore of Lake Ontario and in the St. Lawrence and Susquehanna river valleys as absolute losses to the League's population akin to actual deaths or captivities.[2] Instead, these people are integrated into estimates of the larger Iroquois collectivity in keeping with its actual history.

The population estimates presented here indicate the importance of avoiding, as archaeologists Brenda Baker and Lisa Kealhofer recommend, the facile assumption that "epidemic diseases rapidly swept across the New World, decimating populations and destroying cultural and biological continuity within extant groups." Iroquois people need to be given more credit for developing innovative responses to the undeniable crises caused by unrelenting waves of epidemic diseases (outbreaks occurred roughly once every three years between 1634 and 1701). Historical demographic research has shown that Native American populations with even a 1 percent rate of annual growth could recover completely from a forty percent population loss within thirty-five years.[3] Seventeenth-century Iroquois military campaigns naturalized large numbers of indigenous aliens (and some Europeans) as members of Iroquois nations.

Additionally, fragments of documentary evidence suggest that Iroquois people had developed quarantining practices to blunt the potential impact of mortality from disease by the 1670s, and perhaps also a degree of genetic immunity that improved the likelihood of individuals surviving epidemics. Iroquois concern for postepidemic demographic recovery might also inform our assessment of European reports of the particularly indulgent and protective attitude of Iroquois people toward their children during the seventeenth century.[4] Although the seventeenth century ended on a slight downturn, the overall trend of postepidemic Iroquois population recovery continued during the eighteenth century. At least 11,000 Iroquois people were reported alive on the eve of the Revolutionary War.[5]

Contemporary seventeenth-century observers often reckoned Native American populations in terms of the number of "warriors," or men of fighting age (approximately fifteen to fifty years of age). Such estimates originated only occasionally from direct observation, and were also susceptible to manipulation for political interests. Following standard practice, warrior counts have been multiplied by a conservative factor of four to produce total estimated group numbers.[6] Contemporary estimates indicating a range of numbers have been split at their midpoint for purposes of calculation. For example, an estimate of 300 to 400 warriors has been calculated as 350 warriors. References in the leftmost column indicate that all data for that year originate from the source(s) cited. "E" indicates a documented outbreak of epidemic disease in a particular year for a given nation; if all communities in Iroquoia were affected, then the indicator appears in the leftmost column. All figures cited in the middle six columns represent warrior counts unless otherwise indicated by italics. Figures in italics denote estimates of total group number. The estimated total population figure in the rightmost column represents the sum total of estimated group numbers for the calendar year.

SEVENTEENTH-CENTURY IROQUOIS POPULATION CHANGE

DATE	MK	OE	ON	CY	SE	MULTI	TOTAL
1634 E[7]							
1637 E[8]							
1639 E[9]							
1640[10]	*2,835*	*1,000*	*2,000*	*2,000*	*4,000*		*11,835*
1643	750 [11]						
1646	E [12]						
1649 E[13]							
1650[14]	*1,734*	*600*	*1,200*	*1,200*	*4,000*		*8,734*
1653	600 [15]						
1660[16]	500 [17]	100	300	300	1,000		*8,800* [18]

DATE	MK	OE	ON	CY	SE	MULTI	TOTAL
1661							8,000 [19]
1662		E [20]	E [21]		E [22]		
1665 [23]	350	140	300	300	1200		9160
1666	3,000 [24]					105 [25]	
1667						600 [26]	
1668					E [27]	600 [28]	8600 [29]
1669 E[30]		160 [31]		300 [32]	1100 [33]	700 [34]	
1670 [35]	1,985	600	1,300	1200	4,000	1,000 [36]	10,085
1671						900 [37]	8,900 [38]
1672	E [39]			300 [40]		900 [41]	
1673	400 [42]				800 [43]	1,100 [44]	
1674						1,180 [45]	
1675						1,180 [46]	12,000 [47]
1676	300 [48]				E [49]	1,350 [50]	
1677	300 [51]	200 [52]	350 [53]	300 [54]	1,000 [55]	1,350 [56]	9,950
1678						E [57]	
1679 [58]	400 [59] E [60]	150 E [61]	300 E [62]	300	300		
1680 [63]	1,000	800	1,400	1,200	4,000	1,600 [64]	10,000 [65]
1681 E[66]	300 [67]	180 [68]	300 [69]	300 [70]		1,600 [71]	9,920 [72]
1682					1,500 [73]	1,555 [74]	11,055 [75]
1683						1710 [76]	
1684					1,500 [77]		
1685 [78]	200	150	300	200	1,200	1,604 [79]	9,804 [80]
1686						1,410 [81]	
1687						E [82]	
1688 E[83]						616 [84]	
1689 [85] E[86]	270	180	500	300	1,300	600 [87]	10,800
1690 [88] E[89]	1,000	720	2,000	1,280	4,000	400 [90]	9,400 [91]
1691 E[92]							8,800 [93]
1692	130 [94]					721 [95]	
1694						720 [96]	7,100 [97]
1695						701 [98]	
1696 E[99]					1,000 [100]		10,700 [101]
1697							6300 [102]
1698	400 [103]	150 [104]	300 [105]	300 [106]	600 [107]	1,163 [108]	6,963 [109]
1699						1300 [110]	5700 [111]
1700 [112]	620	280	1,000	800	2,400	1,500 [113]	6,600 [114]
1701	100 [115]						6,400 [116]

NOTES

PREFACE

1. *LIR*, 172–73 ("Drafft of this . . . ," 172); *NYCD* 4:252–53 (all other quotes, 252); G. Malcolm Lewis, "Maps, Mapmaking and Map Use by Native North Americans," in Woodward and Lewis, *History of Cartography,* vol. 2, book 3, 77; Lewis, "First Nations Mapmaking," 9–10. The map itself lacks attribution, but I have inferred Onondaga authorship on the basis of the documented presence of Onondaga leaders in Albany during the same week the map was produced and their discussion of the "Circumstances" of their "Country" with New York governor Benjamin Fletcher at that time. See A1894, 41:38.

2. Michael Dietler, "Consumption, Agency, and Cultural Entanglement," in Cusick, *Studies in Culture Contact,* 298; Silliman, "Culture Contact or Colonialism?" 59–64; Kurt Jordan, "Colonies, Colonialism, and Cultural Entanglement," in Majewski and Gaimster, *International Handbook of Historical Archaeology,* 31–49.

3. For analogous case studies of identity formation among mobile groups of Native Americans, see Warren, *Shawnees and Their Neighbors,* 13–20; Schutt, *Peoples of the River Valleys,* 1–30. Cf. Brooks, *Common Pot,* 138–39. By focusing on the post-Revolutionary sentiments of Mohawk leader Joseph Brant, Brooks overstates the ostensibly static, territorial nature of Iroquois spatiality.

4. Olive P. Dickason, "'For Every Plant There Is a Use': The Botanical World of Mexica and Iroquoians," in Abel and Friesen, *Aboriginal Resource Use in Canada,* 12–17; James A. Moore, "The Trouble with Know-It-Alls: Information as a Social and Ecological Resource," in Moore and Keene, *Archaeological Hammers and Theories,* 173–87; Dolores Root, "Information Exchange and the Spatial Configurations of Egalitarian Societies," in ibid., 193–212; Agorsah, "Evaluating Spatial Behavioral Patterns," 232–34; Haas, "Wampum as Hypertext."

5. L. Carless Hulin, "The Diffusion of Religious Symbols within Complex Societies," in Hodder, *Meaning of Things,* 94 ("mass media"); Hoffer, *Sensory Worlds,* 32–34 ("sensuous performances," 34); Widlok, "Mapping Spatial and Social Permeability," 392; Dodge and Kitchin, "Code and the Transduction of Space," 171–78; Hamell, "Iroquois and the World's Rim."

6. Wolfe, "Settler Colonialism"; Hoxie, "Retrieving the Red Continent"; Goldstein, "Where Nation Takes Place." My methodological approach owes a debt to the insights of many scholars. See Fixico, "Ethics and Responsibilities"; Wishart, "Selectivity of Historical Representation," 115–16; Echo-Hawk, "Ancient History in the New World"; Ball, "'People Speaking Silently to

Themselves,'" 473–75; Dabulskis-Hunter, *Outsider Research;* Newhouse, "Indigenous Knowledge"; Leslie Brown, "Becoming an Anti-Oppressive Researcher," in Brown and Strega, *Research as Resistance,* 255–86; Colin Calloway, "My Grandfather's Axe: Living with a Native American Past,' in Hurtado, *Reflections on American Indian History,* 3–31; Kent G. Lightfoot, "Oral Traditions and Material Things: Constructing Histories of Native People in Colonial Settings," in Brooks, DeCorse, and Walton, *Small Worlds,* 265–88; Witgen, "Rituals of Possession"; Miller, "Native Historians Write Back." On the distinction between living Iroquois oral traditions and textualized versions available for public study, see Christopher Jocks, "Living Words and Cartoon Translations: Longhouse 'Texts' and the Limitations of English," in Grenoble and Whaley, *Endangered Languages,* 217–33; Hill, "The Clay We Are Made Of," 83–86; White, "Haudenosaunee Worldviews," 5–33.

7. Freidel, *Harvard Guide to American History,* 1:23–25; Smith, "Culture, Commerce, and Calendar Reform," 558–59.

INTRODUCTION

1. Lafitau, *Customs of the American Indians,* 2:221–24, 238; Alfred, *Peace, Power, Righteousness,* xi–xvii. Cf. Fenton, "Structure, Continuity, and Change," 18–21; Fenton, *Great Law and the Longhouse,* 135–40, 725–37. For examples of parallel ceremonies among Native nations bordering Iroquoia, see *JR* 51:223–27; Salley, *Narratives of Early Carolina,* 10–11; Sagard, *Histoire du Canada* 1:54–57; Hennepin, *New Discovery* 2: 566–71. See also Chambers, "Spatial Personas," 1166–67.

2. Michel Foucault, "The Eye of Power," in Gordon, *Power/Knowledge,* 146–49; Darnton, *Great Cat Massacre,* 257–59; Carter, *Road to Botany Bay,* xxiii–xxiv; Alexander von Gernet, "New Directions in the Construction of Prehistoric Amerindian Belief Systems," in Goldsmith et al., *Ancient Images, Ancient Thought,* 133–40; Sioui, *For an Amerindian Autohistory,* 37; Amith, *Möbius Strip,* 6–7, 16–17; Cresswell, *On the Move,* 1–23; Penelope Drooker, "The Ohio Valley, 1550–1750: Patterns of Sociopolitical Coalescence and Dispersal," in Ethridge and Hudson, *Transformation of the Southeastern Indians,* 115–16, 126, 133; Turgeon, "Tale of the Kettle," 4; Williamson, *Powhatan Lords of Life and Death,* 3; Kent G. Lightfoot, "Oral Traditions and Material Things: Constructing Histories of Native People in Colonial Settings," in Brooks, DeCorse, and Walton, *Small Worlds,* 265–88.

3. My thinking on this matter has been influenced by a number of works, but see especially Keith M. Basso, "Wisdom Sits in Places: Notes on a Western Apache Landscape," in Feld and Basso, *Senses of Place,* 56–57; Deborah Doxtator, "Godi'Nigoha: The Women's Mind and Seeing Through to the Land," in *Godi'Nigoha,* 34; Peter Nabokov, "Orientations from Their Side: Dimensions of Native American Cartographic Discourse," in Lewis, *Cartographic Encounters,* 266.

4. Butler, *Becoming America,* 11–16, 67, 119–24, 136–37, 149–50. Cf. Gary Nash, "The Concept of Inevitability in the History of European-Indian Relations," in Pestana and Salinger, *Inequality in Early America,* 267–91.

5. For general discussions of the implications of "authenticity," see Wolfe, *Settler Colonialism,* 163–214; Deloria, *Indians in Unexpected Places;* Raibmon, *Authentic Indians.*

6. Morgan, *League of the Iroquois,* 41–46; George S. Snyderman, "Concepts of Land Ownership among the Iroquois and Their Neighbors," in Fenton, *Symposium on Local Diversity in Iroquois Culture,* 15–34; William N. Fenton, "Locality as a Basic Factor in the Development of Iroquois Social Structure," in ibid., 35–54; Fenton, "Iroquois Confederacy in the Twentieth Century,"

263; William N. Fenton, "Northern Iroquoian Culture Patterns," in Trigger, *Northeast*, 306–7; William A. Starna, "Aboriginal Title and Traditional Iroquois Land Use: An Anthropological Perspective," in Vecsey and Starna, *Iroquois Land Claims*, 31–48; Snow, *Iroquois*, 92; Trigger, "Liberation of Wendake," 7; Cresswell, *On the Move*, 1–36 ("sedentarist metaphysics," 26); Kathleen M. Sydoriak Allen, "Temporal and Spatial Scales of Activity among the Iroquois: Implications for Understanding Cultural Change," in Miroff and Knapp, *Iroquoian Archaeology*, 159–65. For critiques of this perspective, see Hoffman, "Ancient Tribes Revisited," 1; Carter, *Road to Botany Bay*, xiv–xxiv, 321–51; Malkki, "National Geographic"; Chapdelaine, "Sedentarization of the Prehistoric Iroquoians"; Clifford, *Routes*, 52–91; White and Drexler, "Colonial Studies," 750; Amith, *Möbius Strip*, 218; Simpson, "Ethnographic Refusal," 71.

7. Fenton, "Problems Arising," 190; William N. Fenton, "Lewis Henry Morgan (1818–1881): Pioneer Ethnologist," editor's introduction to Morgan, *League of the Iroquois*, v; Naroll, "Causes of the Fourth Iroquois War," 55; Barbara W. Lex, "Altered States of Consciousness in Northern Iroquoian Ritual," in Bharati, *Realm of the Extra-Human*, 282; Bradley, *Evolution of the Onondaga Iroquois*, 1; Richter, *Ordeal of the Longhouse*, 1; Abler, "Iroquois Policy and Iroquois Culture," 483.

8. Elisabeth M. Tooker, foreword to Morgan, *Ancient Society*, xv (quote); Fred W. Voget, "Anthropological Theory and Iroquois Ethnography, 1850–1970," in Foster, Campisi, and Mithun, *Extending the Rafters*, 348–57; Alice B. Myers, preface to Myers, *Households and Families of the Longhouse Iroquois*, xxvii–xxviii; Ortner, "Theory in Anthropology," 126–66.

9. Morgan, *League of the Iroquois*, vi (quote); Parker, *Life of General Ely S. Parker*, 79–88; Resek, *Lewis Henry Morgan*, 27–30; Elisabeth M. Tooker, "Ely S. Parker, Seneca, ca. 1828–1895," in Liberty, *American Indian Intellectuals*, 23–27; Trautmann, *Lewis Henry Morgan*, 37–38; Michaelsen, "Ely S. Parker"; Mann, *Iroquoian Women*, 67–68.

10. Morgan, *League of the Iroquois*, 226–29, 233–59; Wallace, *Death and Rebirth of the Seneca*, 304–36; William N. Fenton, editor's introduction to A. C. Parker, *The Code of Handsome Lake: The Seneca Prophet*, in Fenton, *Parker on the Iroquois*, 34; Parker, *Life of Ely S. Parker*, 255–56; Tooker "On the Development of the Handsome Lake Religion," 38. See also versions of Gaiwi'io in Akweks, "Code of Handsome Lake"; Thomas, "Articles of Kariwiio."

11. Morse, *Report to the Secretary of War*, appendix, 4–5; Thomas S. Abler, "The Kansas Connection: The Seneca Nation and the Iroquois Confederacy Council," in Foster, Campisi, and Mithun, *Extending the Rafters*, 81–93; Hauptman, *Conspiracy of Interests*, 191–212.

12. Parker, *Code of Handsome Lake*, 20, 62–77; Noon, *Law and Government*, 24–31; Hewitt, "Field Studies of the Iroquois," 83–84; Fenton, "Iroquois Suicide," 131; Spoehr, "Changing Kinship Systems," 203–4; Rioux, "Relations Between Religion and Government," 95–96; Tooker, "On the New Religion of Handsome Lake"; St. John, "Dream-Vision Experience of the Iroquois," 132–49; Wonderley, "Iroquois Creation Story Over Time"; Campbell, "Seth Newhouse," 189. Cf. arguments asserting the conservative character of Handsome Lake's socio-spatial reforms prescribed by Gaiwiio in Tooker, "On the New Religion of Handsome Lake"; A. F. C. Wallace, "Handsome Lake and the Decline of the Iroquois Matriarchate," in Hsu, *Kinship and Culture*, 367–76; Lex, "Altered States of Consciousness," 284; Jensen, "Native American Women and Agriculture," 429–30; Tooker, *Lewis H. Morgan*, 4–6; Mann, *Iroquoian Women*, 164, 314–24; Hill, "Clay We Are Made Of," 83–84; Myers, *Households and Families of the Longhouse Iroquois*, 29–31.

13. Parker, "Political Condition of the Ag-wa-nar-she-one," (quotes); Parker, *Analytical History of the Seneca Indians*, 140, 143, 150–52; Mathur, "Iroquois in Ethnography," 16; Abrams, *Seneca People*, 66–76; Armstrong, *Warrior in Two Camps*, 16; Tooker, *Lewis H. Morgan*, 4; Whiteley, "Why Anthropology Needs More History," 502–7; Abler, "Seneca Moieties and Hereditary

Chieftainships," 459; Carlson, *Sovereign Selves,* 43.

14. Morgan, *League of the Iroquois,* 25 (quote), 47, appendix I, 465–74; Bieder, "Grand Order of the Iroquois," 352; Carr, *Inventing the American Primitive,* 158; Deloria, *Playing Indian,* 90–94; Jo Margaret Mano, "Unmapping the Iroquois: New York State Cartography, 1792–1845," in Hauptman and McLester, *Oneida Indian Journey,* 171–95; Wonderley, *Oneida Iroquois Folklore,* 1–4, 25–30; Ben-zvi, "National Approaches and Cultural Evolution"; Ben-zvi, "Where Did Red Go?."

15. Michelsen, "Iroquois Population Statistics"; Hauptman, *Conspiracy of Interests,* 216; William C. Sturtevant, "Oklahoma Seneca-Cayuga," in Trigger, *Northeast,* 539. In 1851, the seven Iroquois communities in New York State had a population of approximately 3,700 people, while the seven Iroquois communities in Canada, Wisconsin, and Kansas numbered approximately 6,000 people. See also Sibley, *Geographies of Exclusion,* ix–xi; Sluyter, *Colonialism and Landscape,* 3–26.

16. Morgan, *League of the Iroquois,* 123 ("habit of traveling"), 143–46 (all other quotes), 444–61.

17. Fenton, "Lewis Henry Morgan," xi, n2; Fenton, "Tonawanda Longhouse Ceremonies," 144; Fenton, "Iroquois Confederacy in the Twentieth Century," 258; William N. Fenton, "Horatio Hale M.A. (Harvard), F.R.S.C (1817–1896)," in Hale, *Iroquois Book of Rites,* 9; Lex, "Altered States of Consciousness," 281 ("dean"); A. F. C. Wallace, "The Career of William N. Fenton and the Development of Iroquoian Studies," in Foster, Campisi, and Mithun, *Extending the Rafters,* 11 ("dean"). Cf. William C. Sturtevant, "A Structural Sketch of Iroquois Ritual," in Foster, Campisi, and Mithun, *Extending the Rafters,* 133–35; Landsman, "Anthropology, Theory, and Research in Iroquois Studies."

18. Fenton, *Great Law and the Longhouse,* 19 (quotes). See also Fenton's related comments in "Iroquois Suicide," 84, 91; "Training of Historical Ethnologists"; "Cultural Stability and Change," 170–71; "Huronia"; "Horatio Hale," 25; introduction to *Iroquois Eagle Dance,* xii–xiii. For other scholars' adoption of this methodology, see Michael K. Foster, "On Who Spoke First at Iroquois-White Councils: An Exercise in the Method of Upstreaming," in Foster, Campisi, and Mithun, *Extending the Rafters,* 183–207; Richter, "Up the Cultural Stream," 363–69; Wonderley, "Effigy Pipes," 213–14; Abler, "Upstream from Coldspring." For an example of "upstreaming" that privileges ethnographic observation over documentary evidence, see Fenton, *Great Law and the Longhouse,* 19. Cf. Abler, *Cornplanter,* 105.

19. *IMC,* 129; Goldenweiser, "Death of Chief John A. Gibson"; Parker, introduction to *Code of Handsome Lake,* 14–15; Hewitt, "Culture of the Indians of Eastern Canada," 179–80; Hewitt, "'League of Nations,'" 206; Hewitt, "Field Researches among the Six Nations," 203; Hewitt, "Field Researches among the Iroquois Tribes," 175; Hewitt, "Field-Work among the Iroquois Indians of New York and Canada," 81; Fenton, "Simeon Gibson"; Fenton, "Twi'-Yendagon'"; Fenton, *Iroquois Eagle Dance,* 207; Fenton, "This Island, the World on a Turtle's Back," 284; Fenton, "Howard Sky"; William N. Fenton, "Return to the Longhouse," in Kimball and Watson, *Crossing Cultural Boundaries,* 115–18; William N. Fenton, "'Aboriginally Yours,' Jesse J. Cornplanter, Hah-Yonh-Wonh-Ish, The Snipe (Seneca, 1889–1957)," in Liberty, *American Indian Intellectuals,* 176–95; Fenton, *Great Law and the Longhouse,* v; Witthoft, *Green Corn Ceremonialism,* 29–30; A. F. C. Wallace, "Cultural Composition of the Handsome Lake Religion," in Fenton and Gulick, *Symposium on Cherokee and Iroquois Culture,* 147–50; Sturtevant, "Structural Sketch of Iroquois Ritual," 135 ("knowledgeable, intellectual, and communicative"); Elisabeth M. Tooker, "Ethnometaphysics of Iroquois Ritual," in Hill, *Symbols and Society,* 105; Annemarie Shimony, "Alexander General, 'Deskahe' (Cayuga-Oneida, 1899–1965)," in Liberty, *American Indian Intellectuals,* 159–75; Mann, *Iroquoian Women,* 312; Foster, "Jacob Ezra Thomas"; Theresa L. McCarthy, "Iroquoian and Iroquoianist: Anthropologists and the

Haudenosaunee at Grand River"; Michelle A. Hamilton, "Borders Within: Anthropology and the Six Nations of the Grand River," in Hele, *Lines Drawn Upon the Water*, 191–203.

20. *NYCD* 7:573; Morgan, *League of the Iroquois*, 346–47; Fenton, "Locality as a Basic Factor," 40; Fenton, "Lore of the Longhouse," 131–32; Fenton, "Structure, Continuity, and Change," 18; Blau, "Historical Factors," 255; Tooker, *Iroquois Ceremonial of Midwinter*, vii; Sally M. Weaver, "The Iroquois: The Consolidation of the Grand River Reserve in the Mid-Nineteenth Century," in Rogers and Smith, *Aboriginal Ontario*, 196–97; Dean Snow, "The Lessons of Northern Iroquoian Demography," in Sullivan and Prezzano, *Archaeology of the Appalachian Highlands*, 264; John Mohawk, "The Power of Seneca Women and the Legacy of Handsome Lake," in Grounds, Tinker, and Wilkins, *Native Voices*, 32; Abler, "Seneca Moieties and Hereditary Chieftainships," 460–61; Wonderley, "Effigy Pipes," 214; Myers, *Households and Families of the Longhouse Iroquois*, 31–34. For critiques of upstreaming methodology in the context of Iroquois scholarship, see Webster, "Northern Iroquoian Hunting," 3; Bradley, *Evolution of the Onondaga Iroquois*, 4, 104; Gail Landsman and Sara Ciborski, "Representation and Politics," 428; Kathleen M. S. Allen, "Iroquois Ceramic Production: A Case Study of Household-Level Organization," in Bey and Pool, *Ceramic Production and Distribution*, 133; Ramsden, "Current State of Huron Archaeology," 104–7; Deer, "La 'loi des condoléances,'" 68; William J. Engelbrecht, "Iroquoian Ethnicity and Archaeological Taxa," in Williamson and Watts, *Taming the Taxonomy*, 51; Hart and Brumbach, "Death of Owasco," 749–50; Stephen Chrisomalis and Bruce G. Trigger, "Reconstructing Prehistoric Ethnicity: Problems and Prospects," in Wright and Pilon, *Passion for the Past*, 430; Simpson, "To the Reserve and Back Again," 114–15. For general critiques of this methodology, see Whiteley, *Deliberate Acts*, 6; Lockhart, *Of Things of the Indies*, 76–77; Michaelson, *Limits of Multiculturalism*, 33–35.

21. Lafitau, *Customs of the American Indians*, 2:117–18; Morgan, *League of the Iroquois*, 40–41; Morgan, *Ancient Society*, 123, 149–50; Fenton, "Problems Arising," 159–251; Robert J. Rayback, "The Indian," in Thompson, *Geography of New York State*, 119–20; Aquila, *Iroquois Restoration*, 112–28; Elisabeth M. Tooker, "Introduction," in Tooker, *Iroquois Source Book* 1: xiii; Richter, *Ordeal of the Longhouse*, 2–4; Grumet, *Historic Contact*, 340; Hill, "Continuity of Haudenosaunee Government," 14. Cf. Sioui, *For an Amerindian Autohistory*, 32; Williamson and Robertson, "Peer Polities Beyond the Periphery," 28; Brown, "Archaeology of Ancient Religion," 465–72; Susan M. Jamieson, "A Brief History of Aboriginal Social Interactions in Southern Ontario and Their Taxonomic Implications," in Williamson and Watts, *Taming the Taxonomy*, 177.

22. Wolf, *Europe and the People without History*, 170 ("failure," "change enough," "state," "more centralized political entities"); Rumrill, "Interpretation and Analysis," 1 ("disasters"); Robert D. Kuhn et al., "The Jackson-Everson Site," in Kuhn and Snow, *Mohawk Valley Project*, 30 ("disintegration of traditional . . . ," "disorder inherent in . . ."); Brandão, *"Your Fyre Shall Burn No More,"* 131 ("European materialist values," "economic clout to withstand . . ."). See also Trelease, *Indian Affairs in Colonial New York*, viii–xii; George R. Hamell, "Gannagaro State Historic Site: A Current Perspective," in Bonvillain, *Studies on Iroquoian Culture*, 94–95; Jennings, *Ambiguous Iroquois Empire*, 176–77, 187, 205–7; Kapches, "Spatial Dynamics of Ontario Iroquois Longhouses," 64–65; Thomas S. Abler, "Beavers and Muskets: Iroquois Military Fortunes in the Face of European Colonization," in Ferguson and Whitehead, *War in the Tribal Zone*, 152; Richter, *Ordeal of the Longhouse*, 86–87, 105–33, 148–49, 162–89; Dennis, *Cultivating a Landscape of Peace*, 256–71; Snow, *Iroquois*, 109, 124, 131–32; Fenton, *Great Law and the Longhouse*, 244–45, 248–53, 258–59, 275, 302, 311–13, 320–30, 357–58; Wonderley, *Oneida Iroquois Folklore*, 14–16; Hopkins, "Impact of European Material Culture." For a comprehensive list of criteria offered by scholars as evidence of Iroquois cultural decline, see

298   NOTES TO THE INTRODUCTION

Jordan, "Seneca Iroquois Settlement Pattern," 24.

23. The claim for an ostensible divergence between "League" and "Confederacy" leadership circa 1660 represents a case study in the pitfalls of "upstreaming" methodology. The notion originated with Fenton's effort to "authenticate" the existence of the League prior to 1851 by means of searching documentary sources for the names of hereditary titled chiefs obtained from nineteenth- and twentieth-century informants. See William N. Fenton, "Problems in the Authentication of the League of the Iroquois," in Hauptman and Campisi, *Neighbors and Intruders*, 261–68; Fenton, *Great Law and the Longhouse*, 8–9, 197n7, 531–32, 546–47. Fenton claimed little success, but he overlooked evidence of the flexibility of names among Iroquois people, even "old sachems." See *JR* 62:59–61, 173, 64:91–93; *NYCD* 9:183; Colden, *History of the Five Indian Nations which are dependent on the Province of New-York*, 1:xxix ("old sachems"); Lafitau, *Customs of the American Indians*, 1:71; Waterman, *"To Do Justice to Him and Myself,"* 39; Cooke, "Iroquois Personal Names," 427; Marianne Mithun, "Principles of Naming in Mohawk," in Tooker, *Naming Systems*, 46, 50, Ganter, *Collected Speeches of Sagoyewatha*, xx, which renders such an approach invalid for the purpose of establishing an "authentic" or comprehensive list. Similar efforts (based on the same flawed assumption of static naming patterns) to replicate Fenton's method and verify the existence of the League through searches of printed primary sources for hereditary chiefs' names appear in Starna, "Seventeenth-Century Dutch-Indian Trade," 7, and Daniel K. Richter, "Ordeals of the Longhouse: The Five Nations in Early American History," in Richter and Merrell, *Beyond the Covenant Chain*, 169–70, and led Richter to the speculative claim of a distinction between the "League" and the "Confederacy" arising during the seventeenth century (with the former confined to ceremonial functions and the latter dealing exclusively with politics). For adoptions of Richter's claim, see Snow, *Iroquois*, 129–34; Fenton, *Great Law and the Longhouse*, 357, 493–95. Cf. Tooker, "United States Constitution and the Iroquois League," 313–17, 332n9; Brandão, *"Your Fyre Shall Burn No More,"* 29, 43; Deer, "La 'loi des condoléances,'" 65–66.

24. Pouchot, *Memoir*, 469 ("intimately linked"); Strong, "Imposition of Colonial Jurisdiction"; Cole Harris, "How Did Colonialism Dispossess?"; Gosden, *Archaeology and Colonialism*, 24–28; Silliman, "Culture Contact or Colonialism"; Amith, *Möbius Strip*, 552. See also White, "Early American Nations," 67; Shoemaker, *Strange Likeness*, 14–15; Ganter, *Collected Speeches of Sagoyewatha*, xix.

25. Charles Thomson, "Commentaries," in Jefferson, *Notes on the State of Virginia*, 207; Morgan, *League of the Iroquois*, 26; Wonderley, *Oneida Iroquois Folklore*, 15 ("lost forever to the home population"); Aquila, *Iroquois Restoration*, 71; Axtell, *Invasion Within*, 277; Richter, "Iroquois versus Iroquois," 10; Richter, *Ordeal of the Longhouse*, 188; Dennis, *Cultivating a Landscape of Peace*, 266–67; Calloway, *New Worlds for All*, 147; Engelbrecht, *Iroquoia*, 167–68. Cf. alternate perspectives on Iroquois mobility in Alfred, *Heeding the Voices of Our Ancestors*, 43–51; Jordan, *Seneca Restoration*, 198–224. See also Oetelaer and Meyer, "Movement and Native American Landscapes."

26. Barnett, *Innovation*, 7–10, 181–85, 313–73; Robert A. Levine, "Properties of Culture: An Ethnographic View," in Shweder and Levine, *Culture Theory*, 67–87; Giddens, *Consequences of Modernity*, 37.

27. Le Roy de la Potherie, *Histoire*, 2:421 ("confused fables"); *JR* 56:33; Eliade, *Myth of the Eternal Return*, 3–18; Victor W. Turner, "Forms of Symbolic Action," in Spencer, *Forms of Symbolic Action*, 4–6; Comaroff, *Body of Power*, 118–20; Bourdieu, "Social Space and Symbolic Power," 23; Wonderley, *Oneida Iroquois Folklore*, xvii–viii; Bonaparte, *Creation and Confederation*, 31.

28. Deborah Doxtator, "Inclusive and Exclusive Perceptions of Difference: Native and Euro-Based Concepts of Time, History, and Change," in Warkentin and Podruchny, *Decentering the*

Renaissance, 38 (quote). See also Boice, "Iroquois Sense of Place," 179–82; Rodney Frey, "Oral Traditions," in Biolsi, *Companion to the Anthropology of American Indians,* 155.

29. Hewitt, "Iroquoian Cosmology, Part I," 184–203, 241, 302–27; Hewitt, "Iroquoian Cosmology, Part II," 482–83, 489–90, 559–98; Kurath, *Iroquois Music and Dance,* 71; Michael K. Foster, "When Words Become Deeds: An Analysis of Three Longhouse Speech Events," in Bauman and Sherzer, *Explorations in the Ethnography of Speaking,* 356; McElwain, *Mythological Tales,* 9; Wright, *Proxemic Analysis,* 36–37; Mary A. Druke, "The Concept of Personhood in Seventeenth and Eighteenth Century Iroquois Ethnopersonality," in Bonvillain, *Studies on Iroquoian Culture,* 63–67; Katsi Cook, "The Women's Dance: Reclaiming Our Powers," in Bruchac, *New Voices from the Longhouse,* 80–81; Hamell, "Iroquois and the World's Rim," 452–53; Natalie Zemon Davis, "Iroquois Women, European Women," in Hendricks and Parker, *Women, "Race" and Writing,* 257; Doxtator, "Inclusive and Exclusive Perceptions of Difference," 39–44; Connelly, "Textual Function of Onondaga Aspect," 284–90; Cornelius, *Iroquois Corn,* 81–82; Alfred, *Peace, Power, Righteousness,* xiv; Paul Williams, Kayanesenh, "Creation," in Haudenosaunee Environmental Task Force, *Words That Come Before All Else,* 2–4; Abler, "Dendrogram and Celestial Tree"; Wonderley, "Iroquois Creation Story Over Time," 1–16.

30. Engelbrecht, "Iroquoian Ethnicity and Archaeological Taxa," 53 (quote); Niemczycki, *Origin and Development of the Seneca and Cayuga Tribes,* 97–100; Chapdelaine, "Sedentarization of the Prehistoric Iroquoians," 197–201; Lenig, *"In Situ* Thought"; Sempowski and Saunders, *Dutch Hollow and Factory Hollow,,* 669–712; Kuhn and Sempowski, "New Approach to Dating the League of the Iroquois"; Robert J. Hasenstab, "Proto-Iroquois," in Peregrine and Ember, *Encyclopedia of Prehistory,* 6:453–54; Funk and Kuhn, *Three Sixteenth Century Mohawk Iroquois Village Sites,* 156–58; Hart and Brumbach, "Death of Owasco," 737–52; Peter Ramsden, "But Once the Twain Did Meet: A Speculation About Iroquois Origins," in Rankin and Ramsden, *From the Arctic to Avalon,* 27–31; Martin, "Languages Past and Present." Snow's "migration hypothesis," which posits an incursion of Iroquoian speakers from modern-day Pennsylvania into modern-day New York and Ontario after 900, most recently articulated in his "Evolution of the Mohawk Iroquois" (in Brose, Cowan, and Mainfort, *Societies in Eclipse,* 20–22), has been heavily criticized. See Chrisomalis and Trigger, "Reconstructing Prehistoric Ethnicity," 423. For Iroquois tradition of their historic point of origin near the falls of the present-day Oswego River, see Schoolcraft, *Notes on the Iroquois,* 49; Beauchamp, *Indian Names in New York,* 34. None of the documentary and archaeological evidence presented above is intended to diminish contemporary Iroquois peoples' belief, recently articulated by Tuscarora scholar Richard W. Hill. Sr., that they "are connected biologically, socially, artistically, and culturally to the most ancient of our ancestors who lived within our aboriginal territories," dating back at least "four millennia" and perhaps longer. See Hill, Sr., "Making a Final Resting Place Final: A History of the Repatriation Experience of the Haudenosaunee," in Kerber, *Cross-Cultural Collaboration,* 10.

31. Anderson, "Climate and Culture Change," 165–66; Clermont, "L'Importance de la Pêche en Iroquoisie," 17; Little, "Inland Waterways in the Northeast"; Hasenstab, "Canoes, Caches, and Carrying Places," 39–42; Williamson and Robertson, "Peer Polities," 27–30; J. V. Wright, "The Prehistoric Transportation of Goods in the St. Lawrence River Basin," in Baugh and Ericson, *Prehistoric Exchange Systems,* 47–71; Susan C. Prezzano, "Warfare, Women, and Households: The Development of Iroquois Culture," in Claasen and Joyce, *Women in Prehistory,* 88–99; Drooker, *View from Madisonville,* 333–37; James W. Bradley, "Change and Survival among the Onondaga Iroquois since 1500," in Brose, Cowan, and Mainfort, *Societies in Eclipse,* 27. For ceramic and lithic analyses of mobility, see MacNeish, *Iroquois Pottery Types;* H. Martin Wobst, "Stylistic Behavior and Information Exchange," in Cleland, *For the Director,* 317–28;

Rutsch, *Smoking Technology,* 20–21; Martha A. Latta, "The Captive Bride Syndrome: Iroquoian Behavior or Archaeological Myth?" in Walde and Willows, *Archaeology of Gender,* 375–82; Allen, "Iroquois Ceramic Production," 136–40; Elizabeth S. Chilton, "The Cultural Origins of Technical Choice: Unraveling Iroquoian and Algonquian Ceramic Traditions in the Northeast," in Stark, *Archaeology of Social Boundaries,* 132–33; Wonderley, "Oneida Ceramic Effigies," 23–25; Hart and Brumbach, "Death of Owasco," 749; Kapches, "Invisible Women." Cf. Birch, "Rethinking the Archaeological Application of Iroquoian Kinship"; Michelaki, "More than Meets the Eye," 147–48

32. Nancy Bonvillain, "Iroquoian Women," in Bonvillain, *Studies on Iroquoian Culture,* 50; Ferdais, "Matrilinéalité et/ou matrilocalité chez les Iroquoiens," 186–87; Brumbach, "Ceramic Analysis," 341, 353; Steckley, "Huron Kinship Terminology," 57; Gretchen L. Green, "Gender and the Longhouse: Iroquois Women in a Changing Culture," in Eldridge, *Women and Freedom in Early America,* 10; Michael Spence, "Comments: The Social Foundation of Archaeological Taxonomy," in Williamson and Watts, *Taming the Taxonomy,* 279–81.

33. Oury, *Marie de l'Incarnation,* 565; Goodenough, "Residence Rules"; Tooker, "Masking and Matrilineality," 1172; Helms, "Matrilocality," 205; Divale, *Matrilocal Residence in Pre-Literate Society,* 21–24; Pasternak, Ember, and Ember, "Extended Family Households," 109–14; Hayden, "Corporate Groups," 3–16; Lewandowski, "Diohe'ko"; Ramsden, "Palisade Extension," 177–83; Mima T. Kapches, "Chaos Theory and Social Movements: A Theoretical View of the Formation of the Northern Iroquoian Longhouse Cultural Pattern," in Bekerman and Warrick, *Origins of the People of the Longhouse,* 86–96; Crawford, Smith, and Bowyer, "Dating the Entry of Corn," 112–19; Cornelius, *Iroquois Corn,* 107–13; Hart, "Maize"; Hart, "Rethinking the Three Sisters"; Engelbrecht, *Iroquoia,* 22–25; Thompson et al., "Phytolith Evidence"; Martin, "Lower Great Lakes Region Maize"; Jane Mt. Pleasant, "The Science Behind the Three Sisters Mound System," in Staller, Tykot, and Benz, *Histories of Maize,* 529–37. Cf. Peregrine, "Matrilocality," 36. Iroquois tradition locates the origin of the "Three Sisters" crops to Toppin Mountain, near present-day Preble, New York. See Masterson, "Foolish Oneida Tale," 54; Lemay, *Life of Benjamin Franklin,* 483. For evidence of the persistence of matrilineal, extended-family households in Iroquoia down to the nineteenth-century, see Abler, *Cornplanter,* 136; Tiro, *Along the Hudson and Mohawk,* 62; Hauptman, "Two Worlds of Aunt Dinah John," 14.

34. Le Roy de la Potherie, *Histoire,* 2:427–29; Wallace, *Iroquois Book of Life,* 24–28; Hertzberg, *Great Tree and the Longhouse,* 4–7, 23–30; Wright, *Proxemic Analysis,* 76; Elisabeth M. Tooker, "Women in Iroquois Society," in Foster, Campisi, and Mithun, *Extending the Rafters,* 119–20; Annemarie Shimony, "Iroquois Religion and Women in Historical Perspective," in Haddad and Findly, *Women, Religion, and Social Change,* 404; Richter, *Ordeal of the Longhouse,* 22–23; Mann, *Iroquoian Women,* 204–5; Hasenstab, "Proto-Iroquois," 456; Snow, "Evolution of the Mohawk Iroquois," 22; Bursey, "Women and Cabin Sites"; Horn-Miller, "Otiyaner," 57–58; Douglas J. Perrelli, "Iroquoian Social Organization in Practice: A Small-Scale Study of Gender Roles and Site Formation in Western New York," in Miroff and Knapp, *Iroquoian Archaeology,* 21–29.

35. B. H. Quain, "The Iroquois," in Mead, *Cooperation and Competition,* 241, 244–45, 272–73; Fenton, "Toward the Gradual Civilization of the Indian Natives," 567; Fenton, "Northern Iroquoian Culture Patterns," 299–300; Wallace, "Handsome Lake," 368; Starna, "Aboriginal Title and Traditional Iroquois Land Use," 34; Grumet, *Historic Contact,* 327–31; Elizabeth S. Chilton, "Mobile Farmers of Pre-Contact Southern New England: The Archaeological and Ethnohistoric Evidence," in Hart, *Current Northeast Paleobotany,* 163.

36. Morgan, *League of the Iroquois,* 315–19; Morgan, *Houses and House-Life,* 128–29; Fenton, "Locality," 41; Wallace, *Death and Rebirth of the Seneca,* 22–23; Dean Snow, "The Evolution

of Mohawk Households, A.D. 1400–1800," in MacEachern, Archer, and Garvin, *Households and Communities,* 296–98; Lisa Fogt and Peter Ramsden, "From Timepiece to Time Machine: Scale and Complexity in Iroquoian Archaeology," in Meyer, Dawson, and Hanna, *Debating Complexity,* 39–45; Mohawk, "Power of Seneca Women," 27–30; Kimberly Williams-Shuker, "Bottom-Up Perspectives of the Contact Period: A View from the Rogers Farm Site," in Miroff and Knapp, *Iroquoian Archaeology,* 206–9. Cf. Susan M. Jamieson, "Precepts and Percepts of Northern Iroquois Households and Communities: The Changing Past," in MacEachern, Archer, and Garvin, *Households and Communities,* 307–14; Adrian O. Mandzy, "The Results of Interaction: Change in Cayuga Society during the Seventeenth Century," in Hayes, Bodmer, and Saunders, *Proceedings,* 147; Gary Warrick, "Evolution of the Iroquoian Longhouse," in Coupland and Banning, *People Who Lived in Big Houses,* 20–21; Jordan, *Seneca Restoration,* 199–205.

37. *NNN,* 302; Blanchard, *Seven Generations,* 163–66 (quote 166); Beauchamp, "Aboriginal Occupation of the State of New York," 22; Douglas B. Carter, "Climate," in Thompson, *Geography of New York State,* 60–74; Ritchie and Funk, *Aboriginal Settlement Patterns,* 359–69; Stanley C. Bond Jr., "The Relationship between Soils and Settlement Patterns in the Mohawk Valley," in Snow, *Mohawk Valley Project,* 17; Brumbach, "Anadromous Fish and Fishing," 35–37; Snow, "Evolution of the Mohawk Iroquois," 23; Engelbrecht, *Iroquoia,* 30–31, 88–91; William J. Engelbrecht "Defense in an Iroquois Village," in Rankin and Ramsden, *From the Arctic to Avalon,* 19. Cf. Snow, "Lessons of Northern Iroquoian Demography," 266; Engelbrecht, *Iroquoia,* 125–26.

38. *JR* 8:21, 10:305–11, 11:131; Klinck and Talman, *Journal of Major John Norton,* 286; Gehring and Grumet, "Observations of the Indians," 110; Kaiontaronkwen (Ernest M. Benedict), "Pageant History of the St. Regis Reservation," in Akweks, *History of the St. Regis Akwesasne Mohawks,* 31; Snow, *Mohawk Valley Archaeology,* 226; Engelbrecht, "Northern New York Revisited," 132; Abler, *Cornplanter,* 130; William Woodworth Rawano:kwas, "Their Bones Are Here, Raotinskionh: The Moatfield Ossuary in Indigenous Context," in Williamson and Pfeiffer, *Bones of the Ancestors,* 1; Peter A. Nabokov, "Native Views of History," in Trigger and Washburn, *Cambridge History,* 21–23; G. Peter Jemison, "Who Owns the Past?" in Kerber, *Archaeology of the Iroquois,* 407; Rayner-Herter, "Niagara Frontier Iroquois," 71, 82.

39. *JR* 62:55; Belmont, "Histoire du Canada," 45; Lafitau, *Customs of the American Indians,* 2:69–70; Beauchamp, "Aboriginal Occupation," 22; Beauchamp, *Indian Names in New York,* 3; Starna, Hamell, and Butts, "Northern Iroquoian Horticulture," 197–99; Doolittle, *Cultivated Landscapes,* 182–90, 456; Engelbrecht, *Iroquoia,* 92–106.

40. Jones et al., "Evolution of Climate"; Campbell and Campbell, "Little Ice Age"; Myers, "Examination of Late Prehistoric McFate Trail Locations," 47; William R. Fitzgerald, "Contact, Neutral Iroquoian Transformation, and the Little Ice Age," in Brose, Cowan, and Mainfort, *Societies in Eclipse,* 44–45; Abel and Fuerst, "Prehistory of the St. Lawrence River Headwaters Region," 38; David S. Brose, "Late Prehistoric Societies of Northeastern Ohio and Adjacent Portions of the South Shore of Lake Erie: A Review," in Genheimer, *Cultures Before Contact,* 109; David S. Brose, "Penumbral Protohistory on Lake Erie's South Shore," in Brose, Cowan, and Mainfort, *Societies in Eclipse,* 60; Mark F. Seeman and William S. Dancey, "The Late Woodland Period in Southern Ohio: Basic Issues and Prospects," in McElrath, Emerson, and Fortier, *Late Woodland Societies,* 602; Bruce G. Trigger, "Maintaining Economic Equality in Opposition to Complexity: An Iroquoian Case Study," in Upham, *Evolution of Political Systems,* 143; Clermont, "L'Importance de la Pêche," 18–20; Hasenstab, "Agriculture, Warfare, and Tribalization," 66–67; Evelyn Cossette, "The Exploitation of Deer among St. Lawrence Iroquoians," in Pendergast and Chapdelaine, *Essays in St. Lawrence Iroquoian Archaeology,*

59. For specific discussion of the incident at the Alhart site, see Niemczycki, "Genesee Connection," 37; Wray et al., *Adams and Culbertson Sites*, 20, 247–48; Engelbrecht, *Iroquoia*, 44, 132n4; Rayner-Herter, "Niagara Frontier Iroquois," 246.

41. *JR* 45:249, 47:37, 48:75, 54:117; Hertzberg, *Great Tree and the Longhouse*, 23–29; Engelbrecht, *Iroquoia*, 35–36; Bursey, "Aggrandizers vs. Egalitarianism," 128–36.

42. *JR* 63:235–37; Parker, *Analytical History*, 71; Fenton, "Fish Drives"; Fenton and Deardorff, "Last Passenger Pigeon Hunts"; Pratt, *Archaeology of the Oneida Iroquois*, 11; Webster, "Northern Iroquoian Hunting," 65–66, 100–114, 153–59; Recht, "Role of Fishing," 6–12; Orlandini, "Passenger Pigeon," 71–73; Green, "Gender and the Longhouse," 13–14; Engelbrecht, *Iroquoia*, 10–17, 27; Abler, *Cornplanter*, 139, 143.

43. *JR* 5:29, 46:95–101; *NYCD* 3:815–17. See also DuVal, *Native Ground*, 115.

44. Cook, *Voyages of Jacques Cartier*, 24–25; Gehring and Starna, *Journey into Mohawk and Oneida Country*, 6, 19; *JR* 9:253–55, 41:67, 43:141, 273, 50:39–41, 51:193, 62:69; Brandão, *Nation Iroquoise*, 103–5; Kip, *Early Jesuit Missions*, 97–98; Lahontan, *New Voyages* 1:142; Charlevoix, *History*, 4:198–99; *NYCD* 4:494; Colden, *History of the Five Indian Nations which are dependent on the Province of New-York*, 1:xxxii; Morgan, *League of the Iroquois*, 116–17; Tooker, "Women in Iroquois Society," 115; Davis, "Iroquois Women," 244.

45. Gehring and Starna, *Journey into Mohawk and Oneida Country*, 6; Charlevoix, *History* 3:163; *LIR*, 173–74; *NYCD* 3:775; Waterman, *"To Do Justice to Him and Myself,"* 17, 47–48; Levy, *Fellow Travelers*, 120–21.

46. *JR* 50:39–41; Gehring, *Delaware Papers*, 320; Hennepin, *Description of Louisiana*, 309; Colden, *History of the Five Indian Nations which are dependent on the Province of New-York*, 1: 29; Blair, *Indian Tribes* 2:92; *RAPQ* (1927–28):36; Magee, "They Are the Life of the Nation."

47. Pouchot, *Memoir*, 451 ("great councils of . . ."); Gehring and Starna, *Journey into Mohawk and Oneida Country*, 19; *JR* 41:229–31, 47:277, 55:265, 64:91; *MCARS* 3:342; *An Account of the Treaty*, 5; *CMRNF* 1:505; Verney, *Good Regiment*, 61, 66; Carla Gerona, "Imagining Peace in Quaker and Native American Dream Stories," in Pencak and Richter, *Friends and Enemies in Penn's Woods*, 50–51.

48. *JR* 44:25–27; Smith, "Myths of the Iroquois," 89–90, 107–10.

49. Beauchamp, *Indian Names in New York*, 53–54, 57; Rydjord, *Indian Place-Names*, 253–70; Gordon, "Onondaga Iroquois Place-Names," 220–24.

50. *JR* 12:161, 41:93–95, 42:207, 49:107, 52:165; Lafitau, *Customs of the American Indians*, 2:36–37, 138; Colden, *History of the Five Indian Nations Depending on the Province of New-York*, 4; Colden, *History of the Five Indian Nations which are dependent on the Province of New-York*, 1:xxv–xxvi; *DHNY* 1:4, 10; *NYCD* 9:652; *WJP* 3:32; Parker, *Seneca Myths*, 283n; Morgan, *League of the Iroquois*, 340; Beauchamp, "French Lake Mounds," 33–47; Brigham, "Sites and Trails of the Mohawk Indians," 86–89; Jones, "Iroquois Population History," 160–63. For an online database of surviving Seneca "trail trees," see www.indiantrailtree.com.

51. Lafitau, *Customs of the American Indians*, 2:130 (quote); *NYCD* 4:198, 232, 236–37, 899; Lahontan, *New Voyages* 2:427; Lewis, "Intracultural Mapmaking by First Nations Peoples."

52. *NYCD* 4:64, 9:479, 622, 652; *IHC* 23:325; *JR* 32:31, 59:149; Robinson, *Maryland Treaties*, 201; Lahontan, *New Voyages* 2:510–14; Hennepin, *Description of Louisiana*, 78; Baugy, "Journal," 43; William N. Fenton, "Captain Hyde's 'Observations'"; Kinietz, *Indians of the Western Great Lakes*, 351; Long, *Voyages and Travels*, 173; Mallery, "Sign Language," 326–27; Beauchamp, *Indian Names in New York*, 78; Hagedorn, "Brokers of Understanding," 383; Westra, "A New Version of Lahontan's 'Hieroglyphic' Message"; Lenik, *Picture Rocks*, 195–98; Scott Meachem, "Markes Upon Their Clubhammers: Interpreting Pictography on Eastern War Clubs," in King and Feest, *Three Centuries of Woodlands Indian Art*, 67–74

53. *DHNY* 1:10; *NNN*, 300–302; van Gastel, "Van der Donck's Description of the Indians," 418–19; Gehring and Starna, *Journey into Mohawk and Oneida Country*, 1, 3, 10, 11, 20–22, 26n13; *JR* 51:183, 56:57; *NYCD* 4:559, 9:390, 435, 479, 602; Oury, *Marie de l'Incarnation*, 648; Kip, *Early Jesuit Missions*, 124. Recent scholarship on elm bark canoes has challenged long-standing assertions of their poor quality and limited use by Iroquois builders. For negative views, see Speck, *Iroquois*, 17; Fenton and Dodge, "Elm Bark Canoe," 192–93; Fenton, "Northern Iroquoian Culture Patterns," 303. Cf. Adney and Chappelle, *Bark Canoes and Skin Boats*, 212–15; Tooker, *Lewis H. Morgan*, 249–51; Engelbrecht, *Iroquoia*, 18.

54. Kinietz, *Indians of the Western Great Lakes*, 342; Webster, "Northern Iroquoian Hunting," 121–24; Junker-Anderson, "Eel Fisheries," 113; Waugh, *Iroquis [sic] Foods*, 42–43, 61, 88–90, 194–95.

55. *NYCD* 1:282, 9:361; *RFF*, 103–4; Gehring and Starna, *Journey into Mohawk and Oneida Country*, 6; Boucher, *Histoire Véritable*, 19; Le Roy de la Potherie, *Histoire*, 2:437; Lafitau, *Customs of the American Indians*, 1:357, 2:97, 127–28, 201, 231; *LIR*, 81; Cox, *Journeys of La Salle*, 1:12; Hulbert and Schwarze, *David Zeisberger's History of the Northern American Indians*, 24; Morgan, *League of the Iroquois*, 346; Beauchamp, "Aboriginal Use of Wood," 139–45, 160–69; Orchard, "Mohawk Burden Straps," 357; Lyford, *Iroquois*, 30–36, 45; Rayback, "Indian," 117–19; Tuck, *Onondaga Iroquois Prehistory*, 3; King, *Thunderbird and Lightning*, 73–77; Tooker, *Lewis H. Morgan*, 178–79, 183, 189–90, 219–20, 255–56; Victor Lytwyn, "Waterworld: The Aquatic Territory of the Great Lakes First Nations," in Standen and McNabb, *Gin Das Winan*, 14; Hasenstab, "Proto-Iroquois," 455; Engelbrecht, *Iroquoia*, 140; R.S. Stephenson, "The Decorative Art of Securing Captives in the Eastern Woodlands," in King and Feest, *Three Centuries of Woodlands Indian Art*, 55–66. See also Merrell, *Into the American Woods*, 128–56.

56. Morgan, *Ancient Society*, 71; Goldenweiser, "On Iroquois Work, 1912," 466–67; Goldenweiser, "Clan and Maternal Family of the Iroquois League," 696–97; Goldenweiser, "On Iroquois Work, 1913–14," 370; Barbeau, "Iroquoian Clans and Phratries," 393–99; Kloos, "Matrilocal Residence and Local Endogamy," 854–62; Charlton, "On Iroquois Incest," 30–38; Tooker, "Clans and Moieties," 362; Tooker, "Women in Iroquois Society," 111–12; Bonvillain, "Iroquoian Women," 51–52; Trigger, "Maintaining Economic Equality," 128; Engelbrecht, *Iroquoia*, 47, 68–69. See also Janet Carsten, "Introduction: Cultures of Relatedness," in Carsten, *Cultures of Relatedness*, 1–26. Cf. Fenton, "Locality as a Basic Factor," 43–49. Fenton noted the aversion of his twentieth-century Iroquois informants for marrying outside their home communities, and despite "numerous exceptions" to this pattern he identified in the "data" (presumably historical sources), he elected to identify his informants' contemporary viewpoint as the "authentic" cultural pattern. See also Alice Myers's assertion of the nonexistence of the "clan" among the Iroquois in her preface to Myers, *Households and Families of the Longhouse Iroquois*, xxxi–xxxiv, which reflects findings from fieldwork conducted at Grand River in the late 1950s.

57. *JR* 43:265.

58. Ibid., 1:263; Du Creux, *History of Canada*, 125.

59. Hertzberg, *Great Tree and the Longhouse*, 57; Trigger, "Iroquoian Matriliny," 56–58; Tooker, "Women in Iroquois Society," 120; David A. Ezzo, "Female Status and the Life Cycle: A Cross-Cultural Perspective from Native North America," in Cowan, *Papers*, 1991), 137–38; Warrick, "Evolution of the Iroquoian Longhouse," 12; Hasenstab, "Proto-Iroquois," 457; Engelbrecht, *Iroquoia*, 113.

60. Lafitau, *Customs of the American Indians*, 1:90, 2:99; Le Roy de la Potherie, *Histoire*, 2:434; Boucher, *Histoire Véritable*, 110–11, 114–15; *IMC*, 191; Denton, *Brief Description of New York*, 19; Benjamin Franklin, "Remarks on the Politeness of the Savages in North America [1783],"

in Franklin, *Bagatelles from Passy,* 7–11; Ganter, *Collected Speeches of Red Jacket,* 12–13; Tiro, *Along the Hudson and Mohawk,* 59; Morgan, *League of the Iroquois,* 327–29; Heckewelder, *History, Manners, and Customs,* 148–49; Smith, "Myths of the Iroquois," 78; Chadwick, *People of the Longhouse,* 81, 123; Canfield, *Legends of the Iroquois,* 155–58; Wolf, *Iroquois Religion,* 86–87; Quain, "Iroquois," 254; Cornelius, *Iroquois Corn,* 104–5; Irving Powless, "The Sovereignty and Land Rights of the Houdenosaunee [*sic*]," in Vecsey and Starna, *Iroquois Land Claims,* 157; Mann, *Iroquoian Women,* 229–30; Engelbrecht, *Iroquoia,* 76, 139–40; Sohrweide, "Onondaga Longhouses," 22. Some precolonial documentary evidence suggests that facial tattooing of totemic clan images may have served as an indicator of adulthood for Iroquois men and possibly a "passport" of sorts for facilitating travel. See Waterman, *"To Do Justice to Him and Myself,"* 97, 141, 151, 153, 158, 166, 169, 180; Sinclair, "Tattooing," 369–70, 393.

61. *JR* 44:299, 54:25, 115, 55:77 ("public criers"), 62:79; *NYCD* 4:50, 80, 918; Du Creux, *History of Canada,* 1:97; Coyne, "Exploration of the Great Lakes," 23; Gehring and Grumet, "Observations of the Indians," 108–10; Lafitau, *Customs of the American Indians,* 1:232–34; Klinck and Talman, *Journal of Major John Norton,* 103; Robert Whallon, "Investigations of Late Prehistoric Social Organization in New York State," in Binford and Binford, *New Perspectives in Archeology,* 223–44; David M. Brose, "A Speculative Model of the Role of Exchange in the Prehistory of the Eastern Woodlands," in Brose and Greber, *Hopewell Archaeology,* 3; Niemczycki, "Seneca Tribalization," 82–83; Wobst, "Stylistic Behavior," 319–28; Trigger, "Prehistoric Social and Political Organization," 28–29; Michael W. Spence, "The Social Context of Production and Exchange," in Ericson and Earle, *Contexts for Prehistoric Exchange,* 187–91; Penelope B. Drooker, "Exotic Ceramics at Madisonville: Implications for Interaction," in Williamson and Watts, *Taming the Taxonomy,* 72–73; Elizabeth S. Chilton, "One Size Fits All: Typology and Alternatives for Ceramic Research," in Chilton, *Material Meanings,* 45, 58–59; Robert D. Kuhn, "Reconstructing Patterns of Interaction and Warfare Between the Mohawk and Northern Iroquoians during the A.D. 1400–1700 Period," in Wright and Pilon, *Passion for the Past,* 160–61; Bohaker, "*Nindoodemag,*" 30–39. See also Heather Lechtman's analogous study, "Technologies of Power: The Andean Case," in Henderson and Netherly, *Configurations of Power,* 245–46.

62. Piddington, *Kinship and Geographical Mobility;* Barsh, "Nature and Spirit of North American Political Systems," 187–94; Anderson, *Imagined Communities,* 22–27; Barnett, "Ways of Relating," 15–16.

63. Parker, *Seneca Myths,* 30, 128–32; Waugh, *Iroquis [sic] Foods,* 46–47, 79; Quain, "Iroquois," 248–49; Hertzberg, *Great Tree and the Longhouse,* 36, 75; Tooker, *Iroquois Ceremonial of Midwinter,* 36; Fenton, *Great Law and the Longhouse,* 49; Cornelius, *Iroquois Corn,* 104; Wonderley, "Oneida Ceramic Effigies," 37–39.

64. Sagard, *Histoire du Canada,* 3:799; *JR* 15:121; Susan M. Kus, "The Social Representation of Space: Dimensioning the Cosmological and the Quotidian," in Moore and Keene, *Archaeological Hammers,* 278–87; Walker and Schiffer, "Materiality of Social Power," 83; de Costa, "Cosmology, Mobility, and Exchange."

65. *JR* 9:275–77, 22:51; *NYCD* 5:274; *LIR,* 84, 88; Lahontan, *New Voyages* 2:459, 474; Hale, *Iroquois Book of Rites,* 95–96; Richter, "War and Culture," 528–59; Sanday, *Divine Hunger,* 125–50; Dennis, *Cultivating a Landscape of Peace,* 106–8; Brandão, *"Your Fyre Shall Burn No More,"* 31–61; Fenton, *Great Law and the Longhouse,* 259–60; Milner, "Warfare," 110–28; Funk and Kuhn, *Three Sixteenth Century Mohawk Iroquois Village Sites,* 157–58; Bradley, "Change and Survival," 27; Traphagan, "Embodiment, Ritual Incorporation, and Cannibalism." Cf. Blick, "Iroquois Practice of Genocidal Warfare."

66. Cf. evidence of hostility arising from unresolved murders as hindering freedom of movement

among the Hurons, Neutrals, and Algonquins in *JR* 8:89, 9:275–77, 21:211; Rotstein, "Trade and Politics," 5.

67. Champlain, *Works,* 2:94; *JR* 8:25, 9:253–55, 12:189, 13:49, 30:231, 35:107–9, 50:37–39; Oury, *Marie de l'Incarnation,* 619–20; *NYCD* 3:440, 9:598, 13:521; *LIR,* 125; *AMD* 15:239, 285; Le Roy de la Potherie, *Histoire,* 2:424; Lafitau, *Customs of the American Indians,* 2:160; Quaife, *Western Country in the Seventeenth Century,* 30; Blair, *Indian Tribes* 2:105; Kinietz, *Indians of the Western Great Lakes,* 356; Knowles, "Torture of Captives," 151; Helen C. Rountree, "The Powhatans and Other Woodland Indians as Travelers," in Rountree, *Powhatan Foreign Relations,* 50; Lewis, "First Nations Mapmaking," 1 ("spatial awareness"). See also Rath's discussion of "death songs" sung by war captives, which recounted their life's exploits and therefore also constituted a means of public information dissemination, in *How Early America Sounded,* 156. On the persistent cultural influences of seventeenth-century adoptees among Iroquois communities in the twentieth century, see Bursey, "Frog Pond Site," 28.

68. William J. Engelbrecht, "Ceramic Patterning between New York Iroquois Sites," in Hodder, *Spatial Organisation of Culture,* 141–52; Engelbrecht, *Iroquoia,* 85, 106, 111–14, 128; James F. Pendergast, "The Introduction of European Goods into the Native Community in the Sixteenth Century," in Hayes, Bodmer, and Saunders, *Proceedings,* 12–15; Snow, "Evolution of the Mohawk Iroquois," 22; Kuhn, "Reconstructing Patterns," 145–66.

69. Hewitt, "Some Esoteric Aspects of the League," 322; Morgan, *League of the Iroquois,* 116–19; Vecsey, "Story and Structure of the Iroquois Confederacy," 93; Hamell, "Iroquois and the World's Rim," 455–59; Dennis, *Cultivating a Landscape of Peace,* 79–82; Lutz, "Iroquois Confederation Constitution," 104–5; John Brown Childs, "Beyond Unity: Transcommunal Roots of Coordination in the Haudenosaunee (Iroquois) Model of Cooperation and Diversity," in Prazniak and Dirlik, *Places and Politics,* 274–84; Engelbrecht, *Iroquoia,* 144. See also Tooker, "League of the Iroquois," 419–22; Fenton, *Great Law and the Longhouse,* 128–31.

70. Brandão, *Nation Iroquoise,* 80–85; Lafitau, *Customs of the American Indians,* 2:173, 230; Hale, *Iroquois Book of Rites,* 106–21; Hewitt, "Requickening Address of the League," 163–66; Wolf, *Iroquois Religion,* 76; Wallace, *Iroquois Book of Life,* 78–79; Shimony, *Conservatism among the Iroquois,* 228–31; Santiemma, "La Ligue des Iroquois"; Wonderley, *Oneida Iroquois Folklore,* 11; Rath, *How Early America Sounded,* 168–70; Paul Williams, "Oral Tradition on Trial," in Standen and McNab, *Gin Das Winaan,* 29–34. For a visual depiction of the thirteen strings of wampum used in the Condolence ceremony, see George G. Heye, "Wampum Collection," Heye Foundation *Indian Notes* 7.3 (July 1930): 323.

71. Vecsey, "Story and Structure of the Iroquois Confederacy," 79 (quote), 91–93; Hanni M. Woodbury, "Introduction," in Gibson, *Concerning the League,* lvi–lvii; Fenton, "Seth Newhouse's Traditional History," 158; Fenton, "Lore of the Longhouse," 132–39; Wallace, *Iroquois Book of Life,* 27; Wallace, "Dekanawideh Myth," 125; Hertzberg, *Great Tree and the Longhouse,* 99–101; Porter, "Traditions of the Constitution," 18; Hall, *Archaeology of the Soul,* 34–35; Cornelius, *Iroquois Corn,* 82–83; Campbell, "Seth Newhouse," 183–202; Bonaparte, *Creation and Confederation,* 101–5.

72. Vecsey, "Story and Structure of the Iroquois Confederacy," 94–97; Klinck and Talman, *Journal of Major John Norton,* 98–105; Hewitt, "Legend of the Founding of the Iroquois League," 132–43; Hewitt, "Constitutional League of Peace," 536–37; Wallace, *Iroquois Book of Life,* 34–64; Scott, "Traditional History of the Confederacy"; Parker, *Constitution of the Five Nations,* 14–28; Francis Boots Ateronhiatakon, "Iroquoian Use of Wampum," in Bruchac, *New Voices from the Longhouse,* 35–37; Ceci, "Value of Wampum," 99–100; Graeber, *Toward an Anthropological Theory of Value,* 117–26. I have chosen in this study to employ "Wendat" and "Wendake" to replace the more commonly used descriptors of "Huron" and "Huronia"

(respectively). See *JR* 16:227; Sioui, *Les Wendats*, 11–15.

73. Woodbury, "Introduction," xxxiii–xxxiv (quote xxxiii), xxv–xlvi, 537–701; Hale, "Iroquois Condoling Council"; Hale, *Iroquois Book of Rites*, 191–213; Beauchamp, "Iroquois Condolence," 313–16; "Ancient Rites of the Condoling Council"; Hewitt, "Requickening Address of the Iroquois Condolence Council"; Hewitt, "Requickening Address of the League," 166–79; Fenton, "Iroquois Condolence Council"; Fenton, *Great Law and the Longhouse*, 137–39, 163–79, 725–37; Foley, "Iroquois Condolence Business," 47–53; John Bierhorst, "The Ritual of Condolence: An Iroquois Ceremonial," in Bierhorst, *Four Masterworks*, 112–18; Tooker, "League of the Iroquois," 437–40; Michelsen, "Account of an Iroquois Condolence Council"; Barreiro, "Chief Jacob Thomas"; Alfred, *Peace, Power, Righteousness*, xx–xxiii.

74. Cook, *Voyages of Jacques Cartier*, 60–61; Lafitau, *Customs of the American Indians*, 2:174, 244–45. For narrated versions of the "Edge of the Woods," see Hewitt, *Mohawk Form of Ritual Condolence*, 83–122; Boyce, "Glimpse of Iroquois Culture," 288; Hale, *Iroquois Book of Rites*, 191; Beauchamp, "Civil, Religious, and Mourning Councils," 355–57; Fenton, "Seth Newhouse's Traditional History," 148; Fenton, "Roll Call of the Iroquois Chiefs," 48; Karin E. Michelsen, "Mohawk Text: The Edge of the Forest Revisited," in Mithun and Woodbury, *Northern Iroquoian Texts*, 26–33; "The Edge of the Woods, Delivered by Chief Jake Swamp," in Jemison and Schein, *Treaty of Canandaigua*, 13–14; Abler, *Cornplanter*, 104; Ganter, "Make Your Minds Perfectly Easy." See also van Gennep, *Rites of Passage*, 15–21, 146–47; Turner, *Dramas, Fields, and Metaphors*, 14–16; Smith, *To Take Place*, 103–10.

75. *AMD* 17:199 (quote); Hewitt, "Review," 433; Hewitt, "Some Esoteric Aspects," 325; Strawn, "Public Speaking in the Iroquois League," 61–67; Lex, "Altered States of Consciousness," 285–87; Lynch, "Iroquois," 97; Bradley, *Evolution of the Onondaga Iroquois*, 175; Donald P. St. John, "Iroquois," in Sullivan, *Native American Religions*, 137; Michael K. Foster, "Iroquois Interaction in Historical Perspective," in Darnell and Foster, *Native North American Interaction Patterns*, 24–25; Wallace Chafe, "Seneca Speaking Styles and the Location of Authority," in Hill and Irvine, *Responsibility and Evidence in Oral Discourse*, 72–87; Lutz, "Iroquois Confederation Constitution," 118–19; Taiaiake Alfred, "The People," in Haudenosaunee Environmental Task Force, *Words that Come Before All Else*, 11–12. See also Albert and Le Tourneau, "Ethnogeography and Resource." For a case study of Iroquois ritual innovation in a context of spatial mobility, see George Abrams's discussion of the ceremony attending the 1965 relocation of the Coldspring Longhouse on the Allegany Seneca reservation, "Moving the Fire: A Case of Iroquois Ritual Innovation," in Tooker, *Iroquois Culture, History, Prehistory*, 23–24.

76. Tilley, *Phenomenology of Landscape*, 31–33.

77. *JR* 45:233; *NYCD* 4:258–59, 395; Charlevoix, *History*, 3:45; Calder, *Colonial Captivities, Marches, and Journeys*, 203; Beauchamp, *Moravian Journals*, 80–81; Wesley and Faries, *Stories from the James Bay Coast*, 1–9; Ellis, *Âtalôhkâna nesta tipâcimôwina*, 177; Morgan, *League of the Iroquois*, 414–31; Joseph D. McGuire, "Trade and Trade Routes," in Hodge, *Handbook of American Indians North of Mexico*, 2:799–801; Meyer, "Indian Trails of the Southeast"; Lounsbury, *Iroquois Place-Names*, 25; Hertzberg, *Great Tree and the Longhouse*, 30–32; J. V. Wright and R. Fecteau, "Iroquoian Agricultural Settlement," in Harris, *Historical Atlas of Canada: From the Beginning to 1800* , Plate 12; J. V. Wright and Roy L. Carlson, "Prehistoric Trade," in Harris, *Historical Atlas of Canada: From the Beginning to 1800*, Plate 14; Engelbrecht, *Iroquoia*, 142, 175; John J. Bukowczyk, "Trade, War, Migration, and Empire in the Great Lakes Basin, 1650–1815," in Bukowczyk et al., *Permeable Border*, 10–13; Brooks, *Captives and Cousins*, 304.

78. *NYCD* 4:78–79, 120; Hale, *Iroquois Book of Rites*, 141 ("*kanonsionni*," "people of the extended lodge"); Hewitt, "Review," 432; Gehring and Starna, *Journey into Mohawk and Oneida Country*, 16–17, 46n111; David Cusick, "Sketches of the Ancient History of the Six Nations," in

Beauchamp, *Iroquois Trail,* 35–36; Speck, *Iroquois,* 36; Hertzberg, *Great Tree and the Long-house,* 33, 100–105; Abler, "Longhouse and Palisade," 18; Fenton, "Northern Iroquoian Culture Patterns," 320; Tooker, "League of the Iroquois," 429; Boice, "Iroquois Sense of Place," 184; Wright, *Proxemic Analysis,* 74–75; Graymont, *Iroquois in the American Revolution,* 13–14; "Glossary of Figures of Speech in Iroquois Political Rhetoric," in Jennings et al., *History and Culture of Iroquois Diplomacy,* 118; Powless, "Sovereignty and Land Rights," 159–60; Mima Kapches, "The Iroquoian Longhouse: Architectural and Cultural Identity," in Locock, *Meaningful Architecture,* 253–70.

79. Reynolds, "Persuasive Speaking," 214–18; Campisi, "Iroquois," 168–70; Michael K. Foster, "Another Look at the Function of Wampum in Iroquois-White Councils," in Jennings et al., *History and Culture of Iroquois Diplomacy,* 99–114; Pomedli, "Eighteenth-Century Treaties."

80. Cook, *Voyages of Jacques Cartier,* 103–4; Henry Fleet, "A Brief Journal of a Voyage Made in the Bark Virginia, to Virginia and other Parts of the Continent of America," in Neill, *Founders of Maryland,* 30–31; Gehring and Starna, *Journey into Mohawk and Oneida Country,* 14; *JR* 38:259–61; *NYCD* 3:394, 439; Lewis, "First Nations Mapmaking," 9.

81. *JR* 67:39–41, 68:277–79; *NYCD* 4:661, 6:359–60, 594, 714, 856, 7:541; 8:115; *WA,* 75–76, 226–27, 234–35; Wolf, "Facing Power," 586.

82. On the Niagara portage, see McCarthy, "Lewiston Portage Site," 9; Dunnigan, "Portaging Niagara," 179; Scott and Scott, "Lower Landing Archaeological District," 58. On the Lake Champlain–Richelieu River corridor, see Jennings, *Ambiguous Iroquois Empire,* 30–31; Gray, "Narratives and Identities," 119–56; Bukowczyk, "Trade, War, Migration, and Empire," 15.

83. *DHNY* 1:381; Benson, *America of 1750,* 1:143, 331, 333; *WJP* 3:619, 11:948–51; Aquila, "Iroquois as Geographic Middlemen"; Richter, *Ordeal of the Longhouse,* 209; Heidenreich, "Changing Role of Natives," 33–36; Balvay, "Les relations entre soldats français," 24; D. W. Meinig, "The Colonial Period, 1609–1775," in Thompson, *Geography of New York State,* 135–37; Kammen, *Colonial New York,* 299–300; Kim, *Landlord and Tenant,* 134–37; William Chazanof, "Land Speculation in Eighteenth Century New York," in Frese and Judd, *Business Enterprise in Early New York,* 55–7; Preston, "Texture of Contact," 24–28; Bailyn, *Voyagers to the West,* 573–637; Schmidt, "Mapping an Empire"; Gronim, "Geography and Persuasion."

84. *LIR,* 102 (quote); *NYCD* 4:890, 10:908; Nabokov, *Indian Running,* 18 (80 miles in relay). See also Morgan, *League of the Iroquois,* 441 (100 miles by runners, possibly in relay); Lahontan, *New Voyages* 1:141 (15 miles per day for an individual on foot); Cox, *Journeys of La Salle,* 1:135, and Murray, *Selected Manuscripts,* 21 (25–30 miles per day for an individual on foot); Swartz, "Reevaluation of Late Woodland Cultural Relationships," 46 (15–30 miles per day for an individual on foot; 50–140 miles per day by canoe); Warrick, "European Infectious Disease," 270 (8–18 miles per day for an individual on foot; 13–17 miles per day by canoe). For evidence of canoe travel speeds of 90 miles per day (downstream, with the current) see *JR* 44:111; Hennepin, *New Discovery* 1:37, 234; Coolidge, "French Occupation of the Champlain Valley," 149. For estimates of canoe travel speeds of 45 miles per day downstream and 20 miles per day upstream, see *JR* 44:239. Cf. the much slower rates of official communication between western Europe and North America in Steele, *English Atlantic,* 274–78; Richard D. Brown, "Early American Origins of the Information Age," in Chandler and Cortada, *Nation Transformed by Information,* 39–42; Headrick, *When Information Came of Age,* 182–89; Jaenen, *French Regime in the Upper Country,* 17n13; Jane E. Harrison, "'Adieu pour cette année': Seasonality and Time in New France," in Johnston, *Essays in French Colonial History,* 94–96; Banks, *Chasing Empire Across the Sea,* 218–21.

85. Trigger, "Early Native North American Responses," 1214; Richard L. Haan, "Covenant and Consensus: Iroquois and English, 1676–1760," in Richter and Merrell, *Beyond the Covenant Chain,*

54; Richter, *Ordeal of the Longhouse,* 7. See also Todorov, *Conquest of America,* 61–62, 80, 87, 116; Pratt, *Imperial Eyes,* 6.

1. ON THE JOURNEY, 1534–1634

1. Cook, *Voyages of Jacques Cartier,* 59–61 (quotes). Cf. the estimate of 3,500 persons residing at Hochelaga in 1535 in Blanchard, *Seven Generations,* 86. I use the term "Laurentian Iroquois" to illustrate the connection of these communities to kinfolk in Iroquois territory in modern-day upstate New York, and to highlight the origins of these communities to explain the return of Iroquois people to territory traditionally claimed as their own after circa 1667. These claims derived in part from use in hunting and in part as a result of the amalgamation of at least some of the Iroquoian populations first encountered by Jacques Cartier on the St. Lawrence River in 1534 with the Mohawk and Onondaga nations later in the sixteenth and early seventeenth centuries. For an introduction to the voluminous scholarly literature on this question, see Kuhn, Funk, and Pendergast, "Evidence for a St. Lawrence Iroquoian Presence," 77–86; Pendergast, "Confusing Identities," 150; William Engelbrecht, "Northern New York Revisited," in Wright and Pilon, *Passion for the Past,* 131–33. For one French "league" as the rough equivalent of three statute miles (the definition employed in this study), see Heidenreich, "Measures of Distance," 121; Latta, "Identification of the 17th Century French Missions," 157; Fischer, *Champlain's Dream,* 629. Cf. the range of metric equivalencies for the estimated measure of a "league" in seventeenth-century documentary sources in Chardon, "Linear League," 146 (4.44km); William Engelbrecht and Lynne Sullivan, "Cultural Context," in Sullivan, *Reanalyzing the Ripley Site,* 26 (4.875 km); Dechêne, *Habitants and Merchants,* 289 (4.91 km); Finlayson, *Iroquoian People,* 1:15 (5.5375 km). Hochelaga is believed to have been located near the vicinity of modern-day Montreal. For discussion of potential archaeological sites, see Moira T. McCaffrey and Bruce Jamieson, "The Dawson Archaeological Site: An Overview," in McCaffrey, *Wrapped in the Colours of the Earth,* 41–51; Tremblay, *St. Lawrence Iroquoians,* 36–37. Cf. Wiseman's interpretation in *Reclaiming the Ancestors,* 226–38.

2. On the significance of so-called protohistory, the period between the initial arrival of European material culture into indigenous communities and the subsequent development of regular contact with European personnel, see also Trigger, *Natives and Newcomers,* 116–18; Gregory A. Waselkov, "Historic Creek Indian Responses to European Trade and the Rise of Political Factions," in Rogers and Wilson, *Ethnohistory and Archaeology,* 123–25; David M. Stothers, "The Protohistoric Time Period in the Southwestern Lake Erie Region: European-Derived Trade Material, Population Movement, and Cultural Realignment," in Genheimer, *Cultures Before Contact,* 52; William C. Noble, "The Protohistoric Period Revisited," in Wright and Pilon, *Passion for the Past,* 179–91.

3. Alfred, *Peace, Power, Righteousness,* xx.

4. *JR* 3:39, 291n3 ("Canadian savage"); Hoffman, "Account of a Voyage," 14 (all other quotes); 54–55n30; Cook, *Voyages of Jacques Cartier,* 10, 47, 112, 166; Schlesinger and Stabler, *André Thevet's North America,* 15, 40; Lafitau, *Customs of the American Indians* 2:62; Harrington, "Marine Mammals"; Hoffman, *Cabot to Cartier,* 14, 63; Martijn, "Iroquoian Presence," 48–49; Pendergast, "Native Encounters with Europeans," 104; Michel Plourde, "Iroquoians in the St. Lawrence Estuary: The Ouellet Site Seal Hunters," in Pendergast and Chapdelaine, *Essays in St. Lawrence Iroquoian Archaeology,* 101–19; Roland Tremblay, "Iroquoian Beluga Hunting on Île Verte," in ibid., 121–37; Claude Chapdelaine, "The Iroquoians of the St. Lawrence Valley," in McCaffrey et al., *Wrapped in the Colours of the Earth,* 63–65. Cf. Quinn, *Sources for the*

Ethnography of Northeastern North America, 17–18; John A. Dickinson, "Les précurseurs de Jacques Cartier," in Braudel and Jourdin, *Le Monde de Jacques Cartier*, 137; Ralph Pastore, "The Sixteenth Century: Aboriginal Peoples and European Contact," in Buckner and Reid, *Atlantic Region to Confederation*, 27.

5. Cook, *Voyages of Jacques Cartier* (map on unnumbered page following xli), 24 (quote); James A. Tuck, "European-Native Contacts in the Strait of Belle Isle, Labrador," in Hacquebord and Vaughan, *Between Greenland and America*, 63–64; Junker-Anderson, "Eel Fisheries"; Cossette, "Exploitation of Deer," in Pendergast and Chapdelaine, *Essays*, 59–73; Chapdelaine, "La Transhumance et les Iroquoiens"; Roland Tremblay, "A Middle Phase for the Eastern Saint Lawrence Iroquoian Sequence: Western Influences and Eastern Practices," in Williamson and Watts, *Taming the Taxonomy*, 94–98; Morin, "Early Late Woodland Social Interaction." Stadacona was located near modern-day Quebec.

6. Cook, *Voyages of Jacques Cartier*, 24–25 (quotes); Hoffman, *Cabot to Cartier*, 204; Schlesinger and Stabler, *Andre Thevet's North America*, 14. Cf. Snow, *Mohawk Valley Archaeology*, 143, who identifies the Toudamans as Mohawks.

7. Cook, *Voyages of Jacques Cartier*, 26 (quotes).

8. Ibid., 26–27 (quotes).

9. Ibid., 79 (quote); Lescarbot, *History of New France*, 2:121; Marcel Trudel, "Donnacona," *DCB* 1:275; Roger Schlesinger, "André Thevet and the Amerindians of New France," in Boucher, *Proceedings*, 6–13; Seed, *Ceremonies of Possession*, 56–57; Shoemaker, *Strange Likeness*, 14–26; Melanie Perreault, "American Wilderness and First Contact," in Lewis, *American Wilderness*, 15–33.

10. Cook, *Voyages of Jacques Cartier*, 35–38, 42–50, 54 (quotes).

11. Ibid., 55–66 (quotes 62–66); Trudel, *Beginnings of New France*, 24; Hoffman, *Cabot to Cartier*, 150–57; Eccles, "St. Malo's Sailor"; Forbes, "Two and a Half Centuries of Conflict," 4. Cf. Conrad Heidenreich, "History of the St. Lawrence–Great Lakes Area to A.D. 1650," in Ellis and Ferris, *Archaeology of Southern Ontario*, 476, who asserts a Wendat affiliation for the Agojoudas but fails to address critical issues concerning the English translation of Cartier's original French-language documentation.

12. Cook, *Voyages of Jacques Cartier*, 54, 66–81 (quotes 78); Richard Hosbach, "How the Saint Lawrence Iroquois Cured Cartier's Frenchmen: The First Native Northeastern Medical Prescription," in Hayes, Bodmer, and Saunders, *Proceedings*, 115–31.

13. Cook, *Voyages of Jacques Cartier*, 80–87 (quotes 81–82).

14. Ibid., 96; Peter Cook, "Kings, Captains, and Kin: French Views of Native American Political Cultures in the Sixteenth and Early Seventeenth Centuries," in Mancall, *Atlantic World and Virginia*, 317–26. See also Brian Slattery, "Paper Empires: The Legal Dimensions of French and English Ventures in North America," in McLaren, Buck, and Wright, *Despotic Dominion*, 57–64. Cf. Gregory Evans Dowd, "Domestic, Dependent Nations: The Colonial Origins of a Paradox," in Soderlund and Parzynski, *Backcountry Crucibles*, 127–28.

15. Cook, *Voyages of Jacques Cartier*, 98–105 ("Saguenay," 102; "with certaine little . . . ," 104).

16. Ibid., 98–105 ("what they should doe," 105), 160, 163, 166 (all other quotes); Barkham, "Note on the Strait of Belle Isle," 51–58. In 1723, a Iroquois speaker recounted a traditional narrative of early contact with a "Spaniard," suggesting possible memory of this incident among descendants of sixteenth-century Laurentian adoptees. Cf. Richter, *Ordeal of the Longhouse*, 278–79.

17. S. Barkham, "Documentary Evidence for 16th Century Basque Whaling Ships in the Strait of Belle Isle," in Story, *Early European Settlement*, 53–62; James A. Tuck, "A Sixteenth Century Whaling Station at Red Bay, Labrador," in ibid., 47; Douglass and Bilbao, *Amerikanuak*, 54–55, 70–73; Chapdelaine and Kennedy, "Origin of the Iroquoian Rim Sherd," 41–43; Martijn,

"Iroquoian Presence," 57; Turgeon, "Basque-Amerindian Trade," 81–87; Turgeon, "French Fishers," 608; Martijn, Barkham, and Barkham, "Basques?" 198–99; Sayers, "Etymology of *Iroquois.*" See also Tuck, "European-Native Contacts," 66, who asserts the possibility of the Red Bay rim sherd's association with Agona's Stadaconan party at Belle Isle in 1542. The authenticity of this rim sherd has been disputed on the basis of trace element analysis indicating its production from clay outside known Laurentian Iroquois settlement sites. On the limits of trace element analysis for determining exchange patterns in the archaeological record, see Claassen and Sigmann, "Sourcing Busycon Artifacts," 346.

18. Champlain, *Works,* 2:117; Quinn, *New American World,* 1:217–18; Wright, *Walker Site,* 111; Fitzgerald, *Lest the Beaver Run Loose,* 273; John A. Dickinson, "Old Routes and New Wares: The Advent of European Goods in the St. Lawrence Valley," in Trigger, Morantz, and Dechêne, *Le Castor Fait Tout,* 31–41; Bradley, *Evolution of the Onondaga Iroquois,* 58–60, 90–97; J. V. Wright and Roy L. Carlson, "Prehistoric Trade," in Harris, *Historical Atlas of Canada,* Plate 14; Guldenzopf, "Colonial Transformation of Mohawk Iroquois Society," 3; Kraft, "Sixteenth and Seventeenth Century Indian/White Trade Relations"; Snow, *Mohawk Valley Archaeology,* 197; James F. Pendergast, "The Introduction of European Goods into the Native Community in the Sixteenth Century," in Hayes, Bodmer, and Saunders, *Proceedings,* 12–15; Jacqueline E. M. Crerar, "Assets and Assemblages: The Neutral Economic Approach to Inter-Cultural Relations," in ibid., 46; Martha L. Sempowski, "Early Historic Exchange between the Seneca and the Susquehannock," in ibid., 60–61; Turgeon, "French Beads," 72–77; Drooker, "Two Noded Pipes." See also Bernard Allaire, "L'arrivée des fourrures d'origine Canadienne à Paris (XVIe–XVIIe siècles)," in Lestringant, *La France-Amérique,* 246–47, who argues that no substantial amounts of Canadian peltry reached Paris markets until after 1580.

19. *JR* 15:33; Ferland, *Cours d'Histoire du Canada,* 1:387; J. Bradley and S. Terry Childs, "Basque Earrings and Panther's Tails: The Form of Cross-Cultural Contact in Sixteenth Century Iroquoia," in Ehrenreich, *Metals in Society,* 7–18; William R. Fitzgerald, "Contact, Neutral Iroquoian Transformation, and the Little Ice Age," in Brose, Cowan, and Mainfort, *Societies in Eclipse,* 38–39.

20. Le Blant and Beaudry, *Nouveau Documents,* 246–47; Quinn and Quinn, *English New England Voyages,* 177; Quinn, *New American World,* 4:305; Baxter, *Memoir of Jacques Cartier,* 377–78; Champlain, *Works,* 1:188, 5:78; *JR* 4:207–9, 6:151, 8:27–29; Donald Lenig, "Of Dutchmen, Beaver Hats, and Iroquois," in Funk and Hayes, *Current Perspectives in Northeastern Archaeology,* 73; Pendergast, "Were the French on Lake Ontario?"; Bruce Trigger and Gordon M. Day, "Southern Algonquian Middlemen: Algonquin, Nipissing, and Ottawa, 1550–1780," in Rogers and Smith, *Aboriginal Ontario,* 68; Turgeon, "Basque-Amerindian Trade," 83; Snow, *Mohawk Valley Archaeology,* 143; Trigger, *Natives and Newcomers,* 144–48; William R. Fitzgerald, "A Late Sixteenth Century European Trade Assemblage from Northeastern North America," in Hook and Gaimster, *Trade and Discovery,* 29–32; Cassedy, Webb, and Bradley, "Vanderwerken Site"; Warrick, "Precontact Iroquoian Occupation," 456.

21. Quinn, *North America,* 577; Havard and Vidal, *Histoire de l'Amérique Française,* 37–39; John Dickinson, "Une mystérieuse disparition," in Landry, *Pour le Christ et le Roi,* 82–85; Bernard Allaire, "The European Fur Trade and the Context of Champlain's Arrival," in Litalien and Vaugeois, *Champlain,* 50–52; Tremblay, *St. Lawrence Iroquoians,* 118–25. For eyewitness descriptions of abandoned former Laurentian Iroquois settlements in documentary sources circa 1611 to 1676, see Champlain, *Works* 2:176, 3:59, 63; *JR* 9:59; Du Creux, *History of Canada,* 1:370; *CMRNF* 1:253.

22. Colden, *History of the Five Indian Nations Depending on the Province of New-York,* 3–6 (quotes); Pendergast, "Ottawa River Algonquin Bands," 80–96. Cf. versions of the story in Blair,

Indian Tribes 1:146–47; Le Roy de la Potherie, *Histoire,* 1:175–76. Alternative interpretations include the possibility is that the "Iroquois" in the narrative may refer to Laurentian Iroquois ancestors of the seventeenth-century Iroquois individuals who first related the account to Europeans. For evidence of "symbolic synthesis" between the residents of Hochelaga and the residents of the Oneida Vaillacourt site (occupied circa 1525–1555), see Wonderley, "Iroquois Ceramic Iconography," 73.

23. *JR* 5:288–90n52, 22:215–17, 29:173; *MNF* 5:815; Adams, *Explorations of Pierre Esprit Radisson,* 45–48; Charlevoix, *History,* 2:127–28; Pendergast and Trigger, *Cartier's Hochelaga,* 72–84; Pratt, *Archaeology of the Oneida Iroquois,* 172–75; Bradley, *Evolution of the Onondaga Iroquois,* 56–64, 83–87; Heidenreich, "History of the St. Lawrence–Great Lakes Area," 482–83; Kuhn, Funk, and Pendergast, "Evidence for a St. Lawrence Iroquoian Presence"; Snow, *Mohawk Valley Archaeology,* 180, 198–99, 216; Snow, "Mohawk Demography," 163, 171–72; Maurice Ratelle, "Location of the Algonquins from 1534 to 1650," in Clément, *Algonquins,* 43; Warrick, "Precontact Iroquoian Occupation of Southern Ontario," 456; Lenig, "*In Situ* Thought," 66–67; Funk and Kuhn, *Three Sixteenth Century Mohawk Iroquois Village Sites,* 157; Claude Chapdelaine, "A Review of the Latest Developments in St. Lawrence Iroquoian Archaeology," in Wright and Pilon, *Passion for the Past,* 63–75; Wonderley, "Effigy Pipes," 215–34. For Mohawk oral tradition of a movement led by a woman named Gaihonariosk from the vicinity of modern-day Quebec (Stadacona?) to the Mohawk River valley, "where the climate seemed to her more temperate and the lands more suitable for cultivation," see Lafitau, *Customs of the American Indians,* 1:86. This tradition aligns well with evidence of the St. Lawrence River valley as the northern limit of maize agriculture in North America (see Hoffman, *Cabot to Cartier,* 202) and the primary role accorded to Iroquois women in decisions regarding village relocation. For "Iroquois" as "Mohawks" in French sources, see Lescarbot, *History of New France,* 3:114, 117, 267–68; Du Creux, *History of Canada,* 1:370; Le Blant and Beaudry, *Nouveau Documents sur Champlain,* 350–51.

24. For the Ottawa River valley Algonquins, see Speck, "Boundaries and Hunting Groups," 107; Pendergast, "Ottawa River Algonquin Bands," 107–10. For the Wendats, see Peter Ramsden, "The Hurons: Archaeology and Culture History," in Ellis and Ferris, *Archaeology of Southern Ontario,* 382–83; Sioui, *Huron-Wendat,* 70, 87–88; Abel, "Recent Research on the Saint Lawrence Iroquoians," 137–39. For the Abenakis, see Rand, *Legends of the Micmacs,* 137–41, 169–78, 200–222; *JR* 62:265–67; Richter, "Rediscovered Links," 82; Hamilton, *Adventure in the Wilderness,* 83–84; Pratt, "St. Lawrence Iroquoians," 43–44; Pendergast, "Native Encounters with Europeans," 100–102; Claude Chapdelaine, Richard Boisvert, and Greg Kennedy, "Les Iroquoiens du Saint-Laurent et le basin de la rivière Connecticut," in Chapdelaine, Clermont, and Marquis, *Étude du reseau d'interactions,* 49–58; Wiseman, *Voice of the Dawn,* 59–60, 66; James B. Peterson et al., "St. Lawrence Iroquoians in Northern New England: Pendergast was 'Right' and More," in Wright and Pilon, *Passion for the Past,* 88–117; James B. Peterson et al., "St. Lawrence Iroquoians in Northern New England: Intruders in the 'Dawnland'?" in Rankin and Ramsden, *From the Arctic to Avalon,* 109–28; Stewart and Cowie, "Dietary Indications." Cf. Gordon M. Day, "The Eastern Boundary of Iroquoia: Abenaki Evidence," in Foster and Cowan, *In Search of New England's Native Past,* 117–19.

25. Champlain, *Works,* 1:153–61, 2:186, 196; Sagard, *Histoire du Canada,* 3:803; *JR* 16:227–29, 35:251, 43:261, 53:243; Le Roy de la Potherie, *Histoire* 2:424; Blair, *Indian Tribes,* 1:84–85; Patricia Galloway, "Confederacy as a Solution to Chiefdom Dissolution: Historical Evidence in the Choctaw Case," in Hudson and Tesser, *Forgotten Centuries,* 414 (quote); Trigger, "Sixteenth Century Ontario," 208–10; Steckley, "Clans and Phratries," 29–34; Jamieson, "Examination of Prisoner Sacrifice"; Jamieson, "Place Royale"; Mary A. Druke, "Linking Arms: The Structure of

Iroquois Intertribal Diplomacy," in Richter and Merrell, *Beyond the Covenant Chain,* 29–39; Michael K. Foster, "Iroquois Interaction in Historical Perspective," in Darnell and Foster, *Native North American Interaction Patterns,* 25, 35–36; Chapdelaine, "Mandeville Site"; Stewart, "Faunal Findings from Three Longhouses"; Sioui, *Huron-Wendat,* 87; Stothers, "Protohistoric Time Period," 70; Parker, *Archeological History,* 637–68, 667; Junker-Anderson, "Eel Fisheries," 106–9; Recht, "Role of Fishing," 19–20; Victor P. Lytwyn, "Torchlight Prey: Night Hunting and Fishing by Aboriginal People in the Great Lakes Region," in Nichols, *Actes du Trente-Deuxième,* 304–17; Kuhn, "Reconstructing Patterns of Interaction and Warfare," 148–50; Bradley, "Change and Survival," 31; Janet Young, "Bilateral Differences in Femoral Torsion: Identifying Reasons for Its High Incidence Amongst the St. Lawrence Iroquoians of the Roebuck Site," in Wright and Pilon, *Passion for the Past,* 167–77; Blum, *Ghost Brothers,* 216–24; Sioui, *Histoires de Kanatha,* 167–76. See also Brooks, *Captives and Cousins,* 98–101. For evidence of cross-cultural linguistic capacity among Iroquoian and Algonquian populations, see Champlain, *Works,* 2:94; *JR* 5:113–15, 227, 233, 9:65, 14:15, 125, 33:109, 43:297–99.

26. Schoolcraft, *Notes on the Iroquois,* 51 ("scatter[ed]"); Michael Spence, "Comments: The Social Foundations of Archaeological Taxonomy," in Williamson and Watts, *Taming the Taxonomy,* 277 ("cultural seeds"); Noon, *Law and Government,* 28; Mathur, "Iroquois in Ethnography," 14. For an important distinction between "assimilative" adoption (the wholesale integration of an individual into a group, with an expectation of loyalty to the adopting lineage) and "associative" adoption (in which the adoptee retains his or her former identity alongside a new, fictive affiliation), see Lynch, "Iroquois Confederacy," 87–89; Engelbrecht, *Iroquoia,* 162; Ramsden, "Palisade Extension," 177–83; Doxtator, "What Happened to the Iroquois Clans?" 62.

27. *JR* 10:11, 16:227–29, 19:1–7, 135, 20:43; *MNF* 5:816; Heidenreich, *Huronia,* 84–85; Trigger, *Children of Aataentsic,* 30, 156–57, 174, 587; Elisabeth M. Tooker, "Wyandot," in Trigger, *Northeast,* 404–5; Ramsden, "Hurons," 361–63, 382; Richard E. Sutton, "New Approaches for Identifying Prehistoric Iroquoian Migrations," in Bekerman and Warrick, *Origins of the People of the Longhouse,* 75–83; Allen, "Wa-nant-git-che-ang"; Garrad, "Commemorating the 350th Anniversary of the Dispersal of the Wyandots," 3.

28. For the southward movement of the Susquehannocks, see John Witthoft, "Ancestry of the Susquehannocks," in Witthoft and Kinsey, *Susquehannock Miscellany,* 22–29; Turnbaugh, *Man, Land, and Time,* 236–40; Bruce E. Rippeteau, "The Upper Susquehanna Valley Iroquois: An Iroquoian Enigma," in Engelbrecht and Grayson, *Essays in Northeastern Anthropology,* 136–46; Kent, *Susquehanna's Indians,* 15–21; Brashler, "Middle 16th Century Susquehannock Village"; Grumet, *Historic Contact,* 301–4; Susan C. Prezzano and Christina B. Rieth, "Late Prehistoric Cultures of the Upper Susquehanna Valley," in Sullivan and Prezzano, *Archaeology of the Appalachian Highlands,* 174; Jeffrey L. Hantman, "Monacan Archaeology of the Virginia Interior, A.D. 1400–1700," in Brose, Cowan, and Mainfort, *Societies in Eclipse,* 122–23; Robert D. Wall, "The Chesapeake Hinterlands: Contact Period Archaeology in the Upper Potomac Valley," in Blanton and King, *Indian and European Contact in Context,* 74–77, 96–97; Lauria, "Mythological Giants," 21–22; Wall and Lapham, "Material Culture," 169–71; Rice, *Nature and History in the Potomac Country,* 45–50. Scholars have suggested precontact connections of the Susquehannocks with future Iroquois League nations on the basis of linguistic and archaeological evidence. Though no consensus exists, the weight of evidence favors precontact affinities between the historically known Susquehannocks and the Mohawks, Oneidas, and Onondagas. See Mithun, "Stalking the Susquehannocks," 5–10; Swartz, "Reevaluation of Late Woodland Cultural Relationships," 46–51; Michael Foster, "Language and the Culture History of North America," in Goddard, *Languages,* 106; Henry, "Cultural Change and Adaptation,"

99–105. For the southward movement of peoples from the Lake Erie shoreline, see Mayer-Oakes, *Prehistory of the Upper Ohio Valley,* 72; Brose, "Late Prehistoric Societies," 97–99; Brose, "Penumbral Protohistory," 59–65; O'Donnell, *Ohio's First Peoples,* 26–27. Brose associates some of the people involved in this southward movement with the historically known Wenros in his *Archaeological Investigations in Cuyahoga Valley,* 225, although his model for this population shift has been challenged: see Jeff Carskadden and James Morton, "Fort Ancient in the Central Muskingum Valley of Eastern Ohio: A View from the Philo II Site," in Genheimer, *Cultures Before Contact,* 183–86; Redmond and Ruhl, "Rethinking the 'Whittlesley Collapse,'" 77–78. For the eastward movement of the Neutrals, see Paul A. Lennox and William R. Fitzgerald, "The Culture History and Archaeology of the Neutral Iroquoians," in Ellis and Ferris, *Archaeology of Southern Ontario,* 425–38; Jamieson, "Regional Interaction," 77–81; Fitzgerald, "Contact," 38. Evidence of direct late-sixteenth-century Neutral Iroquois interactions with peoples in the Sandusky River area, the Ohio River valley, and the Susquehanna River valley suggests that this eastward shift of Neutral population aimed in part at greater access to the Mid-Atlantic and indigenous "Fort Ancient" exchange axes (the latter included contacts with peoples ranging from modern-day northeast Iowa to Tennessee and Alabama). See Bowen, *Sandusky River Area,* 27; Penelope B. Drooker, "The Ohio Valley, 1550–1750: Patterns of Sociopolitical Coalescence and Dispersal," in Ethridge and Hudson, *Transformation of the Southeastern Indians,* 120–22; Fox, *"Thaniba Wakondagi"*; Fox, "North-South Copper Axis." Drooker provides evidence of direct Iroquoian contact with Fort Ancient peoples at Madisonville after 1580, though the precise affiliation of the ceramic evidence remains unresolved; she cites possible Neutral, Seneca, or Susquehannock identities for the Iroquoian visitors to Madisonville in *View from Madisonville,* 326–37; Penelope B. Drooker, "Exotic Ceramics at Madisonville: Implications for Interaction," in Williamson and Watts, *Taming the Taxonomy,* 78–79. See also Martha L. Sempowski, "Spiritual Transformation as Reflected in Late Prehistoric Human Effigy Pipes from Western New York," in Wright and Pilon, *Passion for the Past,* 263–81.

29. *NYCD* 9:665 (quote); Wray, Sempowski, and Saunders, *Tram and Cameron,* 28–32; Rumrill, "Mohawk Glass Trade Bead," 8. It is likely that the African woman who died at the Seneca Tram site had spent time at Spanish St. Augustine (see Deagan, *Spanish St. Augustine,* 32–33). She may have been among the 250 Africans liberated from St. Augustine by Sir Francis Drake and later abandoned at Roanoke following the evacuation of that colony's English settler population in July 1586 (see Quinn, *Roanoke Voyages,* 1: 254–55; Kupperman, *Roanoke,* 91–92; Kelsey, *Sir Francis Drake,* 276–77).

30. Bradley, *Evolution of the Onondaga Iroquois,* 111; Hill, "Historical Position of the Six Nations," 103; Bishop, "Locke's Theory of Original Appropriation," 320–35.

31. Engelbrecht, *Iroquoia,* 130–36 ("cannot dig up . . . ," 131); Beauchamp, *Indian Names in New York,* 34; Schoolcraft, *Notes on the Iroquois,* 49; Parker, *Archeological History,* 482, 690; Richard E. Hosbach, "A Gyneco-Android Subset of Native Iroquoian El Rancho Pipes: A New Pipe Designation with the Philosophical Concept of Sexual Duality as Its Basic Motif," in Hayes, Bodmer, and Sempowski, *Proceedings,* 87–91; Wonderley, "Effigy Pipes," 228–34; Wonderley, "Archaeological Research," 20. For documented seventeenth-century Iroquois oral tradition dating the formation of the League prior to the arrival of Europeans, see *JR* 41:87 (1654); *WA,* 24 (1694). See also Pouchot, *Memoir,* 391–92, for an explicit geographical reference to the south branch of Sandy Creek (near present-day Pinckney, New York) as the site of Iroquois origin. Cf. William A. Starna, "Retrospecting the Origins of the League," 305–21.

32. Sagard, *Long Journey to the Country of the Hurons,* 158; *JR* 16:227–29, 21:193, 33:95–97, 45:243; Gibson, *Concerning the League,* 90–94 (Jigonsaseh), 139 (wampum), 297–98 (Tree of Peace),

328–30 (wampum), 459–60 ("dish with one spoon"); Parker, *Life of General Ely S. Parker,* 44–46, 190–91, 321–22; Beauchamp, *Iroquois Folklore,* 137–43; Paul A. W. Wallace, "Dekanawideh," *DCB* 1:253; Engelbrecht, "Iroquois"; Monte Bennett, "Glass Trade Beads from Central New York," in Hayes, *Proceedings of the 1982 Glass Trade Bead Conference,* 51–58; Abraham Rotstein, "The Mystery of the Neutral Indians," in Hall, Westfall, and McDowell, *Patterns of the Past,* 15; Rumrill, "Mohawk Glass Trade Bead Chronology," 8; Ramsden, "Hurons," 363; Martha L. Sempowski, "Early Historic Exchange Between the Seneca and the Susquehannock," in Hayes, Bodmer, and Saunders, *Proceedings,* 60–61; Victor P. Lytwyn, "A Dish with One Spoon: The Shared Hunting Grounds Agreement in the Great Lakes and St. Lawrence Valley Region," in Pentland, *Papers,* 210–11; Mann, *Iroquoian Women,* 119–26; Robertson, "Mourning, Curing, Feasting, or Industry?"; Sempowski and Saunders, *Dutch Hollow and Factory Hollow,* 709–12; Snow, "Evolution of the Mohawk Iroquois," 23; Bradley, "Change and Survival," 27. The Bay of Quinté is now part of Tyendinaga Mohawk Territory.

33. *JR* 58:185 (quotes); Lynn Ceci, "Tracing Wampum's Origins: Shell Bead Evidence from Archaeological Sites in Western and Coastal New York," in Hayes and Ceci, *Proceedings,* 72; Martha L. Sempowski, "Fluctuations through Time in the Use of Marine Shell at Seneca Iroquois Sites," in ibid, 86–88; Kuhn and Sempowski, "New Approach to Dating," 311–12; Carpenter, *Renewed,* xviii–xx; Bonaparte, *Creation and Confederation,* 101–5; Mason, *Inconstant Companions,* 125–28; Jones, "Iroquois Population History," 355, 357. On postcontact internment of European trade goods in Iroquois graves, see Ritchie, *Archaeology of New York State,* 321; Sempowski, "Differential Mortuary Treatment"; Snow, "Evolution of the Mohawk Iroquois," 24. On the enhancement of social solidarity through condolence practices, see David G. Mandelbaum, "Social Uses of Funeral Rites," in Feifel, *Meaning of Death,* 189; Rosenblatt, Walsh, and Jackson, *Grief and Mourning,* 6–8; Richard Huntington and Peter Metcalf, "Introduction," in Huntington and Metcalf, *Celebrations of Death,* 1–2; Maurice Bloch and Jonathan Parry, "Introduction," in Bloch and Parry, *Death and the Regeneration of Life,* 11–15, 41; Robert L. Hall, "Calumet Ceremonialism, Mourning Ritual, and Mechanisms of Inter-Tribal Trade," in Ingersoll and Bronitsky, *Mirror and Metaphor,* 29–31; Carr, "Mortuary Practices," 105–7; Drooker, "Ohio Valley," 120. Cf. Braun and Plog, "Evolution of 'Tribal' Social Networks," 512.

34. *JR* 13:39, 139, 17:195–201, 18:217–19 ("widow," "women," 217); Du Creux, *History of Canada,* 1:395 ("to a poor old woman"); *IMC,* 81 ("mother"); Willoughby, "A Mohawk (Caughnawaga) Halter." For general comments on late-sixteenth- and early-seventeenth-century warfare, see Schlesinger and Stabler, *André Thevet's North America,* 38; Champlain, *Works,* 1:103, 137, 2:50–51, 267–68, 300–303, 306–7, 3:59; Colden, *History of the Five Indian Nations Depending on the Province of New-York,* 8; Charlevoix, *Journal of a Voyage to North-America,* 1:288.

35. On the origins of the Dutch presence in the Hudson River valley after 1611, see *NYCD* 4:353; Victor Enthoven, "Early Dutch Expansion in the Atlantic Region," in Postma and Enthoven, *Riches from Atlantic Commerce,* 36–38; Haefeli, "On First Contact," 415–19. For an evocative statement of Iroquois conceptions of a sentient "Tree of Peace," see *An Account of the Treaty,* 8.

36. Champlain, *Works,* 1:100 (quotes); *MNF* 1:667; Quinn, "Henri Quatre"; Eric Thierry, "La paix de Vervins et les ambitions françaises en Amérique," in Labourdette, Possou, and Vignal, *Le Traité de Vervins,* 373–86; Trigger and Day, "Southern Algonquian Middlemen," 68; Heidenreich, "Changing Role of Natives," 31. On the *pays d'en haut,* see White, *Middle Ground,* x–xv; Skinner, *Upper Country.*

37. Champlain, *Works,* 1:99–103 (quote 103); Lescarbot, *History of New France,* 2:86–87; *NYCD* 4:352, 9:78; Le Roy de la Potherie, *Histoire,* 2:446; Girard and Gagné, "Première Alliance Interculturelle," 7–11; Havard and Vidal, *Histoire de l'Amérique Française,* 47; Alain Beaulieu, "The

Birth of the Franco-American Alliance," in Litalien and Vaugeois, *Champlain,* 153–61. See also Moussette, "Encounter in the Baroque Age"; Blum, *Ghost Brothers,* 3–10.

38. Champlain, *Works,* 1:103 ("greater number"), 137 ("infest[ed]"), 141–43, 159–64, 170, 178–80 (all other quotes), 188; Pastore, "Sixteenth Century," 29; Bruce J. Bourque and Ruth H. White-head, "Trade and Alliances in the Contact Period," in Baker et al., *American Beginnings,* 136.

39. Champlain, *Works,* 2:69 (quotes); Sowter, "Algonkin and Huron Occupation of the Ottawa Valley," 65–66, 92–94; William J. Eccles, "Sovereignty-Association, 1500–1783," in Eccles, *Essays on New France,* 160; Gilbert A. Stelter, "Military Considerations and Colonial Town Planning: France and New France in the Seventeenth Century," in Bennett, *Settlements in the Americas,* 218. For evidence of concerted Dutch competition in the St. Lawrence valley after 1605, sub-sequent to their presence in the Grand Banks fishery for several decades, see Murray, "Early Fur Trade," 367; Howard Vernon, "The Dutch, the Indians, and the Fur Trade in the Hudson Valley, 1609–1664," in Hauptman and Campisi, *Neighbors and Intruders,* 200; Kupp, "Dutch Influences in Canada, III," 15; Cornelius Jaenen, "Champlain and the Dutch," in Litalien and Vaugeois, *Champlain,* 241; Gehring, "Dutch among the People of the Long River," 4.

40. Champlain, *Works,* 2:67–105 (quotes 97–100); Charlevoix, *History,* 2:12–19; Fischer, *Champlain's Dream,* 264, 614–15.

41. Champlain, *Works,* 2:121; Barkham, "Documentary Evidence," 56. For evidence of Native peoples' desire to limit French spatial mobility, see Champlain, *Works,* 2:19, 286–88, 3:100; Sagard, *Long Journey,* 51, 75, 257, 260; *JR* 6:19, 8:41, 81, 9:247, 10:77, 223–25, 12:247, 15:151, 20:19, 56:171–73; Heidenreich, "Changing Role of Natives," 31–32.

42. Champlain, *Works,* 2:122–34 (quotes); Fischer, *Champlain's Dream,* 264.

43. Barbour, *Complete Works of Captain John Smith,* 1:149–50 ("mortall"), 166 ("great," "very populous"), 226–27, 230–31, 232 ("river of Cannida"), 2:11n2, 12, 107, 119 ("had conference," "Targets, Baskets, Swords . . . ," "dexteritie in their small boats"), 171 ("greene wounds"), 172; Barbour, *Jamestown Voyages,* 2:267. Pendergast, in *Massawomecks,* 68–71, makes a case for the Massawomecks as a distinct Iroquoian group. Scholars adopting Pendergast's con-clusions include Helen C. Rountree, "Summary and Implications," in Rountree, *Powhatan Foreign Relations,* 217; Sempowski, "Early Historic Exchange," 52; Gallivan, *James River Chief-doms,* 11; Williamson, *Powhatan Lords,* 34, 41, 55; Sorg, "Linguistic Affiliations"; Van Zandt, *Brothers among Nations,* 71–73, 167. Cf. Hoffman, *Observations on Certain Ancient Tribes,* 196–99 (who associates the Massawomecks with the historically known Erie nation, a claim rejected by Marian E. White; see Marian E. White, "Erie," in Trigger, *Northeast,* 412); Roun-tree, *Pocahontas,* 42 (who identifies the "Massawomecks or Pocoughtraonacks" as "probably a western branch of the Susquehannocks living in the Appalachian Mountains" on the basis of Susquehannock-like ceramic evidence dated to the late sixteenth–early seventeenth cen-tury originating in the panhandles of the modern-day states of Maryland and West Virginia); James D. Rice, "Escape from Tsenacommacah: Chesapeake Algonquians and the Powhatan Menace," in Mancall, *Atlantic World and Virginia,* 107, 117–18, 127, 130 (who distinguishes the "Iroquoian" Massawomecks from the Five Nations and Susquehannocks, but does not cite Pendergast). John Smith's 1612 *Map of Virginia* depicts the Massawomecks in three "King's houses" at the base of a lake northwest of Chesapeake Bay. Aside from the westward orienta-tion of the villages, which might be attributed to poorly translated cartographic information from Native informants, Smith's representation may plausibly be interpreted as the earli-est, albeit unwitting, mapping of three of the four westernmost nations of the emerging League (Senecas, Cayugas, and Onondagas) near the south shore of Lake Ontario. On the 1612 Smith map, see William P. Cumming, "Early Maps of the Chesapeake Bay Area: Their Relation to Settlement and Society," in Quinn, *Early Maryland in a Wider World,* 281–83; Lisa

Blansett, "John Smith Maps Virginia: Knowledge, Rhetoric, and Politics," in Applebaum and Wood, *Envisioning an English Empire,* 87–91. On the role of Native informants in the early modern mapping of North America, see Lewis, "First Nations Mapmaking." For arguments supporting an identification of the Massawomecks with Iroquois nations, see Jefferson, *Notes on the State of Virginia,* 97, 205–6; Morgan, *League of the Iroquois,* 7; Fowke, *Archeologic Investigations,* 72; Semmes, *Captains and Mariners,* 90; Weslager, *Nanticoke Indians,* 27; Bradley, *Evolution of the Onondaga Iroquois,* 99; Potter, *Commoners, Tribute, and Chiefs,* 176–79; Hatfield, *Atlantic Virginia,* 12, 19–20. Rountree and Davidson, *Eastern Shore Indians,* 45, describe the identity of the Massawomecks as "uncertain" but lean against an Iroquois equivalency on the basis of the Massawomecks' use of "birchbark" canoes. This claim is not conclusively established by the evidence, however. Smith's phrase "luted with gumme" could imply the use of tree resin, as was common in the construction of birchbark canoes, or moistened "oakum" (crushed fibers of red elm bark) characteristic of Iroquois elm bark canoes. On "oakum," see Lafitau, *Customs of the American Indians,* 2:125; Benson, *America of 1750,* 1:363–64 (quote 364); Pilkington, *Journals of Samuel Kirkland,* 33. Even assuming that the "Massawomekes" Smith encountered in 1607 were in fact using birchbark canoes, given the range of paper birch trees used in their construction (*Betula papyrifera* Marshall, which seldom grows naturally where average July temperatures exceed 21° C), the Iroquois were much more likely to have had access to them through trade (see Lafitau, *Customs of the American Indians,* 2:126), or through their own procurement and construction (*NYCD* 4:559), than another population residing to the south of Iroquoia. See Safford, Bjorkborn, and Zasada, "*Betula papyrifera* Marsh."

44. *NNN,* 7, 22–23; Ruttenber, *History of the Indian Tribes,* 14–15; Brasser, *Riding on the Frontier's Crest,* 11; Lenig, "Of Dutchmen, Beaver Hats, and Iroquois," 71, 78; Wray, "Volume of Dutch Trade Goods," 103 ("tidal wave"); Kenyon and Fitzgerald, "Dutch Glass Beads in the Northeast," 26; Bradley, *Evolution of the Onondaga Iroquois,* 103; Burke, *Mohawk Frontier,* 2–3; Paul R. Huey, "The Dutch at Fort Orange," in Falk, *Historical Archaeology in Global Perspective,* 27; Gehring and Starna, "Dutch and Indians in the Hudson Valley," 6–7; Snow, *Mohawk Valley Archaeology,* 239; Sempowski, "Early Historic Exchange," 59–60; Margriet de Roever, "Merchandises for New Netherland," in van Dongen et al., *One Man's Trash,* 77; Sempowski and Saunders, *Dutch Hollow and Factory Hollow,* 671, 689; Lenig, "Patterns of Material Culture," 50–53; Clark, "Gender at an Early Seventeenth Century Oneida Village," 373–79.

45. van Loon, "Tawagonshi," 22 ("Tawagonshi treaty"); Brasser, *Riding the Frontier's Crest,* 11–12; Rink, *Holland on the Hudson,* 33–34; Gehring and Starna, "Dutch and Indians in the Hudson Valley," 10; Merwick, *Shame and the Sorrow,* 19. For the academic critique, noteworthy for its attempt to foreclose future discussion, see Gehring, Starna, and Fenton, "Tawagonshi Treaty of 1613"; "Descriptive Treaty Calendar," in Jennings et al., *History and Culture of Iroquois Diplomacy,* 158. Cf. Benjamin, "Tawagonshi Agreement of 1613." For claimed alternative dates for the Tawagonshi treaty, see van Schaick, "Showdown at Fort Orange," 41 (1617); Vernon, "Dutch, the Indians, and the Fur Trade," 200 (1618); Blanchard, *Seven Generations,* 121 (post 1624).

46. Richter, "Rediscovered Links," 81 (quote); *NYCD* 1:79–80; *NNN,* 47–48; *WA,* 95; Kupp, "Dutch Influences in Canada II," 15; Gehring and Starna, "Dutch and Indians in the Hudson Valley," 13; Jaenen, "Champlain and the Dutch," 241; Otto, *Dutch-Munsee Encounter in America,* 54–55, 61–62, 70. See also a 1660 Mohawk description of their "old friendship" with the Dutch having existed "for more than thirty years" (*FOCM,* 503), the sworn testimony of a Dutch settler in 1698 attesting to regular renewals of the Dutch-Iroquois alliance at Albany after 1639 (*NYCD* 4:352), a 1699 claim by Dutch authorities in Albany characterizing the alliance as so old "that

there is none now living that can remember the beginning of it" (ibid., 4:568), and a 1701 Mahican claim dating the origin of their "covenant chain" with the Dutch to "ninety years ago" (ibid., 4:902). Richter's claim that the "western Iroquois tribes" were not brought into the "Covenant" until 1642 ("Rediscovered Links," 55) is at odds with documentary evidence of the *kaswentha* tradition and of direct trade at Fort Orange by League nations residing west of the Mohawks after 1622 (*NNN*, 68, 70, 72; Gehring and Starna, *Journey into Mohawk and Oneida Country*, 1, 18). For documented recitations of the *kaswentha* tradition from 1656 to 1744, see *JR* 43:107–9 (1656), 44:207 (1658); *WA*, 9; Richter, "Rediscovered Links," 76 (October 3, 1678), 81 (July 7, 1689); *NYCD* 3:775 (June 12, 1691); *WA*, 24 (May 15, 1694); *Account of the Treaty*, 7 (August 25, 1694); *Propositions Made by the Five Nations*, 4–5 (August 1, 1698); *NYCD* 4:733 (September 8, 1700), 909 (July 30, 1701), 5:667 (1722); Richter, *Ordeal of the Longhouse*, 278–79 (1723); Kalter, *Benjamin Franklin*, 94–95 (1744). Cf. the unconvincing claims of the origin of *kaswentha* in a late-nineteenth-century "verbalization" of "an ancient assumption of autonomy" in Muller, "Two 'Mystery' Belts," 131, and Miller, *Compact, Contract, Covenant*, 50.

47. Hill, "Oral Memory of the Haudenosaunee." Differences in oral tradition from the written document are primarily associated with the latter's provision for land sales. On *kaswentha*, see ibid., 27–28; Francis Boots Ateronhiakaton, "Iroquoian Use of Wampum," in Bruchac, *New Voices from the Longhouse*, 37–38; Howard R. Berman, "Perspectives on American Indian Sovereignty and International Law, 1600–1776," in Lyons et al., *Exiled in the Land of the Free*, 135; Monture-Angus, *Journeying Forward*, 39; George-Kanentiio, *Iroquois Culture and Commentary*, 118–21; Ransom and Ettenger, "Polishing the Kaswentha," 222; Alfred, *Wasásé*, 266; Salli M. Kawennotakie Benedict, "Made in Akwesasne," in Wright and Pilon, *Passion for the Past*, 441–42; King, "Value of Water," 459–61. For visual representations of "Two Row" belts, see Heye, "Wampum Collection," 320–21; Tehanetorens, *Wampum Belts*, 10–11; Paul Williams, "Wampum of the Six Nations Confederacy at the Grand River Territory, 1784–1986," in Hayes and Ceci, *Proceedings*, 200–201. Significantly, there is no mention of *kaswentha* in Jennings et al., *History and Culture of Iroquois Diplomacy*, widely regarded as the standard scholarly reference work on the subject.

48. Champlain, *Works*, 2:138–42, 186–89, 193–98, 205, 217, 239–309, 4:118–19; *JR* 20:19; Trigger, *Children of Aataentsic*, 367; Noble, "Tsouharissen's Chiefdom," 133–35; William C. Noble, "Frenchmen in Neutralia: Inter-Ethnic and Inter-Tribal Policies, Politics, and Practices of Contact," in Hayes, Bodmer, and Saunders, *Proceedings*, 26.

49. *NYCD* 1:13–14 ("kettles, beads, and merchandise," 14); Champlain, *Works*, 3:31 ("ancient"), 54–55; Jacobs, "Truffle Hunting." Cf. Le Tac, *Histoire Chronologique de la Nouvelle France*, 93; LeClercq, *First Establishment of the Faith in New France*, 1:98; Trigger, *Children of Aataentsic*, 346; Kupp, "Dutch Influences in Canada, III," 15; Huey, "Dutch at Fort Orange," 29; Funk, *Archaeological Investigations*, 1:85; Gehring, "Dutch among the People of the Long River," 9–10. Cahiagué was located near modern-day Hawkestone, Ontario. See Tooker, *Ethnography of the Huron Indians*, 149–50; Heidenreich, *Huronia*, Map 17; Latta, "Identification of the 17th Century French Missions in Eastern Huronia," 147–71. These sources will be used for other descriptions of Wendat town identities, affiliations, and locations cited below unless otherwise noted.

50. Champlain, *Works*, 3:55 ("very wide detour," "thickly populated"), 4:244–45 ("Antouhono-rons," 244), 248, 283; Barbour, *Complete Works of Captain John Smith*, 1:149–50; *JR* 45:203–5; Noble, "Tsouharissen's Chiefdom," 138–39; Grumet, *Historic Contact*, 307 (Susquehannock population estimate). In the explanatory note to his 1632 map of New France, Champlain stated that the "Iroquois and the Antouhonorons together make war against all other nations" (*Works*, 6:250). Pendergast (*Massawomecks*, 65–66) interprets this as Champlain

identifying the "Iroquois" and the "Antouhonorons" as distinct Iroquoian groups. He also argues (ibid., 68–69) for equating Champlain's "Antouhonorons" with Smith's "Massawomeks" on the basis of Champlain's statement of the spatial extent of a single documented "Antounohonoron" movement (Champlain, *Works*, 4:304). Cf. Steckley, "Tale of Two Peoples," for an argument (based on linguistic evidence) identifying the "Antouhonorons" as a separate group. Yet these claims are at odds not only with the evidence associated with League formation discussed above, they assume the permanent and relatively recent character of the "Antouhonoron" movement (which is not necessarily supported in the original documentary source), and both Pendergast and Steckley overlook the consistent use of the term "Iroquois" by Champlain (and other seventeenth-century French authors) to denote the historically known Mohawk nation. Thus, "Antouhonoron" is best understood as a French collective reference for the western four nations of the Iroquois League during Champlain's time, just as "Massawomek" served the English in the Chesapeake Bay region, and "Sinneken" served the Dutch (see Gehring and Starna, *Journey into Mohawk and Oneida Country*, 23n1). Cf. Heidenreich, *Huronia*, 39–40; Trigger, *Children of Aataentsic*, 227; Jack Campisi, "Oneida," in Trigger, *Northeast*, 490. On the Fugle site, see Sempowski and Saunders, *Dutch Hollow and Factory Hollow*, 674–75. Such caution on the part of the Senecas appears to have been warranted. Despite early seventeenth-century ceramic evidence of Seneca exchange with their eastern Iroquois neighbors, archaeologists have noted the comparative scarcity of wampum from Hudson River sources (a crucial indicator of League communications and ceremonialism) on Seneca sites until the early 1640s, after which recovered quantities of wampum increase dramatically. See Engelbrecht, *Iroquoia*, 156; Haas, "Wampum as Hypertext."

51. Bradley, *Evolution of the Onondaga Iroquois*, 113, 116, 223n3; Beauchamp, *Indian Names in New York*, 52; Fischer, *Champlain's Dream*, 615–16. Kaneenda was located near the present site of the Carousel Mall in Syracuse, New York.

52. Champlain, *Works*, 3:56–81 (quotes), 105–14; Le Tac, *Histoire Chronologique*, 95–97; *NYCD* 9:702; Marshall, "Champlain's Expedition Against the Onondagas in 1615," in *Historical Writings of the Late Orsamus H. Marshall*, 19–66; Pratt, *Archaeology of the Oneida Iroquois*, 50–66, 91–93; Stothers, "Protohistoric Time Period," 68–69. Cf. arguments identifying the Oneidas as Champlain's target in 1615 in Trigger, *Children of Aataentsic*, 306, 312–15; Snow, *Mohawk Valley Archaeology*, 239. See also Fenton, *Great Law and the Longhouse*, 243, who identifies the targeted group simply as "Iroquois."

53. Charlevoix, *History*, 2:27–29 ("with loss and shame," 29); Sagard, *Histoire du Canada*, 2:417, 3:804 ("friends and relatives"); Champlain, *Works*, 3:99–100; *JR* 21:211; Noble, "Frenchmen in Neutralia," 26–27.

54. On Brûlé's narrative, cf. McCracken, "Susquehannocks, Brûlé, and Carantouannais"; Twigg, "Revisiting the Mystery."

55. Champlain, *Works*, 3:213–24 (quotes); Sagard, *Histoire du Canada*, 2:429–31; Noble, "Frenchmen in Neutralia," 27–28.

56. Gehring and Starna, "Dutch and Indians in the Hudson Valley," 16 ("cut out the . . ."); *VRBM*, 302–4; Du Creux, *History of Canada*, 1:358; van Laer, "Early Dutch Manuscripts," 231; Jaenen, "Champlain and the Dutch," 242–43.

57. Champlain, *Works*, 5:74–75 (quotes)

58. Ibid., 76–80 (quotes); Sagard, *Histoire du Canada*, 4:846; *JR* 4:171, 261n24; Elsie M. Jury, "Miristou," *DCB* 1:508–9; *MNF* 2:840–41. Cf. *NYCD* 9:702.

59. Champlain, *Works*, 5:117–18, 130–33 (quotes).

60. Charlevoix, *History*, 2:32–33 (quotes). Charlevoix's likely source was LeClercq's *First Establishment of the Faith in New France*, 1:177–79. Although LeClercq's claimed authorship of this book

has been convincingly refuted by Hamilton ("Who Wrote *Premier Établissement?*"), those responsible for forgery of the text may well have had access to the now-lost annual letters of the Récollets from New France circa 1615–29. The information pertaining to the 1622 Iroquois attacks in the book does not lend significant support to the forgers' contemporary anti-Jesuit purposes in preparing the narrative. See also Frédéric Gingras, "Poulain, Guillaume," *DCB* 1:552; Goldstein, *French-Iroquois Diplomatic and Military Relations*, 57; Charles A. Martijn, "The 'Fort Des Hiroquois' of Brother Sagard in 1623," in Pendergast and Chapdelaine, *Essays in St. Lawrence Iroquoian Archaeology*, 139–61. Cf. Trigger, *Children of Aataentsic*, 349.

61. Sagard, *Long Journey*, 74, 152–53 (quotes); Trigger, *Children of Aataentsic*, 417–18.

62. Sagard, *Long Journey*, 158 (quotes), 261; Champlain, *Works*, 3:227; *JR* 8:151, 21:193; Blair, *Indian Tribes* 1:148; Rotstein, "Mystery of the Neutral Indians," 19–20; Noble, "Frenchmen in Neutralia," 27; Sioui, *Huron-Wendat*, 170.

63. LeClercq, *First Establishment of the Faith*, 1:212 ("all the ordinary . . ."); *DHNY* 3:35; Trudel, *Beginnings of New France*, 148. For discussion of the trade fair in New France, held at Quebec in 1624, after being held at Trois-Rivières from 1620 to 1622, then at Cap-de-la-Victoire (near the mouth of the Richelieu River) in 1623 and again from 1625 to 1629, see André Vachon, "Laviolette," *DCB* 1:432.

64. Cf. Fenton, *Great Law and the Longhouse*, 129.

65. *DHNY* 3:50–51 (quotes 51); *NYCD* 3:473; Otto, *Dutch-Munsee Encounter*, 78; Trigger, "Mohawk-Mahican War"; Starna and Brandão, "From the Mohawk-Mahican War to the Beaver Wars."

66. Sagard, *Histoire du Canada*, 3:803 ("well-known"); Brasser, *Riding on the Frontier's Crest*, 13.

67. *JR* 7:217, 9:175, 10:75, 14:101, 28:113–15; Champlain, *Works*, 5:214–15; Grassmann, *Mohawk Indians*, 41n5; Gehring and Starna, *Journey into Mohawk and Oneida Country*, 22; Brasser, *Riding on the Frontier's Crest*, 13; Paul R. Huey, "Dutch Sites of the 17th Century in Rensselaerswyck," in Orr and Crozier, *Scope of Historical Archaeology*, 71. On shell wampum, see Ceci, "Value of Wampum"; George L. Hamell, "Wampum: Light, White and Bright Things Are Good to Think," in Van Dongen et al., *One Man's Trash*, 41–51.

68. *NNN*, 84–85 (quotes); *VRBM*, 306; Champlain, *Works*, 5:208; Snow, *Mohawk Valley Archaeology*, 241; Rumrill, "Mohawk Glass Trade Bead Sequence," 9–10.

69. Champlain, *Works*, 5:214–22 (quotes), 227–28; *MNF* 2:814; van Laer, *Documents Relating to New Netherland*, 52–55, 109, 192. Cf. Merwick, *Shame and the Sorrow*, 122–23.

70. Champlain, *Works*, 5:222–26 (quotes).

71. Ibid., 229–30 (quote 230). The identity of the Indians blamed for the death of Magnan and Cherououny is given as "Ouentouoronons" in the document. Note the striking similarity of this ethnonym to "Antouhonorons," the term the French employed to denote the people known historically as the western four nations of the League. Biggar (ibid., 230n1) identifies them as "probably Onondagas." Le Tac (*Histoire Chronologique*, 139–40) describes the murderers as non-Mohawk "Iroquois." Cf. J. N. B. Hewitt's identification of this name as a synonym for "Seneca," in Hodge, *Handbook of American Indians*, 2:507, 1112.

72. *WJP* 10:67 (quote); *JR* 21:21, 58:185. See also *NYCD* 7:386.

73. Champlain, *Works*, 5:308–12 (quotes).

74. Van Laer, *Documents Relating to New Netherland*, 212–15 ("come to an agreement . . ."); Champlain, *Works*, 5:231–32, 6:3; *NNN*, 89, 131; Eekhof, *Jonas Michaëlius*, 109–10; Gehring and Starna, "Dutch and Indians in the Hudson Valley," 18; Thomas, "In the Maelstrom of Change," 196. See also Abraham I. Pershits, "Tribute Relations," in Seaton and Claessen, *Political Anthropology*, 149–54.

75. Du Creux, *History of Canada*, 1:46–47, 52–53; Champlain, *Works*, 5:304–5; Le Tac, *Histoire Chronologique*, 142; "Memorandum Relating to the Surrender of Québec," in Doughty, *Public*

Archives of Canada, appendix D, 22; John S. Moir, "Kirke, Sir David," *DCB* 1:405; Trigger, *Children of Aataentsic,* 445–62.

76. Champlain, *Works,* 5:195; Sagard, *Histoire du Canada,* 4:846; *JR* 5:51, 195, 6:151, 8:27–29; Moir, "Kirke, Sir David," 405; Jean Hamelin, "Nicollet de Belleborne, Jean," *DCB* 1:517; Bernard Allaire, "The Occupation of Québec by the Kirke Brothers," in Litalien and Vaugeois, *Champlain,* 245–57. See also Sempowski and Saunders, *Dutch Hollow and Factory Hollow,* 671, for evidence of an adult male Caucasian skeleton interred underneath the remains of an adult Seneca man in a Seneca cemetery dating to circa 1605–25, along with skeletal evidence of three female children of mixed Native and European ancestry in the same cemetery, which suggests close ties between the Senecas and at least one European trader. Given the chronology of the site, this individual might have been Dutch or one of the French traders whom Récollet missionary Joseph de La Roche Daillon claimed frequented Neutralia prior to 1626 (see Sagard, *Histoire du Canada,* 3:809).

77. Henry Fleet, "A Brief Journal of a Voyage Made in the Bark Virginia, to Virginia and other Parts of the Continent of America," in Neill, *Founders of Maryland,* 30 (quote); J. Frederick Fausz, "'To Draw Thither the Trade of Beavers': The Strategic Significance of the English Fur Trade in the Chesapeake, 1620–1660," in Trigger, Morantz, and Dechêne, *Le Castor Fait Tout,* 51; Stewart and Wedel, "Finding of Two Ossuaries"; Christian F. Feest, "Nanticoke and Neighboring Tribes," in Trigger, *Northeast,* 249–50.

78. Fleet, "Brief Journal," 25–33 ("Massomacks," 25; "Hereckeenes," "Cannida," 31); Morrison, "Virginia Indian Trade," 224 ("Massawomeckes," "skins"); *AMD* 5:184–206 ("Dutch cloth," 198) ("Spanish axes," 206); Andrew White, S.J., *A Relation of the Colony of the Lord Baron or Baltimore, in Maryland, Near Virginia* (1677; in Force, *Tracts and Other Papers,* vol. 4, no. 12, 20–21; Gehring and Starna, *Journey into Mohawk and Oneida Country,* 7; MacCord, "Susquehannock Indians," 239; Isaac, "Kent Island," 93–119, 210–32; Franics Jennings, "Susquehannock," in Trigger, *Northeast,* 363; J. Frederick Fausz, "Merging and Emerging Worlds: Anglo-Indian Interest Groups and the Development of the Seventeenth-Century Chesapeake," in Carr, Morgan, and Russo, *Colonial Chesapeake Society,* 59–73; Sempowski, "Early Historic Exchange," 59–61; Boza Arlotti, "Evolution of the Social Organization of the Susquehannock," 47.

79. *JR* 8:115; William C. Johnson, "The Protohistoric Monongahela and the Case for an Iroquois Connection," in Brose, Cowan, and Mainfort, *Societies in Eclipse,* 67–82; Sempowski and Saunders, *Dutch Hollow and Factory Hollow,* 675; Richardson, Anderson, and Cook, "Disappearance of the Monongahela"; Herbstritt, "Foley Farm"; Means, *Circular Villages of the Monongahela Tradition,* 18–23.

80. *JR* 5:27–55 ("most sensitive and private parts," 53; "Flemish Captain," 55), 95 ("wrestle and see . . ."), 97, 6:259, 7:85, 97, 127, 171 ("sorcerer"), 9:95–99; *VRBM,* 248 (all other quotes).

81. *JR* 5:215 (quotes), 251, 6:145.

82. *MNF* 2:367–68, 371, 381–82 ("give trouble," "free movement"); *CMRNF* 1:113 (all other quotes); Champlain, *Works,* 6:376, 378–79.

83. *JR* 5:35, 43, 55, 93, 107, 131, 133, 177–79, 199, 203, 209 (quotes), 8:29, 11:195, 15:31; Du Creux, *History of Canada,* 1:145–46; William W. Fitzhugh, "Cultures, Borders, and Basques: Archaeological Surveys on Québec's Lower North Shore," in Rankin and Ramsden, *From the Arctic to Avalon,* 53–70. For an important discussion of the significant differences between the versions of the *Relations* in *JR* and *MNF,* see Codignola, "Battle Is Over."

84. *JR* 5:239, 291–92n58, 6:11 ("great caution," "pass by in . . ."), 8:79, 93–95, 125 ("female soothsayer," "pyromancy"), 127, 9:115–17, 10:305–11, 12:143–45, 13:179, 14:9, 53, 101–3, 19:83, 21:211; Du Creux, *History of Canada,* 1:181 ("supplies of Indian corn . . ."). For a description of the route from Georgian Bay to the Lachine Rapids, see Rumney, "Ottawa-Nipissing Canoe Route."

85. Champlain, *Works,* 4:200–201; Sagard, *Long Journey,* 60; Trigger, *Children of Aataentsic,* 473–76.

86. *VRBM,* 243, 303–4 ("head chief," 303), 330; Gehring and Starna, *Journey into Mohawk and Oneida Country,* 1, 23n1 ("Sinnekens"); *NYCD* 1:78 ("four thousand beaver skinnes"), 3:19; Rink, *Holland on the Hudson,* 99–106, 121–25; Huey, "Dutch at Fort Orange," 33–34; Lenig, "Patterns of Material Culture," 55–57; Gehring, "Dutch and the People of the Long River," 13–15; Merwick, *Shame and the Sorrow,* 81–102. Cf. the list of annual peltry volumes at Fort Orange in *NNN,* 78, which demonstrates growth from approximately 4,700 skins per year in 1624 to over 10,000 skins per year in 1628. According to Jacobs, the volume of peltry remained stable at roughly 1628 levels until declining after 1633 (see Jacobs, *New Netherland,* 198–99). Cf. Matson's assertion of peltry volumes at Fort Orange averaging 15,000 skins annually between 1630 and 1635 in Matson, *Merchants and Empire,* 15. On Rensselaerswyck, see Jaap Jacobs, "Dutch Proprietary Manors in America: The Patroonships in New Netherland," in Roper and van Ruymbeke, *Constructing Early Modern Empires,* 311–21.

87. *JR* 6:57–59, 145, 7:213–15 ("Hiroquois," 213), 7:223–25, 8:69, 115–17 ("wish[ed] to become . . . ," 117), 149–51; Bruce Trigger, "Amantacha," *DCB* 1:59; Sulte, "Trois-Rivières d'Autrefois," 27. Note that the 1634 Wendat rendering of Iroquois ethnonyms recorded by Le Jeune as "Sonontoen[s], Onontaehronons, Ouioenrhonons, Ouiochrhonons, and Agnierrhonons" (*JR* 8:17) transposes the expected sequence of the Onondagas (Onontaehronons) and Cayugas (Ouioenrhonons) in this delineation of the League nations proceeding west to east from Seneca country.

88. Hewitt, "Some Esoteric Aspects of the League of the Iroquois," 322 (quote); Morgan, *League of the Iroquois,* 116–19; Vecsey, "Story and Structure of the Iroquois Confederacy," 93; Hamell, "Iroquois and the World's Rim," 455–59; Dennis, *Cultivating a Landscape of Peace,* 79–82; Lutz, "Iroquois Confederation Constitution," 104–5; John Brown Childs, "Beyond Unity: Transcommunal Roots of Coordination in the Haudenosaunee (Iroquois) Model of Cooperation and Diversity," in Prazniak and Dirlik, *Places and Politics,* 274–84; Engelbrecht, *Iroquoia,* 144. Cf. Wallace, *White Roots of Peace,* 55–56; Fenton, *Great Law and the Longhouse,* 72; Mann, *1491,* 329–37.

89. See also analogous discussions of similar processes among the Narragansetts (William A. Turnbaugh, "Assessing the Significance of European Goods in Seventeenth Century Narragansett Society," in Rogers and Wilson, *Ethnohistory and Archaeology,* 135), Choctaws (Galloway, *Choctaw Genesis,* 338–60), Creeks (Womack, *Red on Red,* 30–31), and Pueblos (Winifred Creamer, "The Origins of Centralization: Changing Features of Local and Regional Control during the Rio Grande Classic Period, A.D. 1325–1540," in Haas, *From Leaders to Rulers,* 56–58).

2. THE EDGE OF THE WOODS, 1635–1649

1. Gehring and Starna, *Journey into Mohawk and Oneida Country,* 12–13 (quotes), 14; Hagerty, *Wampum, War and Trade Goods,* 30; Wonderley, *Oneida Iroquois Folklore,* 6–7. Oneyutte-hage was located near modern-day Munnsville, New York.

2. Alfred, *Peace, Power, Righteousness,* xx. The spatial expansion of Iroquoia after 1635 stands in stark contrast to the experience of many neighboring Native peoples, especially the Wendat Confederacy, whose constituent nations, despite a pre-epidemic population of 20,000 to 30,000 people, occupied an ever-declining settlement area until their defeat and dispersal by the Iroquois after 1649. See *JR* 8:117, 18:233, 21:201, 28:275, 291, 33:65, 125–27, 40:23; Gehring

and Starna, *Journey into Mohawk and Oneida Country,* 11; Gendron, *Quelques Particularitez,* 9–10; Le Roy de la Potherie, *Histoire,* 2:442; *NNN,* 302; Brandão, *Nation Iroquoise,* 51; Finlayson, *Iroquoian Peoples,* 1:8; Wright, "Ceramic Vessels," 44–45; Trigger, *Children of Aataentsic,* 162–64; Gary Warrick, "Trends in Huron Family, Household, and Community Size, A.D. 900–A.D. 1650," in MacEachern, Archer, and Garvin, *Households and Communities,* 277–86; Ferris, "In Their Time," 73.

3. For another document possibly created on this expedition, see van Loon, "Letter from Jeronimus de la Croix." Gehring and Starna dismiss this document as "bogus" in "Case of Fraud," but their critique (256–58) does not rule out the possibility that this document represented a later copy of an original letter (as was the case with the Tawagonshi treaty and even with the Van den Bogaert journal itself).

4. Gehring and Starna, *Journey into Mohawk and Oneida Country,* 1–6 (quotes).

5. Ibid., 7 (quotes).

6. Ibid., 8–14 (quotes). For a 1671 description of the use of maize kernels as a mnemonic tool in Oneida country, see *JR* 55:45.

7. Gehring and Starna, *Journey into Mohawk and Oneida Country,* 14–17 (quotes). According to Hagerty, *Wampum,* 114–16, one "hand" of wampum was roughly equivalent to forty strung beads of wampum (roughly ten inches long), and converted to ten contemporary Dutch stivers (or half a guilder). Thus, the Oneidas were seeking a price of two guilders per pelt, which threatened a sizable cut in Dutch profit margins, given the relatively stable price of six to seven guilders per pelt in Europe circa 1630–46. Cf. Gehring and Starna, *Journey into Mohawk and Oneida Country,* 33n31, who define a "hand" as a European measure equivalent to four inches.

8. Gehring and Starna, *Journey into Mohawk and Oneida Country,* 18–22 (quotes).

9. Ibid., 4, 8 ("very sick"), 10, 17; *JR* 7:220, 8:23–25, 31, 42, 59, 73, 87–89, 9:251–53; *MNF* 2:800, 3:860; Du Creux, *History of Canada,* 1:194; Hosmer, *Winthrop's Journal,* 1:118; Charlevoix, *History,* 2:94; Trigger, "Amantacha"; Susan Johnston, "Epidemics: The Forgotten Factor in Seventeenth Century Native Warfare in the St. Lawrence Region," in Cox, *Native People, Native Lands,* 14–15; Robert Larocque, "Secret Invaders: Pathogenic Agents and the Aboriginals in Champlain's Time," in Litalien and Vaugeois, *Champlain,* 269. For the "virgin soil" character of this epidemic among the Iroquois, see Snow and Lanphear, "European Contact and Indian Depopulation," 23–24. Cf. Dobyns, "More Methodological Perspectives," 295–96; Snow and Lanphear, "Rejoinder to Dobyns," 299–304. Snow, in his "Mohawk Demography," 174, estimates Mohawk losses at 63 percent based on archaeological evidence of subsequent changes in Mohawk housing patterns. This rate of depopulation is comparable to the rate of 60 percent posited for Wendake (circa 1634–39) in Warrick, "European Infectious Disease," 263, 267. For an important critique of Warrick's method in obtaining this ratio, which suggests an inflated depopulation rate, see Ferris, "In Their Time," 74–75. See also the opinion of Norman C. Sullivan, "Contact Period Huron Demography," in Paine, *Integrating Archaeological Demography,* 339, who suggests that the first "serious event of population disruption" among the Wendats did not occur until 1639–40, when four successive waves of disease caused estimated population losses of 48–58 percent. For descriptions of possible quarantine practices in seventeenth- and eighteenth-century Iroquoia, see *JR* 52:165, 54:57, 58:215–17, 231, 59:243, 62:99; Lafitau, *Customs* 2: 206. For evidence of Iroquois people apparently surviving smallpox, see Waterman, *To Do Justice to Him and Myself,* 141, 157.

10. *JR* 43:287, 56:33, 58:185, 209–11; Lafitau, *Customs of the American Indians,* 1:311–12; Starna, "Seventeenth-Century Dutch-Indian Trade," 7 ("socialization process," "hobbled given the . . ."); Starna, "Biological Encounter," 511–19; Ramenofsky, *Vectors of Death,* 71–100;

Snow, *Iroquois,* 94, 304 ("repackaging"), 362. See also analogous discussions in Ewen, "Continuity and Change," 41–42; Lisa Kealhofer and Brenda J. Baker, "Counterpoint to Collapse: Depopulation and Adaptation," in Baker and Kealhofer, *Bioarchaeology of Native American Adaptation,* 209–10; Kelton, "Avoiding the Smallpox Spirits," 45; Martelle, "Some Thoughts"; Francis Brooks, "The Impact of Disease," in Raudzens, *Technology, Disease, and Colonial Conquests,* 145–60. Abundant contemporary evidence attests to unity among the constituent nations of the League and to the persistence of persuasive, consultative authority exercised by elder male leaders within a given clan, town, or nation in collaboration with younger men. See Lahontan, *New Voyages* 2:422; Le Roy de la Potherie, *Histoire* 2:435–37; Oury, *Marie de l'Incarnation,* 808, 839, 917; *LIR,* 41; *JR* 51:119–123, 237, 52:179, 53:213–35, 54:113, 119, 265, 57:137–39, 58:179, 61:27, 62:59; *NYCD* 4:118, 195, 276, 279, 729, 801, 9:170, 228, 255; *AMD* 17:14; Belmont, "Histoire du Canada," 35; Sivertsen, *Turtles, Wolves, and Bears,* 32.

11. Gehring and Starna, *Journey into Mohawk and Oneida Country,* 16; *VRBM,* 330. No record exists of Bogaert's return to Iroquoia in an official capacity after 1635, but in 1647 he fled to Mohawk country to escape a sodomy charge and subsequently died in a mysterious fire. See Gehring, *Delaware Papers (Dutch Period),* 22.

12. *JR* 8:59–61, 9:65–67, 121, 225, 241, 253–59, 263, 271, 295–99 (quote 299), 10:51, 75–77, 81, 227–29, 245, 11:69–71, 185, 215, 12:181–83, 13:7, 83, 17:223–25, 21:269–73; Speck, "Montagnais and Naskapi Tales," 12, 22, 30.

13. *JR* 8:303–4n38, 13:37–83 (quotes), 15:169, 249n12. See also Wallace's interpretation in *Death and Rebirth of the Seneca,* 104–7. Scanonaenrat was located near modern-day Orr Lake, Ontario.

14. *JR* 5:211, 8:49, 9:219 ("exterminated," "all one people," "daughters"), 235, 237, 255, 295–99 ("madness," 299), 11:95, 19:27, 29–35 ("Anne Thérèse"), 29, ("long sickness"), 31, 287, 21:119 (French population estimate); Du Creux, *History of Canada,* 2:414; *MNF* 2:802–3, 3:826, 4:764. For discussions of assimilative processes at work in early French colonialism, see Stanley, "Policy of 'Francisation'"; Sara E. Melzer, "The Underside of France's Civilizing Mission: Assimilationist Policies in New France," in Koch, *Classical Unities,* 151–64; Belmessous, "Assimilation and Racialism"; Ingersoll, *To Intermix with Our White Brothers,* 23–27, 53–73. Cf. Pestana, *English Atlantic,* 229–32 for an estimate of approximately 19,000 English settlers in the New England region circa 1640.

15. *JR* 12:53–55 ("Admiral," "all the news . . ."), 153–61 (all other quotes), 30:281, 50:21; *MNF* 3:863.

16. *JR* 7:73, 9:241, 245, 275–77, 10:75–77, 12:187–89, 247, 257 ("iron arrow-heads"), 18:183 ("javelins"), 21:37, 24:291, 25:27, 265, 26:71.

17. *NNN,* 274 (quote); Champlain, *Works,* 5:313–18; *VRBM,* 426, 565–66, 626; *MaHSC* ser.4, 6:159; Boucher, *Histoire Véritable,* 123, 164; Du Creux, *History of Canada,* 1:142; O'Shea, "Springfield's Puritans and Indians"; Cf. Charlevoix, *History,* 2:32, for evidence of the short-lived illegal French trade of firearms at Tadoussac in 1620. For archaeological evidence of firearms in Iroquoia after 1640, see Snow, *Mohawk Valley Archaeology,* 299; Jan Piet Puype, "Dutch and Other Flintlocks from Seventeenth Century Iroquois Sites," in Hayes, *Proceedings of the 1984 Trade Gun Conference,* 69–91; Vernon, "Dutch, the Indians, and the Fur Trade," 204; Wray, "Volume of Dutch Trade Goods," 106; Lowensteyn, "Role of the Dutch," 23; Given, *Most Pernicious Thing,* 57–68; Fenton, *Great Law and the Longhouse,* 245. For the Mohawks' role as the League's eastern doorkeepers, see Gibson, *Concerning the League,* 267–69; Fenton, "Structure, Continuity, and Change," in Jennings et al., *History and Culture of Iroquois Diplomacy,* 16–17.

18. *JR* 12:99–105, 199–217 (quotes). On Iroquois pictographic writing, see Beauchamp, "Aboriginal Use of Wood," 135–36, and the evidence discussed below (note 37). Mohawks killed as many

as twenty members of Sassacus's embassy in July 1637, plundered an estimated "five hundred pounds'" worth of the Pequot leader's wampum, and sent the Pequots' severed head and hands to William Pynchon. This act quelled widespread fears in New England of a rumored "Conglutination" between the Mohawks and the Pequots during the Pequot War. See Dunn, Savage, and Yaendle, *Journal of John Winthrop,* 226–27, 229 ("five hundred pounds"); *WP* 3:436 ("Conglutination"); *MaHSC* ser.4, 6:201, 204–5, 239; Bradford, *Bradford's History,* 430; Neal Salisbury, "Toward the Covenant Chain: Iroquois and Southern New England Algonquians, 1637–1684," in Richter and Merrell, *Beyond the Covenant Chain,* 61–62, 181n7; Lipman, "'Meanes to Knitt Them Togeather,'" 24–25.

19. *JR* 15:159, 16:253, 17:25–31, 75–77 (quotes), 213, 21:231–33, 39:141, 57:197; Du Creux, *History of Canada,* 1:254; McCarthy and Newman, "Seneca Indian Find," 137; White, *Iroquois Culture History,* 39–40; Marian E. White, "Neutral and Wenro," in Trigger, *Northeast,* 409–10; Ridley, "Wenro in Huronia," 10–20; William Engelbrecht, "The Kleis Site Ceramics: An Interpretive Approach," in Foster, Campisi, and Mithun, *Extending the Rafters,* 336–37; MacDonald, "Neutral Freelton Village Site," 21; Garrad, "Survival of the Wenro"; Crerar, "Assets and Assemblages," 46; Granger, "Orchid Site," 36–37; Arthur J. Ray, "The Fur Trade in North America: An Overview from a Historical Geographical Perspective," in Novak et al., *Wild Furbearer Management,* 22. For an argument stressing the indeterminate nature of indigenous national identities on the Niagara Frontier, see Rayner-Herter, "Niagara Frontier Iroquois," 7–10, 314.

20. The surplus wampum that facilitated François's journey to Oneida country may have originated from the plunder of the Pequots or from Mohegan and Narragansett tribute payments to the Mohawks after 1637 (the latter conducted via Pynchon's post at Springfield). See Dunn, Savage, and Yaendle, *Journal of John Winthrop,* 328–29; *VRBM,* 483–84; *WP* 4:258–59, 418, 432, 443; *MaHSC* ser.4, 6:159, 174, 357–59, 372–73; 7:411; ser.5, 1:331; *RCNP* 9:19, 75–76, 116; Oldmixon, *British Empire in America,* 1:224; Chapin, *Sachems of the Narragansetts,* 63.

21. *JR* 12:85, 13:265, 15:37, 43, 125, 167, 171–73, 183, 187, 16:215, 17:101–11, 223, 18:33, 43–45, 217–19, 19:81, 27:289 ("child[ren]"), 297 ("so that their . . ."); *MNF* 4:781; Snow, "Mohawk Demography," 163–64, 171–72. For subsequent references to the Oneidas as the "children" or "daughters" of the Mohawks, which date to 1694, see *LIR,* 60–61; *NYCD* 3:277, 4:85. See also Pratt, *Archaeology of the Oneida Iroquois,* 137.

22. *JR* 16:215 ("forts"), 18:217–19, 20:167, 259, 271–73, 21:63–65, 117, 247, 22:249, 253, 24:269, 26:301–7, 27:37, 55.

23. *JR* 17:49, 20:35, 57, 79 ("long javelin"), 95 ("our first and good Christian"), 21:211, 22:251; Du Creux, *History of Canada,* 1:246–56, 305–11; Campeau, *La Mission des Jésuites,* 55; Hawkins, "Recreating Home?"; Steckley, *De Religione,* 131. Contarea was located near modern-day Orillia, Ontario.

24. *JR* 14:127, 205–29, 286–87n12, 16:75–111, 17:233–35, 18:23–145, 21:125, 177–85; Ronda, "Sillery Experiment"; Garrad, "Attack on Ehwae," 108–11; Charles Garrad and Conrad Heidenreich, "Khionontateronon (Petun)," in Trigger, *Northeast,* 394–96. Ehwae was located near modern-day Creemore, Ontario.

25. *JR* 21:21–23 (quotes).

26. Ibid., 25–33 (quotes). Cf. dating of these men's capture to February 1641 in André Vachon, "Godefroy de Normanville, Thomas," *DCB* 1:341; Raymond Douville, "Marguerie de la Haye, François," in ibid., 1:489; *MNF* 3:843, 851.

27. *NYCD* 9:598 ("passports"); *JR* 21:31–33 (all other quotes), 46:225.

28. *JR* 21:35–37 (quotes).

29. Ibid., 21:39–41 (quotes); Charlevoix, *History,* 2:124–25.

30. *JR* 21:43–47 (quotes).

31. Ibid., 21:49–55 (quotes). This revised offer may have represented an effort by the Mohawks to eliminate the need for subsequent travel to Trois-Rivières, the site of the annual French trade fair circa 1632–60 (see Desrosiers, "Les Trois-Rivières," 85; André Vachon, "Laviolette," *DCB* 1:432), in order to establish more effective competition with the Dutch summer trading season (or *handelstijd*) at Beverwijck (see Merwick, *Possessing Albany,* 77–103; Jacobs and Shattuck, "Beaver for Drink," 101).

32. *JR* 21:55–65 (quotes).

33. Ibid., 21:51 ("who had been naturalized . . ."), 55 (all other quotes).

34. Ibid., 21:61 (quote).

35. Ibid., 22:251–69 (quotes); Du Creux, *History of Canada,* 1:337–39; *MNF* 5:822; RAB, nos. 39423, 39424, 73931, 86845, 86854, 86895, 87022, 87025, 89304.

36. Dollier de Casson, "Histoire de Montréal," 4 ("dyke," "fury"); *JR* 22:17, 35 ("war in the fashion . . . ," "either won over . . ."), 127, 211, 269 ("as well as . . ."), 277–81, 24:281–83; Oury, *Marie de l'Incarnation,* 167–68 ("keep the way free"); "Memoires de Feu Monsieur Boucher," 398; Du Creux, *History of Canada,* 1:370; Le Clercq, *First Establishment of the Faith,* 2:13; Stelter, "Military Considerations," 221–22; Woodward, "Metal Tomahawk," 2–8; Carpenter, *Renewed,* 94.

37. Oury, *Marie de l'Incarnation,* 166–69 (quotes); *JR* 22:269–73, 26:187–93, 31:21–51; Du Creux, *History of Canada,* 1:342. On Thérèse Kionhreha, see Campeau, *La Mission des Jésuites,* 86; *MNF* 5:826. Cf. Thomas Grassmann, "Oionhaton, Thérèse," *DCB* 1:523–24, who identifies this individual with Kionhreha; evidence suggests that she may actually have been a sister or cousin of Kionhreha (see *MNF* 4:788, 6:741, 8:985). The association of specific colors associated with the intended fates of captives in this account differs from the 1637 incident discussed above, but aligns with a description of an incident occurring in 1682 (see *JR* 62:87). See also the account of Jesuit Pierre Millet's 1688 capture, after which his face was painted both black and red (*JR* 64:91) and Haefeli, "On First Contact," 425. The August 1642 attack on the Wendat party escorting Jogues occurred on the St. Lawrence River near modern-day Sorel, Quebec.

38. *JR* 18:229, 245, 22:93, 127, 249, 24:225, 267–73 (quotes), 25:105–15, 27:237–45; Trigger and Day, "Southern Algonquian Middlemen," 72.

39. "The Memoir of Lamothe Cadillac," in Quaife, *Western Country in the 17th Century,* 30 (quotes); *JR* 21:63, 75, 24:205–9, 279–87, 293–97, 26:55, 31:89; Blair, *Indian Tribes,* 1:146; Williams, "Class Act," 407, 415.

40. *IMC,* 18 ("aunt"), 35–36 ("formerly captured and . . ."); *MNF* 2:853 ("Ondessonk"); Du Creux, *History of Canada,* 1:376 ("old woman, who . . . ," "take the place . . ."); Trigger, *Children of Aataentsic,* 646. The Iroquois later conferred the name "Ondessonk" to Jesuits Simon Le Moyne and Thierry Beschefer (see *JR* 41:89, 97, 109, 42:43, 44:127, 50:129, 171). Ossernenon was located near modern-day Auriesville, New York.

41. Du Creux, *History of Canada,* 1:377–80 (quotes); *JR* 31:81–85; Day, "Identity of the Sokokis," *Ethnohistory* 12 (1965): 242–43; Trigger, *Children of Aataentsic,* 646. The Sokokis' home village was then located near modern-day Northfield, Massachusetts.

42. *JR* 31:87–89 (quote 87)

43. *VRBM,* 416, 483–84, 508–9 ("three very fine blankets," "*Sader Juchta,*" "great friendship"), 625 ("the cruel war . . ."); Hosmer, *Winthrop's Journal,* 2:33; *NYCD* 4:352; *IMC,* 32; van Laer, "Arent van Curler," 24; Bradley, "Visualizing Arent van Curler," 3–5. On the increasing importance of blankets and other cloth goods in the Dutch-Iroquois trade, see Baart, "Cloth Seals at Iroquois Sites," 77–80.

44. van Laer, "Arent van Curler," 27–28 (quotes); Gehring and Starna, *Journey into Mohawk and Oneida Country,* 10, 13–14, 20, 39–40n69.

45. *JR* 15:47, 31:89 ("to visit some . . . ," "the triumphs of . . ."); Du Creux, *History of Canada,* 1:380–81 (all other quotes); van Laer, "Arent van Curler," 28; Otto, *Dutch-Munsee Encounter,* 119.

46. Du Creux, *History of Canada,* 1:381.

47. Ibid., 1:382–85 (quotes), 396n1; *ERNY* 1:166, 436.

48. *JR* 24:305 ("Iroquois by affection," "partly in French . . ."); *IMC,* 20–21 ("to take, if they can . . .").

49. *JR* 22:269, 297–99, 23:25–27, 33–35, 159, 197, 267, 24:185, 25:35–39, 109, 117–21, 149–51, 157–59, 191–93, 261, 26:29–51, 53–73, 237–49, 275, 27:63–65, 89, 175, 28:43–45 ("pitiless," "age, sex, or condition . . . ," 43), 57 ("the fury of . . . ," "who depopulates the . . ."); Du Creux, *History of Canada,* 1:388.

50. *MNF* 2:807–8, 5:642, 759–60, 820–21; 6:42 ("constant warfare") 48; 7:305, 444, 854; *JR* 12:203 ("edge of the woods," "lurked"), 24:231, 253, 265, 279 ("tilling the soil"), 27:221–27 ("Goblins," 221), 32:105, 159; *IMC,* 43, 48–55 ("quite dear," 54); *ERNY* 1:168; Gehring, *Correspondence, 1647–1653,* 87–91; Du Creux, *History of Canada,* 1:395–96; Dollier de Casson, "Histoire du Montréal," 25; Belmont, "Histoire," 23–24; Bertrand, *Histoire de Montréal,* 1:29–31; Marie-Claire Daveluy, "Chomedey de Maisonneuve, Paul de," *DCB* 1:218; Leopold Lamontagne, "Le-neuf de la Poterie, Jacques," *DCB* 1:467; Lanctot, *Montréal under Maisonneuve,* 29; Dickinson, "La Guerre Iroquoise," 51; Gélinas, "La Nature des Attaques Iroquoises," 121–22; Dechêne, *Habitants and Merchants,* 5–6; Dubé, *Chevalier de Montmagny,* 169–70.

51. Dollier de Casson, "Histoire du Montréal," 32 ("butcherings"); Charlevoix, *History,* 2:174 ("boasted aloud that . . ."); Du Creux, *History of Canada,* 1:396 ("lurking in the woods"); *NYCD* 3:574 ("plyed," "over a door . . ."); *JR* 26:35–37, 55, 27:63; *MNF* 6:782–83; Jean Hamelin, "Legardeur de Repentigny, Pierre," *DCB* 1:447; Eccles, "Sovereignty-Association," 161.

52. Du Creux, *History of Canada,* 1:397–400 (quotes). Cf. *JR* 26:59–73.

53. Robie, "Kiotsaeton's Three Rivers Address"; Fenton, "The Earliest Recorded Description: The Mohawk Treaty with New France at Three Rivers, 1645," in Jennings et al., *History and Culture of Iroquois Diplomacy,* 127–53; Lytwyn, "A Dish with One Spoon," in Pentland, *Papers,* 212–14; Warkentin, "In Search of the 'The Word of the Other,'" 1–2; Johnston, "Covenant Chain of Peace," 40–81; Rasmussen, "Negotiating Peace."

54. *JR* 27:253–63 (quotes). Cf. Oury, *Marie de l'Incarnation,* 251–58, Du Creux, *History of Canada,* 2:408–13; Charlevoix, *History,* 2:179–82.

55. Oury, *Marie de l'Incarnation,* 255–56 ("allies," 255); *DHNY* 4:117–18 ("glittering yellow paint," 117): *JR* 27:255–59; van Laer, *Council Minutes,* 280; van der Donck, *Description of New Netherland,* 39–40; *VRBM,* 483–84; O'Callaghan, *History of New Netherland* 1:355–56; Johnson, *Instruction for Johan Printz,* 116; Feister, "Linguistic Communication," 36; Evan Haefeli, "Kieft's War and the Cultures of Violence in Colonial America," in Bellesiles, *Lethal Imagination,* 17–40; Meuwese, "'For the Peace and Well-Being of the Country,'" 414; Otto, *Dutch-Munsee Encounter,* 113–25; Merwick, *Shame and the Sorrow,* 135–79. Cf. Anthony F. Buccini, "Swan-nekens Ende Wilden: Linguistic Attitudes and Communication Strategies among the Dutch and Indians in New Netherland," in Prins et al., *Low Countries and the New World(s),* 17.

56. *JR* 27:251; Oury, *Marie de l'Incarnation,* 260.

57. *JR* 27:261–63 (quote); Hamell, "Strawberries," 77; Bradley, "Change and Survival," 34. Kiot-saeton's references to mutual visibility may have reflected a contemporary concern for the mutual visibility of allied League settlements to facilitate defense and communications. See Jones, "Using Viewshed Analysis," 527.

58. *JR* 27:265, 277–79 ("orders from the . . ."), 28:149–51, 315n16, 29:247–51; Oury, *Marie de*

l'Incarnation, 250–52 (all other quotes); Trigger, *Children of Aataentsic,* 648.

59. *JR* 27:279 (quotes); *JJ,* 4.

60. *JR* 27:281–89 (quotes).

61. Ibid., 27:287–301 (quotes).

62. Dollier de Casson, "Histoire du Montréal," 34 ("patched-up"); *JR* 27:79, 303 ("as pledges of . . ."), 28:279–83 (all other quotes); *JJ,* 4–5; Charlevoix, *History,* 2:183; Trudel, *Beginnings of New France,* 212–14.

63. *JR* 28:155, 169–71, 205, 277, 281, 283–87, 29:147–51 (quotes), 153–55, 251–55; *JJ,* 4, 29–31, 36–37, 53; Du Creux, *History of Canada,* 2:435–36; Charlevoix, *History,* 2:183, 193.

64. *JR* 28:293.

65. Oury, *Marie de l'Incarnation,* 280–81 ("to ask after . . . ," 281); *JR* 26:29, 28:293–301 (all other quotes), 29:95.

66. *JR* 28:137 ("engineer of New France"), 29:49–51 (all other quotes); Du Creux, *History of Canada,* 2:440.

67. *JR* 29:53 ("one of the great . . ."), 55–57 (all other quotes).

68. Du Creux, *History of Canada,* 2:440–43 (all quotes); *JR* 29:57–59, 294n6; Oury, *Marie de l'Incarnation,* 281.

69. *JR* 8:117, 18:133, 28:137 (quote), 213, 29:59–61; *JJ,* 57; *MNF* 6:529–38; Gendron, *Quelques Particularitez,* 9–10; Margry, *Découvertes,* 1:37–41; Hunter, "Erie Stone," 3. Cf. Crouse, "Contributions of the Canadian Jesuits," 25–28, 60–61; Heidenreich, "Seventeenth Century Maps," 86; Heidenreich, "Analysis of the 17th Century Map"; Steckley, "Early Map 'Novvelle France.'"

70. Schmidt, "Mapping an Empire," 551–52 (quote 552). Cf. Frijhoff, "Jesuits, Calvinists, and Natives," 53–54. For evidence of analogous Wendat and Neutral hostility to perceived spatial reconnaissance by French missionaries, see Sagard, *Histoire du Canada,* 3:801–2; *JR* 8:81, 21:189–91, 209; "Letter of Joseph-Marie Chaumonot to Father Philippe Nappi," 5.

71. *JR* 28:225, 231 ("who were going . . ."), 29:63, 229–33, 30:175, 193–95, 227–29, 31:115–17, 289–90n6, 32:19–27, 245, 39:175–237; *JJ,* 62, 65 ("Otrih8re, huron yroquoisé"), 86, 95; Du Creux, *History of Canada,* 2:444–48 ("as a warning . . . ," 445); Oury, *Marie de l'Incarnation,* 323–24; *ERNY* 1:437. Cf. Charlevoix, *History,* 2:195–96, 273. I base my association of this "Otrih8re," who escorted Jogues to his death in Mohawk country in 1646, with the individual later identified as Otreouti on evidence of a contemporary description of his status as a Wendat "renegade" engaging in attacks on French settlers (see Marshall, *Word from New France,* 263 [quote]; cf. Oury, *Marie de l'Incarnation,* 667), his recapture by the Mohawks near Montreal in November 1650, and his dramatic 1661 murder of Sulpician priest Jacques Le Maistre (see *JR* 46:189, 217–19), which echoed documented Wendat expressions of hostility toward baptism during the 1640s, especially prominent at Ossossané (see *JR* 19:189, 225, 231) and during the 1649 executions of Brébeuf and Lalemant. For the pronunciation of "8" in transcriptions of Huron names as "oua," see Steckley, "Clans and Phratries," 30. For evidence of the routine nature of captive distribution among League nations, which helps to explain the presence of Otreouti and Thérèse Kionhreha, whom Jogues encountered in Mohawk country in 1646 (see *JR* 29:55) among the Onondagas after their initial capture by the Mohawks, see *JR* 40:225, 51:213, 62:85–87. Cf. Thomas Grassmann, "Otreouti," *DCB* 1:525–26.

72. *JR* 28:225, 29:229; 30:161, 165, 187, 191–93, 221 ("their former routes," "approaches"), 227 ("sent presents to . . ."), 229, 233–51, 281, 291–95, 31:21, 269 ("perpetrat[ing] such tricks"), 32:169–71, 33:45; *JJ,* 79, 81, 85, 92, 94–95; *MNF* 7:43–44; Oury, *Marie de l'Incarnation,* 325; Du Creux, *History of Canada,* 2:448–53; Dollier de Casson, "Histoire du Montréal," 35–38; Gélinas, *Role of Fort Chambly,* 9; Trudel, *Beginnings of New France,* 257 (population of New France circa 1645).

73. *JR* 30:161 ("and knowing every . . ."), 231, 233–35 ("seized persons and baggage"), 277 ("soon married"), 281; *JJ*, 80; Du Creux, *History of Canada,* 2:450; *MNF* 6:768, 774, 7:825, 845; Oury, *Marie de l'Incarnation,* 326.

74. *JR* 30:289 (quotes). For other evidence of baggage abandonment as an escape tactic by Native peoples, see Champlain, *Works,* 2:100; *JR* 30:289, 40:101, 43:143, 62:103; Blair, *Indian Tribes,* 1:175–76; *NYCD* 9:557, 628–29. Cf. Brandão, *"Your Fyre Will Burn No More,"* 53–58, who argues for the absence of any economic motives in seventeenth-century Iroquois warfare. For critiques of Brandão, see Abler, "Iroquois Policy," 485–86; Greer, *Mohawk Saint,* 214n12; Ferris, *Archaeology of Native-Lived Colonialism,* 116–18.

75. *JR* 30:195, 253, 32:29, 185, 33:59 ("robbers more cruel . . ."), 117–23 ("a Huron by birth . . . ," 119).

76. *JR* 33:65–67, 71–73 (quote 71), 81–85, 89–97, 103–13, 125–37, 165–67, 39:141; *MNF* 5:836, 6:743, 772; Dollier de Casson, "Histoire de Montréal," 39–40; Michael Dean Mackintosh, "New Sweden, Natives, and Nature," in Pencak and Richter, *Friends and Enemies in Penn's Woods,* 3–17; Fur, *Colonialism in the Margins,* 90–98.

77. *JR* 30:273 ("a great malady"), 33:123 ("averse"), 34:57; *JJ,* 128; Charlevoix, *History,* 2:210–11, 218–25; Susan Johnston, "Epidemics: The Forgotten Factor in Seventeenth Century Native Warfare in the St. Lawrence Region," in Cox, *Native People, Native Lands,* 24; Sider, *Living Indian Histories,* 15–16 ("civil war"); Sioui, *For an Amerindian Autohistory,* 46; Carpenter, *Renewed,* 118–34; Blum, *Ghost Brothers,* 57–61. For analyses that largely follow Jesuit interpretations, see Tooker, "Iroquois Defeat of the Hurons"; Otterbein, "Why the Iroquois Won"; Otterbein, "Huron vs. Iroquois"; Trigger, *Children of Aataentsic,* 751–66; White, *Middle Ground,* 1–5; Richter, *Ordeal of the Longhouse,* 61–62; Fenton, *Great Law and the Longhouse,* 245–46; Dean Snow, "Iroquois-Huron Warfare," in Chacon and Mendoza, *North American Indigenous Warfare,* 149–59.

78. *NNN,* 273–74, 303 ("exceedingly fond," "sparing no expense . . ."); Venema, "Court Case of Brant Aertz van Slichtenhorst," 6 (all other quotes); *LIR,* 144; Gehring, *Council Minutes,* 43; Gehring, *Correspondence,* 33; *RCNP* 9:113, 116, 143; Kevin Moody, "Traders or Traitors: Illicit Trade at Fort Orange in the Seventeenth Century," in Fisher, *Peoples, Places, and Material Things,* 25–38; Venema, *Beverwijck,* 44, 182, 254, 275–77, 448; Jacobs, *New Netherland,* 205, 208–9.

79. Du Creux, *History of Canada,* 2:505–9; *JR* 33:259–63 (quotes), 34:87–99, 39:239–43; Charlevoix, *History,* 2:210–13; Léon Pouliot, "Daniel, Antoine," *DCB* 1:247; Trigger, *Children of Aataentsic,* 693; Major, "Les Jésuites chez les Hurons." Teanaustayé, the host community of the St. Joseph II Jesuit mission, was located near modern-day Hillsdale, Ontario.

80. *JR* 34:25–35 ("wretched Huron renegade[s]," 27, 123–37, ("considerable breaches," 125–27), Du Creux, *History of Canada,* 2:517 ("most"). Taenhatenteron was located near modern-day Sturgeon Bay, Ontario, and the St. Louis mission near modern-day Victoria Harbour, Ontario.

81. *JR* 34:127 ("driving forth . . ."), 141–43 ("Huron Infidels . . ."), 197, 203–18, 225, 39:245–63; Du Creux, *History of Canada,* 2:517 ("most"), 518–42; Oury, *Marie de l'Incarnation,* 387–88; Charlevoix, *History,* 2:218–25; Kidd, *Excavation of Ste.-Marie I,* 4–14; Jury and Jury, *Sainte-Marie among the Hurons,* 10–18; Saunders, Knight, and Gates, "Christian Island"; Jackson et al., "Winter of Discontent"; Williamson and Pfeiffer, *Bones of the Ancestors,* 113. For the location of St. Ignace II, cf. Thomas Grassmann, "Annenraes," *DCB* 1:66; Léon Pouliot, "Lalemant, Gabriel," ibid., 413, who asserts a location halfway between the modern-day towns of Coldwater and Vasey, Ontario; Latta, "Search for St. Ignace II." For an estimate of the French population in Wendake circa 1645–50 as sixty men (priests, *donnés,* servants, and soldiers), see Kidd, *Excavation of Ste.-Marie I,* 13; Jury and Jury, *Sainte-Marie among the Hurons,* 16. Cf. Pouliot's

estimate of forty-two men (sixteen Jesuits, four lay brothers, and twenty-two *donnés*) in "Lalemant, Jerôme," *DCB* 1:414.

82. *JR* 21:181, 33:83, 34:223, 35:19–21, 107–71 ("put to death," "they deemed unable . . ." 111), 40:15–23; *NYCD* 5:274 (Teganissorens quotes); Du Creux, *History of Canada,* 2:543–55; Thomas, "In Search of Etharita," 93–97; Garrad, "Chabanel and Honare,enhak."

3. REQUICKENING, 1650–1666

1. *JR* 42:85–87 (quotes); Bradley, *Evolution of the Onondaga Iroquois,* 206; Grumet, *Historic Contact,* 390.

2. *JR* 35:207–11; *MNF* 6:758–59; Jean-Jacques Le Febvre, "Grandmaison, Éléonore de," *DCB* 1:344–45; Tehariolina, *La Nation Huronne,* 58–59; Sioui, *For an Amerindian Autohistory,* 86–88; Tanguay, "Les Règles d'alliance," 21–22.

3. My estimate is based on the documented presence of at least 600 Tahontaenrat Wendats in Seneca country in 1651 (Warrick, *Population History,* 238), 600 Wendats in Onondaga country in 1656 (*JR* 44:41), and at least 350 Attignawantan Wendats in Mohawk country in 1657 (Warrick, *Population History,* 240; cf. Snow's estimate of 570 Wendats in Mohawk country at this time in Snow, *Mohawk Valley Archaeology,* 410). See also Jesuit Simon Le Moyne's estimate of "more than a thousand" Christian Wendats held captive in Iroquois in 1654 (*JR* 41:133). Contemporary evidence of the ability of Iroquois war parties to secure approximately five female and/or juvenile captives per warrior (see ibid., 53:39–41) also lends support to the argument for large numbers of Wendats incorporated into European settlements after the campaigns of 1649–1650. Other documentary evidence indicates that at least an additional 210 Wendats were either captured by Iroquois warriors or relocated voluntarily to Iroquoia from 1650 to 1660 (see *JJ,* 145–46, 151–52, 157–58, 165–66, 168, 178–79, 182, 188, 215, 287–88, 312; *JR* 35:59, 36:141–43, 179, 37:93, 99, 101, 111, 203, 38:45, 49, 61, 171, 191, 42:59, 43:33, 41–43, 49–53, 55, 117, 123–25, 135, 187, 207, 255, 44:69, 107, 185, 189, 289–91, 45:165, 46:121, 48:85–89; *MNF* 6:773, 8:936, 938–40, 942, 971, 986–88, 996, 998–99, 9:652–53; Adams, *Explorations of Radisson,* 52–53; Oury, *Marie de l'Incarnation,* 583–84; *NYCD* 3:123). Additionally, at least another 76 Wendats are known to have been killed by Iroquois warriors during that decade (see *JJ,* 140–41, 151–53, 165, 170, 174–75, 283–84; *JR* 35:47–49, 36:123, 179, 37:93, 99, 103–5, 111–13, 115–17, 38:45, 57–59, 177; 41:199, 42:43–45, 43:43, 57–59, 73–75, 99, 105–7, 115–25, 165, 44:71–77, 117, 149, 155, 167–69, 185, 45:85–89, 155–57, 245–61, 46:25–33, 89–101, 145; *MNF* 4:765–66, 788, 7:829, 8:935–37, 941, 961–62, 971, 985, 987–88, 9:651; Adams, *Explorations of Radisson,* 52, Oury, *Marie de l'Incarnation,* 584; Du Creux, *History of Canada* 2:565–66. Subtracting the number of Wendats killed from the number adopted into (or relocated voluntarily to) Iroquois settlements adds a net sum of at least 134 more individuals to the baseline estimate of 1,555 Wendat adoptees (see Brandão,"*Your Fyre Will Burn No More,*" 77). Finally, one must also consider the evidence of at least 1,100 more Wendats likely to have been alive in 1651 and who are accounted for in neither the archaeological record of Wendats who died on Christian Island circa 1649–1650 (Williamson and Pfeiffer, *Bones of the Ancestors,* 113), nor in contemporary estimates of Wendat refugee communities in the upper Great Lakes and the St. Lawrence valley. See *JR* 41:139, 45:243, 54:169, 283; Warrick, *Population History,* 236–40; Trigger, *Children of Aataentsic,* 750, 826–40.

4. White, *Middle Ground,* 1–10 ("shattered," 2); Snow, *Iroquois,* 117 ("rampage"); Richter, *Ordeal of the Longhouse,* 62 ("virtually every Indian . . ."); Hinderaker, *Elusive Empires,* 12–13; Fenton, *Great Law and the Longhouse,* 245–47.

5. *JR* 35:187–91, 199–201, 36:123, 143, 181–87, 41:57; *MNF* 8:938; Du Creux, *History of Canada,* 2:566–67; Dollier de Casson, "Histoire du Montréal," 41; Pouchot, *Memoir,* 470; Sowter, "Algonkin and Huron Occupation," 95–99, 103–4; Coyne, "Jesuits' Mill or Mortar"; Garrad, "Commemorating the 350th Anniversary." On the Wendat refugee colony at Isle d'Orléans opposite Quebec, see *JR* 35:207–11; *MNF* 6:758–59; Le Febvre, "Grandmaison, Éléonore de"; Tehariolina, *La Nation Huronne,* 58–59; Sioui, *For an Amerindian Autohistory,* 86–88; Tanguay, "Les Règles," 21–22. On the Wendat dispersal into the upper Great Lakes and their amalgamation with refugee Tionnontatés, see *MNF* 8:935–36; "Tionnontates," 16–18; Ronald J. Mason, "Huron Island and the Island of the Poutouatomis," in Johnson, *Aspects of Upper Great Lakes Anthropology,* 154–55; Elisabeth M. Tooker, "Wyandot," in Trigger, *Northeast,* 398–406; Susan M. Branstner, "Tionontate Huron Occupation of the Marquette Mission," in Walthall and Emerson, *Calumet and Fleur-de-Lys,* 179–80. For evidence of Wendat refugees relocating to Susquehannock country, see *MNF* 8:935, 999.

6. *JR* 19:269n5, 35:47–49, 51, 59, 179, 217–23 (quotes 221–23), 247–55, 275; *JJ,* 137, 140–41, 145–46; Du Creux, *History of Canada,* 1:301–4, 2:565–66; Oury, *Marie de l'Incarnation,* 394; *MNF* 4:765–66; 6:773 ("Otrihouré [Huron, mais Iroquoisé]); Charlevoix, *History,* 2:258; Grassmann, *Mohawk Indians and Their Valley,* 152; Lucien Campeau, "Le Coq, Robert," *DCB* 1:441; *MNF* 2:836.

7. Gehring, *Council Minutes,* 43 (quote); Gehring, *Correspondence,* 110.

8. *JR* 13: 55; 15: 169; 17: 87–89; 21: 187–91, 195, 195, 209; 22: 223–25; 27: 21–29; 30: 95; 35: 215; 36: 117–23, 133, 141–43, 177–79 (quote 177); 37: 97; 38: 45, 179; 44: 21; 45: 243, 139, 141–43, 177, 179; *JJ,* 150–5, 161; Du Creux, *History of Canada* 2: 567; Blair, *Indian Tribes,* 1:149–50; *MNF* 5: 816; 6: 754–55, 773; 8: 997; Sagard, *Histoire du Canada* 3: 802; Wright, *Neutral Indians,* 57, 138; Marian E. White, "On Delineating the Neutral Iroquois," 66; Lennox, *Bogle I and Bogle II Sites,* 272; Lennox, *Hood Site,* 74, 93, 97, 135; Kenyon, *Grimsby Site,* 233–34; Ferris, "Beyond the Frontier"; David M. Stothers, "Late Woodland Models for Cultural Development in Southern Michigan," in Halsey and Stafford, *Retrieving Michigan's Buried Past,* 207. For Iroquois oral tradition related to the origin of their war with the Neutrals, see Lafitau, *Customs of the American Indians* 2:105–6. For references to Neutral adoptees living among the Iroquois *circa* 1668 to 1780, see *JR* 52:19, 56:51; Wright, *Neutral Indians,* 58. For nineteenth-century evidence of Neutral identity surviving among the Senecas, see Morgan, *League of the Iroquois,* 76; Lloyd, *League of the Iroquois* 2:181; Parker, *Analytical History,* opp.136; Frank H. Severance, "Preface," in Parker, *Life of General Ely S. Parker,* vii–ix; George R. Hamell, "Gannagaro State Historic Site: A Current Perspective," in Bonvillain, *Studies on Iroquois Culture,* 95–97.

9. *JR* 20:61, 308n27, 54:227. The identity of the "Fire Nation" is a matter of dispute. Linguist Ives Goddard equates "Fire Nation" exclusively with Mascoutens in Trigger, *Northeast,* 671. David Brose, "Late Prehistory of the Upper Great Lakes Area" (in Trigger, *Northeast,,* 579), and Michelaki ("More than Meets the Eye," 144–48), dispute the idea of any specific ethnic identification for "Fire Nation." Clifton, in *Prairie People,* 18–19, notes that the Wendats, Neutrals, and Tionnontatés all used "Fire Nation" as a blanket term for all Algonquin-speaking populations of modern-day lower Michigan but never for the Potawatomis specifically. See also David A. Baerreis, Erminie Wheeler-Voegelin, and Remedios Wycoco-Moore, "The Identity of the Mascoutens," in Horr, *Indians of Northeastern Illinois* , 249–51, 267–70. Cf. Deale, "History of the Potawatomis," 305, who interprets the "Fire Nation" as Potawatomis owing to their taking refuge in 1641 with other nations at Sault Ste. Marie (*JR* 23:225) and the description of their location in 1643 as more distant from Wendake than the Neutrals (*JR* 27:25). For linguistic evidence supporting a Potawatomi identity for the "Fire Nation," see Steckley, "Finding a Home for Two Tribes," 128.

10. Fitzgerald, "Refinement of Historic Neutral Chronologies," 31;Warrick, *Population History,* 238; Saunders and Sempowski, *Dutch Hollow and Factory Hollow,* 3; Grumet, *Historic Contact,* 412; Fenton, *Little Water Medicine Society,* xiii–xiv, 188–89. Sempowski, in personal correspondence to the author (April 5, 2007), suggested that the population of Gandougarae (known archaeologically as the Wheeler-Station site) was less than 800 people. For discussion of the possible cultural influences of these Neutral adoptees, see Williamson and Veilleux, "Review of Northern Iroquoian Decorated Bone and Antler Artifacts," 13–16; Pearce, "Turtles from Turtle Island," 100–101.

11. Blair, *Indian Tribes,* 1:151 ("other bones to gnaw"); *JR* 36:141, 247–48n49, 37:95–111; Hodge, *Handbook of American Indians,* 1:112; Cadzow, *Archaeological Studies,* 21, 62–96; Heisey and Witmer, "Of Historic Susquehannock Cemeteries," 99; Kent, *Susquehanna's Indians,* 37; Grumet, *Historic Contact,* 309 ("one of the . . ."). Given the name of the Susquehannock town (Atrakwae, located near modern-day Washington Boro, Pennsylvania), other documentary references to the "Akhakvaeronnons" (see *JR* 18:233; Engelbrecht and Sullivan, "Cultural Context," 26), and subsequent evidence of "Trakwaehronnon" captives among the Iroquois circa 1660 (see *JR* 45:207), the term "Kahkwas," recently identified as a separate, possibly Neutral-affiliated Iroquoian group located near the Niagara peninsula and ostensibly dispersed by the Senecas in 1652 (see Heidenreich "Analysis of the 17th Century Map," 100; Pendergast, "Kakouagoga or Kahkwas"), may actually refer to the Susquehannocks. See *JR* 38:61–63, 189–91; Myers, *Narratives of Early Pennsylvania,* 140, 157; *AMD* 3:276–77; Steckley, "Tale of Two Peoples," 13; Rountree and Davidson, *Eastern Shore Indians of Virginia and Maryland,* 91. Cf. the intriguing discussion of Iroquois oral tradition regarding the war with the Kahkwas in Parker, *Archeological History,* 550, and Wonderley, *At the Font of the Marvelous,* 14–42. The problem in linking the traditional and documentary evidence in this case lies in the dating of the site in question (the "Buffam Street Site," on Buffalo Creek, near modern-day Buffalo, New York) Current research dates this site to an early sixteenth century Iroquoian occupancy, long before the chronology claimed by Pendergast. See Rayner-Herter, "Niagara Frontier Iroquois," 70–74, 298.

12. Du Creux, *History of Canada,* 2:622 ("the plague of the country . . ."); *NYCD* 1:548 ("the insolence of . . ."), 9:5–6; *JR* 36:75–111, 83, 129, 131, 227–29, 37:95, 259, 38:35–37, 293n1; *MNF* 8:1–14, 56–58; *JJ,* 159; Charlevoix, *History,* 2:213–17; Gehring, *Correspondence,* 27; *RCNP* 9:113, 199–203, 422–23; *WP* 6:90–91; Ward, *United Colonies of New England,* 95–98; Cohen, "Hartford Treaty"; Venema, *Beverwijck,* 43–44; Huey, "Dutch at Fort Orange," 36–39; Charles T. Gehring, "Encountering Native Americans in Unexpected Places: Slichtenhorst and the Mohawks," in Saunders and Zuyderhoudt, *Challenges of Native American Studies,* 286–87; Merwick, *Shame and the Sorrow,* 229–30. New Netherland's settler population consisted of 2,500 people in 1645 (Otto, *Dutch-Munsee Encounter,* 107), while the population of New France only reached 1,000 in 1648 (Dubé, *Chevalier de Montmagny,* 238).

13. *JJ,* 150–60, 163, 165–66, 170; *JR* 35:201; 36:83, 117–35, 139–43, 147–49, 165, 177–87, 195, 37:67–71 (quote 67), 93–105, 38:45, 49–51; *MNF* 8:969, 981–82, 999–1000; Du Creux, *History of Canada,* 2:597, 627–28; Charlevoix, *History,* 2:245; Gérard E. McNulty and Louis Gilbert, "Attikamek (Tête de Boule)," in Helm, *Subarctic,* 791–92.

14. *JR* 38:63 ("wanton [Iroquois] rascals . . ."), 40:85 ("continually laying ambuscades . . ."), 89 ("fragments of human bodies"); Du Creux, *History of Canada,* 2:628; Dollier de Casson, "Histoire du Montréal," 42 ("always had men . . ."), 46–47; Oury, *Marie de l'Incarnation,* 390, 477–79. Cf. Gilles Paquet and Jean-Pierre Wallot, "Nouvelle-France/Quebec/Canada: A World of Limited Identities," in Canny and Pagden, *Colonial Identity in the Atlantic World,* 100.

15. Adams, *Explorations of Pierre Esprit Radisson,* 1–36 (quotes); Wykoff, "Land of the Eries";

Fournier, *Pierre-Esprit Radisson*, 11–39; Blum, *Ghost Brothers*, 216–37. Cf. Dickinson, "La Guerre Iroquoise," 54n7, who dates Radisson's capture to 1650 on the basis of an absence of evidence of captures recorded at Trois-Rivières in 1651.

16. *JR* 37:99–105, 111–13, 117–19, 125, 135–45, 203, 38:45–63 ("Squad of Hurons," "swell their troops," 51; "wretches," "hide in the woods . . . ," 63), 171, 175–77, 40:97, 101; *JJ*, 169–71, 174, 177–79, 181–82; Du Creux, *History of Canada*, 2:624–25; Dollier de Casson, "Histoire du Montréal," 44–50; Charlevoix, *History*, 2:245–46; Belmont, "Histoire," 26.

17. *JR* 38:179, 183, 189, 40:85, 91, 165–69 (quotes 165); *JJ*, 185; *MNF* 8:940.

18. *JR* 36:181–87, 37:107–11, 38:53–55, 177, 183, 189–95, 197, 40:85, 97, 101–21 (all other quotes 113–21), 147–51, 155–57, 169–71, 41:43; *JJ*, 171–73, 182, 185, 188–89; Dollier de Casson, "Histoire du Montréal," 52–54; "Memoires de Feu Monsieur," 399.

19. *JR* 38:189–95, 40:95, 159, 179–81 (quotes 181); *JJ*, 190; Belmont, "Histoire du Canada," 27–28. The discussion of women's authority over the "sweat-house" in this context, along with evidence of Seneca warrior Saouaondanoncoua's decision to marry an Onondaga woman in order to be free to continue attacking the Wendats after a Seneca-Wendat truce prior to 1634 (see *JR* 13:45), represents a significant discrepancy with Lafitau's oft-cited assertion (in *Customs of the American Indians*, 2:99) concerning the formation of war parties to serve the interests of the warriors' father's clan. On the presence of sweat lodges on precontact Ontario Iroquois sites, which archaeologists generally interpret as an instrument of promoting the social integration of in-marrying men residing in matrilineal longhouses, see Macdonald and Williamson, "Sweat Lodges and Solidarity," 72. For evidence of sweat lodges in Wendake during the early seventeenth century, see Champlain, *Works*, 3:153; Sagard, *Long Journey*, 197–98; *JR* 13:203, 14:65, 26:175–77, 245. For Bressani's post-Mohawk captivity (1653) description of Iroquois sweats in separate "cabins" large enough to hold fifteen to twenty persons "seated like Apes," see *JR* 38:253–55 (quote 253). See also Fenton, "Contacts," 513–14.

20. *JR* 40:115–17 (quotes); Bruce Trigger, "Tekarihogen," *DCB* 2:624–25; *MNF* 8:997; Elisabeth M. Tooker, "League of the Iroquois," in Trigger, *Northeast*, 424, 427.

21. *JR* 40:157–63, 185–95 (quotes 185).

22. Ibid., 123–55 ("who were going . . . ," 149–51), 41:47–49; "Memoires de Feu Monsieur Boucher," 400 ("Anciens"); Du Creux, *History of Canada*, 2:637–42. For evidence of Poncet's cassock in Onondaga country in 1657, see *JR* 43:273.

23. *JR* 38:197, 40:119, 41:43, 177–79 ("widows and girls . . . ," 179); Du Creux, *History of Canada*, 2:657 ("treat more freely . . ."), 681–82 ("others of the . . . ," 681).

24. *JR* 41:219–21 (quotes 219); *JJ*, 191.

25. Cf. Wolf, *Europe and the People without History*, 169; Brandão, *"Your Fyre Shall Burn No More,"* 106–10; Fenton, *Great Law and the Longhouse*, 247–48; Patricia C. Albers, "Marxism and Historical Materialism in American Indian History," in Shoemaker, *Clearing a Path*, 115–17. For Onondaga country as the League's "smokehole," see Gibson, *Concerning the League*, 270–71; William Fenton, "Structure, Continuity, and Change," in Jennings et al., *History and Culture of Iroquois Diplomacy*, 15; "Glossary," in ibid., 119.

26. *JR* 38:199 ("large Porcelain collars . . ."), 41: 19–21, 43, 47–49 ("secret," "where were already . . ."), 225–27 ("seminarists," "wretched [Mohawk] country"); *JJ*, 191–92; *FOCM*, 76–78.

27. *JR* 41:21–23, 51–55 (quotes); *JJ*, 194–95. Cf. *MNF* 8:678.

28. *JR* 36:123, 181–87, 41:57 (quotes).

29. Ibid., 41:139, 63–65 (quotes).

30. Ibid., 38:179, 294n12, 41:67–71 ("surgeon," 67), 77–79, 111; *MNF* 9:704 ("grand chief"); *JJ*, 183–84. The surgeon may have been Louis Chartier. See Antonio Drolét, "Chartier, Louis," *DCB* 1:201. Documentary evidence establishes Sagochiendagehté as the uncle of Onondaga leader

Garacontié (rather than as the same individual), and also indicates that the nephew assumed his uncle's diplomatic responsibilities in 1658. See *JR* 41:99, 47:73; *MNF* 9:673. Cf. Bruce Trigger "Garakontié, Daniel," *DCB* 1:322–23); Clermont, "Une Figure Iroquoise," 103. Sources identify the (non-Seneca) Indians captured by the Tionnontatés and Odawas as "Wolves," a long-standing French appellation for the Mahicans (see Ted J. Brasser, "Mahican," in Trigger, *Northeast,* 211). Yet this appellation could also apply to either the Seneca or Mohawk Wolf clan, or to a Mahican adoptee among either the Senecas or Mohawks. For evidence of one Mahican "naturalized" among the Mohawks circa 1660, see *JR* 46:87.

31. Du Creux, *History of Canada,* 2:661 (quotes). For other evidence of the increasing frequency of emetic discourse in seventeenth-century Iroquois Condolence ceremony rhetoric (an indigenous Iroquois practice that may have been extended into condolence diplomacy as a result of the influence of adoptees from the west and south), see *JR* 42:51–53, 44:111–15, 45:83; *An Account of the Treaty . . . ,* 12–13; *Propositions Made by the Five Nations,* 5; Blair, *Indian Tribes* 2:51; Herrick, *Iroquois Medical Botany,* 110, 228; Jerald T. Milanich, "Origins and Prehistoric Distributions of Black Drink and the Ceremonial Shell Drinking Cup," in Hudson, *Black Drink,* 83–119.

32. *JR* 41:69–75 (quotes); Du Creux, *History of Canada,* 2:662–64; Gendron, *Quelques Particularitez du pays des Hurons,* 8; Amandus Johnson, "The Indians and Their Culture, as Described in Swedish and Dutch Records from 1614 to 1664," in Hodge, *Proceedings,* 278; White, "Ethnic Identification and Iroquois Groups," 25–27; William Engelbrecht, "The Kleis Site Ceramics: An Interpretive Approach," in Foster, Campisi, and Mithun, *Extending the Rafters,* 336–37; Engelbrecht, "Erie," 2; Gramly, *Two Early Historic Iroquoian Sites,* ix; William A. Fox, "Horned Panthers and Erie Associates," in Wright and Pilon, *Passion for the Past,* 299; Fur, *Colonialism in the Margins,* 148. For oral tradition of Erie residency near modern-day Buffalo, New York, see Ketchum, *Authentic and Comprehensive History of Buffalo,* 1:7.

33. *JR* 41:81 (quotes).

34. Ibid., 19:211–13 (quote 213), 41:37; Du Creux, *History of Canada,* 2:679–80; Mark Meuwese, "From Intercolonial Messenger to 'Christian Indian': The Flemish Bastard and the Mohawk Struggle for Independence from New France and Colonial New York in the Eastern Great Lakes Borderland, 1647–1687," in Hele, *Lines Drawn Upon the Water.* Canaqueese's embassy coincided with growing Mohawk discontent over increasing prices and scarce goods (particularly ammunition) at Dutch Fort Orange as well as Mohawk outreach to English traders and officials, possibly via the Narragansetts, who may have included the Mohawks in their "covenant" with the United Colonies of New England. See Gehring, *Council Minutes,* 116; Gehring, "Undiscovered van Rensselaer Letter," 13, 28; *FOCM,* 146–47, 150; *RCNP* 10:282 ("covenant"); *WP* 6:254; *PP* 2:32, 35, 55, 94, 107; Bartlett, *Records of the Colony of Rhode Island,* 1:295; Rhode Island Historical Society, *Collections,* 2:158–60; Moloney, *Fur Trade in New England,* 56–60; William S. Simmons, "Narragansett," in Trigger, *Northeast,* 194; Thomas Grassmann, "Flemish Bastard," *DCB* 1:307–8; Vaughan, *New England Frontier,* 171–72; Venema, *Beverwijck,* 171. For documentary evidence of Mohawk-Dutch sexual relations, intermarriage, and individuals of Dutch-Mohawk ancestry in seventeenth-century New Netherland and New York, see *JR* 50:183; *IMC,* 43, 196–97; *FOCM,* 454; *AMD* 17:201; *MCARS* 3:264; *NYCD* 3:323, 325, 328, 431; *LIR,* 29, 31, 45, 80, 111–13, 120, 127, 131–33, 139–40, 146, 156–57; Paltsits, *Executive Council Minutes* 2:668; James and Jameson, *Journal of Jasper Danckaerts,* 201–11; Pearson, *History of the Schenectady Patent,* 17, 169, 188–89; Sivertson, *Turtles, Wolves, and Bears,* 1–10; Hagedorn, "Brokers of Understanding," 381–82; Bradley, "Visualizing Arent van Curler," 7; Staffa, *Schenectady Genesis,* 33–34, 38, 49–50, 72; Ferguson, *Schoharie Mohawks,* 16–19; and the discussion of Dutch adultery cases adjudicated at Fort Orange in Meuwese, "'For the

Peace and Well-Being of the Country'" 351–53. Cf. Rothschild's assertion, based exclusively on archaeological evidence, of the limited Dutch sexual interest in Mohawk women (and vice versa) in *Colonial Encounters in a Native American Landscape,* 217–20.

35. *JR* 41:87–89 (quotes).

36. Ibid., 41:99–109 (quotes), 199.

37. Ibid., 41:109–19 (quotes). Cf. Oury, *Marie de l'Incarnation,* 542. Kionhreha's adoptive Neutral "daughter" reportedly died on December 7, 1655, at Onondaga of a consumptive fever. See *JR* 41:103, 42:131.

38. *JR* 41:37–39 ("captive church," "old time Hurons," "both sexes"), 119–29 ("beautiful prairies . . . ," 127), 256n6, 42:203–5, 215. For Otihatangué, see ibid., 41:97, 42:71–73, 43:145; Bradley, *Evolution of the Onondaga Iroquois,* 118, 225n9; Recht, "Role of Fishing," 14–15. For "La Famine," see *NYCD* 3:431n1, 9:172n1; *JR* 42:295n1; Olds, "Journal of Chevalier de Baugy," 31; Bernard Weilbrenner, "Morel de la Durantaye, Olivier," *DCB* 2:488.

39. *JR* 41:131–35, 201–3 (quotes).

40. Oury, *Marie de l'Incarnation,* 546 (quote). For evidence of the role of clan matrons in seventeenth-century public councils, see *JR* 2:297–98n33, 54:281, 55:265, 64:91. See also Morgan, *League of the Iroquois,* 321–27.

41. *JR* 41:42, 83 (quote). For a traditional account of the Genesee River as the boundary between the Eries and the Senecas, see Morgan, *League of the Iroquois,* 337.

42. *JR* 41:107, 109, 42:73–75, 97–99, 111–13, 137–39, 177–83 (quotes), 187–89, 203, 47:59; *MNF* 4:788; Du Creux, *History of Canada,* 2:713; Johnson, "Indians and Their Culture," 278; Parker, *Analytical History of the Seneca Indians,* 47–48; Mayer-Oakes, *Prehistory of the Upper Ohio Valley,* 72; Guthe, *Late Prehistoric Occupation in Southwestern New York,* 20, 51–52; White, *Iroquois Culture History,* 41–49; Marian E. White, "Erie," 414; Engelbrecht and Sullivan, "Cultural Context," 23–27. On Gentaienton and its potential location within the bounds of modern Cattaraugus Seneca Territory, see *JR* 43:197, 58:75, 61:195; M. Raymond Harrington, "A Midcolonial Seneca Site in Erie County," in Parker, *Archeological History of New York,* 207–37. See also ibid, 117, 126, 135, 146, 493–94, 555–56. On the potential location of Rigué, see Carpenter, Peirman, and Schoff, "28th Street Site." On the Erie survivors as Westos, see Cheves, "Shaftesbury Papers," 457; Neill, *Virginia Carolorum,* 245–46, 327; MacCord, "Ricahecrian Identity"; Bowne, *Westo Indians,* 32–53; Fur, *Colonialism in the Margins,* 148.

43. Pearson, *Early Records of the City and County of Albany,* 217 (quotes).

44. Oury, *Marie de l'Incarnation,* 562 (quote), 564; Du Creux, *History of Canada,* 2:690–96; *JR* 42:63; *MNF* 8:977, 983; Marcel Moussette, "1655."

45. Du Creux, *History of Canada,* 2:696–97 (quotes 697); *JR* 42:49; Oury, *Marie de l'Incarnation,* 564, 582.

46. *JR* 42:37–47 (quotes).

47. Ibid., 41:229–31 ("Chieftainess," 229), 42:49–55 (all other quotes).

48. Ibid., 42:55–57 (quotes); Oury, *Marie de l'Incarnation,* 565–66; Du Creux, *History of Canada,* 2:698–702; R. White, "'Although I am Dead, I am not Entirely Dead. I Have Left a Second of Myself': Constructing Self and Persons on the Middle Ground of Early America," in Hoffman, Sobel, and Teute, *Through a Glass Darkly,* 406.

49. *JR* 42:59–93 (quotes 85–95), 219, 223–25, 295n3; Du Creux, *History of Canada,* 2:706; *MNF* 6:741.

50. *JR* 38:175, 42: 101–11 (quotes),169, 295n5, 54:269–71.

51. Ibid., 42:115–21 (quotes).

52. *MaHSC* ser. 4, 6:477 ("taking away by . . ."); Pearson, *Early Records of the City and County of Albany,* 237 (all other quotes); *CJVR,* 21; *NYCD* 12:98; Paul Otto, "Peach War (1655–1657)," in

Gallay, *Colonial Wars of North America*, 546–47. Cf. Strong, "Mohawk Sovereignty,"

53. *JR* 43:99, 167, 44:101–3 (quotes 103).

54. Ibid., 43:99, 103–11 (quotes), 251.

55. Ibid., 42:131–33, 139–47, 151, 171–75, 185–89 ("general affairs of . . . ," 189), 191–99, 201 ("break entirely"), 43:111–13; Adams, *Explorations of Radisson*, 63.

56. *JR* 43:129 (quotes). For the French seigneury at Gannentaha, see ibid., 41:245–47. On seigneurial land tenure in New France, see Munro, *Documents*, xv–cxvi; Harris, *Seigneurial System in Early Canada*. For an overview of the Gannentaha mission, see Campeau, *Gannentaha*.

57. *JR* 43:129 (quotes).

58. Ibid., 43:99, 115–125 ("scattered in all . . . ," 117; "a large number . . . ," 119), 135–37, 141; *JJ*, 196–98; Blair, *Indian Tribes*, 1:152–57, 193 (all other quotes).

59. *JR* 43:187 (quote), 251; *MNF* 8:985–86, 9:694; Mason, *Rock Island*, 15–17; Daniel G. Cude, "Identifying the Ojibway of Northern Lake Superior and the Boundary Water Region, 1650–1750," in Nichols, *Actes du Trente-Deuxième Congrès des Algonquinistes*, 82–86. Tionnontatés represented the majority among the refugee Wendat population in the upper Great Lakes after 1650. See Tooker, "Wyandot," 404–5.

60. Trigger, *Children of Aataentsic*, 806 (quotes).

61. *JR* 41:213–19, 42:257, 263–67, 297n16, 43:99, 115, 129 (quotes).

62. Ibid., 43:157–69 (quotes); *NYCD* 9:680; Metz, *Sainte Marie among the Iroquois*, 90–99. A reconstructed version of the Ste. Marie de Gannentaha mission currently exists in Liverpool, New York. This site is approximately 800 yards northwest of the actual location of the short-lived mission: the parking lot of the LeMoyne Manor Restaurant. See McDowell-Loudan, "Ste-Marie de Gannentaha."

63. *JR* 43:171–77 (quotes).

64. Stokes, *Iconography of Manhattan Island*, 4:169 ("4000 beavers"); *JR* 43:177–85 (all other quotes), 44:151; *MNF* 9:651.

65. *JR* 42:225–45, 251 (quote), 255; *JJ*, 200–202; Du Creux, *History of Canada*, 2:741–53; Charlevoix, *History*, 2:273–75; J. Monet, "Garreau, Léonard," *DCB* 1:325. Cf. Blair, *Indian Tribes*, 1:157–58, for Perrot's identification of the murderer of Garreau as a "French renegade" with Canaqueese's party.

66. *JR* 42:253–57 (quotes); *JJ*, 201–2. For League tradition regarding three advance warnings to nations targeted for "inclusion in the Great Peace," see A. C. Parker, "The Constitution of the Five Nations," in Fenton, *Parker on the Iroquois*, 54.

67. *JR* 42:261, 43:27–29 (quote 27), 45, 187; *JJ*, 204, 206.

68. *JR* 43:35, 199–207 (quotes); *JJ*, 209.

69. *JR* 43:33–43, 51 ("Tribe of the Rock"), 191 ("Cord nation," "Bear nation"), 201–7 (all other quotes), 225–31, 253; *JJ*, 209–13; Conrad Heidenreich, "Huron," in Trigger, *Northeast*, 387.

70. *JR* 43:43 ("young and very resolute . . ."), 45–47, 187–89 (all other quotes); *JJ*, 214–15.

71. *JR* 43:33, 47–49 ("little children," 49), 53, 187, 191–97 (all other quotes), 255, 44:185; *JJ*, 215.

72. *FOCM*, 150, 304–5 (quotes).

73. Ibid., 305–6 (quotes), 515n, 518; Gehring, *Correspondence*, 107; *RGCMB* 3:436–37.

74. *JR* 43:51–53, 55–59, 69–77, 165, 44:69–77 (quotes 65–67), 149, 185, 189–93; *JJ*, 217–20; Adams, *Explorations of Radisson*, 52–53; Fournier, *Pierre-Esprit Radisson*, 63.

75. Huey, "Archaeological Testing"; Sohrweide, "Onondaga Longhouses," 18–20; Engelbrecht, *Iroquoia*, 165.

76. *JR* 43:257–89 (quotes). See also claims of "Twelve different Nations" of captives among the Onondagas in 1657 (ibid., 44:43), captives of eight to ten different nations throughout Iroquoia in 1660 and 1662 (ibid., 45:207, 47:193), and a claim of sixteen different nations of

adopted captives in Iroquoia in 1671 (ibid., 63:165).

77. Ibid., 43:293–95 (quotes).

78. Webb, *1676*, 254; Starna and Watkins, "Northern Iroquoian Slavery"; Rushforth, "'A Little Flesh We Offer You,'" 786–87. The best refutation of these assertions may be found in descriptions of so-called Iroquois slavery by contemporary French observers in *JR* 41:95–97, 43:299–301, 307–9, 44:47, 203–5, 47:57, 54:93; Boucher, *Histoire Véritable*, 102, 133; Coyne, "Exploration of the Great Lakes," 27; Le Roy de la Potherie, *Histoire* 2:424, 442; Pouchot, *Memoir*, 470. See also Trigger, *Children of Aataentsic*, 830–31.

79. *JR* 47:181–83 (quotes). For evidence of captives being killed after a probationary period, or for specific reasons such as disobedience, illness, leaking intelligence, twin births, or mercy killings of infant orphans, see ibid., 42:43–45, 73–75, 137–39, 187–89, 43:295, 303, 44:39, 73, 49:107. Seemingly random or capricious slayings of captives, especially children, may have been related to aspects of the "mourning-war" complex. See, for example, the description of two Wendat children "slaughtered by those to whom they had been given" prior to 1655 (ibid., 42:81), the November 1655 ritual torture and execution of an Erie boy (aged nine or ten) (ibid., 42:97–99; Du Creux, *History of Canada*, 2:713), the February 1656 torture and execution of a young Erie man after his voluntary surrender to the Onondagas (*JR* 42:191–95), the August 1657 murder of a Christian Wendat woman who refused to engage in sexual relations with her Onondaga captor (ibid., 44:73), the late 1657 reports of planned executions of captive women among the Onondagas (ibid., 43:303), and Onondaga burnings of Wendat women and children in "slow fires" (ibid., 44:155 [quote], 167–69). For evidence of adoptees' freedom of movement, see ibid., 44:47, 47:197, 52:165. For evidence of captive labor, including common labor undertaken by Iroquois people with members of adopted nations, see ibid., 41:95–97, 125, 42:71–73, 187–89, 46:113–15. For descriptions of Tahontaenrat healing rituals in Seneca country, see ibid., 58:229, 237. For a 1687 description of a Seneca False Face mask, see ibid., 63:289. For arguments favoring the introduction of False-Face healing to Iroquoia via Wendat and/or Neutral adoptees, see Blau, "Function and the False Faces"; Fox, "Horned Panthers," 287–88. For assertions of the indigenous character of False Face masking among League nations, see Parker, "Secret Medicine Societies," 181; Fenton, *False Faces of the Iroquois*, 67–78. For evidence of male adoptees becoming titled headmen, see *JR* 42:57; Lafitau, *Customs of the American Indians*, 2:171–72. For evidence of adoptees as self-made chiefs, see the examples of Agariata, a Neutral adoptee reported as the leader of a Mohawk war party in 1666 (*JR* 50:199; *JJ*, 349), Atogwatkann/Adogodquo, aka "The Large Spoon," an Algonquin adoptee who negotiated on behalf of the Mohawks circa 1658–1663 (*JR* 44:231–33, 45:91–95, 99–105; *JJ*, 239–41; *NYCD* 13:309), and the discussion of Otreouti elsewhere in this study. For evidence of female adoptees' authority, see *JR* 62:61–65.

80. *JR* 42:135, 141, 151, 43:251, 307–9, 47:195, 56:51; Bruce Trigger, "Maintaining Economic Equality in Opposition to Complexity: An Iroquoian Case Study," in Upham, *Evolution of Political Systems*, 140–41 (quote 141). Cf. *JR* 43:251; Boucher, *Histoire Véritable*, 134, for rare evidence of Wendat adoptees promoting Christianity among their Mohawk hosts.

81. *JR* 33:107–9, 43:297–99 ("as slaves," "Iroquois language"), 44:203–5 ("husbands separated from . . ."), 52:179; Blair, *Indian Tribes*, 1:146, 149–50; Lafitau, *Customs of the American Indians*, 1:338, 350, 2:153–55, 171–72; Charlevoix, *History*, 3:16. For evidence of assimilative adoptions among the constituent League nations, see Engelbrecht, *Iroquoia*, 163 (Senecas, Cayugas, and Mohawks); *JR* 40:139, 42:42 (Mohawks), 43:307–9, 44:33, 39–43 (Onondagas), 47:187, 51:123 (Oneidas); Adrian Mandzy, "Rogers Farm Site," 19 (Cayugas).

82. *JR* 45:207 (quotes). For evidence of associative adoptions among the constituent League nations, see ibid., 44:21, 25–27, 54:81; Oury, *Marie de l'Incarnation*, 543–44 (Tahontaenrat

Wendats in Seneca country). For evidence of a separate Attignawantan Wendat (Bear nation) settlement of approximately 570 people among the Mohawks (established in 1657
on the north side of the Mohawk River, opposite extant Mohawk villages then on the
south side of the river), see *JR* 43:187, 45:205–9, 46:109–11, 47:57, 49:107; Kuhn and Snow,
Mohawk Valley Project, 2–3, 30–31, 75–91; Kuhn, "Cromwell Site," 33–34; Snow, *Mohawk
Valley Archaeology,* 361, 364–65, 403–10 (population estimate 410). For evidence of the
Ahrendahronon Wendats (Rock nation) settling among the Onondagas, see *JR* 44:69, 185;
Steckley, "Wendat Dialects," 35. For Christian Wendat segregation from the principal Onondaga village after the mid-1650s, see *JR* 40:225–27, 41:37–39, 103–5, 42:81, 43:365, 54:43.
For circumstantial evidence of Christian Wendat segregation in Oneida country, see ibid.,
49:131–33 (the reference may describe a menstrual hut). For evidence of the Attigneengno-
nahac Wendats (Cord nation) electing to remain at the Isle d'Orléans, see ibid., 43:57–59,
191–93, 44:69, 149, 189–91; *JJ,* 219–20; Charlevoix, *History,* 2:280. For archaeological evidence
of persistent Wendat burial practices, especially that of wooden "tombs" or mausoleums
placed over graves (see Le Roy de la Potherie, *Histoire* 2: 423 and Kinitiez, *Indians of the
Western Great Lakes,* 410) in Seneca settlements post-dating 1650, see Houghton, *Archaeology of the Genesee,* 54–59; White, "Orchid Site Ossuary," 38; University of the State of
New York, *Sullivan-Clinton Campaign,* 176. On the significance of Wendat culture to the
nineteenth-century Handsome Lake religious movement in Iroquoia, see the discussion in
Bursey, "Frog Pond Site," 28.

83. *JR* 44:47 ("in the center . . . ," "a great number . . . ," "very populous"), 43:61, 287 (all other
quotes).
84. Ibid., 43:67–71 ("shackled together," 69), 44:63–65 ("the stumbling block"), 155–57, 193–95,
197–201; Dollier de Casson, "Histoire du Montréal," 68; Oury, *Marie de l'Incarnation,* 604; *JJ,*
223–25; *MNF* 9:675, 704; Marie-Claire Daveluy, "Ailleboust de Coulonge, et d'Argentay, Louis
d,'" *DCB* 1:46.
85. *JR* 44:85–91, 201, 207–13 (quotes); *JJ,* 229–32.
86. *JR* 44:149–51, 213–17 (quotes); Adams, *Explorations of Radisson,* 71; Oury, *Marie de
l'Incarnation,* 603–4; Charlevoix, *History,* 3:13–16.
87. *JR* 44:95, 149–53, 155–61, 173–83, 221, 311–15; *JJ,* 234; Adams, *Explorations of Radisson,* 72–77;
MNF 9:178–82; Le Roy de la Potherie, *Histoire* 2:446 (cannon at Gannentaha).
88. *MNF* 9:650; *CJVR,* 324–26; Wray, "Volume of Dutch Trade Goods," 106–7; Puype, "Dutch and
Other Flintlocks," 68; Baart, "Cloth Seals at Iroquois Sites," 80–83; Huey, "Archaeology of 17th
Century New Netherland," 100–101. Cf. Bradley, *Evolution of the Onondaga Iroquois,* 175.
89. *JR* 10:320–21n4, 44:95–97 (quotes); *JJ,* 235–36.
90. *JR* 44:99–101 (quotes), 223–25.
91. Ibid., 101–7, 111, 225–31; *JJ,* 237–38; *FOCM,* 400–402 (quotes); *NYCD* 12:99, 13:13, 122.
92. *JR* 44:107–9 ("all or none," 109), 117, 233 ("Atogwatkann, called La Grande . . ."); *MNF* 9:203; *JJ,*
239–41.
93. *JR* 44:109–13. A fourth Wendat accompanying Otreouti's embassy escaped. This individual's
reported name, "le Roy du Suede" (King of Sweden; see ibid., 44:109–11), suggests some
former association on his part with the Swedish settlement on the Delaware River, possibly
originating from ties of trade established on the Wendat Charles Ondaaiondiont's three-day
visit to the Dutch and Swedes on the Delaware River during June 1647 negotiations with
the Susquehannocks (see ibid., 33:129–37) and/or residency among the Susquehannocks as
refugees after 1649 (see ibid., 36:141, 45:243). See also Lorraine E. Williams, "Indians and
Europeans in the Delaware Valley, 1620–1655," in Hoffecker et al., *New Sweden,* 114–19.
94. *JR* 44:115–19 ("matters shall be . . ." 115; "iron bars," 119), 45:89; *JJ,* 241–43; *MNF* 9:673–74, 706.

95. *JR* 44:117–19 (quotes), 315–17; *JJ*, 243–44; *MNF* 9:647, 694; Oury, *Marie de l'Incarnation*, 566, 604.

96. *JR* 44:49, 237 ("nearly everywhere . . ."), 249–51, 45:99, 219–23, 46:145, 47:149; Cadillac, "Memoir," in Quaife, *Western Country*, 10; Colden, *History of the Five Indian Nations Depending on the Province of New-York*, 15; Overstreet, "Oneota Prehistory and History," 287–90.

97. *JR* 44:121–25 (quotes); *JJ*, 244–49; *FOCM*, 411.

98. *JR* 44:125–29 (quotes), 45:79, 87.

99. Ibid., 45:81–89 (quotes); *JJ* 251–56.

100. *JR* 45:91–95 (quotes); Du Creux, *History of Canada*, 2:694; Dickinson, "La Guerre Iroquoise," 52; Moussette, "1655," 277, 285.

101. Charlevoix, *History*, 3:34 ("children to repeople . . ."); *JR* 45:31, 35, 97–99 (all other quotes), 107–9, 113–17; *JJ*, 257–58, 262, 266–67; Oury, *Marie de l'Incarnation*, 614–15, 619–20. For the population of New France circa 1658, see Trudel, *Beginnings of New France*, 257.

102. *JR* 45:31–35, 109, 47:93 ("through which," "easily pass"); *FOCM*, 453–54 (all other quotes 454); *JJ*, 262. For the decline of peltry volumes in New Netherland after 1657, see *CJVR*, 104, 106–7; Burke, *Mohawk Frontier*, 7–11; Venema, *Beverwijck*, 159, 178, 203, 206; Jacobs, *New Netherland*, 212–13. This decline in peltry volumes in New Netherland may reflect Mohawk redirection of their trade toward John Pynchon's post at Springfield (see Salisbury, "Toward the Covenant Chain," 65). For a colorful account of the frenzied competition at Beverwijck during *handelstijd* (the annual trading season spanning May to November), see Merwick, *Possessing Albany*, 77–103.

103. *FOCM*, 454–59 (quotes); Grassmann, *Mohawk Indians*, 210; *CJVR*, 186; *NYCD* 13:123, 164, 179–84. "Kaghunawage" was the Mohawk Turtle clan village on the south side of the Mohawk River, known to archaeologists as the Freeman site.

104. *JR* 45:41–43 ("destruction of two . . ."), 49, 97 ("squads"), 217–19, 237.

105. Ibid., 45:157, 245–61 (quote 249). For the location of Dollard's palisade near modern-day Orleans, Ontario, see Lee, "Long Sault of the Ottawa," 97–98. Cf. Sowter, "Algonkin and Huron Occupation," 66–68. On the distinction between the "Long Sault" of the Ottawa River and the "Long Sault" of the St. Lawrence River, see Lahontan, *New Voyages* 1:68n, 217n.

106. Oury, *Marie de l'Incarnation*, 622–27 (quote 624); *JR* 46:23–61, 121; *MNF* 9:689; Dollier de Casson, "Histoire du Montréal," 81–86; Belmont, "Histoire du Canada," 30–31; Bertrand, *Histoire de Montréal*, 1:71–76; André Vachon, "Taondechoren, Louis," *DCB* 1:632–33; André Vachon, "Dollard des Ormeaux, Adam," ibid., 266–75; Dickinson, "La Guerre Iroquoise," 42–43, 49–50, 52.

107. *JR* 45:153–59, 245, 46:61, 85–101 ("Iroquoised Hurons," 91), 121–23 (all other quotes); *JJ*, 282–85; Oury, *Marie de l'Incarnation*, 627.

108. *FOCM*, 463–64, 503 ("enjoyed for more . . ."), 515–18; Gehring, *Delaware Papers (Dutch Period)*, 197, 234; "Virginia and Maryland, or the Lord Baltimore's Printed Case [1655]," Force, *Tracts* 2:5; Georges-Émile Giguère, "Albanel, Charles," *DCB* 1:48; Adair, "Dollard des Ormeaux"; Chevalier, "Myth and Ideology"; Dickinson, "Annaotaha et Dollard"; Webster, "Susquehannock Animal Economy," 57–58; Custer, "Analysis of Grave Good Assemblages," 38–40; Fur, *Colonialism in the Margins*, 176. For official Dutch efforts from 1660 to 1664 to respond to Iroquois complaints of abuses by mobile Dutch brokers, see O'Callaghan, *Laws and Ordinances*, 383, 425–27, 463–64; Sullivan, *Punishment of Crime*, 160.

109. *JR* 45:181–201 (quotes), 205; Oury, *Marie de l'Incarnation*, 648–49; Boucher, *Histoire Véritable*, 5, 152–53.

110. *JR* 46:165–67, 171–75, 179, 205 ("from Tadoussac to Montréal . . ."), 207 (all other quotes), 209–21, 251, 47:35–49, 69, 155–57, 50:55–67; *JJ*, 293, 299, 303; Oury, *Marie de l'Incarnation*,

666–67; Dollier de Casson, "Histoire du Montréal," 88–94; Gustave Lanctot, "Brigeac, Claude," *DCB* 1:130; *MNF* 9:659; André Vachon, "Godefroy de Vieuxpont, Jacques de," *DCB* 1:341; Olga Jurgens, "Vignal, Guillaume," ibid., 1:661–62; Raymond Douville, "Hertel de la Fresnière, Joseph-François," ibid., 2:282–84; Melanie Perreault, "Messier, dit St. Michel," ibid., 2:469–70; Claude Perreault, "Cuillerier, René," ibid., 2:164–65. For the 1661 killing and beheading of the son of Jean de Lauson, who in 1652 had overseen the ritual torture and execution of Mohawk headman Aontarisati at Trois-Rivières, see Oury, *Marie de l'Incarnation,* 479, 665–66; J. Monet, "Lauson, Jean de, Junior," *DCB* 1:429–31; *MNF* 6:763.

111. *JR* 46:145, 189, 251 ("the great scourge of . . ."), 285–91 ("Squirrel nation," 289), 293 "no Pirates so dangerous . . ."), 47:139, 56:115. The identity of the "Squirrel nation" is unclear. Their documented location in 1661, according to Toby Morantz (personal communication to the author, April 23, 2007), places them on the border between Attikamekw and Cree territory. For Cree oral tradition of Iroquois attacks, see Wesley and Faries, *Stories from the James Bay Coast,* 1–9; Ellis, *Âtalôhkâna nesta tipâcimôwina,* 177.

112. *AMD* 1:400, 406–7, 417–18, 3:403, 411, 420, 434, 441; Oury, *Marie de l'Incarnation,* 666; *JR* 46:155, 47:69, 111, 215; Gehring, *Delaware Papers (Dutch Period),* 236, 243, 264, 306–7, 312, 314, 334; McIlwaine, *Journals,* 15–16; Ives Goddard, "Delaware," in Trigger, *Northeast,* 222–23; Francis Jennings, "Indians and Frontiers in Seventeenth-Century Maryland," in Quinn, *Early Maryland,* 222–24; Kraft, *Lenape-Delaware Heritage,* 434–36; Fur, *Colonialism in the Margins,* 224, 232. The Mohawks were reportedly in a "confederacye" with the Pocumtucks and Squakheags as late as 1659. See *RCNP* 10:222.

113. *JR* 46:179–81, 223–37 (quotes), 47:93, 50:63–67; *JJ,* 299–300.

114. *JR* 46:155, 181, 239, 245 ("prowling about our . . . ," "captives of their . . ."), 47:69–73 ("avenge the insult . . . ," 73).

115. *JR* 47:75–83 (quotes).

116. Hennepin, *Description of Louisiana,* 310 ("crying 'Hay, hay' . . ."); *JR* 46:189, 217–19 ("[c]lothed in this precious spoil . . . ," 219), 47:97 (all other quotes); Dollier de Casson, "Histoire du Montréal," 89–91; Belmont, "Histoire du Canada," 31.

117. *JR* 47:101–7 (quotes), 183, 241–43.

118. *CJVR,* 225; *NYCD* 13:203, 219, 244, 14:296; van Laer, "Albany Notarial Papers, 1666–1693," 2; Parker, *Archeological History,* 692; Huey, "Dutch Sites," 71; Pearson, *History of the Schenectady Patent,* 11–17; Burke, *Mohawk Frontier,* 19, 31, 68–73; Bradley, "Visualizing Arent van Curler," 7–13; Ferguson, *Schoharie Mohawks,* 17–20.

119. *JR* 46:147–49 (quotes); Oury, *Marie de l'Incarnation,* 672; *CMRNF* 1:155–56; Trudel, *Histoire de la Nouvelle-France,* 167. For the population of New France circa 1663, see Trudel, *Beginnings of New France,* 257.

120. *JR* 47:155, 157 (quote), 191–93, 201–3, 277 ("Otourewati"), 287–91, 303, 48:89–111, 279, 49:119–35; *JJ,* 306 ("Ot8re8ati"), 311–12; Dollier de Casson, "Histoire du Montréal," 95–96; Marie-Claire Daveluy, "Closse, Raphael-Lambert," *DCB* 1:231.

121. *JR* 47:139–53 (quotes), 193, 50:63; Brandão, *Nation Iroquoise,* 71–73. Cherokee and Chickasaw oral tradition, along with evidence of an artificially deformed skull among human remains in a contemporary Seneca site, strongly suggests the identity of the nations sustaining Iroquois attacks at this time. For eighteenth-century Chickasaw tradition of displacement by musket-bearing Iroquois warriors, see Moore, *Nairne's Muskohogean Journals,* 37. For nineteenth-century Cherokee oral tradition of dislocation from the lower Ohio River valley during the mid-seventeenth century, see Klinck and Talman, *Journal of Major John Norton,* 46, 263; Moulton, *Papers of Chief John Ross,* 1:112. For evidence of consciousness of Cherokee ancestry among the Onondagas circa 1845, see Schoolcraft, *Notes on the Iroquois,* 443. For evidence

of artificially deformed skulls on seventeenth-century Seneca sites, see Cornwell, "Artificially Deformed Skull"; Sublett and Wray, "Some Examples of Accidental and Deliberate Human Skeletal Modification," 19, 23. For skull modification as a cultural practice among southeastern nations, see Williams, *Adair's History*, 9–10. For the association of the Ontôagannhas with the Shawnees then residing in western Kentucky, see *JR* 47:316n9, 56:63; Charles Callender, "Shawnee," in Trigger, *Northeast*, 634. Cf. Steckley, "Early Map," 20. For evidence of possible Iroquois attacks on the Quapaws, see Shea, *Discovery and Exploration of the Mississippi Valley*, 47; DuVal, *Native Ground*, 67. For evidence of possible Iroquois attacks on the ancestors of the Illinois people prior to the League's post-1684 campaign against the Illinois Confederacy, see *JR* 18:231, 42:221, 44:246, 50:289, 51:49, 54:165–67, 187–89, 58:23; *NYCD* 9:162–63; Charles Callender, "Illinois," in Trigger, *Northeast*, 678; Robert L. Hall, "Rethinking Jean Nicolet's Route to the Ho-Chunks in 1634," in Jeske and Charles, *Theory, Method, and Practice*, 240; Calloway, *One Vast Winter Count*, 235; Ehrhardt, *European Metals*, 83–104.

122. *JR* 47:139–43 (quote 141), 147–49, 279, 48:75–77; *JJ*, 307–8; *CJVR*, 358; *RCNP* 10:282; Blair, *Indian Tribes*, 1:178–81; Charlevoix, *History*, 3:64–65; Schmalz, "Role of the Ojibwa," 333; Conway, "Ojibwa Oral History," 19–20; Mason, *Inconstant Companions*, 137–42; Calloway, *One Vast Winter Count*, 230.

123. Alsop, *Character of the Province of Maryland*, 79 ("Barken City"); *JR* 48:77–81 (all other quotes 77–79); *AMD* 1:471–72; Gehring, *Delaware Papers (Dutch Period)*, 320–21, 334. The document printed in *Delaware Papers (Dutch Period)*, 334, contains the phrase "the Minquas [Susquehannocks] would assist the Sinnecus against the Minquas." Gehring, in personal correspondence to the author (October 26, 2006), checked the original manuscript and reported that the first mention of "Minquas" actually reads as "Maquas" (Mohawks).

124. *JR* 47:303 ("Le Fer," "the most renowned"), 48:25–27, 83, 99–111, 49:139–41, 149; *JJ*, 318; *CJVR*, 358 ("infest[ed] the Maquas trail . . ."); *NYCD* 2:371–72, 13:257–58, 308, 355–56; *MaHSC* ser.5, 1:399–400, 8:88–89; Taylor, "Fort Hill Bluff Site"; Gordon M. Day, "The Ouragie War: A Case History in Iroquois-New England Indian Relations," in Foster, Campisi, and Mithun, *Extending the Rafters*, 42; Bruchac and Thomas, "Locating 'Wissatinnewag,'" 56–63. Fort Hill was located near modern-day Hinsdale, New Hampshire.

125. *JR* 47:307, 48:233, 49:141 (quotes), 149, 51:243; *AMD* 1:511, 522–25, 539–40, 3:498–503, 549; *PA* ser. 2, 5:549–50; Fur, *Colonialism in the Margins*, 233.

126. *NYCD* 9:9–15, 20–21; *JR* 48:153–79 ("great treasure," 175); Du Creux, *History of Canada*, 1:5–7, ("Map of New France" opposite 68); Boucher, *Histoire Véritable*, 20, 24–26, 37–38, 48–49, 86–87; Massicotte, "La Milice de 1663"; André Vachon, "Gaudais-Dupont, Louis," *DCB* 1:325–26; *MNF* 9:674, 691; André Vachon, "Monts, Sieur de," *DCB* 1:511–12; Leslie Choquette, "Proprietorships in French North America," in Roper and Van Ruymbeke, *Constructing Early Modern Empires*, 124–25.

127. *JR* 48:235, 49:109–17, 137, 143–49 (quotes); *JJ*, 326.

128. *JR* 33:63–65, 48:237–39, 49:137, 149–53 (quotes); Oury, *Marie de l'Incarnation*, 727–28.

129. Christoph and Christoph, *Books of General Entries*, vol. 1, 47–48 (quotes); Smith, "Captain Thomas Willett," 413–14.

130. Ibid., 48–49; *NYCD* 3:67–68 (depiction of Canaqueese's mark, signed as "Smith John," 68), 104, 111; Smith, *History of the Province of New York*, 1:21–34; *ERNY* 1:560–62.

131. *JR* 49:173, 50:21, 37–43, 203, 307–11, 51:79, 56:183–85; *MaHSC* ser. 4, 6:531–32; ibid. ser. 5, 1:399–400; *PP* 1:45–46, 50, 53–54, 56; *CSPC* 5:246, 321; *PA* ser. 2, 5:550; *DHNY* 1:76; Blair, *Indian Tribes*, 1:175–76; Oury, *Marie de l'Incarnation*, 741–42; Day, "Ouragie War," 42–43.

132. *NYCD* 9:25 ("carry war even . . . ," "firesides in order . . ."); Jaenen, *French Regime in the Upper Country of Canada*, 59 (all other quotes); Charlevoix, *History*, 3:80; Philippe Jacquin, "The

Colonial Policy of the Sun King," in *Sun King*, 78–79; Petrovich, "Perception and Reality," 76–77.

133. *JR* 49:161, 163, 169, 213–39 ("groaning under . . . ," 213; "destruction of the Iroquois," 237), 253–55, 257–67 ("Of the Iroquois Country . . ."), 50:81–91 (all other quotes 89); Oury, *Marie de l'Incarnation*, 740, 754–55; *JJ*, 333–35; Charlevoix, *History*, 3:81; Audet, "A Propos du Regiment de Carignan," 257–60; *NYCD* 9:32n1; Faillon, *Histoire de la colonie Française*, 3:125; Coolidge, "French Occupation of the Champlain," 158–59; Verney, *Good Regiment*, 4, 18–20, 27; Bosher, "Imperial Environment of French Trade," 58; Gélinas, *Role of Fort Chambly*, 13.

134. *JR* 43:239 ("customary marauding expeditions"); *JJ*, 239; Dollier de Casson, "Histoire du Montréal," 99–100; Blair, *Indian Tribes*, 1:198–99; Jean-Jacques LeFebvre, "Le Moyne de Longueuil et de Châteauguay, Charles de," *DCB* 1:463–65. For renderings of Le Moyne's adoptive Onondaga name, see *NYCD* 4:121; Belmont, "Histoire," 37; *An Account of the Treaty*, 11.

135. *NYCD* 9:37–38 (quotes 37); *JR* 49:177–81, 50:127–31; *JJ*, 339–40.

136. *JR* 49:179–81 ("La Grand geule"), 50:127 ("fickle and perfidious"); *JJ*, 340; *NYCD* 3:121–25 (all other quotes), 9:39.

137. *NYCD* 9:30 ("interven[ing]"); Jaenen, *French Regime*, 15 ("as far as . . . ," "Mexico"); *JR* 50:135 ("try unknown routes"); *DHNY* 1:72.

138. *JR* 50:135 (quote), 155, 181–85; *CSPC* 5:349–50; *NYCD* 3:128–33, 4:405.

139. *DHNY* 1:72–74 (quotes); *JJ*, 340–43; Dollier de Casson, "Histoire du Montréal," 101; Verney, *Good Regiment*, 42–52; Gélinas, *Role of Fort Chambly*, 10. For a lengthy contemporary poem satirizing Courcelles's failed enterprise, see "Vers Burlesque"; André Vachon, "Chartier de Lotbinière, René-Louis," *DCB* 2:136.

140. *JR* 50:135–37 (quote 137), 189–91; *NYCD* 3:125–27, 9:44–47; *DHNY* 1:75–76; *PP* 1:55–56; Verney, *Good Regiment*, 61. French officials apparently interviewed the Senecas for information on their clan organization at Quebec in July 1666. See *NYCD* 9:47–51. Cf. Charlevoix, *Journal* 2:107–8, who claims that a delegation of Iroquois visited Paris in 1666.

141. *NYCD* 3:117, 120–21 ("the French and Mowhawks," 121), 129–30, 137–38; *DHNY* 1:78–83 ("the Interest of Europe," "barbarous Indyans . . . ," 83); *LIR*, 29–31 (all other quotes), 33–35; *PP* 1:57–65; *CSPC* 5:389, 399, 401; *MaHSC* ser. 5, 8:96–102.

142. *LIR*, 31–33 (quote 32); *JR* 50:167, 193, 197, 199; *JJ*, 346; Dollier de Casson, "Histoire du Montréal," 102; Le Roy de la Potherie, *Histoire*, 1:271–72; Coolidge, "French Occupation of the Champlain Valley," 168; Verney, *Good Regiment*, 61–63. Cf. Thomas Grassmann, "Agariata," *DCB* 1:40–41, who does not mention Agariata's Neutral origins.

143. Le Roy de la Potherie, *Histoire* 1: 272 ("cried out in . . . ,"); *JR* 50:139–41 ("more tractable," 141), 197–99 (all other quotes); Oury, *Marie de l'Incarnation*, 770–71, 774; *RAPQ* (1930–31): 46–50, 60; Charlevoix, *History*, 3:88–89; Verney, *Good Regiment*, 66. For "Onnonkenritiwi" as one of the eight hereditary Seneca titles, see Tooker, "League of the Iroquois," 425; Fenton, *Great Law and the Longhouse*, 194, 411. Cf. Morgan, *League of the Iroquois*, 74. The individual present at Quebec in 1666 may have been the same Seneca leader Jesuits identified in 1656 (*JR* 44:23; *MNF* 9:651) and in 1672 (*JR* 56:61).

144. *PP* 1:61 ("Sunnuck"); *MaHSC* ser.5, 8:102–3 ("many hundreds," "chief sachems," "Lake Hieracoies"); *LIR*, 145 ("out a hunting"); *JR* 50:143–45 (all other quotes).

145. *JR* 50:143 (quote); Kip, *Early Jesuit Missions*, 83. For accounts of four Mohawk "forts" destroyed, see *DHNY* 1:77; Oury, *Marie de l'Incarnation*, 776. Cf. the assertion of five Mohawk villages destroyed in "Memoires de Feu Monsieur Boucher," 403, and six villages destroyed in Gélinas, *Role of Fort Chambly*, 14.

146. *JR* 50:145 ("the mutilated bodies"), 203 ("large cabins"); *DHNY* 1:57–84 ("Andaraque," 77); *PP* 1:71; *JJ*, 351–52; Oury, *Marie de l'Incarnation*, 773–76; Charlevoix, *History*, 3:90–92; Colden,

History of the Five Indian Nations Depending on the Province of New-York, 17–18; André Vachon, "Duquet de la Chesnaye, Pierre," *DCB* 1:298; Verney, *Good Regiment,* 71–83. The estimate of 100 Mohawk longhouses destroyed, measured against a contemporary estimate of the Mohawk population at 3,000 people (see Oury, *Marie de l'Incarnation,* 775), roughly corroborates the ratio of 30 to 40 people per longhouse advanced by Snow (see "Mohawk Demography," 165). For contemporary Iroquois recollections of the 1666 French invasion of Mohawk country, see *NYCD* 4:121, 352. Cf. the garbled version related by New York Governor Thomas Dongan in 1687 (ibid., 3:395).

147. *JR* 50:147, 203–5 (quotes); *NYCD* 9:56; Oury, *Marie de l'Incarnation,* 774, 776; *PP* 1:71–72.

148. Bradley, *Evolution of the Onondaga Iroquois,* 186 ("dilution," "ethnic identity"); Parker, *Analytical History of the Seneca Indians,* 50–51 ("dynamic ideals," "moral force").

149. Cf. Snow, "Mohawk Demography," 165–66, 176.

4. Six Songs, 1667–1684

1. *JR* 51:201–3 (quotes). See also the description of firearms used in a 1794 Edge of the Woods welcome offered by Senecas to a Pennsylvania surveyor in Abler, *Cornplanter,* 104.

2. Hennepin, *New Discovery,* 1:341 ("*Atsientatsi,*" "Black Gowns"); *IMC,* 189; Snow, *Mohawk Valley Archaeology,* 411, 413, 425–28. Tionnontogouen is known to archaeologists as the White Orchard site.

3. Hennepin, *New Discovery,* 2:583 (quotes); *LIR,* 144–45. In 1679, Jesuits resided at seven of the thirteen extant Five Nations towns (*JR* 61:237, 270n13). The League's two doorkeepers, the Mohawks and the Senecas, placed clear restrictions on Jesuit residency within their national homelands between 1667 and 1684. On the Jesuits in Mohawk country, see *JR* 51:87, 179, 201, 219, 53:139, 55:41, 56:27, 57:25, 81, 89, 61:165. On the Jesuits in Seneca country, see ibid., 57:191–95, 58:237, 59:251, 61:21, 165; Bihler, "Jesuit Mission." On Hennepin, see Jaenen, "Missionaries as Explorers," 40–45.

4. Greer, *Mohawk Saint,* 55 ("dissident Mohawks"), 93 ("uncoordinated drift"), 99 ("a breakaway group . . ."); Vecsey, *Paths of Kateri's Kin,* 85 ("christened Iroquois," "eschewed kinship with . . .," "fled," "ostracism"). This perspective has a long pedigree: see *JR* 47:320n28; *NYCD* 4:351; Kip, *Early Jesuit Missions,* 134; Colden, *History of the Five Indian Nations Depending on the Province of New-York,* 39n–40n; Charles Thomson, "Commentaries," in Jefferson, *Notes on the State of Virginia,* 207; Morgan, *League of the Iroquois,* 26; Pritchard, "For the Glory of God," 142; Aquila, *Iroquois Restoration,* 71; Axtell, *Invasion Within,* 277; Richter, *Ordeal of the Longhouse,* 199–209; Dennis, *Cultivating a Landscape of Peace,* 167–68; Brandão, "*Your Fyre Shall Burn No More,*" 121–22; Fenton, *Great Law and the Longhouse,* 404; Wonderley, "Iroquois Creation Story," 9; Blum, *Ghost Brothers,* 44–46; Carpenter, *Renewed,* 135–36; Shannon, *Iroquois Diplomacy,* 37. Cf. a detailed satellite image depicting locations of precontact Laurentian Iroquoian archaeological sites and the contemporary Iroquois communities of Tyendinaga, Akwesasne, Kahnawake, and Kanesatake in Tremblay, *St. Lawrence Iroquoians,* 34–35.

5. Alfred, *Peace, Power, Righteousness,* xxii ("keep listening to . . ."); *JR* 51:123 ("Iroquois in temper . . ."), 187, 257, 52:53–55, 63:165 ("sixteen nations"). For evidence of the success of the Iroquois efforts to assimilate alien adoptees by 1667, as demonstrated by intermarriage between ethnic Iroquois and adoptees and children born of these unions, as well as the coresidency of adoptees and ethnic Iroquois in Iroquois towns, see *JR* 51:131, 187, 211, 219, 231, 251–53, 257, 52:23, 165, 179, 195, 58:221–23, 62:61–65, 63:151; Oury, *Marie de l'Incarnation,*

786–87. Cf. evidence of ongoing spatial segregation of Wendat adoptees in Onondaga country circa 1668–70 (*JR* 52:165, 54:45), in Mohawk country circa 1667–79 (Snow, *Mohawk Valley
Archaeology*, 411–15), and most visibly at the Seneca town of Gandougaraé (home to the
Tahontaenrat adoptees and referred to as the St. Michel mission) circa 1669–87 (Coyne, "Exploration of the Great Lakes," 34–35; *JR* 52:53–55, 54:81–93, 121, 55:79, 56:59–69, 57:191, 58:229;
Olds, "Journal of Chevalier de Baugy," 40; Houghton, *Archeology of the Genesee Country*,
54–59; White, "Orchid Site Ossuary," 20). Thanks to my colleague Kurt Jordan for sharing his
knowledge of the Senecas' archaeological record.

6. Charlevoix, *History*, 3:117 (quote); *JR* 63:185; Le Roy de la Potherie, *Histoire*, 2:440; Kip, *Early
Jesuit Missions*, 102, 120.

7. *MaHSC* ser. 5, 8:107 ("French scutchion"); *PP* 1:69–72 (all other quotes); *NYCD* 9:56, 58; *DHNY*
1:77.

8. *NYCD* 3:151–53 (quote 153); *JR* 50:209; *JJ*, 353; Oury, *Marie de l'Incarnation*, 786.

9. *NYCD* 3:148 ("subordinate"), 156–58; *JR* 50:211–13 ("families as hostages," 211), 51:181; *JJ*, 355;
"First Publication of a Jesuit Letter," 8; van Laer, "Documents Relating to Arent van Curler's
Death," 30–32; John Dickinson, "Vivre en Canada," in Landry, *Pour Le Christ et Le Roi*, 112–16.
Van Curler drowned near the Bay of Perou, opposite modern-day Essex County, New York.

10. *JR* 50:215, 51:83, 179–87 (quotes); *JJ*, 356.

11. *JR* 51:189–207 (quotes).

12. Ibid., 51:201 ("assurance of peace"), 207–9 ("Orator," "gesticulations," 207); *RGCMB* 4, pt. 2:
359–60; *MaHSC* ser.5, 8:98–99. In 1698, Jesuits at Quebec reported that they received 24,000
livres annually from the French Crown for the support of their "Iroquois mission." See *NYCD*
4:349.

13. *JR* 51:119–39, 187, 197, 211–15, 221–35; Jaenen, *French Regime in the Upper Country*, 59–65
("two Black Robes," 62; "gunsmith to . . . ," 63); *RAPQ* (1930–31): 74, 89; *NYCD* 9:60; *AMD* 5:13;
Blair, *Indian Tribes*, 1:226; Oury, *Marie de l'Incarnation*, 787.

14. *JR* 52:119 ("their ears with . . . ," "'I do not hear'"), 153 ("prayers," "most superstitious," "suffer
any opposition . . ."), 53:213–17, 56:61 ("brain"), 59:77.

15. Blair, *Indian Tribes*, 1:203 ("dispersed"); *WJP* 12:172 ("original Owners"); *JR* 48:167–79,
51:263–65, 56:43, 63:151; Hoffman, *Cabot to Cartier*, 202; *JDCSNF* 1:558, 2:124, 337; Massicotte,
"La Foire des Pelleteries." See also Drooker, "Fort Ancient Cultures," 105–6; Lightfoot, *Indians, Missionaries, and Merchants*, 178–80. Cf. a 1763 claim by British Indian Department
superintendent Sir William Johnson (*NYCD* 7:573) that the Iroquois held title as "Original
Proprietors" to lands south of the St. Lawrence River and Lake Ontario, and that their claims
north of those bodies of water derived from "conquest."

16. Vecsey, *Paths of Kateri's Kin*, 88 (quote). For subsequently recorded Iroquois tradition sanc-
tioning movement from League settlements to new areas, subject to orders of recall from
League leaders (which may be best considered as an ex post facto explanation for these
movements rather than direct evidence of seventeenth-century practice), see Arthur C.
Parker, "Constitution," in Fenton, *Parker on the Iroquois*, 50.

17. *JR* 51:237 (quotes), 52:153; *JDCSNF* 1:129–30. Cf. Richter, *Ordeal of the Longhouse*, 169–70,
who interprets this 1668 passage as evidence of the decline of the traditional League and
the rise of what he terms "informal meetings" of an evolving parallel body of nonhereditary
leaders he terms the "Confederacy," a claim based on the perceived absence of documentary
evidence of League titleholders in the documentary record.

18. *JR* 50:217, 52:23–27, 61:195–99, 63:149–59 (quotes); *JJ*, 355, 357, 360; Roy Wright, "The People of
the Panther: A Long Erie Tale," in Foster, *Papers in Linguistics*, 66–68; Bruce Trigger, "Native
Resettlement, 1635–1800," in Harris, *Historical Atlas of Canada*, Plate 47. For the origin of the

name "Sault St. Louis," see *JR* 18:227–29.

19. Coyne, "Exploration of the Great Lakes," 39 ("Iroquois du Nord"); Vachon, "Dollard des Ormeaux," 270 ("dispersed"); *RFF,* 85–90, 100, 473–82; Dollier de Casson, "Histoire du Montreal," 110; *JR* 50:197–99, 51:177, 257, 297, 52:47; *NYCD* 4:395; Vachon, "Dollard des Ormeaux," 270; Richter, *Ordeal of the Longhouse,* 120–21; White, *Middle Ground,* 47; Ferris, "In Their Time," 114. For a circa 1682 report that claimed the Iroquois preferred to trap beaver rather than employ firearms, see "Account of Iroquois Indians." Cf. claims of beaver depletion in the domestic hunting territories of League nations after 1667 in *NYCD* 9:80; *RFF,* 103; Norton, *Fur Trade in Colonial New York,* 15, 28, 33–34; A. J. Ray, "The Fur Trade in North America: An Overview from a Historical Geographical Perspective," in Novak et al., *Wild Furbearer Management,* 22; Kuhn and Funk "Boning Up on the Mohawk," 52; Krech, *Ecological Indian,* 176.

20. Gookin, *Historical Collections,* 20 (quotes); Oury, *Marie de l'Incarnation,* 808, 828; *NYCD* 3:172, 13:436; Paltsits, *Minutes,* 2:387–89; *MCARS* 1:75; *CJVR,* 413; Sanson, *America,* 40; *JR* 51:169, 249, 52:123, 127–31; Christoph and Christoph, *Books of General Entries,* vol. 1, 175.

21. Oury, *Marie de l'Incarnation,* 802 (quotes).

22. *JR* 50:237–41, 51:83, 131, 169–75, 213–17 ("thousand [other] acts . . . ," 217), 219, 245, 52:139–41, 53:33–35, 241, 54:113–19; Oury, *Marie de l'Incarnation,* 786–87, 807–8, 863–65 ("one of the most prominent," 863; "join together to . . . ," 865), 939; Coyne, "Exploration of the Great Lakes," 7, 19, 33, 49 ("a mockery of . . ."); Blair, *Indian Tribes,* 1:204–7; Dollier de Casson, "Histoire du Montreal," 108; *NYCD* 3:162–63, 9:883; van Laer, "Documents Relating to Arent van Curler's Death," 31n; *MCARS* 1:186; Steckley, *De Religione,* 129–37; Charlevoix, *History,* 3:111, 149–51. For further evidence of Iroquois resistance to the Jesuits and for abuses of missionaries in Iroquoia after 1667, see *JR* 51:129, 137, 231, 52:119–21, 149, 157, 161, 181, 183, 197, 53:241, 245, 295–97, 54:57–59, 117, 55:297, 56:53, 58:199–201; Oury, *Marie de l'Incarnation,* 839–40.

23. Charlevoix, *History,* 3:123–24 (quotes); *JR* 57:249–51; Blair, *Indian Tribes,* 1:307, 334–36; Branstner, "Tionontate Huron Occupation," 180.

24. *JR* 52:199–203, 53:247 (quote), 255, 54:115, 55:97, 141–43, 159–61, 169, 56:115, 145, 57:203, 207–9; Coyne, "Exploration of the Great Lakes," 43–45; Burnham, *To Please the Caribou.*

25. Coyne, "Exploration of the Great Lakes," 3–9 (quotes); Blair, *Indian Tribes,* 1:207; Donnelly, "Belmont's History of Brandy," 53, 57; Dollier de Casson, "Histoire du Montreal," 112.

26. Coyne, "Exploration of the Great Lakes," 13–27 (quotes); *JR* 44:23, 53:153, 245, 54:107–13; George R. Hamell, "Gannagaro State Historic Site," in Bonvillain, *Studies on Iroquois Culture,* 94; Engelbrecht, *Iroquoia,* 100. Gandagan is known to archaeologists as the Marsh site.

27. Gookin, *Historical Collections,* 40–42 ("praying Indian," 40), 77–78, 85; *NYCD* 13:465 ("Kinaquariones"); *JR* 51:295, 52:123, 127–31, 135–37, 53:137–57, 243, 63:177; *CJVR,* 413; *PP* 1:80–81; Paltsits, *Minutes,* 1:377–78; Christoph and Christoph, *Books of General Entries,* vol. 1, 215, 304; Brasser, *Riding on the Frontier's Crest,* 22; Bourque, *Twelve Thousand Years,* 138–40. On the identity of the murderers of the Mahicans in the St. Lawrence valley, see Oury, *Marie de l'Incarnation,* 863–64 ("Loups," 863). Cf. *JR* 53:241, 54:113–15. Kinaquariones was located near modern-day Schenectady, New York.

28. Coyne, "Exploration of the Great Lakes," 19; *JR* 52:157–61 ("destined for the flames," 161), 167–71, 53:243, 247, 251–55, 54:23–25, 75–77 ("Ambassador," 77); Blair, *Indian Tribes,* 1:226 ("considerably augmented"); Jones, "Iroquois Population History," 82. For Iroquois-reported dreams related to the Susquehannock conflict, see *JR* 52:155, 53:253, 289–93, 56:35–37.

29. *JR* 54:117–21 ("in the direction of the Huron country," 119); Coyne, "Exploration of the Great Lakes," 27–39 (quotes); *JR* 54:117–21. On Iroquois consumption of dog meat in preparatory feasts for the torture of captives and military campaigns, see *JR* 62:75; *LIR,* 164; Blau, "Iroquois

White Dog Sacrifice"; Fenton, *Iroquois Eagle Dance*, 106–7, 177–78.

30. Coyne, "Exploration of the Great Lakes," 39–69 (quotes). The Sulpicians spent the winter of 1669–70 near modern-day Turkey Point, in Norfolk County, Ontario.

31. *JR* 52:197, 53:41, 255–57, 54:47, 219–27 ("under the guidance . . . ," "six large cabins," 219). Cf. ibid., 53:39–41, for the claim that the Iroquois took 100 Fox women and children prisoners in the attack. For the location of the Fox village near modern-day Manawa, Wisconsin, see ibid., 54:227, 307–8n12, 55:321n10.

32. *JR* 54:263–65 (quotes). Subsequent French reports of the incident altered, perhaps deliberately, the identification of the Senecas' victims from Foxes to Potawatomis (the latter were then arguably allied to the French), or rendered the identity of the victims even more vaguely as "upper Algonquins" (see *JR* 53:139), which enabled Courcelles to characterize them as French-allied "Outaouak Algonquins." Yet Allouez's firsthand account of the incident clearly identified the group attacked as "Outagamis" (*JR* 54:219) or Fox (see Charles Callender, "Fox," in Trigger, *Northeast*, 646). Cf. Perrot's 1667 ceremony of possession at Sault Ste. Marie in which he asserted Louis XIV's protection over all nations of the upper Great Lakes despite the Native leaders in attendance agreeing only to an alliance with the French king, discussed in Blair, *Indian Tribes*, 1:346–47; Colden, *History of the Five Indian Nations Depending on the Province of New-York*, 19.

33. *JR* 53:39, 54:219–21, 265–67 ("Elders," "young men," 265); Dollier de Casson, "Histoire du Montreal," 113; Charlevoix, *History*, 3:161–62.

34. *JR* 51:239–41, 52:161–63, 181–83, 53:41, 47–57 ("in the name . . . ," "whom Onontio had . . . ," 47–49), 257, 267, 295, 54:37–39, 47, 111–13, 269–73, 55:59 ("very well-known"), 56:143; Oury, *Marie de l'Incarnation*, 808–9. Jesuits identified the Senecas' Fox targets as "Ontougannha" (see *JR* 53:47), a term elsewhere used to denote the Shawnees and in this instance an apparent erroneous rendering of "Outagami."

35. *JR* 53:41 ("umpire in their quarrels"); *NYCD* 9:84–85 (all other quotes); Belmont, "Histoire," 34. For evidence of the lower prices of trade goods at Albany compared to those at Montreal, see *CMRNF* 1:179–80, 255, 263 (circa 1676–77); *NYCD* 9:36–37 (circa 1665), 408–9 (circa 1689).

36. *NYCD* 9:63–67 (quotes); *CMRNF* 1:205; *RFF*, 102.

37. *NYCD* 9:80–84 (quotes); Oury, *Marie de l'Incarnation*, 939.

38. *MCARS* 1:186, 255–57 (quotes), 259–60; *CJVR*, 440; *JR* 53:255, 54:281; Paltsis, *Executive Council Minutes*, 1:381; *PP* 1:84, 93–95; *MaHSC* ser.3, 10:79; *NYCD* 13:458; Christoph and Christoph, *Books of General Entries*, vol. 1, 436; *DHNY* 4:115; Gookin, *Historical Collections*, 34–36.

39. *JR* 53:247, 54:115, 287, 55:33–35 ("throng[s] of Savages . . . ," "Chiefs"), 55, 115, 261–67, 287, 57:47, 53–63, 67, 60:69–71, 63:157–59 ("cabins," "very fine," 159), 161–67 ("the word[s] from . . . ," 163); Charlevoix, *History*, 3:163; van Laer, "Albany Notarial Papers, 1667–1687," 11–12; *MCARS* 1:259–60; E. M. Jury, "Atironta, Pierre," *DCB* 1:71; Christian Morrissonneau, "Huron of Lorette," in Trigger, *Northeast*, 389.

40. *JR* 54:277–83 ("degraded her from . . . ," 283), 55:261–67, 56:29 ("all in readiness"), 57:55, 71. For evidence that nonliterate Iroquois couriers verified the contents of letters they carried to and from Jesuits by comparing recitations of their content by both writers and recipients, see Oury, *Marie de l'Incarnation*, 918.

41. *JR* 53:55–57, 55:35 ("people gathered from . . . ," "different Iroquois nations . . ."), 56:21, 45–47, 63:165 ("made but one," "sociability, visits, hospitality . . ."), 167. For Jesuit characterizations of the Christian devotion manifested by early relocatees to the St. Lawrence valley, see *JR* 52:25–27, 54:283, 56:21–23, 57:73–75, 58:75–77, 63:149, 155–57, 163–67.

42. *JR* 63:167–75 (quotes); Cushner, *Why Have You Come Here?*, 152–53.

43. *JR* 55:105–15 (quotes), 57:21–23, 203; *RFF*, 103–4; *NYCD* 9:89, 91; Margry, *Découvertes*, 1:56, 80,

96–99; Leavelle, "Geographies of Encounter."

44. *JR* 56:55–57, 67–69, 57:21–25 (quotes), 169–71, 203, 58:49–53; *RAPQ* (1926–27): 35; *NYCD* 9:95–96, 110; Quaife, *Western Country,* 67–69. On the 1671 Iroquois peace with the Mahicans, see *LIR,* 36; *CJVR,* 449; *PP* 1:102–6; Paltsits, *Minutes,* 2:748–49; *MCARS* 1:303; *NYCD* 13:464–65; Christoph, *Administrative Papers,* 182–83; Keppler, "Peace Tomahawk Algonkian Wampum."

45. *NYCD* 9:95–103 (quotes).

46. Beauchamp, *Indian Names in New York,* 64 ("Cataraqui," "fort in the water"); *NYCD* 9:104–18 (all other quotes); *JR* 57:27–31; *RAPQ* (1926–27): 26–52; *RFF,* 108–14, 174; *NYCD* 3:510, 4:449; Eccles, *Frontenac,* 56; Adams, "Iroquois Settlement at Fort Frontenac," 8. Claude Bernou's map, "Carte d'une Grande Partie du Canada," has been dated to circa 1680–86. See Heidenreich, "Seventeenth Century Maps," 93–94; Trigger, *Children of Aataentsic,* 838–39.

47. *JR* 55:267–69, 297, 57:25 ("compatriots," "good reception"), 47, 53, 63–77 ("nearly fifty," 71), 273, 58:14, 131, 147–51, 197–99, 296n19, 60:69 ("recruits"), 71–103. In 1674, Lorette housed 210 persons in a dozen "cabins" (ibid., 58:149), at least 52 of whom were Iroquois (ibid., 58:131–33). In 1675 and 1676, the Jesuits reported 300 souls (possibly representing a majority of Iroquois) at Lorette (ibid., 60:27, 145).

48. Ibid., 57:27–29 ("to provide themselves," "stuffs," 27), 81–85 ("malignant fever," 81), 91, 99–103, 139, 179, 193, 58:75–89 ("countrymen," 81), 63:175; Lafitau, *Customs of the American Indians,* 2:55 ("between sheets of bark"); Paltsits, *Minutes,* 2:737–39. On the Third Anglo-Dutch War, see Shomette and Haslach, *Raid on America.*

49. *JR* 57:105–11 ("who are not . . . ," "of the black . . . ," 109), 145, 58:171–75 ("elder," "Assendassé," 171), 59:75–77, 63:177–79.

50. Ibid., 57:141–45 ("solicitations," "compel his wife," 141; "made themselves drunk . . . ," 145), 59:237, 241 (all other quotes), 62:69–71.

51. Ibid., 57:317n3, 58:201, 207–9, 63:175–81 (quotes 175); *NYCD* 9:116–17.

52. *JR* 58:13, 115–23 ("lake of the Two Mountains," 115), 133 ("nevertheless adopted one . . ."), 137, 241, 247–53, 295n17, 59:41, 45, 60:29, 69, 61:207–9 ("a good deal for . . . ," 209), 63:183–85 ("recipients of charity," 185); Christoph, Scott, and Stryker-Rodda, *Kingston Papers,* 2:532; *NYCD* 9:118; Munro, *Documents,* 39–40; *CMRNF* 1:274.

53. *JR* 58:15, 181–89 ("several embassies from . . . ," 185), 211 ("deputed with all . . ."), 237 ("superstitions," "a considerable impediment . . ."), 62:199–201; *NYCD* 13:479 ("renew the peace"); Gehring and Grumet, "Observations of the Indians," 109–10.

54. *JR* 58:225–27, 59:145 ("the nations whom . . ."), 245, 251, 312n35, 60:185–87, 61:27, 62:209; *AMD* 2:376, 378 ("Cynicoes Indians"); *IMC,* 191; Blair, *Indian Tribes,* 1:226–27; Alvord and Bidgood, *First Explorations of the Trans-Allegheny Region,* 210–26; Gookin, *Historical Collections,* 37–40; *RGCMB* 4, pt. 2: 360–61.

55. *JR* 59:251 (quotes), 60:173, 185; *NYCD* 9:119, 122–24, 127; *RFF,* 116, 120–22.

56. *AMD* 2:428–30 (Maryland Assembly quotes), 15:58, 78; *NYCD* 13:491 (Andros quotes); Christoph and Christoph, *Andros Papers,* 1:132. For evidence of Susquehannock leaders fluent in the Mohawk language circa 1676, see A1894 25:124.

57. *MaHSC* ser. 4, 6:298 ("head (or heads) . . ."); ibid., ser. 4, 7:577; Christoph and Christoph, *Books of General Entries,* vol. 2, 79–80; "A New and Further Narrative of the State of New England, Being a Continued Account of the Bloody Indian War" (1676), in *King Philip's War Narratives,* 8; *NYCD* 13:491–92; *PP* 1:150–52; *MCARS* 2:17, 37. For the destruction of Pynchon's trading post, see "The Present State of New-England, with Respect to the Indian War" (1675), in *King Philip's War Narratives,* ; Oberg, *Uncas,* 181–82.

58. *PRCC* 2:397 ("40 or 50 miles"), 398 ("destroy these bloody . . ."), 406–7 ("3000 or more . . . ," 406); Christoph and Christoph, *Books of General Entries,* vol. 2, 93 (all other Andros quotes);

"Account of Iroquois Indians"; Andrews, *Narratives of the Insurrections,* 47–48; *MCARS* 2:56, 64–65; *NYCD* 3:242, 254, 257–67, 13:509; *NYSA,* A1894, 25:90, 116; *MaHSC* ser. 4, 6:309; *CMRNF* 1:243–44; *JR* 60:133–35; "New and Further Narrative," 8; Christoph and Christoph, *Andros Papers,* 1:330–31; "John Paine's Journal," 188. For a description of a ceremonial wampum head ornament, reportedly a gift of the "Muh-hogs," that was recovered from King Philip's body in August 1676, see Church, *Diary,* 170. Cf. Increase Mather's unique, uncorroborated claim that King Philip surreptitiously killed Mohawks during the winter of 1675–76 in an effort to frame the English and win over the Mohawks as allies in "An Earnest Exhortation to the Inhabitants of New-England" (1676), in Slotkin and Folsom, *"So Dreadfull a Judgment,"* 129.

59. *NYCD* 3:255 (quotes); "New and Further Narrative," 13; *MeHSC* ser. 2, 6:166–67; *PRCC* 2:404, 406–7, 461–62; Christoph and Christoph, *Andros Papers,* 1:352, 355; *JR* 60:133, 185–87; Drake, *History of the Indian Wars,* 2:227; *LIR,* 165–66; Drake, *King Philip's War,* 122–23; Oberg, *Uncas,* 188.

60. *NYCD* 13:497 (quotes), 500; *AMD* 2:481, 15:97; Gehring, *Delaware Papers (English Period),* 18, 104.

61. *AMD* 5:134–35, 15:120–21 ("Old Fort about . . . ," "peace with . . ."); Christoph and Christoph, *Books of General Entries,* vol. 2, 130–32 ("wholly out of . . . ," 130); *PA* ser. 2, 7:782, 786–87; *MCARS* 2:245–46; *AMD* 5:152–53 ("confederat[ion]," "Sennico and Susquehannoh Indians," "the bloodiest people"); Landis, "Location of the Susquehannock Fort," 114–15. The Susquehannocks' settlement was opposite modern-day Washington Borough, Pennsylvania.

62. Christoph and Christoph, *Andros Papers,* 2:53; *AMD* 5:135 ("Mischief done by . . ."), 147–48 ("robb[ing] divers plantations"); *PRCC* 2:480 ("common [Algonquian] enemie"), 489, 495; *NYCD* 13:504 ("Eastward," "as friends," "Christians"); *RGCMB* 5:123.

63. Christoph and Christoph, *Andros Papers,* 2:160–61, 3:25–26; *NYCD* 4:252–53.

64. *LIR,* 40–41 ("Mahicanders and North Indians," "while we are . . ."); *NYCD* 3:242, 13:502, 508–13, 517, 521 ("but one"); *PRCC* 2:92–93, 502; Drake, *History of the Indian Wars,* 2:226–29 ("Blind Will," 228); *RGCMB* 5:134, 138, 165–67; *MCARS* 2:199n; *CNYCM,* 29; Drake, *Indian Captivities,* 60–62.

65. *AMD* 2:25–27, 5:243–51 ("divers murders and outrages," "Cinnigos and divers . . ." 243), 15:149–53; *NYCD* 13:507–8; Semmes, *Captains and Mariners,* 468–85; Robinson, "Tributary Indians"; Rountree and Davidson, *Eastern Shore Indians,* 99–121.

66. *LIR,* 42–48 ("Christians and Indians," 43; "Capt[ain]," "som[e] hoggs and beasts," 44; "up the axe," "Intertein," 48); *JR* 61:25 ("bloody flux"), 31; *MCARS* 2:257; *AMD* 5:251–60, 263, 15:164–69.

67. Christoph and Christoph, *Andros Papers,* 2:182–83 ("behind Virginia," 183); *WA,* 8 (all other quotes); Richter, "Rediscovered Links," 46–47; *NYCD* 13:516; *LIR,* 56. For evidence of long-standing Iroquois memory of seventeenth-century Susquehannock adoptions, see Abler, *Cornplanter,* 113.

68. *JR* 54:169, 283, 55:171, 56:115, 57:249, 60:135, 173 ("after the missionaries . . . ," "their chapels and . . ."), 185–87, 211 ("gave valuable presents," "Nadoussiens," "lure all our savages . . ."); *NYCD* 9:126 ("to reconcile the minds . . ."), 13:499–500; Houghton, "Seneca Nation," 431, 436 (Bunce Site); Coyne, "Exploration of the Great Lakes," 71; Christoph and Christoph, *Andros Papers,* 1:432–33; *RAPQ* (1926–27): 93; Eccles, *Frontenac,* 81. For the Tionnontaté population estimate, see Branstner, "Tionontate Huron Occupation," 195.

69. Margry, *Découvertes,* 1:319–20; *JR* 63:195.

70. Margry, *Découvertes,* 1:321 ("Marie-Félix," "like slaves"); *JR* 59:285 ("being low in . . ."), 63:191 ("a league and . . ."). For evidence of analogous distances and rationales for village relocation elsewhere in Iroquoia, see *JR* 62:55; Belmont, "Histoire," 45; Engelbrecht, *Iroquoia,* 106, 126.

71. *JR* 59:269–85 ("a captain of the . . . ," "in the name of the . . . ," 277), 289, 60:145–47, 62:69,

63:189, 199 ("Hot Powder," "all the noise . . . ," "see for themselves"); *CMRNF* 1:257. For evidence of other recruiting missions and the ongoing visits by Iroquois people to the Laurentian settlements, see *JR* 59:261–63, 60:291–93, 61:65, 63:195–97.

72. *JR* 59:283 ("captain of the . . ."), 289, 60:177 ("the best mind . . ."), 63:199; *LIR,* 47 ("Canondondarwe"); Christoph and Christoph, *Andros Papers,* 2:53; Colden, *History of the Five Indian Nations Depending on the Province of New-York,* 51. Canondondarwe appears to have served as Wolf clan speaker for Tionnontogouen circa 1677–85, see *NYCD* 13:524 ("Cannonundawa"); *AMD* 15:165 ("Cannondondawe"), 17:200 ("Cannondowane"); *MCARS* 2:469; *LIR,* 88; Colden, *History of the Five Indian Nations Depending on the Province of New-York,* 51 ("Connondowe").

73. *JR* 12:272–73n11, 59:285–87, 316n51, 60:275–77 ("captains," "4 captains . . . ," 277), 287–89, 293 (Tiwates'kon), 61:57–59, 201; Louise Tremblay, "La Politique Missionaire," 50–51.

74. *JR* 63:195 (quotes).

75. Ibid., 60:309, 61:53 ("inclination," "quite contrary dispositions," "fully determined . . ."), 55 ("lofty sentiments . . ."), 239, 62:169, 175–77, 63:201–5, 217–19; Kip, *Early Jesuit Missions,* 86–87 ("Iroquois nation," 87). The most significant works among the voluminous literature on Kateri Tekakwitha include Greer, *Mohawk Saint;* Koppedrayer, "Making of the First Iroquois Virgin"; Shoemaker, *Negotiators of Change,* 49–71; Holmes, "Narrative Repatriation."

76. *RFF,* 91 ("very great wanderings"), 93–94 ("frequent journeys," "instability"), 95, 97, 101; Hennepin, *New Discovery,* 1:46–49 ("Forty cottages," 48; "through their vast . . . ," "two hundred leagues . . . ," 49), 74, 2:539 ("Ganneousekaera"); Hennepin, *Description of Louisiana,* 59; *JR* 62:169, 275n16; Margry, *Découvertes,* 1:296–98; Donnelly "Belmont's History of Brandy," 52–53, 57; Eccles, *Frontenac,* 70; Tremblay, "La Politique Missionaire," 57.

77. Margry, *Découvertes,* 1:294 ("barque," "bridle"); *JR* 59:201–3 ("a goodly number . . . ," 201), 60:167; *NYCD* 3:247, 9:128, 13:503; *MCARS* 2:211; Hennepin, *New Discovery,* 1:42–43. For a description of French "barques," see *NYCD* 9:613n1.

78. Richter, "Rediscovered Links," 76 (quotes). Cf. *WA,* 9.

79. *NYCD* 3:260, 13:531–32 (quotes).

80. Hennepin, *Description of Louisiana,* 65 ("brigantine"), 67 ("little village"), 69 ("Fresh seas"), 73 ("very fine road," "house defended by . . ."); Hennepin, *New Discovery,* 1:78–80 ("a great Hanger . . . ," 80); Cox. *Journeys of Réné Robert Cavelier,* 1:2–3, 94–95 ("strait of communication," 94); Margry, *Découvertes,* 1:441–42 ("umbrage," 442), 575–76, 2:12–14; Roberts, *Encyclopedia of Historic Forts,* 569. For claims of a fortified storehouse constructed by La Salle at Niagara in 1676, see *NYCD* 9:126; *JR* 60:135, 319n21. No mention of this structure appears in the accounts of the 1678–79 construction of Fort de Conty.

81. Hennepin, *Description of Louisiana,* 76–87 ("Tegarondies," 76; "strict watch," 83); Hennepin, *New Discovery,* 1:81–93; Margry, *Découvertes,* 1:576–78, 2:8; Jordan, "Seneca Iroquois Settlement Pattern," 29; Calnan, "Moïse Hillaret." Tegarondies is known to archaeologists as the Rochester Junction site.

82. Hennepin, *New Discovery,* 1:101 ("very busie . . ."), 102–3, 107 ("a great many . . . ," "Warlike Expedition"); Hennepin, *Description of Louisiana,* 90–91. For identification of the "Tintoha" as the Teton Sioux, see Hennepin, *New Discovery,* 1:107n1, 223, 225; Margry, *Découvertes,* 1:481; Anderson, *Kinsmen of Another Kind,* 23–24; Raymond J. DeMallie, "Sioux Until 1850," in DeMallie, *Plains,* 720, 725.

83. Hennepin, *New Discovery* 1:101 ("remove the jealousie . . ."); Christoph and Christoph, *Andros Papers,* 3:544; Cox, *Journeys of Réné Robert Cavelier,* 1:116; *NYCD* 9:163; Charlevoix, *History,* 3:204. For a brief April 1679 reference by Andros to Iroquois reports of French efforts to send a "Garrison of settlement" into an Iroquois town south of Lake Ontario (which likely represented garbled intelligence of either La Salle's activities or a visit by French traders

from Fort Frontenac to Seneca country), see *NYCD* 3:278.

84. *IHC* 23:11–15 (quotes). I contend, on the basis of La Salle's prior familiarity with Seneca country, that his "Sanchioragon" is a version of "Gandachiaragou," which the Jesuits assigned to the large western (Dann site) Seneca village in 1668 (see *JR* 54:81). This claim is at odds with extant archaeological interpretation of the terminal point of occupancy for Dann. Cf. Jordan, "Seneca Iroquois Settlement Pattern," 29.

85. Hennepin, *New Discovery,* 1:134 (quotes), 158–59; Margry, *Découvertes,* 1:491, 495, 2:93–102.

86. *NYCD* 13:536 ("or others in . . ."); *AMD* 15:175–76 ("scour[ed] the heads . . . ," 176), 183–87 ("foreign Indians," 187), 213–14 ("easily distinguish . . . ," 213), 238–42 ("will never cease . . . ," 241), 251–52, 383, 17:5; *LIR,* 56; *WA,* 9; Colden, *History of the Five Indian Nations Depending on the Province of New-York,* 22–28; James and Jameson, *Journal of Jasper Danckaerts,* 137.

87. *LIR,* 48–55 (quotes).

88. Ibid., 53–61 (quotes); *CVSP* 1:12; Colden, *History of the Five Indian Nations Depending on the Province of New-York,* 28–31.

89. *AMD* 5:272 ("Susquahannough Fort"), 15:283 ("Senniquo"), 285–87, 293, 300–306, 311; Hennepin, *Description of Louisiana,* 267 ("eight hundred men . . ."); Hennepin, *New Discovery,* 1:341 ("four hundred Leagues"); *NYCD* 9:191.

90. Margry, *Découvertes,* 1:504–8 ("un Jésuite," 508), 586; Cox, *Journeys of Réné Robert Cavelier,* 1:8–9 ("protection," "greatly irritated," 9), 117; Hennepin, *New Discovery,* 1:338–39; *NYCD* 9:161–62; Callender, "Illinois," 673. Tamaroa was located in the modern-day state of Missouri, across the Illinois River from present-day Cahokia, Illinois.

91. Cox, *Journeys of Réné Robert Cavelier,* 1:12–13 ("six packets of . . . ," "eaten his [French] children"); Hennepin, *Description of Louisiana,* 267 ("who had only . . .").

92. Cox, *Journeys of Réné Robert Cavelier,* 1:10–13, 118–20, 129–30 ("Ozage," 129); Margry, *Découvertes,* 1:510–13, 519–20, 527–28 ("three thousand beavers," "contrary to the . . . ," 527), 532; Lahontan, *New Voyages,* 2:486–88; Hennepin, *New Discovery,* 1:340–41; *NYCD* 9:163. On the possible expedition against the Otoes circa 1681–82, see Lahontan, *New Voyages,* 1:198–99; "The Prehistoric and Historic Habitat of the Missouri and Oto Indians," in *Oto and Missouri Indians,* 17–19; O'Brien, *Paradigms of the Past,* 463.

93. *NYCD* 9:147 ("embarassed Sieur de . . ."); *RGCMB* 5:299–300 ("invasions, depredation, and . . . ," 299); *NYCD* 3:271–76, 13:519–31 ("should be held . . . ," 525); Christoph and Christoph, *Books of General Entries,* vol. 2, 244; *RCNP* 10:366–67, 390, 395, 398, 404; *JR* 63:213–15; Le Roy de la Potherie, *Histoire,* 1:298; Clifton, *Prairie People,* 19–20.

94. *PP* 1:179–83 ("many hard things," 181; "the eastward side . . . ," 182; "near £90," 183); *RGCMB* 5:319–21 (all other quotes 320). Bridenbaugh misdates this conference to 1683.

95. *RGCMB* 5:320 ("covenant," "Governor of Cannida . . ."); *WA,* 9–10 ("to go to Canada . . . ," 10); Richter, "Rediscovered Links," 56; *NYCD* 9:136.

96. *MCARS* 2:422–23 (quotes).

97. *NYCD* 9:129 ("carry[ing] their peltries . . ."), 132–39, 150 ("constitutes their wealth . . ."); *JR* 62:185.

98. *NYCD* 9:142 ("in the bush"), 159–60 ("double," 160); *MCARS* 3:143–44 (all other quotes 143), 251–52.

99. *NYCD* 9:145–47 (quotes), 150.

100. Ibid., 9:147 ("satisfaction," "explain their conduct"); Hennepin, *Description of Louisiana,* 260–64 ("spoke for his . . . ," 263); Hennepin, *New Discovery,* 1:316–17, 326–28.

101. *NYCD* 9:163–64 ("influential," 163), 176 ("Feast of the Dead"); Belmont, "Histoire," 34 ("Hannonsache"); *JR* 62:93–95, 213, 63:223 ("kept all Canada . . ."); Roberts, *Encyclopedia of Historic Forts,* 416–17, 421. Fort de Buade was located near modern-day St. Ignace, Michigan.

102. *AMD* 17:198–99 ("Speaker," 198); *NYCD* 3:445, 9:169 ("at the fort . . ."), 170 ("men [as well] as women"), 190, 255.

103. Dubé, *La Nouvelle France,* 36–37 (quote 36).

104. *NYCD* 9:174 ("Téchoueguen, or la Famine"); Belmont, "Histoire," 34 ("put Onontio into the kettle"). La Famine was located near modern-day Selkirk Shores State Park, New York.

105. *NYCD* 3:442, 9:175, 177, 183, 191 (quotes); Belmont, "Histoire," 34.

106. *NYCD* 9:177–82 (quotes); *JR* 62:71–93.

107. *JR* 62:73 ("alive"), 79 ("largest in the . . ."), 95 ("have never had . . ."), 151–53 ("annihilate," "make Iroquous," "strengthening themselves with," 153), 185; *AMD* 17:5 ("Southern Indians"); Cox, *Journeys of Réné Robert Cavelier,* 1:31; Bradley, *Evolution of the Onondaga Iroquois,* 206; Bowne, *Westo Indians,* 89–107. The Onondaga town hosting Lamberville in 1682 is known to archaeologists as the Weston site.

108. *NYCD* 9:183–89 (quotes); *CMRNF* 1:289; Dubé, *La Nouvelle France,* 107.

109. *AMD* 5:280–81, 322, 331, 348–49, 7:110–11, 15:353–54, 358–59 ("Sinniquos," 359), 373–76, 380, 383, 385, 406, 408, 410, 418, 17:4–6 ("make an end," 4).

110. Ibid., 17:8–10, 12–15 ("Zachaiah fort," 12; "great men," 13; "into the fort . . . ," "the Pascattoway Indians . . . ," "could not be . . . ," 14), 19–21, 25, 29–30, 200–202; Feest, "Nanticoke and Neighboring Tribes," 243. Zachaiah Fort was located approximately four miles southeast of modern-day La Plata, Maryland.

111. *AMD* 5:348–49 ("well within the power," 349), 7:270, 334–35, 370–72, 17:78, 98–103, 110, 115, 197–200, 204–5, 208–9; *NYCD* 3:321–28, 13:555–65 ("not detained but . . . ," 564); *MCARS* 3:264–66, 271–73, 307 ("suddenly died," "Maryland Indians"); *JR* 62:67; Gehring, *Delaware Papers (English Period),* 355; *PA* ser. 1, 5:729; *LIR,* 61–65; Christoph and Christoph, *Books of General Entries,* vol. 2, 260.

112. *JR* 62:157–65 (quotes); Dubé, *La Nouvelle France,* 57–58; *NYCD* 9:210; *CMRNF* 1:551.

113. *NYCD* 9:200, 204 ("Montreal rascals"), 215–16 (all other quotes 215).

114. *JR* 61:159 ("only Crosses, rebuffs . . . ," "regarded them as . . ."), 62:67, 223–25 ("so haughty that . . ."), 63:57; Hennepin, *Description of Louisiana,* 310–11.

115. Margry, *Découvertes,* 5:7 (quote); *NYCD* 9:197–98, 201; *JR* 62:209; Blair, *Indian Tribes,* 2:13–16.

116. *DHNY* 1:398–99 (quotes); *NYCD* 3:334, 447; *JR* 62:169, 257.

117. *JR* 62:167 ("in a very high . . ."), 169 ("Indian corn"), 171–83 ("very fickle," 171), 187 ("savage women," "sometimes propound to . . ."), 243, 249–51, 63:227; *NYCD* 9:209 ("good Iroquois soldiers"); Dubé, *La Nouvelle France,* 63 ("180 *arpents*"); Colden, *History of the Five Indian Nations Depending on the Province of New-York,* 40n; Smith, *History of the Province of New York,* 1:56 ("Praying Indians"). For evidence of persistent national diversity among Iroquois residents of the Laurentian settlements, see Waterman, *"To Do Justice to Him and Myself,"* 155, 192.

118. *JR* 62:169, 179–81, 185 ("disputes"), 245 ("a truly Christian"), 247 (all other quotes), 253; Belmont, "Histoire," 35.

119. *JR* 62:255–57 (quotes); *NYCD* 9:206, 212–13; Dubé, *La Nouvelle France,* 63; Lahontan, *New Voyages,* 1:55–56.

120. Belmont, "Histoire," 35 ("Captain"); *NYCD* 9:202–3 (all other quotes).

121. Belmont, "Histoire," 35–36 (quotes).

122. *NYCD* 9:202, 226–27 (quotes); *JR* 61:21, 62:99, 103–7, 225–31, 272n9; Belmont, "Histoire," 17.

123. *PWP* 2:260–61, 423 ("Sachems of the . . ."), 424, 429, 479, 481–82 ("had nothing to do . . . ," 482); Hall, *Narratives of Early Maryland,* 440 ("great expence of . . ."); *NYCD* 9:227.

124. *DHNY* 1:393–95 (quotes); *LIR,* 69–71; *MCARS* 3:379–81.

125. *PWP* 2:87 ("put a stop . . ."); *DHNY* 1:95–97 (all other quotes).

126. *PWP* 2:468, 498–99, 3:132 ("hinder"), 159; *LIR,* 112–14; *DHNY* 1:399; Richter, "Rediscovered

Links," 63–66; *NYCD* 9:218. Penn did not vacate Dongan's Iroquois deed until January 1697, when he obtained a 1,000-year lease from the former New York governor for a payment of £100 (see *PWP* 3:477–78).

127. *NYCD* 9:228 ("censure," "apprehension of losing . . ."); *LIR*, 70–71 ("young men," 70); *VECJ* 1:52–54 ("Senecas," "Mattapony Indian Town," "Chickahominy fort," "riffl[ing]," 53), 496; *AMD* 17:229, 369 ("Eastern Shore"); McIlwaine, *Journals of the House of Burgesses of Virginia,1659/60–1693*, 205.

128. *NYCD* 9:228 (quotes); Lahontan, *New Voyages*, 1:58. See also Lahontan, *New Voyages*, 2:488–94, for Lahontan's vivid description of a winter 1683–84 Iroquois campaign against the Fox, and Peyser and Brandão, *Edge of Empire*, 41, for an account of a large-scale Iroquois attack on the Mascoutens circa 1683.

129. *NYCD* 3:444–45, 451 ("fifteen or sixteen . . . ," "Scious"), 9:230, 232; Dubé, *La Nouvelle France*, 130–33, 161–68, 175–81, 184–88, 193; Cox, *Journeys of Réné Robert Cavelier*, 1:31–32, 59; Margry, *Découvertes*, 1:614; Peyser and Brandão, *Edge of Empire*, 43; Roberts, *Encylopedia of Historic Forts*, 268. Fort St. Louis was located near modern-day Utica, Illinois.

130. *NYCD* 3:447–48 ("forbid those at . . . ," 448), 451, 9:223, 226 ("ambassador," "suite"), 239–40, 258; *MCARS* 3:463.

131. *NYCD* 9:229–31 (quotes); Perrot, Blair, *Indian Tribes*, 1:231–32.

132. *NYCD* 9:230, 252–55 (quotes).

133. *MCARS* 3:470 ("weaken themselves"); *NYCD* 3:449 ("voluntarily given up . . . ," "Indyan Castles," "the coates of armes . . ."), 9:253 ("joy," "flesh," "as good as . . .").

134. *NYCD* 9:228 ("ragged ship's flag," "armorial bearings of . . . ," "public chest," "the light"), 247 ("rhodomontade"); Richter, "Rediscovered Links," 63–65 ("Duke of York's armes . . . ," "catched at [them] . . . ," 64); Dubé, *La Nouvelle France*, 243 ("bourgs"); *NYCD* 9:257 ("drunken man," "proclamations," "Duke of York's . . ."); Colden, *History of the Five Indian Nations which are dependent on the Province of New-York*, 51 ("cannot defend us . . ."); Olds, "Journal of Chevalier de Baugy," 42–43 ("the arms of England," 42; "great friend of the English," 43); Belmont, "Histoire du Canada," 45 ("Ganonkentahaoui"); Jordan, "Seneca Iroquois Settlement Pattern," 29. For evidence of Senecas preserving a French flag into the early nineteenth century, see Abler, *Cornplanter*, 181.

135. *NYCD* 3:417–18 (quotes 417), 444, 543–44.

136. Ibid., 3:347, 350, 394, 9:233, 241, 254 , 256–57 (quotes); 259, 261; Colden, *History of the Five Indian Nations which are dependent on the Province of New-York*, 50.

137. *NYCD* 3:450 ("towards the 20th . . . ," "chastisement of those . . ."); Lahontan, *New Voyages*, 1:71 ("Needles, Knives, Powder . . ."); Dubé, *La Nouvelle France*, 219 ("Iroquois chrestiens"); Mourin, "Porter la Guerre Chez les Iroquois," 12–14.

138. *NYCD* 9:229, 232, 240–42 ("Brandy and Tobacco," 241), 254, 256–57 ("pensioner," 257), 260; *JR* 63:241–43 (all other quotes); Charlevoix, *History*, 3:249.

139. *NYCD* 3:347, 9:242 ("furious rage," "had granted them . . . ," "conclude affairs"), 257–58 (all other quotes); Charlevoix, *History*, 3:252; Colden, *History of the Five Indian Nations which are dependent on the Province of New-York*, 50–51.

140. Lahontan, *New Voyages*, 1:72–73 ("dismiss," 72; "dissatisfied," "threw out all . . . ," 73); *NYCD* 9:242, 245 (all other quotes); Blair, *Indian Tribes*, 1:233–40; Belmont, "Histoire," 37.

141. *NYCD* 9:237–38 (quote 237), 243. Cf. versions in Dubé, *La Nouvelle France*, 226–29; *DHNY* 1:117–20.

142. Lahontan, *New Voyages*, 1:74–75 (quotes); *NYCD* 9:242; Charlevoix, *History*, 3:256; *CMRNF* 1:553.

143. Lahontan, *New Voyages*, 1:75–79 (quotes). Senecas at Ganondagan greeted Hennepin with

a calumet ceremony in May 1681 (see Hennepin, *New Discovery*, 1:326). Lahontan claimed in 1684 (*New Voyages*, 1:58) that League meetings included a "Union Feast," where all "Deputies" from the "five Cantons" joined to "smoak in the great Calumet, or Pipe of the Five Nations." For general discussion of the calumet ceremony's relationship to freedom of movement among indigenous peoples of the upper Great Lakes and continental interior, see Le Roy de la Potherie, *Histoire*, 1:226–30; Blair, *Indian Tribes*, 1:182–86, 2:72–73, 96n; *JR* 58:97–99, 59:129–37; *IHC* 23:9, 389–91; Cox, *Journeys of Réné Robert Cavelier*, 1:118; Hennepin, *New Discovery*, 1:228; *An Account of the Treaty . . .*, 16–17; Lahontan, *New Voyages* 1:169, 189; Le Sueur, "History of the Calumet," 11; Rob Mann, "Smokescreens: Tobacco, Pipes, and the Transformational Power of Fur Trade Rituals," in Rafferty and Mann, *Smoking and Culture*, 165–83. Cf. Fenton, *Iroquois Eagle Dance*, 153–72.

144. *NYCD* 9:259 ("venal being"), 702–3; Lahontan, *New Voyages*, 1:79–85 (all other quotes); *JR* 63:245.

145. *NYCD* 9:237–38, 247–48 ("sycophant who seeks . . . ," "fooled," "most shameful manner"), 259–61; Lahontan, *New Voyages* 1:86 ("no more than . . ."), 88 ("great Stakes . . ."); Blair, *Indian Tribes*, 1:242–43; Hennepin, *New Discovery*, 2:550–51. For a description of Otreouti echoing that given by De Meulles, see Hennepin, *Description of Louisiana*, 307.

146. *NYCD* 3:323 ("all [the] Indians . . ."), 9:249 (all other quotes), 260–61; *LIR*, 75.

5. Over the Forest, Part 1, 1685–1693

1. *NYCD* 4:82.
2. Alfred, *Peace, Power, Righteousness*, xxiii; Gibson, *Concerning the League*, xlv–xlvi, xlix; Dan Longboat, "Haudenosaunee Meet the World Eaters in the Fur Trade: Capitalism vs. the Natural World," in Johnston, *Aboriginal People and the Fur Trade*, 86–89.
3. *RFF*, 153 (quote); *NYCD* 9:269–72.
4. *LIR*, 76, 79–81 (quotes); Lahontan, *New Voyages*, 1:91–95.
5. *VECJ* 1:71–72 ("two Indians from . . . ," 71), 369, 506; *LIR*, 83–89 ("troops," 87); *AMD* 17:365–69; Richter, "Rediscovered Links," 59–60; Colden, *History of the Five Indian Nations Depending on the Province of New-York*, 43–44; Tinling, *Correspondence of the Three William Byrds*, 1:44, 55; *CSPC* 12:114; *CNYCM*, 43; *NYCD* 3:454; Christian F. Feest, "Nanticoke and Neighboring Tribes," in Trigger, *Northeast*, 249–50. League war parties also targeted Siouan nations such as the Tuteloes and Saponis at this time. See Dixon, "A Saponi by Any Other Name," 71; Vest, "An Odyssey Among the Iroquois," 126-27.
6. *NYCD* 3:363 ("King's Dominions"); *LIR*, 83–84 (all other quotes); Peyser and Brandão, *Edge of Empire*, 9. Cf. evidence of a similarly strong beaver trade in New France in 1685 (the final year before the issue of a limited number of fur trade licenses) in *NYCD* 9:287; Lahontan, *New Voyages*, 1:99–101.
7. *LIR*, 84 (quotes); *NYCD* 3:445; Severance, *Old Frontier of France*, 1:96-106.
8. Lahontan, *New Voyages*, 1:91 ("smuggling"), 99; *NYCD* 3:461, 476, 9:274–81 (all other quotes), 286–90; *RFF*, 155; *LIR*, 93–94.
9. *NYCD* 9:274, 283–85 (quotes).
10. Ibid., 3:456, 9:293–96, 313 (quotes); *LIR*, 100.
11. *NYCD* 9:287–89 (quotes), 290, 300, 306; Margry, *Découvertes*, 5:22–25; *WHSC* 16:127–30; *RFF*, 160; Roberts, *Encyclopedia of Historic Forts*, 423–24.
12. *LIR*, 97–100, 103–4 (quotes); *NYCD* 3:418, 455, 9:296–97, 299; *DHNY* 1:404–5; Lahontan, *New Voyages*, 1:103; Richter, "Rediscovered Links," 67, 76–77; *CLNY* 1:211; Christoph, *Dongan*

Papers, 34–42.

13. *NYCD* 3:463, 488–89, 9:297–98, 302 ("Antoine L'Epinart . . ."), 308, 318–20; Richter, "Rediscov-ered Links," 77–78 (all other quotes 77); *LIR*, 106–7.

14. *NYCD* 3:442, 444, 9:298–301 ("colony must be put down . . . ," "if war [against the Iroquois] . . . ," "unwilling that we . . . ," "corn fields at . . ."), 324–25 ("submit themselves," 324); Olds, "Journal of Chevalier de Baugy," 10–11.

15. *NYCD* 3:393–95, 454, 9:297, 303–5 ("Memoir in Proof . . ."), 306, 308–9, 377–84, 394–95, 418. The 1686 French "Memoir" cited the discoveries of Cartier, Champlain's (claimed) multiple military victories over the Iroquois, the Gannentaha mission and fort in Onondaga country circa 1656–58, the 1666 Talon treaty, and the 1669 act of possession by Dollier de Casson and Bréhant de Galinée.

16. *LIR*, 109–11 (quotes), 135–36; *NYCD* 3:395, 395n, 476; Richter, "Rediscovered Links," 78; Robin-son, *Toronto*, 49-50; Charles Callender, "Miami," in Trigger, *Northeast*, 688; Sivertsen, *Turtles, Wolves, and Bears*, 31-32.

17. *NYCD* 3:392–94, 396 ("the arms of . . . ," "castle"), 416, 464; *LIR*, 110–12 (all other quotes), 113–17; Lahontan, *New Voyages*, 1:137; Richter, "Rediscovered Links," 79; NYSA, A1894, 35:54 (April 7, 1687 [O.S.]). Cf. McConville, *King's Three Faces*, 233.

18. *NYCD* 3:388–89, 9:300, 313–16, 321–22, 358–59; *CMRNF* 1:352–62, 372–81; *LIR*, 117; Blair, *Indian Tribes*, 1:245, 249–51; Mourin, "Porter la Guerre," 11-12.

19. *NYCD* 3:44, 9:324–25, 338; *LIR*, 114–16 (quote 114), 118, 122; Richter, "Rediscovered Links," 68, 79; *JR* 64:249; Bradley, *Evolution of the Onondaga Iroquois*, 113, 118, 223n3, 224n8.

20. *NYCD* 9:315, 328, 337, 358 (quotes 328); *LIR*, 125–26, 137–39; Cox, *Journeys of Réné Robert Cavelier*, 1:38; *JR* 63:283, 64:241, 249; Catalogne, "Recueil," 13–14; Billings, *Papers of Baron Howard*, 313–14, 322–23; Lahontan, *New Voyages*, 1:120.

21. NYSA A1894, 35:171 (June 24/July 4, 1687) ("as subjects of . . . ," "molest or disturb . . ."); *LIR*, 119–20 (all other quotes), 123, 131.

22. *LIR*, 120n ("in case any . . ."), 122, 124, 127, 131; *NYCD* 3:444, 465 (all other quotes), 503–4, 533–34; *PA* ser. 1, 1:104–5. Cf. documented recitations of the Tawagonshi tradition (most of which occurred in Albany) from 1656 to 1701: 1656 (*JR* 43:107–9); 1658 (ibid., 44:207); July 8, 1687 (Richter, "Rediscovered Links," 68); July 7, 1689 (ibid., 81); June 12, 1691 (*NYCD* 3:775); May 15, 1694 (*WA*, 24); August 25, 1694 (*Account of the Treaty*, 7); August 1, 1698 (*Propositions Made by the Five Nations of Indians*, 4–5); September 8, 1700 (*NYCD* 4:733); July 30, 1701 (ibid., 4:909). For a 1691 English claim of an Iroquois surrender of territory "in the time of the Dutch," see ibid., 3:797.

23. *LIR*, 126–27 ("messengers who have . . . ," 126); Olds, "Journal of Chevalier de Baugy," 15 ("Christian Iroquois"); *JR* 63:269; *NYCD* 3:431 ("Krynne the Maquase"), 433, 435, 9:331 ("domi-ciled," "various missions"), 340 ("old Carignan officers"), 342, 359–60 ("dragoons in France," 359); Belmont, "Histoire," 44.

24. Lahontan, *New Voyages*, 1:124; *NYCD* 3:480, 523, 9:77n1, 315, 331–32, 341 ("most disorderly"), 360–63 (all other quotes 360–61); Olds, "Journal of Chevalier de Baugy," 14, 18–20, 29; Cata-logne, "Recueil," 13; *JR* 64:241–49; Canada, *Censuses of Canada* 4:16-21. Denonville eventu-ally shipped at least thirty-six (*JR* 63: 281) and possibly as many as sixty (*IHC* 23:134–35; *NYCD* 3:514) Iroquois men to France in 1687. Individuals described as "Chief captains" and "principal warriors" may have accounted for twenty-seven or twenty-eight of the so-called Iroquois *galériens* (*NYCD* 3:560 ["principal warriors"], 579, ["Chief captains"], 621). Twenty-one survivors boarded ships bound to New France in 1689 (*CMRNF* 1:454; Lahontan, *New Voyages* 1:233), but only thirteen are known to have survived the voyage back to North America (*JR* 64:241–43; Richter, "Rediscovered Links," 70). Cf. Olive P. Dickason, "Amerindians

in Renaissance Europe," in Gough and Christie, *New Dimensions in Ethnohistory*, 12–13. Otondiata (modern-day Grenadier Island, opposite Leeds County, Ontario) was the site of an Iroquois eel-fishery; it also marked the final portage between Montréal and Lake Ontario. See *NYCD* 9:77n, 83.

25. Lahontan, *New Voyages*, 1:121–22 (quotes); *NYCD* 9:341; Olds, "Journal of Chevalier de Baugy," 27; *JR* 64:247–49; *WJP* 10:12.

26. Olds, "Journal of Chevalier de Baugy," 20–22, 29–33 ("enraged because their . . . ," "slip[ped] into the . . . ," 29–30), 37 ("Huron of Missilimaki," "boatman"), 38, 40; Belmont, "Histoire," 42–43 ("Garistatsi and Gannagenroguen . . ."); *NYCD* 3:431, 433, 446–47 ("were resolved not to . . . ," 447), 9:364–66; *JR* 63:275; Cox, *Journeys of Réné Robert Cavelier*, 1:39 (all other quotes); *IHC* 23:134; Blair, *Indian Tribes*, 1:251, 255; Grumet, *Historic Contact*, 406; Mohawk, *War against the Seneca*, 11. For evidence of Seneca women participating in the defense of their homelands in 1779, see Graymont, *Iroquois in the American Revolution*, 212.

27. *NYCD* 3:431–32, 479 ("hoop and hollow," "fought very well . . ."), 9:337–38, 364–65 ("three columns," 364); Lahontan, *New Voyages*, 1:127–30 ("their own country," 130); Olds, "Journal of Chevalier de Baugy," 34–37 ("The reason why . . . ," "because they wore . . . ," 37); *WHSC* 16:140; *JR* 63:273–75; Belmont, "Histoire," 41–45; Cox, *Journeys of Réné Robert Cavelier*, 1:39; Marshall, *Narrative of the Expedition*, 157–59; *LIR*, 133; Blair, *Indian Tribes*, 1:255; Babcock, "Places of Special Historical Interest"; Selden, "Denonville's Army"; Jemison, "Ganondagan Lives On," 3. Cf. inflated casualty estimates for the July 13, 1687, battle reported in Lahontan, *New Voyages*, 1:128–29; *LIR*, 129–30.

28. Belmont, "Histoire," 45 ("famous Babylon"); Lahontan, *New Voyages*, 1:130–31 ("fruitless adventure," 130); *NYCD* 3:431–32 ("out-fields," 432), 9:338 (all other quotes); Olds, "Journal of Chevalier de Baugy," 28, 38–39.

29. Margry, *Découvertes*, 5:26–27 ("the largest of . . . ," 27); Olds, "Journal of Chevalier de Baugy," 42–44 ("board written upon," "hatchet," 43); *NYCD* 3:435, 437, 476, 481, 9:367 ("Gannounata"), 338 (all other quotes); Belmont, "Histoire," 45; Lahontan, *New Voyages*, 1:125–26; Blair, *Indian Tribes*, 1:252; *JR* 63:275–77, 283, 289; Viele, *Viele Records*, 21, 29–30.

30. *NYCD* 9:339, 365–68 (bushel estimate 368n1); Olds, "Journal of Chevalier de Baugy," 39–44; Belmont, "Histoire," 45–46; Blair, *Indian Tribes*, 2:58; *LIR*, 112.

31. *NYCD* 9:300, 302, 339 ("a secure asylum . . ."), 367–69 ("Iroquois," 368); Lahontan, *New Voyages*, 1:132 ("either destroy'd or . . ."), 139–40n2, 149, 220 ("General and Chief Counselor," "totally routed"); William N. Fenton, "Kondiaronk," *DCB* 2:320-23; Tooker, "Wyandot," 405; Trigger, *Children of Aataentsic*, 30.

32. Catalogne, "Recueil," 16 (quotes); *NYCD* 9:369, 480, 518; Belmont, "Histoire," 46–47; *JR* 63:277–83; *IHC* 23:134; Olds, "Journal of Chevalier de Baugy," 45–51; *WHSC* 16:128; Le Roy de la Potherie, *Histoire*, 2:484; Blair, *Indian Tribes*, 1:252–53n.

33. Cf. Jennings, *Ambiguous Iroquois Empire*, 187, 191; Richter, *Ordeal of the Longhouse*, 195.

34. *JR* 63:279, 64:33 ("corn and bark houses"); Lahontan, *New Voyages*, 1:121 ("unfavorable Issue of . . ."); *NYCD* 3:478–79, 482, 9:375–77 ("Termination of the . . . ," 375), 388, 392, 447 ("trifling impression," "Not one of . . . ," "as two arrows . . ."); Marshall, *Narrative of the Expedition*, 157. Examples of contemporary French boasting appear in *NYCD* 9:336, 369; Olds, "Journal of Chevalier de Baugy," 50.

35. Lahontan, *New Voyages*, 1:136 ("a thousand Iroquese"); *NYCD* 3:480–81 ("composed of all . . . ," 480), 9:347, 352–54, 369–70, 389–90; *RFF*, 164–74 ("inspired by the . . . ," 166), 180; *JR* 64:257 ("who had been . . ."); *LIR*, 133; Olds, "Journal of Chevalier de Baugy," 50; Belmont, "Histoire," 47–48; Rochemonteix, *Les Jésuites*, 3:621–27; Catalogne, "Recueil," 18–19.

36. Lahontan, *New Voyages*, 1:142 (quote); *JR* 63:279, 64:249–55, 281n34; *RFF*, 180.

37. *NYCD* 3:431–39 ("Captain," "would have peace . . . ," "Christian Indians at . . . ," "Native Coun-
    try," 439), 444, 483 ("General," "Cryn and his company"), 488 ("esteem"), 530, 9:354.
38. Ibid., 3432–38 ("first Castle," 432), 444, 478 ("Brethren, sisters, uncles . . ."), 527, 534, 9:352–54;
    Catalogne, "Recueil," 17.
39. Belmont, "Histoire," 47 (quote); *JR* 63:279, 289, 64:255–57; *NYCD* 9:353; *LIR,* 139–40; *PRCC*
    3:438–39.
40. *NYCD* 3:428–30 (quotes), 473–77, 503–4, 514–17, 529, 532; Dongan to William Blathwayt, Sep-
    tember 21, 1687 (O.S.), BP-CW, vol. 11; Christoph and Christoph, *Books of General Entries,* vol.
    2, 394; *LIR,* 137, 141; *JR* 63:291–93.
41. Blair, *Indian Tribes,* 2:35; *NYCD* 3:466–72, 507–9, 512–13, 517–18, 9:155 (1681 valuation of beaver
    pelts between 3 and 4 livres each, depending on quality), 337, 347, 355–56 ("to make war,"
    "general peace"), 370–71, 399 (peltry loss estimate), 403 (Michilimackinac estimate); Demers,
    "French Colonial Legacy," 40.
42. *NYCD* 3:442 (quote), 483, 9:408–9; *CMRNF* 1:476–77.
43. *NYCD* 3:439 ("bury the hatchet"); Blair, *Indian Tribes,* 1:255 ("make their excuses . . ."); Lahon-
    tan, *New Voyages,* 1:140–42 ("Iroquese Beaver-hunters," 140); Grumet, *Historic Contact,* 407;
    Sempowski and Saunders, *Dutch Hollow and Factory Hollow,* 3.
44. Whitmore, *Andros Tracts,* 7:76–78 (quote 77); *NYCD* 3:477, 479, 481, 484–86, 511, 579 (expense
    estimate), 699; *LIR,* 137, 143; *PA* ser. 1, 1:104; Peter Schuyler, "Account of Sundry Disbursements
    for Sundry Gifts and Presents made to ye Indians and Reliefe of Christian Prisoners," March
    12, 1687/88 (O.S.), BL 189, HEHL.
45. *NYCD* 3:480–81 ("among [all] the . . . ," 480), 517, 520–36 (all other quotes), 560–61, 9:389, 391,
    453; *LIR,* 140; Edward Randolph to John Povey, October 2, 1688 (O.S.), BL 139, HEHL.
46. *NYCD* 3:510 (quote), 565, 9:391; Belmont, "Histoire," 20; *IHC* 23:323–24; Lahontan, *New Voy-
    ages,* 1:152–56.
47. *CMRNF* 1:445–46; Richter, "Rediscovered Links," 81–82; Lahontan, *New Voyages,* 1:157–61;
    NYCD 3:611; Belmont, "Histoire," 49; Trowbridge, *Meearmeear Traditions,* 75–76. The incident
    depicted in the Miami oral account aligns best with an incident dated to the spring of 1687
    (Belmont, "Histoire," 38), though it could also refer to large-scale Iroquois attacks on the
    Miamis in 1681 (*NYCD* 9:163) or 1682 (*JR* 62:71–73). Cf. White, *Middle Ground,* 3–5; Rafert,
    Miami Indians of Indiana, 9–11.
48. Belmont, "Histoire," 48–49 ("ninety-one slaves," 49); *NYCD* 3:565 ("many more will . . .");
    Simms, *History of Schoharie County,* 23–35 (all other quotes); Brasser, *Riding the Frontier's
    Crest,* 13; Sivertsen, *Turtles, Wolves, and Bears,* 75. See also *History of Montgomery and Fulton
    Counties,* 34; Becker, *Native Americans,* ix–xi, 1.
49. Belmont, "Histoire," 48–49 ("Big Mouth," 48); *NYCD* 3:569, 9:384–86 ("wished only to . . . ,"
    "to observe a . . . ," 384–85), 390–91 ("exterminate," 390), 402; *JR* 64:255–57; *CMRNF* 1:454.
50. *NYCD* 3:534.
51. Ibid., 3:556, 561, 570 ("prevent some blow . . ."), 722 ("advantageous pass"), 9:386–88, 391, 396,
    402; Catalogne, "Recueil," 20; Belmont, "Histoire," 49; Lahontan, *New Voyages,* 1:143; *RFF,* 175.
52. *NYCD* 9:391 ("ambassadors"), 393; Lahontan, *New Voyages,* 1:149, 220–22 (all other quotes); *JR*
    64:257–59, 281n35.
53. *NYCD* 9:394 ("a snare laid . . ."), 402; Lahontan, *New Voyages,* 1:149, 221–22 ("old Iroquese
    Slave . . . ," 222); Blair, *Indian Tribes,* 1:252-55, 2:38–42 (all other quotes).
54. *NYCD* 3:554–55, 9:392–93, 396, 400, 403 ("added considerably to . . ."), 404–5, 411, 427; *CMRNF*
    1:432, 2:25, 27 ("The uncertainty we . . .").
55. *NYCD* 3:557–61, 565, 620; *WHSC* 16:134; *IHC* 23:324; Richter, "Rediscovered Links," 79; La-
    hontan, *New Voyages,* 1:207–8; Billings, *Papers of Lord Howard of Effingham,* 416–17; *RAPQ*

(1927–28): 21.

56. Richter, "Rediscovered Links," 80 (quote); *NYCD* 3:408, 9:422, 427–28; *CMRNF* 1:455–61, 463–64; Belmont, "Histoire," 49.

57. *NYCD* 3:575 ("utter Ruin of . . ."), 611–12, 618 ("engage them to . . ."), 619 ("Presents to be . . ."), 645, 726, 4:183, 186, 197, 9:433; *PRCC* 3:460 ("how matters stand . . ."); Richter, "Rediscovered Links," 82–83; *LIR,* 37-38, 124; *MeHSC* ser. 2, 9:38–39, 50–53. For an analogous example of widespread fear of Native attacks among Anglo-American settler populations, see Dowd, "Panic of 1751."

58. *PRCC* 3:460–63 ("tree of love . . . ," 462); Richter, "Rediscovered Links," 81 (all other quotes); *LIR,* 147–49; *NYCD* 3:599.

59. *JR* 64:67–93 (quotes); Belmont, "Histoire," 50; *NYCD* 3:714; Tooker, "League of the Iroquois," 424; Fenton, *Great Law and the Longhouse,* 193.

60. Belmont, "Histoire," 50 (quote); *JR* 64:71–73; Catalogne, "Recueil," 22.

61. Lahontan, *New Voyages,* 1:224–25 (quotes); Catalogne, "Recueil," 24–25; *NYCD* 3:621, 9:428–29, 431–32, 434–35; *JR* 64:33; Stephen van Cortlandt to William Blathwayt, December 18, 1689 (O.S.), BP-CW, vol. 9. Cf. Richter, "Rediscovered Links," 83n15; and Eccles, *Frontenac,* 192–94, who date the event to July 26, 1689 (its O.S. equivalent). Subsequent genealogical research has established that at least 42 French settlers were killed in the attack on Lachine, and the fate of another 41 Lachine residents is unknown. At least 17 French settlers were captured in the attack. See Girouard, *Lake St. Louis,* 117–39; Lamarche, "Les habitants de Lachine." For evidence of Lachine captives adopted by Iroquois families, see Catalogne, "Recueil," 53; Franquet, *Voyages,* 39.

62. Belmont, "Histoire," 50–51 ("shouted ninety times . . . ," "You deceived us . . ."); Blair, *Indian Tribes,* 2:42–43 ("covered with corpses," 43); Le Roy de la Potherie, *Histoire,* 2:448–49.

63. Richter, "Rediscovered Links," 84 ("Fort, Church"); Lahontan, *New Voyages,* 1:224 ("general Consternation"); *NYCD* 3:621, 9:438, 441, 451.

64. *RFF,* 177–83 (quote 179); Lahontan, *New Voyages,* 1:224–33; *NYCD* 9:435, 446; Le Roy de la Potherie, *Histoire,* 2:449; *RAPQ* (1927–28): 29; *LIR,* 162.

65. *RAPQ* (1927-28): 12–16; Rochemonteix, *Les Jesuites* 3:225–36.

66. *NYCD* 3:599 ("very slender trade"), 693, 9:463 ("their minds full . . ."); Lahontan, *New Voyages,* 1:208–9 ("hang'd," 209), *JR* 64:35 ("incomparably more advantageous"); Blair, *Indian Tribes,* 2:42; *RAPQ* (1927–28): 21.

67. *WHSC* 16:134–38 (quotes); Richter, "Rediscovered Links," 71n66; Blair, *Indian Tribes,* 2:77.

68. *JR* 64:27–39 ("master[s] of everything," 39); Blair, *Indian Tribes,* 2:51–79 (all other quotes); *NYCD* 9:450; Richter, "Rediscovered Links," 70.

69. Lahontan, *New Voyages,* 1:231 ("all things in . . ."); Belmont, "Histoire," 51–52 ("spilling their members . . . ," 52); *RFF,* 175; *CMRNF* 1:454; *RAPQ* (1927–28): 21; *NYCD* 9:431, 435–36, 439, 448, 466; Richter, "Rediscovered Links," 84; Foreman, *Indians Abroad,* 32–33. Cf. Catalogne, "Recueil," 52, which misdates the Iroquois attack to 1693.

70. *NYCD* 3:621, 9:433 ("enemy"), 435, 438, 453 ("Iroquois allies"); *LIR,* 150–58; Richter, "Rediscovered Links," 82.

71. *WA,* 14 (quote); *NYCD* 3:733–34, 9:464–65; Richter, "Rediscovered Links," 69–70, 83–84; Catalogne, "Recueil," 27.

72. Richter, "Rediscovered Links," 70–72 (quotes).

73. *NYCD* 9:463–65 (quote 465); *WA,* 15–16; Richter, "Rediscovered Links," 70–72.

74. Blair, *Indian Tribes,* 2:74, 78; *NYCD* 9:423–24.

75. *NYCD* 3:734, 9:465–67 (quotes); Belmont, "Histoire," 52; *CMRNF* 1:598; Van Cortlandt to Blathwayt, December 18, 1689 (O.S.).

76. *NYCD* 3:735, 9:467–69 ("slaughtered," 468); Whitmore, *Andros Tracts*, 3:114–16 ("houses," 116), 478; *DHNY* 1:302–11; *LIR*, 158–60; Belmont, "Histoire," 52; *JR* 64:61; Lincoln, *Narratives of the Indian Wars*, 204–5; Thomas, *Diary of Samuel Sewall*, 1:251; Staffa, *Schenectady Genesis*, 72 (population figure, 86–89), 98–99. The list of "Killed and Destroyed" at Schenectady (*DHNY* 1:304–5) provides the oft-cited figure of sixty persons killed. But this total estimate does not agree with the information reported within the document, which identifies only fifty-six persons killed: twenty-two adult white men (seven of whom were "burnt" by the French and allied Laurentians), seven adult white women (one "burnt" and another scalped), fourteen white children (one female and one male "burnt"), eleven "Negroes" (whose gender was not specified, two of whom were "burnt"), one "French girl Prisoner among ye Mohogs" (evidently not a Schenectady resident), and one "Maquase Indian" (apparently the lone Laurentian casualty; cf. *NYCD* 9:469). Cf. Reynolds, *Albany Chronicles*, opp.120; Burke, *Mohawk Frontier*, 106–7, 201–5.

77. *DHNY* 1:303–9 ("quite to Canida," 306); *NYCD* 3:700, 710 ("French Indian prisoner"), 727–29 ("backwardness," 728), 4:184n1; Whitmore, *Andros Tracts*, 3:116 ("kindred"), 118 ("Relations"); *CMRNF* 2:28; Sivertsen, *Turtles, Wolves, and Bears*, 20, 25.

78. Whitmore, *Andros Tracts*, 3:119 (quote); Robert Livingston to Sir Edmund Andros, April 19, 1690 (O.S.), BL 214; *NYCD* 3:636-48, 665-84, 692–93, 708, 710, 716, 9:469; John M. Murrin, "English Rights as Ethnic Aggression: The English Conquest, the Charter of Liberties of 1683, and Leisler's Rebellion in New York," in Pencak and Wright, *Authority and Resistance*, 56–94.

79. *NYCD* 3:694 ("the principal land . . ."), 695–96, 701, 706 (all other quotes), 716–17, 725.

80. Ibid., 3:713–14 (quote 714), 731, 9:471–74; *MeHSC* ser. 2, 5:63–64; Richter, "Rediscovered Links," 81n11; Le Roy de la Potherie, *Histoire*, 2:461–62; Gallay, *Colonial Wars*, 202–3, 343–44, 404–5.

81. Lahontan, *New Voyages*, 1:237–39 ("an Interpreter of . . . ," "ancient men," "young Barbarians," 238); *RAPQ* (1927–28): 61–62 ("intervention," "our Indians of . . . ," 62); *NYCD* 3:728–29, 732–36 ("agent," 732; "spared the lives of . . . ," 735), 4:214, 9:466, 469–70, 499, 502, 515–16; Catalogne, "Recueil," 27; Belmont, "Histoire," 53. Cf. Lahontan's claim (*New Voyages*, 238) that the Onondaga capture and execution of members of the French embassy amounted to retaliation for Kondiaronk's assault of their ambassadors in 1688. Chevalier d'Aux remained among the Onondagas long enough to receive the adoptive name "Dionakarondé." Sent by officials at Albany to New York, he remained in confinement there until his 1692 parole by Sloughter. He was then transferred to Boston, from where he was either ransomed or escaped back to New France in September 1692. See *NYCD* 3:855, 4:121 ("Dionakarondé"), 214, 9:515–16, 533; *MPHSC* 33:53; *CMRNF* 2:118. For Millet's Oneida title, see Tooker, "League of the Iroquois," 424; Fenton, *Great Law and the Longhouse*, 294–95; St.-Arnaud, *Pierre Millet*, 144–69. Fellow Jesuit Jean de Lamberville received the Onondaga name "Teiorhensere," which he translated as "the Dawn of the Day," circa 1685. See *NYCD* 3:453 (quotes), 4:95; Colden, *History of the Five Indian Nations Depending on the Province of New-York*, 50.

82. *NYCD* 4:50, 80 ("faithfully"), 87 (all other quotes); *A Journal Kept by Coll. Stephen Courtland*, 12.

83. Richter, "Rediscovered Links," 84 ("the Priest at . . ."); *JR* 64:93–105 (all other quotes 103), 119, 133; *NYCD* 3:715, 732, 9:466.

84. Van Cortlandt to Blathwayt, June 5, 1690 (O.S.), BP-CW, vol. 9 ("600 Christians and . . ."); *MaHSC* ser. 5, 8:305 ("firmly settle the . . .").

85. *NYCD* 4:193–96 ("all things confused," 193), 9:513–14; *MaHSC* ser. 5, 8:306, 308–9 ("very mortall," 309), 311–18; Le Roy de la Potherie, *Histoire*, 2:480.

86. *NYCD* 9:474, 479–80 (all quotes 479); *CMRNF* 2:30; *RAPQ* (1927–28): 38.

87. Lahontan, *New Voyages*, 1:239–41 (quote 240).

88. *NYCD* 4:196, 9:481; *MaHSC* ser. 5, 8:321. Cf. inflated casualty estimates in *NYCD* 3:752–53; *CMRNF* 2:31; *MeHSC* ser. 2, 5:151

89. *NYCD* 9:460 ("incensed"), 481 ("negligence"), 514 ("destroyed all the . . ."); *MaHSC* ser. 5, 8:311 ("want of the . . . ," "the most skillful . . ."), 319; *JR* 64:97–99 ("more Masters of . . . ," 99); Belmont, "Histoire," 52; *CMRNF* 2:31, 56; Le Roy de la Potherie, *Histoire*, 2:480. For estimates of Iroquois smallpox deaths in 1690, see *NYCD* 9:461 ("more than three hundred"), 490 (100–500), 514 ("three hundred Senecas, Cayugas, and Onondagas, and ninety young Mohawks and Oneidas").

90. *NYCD* 3:761, 778, 808, 9:455–62, 480, 482, 485–90, 499, 502, 528; *RFF*, 183; *JR* 64:41–53; *CMRNF* 2:19–23; Catalogne, "Recueil," 28–33; Belmont, "Histoire," 53; Lahontan, *New Voyages*, 1:242–50; *WHSC* 5:66; Richter, "Rediscovered Links," 85; Brasser, *Riding on the Frontier's Crest*, 24–25; Baker and Reid, *New England Knight*, 95-106; McLay, "Wellsprings of a 'World War'."

91. *JR* 64:57–63 ("Dutch," 59; "most reasonable men," 63); *NYCD* 3:777, 9:499, 500–503 ("scattered themselves in . . . ," 502), 515–17 (all other quotes); Belmont, "Histoire," 53.

92. *NYCD* 9:500–503 ("more confused than . . . ," 502), 516–18 ("Squaws busy at . . . ," 517); *RAPQ* (1927–28): 36, 62; Belmont, "Histoire," 53; Le Roy de la Potherie, *Histoire*, 2:484–85. Cf. *JR* 62:275n.

93. Catalogne, "Recueil," 38–41 ("*Osquenon*, by which . . . ," "*Sadreyo*, by which . . . ," 40); Lahontan, *New Voyages*, 1:234n ("pay of a..."); *NYCD* 9:502, 517–18 (all other quotes).

94. *NYCD* 9:499, 502, 516 ("fishing and hunting . . ."); *MeHSC* ser. 2, 5:150–51 ("Enemy," 150); Catalogne, "Recueil," 33–34 ("*dix écus*," 34); Peyser, *Letters from New France*, 45–54; *RAPQ* (1927–28): 69; Lozier, "Lever des chevelures," 518.

95. *NYCD* 3:771-77 (quotes); Richter, "Rediscovered Links," 78–80.

96. *NYCD* 3:777–82 (quotes). Cf. *WA*, 16–17.

97. *NYCD* 3:781, 785, 790, 801, 9:502, 524.

98. Ibid., 3:783 (quotes), 800.

99. Ibid., 801–2 (quotes 802), 4:209, 9:520, 525. French observers identified the presence of Onnonouagaren among the Mohawks who attacked La Prairie. The closest approximation of his name in Schuyler's papers is "Kanagaragayda" (see ibid., 3:802).

100. Ibid., 3:802–5 ("halfe moon," 804), 9:520–23 ("the most obstinate," "since the foundation . . . ," 520), 526; Belmont, "Histoire," 54; *RFF*, 185; Le Roy de la Potherie, *Histoire*, 2:486–88.

101. *RAPQ* (1927–28): 65, 68–70 (quote 69); Richter, "Rediscovered Links," 85; Catalogne, "Recueil," 43; *NYCD* 3:805, 814; *IHC* 23:326. Cf. inflated estimates of Anglo-American and Mohawk casualties at La Prairie in *RAPQ* (1927–28): 65; *NYCD* 9:504, 525–26; Lahontan, *New Voyages*, 1:262–63; Blair, *Indian Tribes*, 1:81.

102. *NYCD* 3:799 ("draw away many . . . ," "so weakened the . . ."), 805-8 (all other quotes); Catalogne, "Recueil," 45.

103. *NYCD* 9:510–11 (quotes 511), 526; Blair, *Indian Tribes*, 2:81-83, 102-3, 114; Le Roy de la Potherie, *Histoire*, 2:490; Quaife, *Western Country*, 71; Peyser, *Letters from New France*, 43–48, 71–72; Nassaney et al., "The Search for Fort St. Joseph," 109-11.

104. *NYCD* 3:791, 794, 834–36 (quotes); *WA*, 17.

105. Catalogne, "Recueil," 47 ("Le Fer"); Belmont, "Histoire," 54 ("slaughtered"); *NYCD* 9:531, 534. Belmont misdates the Mohawk attack on the Kahnawake hunters to October 1691.

106. *NYCD* 3:815-17 (quotes), 841, 9:476-77, 514; van Cortlandt to Blathwayt, January 7, 1691 (O.S.), BP-CW, vol. 9; *CMRNF* 1:505; Le Roy de la Potherie, *Histoire*, 2:462; Catalogne, "Recueil," 47–48; Sivertsen, *Turtles, Wolves, and Bears*, 5-7; Staffa, *Schenectady Genesis*, 33–34, 38, 49–50.

107. *JR* 63:245, 64:113; Parmenter, "After the Mourning Wars," 80. Cf. Eccles, *Frontenac*, 245–51;

Richter, *Ordeal of the Longhouse*, 169–73, *Facing East*, 158-59, 167-68.

108. "The Examination of Joachim Lebert, a French Man of Canada, and Native of Montréal, taken before his Excellency Benjamin Fletcher at Albany," in *Narrative of an Attempt*, 8 (quote); Blair, *Indian Tribes*, 2:85–89; *NYCD* 9:531. Cf. Catalogne, "Recueil," 28 (which misdates the July 1692 engagement at the Long Sault of the Ottawa River to 1690), 48 (which misdates the Toniata Island incident to 1694).

109. *JR* 64:127–29 (quote 127), 145, 65:31; Kip, *Early Jesuit Missions*, 120–32; *NYCD* 9:535, 556–57; Le Roy de la Potherie, *Histoire*, 2:496; *RAPQ* (1927–28): 138; *CMRNF* 2:122. For a circa 1753 description of the four "fetes" celebrated annually "in honor of the four savage martyrs of the village of [Sault] St. Louis," see Gallup, *Memoir of a French and Indian War Soldier*, 40-41.

110. Catalogne, "Recueil," 48 (quotes); Belmont, "Histoire," 54–55; Le Roy de la Potherie, *Histoire*, 2:495; Lahontan, *New Voyages*, 1:224n2, 266–70.

111. *NYCD* 3:815–16 ("present of 1000 . . . ," 816), 840–42, 844; *WA*, 17–18 (all other quotes 17).

112. *NYCD* 3:842–44 (quotes), 9:535–36; Lahontan, *New Voyages*, 1:270–71. Cf. Belmont, "Histoire," 55.

113. *NYCD* 9:555, 557, 567, 580; Le Roy de la Potherie, *Histoire*, 2:498, 509; "The Examination of Andries Casparus and Cornelius Claese van den Bergh, both Dutchmen, taken before his Excellency Benjamin Fletcher, Governor, who have made their escape from Canada, who were Prisoners there, and have been 32 days by the way" [to Albany], in *Narrative of an Attempt*, 7–8.

114. *LIR*, 162–67 (quotes).

115. *NYCD* 9:556 (quotes).

116. Le Roy de la Potherie, *Histoire*, 2:492–94, 501–2; Gervais and Lusignan, "De Jeanne d'Arc à Madeleine de Verchères," 198-205; Lanctot, *History of Canada*, 2:127; André Vachon, "Jarret de Verchères, Marie-Madeleine," *DCB* 3:309–11; Coates and Morgan, *Heroines and History*, 17-40, 258-66. Cf. Belmont, "Histoire," 55–56.

117. *NYCD* 9:539–43 ("nearly half," 539); *JR* 64:109–13 (all other quotes 109).

118. *NYCD* 9:557–58 (quotes 557).

119. Ibid., 550–51, 558 (quotes). Cf. Frontenac's inflated claim of "nearly 400" Mohawks captured in *RAPQ* (1927–28): 152 (quote), 159.

120. Le Roy de la Potherie, *Histoire*, 2:503 ("a great victory . . ."); *NYCD* 4:16-17, 9:559 (all other quotes); Catalogne, "Recueil," 45–46.

121. *NYCD* 4:6–7, 16–19 ("extreme bad cold . . . ," "not be perswaded . . . ," 18–19), 9:551–52, 559–61 (all other quotes); Belmont, "Histoire," 55; Van Cortlandt to Blathwayt, March 26, 1693 (O.S.), BP-CW, vol. 9; *A Journal Kept by Coll. Stephen Courtland*, 9 (French casualty estimate); Mourin, "Porter la Guerre," 16-19.

122. *NYCD* 9:552–53, 563–64; *RAPQ* (1927–28): 90–91 (quote 91).

123. *NYCD* 3:846, 4:222; *Narrative of an Attempt*, 1–3. Five years later, the Earl of Bellomont reported his inability to procure any of the "printed accounts of [Fletcher's] great exploits which he published and sent to England." Fletcher apparently "made it his business to get up all the printed copies" before he left New York, which in Bellomont's view amounted to a tacit admission on Fletcher's part that he had "imposed a romance instead of a true narrative." See *NYCD* 4:426.

124. *NYCD* 4:13–15, 20–24 ("supine and careless," "French and their . . . ," "all one heart . . . ," "Cajenquiragoe," "Lord of the . . . ," "speedy arrival," 20–22), 38, 222 (all other quotes), 464; *Narrative of an Attempt*, 9–12. Cf. *WA*, 18.

125. *RAPQ* (1927–28): 152 ("scatter-brained"); *NYCD* 4:55 ("mostly destroyed"), 59; *A Journal Kept by Coll. Stephen Courtland*, 6–7, 9; Sivertsen, *Turtles, Wolves, and Bears*, 36.

126. *NYCD* 3:783, 9:553, 562, 553–54, 565–66 (quotes), 572; *CMRNF* 2:150; Belmont, "Histoire," 55–56; Le Roy de la Potherie, *Histoire*, 2:506–8; Yves F. Zoltvany, "Chabert de Joncaire, Louis Thomas," *DCB* 2:125–27.

127. *LIR*, 170–71 ("Secret Intrigues," "French Indians"); *NYCD* 4:41, 49–50, 53–54 ("usual Supplies and . . ."), 63; *PP* 1:268–79; *CNYCM*, 86; Hagedorn, "Brokers of Understanding," 383 ("marks and figures"). The two incarcerated Indians escaped from custody in Springfield in early August 1693.

128. *NYCD* 4:38–45 (quotes). Cf. *WA*, 18–20.

129. Blair, *Indian Tribes*, 2:90–97 (quotes); *NYCD* 4:90, 96–97, 9:554, 569–70; *LIR*, 168–69; *CNYCM*, 74–75; *AMD* 8:464–69, 19:519–20; *WA*, 23; *Account of the Treaty*, 27, 38. On the natural abundance of the Detroit region at this time, see George L. Cornell, "American Indians at Wawiiatanong: An Early American History of Indigenous Peoples at Detroit," in Hartig, *Honoring our Detroit River*, 11-18.

130. Blair, *Indian Tribes*, 2:96 ("collars, redstone calumets . . ."); *NYCD* 4:66, 9:554–55, 567–70 ("prodigious heap of . . . ," 568); *RAPQ* (1927–28): 154 (peltry estimate); Le Roy de la Potherie, *Histoire*, 2:510.

131. *NYCD* 4:37, 47–50, 55–62 (quotes); *Narrative of an Attempt*, 8.

132. *NYCD* 3:783, 4:62–63, 77–78, 86–87, 9:554 ("good faith," "adherents were not . . ."), 572 (all other quotes), 581.

133. Ibid., 4:55 (quote).

6. OVER THE FOREST, PART 2, 1694–1701

1. Le Roy de la Potherie, *Histoire*, 2:663–64 (quotes 663).

2. Alfred, *Peace, Power, Righteousness,* xxiii; Gibson, *Concerning the League,* xlv–xlvi, xlix; Ganter, *Collected Speeches of Sagoyewatha,* 141 (quote).

3. Blair, *Indian Tribes,* 2:103–11 (quotes).

4. *NYCD* 9:577–78 ("Chiefs of the . . . ," 577); Le Roy de la Potherie, *Histoire*, 2:516 (all other quotes).

5. Boyd, *Indian Treaties,* 310 (quotes); *NYCD* 4:82.

6. *NYCD* 4:78–80 ("the whole house . . . ," 78; "even to the . . . ," 79), 89–90 ("Praying Indians," "a free pass," 89), 93–94 ("Agoiandres Iroquois," 93), 97, 9:578; Le Roy de la Potherie, *Histoire*, 2:517 ("belts from all . . .").

7. *NYCD* 9:578 ("the proudest nation . . ."), 584 ("the brink of . . ."); Le Roy de la Potherie, *Histoire*, 2:515.

8. *NYCD* 4:85–96 ("truckl[ing] to the . . . ," 89); *WA*, 21 (all other quotes).

9. *NYCD* 4:84 ("humour of making . . ."), 99; *ARMA* 7:437–38 ("fresh troubles," 438); Fletcher to Blathwayt, March 28, 1694 (O.S.), BP-CW, vol. 8.

10. *WA*, 23–24 (quotes); *NYCD* 4:107–8. Wraxall claimed that no record of a reply by Anglo-American authorities appeared in the version of the records he consulted in preparing his *Abridgment*. But on August 25, 1694, the speaker of the Iroquois delegation in Albany claimed that they had come to answer Fletcher's question of "the 7th of May [O.S.] last," which they reported as "Who will be for you and against you" [*sic*]. See *Account of the Treaty*, 5–6 (quotes).

11. Catalogne, "Recueil," 50 ("Sieur de la Chauvignerie"); *NYCD* 4:94, 9:579–81 (all other quotes); *JR* 64:243–45; Severance, *An Old Frontier of France,* 2:154–55. For a possible rendering of Louis Maray de la Chauvignerie's adoptive Onondaga name ("Diondori"), see *NYCD* 4:657.

12. *NYCD* 9:581–84.

13. Catalogne, "Recueil," 51.

14. *JR* 64:143 (quote); *NYCD* 4:64–65, 113, 9:613–16; *ARMA* 7:439; *RAPQ* (1927–28): 185; Brown, "'Great Massacre of 1694.'"

15. *MaHSC* ser. 4, 1:102–10 (quotes 106); *Account of the Treaty,* 3–5. Cf. *WA,* 25–27, which contains information on only the first five days of the conference. For a contemporary street map of Albany, see Miller, *Description of the Province and City of New York.*

16. Havard, *Great Peace,* 144 ("protective aura," "space of internal . . ."); *Account of the Treaty,* 6–10 (all other quotes); *NYCD* 4:716, 729; Jennings et al., *History and Culture of Iroquois Diplomacy,* 122. Fletcher later claimed that d'Aux had escaped from prison and had been pursued, albeit unsuccessfully. See *Account of the Treaty,* 25.

17. *Account of the Treaty,* 11–15.

18. Ibid., 16–22 (quote 19).

19. *NYCD* 4:113–16 ("the ax," 115; "make war against . . . ," 116); 9:584–85, 591, 600 ("told no news"), 611; *RAPQ* (1927–28): 186.

20. *NYCD* 4:115–17 ("hatchet," "kill Cayenquiragoe . . . ," 115), 9:586 ("Upper Nations"); *RAPQ* (1927–28): 195–97; Fletcher to Blathwayt, November 19, 1694 (O.S.), BP-CW, vol. 8; *CMRNF* 2:123–24, 180; Peyser, *Letters from New France,* 58–59; *MPHSC* 33:71.

21. Quaife, *Western Country,* 15–16 (quote 15); *NYCD* 4:124, 9:594–96, 599, 601; Catalogne, "Recueil," 54.

22. *NYCD* 4:120, 125, 9:595n.1, 596–99 (quotes), 600, 642, 666; Le Roy de la Potherie, *Histoire,* 2:558.

23. *NYCD* 4:120–21 (quotes); *JR* 64:143; Le Roy de la Potherie, *Histoire,* 2:530–40; St.-Arnaud, *Pierre Millet,* 169–70.

24. *NYCD* 4:121–22 (quotes); *RFF,* 187; Day, *Identity of the St. Francis Indians,* 24–26.

25. *NYCD* 9:601–5 (quotes); Margry, *Découvertes,* 5:60–62, 71–72; Le Roy de la Potherie, *Histoire,* 2:576–78; Idle, *Post of the St. Joseph River,* 17. .

26. *NYCD* 9:589 ("tampering with the . . . "), 605–6 (all other quotes).

27. Ibid., 9:606–8 (quotes); Quaife, *Western Country,* 10; Irwin, "Contesting World Views." Cadillac identified the "Sable" and "Nassakueton" (or "Fork") Odawa bands at Michilimackinac as having been displaced by Iroquois attacks from former areas of residency to Michilimackinac, where they lived with the Sinago and Kiskakon bands. Cf. Johanna E. Feest and Christian Feest, "Ottawa," in Trigger, *Northeast,* 772–73.

28. *NYCD* 9:619–21 (quotes); Quaife, *Western Country,* 67–69. On subsequent Fox ties with Senecas, see Hunter, "Refugee Fox Settlements among the Senecas"; Charles Callender, "Miami," in Trigger, *Northeast,* 689.

29. *NYCD* 4:124 (quotes), 9:672.

30. Blair, *Indian Tribes,* 2:132–34 (quotes); Le Roy de la Potherie, *Histoire* 2:563. Cf. Cadillac's retrospective accounts of the incident (in *RAPQ* [1928–29]: 342; *MPHSC* 33:103; Peyser, *Letters from New France,* 65), which imply that the Lake Erie canoe battle occurred in 1697, but contextual evidence in the Perrot reports (cited by Le Roy de la Potheire) establishes the 1695 date convincingly.

31. *NYCD* 4:123–26, 9:599, 602–3 (quote 603).

32. Ibid., 9:591–94 ("useless," 591), 609 ("including Regulars, Militia . . ."), 618 ("discovered"), 633, 635; *RFF,* 186, 188–89, 193; *RAPQ* (1928–29): 275.

33. *NYCD* 9:609, 611–12 (quotes 612), 618, 622; *RAPQ* (1928–29): 283.

34. Quaife, *Western Country,* 11 ("intriguing," "evil-disposed"); *NYCD* 9:630–32, 644 (all other quotes); *RAPQ* (1928–29): 279, 283.

35. *NYCD* 9:531–34 ("sure depots for . . . ," 532), 538, 645 ("the Great Kettle . . . ," "keep alive the . . ."); *RFF*, 186 ("harass the Iroquois . . ."); Lahontan, *New Voyages,* 1:271–73.

36. *ARMA* 7:479–80 (quotes); *WA,* 27.

37. *NYCD* 4:430 ("Disgusted"); *WA,* 27–28 (all other quotes).

38. *NYCD* 4:151–52, 158, 9:620–30 (quotes), 642; *LIR,* 172–74.

39. *RAPQ* (1928–29): 304 ("trad[ing] with New York . . ."), 312; *NYCD* 9:646–47 (all other quotes); Le Roy de la Potherie, *Histoire,* 2:548 (peltry value estimate). Cf. *RAPQ* (1928–29): 321 for another report of the incident claiming fifty Senecas killed and thirty-four captured.

40. *NYCD* 9:641–42 (quotes).

41. Cf. Eid, "Ojibwa-Iroquois War"; Schmalz, *Ojibwa of Southern Ontario,* 18–34; Donald B. Smith, "Important Evidence: Nineteenth Century Anishnabeg Perspectives on the Algonquian-Iroquois Wars in Seventeenth Century Southern Ontario," in Johnston, *Aboriginal People and the Fur Trade,* 122–28. Eid, Schmalz, and Smith use nineteenth-century oral tradition related by upper Great Lakes Algonquians to reconstruct a series of successful campaigns, which supposedly expelled the Iroquois from the north shore of Lake Ontario and by 1700 "soundly crushed the Five Nations Iroquois" (Eid, "Ojibwa-Iroquois War," 297). These scholars make virtually no effort, however, to align evidence from oral narratives with specific events in the documentary and archaeological record. While not disputing that the Iroquois suffered casualties in engagements with the peoples of the upper Great Lakes during the 1690s, this evidence challenges historian D. Peter MacLeod's claim that oral evidence in this case has "forced a revision of long-standing opinions" regarding the course of Iroquois warfare during the 1690s (see MacLeod, "Anishnabeg Point of View," 208).

42. *NYCD* 9:636–38 (quotes); *RAPQ* (1928–29): 296.

43. *NYCD* 4:158 ("though monsters . . ."), 168–70 (all other quotes), 171–72, 181–86, 197–98, 207–8, 229–30; *DHNY* 1:323.

44. *DHNY* 1:323–24 (quotes); *NYCD* 4:431–32.

45. *RAPQ* (1928–29): 274 (quote); *NYCD* 9:640–50; *JR* 65:25; Mourin, "Porter la Guerre," 21–22.

46. Van Cortlandt to Blathwayt, March 21, 1696/97 (O.S.), BP-CW, vol. 9 ("to the head . . ."); *NYCD* 9:650–52 ("a descriptive drawing . . . ," 652), 665 ("within three or four . . ."); Catalogne, "Recueil," 55; *JR* 65:25.

47. *JR* 65:25–27 ("burn[ing] at a . . . ," 27); *NYCD* 4:173–74, 9:653–55 (all other quotes); Catalogne, "Recueil," 55; *RAPQ* (1928–29): 307–10, 320, 328.

48. *JR* 65:27 ("tumultuously entered"); *NYCD* 4:242, 9:639–40, 653–57 (all other quotes), 662.

49. *NYCD* 4:174, 176 (quote), 198, 204; *JR* 65:29; *DHNY* 1:345. Cf. Parker, *Archeological History,* 501.

50. *NYCD* 4:204, 232, 235–39 (quotes).

51. Catalogne, "Recueil," 56–57; *RAPQ* (1928–29): 340; *MPHSC* 33:78; *NYCD* 4:177, 243, 245, 252–53, 275, 9:681, 13:502; Christoph and Christoph, *Andros Papers,* 1:404–5.

52. *NYCD* 4:280, 9:665 (quote), 670; *MPHSC* 33:79–80; *JR* 65:31. On the possibility of Tareha as holder of the Oneida title of Odatsedeh in 1697, see a 1698 identification of Odatsedeh as Millet's "adopted brother" (*NYCD* 4:349).

53. *NYCD* 9:669–70 ("family," "for the purpose of . . . ," "a general deputation . . . ," 670), 672, 684 ("Huron deserters"); *CMRNF* 2:219–21; Peyser, *Letters from New France,* 60–61; *MPHSC* 33:76, 82; *RAPQ* (1928–29): 342 (Seneca casualty estimate).

54. *NYCD* 4:279–82 (quotes), 9:670–71, 676; *RAPQ* (1928–29): 341; *MPHSC* 33:79–80.

55. Le Roy de la Potherie, *Histoire,* 2:610 ("Anciens"); *NYCD* 9:678–79 (all other quotes).

56. *NYCD* 4:36 ("no conclusion of . . ."), 9:680 (all other quotes), 685.

57. *NYCD* 4:406, 9:663, 673–76; *MPHSC* 33:81; *RAPQ* (1928–29): 346–47.

58. *CMRNF* 2:227–40; *NYCD* 4:338, 366, 465, 488, 9:677, 680, 685.

59. Van Cortlandt to Blathwayt, May 6, 1698 (O.S.), BP-CW, vol. 9 (quote); Le Roy de la Potherie, *Histoire,* 2:635.

60. *NYCD* 9:681–82 (quotes 681). At least six of the Onondaga prisoners surrendered to the French were eventually repatriated (see ibid., 4:348, 403, 580, 9:695, 710–11).

61. Ibid., 4:305 (quote), 337 (census figures), 9:678, 683–84; Le Roy de la Potherie, *Histoire,* 2:615.

62. *NYCD* 4:266, 305, 333–34, 338–41, 343–44, 348–51, 9:682, 690; van Cortlandt to Blathwayt, July 10, 1698 (O.S.), BP-CW, vol. 9; Kammen, *Colonial New York,* 141.

63. *NYCD* 4:327 ("vacate," value estimate of deed to Mohawk country), 330–31 ("to desert this . . . ," 330), 334, 345–47 (all other quotes), 391, 394, 447–48, 462.

64. Ibid., 9:684–85 (quotes); Le Roy de la Potherie, *Histoire,* 2:618.

65. *Propositions Made by the Five Nations of Indians,* 1–3 (quotes 3); *NYCD* 4:347, 9:685; *WA,* 28–29. Cf. Ferguson, *Schoharie Mohawks,* 33–35.

66. *Propositions Made by the Five Nations of Indians,* 3–21 (quotes); *NYCD* 4:367–70.

67. *NYCD* 4:362–66 (quotes), 370–71, 374–76, 404–6, 418, 426, 430, 9:687, 689–95.

68. Ibid., 4:373 ("face to face," "hinder [them] from . . ."), 9:685–86 ("red jackets," 686); Le Roy de la Potherie, *Histoire,* 2:619–21.

69. *NYCD* 4:401, 407–9, 9:688 (quote), 696–97; Le Roy de la Potherie, *Histoire,* 2:633; *MPHSC* 33:111. Two of the five French prisoners deposited by the Iroquois at Albany had been ransomed by local authorities or had escaped without the permission or knowledge of the Iroquois by May 1699. The Iroquois agreed to the repatriation of the remaining three French prisoners in late June 1699. In September 1699, one of the released French prisoners claimed that Dellius had impregnated her while she was incarcerated in Albany, an act Bellomont equated to the reverend's "insatiable covetousness in procuring two such vast grants of land" from the Mohawks. See *NYCD* 4:561, 572, 581–82 (quote 582). The Iroquois referred to Detroit as "Teuchsagrondie" (Beauchamp, *Indian Names in New York,* 110), a placename that appears to have associations with beaver hunting (see Parker, *Archeological History,* 570).

70. Le Roy de la Potherie, *Histoire,* 2:633–34 ("time of the . . . ," 634); *NYCD* 4:492–94 (all other quotes); Tremblay, "La Politique Missionnaire," 93–94; Trigger, "Native Resettlement, 1635–1800"; David H. Corkran, "Ohensiowanne," *DCB* 2:502. . Cf. *WA,* 31–32.

71. *NYCD* 4:488, 494–95, 9:698, 702–3 (quotes); *CMRNF* 2:321.

72. Le Roy de la Potherie, *Histoire,* 2:624–31 ("considerable," 625); *NYCD* 4:491, 494–98 ("correspondence with the . . . ," 496), 558–61 ("birch canoe," 559); *WA,* 31.

73. *RAPQ* (1928–29): 365–67 ("ancient towns," 367); *NYCD* 4:488 ("most knowing people," "we shall entirely . . ."), 500, 560 ("Brother Corlaer").

74. *NYCD* 4:488, 500–501, 505, 514, 528–29 ("vacating," 528), 532–33, 553–54, 561 ("proposition house," "strung wampum"), 565–66 ("love," "our friends detained by . . . ," "that goods be," 565); Le Roy de la Potherie, *Histoire,* 2:633; *CLNY* 1:412–17.

75. *NYCD* 4:532, 556, 567, 569–70 (quote 569).

76. Ibid., 569–74 ("goods very cheap," 571), 580; *WA,* 33 ("Conestoga a Place . . ."); *AMD* 19:519–20; Evelyn Abraham Benson, "Conestoga Indian Treaties and Traders, 1682–1722," in Coley, Jolly, and Slotter, *Millersville-Penn Manor Community History,* 13.

77. Catalogne, "Recueil," 59–60 ("hunting and fishing . . . ," "calumet," 60); Le Roy de la Potherie, *Histoire,* 2:634–39 (all other quotes).

78. *NYCD* 4:493, 590, 596–97 (quotes 597), 632.

79. *WHSC* 5:67–73 (quotes); Catalogne, "Recueil," 60 (peltry value estimate); *RFF,* 467; *JDCSNF* 4:479–80, 485, 499–503; *NYCD* 4:618, 9:714, 717.

80. *NYCD* 4:556, 579, 606–20 ("General Insurrection of . . . ," 606), 637–38 ("conjunction," "in a short time . . . ," 637), 655–56, 662–63, 676–77 ("South Carolina to . . . ," "bound up in . . . ,"

677), 696 ("Rondax"), 726, 758–59 ("tree of welfare," 758), 836; *MeHSC* ser. 2, 10:43–44, 64–65, 95, 23:22a–22b, 119–20; *CSPC* 18:95–97, 187, 599; Le Roy de la Potherie, *Histoire,* 2:632, 639–40; Calloway, *Western Abenakis of Vermont,* 98–101; Gordon M. Day, "The Eastern Boundary of Iroquoia: Abenaki Evidence," in Foster and Cowan, *In Search of New England's Native Past,* 120; Bourque, *Twelve Thousand Years,* 174; Haefeli and Sweeney, *Captors and Captives,* 85–86.

81. *NYCD* 4:647–54 ("much dejected and . . . ," 647; "near two-thirds," "Canada with their . . . ," 648), 747 (all other quotes).

82. Ibid., 4:647–48.

83. Ibid., 4:654–61, 695–96 (quotes), 9:708.

84. Ibid., 4:694 ("publick treasury"), 9:708–11 (all other quotes).

85. Ibid., 4:690, 692–93 (quotes 692), 748, 792.

86. Ibid., 4:689 ("bewitch'd"), 690 ("full of faction," "very subtile and . . ."), 694, 716; Miller, *Description of the Province and City of New York,* fig.6; Huey, "Schuyler Flatts," 26. For additional evidence of married Iroquois couples with one spouse residing in a Laurentian community, see Waterman, *"To Do Justice to Him and Myself,"* 133.

87. *NYCD* 4:476, 655, 690–91, 693–95 (quotes); *LIR,* 176–78; Cleland, *Rites of Conquest,* 158; Fixico, "Alliance of the Three Fires"; Osborne and Ripmeester, "Mississaugas Between Two Worlds," 262.

88. *NYCD* 4:640, 660–61, 666 ("400 light fuzils," "remove the jealousy . . ."), 685 (all other quotes), 689, 741–42, 753–55, 783, 9:711, 715; *LIR,* 179.

89. *NYCD* 4:713–14, 727–28 (quotes).

90. Ibid., 4:714, 729–33 (quotes), 792; *WA,* 33–34.

91. *NYCD* 4:714, 734–43 ("without any sort of . . . ," 735), 746 (all other quotes), 876, 9:713; *WA,* 34–37.

92. *NYCD* 4:742, 895, 9:715–17 (quotes); *RFF,* 199. For evidence of eight longstanding French adoptees among the Mohawks and three more among the Onondagas circa 1698, see *NYCD* 9:685; Fenton, "Captain Hyde's Observations."

93. *NYCD* 4:767, 782, 798–804 (quotes 798–99).

94. Ibid., 9:711–12 (quotes 712), 718–20.

95. Ibid., 4:745–46, 799–805.

96. Ibid., 4:717 ("quickly comprehended," "an isthmus or neck . . ."), 799 (all other quotes).

97. Ibid., 4:748–51, 768, 782–84, 796, 799, 800–801, 805–7 (quotes 805), 842–43, 873.

98. Ibid., 4:590, 632, 645, 687, 697 ("almost at [his] . . ."), 713 ("Enemies of Government"), 715, 718 ("scandalously weak," "power and greatness"), 724–25, 751–52, 759, 765, 782–84 ("remote nations," 784), 789, 796, 815, 823, 825, 834, 844, 853 ("obstacles"); *CLNY* 1:432–34; *LIR,* 181–82.

99. *RFF,* 200–201 ("store of goods," 201), 203; *MPHSC* 33:97–99; Calder, *Colonial Captivities,* 201–4 ("Biloxi Bay," 201); *NYCD* 4:802 ("to the Southward . . ."), 9:704–8 ("Flat Heads," 706), 713 ("possession of that . . .").

100. *NYCD* 4:767 ("concluded the peace . . . ," "arbiter," "heavy expenses"), 9:713 (all other quotes).

101. Ibid., 4:851, 864, 867–68, 870–73 (quotes); Livingston to Blathwayt, May 23, 1701 (O.S.), BL 149, HEHL.

102. *NYCD* 4:889–91 (quotes). The Onondaga town was then located at the Jamesville Pen site.

103. Ibid., 4:891–92 ("publick meeting of . . . ," 891), 9:721 ("strict neutrality").

104. Ibid., 4:888, 893–94 ("skins," 894), 899 (all other quotes). The document identified the "seven nations" as "Skighquan, Estjage, Assisagh [Mississaugas], Karhadage, Adgenauwe [Ojibwas], Karrihaet, Adirondax" (see *NYCD* 4:899). Cf. *WA,* 39, for Wraxall's claim that some of these names represented "divisional names of the Dowaganhaes Nation—more properly called Castles."

105. *NYCD* 4:881 ("obedience to his . . ."), 896–900 (all other quotes); *WA,* 38–39.

106. *NYCD* 4:904–6 (quotes); *WA,* 39–41; Brandão and Starna, "'Some Things May Slip Out of Your Memory.'"

107. Based on comparison of the representations of Iroquois signatories' names on the document (see *NYCD* 4:910) with contemporary lists of titleholders' names (see Tooker, "League of the Iroquois," 425, and Fenton, *Great Law and the Longhouse,* 193–94), I am identifying "Sonahsowannie" as Seneca titleholder "Shakenjowaneh"; "Tirogaren" as Mohawk titleholder "Deyeonhegwenh" (see also Sivertsen, *Turtles, Wolves, and Bears,* 33); and "Achrireho" as Onondaga titleholder "Arironh." On Mohawk and Seneca "doorkeeping," see Morgan, *League of the Iroquois,* 95; Jennings et al., *History and Culture of Iroquois Diplomacy,* 119; Prezzano, "Warfare, Women, and Households," in Claasen and Joyce, *Women in Prehistory,* 98–99; Irving Powless, Jr., "The Sovereignty and Land Rights of the Houdenosaunee," in Vecsey and Starna, *Iroquois Land Claims,* 159.

108. *NYCD* 4:888 ("800 miles long . . ."), 908–10 (all other quotes); Dunnigan, *Frontier Metropolis,* 19. At least two of the Seneca signatories ("Tohowaragenni" and "Sonessowane") of the July 30, 1701, Albany deed (see ibid., 4:910) had been involved in parallel negotiations in New France since July 1699. See Le Roy de la Potherie, *Histoire,* 2:634 ("Tonaraguennion" and "Tsonhoastsuam"); *NYCD* 9:708 ("Tonareng8enion" and "8hensi8an"). On August 1, 1701, these two Seneca headmen were noted among a group of "Five of the Principal Sachems of the Five Nations" (see *NYCD* 4:907). Seneca Turtle Clan headman "Toarenguenion" signed the August 1701 Montreal treaty (see Havard, *Great Peace,* 119; Guillaud, Delâge, and d'Avignon, "Les signatures amérindiens," 32–33).

109. *NYCD* 4:884, 888 ("fix'd our Indians . . . ," "obedience"), 907–8 ("Five of the . . ."), 911, 915, 916–17 ("hinder," 917); Livingston to Blathwayt, September 3, 1701 (O.S.), BL 217, HEHL; *WJP* 12 (1957): 994–95.

110. *NYCD* 4:917–19 (quotes); Dechêne, *Habitants and Merchants,* 328n41 (Native attendance figure);Johnson, "Les lieux de la Paix de 1701."

111. *NYCD* 4:918–19 (quotes); Le Roy de la Potherie, *Histoire,* 2:618' Lytwyn, "Dish With One Spoon," in Pentland, *Papers,* 215–19; Simpson, "Looking After *Gdoo-naagininaa,*" 36–37. A replica of the document depicting the totemic clan signatures of the Native leaders appears in Margry, *Découvertes,* 5: frontispiece. See also Guillaud, Delâge, and d'Avignon, "Les signatures amérindiens," 28–35.

112. *NYCD* 4:919 ("all Indians), 9:722–25, 737 (all other quotes); Catalogne, "Recueil," 61; Havard, *Great Peace,* 119. There appear to be no League titleholders among the seven Iroquois signatories of the August 1701 Montreal treaty. Four of the signers were Senecas, one of whom ("Tekanoet") was first encountered by the French as a military leader in the Illinois country twenty years earlier. Le Roy de la Potherie described Tekanoet in 1701 as the "Great Chief" of the Senecas (see *Histoire,* 2:644; David H. Corkran, "Tekanoet," *DCB* 2:623–24; Havard, *Great Peace,* 208–9). The other Seneca signers ("Aouenano," "Tonatakout," and "Toarenguenion"), and the Onondaga, Cayuga, and Oneida signers ("Ohonsiowanne," "Garonhiaron," and "Soueouon," respectively) appear to have been civil leaders or speakers. See Havard, *Great Peace,* 190; Bruce G. Trigger, "Tonatakout," *DCB* 2:631; Corkran, "Ohonsiowanne"; Guillaud, Delâge, and d'Avignon, "Les signatures amérindiens," 32–33.

113. Cf. Aquila, *Iroquois Restoration,* 45–69; Haan, "Covenant and Consensus," 53 ("accident"); Richter, *Ordeal of the Longhouse,* 361n44; Brandão and Starna, "Treaties of 1701," 217; Taylor, *American Colonies,* 291 ("partial victory snatched . . ."); Richter, *Facing East from Indian Country,* 170–71; Havard, *Great Peace,* 155, 262n49.

114. My thinking here owes a debt to Rice, "Escape from Tsennacommacah," 140.

115. *NYCD* 4:928 ("overawe"); *JR* 65:211 ("useless"), 223–25 ("dread," 223), 251–53; *RFF,* 204–5 (all other quotes 205). On post-1701 French efforts to extend Iroquois neutrality to settler colonies in eastern North America, see *ARMA* 8:149, 541; *CMRNF* 2:450–51; *NYCD* 9:770, 813.

116. Robert Quary to Sidney, Baron Godolphin, ca. May 1702 (O.S.), BL 28, HEHL (quotes).

117. Catalogne, "Recueil," 64 ("a number of Iroquois . . ."); *NYCD* 4: 918 ("some Indians who . . ."), 989 ("end," "house"); Waterman, *"To Do Justice to Him and Myself,"* 34 ("Rapecke," "Rotsie"); Margry, *Découvertes,* 5:262–65; *JR* 65:223–25, 251–53; Zoltvany, *Philippe de Rigaud de Vaudreuil,* 53. Cf. Richter, *Ordeal of the Longhouse,* 218–19.

118. Blum, *Ghost Brothers,* 90. Cf. Brooks, *Common Pot,* 138–39.

Epilogue

1. Hutchins and Choksi, "From *Calder* to *Mitchell*"; Cappricioso, "Where There's Smoke"; Odato, "Federal Ruling Rejects Plans" (quote).

2. Massey, *For Space,* 4–5 (quotes). See also Michael Warner, "What's Colonial about Colonial America?" in St. George, *Possible Pasts,* 55; Burnard, "Passion for Places"; Wildcat, "Indigenizing the Future," 434.

3. Gronim, "Geography and Persuasion," 375–81; J.B. Harley, "Maps, Knowledge, and Power," in Cosgrove and Daniels, *Iconography of Landscape;* Clarke, "Taking Possession." See also the analogous discussion in Constance Jordan, "Conclusion: Jamestown and Its North Atlantic World," in Appelbaum and Sweet, *Envisioning an English Empire,* 279. For specific references contravening arguments of decline, see evidence of the persistence of multifamily residences among the Iroquois to 1780, in *NYCD* 4:345; Waterman, *"To Do Justice to Him and Myself,"* 108; Wonderley, "Oneida Community," 23. For the persistence of matrilineal kinship reckoning into the nineteenth century, see Glatthaar and Martin, *Forgotten Allies,* 234; Tiro, *Along the Hudson and Mohawk,* 62; *MaHSC* ser. 1, 5:17; Maud, *Visit to the Falls of Niagara,* 117; Hauptman, "Two Worlds of Aunt Dinah," 14. For the persistence of the exclusive speaking of Iroquois languages at the Laurentian communities into the mid-eighteenth century, see *JR* 68:225, 265; Franquet, *Voyages et Mémoires,* 37. See also Baker and Reid, "Amerindian Power."

4. Merlan, "Indigeneity," 304 (quote); Ganter, *Collected Speeches of Sagoyewatha,* 88–92 (Red Jacket quotes 88); Hinderaker, *Elusive Empires,* 267; Hulsebosch, *Constituting Empire,* 11; Taylor, *Divided Ground,* 403–7. See also Hauptman, *Conspiracy of Interests;* Hall, *American Empire;* Beaulieu, "Des Grands Espaces aux Réserves"; Paige Raibmon, "Meanings of Mobility on the Northwest Coast," in Binnema and Neylan, *New Histories for Old,* 375–80; Philip J. DeLoria, "From Nation to Neighborhood: Land, Policy, Culture, Colonialism, and Empire in U.S.-Indian Relations," in Cook, Glickman, and O'Malley, *The Cultural Turn in U.S. History.*

5. Ewers, "Iroquois Indians in the Far West"; Jack A. Frisch, "Iroquois in the West," in Trigger, *Northeast,* 544–46; Robert J. Surtees, "The Iroquois in Canada," in Jennings et al., *History and Culture of Iroquois Diplomacy,* 67–85; Ritzenthaler, "Oneida Indians"; Hauptman and McLester, *The Oneida Indian Journey;* William C. Sturtevant, "Oklahoma Seneca-Cayuga," in Trigger, *Northeast,* 537–43; Hauptman, *Iroquois and the New Deal,* 88–105; Beaver, "Early Iroquoian History"; Charles M. Johnston, "The Six Nations in the Grand River Valley, 1784–1847," in Rogers and Smith, *Aboriginal Ontario,* 167–81; Hill, Gillen, and MacNaughton, *Six Nations Reserve;* Mayer, "Oneida of the Thames"; Hamori-Torok and Heath-Menger, *Unity and Sovereignty?;* Landsman, *Sovereignty and Symbol;* David J. Landy, "Tuscarora Among the Iroquois," in Trigger, *Northeast,* 521; Rayner-Herter, "Niagara Frontier Iroquois," 71, 82; Doran, "Ganienkeh"; Mohawk River Valley Project, *Kanatsiohareke.*

6. Alfred, *Peace, Power, Righteousness,* xiv, 3–4, 58, 147–48.

APPENDIX 1. IROQUOIS SETTLEMENTS, 1600–1701

1. Champlain, *Works,* 3:213–24 (possibly the Seneca village described by Étienne Brûlé in 1616); Wray, "Volume of Dutch Trade Goods," 103; Sempowski and Saunders, *Dutch Hollow and Factory Hollow,* 6, 17–310, 672, 719, 722. Per Dr. Sempowski's request (personal communication to the author, March 25, 2008 and see also Sempowski and Saunders, *Dutch Hollow and Factory Hollow,* 720–21), please note that the representation of Seneca settlement chronology in this appendix relies on the sequence of Seneca sites depicted in *Dutch Hollow and Factory Hollow,* and not on the estimated occupation dates represented therein. .

2. Champlain, *Works,* 3:213–24 (possibly the Seneca village described by Étienne Brûlé in 1616); Sempowski and Saunders, *Dutch Hollow and Factory Hollow,* 6, 583–668, 672–73, 722.

3. Champlain, *Works,* 3:213–24 (possibly the Seneca village described by Étienne Brûlé in 1616); Morgan, *League of the Iroquois,* 314 (identifies name of town at Lima site as "Skä-hasé-ga-o"); Houghton, "Seneca Nation," 417; Parker, *Archeological History,* 595; Wray, "Volume of Dutch Trade Goods," 103–6; Sempowski and Saunders, *Dutch Hollow and Factory Hollow,* 6.

4. Parker, *Archeological History,* 588; Sempowski and Saunders, *Dutch Hollow and Factory Hollow,* 6.

5. *JR* 42:81 (possibly the "village of Sonnontoehronnon Iroquois" burned and abandoned at the "first approach" of an Erie army in 1654); Wray, "Volume of Dutch Trade Goods," 106; Sempowski and Saunders, *Dutch Hollow and Factory Hollow,* 6.

6. Coyne, "Exploration of the Great Lakes," 25 (described in August 1669 by Sulpician missionary René de Bréhant de Galinée as one of two small Seneca towns of 30 houses, each of which was affiliated with a larger town of 150 houses); *JR* 54:79 (one of the Senecas' "four villages" extant in 1670); Sempowski and Saunders, *Dutch Hollow and Factory Hollow,* 6. Cf. *JR* 57:27 for Jesuit Julien Garnier's July 1673 description of only three extant Seneca villages, which may be related to the substantial numbers of Senecas relocating at that time to multinational Iroquois settlements on the north shore of Lake Ontario.

7. Christoph and Christoph, *Books of General Entries,* vol. 1, 48 (possibly one of the two Seneca towns denoted as "Serduntheago" and "Nannadeyo" on sketch of Iroquois towns appended to September 24, 1664, Iroquois treaty with English officials in New York); Coyne, "Exploration of the Great Lakes," 25 (described in August 1669 by Sulpician missionary René de Bréhant de Galinée as one of two large Seneca villages estimated at 150 houses each and located eighteen to twenty miles apart and eighteen to twenty miles south of Lake Ontario; Galinée also noted in 1669 [ibid., 81] that residents of all four Seneca villages had to go "a long distance for water"); *JR* 54:79 (one of the Senecas' "four villages" extant in 1670), 121 ("Gandachiragou," described by Jesuits in 1669), 55:75 (mission of "La Conception" described by Jesuits in 1671), 56:59 ("Gandachiorágon," described by Jesuits in 1672), 57:27 (one of the Senecas' "3 villages," described by Garnier in July 1673 as one of the two Seneca towns composed of the "natives of the country"), 191 (presence of Jesuit Pierre Raffeix in 1673), 58:229, 233, 237–43 (one of the Senecas' "three villages" described by Raffeix in 1674), 59:251 (one of the Senecas' "three different villages" visited by Jesuits in 1675); Houghton, "Seneca Nation," 413–17; Parker, *Archeological History,* 101, 111, 121, 125, 610, 616–17; Cornwell, "Artificially Deformed Skull"; Wray, "Volume of Dutch Trade Goods," 106–7; Sempowski and Saunders, *Dutch Hollow and Factory Hollow,* 6; Ryan and Dewbury, "Eugene Frost Collection."

8. *IMC,* 191 ("Keint:he," small town of twenty-four houses located four miles south of Rochester

Junction visited by Greenhalgh in 1677; described as "well furnished with corne"); *AMD* 15:238 (one of four towns of "Sinniquos" mapped by a Nacochtank adoptee in 1679); Marshall, *Narrative of the Expedition,* 161 ("Gannounata," described by Denonville in 1687); Parker, *Archeological History,* 588–90, 651. Sempowski and Saunders, *Dutch Hollow and Factory Hollow,* 6. Cf. *JR* 61:165 (1679 claim of "3 villages of Sonontouan"); "Account of Iroquois Indians" (1682 claim of "Sineuqes" residing in "3 castles or great settlements, but not fortified").

9. *IMC,* 191 ("Tiottohatton," a large new hilltop settlement of 120 houses visited by Greenhalgh in 1677; described as having "not much cleared ground," but containing the "largest of all the [Iroquois] houses" seen by Greenhalgh on his tour; he described "ordinary" houses at Rochester Junction as 50 to 60 feet in length but noted "some 130 or 140 feet [long] with 13 or 14 fires in one house"; Greenhalgh also noted the presence of a "good store of Corne" growing in an outfield "about a mile to the Northward of the Towne"); Hennepin, *Description of Louisiana,* 76–77 ("Tegarondies," the large western Seneca town described by Hennepin in 1678 and 1679); *JR* 61:165 (possibly one of the "villages of sonontouan" hosting Raffeix and Garnier in 1679); *AMD* 15:238 (one of four towns of "Sinniquos" mapped by a Nacochtank adoptee in 1679); *IHC* 23:11 ("Sanchioragon," described by La Salle [who appears to have used the name for the predecessor village at the Marsh site] in July 1679); *NYCD* 3:435 ("Theodehacto," the "last Sinnekes castle," described in 1687); Olds, "Journal of Chevalier de Baugy," 43 ("Totiakton," described in 1687); Marshall, *Narrative of the Expedition,* 161–62 ("Totiakto," described by Denonville in 1687); Beauchamp, *Indian Names in New York,* 42; Houghton, "Seneca Nation," 411–13; Parker, *Archeological History,* 610, 618–19; Wray, "Volume of Dutch Trade Goods," 109; Sempowski and Saunders, *Dutch Hollow and Factory Hollow,* 6; Jordan, "Seneca Iroquois Settlement Pattern," 28–30. Cf. dated origin of circa 1670–75 in Jordan, "Seneca Iroquois Settlement Pattern," 25; *JR* 61:165 (1679 claim of "3 villages of Sonontouan"); "Account of Iroquois Indians" (1682 claim of "Sineuqes" residing in "3 castles or great settlements, but not fortified").

10. Cox, *Journeys of Réné Robert Cavelier,* 1:3 (1678 Tonty mention of "some cabins of the Iroquois" near Niagara Falls); Hennepin, *Description of Louisiana,* 67 (December 1678 description of a "little village" of Senecas on the Niagara River; see also Hennepin, *New Discovery,* 1:80, 85 [allusion to possible Seneca Wolf Clan (Western Doorkeepers) affiliation of village]), 324–25 (May 1681 Hennepin report that Seneca residents of the village had "withdrawn themselves" to fish, but also noted presence of corn planted there); *NYCD* 9:229 (1684 mention of Seneca presence at Niagara); Lahontan, *New Voyages,* 1:137 (1687 mention of "fifty Iroquese" settled "two leagues" distant from the "waterfall at Niagara"); *LIR,* 124 (1687 description of Niagara as "40 D[utch] miles from the Sinnekes"); Scott, "Historic Contact Archaeological Deposits," 46. Cf. *JR* 61:165 (1679 claim of "3 villages of Sonontouan"); "Account of Iroquois Indians," (1682 claim of "Sineuqes" residing in "3 castles or great settlements, but not fortified"); Beauchamp, *Indian Names in New York,* 47; Parker, *Archeological History,* 630.

11. *NYCD* 4:691 (June 1700 reference to the "furthest castle of the Sinnekes called Sjaunt," site of captivity of a Virginia resident named Charles Smith from circa 1695), 750 (September 1700 claim of an oil spring located "eight miles beyond the Sineks furthest castle"); Parker, *Archeological History,* 661; Sempowski and Saunders, *Dutch Hollow and Factory Hollow,* 6; Jordan, "Seneca Iroquois Settlement Pattern," 31–33. The oil spring referred to in 1700 was located at modern-day Bristol Springs, New York (Parker, *Archeological History,* 162–70, 495; Hamell, "Gannagaro State Historic Site," 95).

12. Wray, Sempowski, and Saunders, *Tram and Cameron,* 177–384; Sempowski and Saunders, *Dutch Hollow and Factory Hollow,* 6.

13. Champlain, *Works,* 3:213–24 (possibly the Seneca village described by Étienne Brûlé in 1616);

Houghton, "Seneca Nation," 417–18; Parker, *Contact Period Seneca Site;* Wray, "Volume of Dutch Trade Goods," 103; Sempowski and Saunders, *Dutch Hollow and Factory Hollow,* 6, 311–582, 722.

14. Houghton, "Seneca Nation," 418–19; Parker, *Archeological History,* 652, 657; Wray, "Volume of Dutch Trade Goods," 103–6; Sempowski and Saunders, *Dutch Hollow and Factory Hollow,* 6.

15. C. F. Hayes III, "The Longhouse at the Cornish Site," in Tooker, *Iroquois Culture,* 91–97; Sempowski and Saunders, *Dutch Hollow and Factory Hollow,* 6.

16. *IMC,* 82 ("Sononteeonon," visited by Pierre Esprit Radisson in 1653); *JR* 42:81 (possibly the "village of Sonnontoehronnon Iroquois" burned and abandoned at the "first approach" of an Erie army in 1654); Wray, "Volume of Dutch Trade Goods," 106; Sempowski and Saunders, *Dutch Hollow and Factory Hollow,* 6. Jones ("Iroquois Population History," 359–60) identifies this site as "one of the largest" of any known Iroquois settlerments circa 1500–1700

17. *JR* 44:25–27 ("St. Michel," home to Tahontaenrat Wendat, Neutral, and Shawnee adoptees, described by Jesuit Joseph Chaumonot in 1656), 52:53–55, 195–97 ("St. Michel," the relocated Tahontaenrat Wendat, Neutral, and Shawnee adoptee community visited by Jesuit Jacques Frémin in 1668); Coyne, "Exploration of the Great Lakes," 25 (described by Galinée in 1669 as a small town consisting of thirty houses), 35 (located in 1669 "half a league" distant from the large Seneca town at the Marsh site); *JR* 54:81–83, 121 ("Gandougaraé," described by Frémin in September 1669 as composed of the "remnants of three different Nations"); Sempowski and Saunders, *Dutch Hollow and Factory Hollow,* 3; Kurt Jordan, personal correspondence to the author, September 14, 2007, and March 26, 2008.

18. *JR* 44:21–25 ("Gandagan," described by Chaumonot as the "principal village" of the Senecas in 1656); *MNF* 9:651 ("Gandagan," home in 1656 to "Annonjenritaoui," described as "the grand chief of the Senecas"); Christoph and Christoph, *Books of General Entries,* vol. 1, 48 (possibly one of the two Seneca towns denoted as "Serduntheago" and "Nannadeyo" on a sketch of Iroquois towns appended to September 24, 1664, Iroquois treaty with English officials in New York); Coyne, "Exploration of the Great Lakes," 19 (description of summer 1669 Susquehannock attack on the town that killed ten Seneca men), 25 (described by Galinée in 1669 as one of two large Seneca villages, estimated at 150 houses each and located eighteen to twenty miles apart and eighteen to twenty miles south of lake Ontario); *JR* 54:79 (one of the Senecas' "four villages" extant in 1670), 81 ("St. Jacques," mentioned in 1671), 115 ("Gandagaro," visited by Frémin and Garnier in September 1669), 55:75 ("St. Jacques," mentioned in 1671), 56:59 ("St. Jacques," mentioned in 1672), 57:27 (one of the Senecas' "3 villages," described in July 1673 by Garnier as one of the two Seneca villages composed of the "natives of the country"), 193–95 (Garnier noted its lack of a chapel at "St. Jacques" in 1673, despite its size, which he estimated as "twice as large as that of St. Michel"), 58:229, 233–35 ("St. Jacques," one of the Senecas' "three villages" described by Raffeix in 1674), 59:251 (one of the Senecas' "three different villages" visited by Jesuits in 1675); Houghton, "Seneca Nation," 420–25, 447; Wray, "Volume of Dutch Trade Goods," 106–7; Sempowski and Saunders, *Dutch Hollow and Factory Hollow,* 6. Cf. Parker, *Archeological History,* 655–56.

19. *JR* 54:79 (one of the Senecas' "four villages" extant in 1670), 55:75, 79 (successor site of St. Michel mission, burned in the spring of 1671); Hoffmann, "McClintock Burial Site"; Sempowski and Saunders, *Dutch Hollow and Factory Hollow,* 3; Jordan, personal correspondence to the author, September 14, 2007, and March 26, 2008.

20. *JR* 56:59 ("St. Michel," described by Jesuits in 1672), 57:27 (one of the Senecas' "3 villages," described in July 1673 by Garnier as composed of the "remnants of several huron nations destroyed by the Iroquois"), 191 (presence of Garnier in 1673), 58:229, 233 (one of the Senecas' "three villages" mentioned in 1674), 59:251 (one of the Senecas' "three different villages"

visited by Jesuits in 1675); *IMC,* 191 ("Canoenada," a small town of thirty houses located four miles south of Ganondagan visited by Greenhalgh in 1677, which he described as "well furnished with Corne"); *JR* 61:165 (possibly one of the "villages of sonontouan" hosting Raffeix and Garnier in 1679); *AMD* 15:238 (one of four towns of "Sinniquos" mapped by a Nacochtank adoptee in 1679); Marshall, *Narrative of the Expedition,* 161 ("Gannogarae," described by Denonville in 1687); *NYCD* 9:366 (1687); Olds, "Journal of Chevalier de Baugy," 40, 42–43 ("Gannounata," described in 1687); Houghton, "Seneca Nation," 436–38, 439–44, 447; Wray and Graham, "New Discoveries On an Old Site"; Sempowski and Saunders, *Dutch Hollow and Factory Hollow,* 3; Jordan, personal correspondence to the author, September 14, 2007;. Cf. *JR* 61:165 (1679 claim of "3 villages of Sonontouan"); "Account of Iroquois Indians" (1682 claim of "Sineuqes" residing in "3 castles or great settlements, but not fortified"); Parker, *Archeological History,* 655. For evidence of an ossuary burial of 28 persons at this site, see White, "Orchid Site Ossuary," 22.

21. *IMC,* 191 ("Canagaroh," hilltop settlement of 150 houses visited by Greenhalgh in 1677); *IHC* 23:11 ("Kanagaro," described by La Salle in 1679); *AMD* 15:238 (one of four towns of "Sinniquos" mapped by a Nacochtank adoptee in 1679); Marshall, *Narrative of the Expedition,* 160 ("Gannagaro," described by Denonville in 1687); *NYCD* 3:434 ("Kohoseraghe," as rendered in Mohawk language in 1687); Houghton, "Seneca Nation," 427–38; Parker, *Archeological History,* 652–54; Hamell, "Gannagaro State Historic Site," 91–93; Jemison, "Ganondagan Lives On," 2–3; Lewis-Lorentz, "From Gannagaro to Ganondagan"; Wray, "Volume of Dutch Trade Goods," 109; Paul R. Huey, "Archaeological Testing for an Electrical Line," 12; Sempowski and Saunders, *Dutch Hollow and Factory Hollow,* 6; Jordan, "Seneca Iroquois Settlement Pattern," 28–30. Cf. dated origin to circa 1670–75 in Jordan, "Seneca Iroquois Settlement Pattern," 25; *JR* 61:165 (1679 claim of "3 villages of Sonontouan"); "Account of Iroquois Indians" (1682 claim of "Sineuqes" residing in "3 castles or great settlements, but not fortified"). Also known as Gannagaro (see Hamell, "Gannagaro State Historic Site," 93) and the Boughton Hill site (see Jordan, "Seneca Iroquois Settlement Pattern," 25).

22. Blair, *Indian Tribes,* 1:255 (autumn 1687 visit of Tionnontaté Wendat embassy to a rebuilt Seneca town, possibly located near some of the Seneca out-fields [east of Ganondagan] spared during the 1687 Denonville expedition); Grumet, *Historic Contact,* 406; Sempowski and Saunders, *Dutch Hollow and Factory Hollow,* 3.

23. *NYCD* 3:805–6 (1691 visit to Albany of Seneca leaders from "Kahesarahera," described at that time as the western limit of the "bounds" of New York); Sempowski and Saunders, *Dutch Hollow and Factory Hollow,* 6; Jordan, "Seneca Iroquois Settlement Pattern," 31–33. I propose that the rendering of "Kahesarahera" in Albany in 1691 represents a close approximation of the Mohawk name "Kohoseraghe" for the Ganondagan community, the predecessor of White Springs (see Beauchamp, *Indian Names in New York,* 61). This name may reflect the location of the League's "western door" at White Springs circa 1691, given the associations of the place-name "Kahesarahera" (translated as "basswood place" in Fenton, "Problems," 229) and League tradition of its western door being "guarded by sheets of slippery bark upon which the enemy would slip if he sought unwarranted and uninvited admittance" (Parker, *Analytical History of the Seneca Indians,* 34–35). On the other hand, it could also represent the place-name for the town at the Snyder-McClure site if the contemporary identification of Kahesarahera as the League's westernmost town was correct and if the Senecas, like the Mohawks did after 1693 (see the discussions of Ft. Plain Cemetery II and Allen IV below) altered the east-west naming patterns of their towns. Cf. Hodge, *Handbook,* 1:640, for translation of Kahesarahera as "a rotten log lying on the top of it." The author walked this site (located on the grounds of White Springs Manor in Geneva, New York) on June 8, 2007. It is located on

elevated ground with a direct view (to the southwest) of Seneca Lake and is in close proximity to a flowing spring.

24. Follett, "Following the Cayuga," 1.5; Grumet, *Historic Contact,* 399; DeOrio, "Preliminary Sequence of the Historic Cayuga Nation"; Niemczycki, "Cayuga Archaeology," 31; Mandzy, "History of Cayuga Acculturation," 106–29.

25. Follett, "Following the Cayuga," 1.6; Grumet, *Historic Contact,* 399; DeOrio, "Preliminary Sequence of the Historic Cayuga"; Niemczycki, "Cayuga Archaeology," 31; Mandzy, "History of Cayuga Acculturation," 64–65.

26. *IMC,* 82 (possibly one of the three villages of "Oiongoiconon[s]" visited by Radisson in 1653); Follett, "Following the Cayuga," 1.6; Grumet, *Historic Contact,* 399; DeOrio, "Preliminary Sequence of the Historic Cayuga"; Mandzy, "History of Cayuga Acculturation," 130–32. Also known as the Garrett site (Niemczycki, "Cayuga Archaeology," 31). The museum collection of artifacts from the so-called Dean site (described in Mandzy, "History of Cayuga Acculturation," 65–66) may be associated with this site. Cf. Wyckoff, "Land of the Eries," 18–21, who argues on the basis of cartographic evidence that Radisson visited three Cayuga villages located on the plains of the upper Chemung River, near modern-day Big Flats, New York. Cf. Marian E. White, William E. Engelbrecht, and Elisabeth Tooker, "Cayuga," in Trigger, *Northeast,* 500; Niemczycki, "Cayuga Archaeology," 31.

27. *IMC,* 82 (possibly one of the three villages of "Oiongoiconon[s]" visited by Radisson in 1653); Grumet, *Historic Contact,* 399. See also Cowin, "Shell Ornaments from Cayuga County."

28. *IMC,* 82 (possibly one of the three villages of "Oiongoiconon[s]" visited by Radisson in 1653); Christoph and Christoph, *Books of General Entries,* vol. 1, 48 (possibly "Canyugo" depicted on a sketch of Iroquois towns appended to September 24, 1664, Iroquois treaty with English officials in New York); *JR* 51:255 (1668 mention of the "St. Joseph" mission), 293 ("Goiogouen," described in 1668), 52:173 (1668 mention of "the mission of Saint Joseph in the country of Oiogouen," located "about twenty leagues" from the Onondagas' town), 179 ("Oiogouen" or St. Joseph; described by Jesuit Étienne de Carheil in 1668 as the "seat" of the Jesuit mission to the Cayugas, then located twelve miles from St. Stephen [René Ménard Bridge Hilltop] and "nearly" eighteen miles from St. René [Rogers Farm]), 54:53 (1670 description of "Goiogouen," or "Saint Joseph, Patron of the whole [Cayuga] Mission"), 109 (August 10, 1669, Frémin visit to Carheil at Oiogouen en route from Seneca country to Onondaga town), 55:67 (1671 description of the "Mission of St. Joseph at Goiogouen"), 56:49–51 (1672 Jesuit description of a single mission "village" in Cayuga country at a location most closely affiliated to Mead Farm suggests terminal dates of circa 1671 for St. Stephen [René Ménard Bridge Hilltop] and St. René [Rogers Farm]), 57:177 (1673 description of the "Mission of St. Joseph at Goiogouen"), 58:225 (1674 description of the "Mission of St. Joseph at Goioguin"); *IMC,* 191 (one of the three unpalisaded Cayuga towns [100 houses in total] visited by Greenhalgh in 1677). Greenhalgh's 1677 description of the three extant Cayuga towns represents them in much greater proximity to one another than Jesuit sources did in 1668. I propose that this reflects the movements after 1671 of the residents of the town of Thiohero/St. Stephen from the René Ménard Bridge Hilltop site to the Young Farm site, and the residents of the town of Onontaré/St. René from the Rogers Farm site to the Lamb site. Cf. Skinner, *Notes on Iroquois Archeology,* 50–51; Follett, "Following the Cayuga," 1.7, 1.8; "Jesuit Mission Site of St. Joseph"; Grumet, *Historic Contact,* 399; DeOrio, "Preliminary Sequence of the Historic Cayuga"; Niemczycki, "Cayuga Archaeology," 31; Mandzy, "History of Cayuga Acculturation," 10, 66, 153–69; Williams-Shuker, "Cayuga Iroquois Households," 14.

29. *JR* 51:293 ("Onontaré," described in 1668), 52:179 (St. René, one of three Cayuga villages described by Carheil in 1668), 54:53 (1670 mention of "Onnontare, which is called the Village of

Saint René"); Hawley, *Early Chapters of Cayuga History,* 21n2, 48n1; Grumet, *Historic Contact,* 399; DeOrio, "Preliminary Sequence of the Historic Cayuga"; Niemczycki, "Cayuga Archaeology," 31; Mandzy, "History of Cayuga Acculturation," 139–52; Mandzy, "Rogers Farm Site," 18–25; Williams-Shuker, "Cayuga Iroquois Households," 14–19.

30. *JR* 51:293 ("Thiohero," mentioned in 1668), 52:179 ("Thiohero," described by Carheil in 1668 as inhabited by Wendat and Susquehannock adoptees), 185 (visited by Carheil in 1668), 54:53 ("Kiohero," or "Saint Estienne," described by the Jesuits in 1670), 56:51 (1672 Jesuit identification of "Lake Tiohero" [Cayuga Lake] as one of the two bodies of water "adjoining our village"; also noted presence of Neutral and Wendat adoptees); Hawley, *Early Chapters of Cayuga History,* 21n2, 48n1; Beauchamp, *Indian Names in New York,* 12; Parker, *Archeological History,* 503; Grumet, *Historic Contact,* 399; DeOrio, "Preliminary Sequence of the Historic Cayuga"; Niemczycki, "Cayuga Archaeology," 31; Mandzy, "History of Cayuga Acculturation," 66–67, 173–76. Also known as the St. Stephen Mission (Williams-Shuker, "Cayuga Iroquois Households," 14).

31. *IMC,* 191 (one of the three unpalisaded Cayuga towns [100 houses in total] visited by Greenhalgh in 1677); Grumet, *Historic Contact,* 399; DeOrio, "Preliminary Sequence of the Historic Cayuga"; Niemczycki, "Cayuga Archaeology," 31–32; Mandzy, "History of Cayuga Acculturation," 169–72. Also known as the Fleming site (Mandzy, "History of Cayuga Acculturation," 169). Cf. *JR* 52:179.

32. *IMC,* 191 (one of the three unpalisaded Cayuga towns [100 houses in total] visited by Greenhalgh in 1677, who noted the Cayugas' intent "the next spring to build all their houses together and Stockado them"); *JR* 61:21 (presence of Carheil at "Oiogouin" in 1678), 165 (presence of Carheil at "goiogoen" in 1679); "Account of Iroquois Indians" (1682 reference to a single Cayuga town); *NYCD* 9:376 (1688 mention of a single Cayuga town as "an Iroquois hamlet of 80 cabins"); Hawley, *Early Chapters of Cayuga History,* 21n2, 48n1; Skinner, *Notes on Iroquois Archeology,* 56–67; Parker, *Archeological History,* 500; Follett, "Following the Cayuga," 1.9, 1.10, 2.1, "Chronology of Indian Affairs," 39; Grumet, *Historic Contact,* 399; DeOrio, "Preliminary Sequence of the Historic Cayuga"; Niemczycki, "Cayuga Archaeology," 31–32; Mandzy, "History of Cayuga Acculturation," 177–96. Also known as the Great Gully site (Engelbrecht, *Iroquoia,* 116).

33. Parker, *Archeological History,* 644; Bradley and Bennett, "Two Occurrences of Weser Slipware"; Bradley, *Evolution of the Onondaga Iroquois,* 116; Bradley, "Change and Survival," 27.

34. Bradley, *Evolution of the Onondaga Iroquois,* 116.

35. Bradley and DeAngelo, "European Clay Pipe Marks," 123; Bradley, *Evolution of the Onondaga Iroquois,* 116.

36. Bradley and DeAngelo, "European Clay Pipe Marks," 123; Bradley, "Dutch Bale Seals," 197–99; Bradley, *Evolution of the Onondaga Iroquois,* 116.

37. *IMC,* 82 ("Nontageya," visited by Radisson in 1653); *JR* 41:99 ("the chief village, Onontagé," visited by Jesuit Simon Le Moyne in 1654), 42:87 (November 5, 1655, description of the town's "carefully cleaned" streets and its "cabin-roofs crowded with children" observing formal reception of the Jesuit embassy); Tanner, "Lot 18 Site"; Bradley and DeAngelo, "European Clay Pipe Marks," 124–26; Bradley, "Dutch Bale Seals," 199; Bradley, *Evolution of the Onondaga Iroquois,* 116.

38. *JR* 43:137, 145 (July 1656 description of the "Village of Onnontaghé"); Bradley and DeAngelo, "European Clay Pipe Marks," 124; Tanner, "Indian Castle Site"; Bradley, *Before Albany,* 43.

39. *JR* 41:245–47 (April 12, 1656 "Concession of Lands in the country of the Onnondageoronons"), 42:95 (November 1655 description of site chosen for the planned "French settlement" at "Ganentaa"), 43:49 (May 17, 1656, presence of Jesuit Joseph-Marie Chaumonot at "Ganentaha,

near Onontagè"), 147 (July 7, 1656, French reconnaissance of location for planned "residence" on the shore of "Lake Ganentaa"), 151, 157, 161, 181, 183, 44:159, 173–83, 187, 217 (accounts of March 20, 1658, French abandonment of Gannentaha), 54:111 (August 20, 1669, visit of Frémin to site of Gannentaha; he reported its "remains" as "in the same condition in which it was" when abandoned in 1658); Parker, *Archeological History,* 647; Grumet, *Historic Contact,* 390.

40. Christoph and Christoph, *Books of General Entries,* vol. 1, 48 (possibly "Nondarowna" depicted on sketch of Iroquois towns appended to September 24, 1664, Iroquois treaty with English officials in New York); *JR* 51:237–39 (1668 description of "Onnontaé, a large village, and the center of all the Iroquois nations," located only "a short day's journey distant" from the Oneidas' town), 52:153 ("the Mission of Saint Jean Baptiste in the country of the Onnontagué," described by the Jesuits in 1668 as "a large village, the center of all the Iroquois tribes, and the place of the general assemblies that they hold each year"), 155 (November 1669 mention of the town of "Onnontagué"), 53:261 (presence of Jesuit Pierre Millet in June 1670), 54:43 (June 1670 Millet description of one "Cabin" affiliated with the town that was "wholly Christian, and occupied exclusively by Huron women, who had formerly come to settle in this country when our Fathers were dwelling" at Gannentaha, circa 1656–58), 55:55 (1671 mention of the "Mission of St. Jean Baptiste at Onnontagué"), 56:39 (1672 description of the "Mission of St. Jean Baptiste at Onnontague"), 57:127 (1673 description of the "Mission of St. Jean Baptiste at Onnontagué"), 58:207 (1674 description of the "Mission of St. Jean Baptiste at Onnontagué"), 59:243 (1675 description of "Onnontagué," the "village of the third [Iroquois] nation"), 60:185 (presence of Jesuit Jean de Lamberville at "Onnontagué," June 18, 1676); *IMC,* 189 (visited by Greenhalgh in 1677; described as a very large, unpalisaded hilltop settlement of 140 houses with land cleared to a distance of two miles around the village; Greenhalgh also noted the presence of an affiliated hamlet of twenty-four houses located two miles beyond the limit of Onondaga fields); *JR* 61:21 (1678 description of "Onnontagué"), 165 (presence of Bruyas at "onnontagé" in 1679); "Account of Iroquois Indians" (1682 reference to a single Onondaga town "seated near the Lake Onontario" [*sic*]); *JR* 62:55–57 (1682 Jesuit statement of nineteen-year duration of Onondaga occupation of this site prior to move to Weston site); Parker, *Archeological History,* 642–44; Bradley and DeAngelo, "European Clay Pipe Marks," 127–28; Bradley, "Dutch Bale Seals," 199; Bradley, *Evolution of the Onondaga Iroquois,* 206; Bradley, *Before Albany,* 184; Richard Hosbach, "Carlos I and Carlos II Coins Found on Two New York Iroquois Sites," in Wright and Pilon, *Passion for the Past,* 193.

41. *JR* 62:55–59 (1682 Lamberville description of Onondaga relocation from Indian Hill town to new town "two leagues" distant at Weston site), 79 (completed town at Weston described by Lamberville in 1682 as "the largest in the Iroquois country"); *NYCD* 9:375 (1688 account of Onondaga settlements described the "beginning" of the Onondaga "cabins" at Techirogouen [the fishing station near modern-day Brewerton, New York], then the "great village of Onnontagué" [at the Weston site], and finally noted a satellite community called "Touenho," consisting of an unspecified number of "other cabins, not far distant from the Village"), 4:60 (1693 description of Onondaga town as one and one-half days' travel from second Oneida town at Upper Hogan); Le Roy de la Potherie, *Histoire,* 2:509 (spring 1693 report of escaped French captive describing "fort" at Onondaga as "built by the English" and consisting of eight bastions and a triple palisade); *NYCD* 9:653 (October 1696 description of the Onondagas' "fort" consisting of a triple palisade in an "oblong" shape, "flanked by four regular bastions"; two of the rows of "stockades" were as thick as "an ordinary [ship]mast," with a "third row, six feet distant, of much smaller dimensions, but between 40 and 50 feet in height"); *RAPQ* (1928–29): 307 (October 1696 description of Onondaga settlement destroyed in 1696 as "nearly 150 leagues" distant from Montreal); Parker, *Archeological History,* 641–42;

Sohrweide, "Onondaga Longhouses," 22–23. For possible evidence of French influence on the architecture of the Weston site, see *JR* 62:243 for a 1683 description of a Jesuit *donné* named Pierre Maizieray who reportedly traveled through different Iroquois communities assisting in house construction during village relocations as well as other "trades."

42. *NYCD* 4:366, 370, 372–73 (1698 descriptions of the "Onnondagoes Castle"), 560–61 (May 1699 reference to single Onondaga town with a specially constructed "proposition house"), 649 (April 1700 description of Onondaga town located "16 miles" distant from nearest body of water, accessed by Livingston on foot from "Kanienda" fishing station [then described as eight miles distant from the Onondaga "castle" (ibid., 4:650, 891)]; Livingston also claimed that firewood was "near being consumed" at Onondaga, fostering speculation that Onondagas would soon "leave their castle" and settle at a location twelve miles east), 660 (May 1700 statement of Onondaga "castle" located 270 miles from Albany), 802 (September 1700 description of Onondaga town located one day's travel on foot west of Oneida town at Collins site), 889–90 (June 1701 description of Onondaga town located one day's travel on foot west of Oneida town at Collins site); Bradley and DeAngelo, "European Clay Pipe Marks," 128–30; Bradley, *Evolution of the Onondaga Iroquois,* 191.

43. Pratt, *Archaeology of the Oneida Iroquois,* 121–24; Bradley and Bennett, "Two Occurrences of Weser Slipware"; Clark, "Gender at an Early Seventeenth Century Oneida Village," 145–50; Jones, "Iroquois Population History," 277 ("one of the most imposing site locations in all of Iroquoia"). Clark's work revises the terminal date of 1595 assigned for this site in Bennett, "Recent Findings," 2; Henry, "Cultural Change and Adaptation," 120.

44. Hosbach and Gibson, "Wilson Site"; Bennett, "Recent Findings," 2.

45. Pratt, *Archaeology of the Oneida Iroquois,* 124–28; McCashion, "Unique Dutch Clay Tobacco Pipe"; Bennett, "Recent Findings," 2.

46. Gehring and Starna, *Journey into Mohawk and Oneida Country,* 14 ("Oneyuttehage," described by Van den Bogaert in 1635); Parker, *Archeological History,* 607; Bennett, "Recent Findings," 2; Bennett, "Longhouse Pattern on the Thurston Site." Cf. Henry, "Cultural Change and Adaptation," 134–35.

47. Bennett and Cole, "Marshall Site"; Bennett, "Recent Findings," 2.

48. McCashion, "Clay Tobacco Pipes of New York State, Part III"; Bennett, "Recent Findings," 2; Bennett, "Stone Quarry Site"; Wonderley, "Importance of Cloth Seals."

49. *IMC,* 82 ("Nojottga," visited by Radisson in 1653); *JR* 44: 29–33 (town visited by Jesuit Joseph Chaumonot in 1656); Bennett, "Recent Findings," 2; Hosbach, "Carlos I and Carlos II Coins," 193; Henry, "Cultural Change and Adaptation," 158; Wonderley, "Importance of Cloth"; Hosbach et al., "Dungey Site"; Neill et al., "Dungey Site."

50. Brandão, *Nation Iroquoise,* 29–30, 49 (possibly the "Oneyoutte" town where French settler Rene Cuillerier was held captive from 1661 to 1663); Christoph and Christoph, *Books of General Entries,* vol. 1, 48 (possibly "Onchyendehunak" depicted on sketch of Iroquois towns appended to September 24, 1664, Iroquois treaty with English officials in New York); Kip, *Early Jesuit Missions,* 85 (1667 description of Oneida town thirty leagues west of western Mohawk town of Tionnontogouen/White Orchard); *JR* 51:121 (1668 Bruyas claim of the extant Oneida town as "thirty leagues" distant from Mohawk country), 221 (1668 mention of "the mission of St. Francis Xavier among the Iroquois Onneiout"), 52:145 (presence of Bruyas at St. François Xavier mission in November 1669), 53:249 (November 1669 Bruyas mention of the "streets of this village"), 55:45 (presence of Bruyas at the "Mission of Saint François Xavier at Onneiout" in 1671), 56:31 (1672 description of the "Mission of Saint François Xavier at Onneiout"), 57:113 (presence of Millet at the "Mission of Saint François Xavier at Onneiout" in 1673), 58:179 (1674 Millet description of the "Onneiout Mission"), 59:241 (1675 description of the "mission

of Onneiout"), 60:183 (1676 description of "Onneiout"); Hagerty, "Iron Trade Knife," 104; Bennett, "Recent Findings," 2. Cf. Bennett's description of the pre-1677 character of the artifact assemblage from this site in his "Moot Site (Sullivan)."

51. *IMC,* 189 (a "newly settled, double stockadoed" town of 100 houses visited by Greenhalgh in 1677; described as having "little cleared ground" and procuring corn from nearby Onondaga [Indian Hills] community); *JR* 61:21 (presence of Jesuit Millet at "Onneiout" in 1678), 165 (presence of Millet at "Onneiout" in 1679); "Account of Iroquois Indians" (1682 reference to a single Oneida town located thirty leagues west of Mohawk country); *NYCD* 4:60 (one of two documented Oneida towns in existence in 1693); Bennett, "Recent Findings," 2. Cf. Grumet, *Historic Contact,* 379–80.

52. *NYCD* 4:60 (one of two documented Oneida towns in existence in 1693); *RAPQ* (1928–29): 307 (October 1696 description of Oneida town burned in 1696 as fifteen leagues east of the Onondaga town at the Weston site); *JR* 65:27 (1696 location of Oneida town given as "12 or 15 leagues from onnontagué"); *NYCD* 9:640 (distance of Oneida town from Onondaga described as "fifteen leagues"), 655–56 (distance from Onondaga town to Oneida town described in 1696 as "fourteen good leagues through the woods, with continual mountains and a number of rivers or large streams to be crossed"); Bennett and Cole, "Upper Hogan Site"; Clark and Owen, "Recent Excavations on the Cody Site"; Bennett, "Recent Findings," 2, 11–12; Bradley, *Before Albany,* 184.

53. *NYCD* 13:502 (November 1696 or 1697 reference to "Kanadagerea Oneidas," possibly the name of the town rebuilt after the 1696 French expedition) (see Christoph and Christoph, *Andros Papers,* 1:404–5, for correct dating of initial reference); *NYCD* 4:372 (September 1698 mention of a single Oneida "castle"), 560–61 (May 1699 reference to single Oneida town), 655 (April 1700 mention of single "Oneyde" town), 802 (September 1700 mention of single "Oneyde" town), 889–90 (July 1701 mention of single "Oneyde" town located over thirty-two miles west-southwest of westernmost Mohawk settlement at Dekanohoge, required crossing of east branch of Unadilla Creek [in modern-day Paris, New York] to reach village); *Catalogue of the Manuscript Maps,* 3:524; Bennett, "Primes Hill Site," 5.

54. Archaeological literature indicates that for much of the seventeenth century, the Mohawks' settlement pattern held strong associations with their three constituent clans. Larger towns, referred to by contemporary European observers as "castles," were often associated with a particular clan (Wolf, Bear, and Turtle moving from west to east), and often had smaller, affiliated "satellite" communities (see Fenton and Tooker, "Mohawk," in Trigger, *Northeast,* 466–67). Beyond this widely shared opinion, little agreement exists concerning the duration and timing of specific Mohawk site occupancies. These disagreements in turn have yielded considerable confusion about the identity of Mohawk settlements documented in historical sources. In the sequence below, I provide an interpretation of the extant data that differs from the following previously published studies: Rumrill, "Interpretation and Analysis"; Rumrill, "Mohawk Glass Trade Bead Chronology"; Snow, *Mohawk Valley Archaeology;* Bradley, *Before Albany;* Starna, "Review Essay," 332. The interpretation presented below owes a substantial debt to Wayne Lenig, whose unpublished paper, "The Swart Collection and Mohawk Archaeology" (2003), discusses a substantial collection of artifacts that has recently come to light and the challenges this new body of evidence poses for many extant assumptions about the Mohawk sequence. See also his earlier remarks in "Patterns of Material Culture," 49. Mr. Lenig generously shared his abundant knowledge of Mohawk archaeology in extensive personal correspondence to the author during March and April 2008.

55. Bradley, *Before Albany,* 16 (an unregistered site). W. Lenig (personal correspondence to the author, April 2008) suggested this site as a potential candidate for the Mohawks' westernmost

"castle" during this time period.

56. Ballard and Ballard, "Contact Mohawk Cemetery"; Lenig, "Of Dutchmen, Beaver Hats, and Iroquois," 77–78; Snow, *Mohawk Valley Archaeology*, 4, 265–78; Bradley, *Before Albany*, 16, 43. Cf. alternate dates of 1610–30 (Rumrill, "Interpretation and Analysis," 7), 1615–30 (Rumrill, "Mohawk Glass Trade Bead Sequence," 15, 17–18).

57. Grumet, *Historic Contact*, 357. W. Lenig (personal correspondence to the author, April 2008) suggested that this site preceded the Failing site in the Mohawks' western settlement sequence. Rumrill ("Mohawk Glass Trade Bead Sequence," 16) notes the difficulty of associating the villages described by Van den Bogaert to archaeological sites.

58. Gehring and Starna, *Journey into Mohawk and Oneida Country*, 9 (possibly "Tenotoge," the Mohawks' fourth "Castle," described by Van den Bogaert in 1634 as consisting of fifty-five houses protected by a triple palisade, with grain storage structures on the opposite side of the Mohawk River); *MNF* 5:593 ("Theontougen," described by Jogues in August 1642); Du Creux, *History of Canada*, 1:382; *JR* 25:69, 31:39–51, 83 (one of three Mohawk towns described by Jogues in 1642–43); *IMC*, 46 ("Theonondiogo," described by Megapolensis in 1644); Bradley, *Before Albany*, 43. Cf. alternate dates of 1615–34 (Snow, *Mohawk Valley Archaeology*, 4, 239–40, 294–97). W. Lenig (personal correspondence to the author, March 2008) suggested this site as the best candidate for Van den Bogaert's "Tenotoge" and disputed Snow's hypothesis that this site represented an ethnic Oneida settlement on the western periphery of Mohawk country. Cf. alternate dates of 1620–35 (Rumrill, "Mohawk Glass Trade Bead Sequence," 16).

59. Gehring and Starna, *Journey into Mohawk and Oneida Country*, 8 ("Cawaoge," a Mohawk "village" described by Van den Bogaert in 1634 as consisting of fourteen houses); Rumrill, "Mohawk Glass Trade Bead Sequence," 16; Bradley, *Before Albany*, 43. Cf. alternate dates of 1634–42 (Snow, *Mohawk Valley Archaeology*, 4, 303, 325–34).

60. Bradley, *Before Albany*, 43. Cf. alternate dates of 1630–46 (Rumrill, "Mohawk Glass Trade Bead Sequence," 25), 1635–55 (Kuhn and Funk, "Boning Up on the Mohawk," 30), 1643–46 (Snow, *Mohawk Valley Archaeology*, 4, 303, 334–59).

61. *JR* 40:127, 135, 139 (possibly one of three Mohawk towns described by Jesuit Joseph Poncet in 1653); Parker, *Archeological History*, 620. W. Lenig (personal correspondence to the author, April 2008) suggested these dates of occupancy for this site. Cf. alternate dates of 1645–50 (Bradley, *Before Albany*, 43), 1666–79 and 1690–93 (Snow, *Mohawk Valley Archaeology*, 4, 426, 443–47).

62. *FOCM*, 459 (September 1659 reference to a single "Third Castle" of the Mohawks); *JR* 45:207 (reference to the Mohawks possessing "three or four wretched Villages" in 1659); Christoph and Christoph, *Books of General Entries*, vol. 1, 48 (depiction of three towns of "Conegehaugah" on sketch of Iroquois towns appended to September 24, 1664, Iroquois treaty with English officials in New York); *JR* 49:257 (1666 mention of "two or three" Mohawk villages), 267 (1666 map depicting three Mohawk villages), 50:203 (one of four Mohawk towns destroyed by the 1666 French expedition); Bradley, *Before Albany*, 43. W. Lenig (personal correspondence to the author, March 2008) suggested this range of dates and identified the site as a possible candidate for one of the four Mohawk towns destroyed in 1666. Rumrill ("Interpretation and Analysis," 29) supports this claim. Cf. alternate dates of 1635–46 (Grumet, *Historic Contact*, 357).

63. *JR* 43:191 (evidence of relocation of a significant number of Huron adoptees to Mohawk country in 1657), 45:207 (reference to the Mohawks possessing "three or four wretched Villages" in 1659), 49:257 (1666 mention of "two or three" Mohawk villages), 267 (1666 map depicting three Mohawk villages), 51:205 (one of the "six villages of the Mohawks" extant in 1667), 211

(Frémin's description of one of the Mohawks "villages" in which he found "forty-five old-time [Huron] Christians"), 52:123 (one of the "seven large Villages" of the Mohawks described by the Jesuits in 1669). W. Lenig (personal correspondence to the author, March 2008) agreed with the author's opinion that this town, composed primarily of Wendat adoptees, was neither burned by the French in 1666 nor visited by Greenhalgh in 1677. Cf. the alternate interpretation that this site represented Greenhalgh's "Canajorha" in Kuhn and Snow, *Mohawk Valley Project,* 3. Cf. alternate dates of 1657–79 (Snow, *Mohawk Valley Archaeology,* 364–65, 403–10, 411–12, 426), 1665–90 (Bradley, *Before Albany,* 184, 186), 1667–80 (Kuhn and Snow, *Mohawk Valley Project,* 29), 1667–82 (Rumrill, "Mohawk Glass Trade Bead Sequence, 33, 35), 1683–93 (Funk and Kuhn, "Boning Up on the Mohawk," 30). See also *NYCD* 13:480 (June 1674 Mohawk claim to have "drawn their three castles into one" in order to "increase their strength and power to resist all enemies," an apparent reference to the Mohawks' three totemic clans rather than to their seven extant settlements at that time).

64. *JR* 51:179 (the "Mission of Sainte Marie," described in 1667), 201–5 ("Tionnontogouen," described by the Jesuits in 1667 as the "capital" of Mohawk country; one of the "six villages of the Mohawks" extant in 1667), 219 (1667 mention of Jesuit mission of Sainte Marie), 52:117 ("Tinniontogouen the principal Village" of the Mohawks, described in October 1668), 123 (one of the "seven large Villages" of the Mohawks described by the Jesuits in 1669), 53:137–39 ("Tionnontogouen," described as four leagues west of Fox Farm/Gandaouagué by Jesuit Jean Pierron in 1669), 57:27 (last documented presence of Jesuit Bruyas at "Tionnontogouen" in July 1673), 81 (location of Jesuit mission of Ste. Marie in 1673), 89 (described as five leagues distant from the other two Mohawk towns hosting Jesuits in 1673; *IMC,* 189 ("Tionondogue," visited by Greenhalgh in 1677; described as a town of thirty houses, built on a hilltop a "bow shot" from the Mohawk River, with a "double stockade" possessing four "ports," each four feet wide); "Account of Iroquois Indians" (one of three extant Mohawk "castles" in 1682, each located four to five leagues distant from one another); *LIR,* 175 (April 1700 mention of "the Place where the great Castle stood called Tionondoge burnt by the French"); McCashion, "Clay Tobacco Pipes of New York State, Part V." Cf. Parker, *Archeological History,* 621. Cf. alternate dates of 1660–90 (Bradley, *Before Albany,* 170, 184), 1667–82 (Rumrill, "Mohawk Glass Trade Bead Sequence," 34), 1667–93 (Snow, *Mohawk Valley Archaeology,* 4, 425–28). See also *NYCD* 13:480.

65. *JR* 52:123 (one of the "seven large Villages" of the Mohawks described by the Jesuits in 1669); *IMC,* 189 (described by Greenhalgh in 1677 as a small hamlet of ten houses, built on flat land close to the Mohawk River, "without Fence," and estimated as 110 miles distant from Albany). W. Lenig (personal correspondence to the author, March 2008) suggested this site as a potential candidate for the unnamed town described by Greenhalgh. See also *NYCD* 13:480. Cf. Grumet, *Historic Contact,* 358.

66. Munsell, *Annals of Albany,* 2:113 (mention of planned 1689 relocation of "Tionnondagé" an "English mile up" the Mohawk River; Le Roy de la Potherie, *Histoire,* 2:503 (the "principal" Mohawk town in 1693); *NYCD* 4:18, 82 (January 1694 mention of "the old Castle called Tionondoge which the French burnt last Spring"; enough of its structures apparently remained to permit a party of Albany messengers to spend the night there en route to Onondaga), 9:550, 558 (one of the three Mohawk towns destroyed by the French expedition of 1693, described as "distant seven or eight leagues" from the other two). W. Lenig (personal correspondence to the author, March 2008) suggested that archaeological evidence of a second occupation of the Crouse site represented a potential identification of this town as documented in contemporary accounts. Cf. Snow's interpretation, *Mohawk Valley Archaeology,* 4, 426, 443–47.

67. *NYCD* 4:59 (one of three rebuilt Mohawk towns described in August 1693), 81–82 (one of four

Mohawk towns described in January 1694), 124 (May 1695 mention of the "uppermost castle" of the Mohawks), 560–61 (May 1699 reference to the "furthermost castle of the Mohogs," then home to the Mohawks' [unnamed] "principal sachem"). W. Lenig (personal correspondence to the author, April 2008) indicated that this town has not been identified archaeologically to date but likely represented the predecessor of the Dekanohage community.

68. *LIR,* 175 (April 1700 description of "Canaoage a Village," located four miles west of "Canajochere" (see Allen IV), and eight miles east of "the Place where the great Castle stood called Tionondoge burnt by the French"); *NYCD* 4:654 (April 1700 reference to Mohawks residing in both "Castles" and "villages"), 655 (April 1700 mention of "a village of the Maquas called Dekanoge," near "Ojeenrudde," a branch of the Mohawk River), 800 (September 1700 mention of "Decanohoge," the "third Castle" of the Mohawks), 802 (September 1700 report of residents of "Decanohoge" being "busie to make houses"), 807 ("Canohogo," described in September 1700), 889 (June 1701 mention of the "furthest castle of the Maquase"); Beauchamp, *Indian Names in New York,* 43. W. Lenig (personal correspondence to the author, March 2008) suggested that archaeological evidence of a second occupation of the Fort Plain Cemetery site represented a potential identification of this town as documented in contemporary accounts. Cf. Snow, *Mohawk Valley Archaeology,* 4; Grumet, *Historic Contact,* 358; Sivertsen, *Turtles, Wolves, and Bears,* 36.

69. Bradley, *Before Albany,* 43; Snow, *Mohawk Valley Archaeology,* 4, 209–16. W. Lenig (personal correspondence to the author, April 2008) suggested that the bead evidence recovered to date indicates an occupation ending no later than 1610. Cf. alternate dates of 1600–15 (Rumrill, "Mohawk Glass Trade Bead Sequence," 8).

70. Lenig, "Patterns of Material Culture," 62; W. Lenig (personal correspondence to the author, April 2008) suggested these dates of occupancy. Cf. alternate dates of circa 1600–1614 (Snow, *Mohawk Valley Archaeology,* 219–32), 1605–25 (Rumrill, "Interpretation and Analysis," 6–7), 1614–24 (Bradley, *Before Albany,* 43), 1615–30 (Rumrill, "Mohawk Glass Trade Bead Sequence," 11, 14–15).

71. Lenig, "Patterns of Material Culture," 62; W. Lenig, (personal correspondence to the author, April 2008) suggested these dates of occupancy. Cf. alternate dates of 1605–25 (Rumrill, "Interpretation and Analysis," 6–7), 1614–24 (Bradley, *Before Albany,* 43; Snow, *Mohawk Valley Archaeology,* 259–65), 1615–30 (Rumrill, "Mohawk Glass Trade Bead Sequence," 14–15, 18–21).

72. Gehring and Starna, *Journey into Mohawk and Oneida Country,* 7 ("Osquage," a Mohawk "village" described by Van den Bogaert in 1634 as consisting of nine houses); Bradley, *Before Albany,* 43. Cf. alternate dates of circa 1525–80 (Snow, *Mohawk Valley Archaeology,* 194–95), 1600–1615 (Rumrill, "Mohawk Glass Trade Bead Sequence," 8, 10).

73. Gehring and Starna, *Journey into Mohawk and Oneida Country,* 5 ("Canagere," the Mohawks' second "Castle," described by Van den Bogaert in 1634 as an unpalisaded hilltop settlement consisting of sixteen houses). W. Lenig (personal correspondence to the author, March 2008) suggested this site as a possible candidate for Van den Bogaert's "Canagere" and also offered a provisional identification of it as the successor to the central Mohawk "castle" (from Coleman-van Deusen). Cf. Snow's interpretation (*Mohawk Valley Archaeology,* 4, 300, 303, 309–22). Cf. alternate dates of 1615–30 (Rumrill, "Mohawk Glass Trade Bead Sequence," 11), 1620–32 (Rumrill, "Interpretation and Analysis," 10).

74. Gehring and Starna, *Journey into Mohawk and Oneida Country,* 7 ("Schanidisse," the Mohawks' third "Castle," described by Van den Bogaert in 1634 as consisting of thirty-two houses on a "very high hill"); Beauchamp, *Indian Names in New York,* 44. W. Lenig (personal correspondence to the author, March 2008) suggested the possibility of this unregistered site (in the vicinity of the Allen site complex) as a possible candidate for Van den Bogaert's

"Schanidisse," but noted that the limited archaeological evidence (including Mohawk-made bone tools and Dutch polychrome beads) suggested an occupancy ending no later than 1640. Cf. Snow's interpretation (*Mohawk Valley Archaeology,* 4, 289–93).

75. Lenig, "Patterns of Material Culture," 61; Bradley, *Before Albany,* 43. Cf. alternate dates of 1634–42 (Snow, *Mohawk Valley Archaeology,* 4, 300, 303, 309–22). W. Lenig (personal correspondence to the author, March 2008) suggested that this site could also represent Van den Bogaert's "Canagere." Cf. alternate dates of 1624–35 (Funk and Kuhn, "Boning up on the Mohawk," 30), and Rumrill's interpretations ("Interpretation and Analysis," 13–16, 17; "Mohawk Glass Trade Bead Sequence," 24–27).

76. *MNF* 5:603 ("Andagaron," described by Jogues in August 1642); *JR* 25:69, 31:39–51, 83 (one of three Mohawk towns described by Jogues in 1642–43); *IMC,* 46 ("Banagiro," described by Megapolensis in 1644); Bradley, *Before Albany,* 43. Cf. alternate dates of 1630–46 (Rumrill, "Mohawk Glass Trade Bead Sequence," 23–24), 1636–42 (Rumrill, "Interpretation and Analysis," 9), 1643–46 (Snow, *Mohawk Valley Archaeology,* 4, 300, 303, 322–25).

77. *JR* 40:127, 135, 139 (possibly one of three Mohawk villages described by Jesuit Joseph Poncet in 1653). W. Lenig (personal correspondence to the author, March 2008) suggested these dates of occupancy for this site. Cf. alternate dates of 1634–42 (Snow, *Mohawk Valley Archaeology,* 4, 303, 460–70).

78. *JR* 40:127, 135, 139 (possibly one of three Mohawk towns described by Jesuit Joseph Poncet in 1653), 45:207 (reference to the Mohawks possessing "three or four wretched Villages" in 1659); Christoph and Christoph, *Books of General Entries,* vol. 1, 48 (depiction of three towns of "Conegehaugah" on sketch of Iroquois towns appended to September 24, 1664, Iroquois treaty with English officials in New York); *JR* 49:257 (1666 mention of "two or three" Mohawk villages), 267 (1666 map depicting three Mohawk villages), 50:203 (one of four Mohawk towns destroyed by the 1666 French expedition); *NYCD* 3:135 ("Andaraque," site of October 17, 1666, French ceremony of possession of Mohawk country); Parker, *Archeological History,* 621. W. Lenig (personal correspondence to the author, March 2008) suggested these dates of occupancy for this site. Cf. alternate dates of 1647–66 (Snow, *Mohawk Valley Archaeology,* 4, 389–401), 1657–65 (Rumrill, "Mohawk Glass Trade Bead Sequence," 31, 38; Bradley, *Before Albany,* 43).

79. *JR* 40:127, 135, 139 (possibly one of three Mohawk towns described by Jesuit Joseph Poncet in 1653). W. Lenig (personal correspondence to the author, March 2008) suggested these dates of occupancy for this site. Cf. alternate dates of 1645–50 (Bradley, *Before Albany,* 43), 1646–59 (Rumrill, "Mohawk Glass Trade Bead Sequence," 29), 1647–66 (Snow, *Mohawk Valley Archaeology,* 4, 375–82).

80. *JR* 40:127, 135, 139 (possibly one of three Mohawk towns described by Jesuit Joseph Poncet in 1653). W. Lenig (personal correspondence to the author, March 2008) suggested these dates of occupancy for this site). Cf. alternate dates of 1646–59 (Rumrill, "Mohawk Glass Trade Bead Sequence," 29), 1647–66 (Snow, *Mohawk Valley Archaeology,* 4, 382–84).

81. *JR* 40:127, 135, 139 (possibly one of three Mohawk towns described by Jesuit Joseph Poncet in 1653); Bradley, *Before Albany,* 43. Cf. dates of 1646–60 (Rumrill, "Interpretation and Analysis," 21), 1647–66 (Snow, *Mohawk Valley Archaeology,* 4, 401–3), 1657–66 (Rumrill, "Mohawk Glass Trade Bead Sequence," 31).

82. *JR* 45:207 (reference to the Mohawks possessing "three or four wretched Villages" in 1659), 49:257 (1666 mention of "two or three" Mohawk villages), 267 (1666 map depicting three Mohawk villages), 50:203 (one of four Mohawk towns destroyed by the 1666 French expedition); Rumrill, "Mohawk Glass Trade Bead Sequence," 30; Bradley, *Before Albany,* 43. Cf. alternate dates of 1627–34 (Snow, *Mohawk Valley Archaeology,* 4, 289–93).

83. *JR* 51:201 (the Mohawks' "second village," described in 1667 as "two leagues distant" from "Gandaouagué"), 205 (one of the "six villages of the Mohawks" extant in 1667), 52:123 (one of the "seven large Villages" of the Mohawks described by the Jesuits in 1669). W. Lenig (personal correspondence to the author, March 2008) suggested this unregistered site as one of the possible candidates for the unnamed towns described by the Jesuits in 1669. See also *NYCD* 13:480.

84. *JR* 51:205 (one of the "six villages of the Mohawks" extant in 1667), 52:123 (one of the "seven large Villages" of the Mohawks described by the Jesuits in 1669), 57:89 (1673 Jesuit description of an unnamed Mohawk town, one of the two nearest to "new Holland," located five leagues east of "Tionnontogouen"); *NYCD* 2:712 ("Kanagaro," described as the second-nearest Mohawk "castle" to "Fort Nassou" [Albany] in 1674); *IMC,* 189 ("Canajorha," described by Greenhalgh, in 1677 as a town of sixteen houses, built on flat land two miles distant from the Mohawk River, with a single "stockade"); "Account of Iroquois Indians" (one of three extant Mohawk "castles" in 1682, each located four to five leagues distant from one another); Beauchamp, *Indian Names in New York,* 43; Parker, *Archeological History,* 620. Cf. alternate dates of 1665–90 (Bradley, *Before Albany,* 184), 1667–79 (Snow, *Mohawk Valley Archaeology,* 4, 411, 419–25), 1667–82 (Rumrill, "Mohawk Glass Trade Bead Sequence," 34). A number of Mohawks from Akwesasne purchased land encompassing this site in 1993 and have since relocated and formed a community known as the Kanatsiohareke. See Porter, *Kanatsiohareke,* 46, 87–88. See also *NYCD* 13:480.

85. W. Lenig (personal correspondence to the author, March 2008) suggested that archaeological evidence of a third occupation at Allen indicates its existence at the time of Frontenac's 1693 expedition. In Lenig's view, the village was not one of the three documented as destroyed by Frontenac, but rather was abandoned by the Mohawks in the aftermath of the expedition. Rumrill ("Interpretation and Analysis," 27–28, 35–36; "Mohawk Glass Trade Bead Sequence," 35–37, 39) supports the idea of an Allen occupation circa 1682–1710. Cf. discussions of post-1694 occupancies of the Allen site in Carse, "Mohawk Iroquois"; Snow, *Mohawk Valley Archaeology,* 4, 390, 449; Bradley, *Before Albany,* 184.

86. *NYCD* 4:59 (one of three rebuilt Mohawk towns described in August 1693), 81–82 (one of four Mohawk towns described in January 1694), 125 (June 1695 mention of "Joseph," a resident of the "second Maquaes Castle"), 372 (September 1698 mention of the "second Moquaes Castle"); *LIR,* 175 (April 1700 mention of "a deserted castle called Iuchnawrede," estimated by Robert Livingston to be located at a point sixteen miles west of "Orachkie" and four miles east of "Canojochere." W. Lenig (personal correspondence to the author, April 2008) suggested these dates of occupancy. Cf. alternate dates of 1647–66 (Snow, *Mohawk Valley Archaeology,* 4, 384–89), 1680–93 (Rumrill, "Interpretation and Analysis," 25, 33–35; Rumrill, "Mohawk Glass Trade Bead Sequence," 35–37), 1690–1700 (Bradley, *Before Albany,* 184).

87. *LIR,* 175 (April 1700 description of "Canajochere the 2d Castle" of the Mohawks, located twenty miles west of the first castle at "Orachkie"); *NYCD* 4:654 (April 1700 reference to Mohawks residing in both "Castles" and "villages"), 800 (September 1700 mention of "Canaedsishore," the "second Castle" of the Mohawks), 802 ("Canijoharie," mentioned September 1700). W. Lenig (personal correspondence to the author, April 2008) suggested the possibility that the diversity of artifacts recovered from the Allen site might indicate a fourth occupation of this historically documented town (the successor of the historically known "Iuchnawrede"). Rumrill ("Mohawk Glass Trade Bead Sequence," 37) supports this contention. See also Carse, "Mohawk Iroquois," 11; Snow, *Mohawk Valley Archaeology,* 4, 390, 449; Bradley, *Before Albany,* 184.

88. Bradley, *Before Albany,* 43; Snow, *Mohawk Valley Archaeology,* 4, 207–8. Cf. alternate dates

of 1595–1615 (Rumrill, "Interpretation and Analysis," 3), 1600–1615 (Rumrill, "Mohawk Glass Trade Bead Sequence," 8).

89. W. Lenig (personal correspondence to the author, March 2008) suggested these dates of occupancy for this site on the basis of European artifacts recovered to date. Cf. alternate dates of 1620–36 (Rumrill, "Mohawk Glass Trade Bead Sequence," 16), 1620–40 (Kuhn, "Cromwell Site," 29), 1624–36 (Rumrill, "Interpretation and Analysis," 8–9; Funk and Kuhn, "Boning Up on the Mohawk," 30), 1627–34 (Snow, *Mohawk Valley Archaeology,* 4, 281–85).

90. Gehring and Starna, *Journey into Mohawk and Oneida Country,* 22 (1635 description of an abandoned town, identified as the easternmost village on the north bank of the Mohawk River destroyed by the Mahicans in either 1625 or 1626); Lenig, "Patterns of Material Culture," 62; Bradley, *Before Albany,* 43; Snow, *Mohawk Valley Archaeology,* 4, 242–49; Brasser, *Riding the Frontier's Crest,* 13–14. Cf. alternate dates of 1605–25 (Rumrill, "Interpretation and Analysis," 3–5, 7), 1615–30 (Rumrill, "Mohawk Glass Trade Bead Sequence," 11–13).

91. Gehring and Starna, *Journey into Mohawk and Oneida Country,* 4–5 ("Oneckegonka," the Mohawks' first "castle," described by Van den Bogaert in 1634 as consisting of thirty-six houses on a "high hill"); Parker, *Archeological History,* 620; Lenig, "Patterns of Material Culture," 58; Bradley, *Before Albany,* 43. Cf. Snow's interpretation in *Mohawk Valley Archaeology,* 281–85. Cf. alternate dates of 1600–1625 (Rumrill, "Mohawk Glass Trade Bead Sequence," 9–10), 1620–40 (Rumrill, "Interpretation and Analysis," 8).

92. Gehring and Starna, *Journey into Mohawk and Oneida Country,* 5 ("Canawarode," a Mohawk "village" described by Van den Bogaert in 1634 as "not worth much"); Lenig, "Patterns of Material Culture," 58; Bradley, *Before Albany,* 43; Snow, *Mohawk Valley Archaeology,* 4, 286–89. Cf. alternate dates of 1615–30 (Rumrill, "Mohawk Glass Trade Bead Sequence," 10–11), 1626–40 (Rumrill, "Interpretation and Analysis," 11).

93. Gehring and Starna, *Journey into Mohawk and Oneida Country,* 5 ("Schatsyerosy," a Mohawk "village" described by Van den Bogaert in 1634 as an unpalisaded settlement of twelve houses that he considered "not worth much"). W. Lenig (personal correspondence to the author, March 2008) suggested that an unregistered site best fits the geographic relationship to "Schatsyerosy" described in the Van den Bogaert journal. Cf. Snow's interpretation in *Mohawk Valley Archaeology,* 304–9.

94. *MNF* 5:600 ("Ossernenon," described by Jogues in August 1642); *JR* 25:69, 28:123, 127–29, 31:39–51, 83 (one of three Mohawk villages described by Jogues in 1642–43); *IMC,* 46 ("Asserué," described by Megapolensis in 1644); Du Creux, *History of Canada,* 1:393–94 (the Mohawks "chief village," site of Jesuit Joseph Bressani's captivity in April–June 1644); *JR* 26:45 (reference to the Mohawks' "first village" as the primary site of Bressani's captivity); Lenig, "Patterns of Material Culture," 61; Bradley, *Before Albany,* 43; Snow, *Mohawk Valley Archaeology,* 4, 304–9. Cf. alternate dates of 1625–50 (Rumrill, "Interpretation and Analysis," 11–12, 17), 1630–46 (Rumrill, "Mohawk Glass Trade Bead Sequence," 21–23).

95. *JR* 29:49 (the Mohawks' "first small village" west of Fort Orange, identified by Jogues as "Oneugiouré, formerly Osserrion," in June 1646); Bradley, *Before Albany,* 43.

96. *JR* 40:127, 135, 139 (one of three Mohawk villages described by Jesuit Joseph Poncet in 1653); *IMC,* 111 ("Caronay," depicted on Adriaen van der Donck's 1656 map of New Netherland); *JR* 42:37–47 (quote 39), 43:209–11 (possibly the "village of Agniée" visited by Jesuit Simon Le Moyne in 1655 and 1656), 44:197, 203, 217, 219 (possibly the Mohawk town identified as "the village of Anié," "Anniequé," and "Agniequé" where Le Moyne spent November 1657 to March 1658); Parker, *Archeological History,* 624; Snow, *Mohawk Valley Archaeology,* 4, 362, 365–71. Cf. alternate dates of 1646–59 (Rumrill, "Mohawk Glass Trade Bead Sequence," 27–29); 1650–57 (Bradley, *Before Albany,* 43).

97. *JR* 45:95, 99–101 (quote 99) (possibly the "Village of agné" visited by Le Moyne in June 1659), 207 (reference to the Mohawks possessing "three or four wretched Villages" in 1659); *FOCM,* 456 (September 1659 description of the Mohawks' "First Castle called Kaghnuwage"); *JR* 49:257 (1666 mention of "two or three" Mohawk villages), 267 (1666 map depicting three Mohawk villages), 50:203 (one of four Mohawk towns destroyed by the 1666 French expedition); Snow, *Mohawk Valley Archaeology,* 4, 362, 371–75; Rumrill, "Mohawk Glass Trade Bead Sequence," 29–30, 32; Bradley, *Before Albany,* 43. Cf. *NYCD* 3:157; *JR* 50:145; Christoph and Christoph, *Books of General Entries,* vol. 1, 48 (depiction of three towns of "Conegehaugah" on sketch of Iroquois towns appended to September 24, 1664, Iroquois treaty with English officials in New York).

98. *JR* 51:187 ("Gandaouagué," described by Jesuit François Le Mercier as the Mohawks' "chief village" in 1667, home town of the Mohawks' "foremost Captain"; Le Mercier also identified this town [a successor to the Printup site] in 1667 as "the one which the late Father Jogues watered with his blood" in 1646), 52:123 (one of the "seven large Villages" of the Mohawks described by the Jesuits in 1669), 53:137–49 (1669 Pierron description of Mahican attack on "Gandaouagué"), 57:89 (1673 identification of Gandaouagué as the Jesuit mission of St. Pierre, located five leagues from "Tionnontogouen"; despite being one of the "two smallest villages in the whole Iroquois country," the Jesuits regarded Gandaouagué as "the first and principal mission that we have among the Iroquois"); *NYCD* 2:712 ("Kaghnewage," described as the nearest Mohawk "castle" to "Fort Nassou" [Albany] in 1674); Gookin, *Historical Collections,* 25 (1674 mention of easternmost Mohawk town located fifty miles from Albany); *JR* 59:237 (1675 description of Bruyas at the "Mission of Agnié," located in "Agnié, the village of the nation nearest to the Dutch"), 60:177 (presence of Bruyas at "Agnié" on July 31, 1676), 179 (presence of Jesuit Jacques de Lamberville at "Gannawagé, a village of Agnié," on May 9, 1676); Hennepin, *New Discovery,* 1:41 (1677 description of "Ganniekez or Agniez," the host village of Bruyas, situated "a large day's journey from New Holland"); *IMC,* 189 (1677 Greenhalgh description of "Cahaniaga": twenty-four houses, double-palisaded with four four-foot-wide "ports," built on the edge of a hill); *JR* 61:21 (one of the two "Agnié villages" hosting Jesuits Jacques de Lamberville and Bruyas in 1678), 165 (one of the "two villages of agnié" hosting Jesuits Jean de Lamberville and François Vaillant de Guelsis in 1679); "Account of Iroquois Indians" (one of three extant Mohawk "castles" in 1682, each located four to five leagues distant from one another); Beauchamp, *Indian Names in New York,* 45; Parker, *Archeological History,* 620. W. Lenig (personal correspondence to the author, March 2008) suggested these dates of occupancy for this site. Cf. alternate dates of 1667–79 (Snow, *Mohawk Valley Archaeology,* 4, 411, 415–19), 1667–82 (Rumrill, "Mohawk Glass Trade Bead Sequence," 33, 35), 1675–90 (Bradley, *Before Albany,* 184). See also *NYCD* 13:480.

99. *JR* 51:201 (unnamed Mohawk community located "two leagues distant" from "Gandaouagué" in 1667), 205 (one of the "six villages of the Mohawks" extant in 1667), 52:123 (one of the "seven large Villages" of the Mohawks described by the Jesuits in 1669), 53:139 ("Ganadagaro," described as the "neighboring fort" to Fox Farm/Ganadaouagué by the Jesuit Jean Pierron in 1669), 57:89 (1673 Jesuit description of an unnamed Mohawk town, one of the two nearest to "new Holland," located five leagues east of "Tionnontogouen" and one of the "two smallest villages in the whole Iroquois country"); *IMC,* 189 ("Canagora," visited by Greenhalgh in 1677; described as a town of sixteen houses built on flat land near the Mohawk River, a "single stockade" and affiliated with "Cahaniaga"); *JR* 61:21 (one of the two "Agnié villages" hosting Jesuits Jacques de Lamberville and Bruyas in 1678), 165 (one of the "two villages of agnié" hosting Jesuits Jean de Lamberville and François Vaillant de Guelsis in 1679); Snow, *Mohawk Valley Archaeology,* 415, 420, 424, 443; Rumrill, "Interpretation and Analysis," 31. W.

Lenig (personal correspondence to the author, March 2008) suggested that the bead types recovered from this site (also known as the Levi Dillenbeck site) indicate a terminal date of occupation "well before 1690."

100. *NYCD* 4:346, 566 (1698 Mohawk petition regarding illegal purchase of Schoharie lands); Simms, *History of Schoharie County,* 23–35; *History of Montgomery and Fulton Counties,* 34; Parker, *Archeological History,* 693; Brasser, *Riding the Frontier's Crest,* 13; Sivertsen, *Turtles, Wolves, and Bears,* 75; Ferguson, "Schoharie Iroquois?" 18n2 (cites mention of "Schoharie Indians" in a 1684 land deed); Ferguson, *Search for the Schoharie Mohawk,* 70–71; Feeguson, *Schoharie Mohawks,* 33–35; Becker, *Native Americans and Their Land,* ix–xi, 1. A small town, known as "Eskahre," consisted of seven or eight "single-unit cabins" located thirty-two miles south of the eastern Mohawk town of "Tionondoroge" on the west bank of the Schoharie Creek near modern-day Middleburgh, New York (Rumrill, "Interpretation and Analysis," 35). Rumrill ("Mohawk Glass Trade Bead Sequence," 37) dates the origin of the site to 1694. Cf. Guldenzopf, "Colonial Transformation of Mohawk Iroquois Society," 46 (who associates the origin of the Schoharie community with "the dispersion resulting from the French attack of 1693"), and Snow's interpretation in *Mohawk Valley Archaeology,* 451–54. W. Lenig (personal correspondence to the author, April 2008) identified the Westheimer Knoll site as a possible location for this historically known Mohawk town. This community and the "Protestant" Mohawk settlement at "Tionondoroge" (Empire Lock) were routinely excluded from contemporary descriptions of Mohawk "castles" after 1689 (see *LIR,* 175).

101. *NYCD* 4:18, 9:550, 558 (one of the three Mohawk towns destroyed by the French expedition of 1693); Grassmann, *Mohawk Indians and Their Valley,* 638–47; McCashion, "Clay Tobacco Pipes of New York State, Part I." W. Lenig (personal correspondence to the author, March 2008) suggested these dates of occupancy for this site. Cf. alternate dates of 1680–93 (Snow, *Mohawk Valley Archaeology,* 431–43), 1682–93 (Rumrill, "Mohawk Glass Trade Bead Sequence," 35), 1690–1700 (Bradley, *Before Albany,* 184). Also known as the Caughnawaga site (Engelbrecht, *Iroquoia,* 117) and the current location of the Kateri Tekakwitha National Shrine.

102. *NYCD* 4:18, 9:550, 558 (one of the three Mohawk towns destroyed by the French expedition of 1693). W. Lenig (personal correspondence to the author, March 2008) suggested that archaeological evidence from a recently discovered and unregistered site in proximity to the Veeder site indicates a fire.

103. *NYCD* 3:771 (1691 statement of intent by "Christian Mohawks" to relocate to "Tionondoroge," a place they described as "56 miles above Albany"), 4:81–82 (one of the four Mohawk towns described in January 1694; referred to as the "Praying Maquase Castle called Tionondoroge," home to a number of "Protestant" Mohawks), 115 (October 1694 mention of the Mohawks' "Praying Indian Castle" at Tionondoge"), 181 (1696 claim of Mohawks residing "not 30 miles above from Albany"), 649 (April 1700 claim of Mohawks residing within sixteen miles of western extent of New York settler population), 654 (April 1700 reference to Mohawks residing in both "Castles" and "villages"); *LIR,* 175 (April 1700 description of "Tiononderoge, where the Praying Maquase Indians have their settlement"; described as forty-eight miles west of Albany, twenty-eight miles west of Schenectady, and four miles east of "Orachkie" [Milton Smith]; *NYCD* 4:889 (June 1701 mention of the "Protestant Maquase Indian Castle"); Moody and Fisher, "Archaeological Evidence," 1; Richter, "'Some of Them,'" 474–75. W. Lenig (personal correspondence to the author, March 2008) suggested this site as a candidate for the historically known town of Tionnonderoge." Cf. Snow's interpretation (*Mohawk Valley Archaeology,* 449). This Mohawk community and the Mohawk settlement on Schoharie Creek were routinely excluded from contemporary descriptions of Mohawk "castles" after 1689 (see *LIR,* 175).

104. *NYCD* 4:59 (one of three rebuilt Mohawk towns described in August 1693), 81–82 (one of

the four Mohawk towns described in January 1694); *WA*, 31 (possibly garbled January 1699 description of "Ornechte, the first Castle of the Mohawk Indians where the Praying Indians live"); *LIR*, 175 (April 1700 description of "Orachkie the first castle of the Maquase," located four miles west of the "Praying Maquase" settlement at "Tiononderoge"); *NYCD* 4:654 (April 1700 reference to Mohawks residing in both "Castles" and "villages"). W. Lenig (personal correspondence to the author, March 2008) suggested a terminal date of 1700 for this site. Cf. alternate dates of 1693–1712 (Snow, *Mohawk Valley Archaeology*, 449, 454–59), 1694–1715 (Rumrill, "Mohawk Glass Trade Bead Sequence," 39), 1700–1715 (Bradley, *Before Albany*, 184). Rumrill ("Interpretation and Analysis," 21) proposes an occupation of this site dating to 1645–57.

105. *NYCD* 4:800 (September 1700 mention of "Ogsadago," the "first Castle" of the Mohawks), 802 (mention of the "first [Mohawk] Castle called Ogsadago"), 906 (July 1701 description of "the first or nearest [Mohawk] castle called Ochniondage" included mention of growing number of [Protestant] "Christians" and their desire to replace the "little Chapell made of barke" with a larger structure); Beauchamp, *Indian Names in New York*, 42. W. Lenig (personal correspondence to the author, March 2008) suggested this site as a possible candidate for the historically known town of "Ogsadago/Ochniondage." Cf. Snow's interpretation (*Mohawk Valley Archaeology*, 449, 454–59).

106. *RFF*, 7–8 (identified as "Kentio" in 1665); *JR* 50:197–99 (1666 mention of Cayugas residing on the north shore of Lake Ontario requesting Jesuit missionaries from French authorities); *RFF*, 89 (leader of community identified as "Roharie" in 1668; fifty "little children" baptized there by Récollets in 1668), 95 (described as "virtually deserted" in June 1677), 99, 101 (described as abandoned by May 1680); Victor Konrad, "The Iroquois Return to Their Homeland: Military Defeat or Cultural Readjustment?" in Ross and Moore, *Cultural Geography of North American Indians*, 197.

107. Coyne "Exploration of the Great Lakes," 39–41 ("Ganastogué Sonontoua Outinaouatoua," described by Galinée in 1669 as consisting of eighteen to twenty "cabins" eighteen to twenty miles inland from Lake Ontario); 45 ("Tinawatawa," described as the site where Galinée reconnoitered with Jolliet on September 24, 1669), 47 (visited by Sulpician Claude Trouvé in November 1669); 81; Robinson, "Montreal to Niagara," 152; Konrad, "Iroquois Return to Their Homeland," 197.

108. *RFF*, 90 (visited by the Sulpician missionary François-Saturin Lascaris d'Urfé in 1671; described as "five leagues" from another north shore settlement); Pritchard, "For the Glory of God," 140n41; *NYCD* 9:112 (mentioned in 1673); Robinson, "Montreal to Niagara," 149; Konrad, "Iroquois Return to Their Homeland," 197.

109. Dollier de Casson, "Histoire du Montréal," 121 (1668 Sulpician visit to "Quinté"); *NYCD* 9:112 ("Kenté," described in 1673); *RFF*, 96 (identified as "Kenté" in 1678); Hennepin, *Description of Louisiana*, 88n; Hennepin, *New Discovery*, 1:77 (1679 mention of "Kenté"; Lahontan, *New Voyages*, 1:70 (1684 mention of "Quinté" seven or eight leagues distant from Fort Frontenac), 121 (1687 mention of town at same distance from Fort Frontenac); Colden, *History of the Five Indian Nations which are dependent on the Province of New-York*, 1:60 (1684 mention of "two villages of the Five Nations" located "about fifteen miles" from Fort Frontenac, consisting of "those Indians that had the most Inclination to the French"); *NYCD* 9:274 (one of "three Iroquois villages" lying "within reach" of Fort Frontenac in 1685); Catalogne, "Recueil," 13 (1687 description of "Quinté" town as "25 leagues" from Fort Frontenac); Belmont, "Histoire," 46 ("Quinté," described by French troops on return from 1687 Denonville campaign); Robinson, "Montreal to Niagara," 148–49; Konrad, "Iroquois Return to Their Homeland," 197.

110. *NYCD* 9:112 ("Ganeious," mentioned in 1673); Hennepin, *New Discovery*, 1:47 (1676 description

of Hennepin and La Salle's effort to persuade portion of "Ganneouse" community, then located "near to Kenté, about nine leagues" from Fort Frontenac to locate in proximity to the fort), 53 (1677 description as located less than nine leagues from Fort Frontenac); Lahontan, *New Voyages,* 1:70 (1684 mention of "Ganneouse" seven or eight leagues distant from Fort Frontenac), 121 (1687 mention of town at same distance from Fort Frontenac); Colden, *History of the Five Indian Nations which are dependent on the Province of New-York,* 1:60 (1684 mention of "two villages of the Five Nations" located "about fifteen miles" from Fort Frontenac, consisting of "those Indians that had the most Inclination to the French"); *NYCD* 9:274 (one of "three Iroquois villages" lying "within reach" of Fort Frontenac in 1685); Olds, "Journal of Chevalier de Baugy," 28 (1687 mention of "Ganecourt," an "Iroquois du Nord" town located "seven leagues" from Fort Frontenac); Belmont, "Histoire," 46 ("Ganeousse," described by French troops on return from 1687 Denonville campaign). Cf. Konrad, "Iroquois Return to Their Homeland," 197.

111. Hennepin, *Description of Louisiana,* 59 (1676 description of "pretty large village" in proximity to Fort Frontenac; mention of land cleared and corn planted); Hennepin, *New Discovery,* 1:47–48 (description of this community as consisting of "about Forty Cottages" located between the fort and the Récollet "House of Mission"), 2:539 (leader of the Ganneious II community circa 1676–81 identified as *"Ganneouse Kaera"*); *RFF,* 128 (1682 Nicolas de la Salle description of the Iroquois village "quite near" Fort Frontenac); *NYCD* 9:274 (one of "three Iroquois villages" lying "within reach" of Fort Frontenac in 1685).

112. *JR* 47:320n28 (description of circa 1669 origins of the Jesuit "residence and mission" of "St. Francis Xavier des Pres" at the extant Iroquois settlement), 58:247 (1674 description of the "Mission to the Iroquois of St. François Xavier at la Prairie de la Magdelaine"), 275 (Jesuit statement of 1669 origins of mission at this town), 59:257 (1675 description of "St. François Xavier at la prairie de le Magdelaine"); Robinson, "Montreal to Niagara," 140; Trigger, "Native Resettlement," Plate 47.

113. *RFF,* 89–90 (described in 1669 as inhabited by "a separate branch of the Senecas"); Dollier de Casson, "Histoire du Montréal," 123 ("Gandasiteiagon," a new, Cayuga-dominated town where the Sulpician d'Urfé spent the winter of 1669–70); Coyne, "Exploration of the Great Lakes," 83 ("Ganatsekiagons," described by Galinée in 1670 as the settlement from which "M. Peré" traveled to Sault Ste. Marie via Lake Simcoe in 1669); *NYCD* 9:112 ("Ganatoheskiagon," described in 1673), 117 ("Gandaschakiagon," described in 1674); *RFF,* 473 (documentation of annual spring trading at this town between Iroquois and Odawas circa 1670–87); *NYCD* 4:694 ("Kanatiochtiage" and "Tchojachiage," two names given in June 1700 for the former site of Ganestiquiagon: a location "upon the Lake of Cadarachqui, near the Sinnekes country," where a group of "Dowaganhaes" relocated [with Iroquois permission in 1700]; Iroquois "tree of peace" reportedly planted there to enable League-mediated trade with Albany); Robinson, "Montreal to Niagara," 149; Konrad, "Iroquois Frontier," 135; Poulton, "Report," 4, 40–41. Cf. Pritchard, "For the Glory of God," 138–39.

114. *JR* 60:69 (Jesuit assertion of Iroquois presence circa 1669–74); Trigger, "Native Resettlement."

115. Gabriel-Doxtator and Van de Hende, *At the Edge of the Woods,* 273 (oral tradition recorded in 1795 of settlement at La Montagne founded by a woman from La Prairie); Dechêne, *Habitants and Merchants,* 325n17 (claims the presence of a "minority of Iroquois" at this mission at the time of its 1671 founding); *JR* 58:115 (1674 Jesuit statement of the suitability of this location for an "Indian colony," noting its proximity to a "route much frequented by the Iroquois and others" in addition to good soil and access to fishing); Pritchard, "For the Glory of God," 140 (documents the relocation of some Cayugas from the Quinté mission to La Montagne in 1680); Tremblay, "La Politique Missionaire," 48–54, 59n16 (notes a majority population of

Iroquois [predominantly Senecas, Cayugas, and Onondagas] at La Montagne by 1681); Canada Department of Agriculture, *Censuses of Canada*, 4:16–17 (1685 census indicated 222 persons residing in thirty-six "cabannes"), 21, 23 (1688 census indicated 181 persons in twenty-six "cabannes"); *NYCD* 9:441 (January 1690 Denonville description of Sulpician mission town of "Iroquois and Hurons" located "three-quarters of a league from the town of Montréal"); Belmont, "Histoire," 53 (May 1691 report of nineteen former residents of "Ganneyouse" hunting in mountains near Chambly); Tremblay, "La Politique Missionnaire," 60 (total population of 212 persons in thirty-five "cabannes" in 1692; total population of 220 persons in forty-three "cabannes" in 1694); *RAPQ* (1927–28): 207 (November 1694 report of destruction of La Montagne by fire); Donnelly, "Belmont's History of Brandy," 53 (report of fifty Indian "cabins" at La Montagne destroyed in September 1694 fire; cf. Tremblay, "La Politique Missionaire," 60, 95, who claims that only forty-three houses were destroyed in the 1694 fire); Canada Department of Agriculture, *Censuses of Canada* 4:40 (1698 census indicated 160 persons residing at La Montagne); Tremblay, "La Politique Missionnaire," 60 (forty-one "cabannes" at La Montagne in 1698); Trigger, "Native Resettlement."

116. *RFF,* 96–97 (mission of "Oriaigon," aka "Teaiagon," mentioned in 1678); Hennepin, *Description of Louisiana*, 66 (late November 1678 purchase of "Indian corn" from resident Iroquois), 88n (1679 mention of "Aogouen" [cf. "Tajajagon,' in Hennepin, *New Discovery*, 1:77]); Margry, *Découvertes*, 1:500 (August 15, 1680, arrival of La Salle at "Téioiagon," described as "sixty leagues" from Fort Frontenac); Belmont, "Histoire," 46 ("Teiaiagon," described by French troops on return from 1687 Denonville campaign); Robinson, *Toronto during the French Regime*, ix, "Montreal to Niagara," 149–50; Pritchard, "For the Glory of God," 138n31; Konrad, "Iroquois Frontier," 133.

117. *JR* 57:47 (1673 mention of an Iroquois woman residing at Lorette), 71 (description of 1673 "migration" of "nearly" fifty persons from a single Mohawk village to Lorette), 60:27–29 (reported presence of "300 souls both Huron and Iroquois" in 1675), 145 (1675 demographics repeated in 1676), 309 (unspecified number of Iroquois residing at Lorette in 1677), 62:257 (documentation of Iroquois present at Lorette in 1683); Lahontan, *New Voyages*, 1:48 (1684 description of Lorette as consisting of 200 families; Iroquois not mentioned); Trigger, "Native Resettlement." Cf. Kip, *Early Jesuit Missions*, 133 (reference to an Iroquois couple residing at Lorette circa 1692); *NYCD* 9:598 (League leaders referred to residents of Lorette in 1695 as "nephews" of the governor of New France, suggesting that there was likely no longer a substantial League-affiliated Iroquois presence there).

118. *JR* 60:275 (presence of Jesuit Pierre Cholenec at "Saint François Xavier du Sault" on January 2, 1677; his description of "22 Huron and Iroquois cabins" at this location, the successor of Kentaké), 63:191 (description of July 1675 beginning of relocation from Kentaké to Kahnawake), 61:165 (January 15, 1678, description of "Saint François Xavier du Sault"), 241 (1679 description of "Saint François Xavier du Sault"), 62:173 (1682 description of St. Francis Xavier du Sault as consisting of sixty cabins and 120 to 150 families); Canada Department of Agriculture, *Censuses of Canada*, 4:16–17 (1685 census indicated 682 persons residing in sixty-eight "cabannes"); *JR* 63:157 (1686 description of town consisting of sixty-one cabins); Catalogne, "Recueil," 17 (description of construction of fortified French garrison at Kahnawake following return of troops from 1687 Denonville expedition); Canada Department of Agriculture, *Censuses of Canada* 4:21, 23 (1688 census indicated 435 persons residing in eighty "cabannes"); Robinson, "Montreal to Niagara," 140; Trigger, "Native Resettlement."

119. *LIR,* 112, 116 (presence of at least one "born Cayouger" among Susquehannock adoptee population documented in June 1687); *NYCD* 3:516 (November 1687 Dongan claim that the Five Nations had "some of there [*sic*] friends" living on the Susquehanna River); *Account of the*

Treaty, 27 (mention by Onondaga speaker of "those Indians that are fled from us and live on the Susquahannah [*sic*] River"); *ARMA* 7:480 (1695 Oneida request for assistance in planned campaign against Fort Frontenac from "the Indians of the southern parts called Rondoges"); *AMD* 19:519–20 (June 1697 description of settlement of "Susquehanna and Seneca Indians" at "Carristaugua"); *NYCD* 4:571 (June 1699 description of Iroquois commerce with Pennsylvania traders at Conestoga, estimated at three days' travel from Iroquoia); Hunter, "Susquehanna Indian Town," 17–18.

120. Richter, "Rediscovered Links," 84; Belmont, "Histoire," 51; *NYCD* 9:441 (accounts of temporary post-August 1689 relocation of Kahnawake community within palisade of Montreal); Lacroix, *Les Origines de La Prairie,* 41; Trigger, "Native Resettlement."

121. *NYCD* 3:781 (1691 claim of Robert Livingston that the "praying Indian castle" in Canada was "very strong stockadoed" with a garrison of twenty French troops); *JR* 64:113 (1692 claim of the two cannons mounted in the town's walls bursting over the winter of 1691–92); *Narrative of an Attempt made by the French of Canada,* 8 (October 1692 claim of a French prisoner in Albany of a garrison of 200 French soldiers at "Ganawagne"); *NYCD* 9:599 (May 1695 plan of Callières to "trace out for the residents of [Kahnawakon] a new fort more commodious than the old one so that they might be more efficiently and more readily assisted in case of attack"); Trigger, "Native Resettlement."

122. Catalogne, "Recueil," 45 (temporary relocation of some residents of Kahnawakon within bounds of Montreal following the August 1691 attack on La Prairie; they rebuilt a "town within the town" and spent the winter of 1691–92 in this location).

123. *NYCD* 4:492 (February 1699 description of the "French Praying Indian Fort" located between "Fort Le Chene" and Montreal), 747 (August 1700 report of "Kachanuage the Praying Indian Castle" located four miles from Montreal); Trigger, "Native Resettlement."

124. *NYCD* 4:493 (February 1699 description of "Canosodage, a castle of the French Praying Indians"); Tremblay, "La Politique Missionaire," 87, 94–95; Trigger, "Native Resettlement."

125. Catalogne, "Recueil," 64 (relocation of a "number of Iroquois families" to the vicinity of Fort Frontenac in 1701); *RFF,* 204; Adams, "Iroquois Settlement at Fort Frontenac," 14.

APPENDIX 2. POSTEPIDEMIC IROQUOIS DEMOGRAPHY, 1634–1701

1. Warrick, *Population History of the Huron-Petun,* 80–89; Ramenofsky, *Vectors of Death,* 91–102; Brandão, *"Your Fyre Shall Burn No More,"* appendixes A, B, E. See also Snow, "Mohawk Demography," 174, who posits a depopulation rate of 63 percent (a decline from a preepidemic population of 7,740 to 2,830 postepidemic) for the Mohawks after their first experience with introduced epidemic disease. Jones, "Iroquois Population History," 86, posits an aggregate depopulation rate of 66 percent for the League as a whole. Cf. Norman C. Sullivan, "Contact Period Huron Demography," in Paine, *Integrating Archaeological Demography,* 339, who suggests a more conservative depopulation ratio of 48 to 58 percent for the Hurons following the smallpox epidemic of 1639–40, which in his view represented "the first serious event of population disruption among the Huron in the period of sustained contact." Both Snow's and Sullivan's ratios are significantly lower than the currently-accepted range of 75–77 percent population decline for all indigenous groups in northeastern North America circa 1492–1650 cited in Alchon, *Pest in the Land,* 99, and Douglas H. Ubelaker, "Population Size, Contact to Nadir," in Ubelaker, *Environment, Origins, and Population,* 699.

2. Cf. Richter, *Ordeal of the Longhouse,* 188. Snow included the Laurentian communities in his "Disease and Population Decline in the Northeast," in Verano and Ubelaker, *Disease and*

Demography in the Americas, 184, table 2, but omitted them from his demographic analysis in *Iroquois,* 110, table 7.1. For critiques of Snow's methodology for estimating Iroquois
population size, see Funk and Kuhn, *Three Sixteenth Century Mohawk Iroquois Village Sites,*
146–54; Carter, "Chains of Consumption," 195–205.

3. Lisa Kealhofer and Brenda J. Baker, "Counterpoint to Collapse: Depopulation and Adaptation," in Baker and Kealhofer, *Bioarchaeology of Native American Adaptation,* 209 (quote);
Thornton, Miller, and Warren, "American Indian Population Recovery," *American Anthropologist* 93 (1991): 37. See also Livi-Bacci, *Concise History of World Population,* 21–24.

4. *JR* 54:45, 57, 58:215–17, 231, 243 (quarantining practices), 53:125, 60:51, 63:205; Waterman, *"To
Do Justice to Him and Myself,"* 141, 157 (evidence suggesting the development of immunities);
JR 16:67–69, 32:147, 42:101–3, 43:271, 309–11, 315, 44:315–17, 52:47–49, 54:93–95, 56:69, 57:117,
58:243; *NYCD* 3:779, 4:738, 9:110–11, 281; Quaife, *Western Country in the Seventeenth Century,*
39; Le Roy de la Potherie, *Histoire,* 2:428 (indulgent attitudes toward children). See also
Kelton's important analogous study, "Avoiding the Smallpox Spirits."

5. Timothy Shannon, "War, Diplomacy, and Culture: The Iroquois Experience in the Seven Years'
War," in Hofstra, *Cultures in Conflict,* 90, 101n22. See also the discussions of archaeological
evidence of Onondaga and Seneca population recovery in Jones, "Iroquois Population History," 58, 67, 78–86.

6. Richter, "War and Culture," 542–43n57; Snow, *Iroquois,* 110, table 7.1; Jones "Iroquois Population History," 35. Cf. Sullivan, "Contact Period Huron Demography," 336, who argues for a
ratio of 5.23 people for each adult Iroquoian male aged fifteen to forty years.

7. *JR* 7:220, 8:42; Ramenofsky, *Vectors of Death,* 99; Dobyns, "More Methodological Perspectives," 295; Jones, *Rationalizing Epidemics,* 75.

8. Ramenofsky, *Vectors of Death,* 99; Dobyns, "More Methodological Perspectives," 295; Snow
and Starna, "Sixteenth-Century Depopulation," 144.

9. Susan Johnston, "Epidemics: The Forgotten Factor in Seventeenth Century Native Warfare in
the St. Lawrence Valley," in Cox, *Native People, Native Lands,* 24; Dobyns, "More Methodological Perspectives," 295; Sullivan, "Contact Period Huron Demography," 339; Robert Larocque,
"Secret Invaders: Pathogenic Agents and the Aboriginals in Champlain's Time," in Litalien
and Vaugeois, *Champlain,* 271–72; Jones, *Rationalizing Epidemics,* 75.

10. Snow, *Iroquois,* 110, table 7.1.

11. *JR* 24:271.

12. Johnston, "Epidemics," 24.

13. Ramenofsky, *Vectors of Death,* 99; Dobyns, "More Methodological Perspectives," 295.

14. Snow, *Iroquois,* 110, table 7.1.

15. *JR* 40:91.

16. Ibid., 45:207.

17. Cf. estimate of 2,304 Mohawks (Snow, *Iroquois,* 110, table 7.1).

18. Cf. estimate of 9,104 people in the Five Nations (ibid.).

19. *JR* 47:105.

20. Ibid., 48:79, 83, 50:63 (an unspecified disease outbreak that reportedly killed "1,000 Iroquois");
Dobyns, "More Methodological Perspectives," 295; Jones, *Rationalizing Epidemics,* 75.

21. *JR* 48:79, 83, 50:63.

22. Ibid., 48:79, 83, 50:63.

23. Ibid., 49:257.

24. Oury, *Marie de l'Incarnation,* 775.

25. *JR* 50:197–99 (report of seventy Cayuga men and thirty-five women and children from
the north shore of Lake Ontario settlement of Quintio in Montréal). In lieu of substantial

documentation of the population of the north shore communities circa 1666–87, I follow Poulton, "Report," in estimating a conservative base population of 100 people per north shore community for each year of its existence. There were five such communities from 1667 to 1668, six from 1669 to 1672, seven from 1673 to 1675, eight from 1676 to 1680, and seven from 1681 to 1687 (see appendix 1). Cf. Konrad, "Iroquois Frontier," 138; Richter, *Ordeal of the Longhouse,* 120–21. I have also used the figure of 100 people per Laurentian community for years lacking documented population counts.

26. Estimate of five extant north shore communities and Laurentian community of Kentaké.
27. *JR* 54:79–81.
28. Estimate of five extant north shore communities and Laurentian community of Kentaké.
29. Total estimate derived from sum of estimated multinational population and report of "[a]ll the Iroquois together" in the Five Nations as "not more than 2,000 men bearing arms" (*JR* 51:139).
30. Ibid., 53:125, 54:45; Ramenofsky, *Vectors of Death,* 99; Dobyns, "More Methodological Perspectives," 295; Jones, *Rationalizing Epidemics,* 75.
31. *JR* 53:247.
32. Ibid., 52:193.
33. Coyne, "Exploration of the Great Lakes," 25.
34. Estimate of six extant north shore communities and Laurentian community of Kentaké.
35. Snow, *Iroquois,* 110, table 7.1 (Five Nations estimate).
36. Total estimate derived from multinational estimate of 400 people in Laurentian settlements (Snow, "Disease and Population Decline," 184, table 2) and estimate of six extant north shore communities.
37. Estimate of six extant north shore communities and Laurentian communities of Kentaké, Notre-Dame-de-Foye, and La Montagne. Cf. report of 150 "souls" at Notre-Dame-de-Foye (*JR* 54:287).
38. Total derived from sum of multinational estimate and report of 2,000 warriors for Five Nations (*NYCD* 9:78).
39. *JR* 57:81–83 (report of fever, headaches, smallpox).
40. Ibid., 56:51.
41. Estimate of six extant north shore communities and Laurentian communities of Kentaké, Notre-Dame-de-Foye, and La Montagne.
42. *JR* 57:91. Cf. ibid., 71, for an account of "nearly" fifty people from a single (unnamed) Mohawk town relocating to the "Huron mission" (likely to the new town at Ancienne Lorette, successor of the mission at Notre-Dame-de-Foy; see ibid., 58:131, 149).
43. Ibid., 58:27.
44. Estimate of seven extant north shore communities and Laurentian communities of Kentaké, Notre-Dame-de-Foye, Ancienne Lorette, and La Montagne. Cf. ibid., 63:179–81 (reported increase of "200 persons" at Kentaké).
45. Total estimate derived from report of total population of 280 people at Kentaké (ibid., 58:249–51, 283), and estimate of seven extant north shore communities and Laurentian communities of Ancienne Lorette and La Montagne. Cf. report of 210 people at Ancienne Lorette, at least 52 of whom were Iroquois (ibid., 58:131–33).
46. Total estimate derived from estimate of seven extant north shore communities, and 1674 figures for Laurentian settlements. Cf. report of 300 people at Ancienne Lorette (ibid., 60:27).
47. *PRCC* 2:406 (Five Nations estimate).
48. *NYCD* 3:255.
49. *JR* 60:175.

50. Total estimate derived from report of total population of approximately 150 people at Anci-
    enne Lorette and 300 people at Kentaké (ibid., 60:27, 145), and estimate of eight extant north
    shore communities and Laurentian community of La Montagne.
51. *IMC*, 189.
52. Ibid.
53. Ibid., 191.
54. Ibid.
55. Ibid., 192.
56. Estimate based on 1676 data.
57. *JR* 63:205.
58. Hennepin, *New Discovery*, 2:511. Cf. *JR* 61:163, 167, for the Jesuits' claim to have baptized over
    4,000 Iroquois during the previous six years, "of whom a goodly part are in possession of
    eternal happiness" (quote 163).
59. *JR* 63:205; *NYCD* 9:129.
60. James and Jameson, *Journal of Jasper Danckaerts*, 181.
61. *LIR*, 55.
62. Ibid., 51–52.
63. Snow, *Iroquois*, 110, table 7.1 (Five Nations estimate).
64. Total estimate derived from estimate of 800 people in Laurentian settlements (Snow, "Dis-
    ease and Population Decline," 184, table 2), and estimate of eight extant north shore com-
    munities. Cf. report of total population of 960 Indians in Laurentian communities (including
    Sillery) (*NYCD* 9:145).
65. Total estimate derived from sum of Five Nations and multinational estimates.
66. *NYCD* 9:154.
67. *AMD* 17:5.
68. Ibid.
69. Ibid.
70. Ibid.
71. Total estimate derived from estimate of 900 people in Laurentian communities of Kahn-
    awake, La Montagne, and Ancienne Lorette (derived from report of 1,167 Indians in Lauren-
    tian communities [including Sillery]) (*NYCD* 9:150), and estimate of seven extant north shore
    communities.
72. Total estimate derived from sum of Five Nations estimates (factoring in an estimate of 1000
    Seneca warriors from 1680 evidence) and multinational estimate. Cf. report of Five Nations
    military strength at 2,000 warriors (*NYCD* 9:162). See also *JR* 62:71 for a description of an
    influx of 700 Illinois captives (mostly children) into Iroquois nations.
73. *JR* 62:163.
74. Total estimate derived from the sum of an estimated 600 people at Kahnawake (based on
    report of sixty "cabins" housing 120–150 "families" at St. François du Sault, with "at least two"
    families per cabin [*JR* 62:173] and using the standard assumption of a five-person nuclear
    family), a report of a total population of 155 people at La Montagne (Louise Tremblay, "La
    Politique Missionaire, 60), and an estimate of seven extant north shore communities and the
    Laurentian community of Ancienne Lorette.
75. Total estimate derived from the sum of report of Five Nations' military strength at 2,500
    "excellent warriors" (*NYCD* 9:196) and multinational estimate. See also *JR* 62:71 (report of
    600 Erie "men, women, and children" relocating to Iroquoia from the frontier of Virginia),
    153 (report of total Iroquois assimilation of "more than nine hundred men armed with mus-
    kets" circa 1680–82), 161 (report of 900 Illinois captives taken circa 1680–82; description of

1,200-man Iroquois expeditionary force departing for another campaign in Illinois country).

76. Total estimate derived from the sum of a reported warrior count of 200 men at Kahnawake (*JR* 62:255; *NYCD* 9:209), a reported total population of 210 people at La Montagne (Tremblay, "La Politique Missionnaire," 60), and an estimate of seven extant north shore communities. Cf. *CMRNF* 1:309 (census total of 1,521 Indians in New France).

77. *NYCD* 9:261.

78. Ibid., 9:282.

79. Total estimate derived from the sum of a census report of total population of 682 people (including 140 "guerriers") at Kahnawake and 222 people at La Montagne (Canada Department of Agriculture, *Censuses of Canada,* 4:16) and an estimate of seven extant north shore communities. Cf. Devine, *Historic Caughnawaga,* 74 (total population of 700 people at Kahnawake); *CMRNF* 1:351 (census total of 1,438 Indians in New France).

80. Total estimate derived from sum of League nation estimates and multinational estimate.

81. Total estimate derived from the sum of a report of 610 people at Kahnawake (based on report of sixty-one "cabins" [*JR* 63:157] and employing the ratio used in calculating the 1682 estimate), plus seven extant north shore communities and the Laurentian community of La Montagne. Cf. *CMRNF* 1:389–90 (census total of 1,436 Indians in New France).

82. Dickinson and Grabowski, "Les Populations Amérindiennes," 59.

83. Jones, *Rationalizing Epidemics,* 75.

84. Canada Department of Agriculture, *Censuses of Canada,* 4:21 (total populations of 435 people at Kahnawake and 181 people at La Montagne).

85. *NYCD* 4:337. Cf. ibid., 701 (for claim that League nations numbered 3,500 men in 1689); *JR* 64:69–71 (Jesuit Pierre Millet report of a 1,700-man multinational Iroquois army in the vicinity of Fort Frontenac at the time of his capture in July 1689).

86. Jones, *Rationalizing Epidemics,* 75.

87. Estimate based on 1688 data (see note 83 above).

88. Snow, *Iroquois,* 110, table 7.1.

89. *NYCD* 4:195, 9:460–61 (estimate of 300 Iroquois deaths from smallpox in September and October 1690); Ramenofsky, *Vectors of Death,* 99; Jones, *Rationalizing Epidemics,* 75.

90. Snow, "Disease and Population Decline," 184, table 2 (multinational estimate).

91. Cf. August 1690 promise by League leaders to provide a total of 1,700 warriors (300 from the Mohawks and Oneidas, and 1,400 from the Onondagas, Cayugas, and Senecas) for a planned invasion of New France (*MaHSC* ser. 5, 8:311). Note also the corroboration between the claimed figure of 1,700 men and Millet's 1689 report (*JR* 64:69–71).

92. Jones, *Rationalizing Epidemics,* 75.

93. Total estimate derived from sum of report of 2,050 warriors in League nations (*NYCD* 9:282) and estimate of 600 people in Laurentian communities of La Montagne and Kahnawakon.

94. *NYCD* 3:815.

95. Canada Department of Agriculture, *Censuses of Canada,* 4:28 (total populations of 509 people at Kahnawakon and 212 people at La Montagne). Cf. description of 160-man war party from Kahnawakon as "nearly their entire force" (*NYCD* 9:538); complaint by Albany officials of French having "draw[n] over 400 of our best Indians" to Laurentian "Praying" towns in recent years (ibid., 3:836).

96. Total estimate based on estimate of 500 people at Kahnawakon (from 1692 data, see note 92 above) and reported population of 220 people at La Montagne (Tremblay, "La Politique Missionnaire," 60).

97. Total estimate derived from sum of report of 1,500 warriors in Five Nations (La Potherie, *Histoire,* 2:515) and estimate of 700 people in the Laurentian communities of La Montagne

and Kahnawakon. Cf. CSPC 14: 361 (report of 1,300 fighting men in the Five Nations).

98. Canada Department of Agriculture, *Censuses of Canada,* 4:34 (total populations of 485 people at Kahnawakon and 216 people at La Montagne). Cf. Dickinson and Grabowski, "Les Populations Amérindiennes," 57, table 3, for a claim of 692 people (including 150 "guerriers") at Kahnawakon.

99. Jones, *Rationalizing Epidemics,* 75.

100. *NYCD* 4:181.

101. Total estimate derived from sum of report that Five Nations could field "scarce 2,500 men" (*NYCD* 4:181) and multinational estimate of 700 people based on 1695 data (see note 95 above).

102. Total estimate derived from sum of report of 1,400 warriors in the Five Nations (*NYCD* 4:768) and estimate of 700 people in the Laurentian communities of La Montagne and Kahnawakon.

103. Hennepin, *New Discovery,* 2:511. Cf. *NYCD* 4:337 (estimate of 110 Mohawk warriors), 345 (report of "thirty-nine houses belonging to the Maquase nation, some of which houses contain one family, some two, and some four").

104. Hennepin, *New Discovery,* 2:511. Cf. *NYCD* 4:337 (estimate of seventy Oneida warriors).

105. Hennepin, *New Discovery,* 2:511. Cf. *NYCD* 4:337 (estimate of 250 Onondaga warriors).

106. Hennepin, *New Discovery,* 2:511. Cf. *NYCD* 4:337 (estimate of 200 Cayuga warriors).

107. *NYCD* 4:337. Cf. Hennepin, *New Discovery,* 2:511 (estimate of 300 Seneca warriors).

108. Total estimate derived from sum of total reported populations of 790 people at Kanatakwente, 160 people at La Montagne, 113 people at Sault-au-Récollet (Canada Department of Agriculture, *Censuses of Canada,* 4:40), and estimate of 100 people at Conestoga. Documentary evidence of a minimal Iroquois presence at Conestoga dates from 1687, but by 1697 we may infer a population of at least 100 people (see the discussion of this community in appendix 1). .

109. Total estimate derived from sum of Five Nations and multinational estimates. The oft-cited April 1698 census (*NYCD* 4:337), which showed such a precipitous Five Nations population decline from 1689 to 1698 that New York governor Bellomont characterized the League as "half destroyed" by King William's War (Ibid., 4:305), was taken at a time when a substantial number of adult Iroquois men were hunting in the upper Great Lakes (*NYCD* 9:678–84; Van Cortlandt to Blathwayt, May 6, 1698 (O.S.), BP-CW, vo1.9; Le Roy de la Potherie, *Histoire* 2:615). Cf. *NYCD* 4:701 for (estimate of League nations' warrior population as 1,100 men); Hennepin, *New Discovery,* 2:511 (estimate of League nations' warrior population as 1,450 men). See also Richter, *Ordeal of the Longhouse,* 188, who claims that "at least 500 of the approximately 2,150 warriors the Five Nations fielded in 1689 had perished, been captured, or *moved to Canadian villages*" (emphasis added).

110. Estimate of 1,200 people at Laurentian communities of Sault-au-Récollet and Kanatakwente based on 1698 data (see note 107 above), and estimate of 100 people at Conestoga.

111. Total estimate derived from sum of multinational estimate and report of 1,100 fighting men in the Five Nations (*CSPC* 17: 135).

112. Snow, *Iroquois,* 110, table 7.1.

113. Total estimate derived from sum of total population estimate of 1,400 people in Laurentian settlements (Snow, "Disease and Population Decline," 184, table 2), and estimate of 100 people at Conestoga. Cf. *NYCD* 4:747 (estimate of 350 warriors at Kanatakwente).

114. Cf. estimates of 1,180 warriors in Five Nations (*NYCD* 4:768) and a total estimate of 7,000 people for the Five Nations (Richter, *Ordeal of the Longhouse,* 356n60).

115. *NYCD* 4:835.

116. Total estimate derived from sum of estimate of Five Nations' military strength at 1,200 warriors (ibid., 9:725), multinational estimate based on 1700 data, and an estimate of 100 people at Cataraqui (see the discussion of this community in appendix 1).

BIBLIOGRAPHY

Abel, Kerry, and Jean Friesen, eds. *Aboriginal Resource Use in Canada: Historical and Legal Aspects.* Winnipeg: University of Manitoba Press, 1991.

Abel, Timothy J. "Recent Research on the Saint Lawrence Iroquoians of Northern New York." *AENA* 30 (2002): 137–54.

Abel, Timothy J., and David N. Fuerst. "Prehistory of the St. Lawrence River Headwaters Region." *AENA* 27 (1999): 1–53.

Abler, Thomas S. *Cornplanter: Chief Warrior of the Allegany Senecas.* Syracuse, N.Y.: Syracuse University Press, 2007.

———. "Dendrogram and Celestial Tree: Numerical Taxonomy and Variants of the Iroquoian Creation Myth." *Canadian Journal of Native Studies* 7 (1987): 195–221.

———. "Iroquois Policy and Iroquois Culture: Two Histories and an Anthropological Ethnohistory." *Ethnohistory* 47 (2000): 483–91.

———. "Longhouse and Palisade: Northeastern Iroquoian Villages of the Seventeenth Century." *Ontario History* 62 (1970): 17–40.

———. "Seneca Moieties and Hereditary Chieftainships: The Early Nineteenth Century Political Organization of an Iroquois Nation." *Ethnohistory* 51 (2004): 459–88.

———. "Upstream from Coldspring: William N. Fenton and the Investigation of Seneca Culture in Time." *Northeast Anthropology* 71 (2006): 1–8.

Abrams, George H. J. *The Seneca People.* Phoenix, Az.: Indian Tribal Series, 1976.

"Account of Iroquois Indians." HM 3028. American Indian File, HEHL.

Adair, E. R. "Dollard des Ormeaux and the Fight at the Long Sault." *CHR* 13 (1932): 121–46.

An Account of the Treaty Between His Excellency Benjamin Fletcher, Captain-General and Governour in Chief of the Province of New-York &c. and the Indians of the Five Nations, viz., the Mohaques, Oneydes, Onnondages, Cajonges, and Sennekes, at Albany. New York: William Bradford, 1694.

The Acts and Resolves, Public and Private, of the Province of the Massachusetts Bay. 21 vols. Boston: Wright & Potter, 1869–1922.

Adams, Arthur T., ed. *The Explorations of Pierre Esprit Radisson, From the Original Manuscript in the Bodleian Library and the British Museum.* Minneapolis, Minn.: Ross & Haines, 1961.

Adams, Nick. "Iroquois Settlement at Fort Frontenac in the Seventeenth and Early Eighteenth Centuries." *OA* 46 (1986): 5–20.

Adney, Edwin T., and Howard I. Chappelle. *The Bark Canoes and Skin Boats of North America.*

Washington, D.C.: Smithsonian Institution Press, 1983.

Agorsah, Emmanuel Kofi. "Evaluating Spatial Behavioral Patterns of Prehistoric Societies." *Journal of Anthropological Archaeology* 7 (1988): 231–47.

Akweks, Aren. "Code of Handsome Lake." In Tehanetorens, ed. *Tales of the Iroquois*, 2 vols., 2: 109–73. 1976. Reprint, Ohsweken, Ont.: Iroqrafts, 1992.

———. *History of the St. Regis Akwesasne Mohawks.* Hogansburg, N.Y.: Akwesasne Counselor Organization, 1947.

Albert, Bruce, and François-Michel Le Tourneau. "Ethnogeography and Resource Use among the Yanomami: Toward a Model of 'Reticular Space.'" *Current Anthropology* 48 (2007): 584–92.

Alchon, Suzanne Austin. *A Pest in the Land: New World Epidemics in Global Perspective.* Albuquerque: University of New Mexico Press, 2003.

Alfred, Taiaiake. *Heeding the Voices of Our Ancestors: Kahnawake Mohawk Politics and the Rise of Native Nationalism.* Toronto: Oxford University Press, 1995.

———. *Peace, Power, Righteousness: An Indigenous Manifesto.* Toronto: Oxford University Press, 1999.

———. *Wasasé: Indigenous Pathways of Action and Freedom.* Peterborough, Ont.: Broadview Press, 2005.

Allen, William Arthur. "Wa-nant-git-che-ang: Canoe Route to Lake Huron through Southern Huronia." *OA* 73 (2002): 38–68.

Alsop, George. *A Character of the Province of Maryland.* 1666. Reprint, ed. Newton D. Mereness, Cleveland: Burrows Bros., 1902.

Alvord, Clarence W., and Lee Bidgood, eds. *The First Explorations of the Trans-Allegheny Region by the Virginians, 1650–1674.* Cleveland: Arthur H. Clark, 1912.

Amith, Jonathan D. *The Möbius Strip: A Spatial History of Colonial Society in Guerrero, Mexico.* Stanford, Calif.: Stanford University Press, 2005.

"Ancient Rites of the Condoling Council." William S. Beauchamp Papers. SC 17369. Box 14, Vol. 1, NYSL.

Anderson, Benedict. *Imagined Communities: Reflections on the Origin and Spread of Nationalism.* Rev. ed. New York: Verso, 1991.

Anderson, David G. "Climate and Culture Change in Prehistoric and Early Historic Eastern North America." *AENA* 29 (2001): 143–86.

Anderson, Gary Clayton. *Kinsmen of Another Kind: Dakota-White Relations in the Upper Mississippi Valley, 1650–1862.* Lincoln: University of Nebraska Press, 1984.

Andrews, Charles M., ed. *Narratives of the Insurrections, 1675–1690.* New York: Charles Scribner's Sons, 1915.

Applebaum, Robert, and John Wood Sweet, eds. *Envisioning an English Empire: Jamestown and the Making of the North Atlantic World.* Philadelphia: University of Pennsylvania Press, 2005.

Aquila, Richard. "The Iroquois as Geographic Middlemen: A Research Note." *Indiana Magazine of History* 80 (1984): 51–60.

———. *The Iroquois Restoration: Iroquois Diplomacy on the Colonial Frontier, 1701–1754.* Detroit: Wayne State University Press, 1983.

Armstrong, William H. *Warrior in Two Camps: Ely S. Parker, Union General and Seneca Chief.* Syracuse, N.Y.: Syracuse University Press, 1978.

Audet, F.-J., ed. "A Propos du Regiment de Carignan." *BRH* 28 (1922): 257–68.

Axtell, James. *The Invasion Within: The Contest of Cultures in Colonial North America.* New York: Oxford University Press, 1985.

Baart, Jan M. "Cloth Seals at Iroquois Sites." *Northeast Historical Archaeology* 34 (2005): 77–88.

Babcock, A. Emerson. "Places of Special Historical Interest in Ellison Park." *RHS-PFS* 7 (1928): 211–13.

Bailyn, Bernard. *Voyagers to the West: A Passage in the Peopling of America on the Eve of the Revolution.* New York: Vintage Books, 1988.

Baker, Brenda J., and Lisa Kealhofer, eds. *Bioarchaeology of Native American Adaptation in the Spanish Borderlands.* Gainesville: University Press of Florida, 1996.

Baker, Emerson W., and John G. Reid. "Amerindian Power in the Early Modern Northeast: A Reappraisal." *WMQ* 61 (2004): 77–106.

———. *The New England Knight: Sir William Phips, 1651-1695.* Toronto: University of Toronto Press, 1998.

Baker, Emerson W., et al., eds. *American Beginnings: Exploration, Culture, and Cartography in the Land of Norumbega.* Lincoln: University of Nebraska Press, 1994.

Ball, Martin W. "'People Speaking Silently to Themselves': An Examination of Keith Basso's Philosophical Speculations on 'Sense of Place' in Apache Cultures." *AIQ* 26 (Summer 2002): 460–78.

Ballard, Gordon, and Graydon Ballard. "A Contact Mohawk Cemetery." NYSAA Chenango Chapter *Bulletin* 9.2 (August 1967): 1–20.

Balvay, Arnaud. "Les relations entre soldats français et Amérindiens: La question de la traite (1683-1763)." *RAQ* 35.2 (2005): 17–28.

Banks, Kenneth. *Chasing Empire Across the Sea: Communications and the State in the French Atlantic, 1713-1763.* Montreal: McGill-Queen's University Press, 2002.

Barbeau, C. M. "Iroquoian Clans and Phratries." *American Anthropologist* 19 (1917): 392–402.

Barbour, Philip L., ed. *The Complete Works of Captain John Smith.* 3 vols. Chapel Hill: University of North Carolina Press, 1986.

———. *The Jamestown Voyages Under the First Charter, 1606-1609.* 2 vols. Hakluyt Society *Works*, Series 2, Nos. 136–137. Cambridge: Cambridge University Press, 1969.

Barkham, Selma. "A Note on the Strait of Belle Isle during the Period of Basque Contact with Indians and Inuit." *Etudes/Inuit/Studies* 4 (1980): 51–58.

Barnett, Clive. "Ways of Relating: Hospitality and the Acknowledgment of Otherness." *Progress in Human Geography* 29 (2005): 5–21.

Barnett, H. G. *Innovation: The Basis of Cultural Change.* New York: McGraw-Hill, 1955.

Barreiro, José. "Chief Jacob Thomas and the Condolence Cane." *Northeast Indian Quarterly* 7 (Winter 1990): 77–79.

Barsh, Russel L. "The Nature and Spirit of North American Political Systems." *AIQ* 10 (Summer 1986): 181–98.

Bartlett, John R., ed. *Records of the Colony of Rhode Island and Providence Plantations in New England.* 10 vols. Providence, R.I.: A. C. Greene and Brother, 1856–65.

Baugh, Timothy G., and Jonathon E. Ericson, eds. *Prehistoric Exchange Systems in North America.* New York: Plenum Press, 1994.

Bauman, Richard, and Joel Sherzer, eds. *Explorations in the Ethnography of Speaking.* Cambridge: Cambridge University Press, 1974.

Baxter, James P., ed. *A Memoir of Jacques Cartier, Sieur de Limoilou.* New York: Dodd, Mead, 1906.

Beauchamp, William S. "Aboriginal Occupation of the State of New York." NYSM *Bulletin* (New York State Education Department, Albany) 32 (1900), 3–167.

———. "Aboriginal Use of Wood in New York State." NYSM *Bulletin* (New York State Education Department, Albany) 89 (1905), 87–272.

———. "Civil, Religious, and Mourning Councils of the New York Indians." NYSM *Bulletin* (New York State Education Department, Albany) 113 (1907): 341–451.

———. "French Lake Mounds, with Notes on Other New York Mounds and Some Accounts of Indian Trails." NYSM *Bulletin* (New York State Education Department, Albany) 87 (1905), 1–82.

———. *Indian Names in New York.* Fayetteville, N.Y.: Recorder Office, 1893.

———. *Iroquois Folklore, Gathered from the Six Nations of New York.* Syracuse, N.Y.: Onondaga Historical Association, 1922.

———, ed. *The Iroquois Trail, or Foot-Prints of the Six Nations in Customs, Tradition, and History.* Fay-
    etteville, N.Y.: Recorder Office, 1892.

———, ed. *Moravian Journals Relating to Central New York, 1745–66.* Syracuse, N.Y.: Diehler Press, 1916.

Beaulieu, Alain. "Des Grandes Espaces aux Réserves: Le Cas des Autochtones de Québec." *Études
    Canadiennes* 62 (2007): 249–62.

Beaver, George. "Early Iroquoian History in Ontario." *OH* 85 (1993): 223–29.

Becker, Mary Druke. *Native Americans and Their Land: The Schoharie River Valley, New York.* West-
    minster, Md.: Heritage Books, 2006.

Bekerman, André, and Gary Warrick, eds. *Origins of the People of the Longhouse: Proceedings of
    the 21st Annual Symposium of the Ontario Archaeological Society.* North York, Ont.: Ontario
    Archaeological Society, 1994.

Bellesiles, Michael A., ed. *Lethal Imagination: Violence and Brutality in American History.* New York:
    New York University Press, 1999.

Belmessous, Salina. "Assimilation and Racialism in Seventeenth and Eighteenth Century French Colo-
    nial Policy." *American Historical Review* 110 (2005): 322–49.

Benjamin, Vernon. "The Tawagonshi Agreement of 1613: A Chain of Friendship in the Dutch Hudson
    Valley." *Hudson Valley Regional Review* 16.2 (1999): 1–20.

Bennett, Monte. "A Longhouse Pattern on the Thurston Site (MSV 1–2)." NYSAA Chenango Chapter
    Bulletin 27.1 (1999): 9–41.

———. "The Moot Site (Sullivan)." NYSAA Chenango Chapter *Bulletin* 14 (1973): 1–25.

———. "The Primes Hill Site: An Eighteenth Century Oneida Station." NYSAA Chenango Chapter *Bul-
    letin* 22.4 (1988): 1–21.

———. "Recent Findings in Oneida Indian Country." NYSAA Chenango Chapter *Bulletin* 21.1 (1984):
    1–12.

———. "The Stone Quarry Site, MSV 4–2: A Mid-Seventeenth Century Oneida Iroquois Station in Cen-
    tral New York." NYSAA Chenango Chapter *Bulletin* 21.2 (1984): 1–35.

Bennett, Monte, and Richard Cole. "The Marshall Site, MSV 7–2." NYSAA Chenango Chapter *Bulletin*
    16.3 (1976): 8–14.

———. "The Upper Hogan Site, Ond 5–4." NYSAA Chenango Chapter *Bulletin* 15.2 (October 1974): 1–24.

Bennett, Ralph, ed. *Settlements in the Americas: Cross-Cultural Perspectives.* Newark: University of
    Delaware Press, 1993.

Benson, Adolph B., ed. *The America of 1750: Travels in North America by Peter Kalm.* 1770. Reprint, 2
    vols., New York: Dover, 1964.

Ben-zvi, Yael. "National Approaches and Cultural Evolution: The Spatial and Temporal U.S. of Lewis
    Henry Morgan's Native America." *Canadian Review of American Studies* 33.3 (2003): 211–29.

———. "Where Did Red Go? Lewis Henry Morgan's Evolutionary Inheritance and U.S. Racial Imagina-
    tion." *CR: New Centennial Review* 7 (2007): 201–29.

Bertrand, Camille. *Histoire de Montréal.* 2 vols. Montreal: Beauchemin, 1935–42.

Bey, George J., III, and Christopher A. Pool, eds. *Ceramic Production and Distribution: An Integrated
    Approach.* Boulder, Colo.: Westview Press, 1992.

Bharati, Agehananda, ed. *The Realm of the Extra-Human: Agents and Audiences.* The Hague: Mouton,
    1973.

Bieder, Robert E. "The Grand Order of the Iroquois: Influences on Lewis Henry Morgan's Ethnology."
    Ethnohistory 27 (1980): 349–61.

Bierhorst, John, ed. *Four Masterworks of American Indian Literature.* New York: Farrar, Strauss, and
    Giroux, 1974.

Bihler, Hugh J. "The Jesuit Mission among the Seneca Iroquois, 1668–1709." United States Catholic
    Historical Society *Historical Records and Studies* 14 (1956): 84–94.

Billings, Warren M., ed. *The Papers of Francis Howard, Baron Howard of Effingham, 1643–1695.* Richmond: Virginia State Library and Archives, 1989.

Binford, Sally R., and Lewis R. Binford, eds. *New Perspectives in Archeology.* Chicago: Aldine, 1968.

Binnema, Ted, and Susan Neylan, eds. *New Histories for Old: Changing Perspectives on Canada's Native Pasts.* Vancouver: University of British Columbia Press, 2007.

Biolsi, Thomas, ed. *A Companion to the Anthropology of American Indians.* Malden, Mass.: Blackwell, 2004.

Birch, Jennifer. "Rethinking the Archaeological Application of Iroquoian Kinship." *CJA* 32 (2008): 194–213.

Bishop, John Douglas. "Locke's Theory of Original Appropriation and the Right of Settlement in Iroquois Territory." *Canadian Journal of Philosophy* 27 (1997): 311–37.

Blair, Emma Helen, ed. *The Indian Tribes of the Upper Mississippi Valley and Region of the Great Lakes.* 2 vols. 1911. Reprint, Lincoln: University of Nebraska Press, 1996.

Blanchard, David S. *Seven Generations: A History of the Kanienkehaka.* Kahnawake Mohawk Territory: Kahnawake Survival School, 1980.

Blanton, Dennis B., and Julia A. King, eds. *Indian and European Contact in Context: The Mid-Atlantic Region.* Gainesville: University Press of Florida, 2004.

Blau, Harold. "Function and the False Faces: A Classification of Onondaga Masked Rituals and Themes." *Journal of American Folklore* 79.314 (1966): 573–79.

——. "Historical Factors in Onondaga Iroquois Cultural Stability." *Ethnohistory* 12 (1965): 250–58.

——. "The Iroquois White Dog Sacrifice: Its Evolution and Symbolism." *Ethnohistory* 11 (1964): 97–119.

Blick, Jeffrey P. "The Iroquois Practice of Genocidal Warfare, 1534–1787." *Journal of Genocide Research* 3 (2001): 405–29.

Bloch, Maurice, and Jonathan Parry, eds. *Death and the Regeneration of Life.* Cambridge: Cambridge University Press, 1982.

Blum, Rony. *Ghost Brothers: Adoption of a French Tribe by Bereaved North America: A Transdisciplinary, Longitudinal, Multilateral Analysis.* Montreal: McGill-Queen's University Press, 2005.

Bohaker, Heidi. "*Nindoodemag:* The Significance of Algonquian Kinship Networks in the Eastern Great Lakes Region, 1600–1701." *WMQ* 63 (2006): 23–52.

Boice, L. Peter. "The Iroquois Sense of Place: Legends as a Source of Environmental Imagery." *New York Folklore* 5 (Winter 1979): 179–88.

Bonaparte, Darren. *Creation and Confederation: The Living History of the Iroquois.* Akwesasne Mohawk Territory: Wampum Chronicles, 2006.

Bonvillain, Nancy, ed. *Studies on Iroquoian Culture. Occasional Publications in Northeastern Anthropology* No. 6. Rindge, N.H.: Franklin Pierce College, 1980.

Bosher, J. F. "The Imperial Environment of French Trade with Canada, 1660–1685." *English Historical Review* 108.426 (1993): 50–81.

Boucher, Philip P., ed. *Proceedings of the Tenth Meeting of the French Colonial Historical Society.* Lanham, Md.: University Press of America, 1985.

Boucher, Pierre. *Histoire Véritable des Moeurs et Productions du Pays de la Nouvelle France, Vulgairement dite le Canada.* 1664. Reprint, Boucherville, Queb.: Société Historique de Boucherville, 1964.

Bourdieu, Pierre. "Social Space and Symbolic Power." *Sociological Theory* 7 (1989): 14–25.

Bourque, Bruce J. *Twelve Thousand Years: American Indians in Maine.* Lincoln: University of Nebraska Press, 2001.

Bowen, Jonathan E. *The Sandusky River Area of North-Central Ohio, 1300–1600.* Upper Sandusky: Sandusky Valley Chapter, Archaeological Society of Ohio, 1994.

Bowne, Eric E. *The Westo Indians: Slave Traders of the Early Colonial South.* Tuscaloosa: University of

Alabama Press, 2005.

Boyce, Douglas W. "A Glimpse of Iroquois Culture History through the Eyes of Joseph Brant and John Norton." *APSP* 117 (1973): 286–94.

Boyd, Julian P., ed. *Indian Treaties Printed by Benjamin Franklin, 1736–1762*. Philadelphia: Historical Society of Pennsylvania, 1938.

Boza Arlotti, Ana Maria. "Evolution of the Social Organization of the Susquehannock Society during the Contact Period in South Central Pennsylvania." Ph.D. diss., University of Pittsburgh, 1997.

Bradley, James W. *Before Albany: An Archaeology of Native-Dutch Relations in the Capital Region, 1600–1664*. NYSM *Bulletin* (University of the State of New York, State Education Department, Albany) 509 (2007).

———. "Dutch Bale Seals from 17th-Century Onondaga Iroquois Sites in New York State." *Post-Medieval Archaeology* 14 (1980): 197–99.

———. *Evolution of the Onondaga Iroquois: Accommodating Change, 1500–1655*. Syracuse, N.Y.: Syracuse University Press, 1987.

———. "Visualizing Arent van Curler: A Biographical and Archaeological View." *De Halve Maen* 78.1 (2005): 3–14.

Bradley, James, and Monte Bennett. "Two Occurrences of Weser Slipware from Early 17th-Century Iroquois Sites in New York State." *Post-Medieval Archaeology* 18 (1984): 301–5.

Bradley, James, and Gordon DeAngelo. "European Clay Pipe Marks from 17th Century Onondaga Iroquois Sites." *AENA* 9 (1981): 109–33.

Brandão, José Antonio, ed. *Nation Iroquoise: A Seventeenth Century Ethnography of the Iroquois*. Lincoln: University of Nebraska Press, 2003.

———. *"Your Fyre Shall Burn No More": Iroquois Policy toward New France and Its Native Allies to 1701*. Lincoln: University of Nebraska Press, 1997.

Brandão, José A., and William A. Starna. "'Some Things May Slip Out of Your Memory and Be Forgott': The 1701 Deed and Map of Iroquois Hunting Territory Revisited." *NYH* 86 (2005): 417–33.

———. "The Treaties of 1701: A Triumph of Iroquois Diplomacy." *Ethnohistory* 43 (1996): 209–44.

Brashler, Janet G. "A Middle 16th Century Susquehannock Village in Hampshire County, West Virginia." *West Virginia Archeologist* 39.2 (1987): 1–30.

Brasser, Ted J. *Riding on the Frontier's Crest: Mahican Indian Culture and Culture Change*. National Museum of Man *Mercury Series* No. 13. Ottawa, Ont., 1974.

Braudel, Fernand, and Michel Mollet du Jourdin, eds. *Le Monde de Jacques Cartier: L'aventure au XVIe siècle*. Montreal: Libre-Expression, 1984.

Braun, David P., and Stephen Plog. "Evolution of 'Tribal' Social Networks: Theory and Prehistoric North American Evidence." *American Antiquity* 47 (1982): 504–25.

Bridenbaugh, Carl, ed. *The Pynchon Papers*. 2 vols. Colonial Society of Massachusetts *Publications* Nos. 60–61. Boston, 1982–85.

Brigham, Robert. "Sites and Trails of the Mohawk Indians." NYSM *Bulletin* (New York State Education Department, Albany) 280 (1929), 86–89.

Brooks, James F. *Captives and Cousins: Slavery, Kinship, and Community in the Southwest Borderlands*. Chapel Hill: University of North Carolina Press, 2002.

Brooks, James F., Christopher N. DeCorse, and John Walton, eds. *Small Worlds: Method, Meaning, and Narrative in Microhistory*. Santa Fe, N.M.: School of American Research Press, 2008.

Brooks, Lisa. *The Common Pot: The Recovery of Native Space in the Northeast*. Minneapolis: University of Minnesota Press, 2008.

Brose, David S. *Archaeological Investigations in Cuyahoga Valley National Recreation Area, Summit and Cuyahoga Counties, Ohio*. Cleveland: Cleveland Museum of Natural History, 1981.

Brose, David S., C. Wesley Cowan, and Robert C. Mainfort Jr., eds. *Societies in Eclipse: Archaeology of the Eastern Woodlands Indians, A.D. 1400–1700.* Washington, D.C.: Smithsonian Institution, 2001.

Brose, David S., and N'omi Greber, eds. *Hopewell Archaeology: The Chillicothe Conference.* Kent, Ohio: Kent State University Press, 1979.

Brown, Craig J. "'The Great Massacre of 1694': Understanding the Destruction of Oyster River Plantation." *Historical New Hampshire* 53 (1998): 68–89.

Brown, James A. "The Archaeology of Ancient Religion in the Eastern Woodlands." *Annual Review of Anthropology* 26 (1997): 465–85.

Brown, Leslie, and Susan Strega, eds. *Research as Resistance: Critical, Indigenous, and Anti-Oppressive Approaches.* Toronto: Canadian Scholars' Press, 2005.

Browne, William H., et al., eds. *Archives of Maryland.* 72 vols. to date. Baltimore: Maryland Historical Society, 1883–.

Bruchac, Joseph, ed. *New Voices from the Longhouse: An Anthology of Contemporary Iroquois Writing.* Greenfield Center, N.Y.: Greenfield Review Press, 1989.

Bruchac, Margaret, and Peter Thomas. "Locating 'Wissatinnewag' in John Pynchon's Letter of 1663." *Historical Journal of Massachusetts* 34 (2006): 56–82.

Brumbach, Hetty Jo. "Anadromous Fish and Fishing: A Synthesis of Data from the Hudson River Drainage." *MIN* 32 (1986): 35–66.

——. "Ceramic Analysis and the Investigation of Matrilocality at the Smith Mohawk Village Site." *NAA* 6 (1985): 341–55.

Buckner, Philip A., and John G. Reid, eds. *The Atlantic Region to Confederation: A History.* Toronto: University of Toronto Press, 1994.

Bukowczyk, John J., et al., eds. *Permeable Border: The Great Lakes Basin as a Transnational Region, 1650–1990.* Pittsburgh: University of Pittsburgh Press, and Calgary: University of Calgary Press, 2005.

Burke, Thomas E., Jr. *Mohawk Frontier: The Dutch Community of Schenectady, New York, 1661–1710.* Ithaca, N.Y.: Cornell University Press, 1991.

Burnard, Trevor. "A Passion for Places: The Geographic Turn in Early American History." *Common-place* 8.4 (July 2008). http://www.common-place.org.

Burnham, Dorothy K. *To Please the Caribou: Painted Caribou Skin Coats Worn by the Naskapi, Montagnais, and Cree Hunters of the Québec-Labrador Peninsula.* Toronto: Royal Ontario Museum, 1992.

Bursey, Jeffrey A. "Aggrandizers vs. Egalitarianism in Agency Theory: Understanding the Iroquoian Economic System, Part 2." *NAA* 27 (2006): 119–48.

——. "The Frog Pond Site (AhGx-359): The Identification of a 17th-Century Neutral Iroquoian Medicine Lodge in Southern Ontario." *CJA* 30 (2006): 1–39.

——. "Women and Cabin Sites: Understanding the Iroquoian Economic System." *NAA* 25.2 (2004): 161–87.

Butler, Jon. *Becoming America: The Revolution before 1776.* Cambridge, Mass.: Harvard University Press, 2000.

Cadzow, Donald A. *Archaeological Studies of the Susquehannock Indians of Pennsylvania.* Safe Harbor Report No. 2. Pennsylvania Historical Commission *Publications* No. 3. Harrisburg, 1936.

Calder, Isabel M., ed. *Colonial Captivities, Marches, and Journeys.* New York: Macmillan, 1935.

Calendar of New York Council Minutes, 1668–1783. Albany: University of the State of New York, 1902.

Calloway, Colin. *New Worlds for All: Indians, Europeans, and the Remaking of Early America.* Baltimore: Johns Hopkins University Press, 1997.

——. *One Vast Winter Count: The Native American West before Lewis and Clark.* Lincoln: University of Nebraska Press, 2003.

——. *The Western Abenakis of Vermont, 1600–1800: War, Migration, and the Survival of an Indian People.* Norman: University of Oklahoma Press, 1990.

Calnan, Joe. "Moïse Hillaret: The First Shipwright on the Great Lakes." *Inland Seas* 58 (2002): 190–207.

Campbell, Celina, and Ian D. Campbell. "The Little Ice Age and Neutral Faunal Assemblages." *OA* 49 (1989): 13–33.

Campbell, William J. "Seth Newhouse, the Grand River Iroquois, and the Writing of the Great Laws." *OH* 96 (2004): 183–202.

Campeau, Lucien. *Gannentaha: Première Mission Iroquoise (1653–1665).* Montreal: Les Éditions Bellarmin, 1983.

——. *La Mission des Jésuites chez les Hurons, 1634–1650.* Montreal: Éditions Bellarmin, 1987.

——, ed. *Monumenta Novae Franciae.* 9 vols. to date. Rome: Institutum Historicum Societatis Iesu, 1966–.

Campisi, Jack. "The Iroquois and the Euro-American Concept of Tribe." *NYH* 63 (1982): 165–82.

Canada Department of Agriculture. *Censuses of Canada, 1665 to 1871.* 5 vols. Ottawa, Ont.: I. B. Taylor, 1876.

Canfield, William W., ed. *The Legends of the Iroquois, Told by the Cornplanter.* New York: A. Wessels, 1902.

Canny, Nicholas P., and Anthony Pagden, eds. *Colonial Identity in the Atlantic World, 1500–1800.* Princeton, N.J.: Princeton University Press, 1987.

Capprecioso, Rob. "Where There's Smoke, There's Fire." *Indian Country Today,* June 21, 2008.

Carlson, David J. *Sovereign Selves: American Indian Autobiography and the Law.* Urbana: University of Illinois Press, 2006.

Carpenter, E. S., K. R. Peirman, and H. L. Schoff. "The 28th Street Site." *PAA* 19 (1949): 3–16.

Carpenter, Roger M. *The Renewed, the Destroyed, and the Remade: The Three Thought Worlds of the Iroquois and the Huron, 1609–1650.* East Lansing: Michigan State University Press, 2004.

Carr, Christopher. "Mortuary Practices: Their Social, Philosophical-Religious, Circumstantial, and Physical Determinants." *Journal of Archaeological Method and Theory* 2.2 (1995): 105–200.

Carr, Helen. *Inventing the American Primitive: Politics, Gender, and the Representation of Native American Literary Traditions, 1789–1836.* Cork, Ireland: Cork University Press, 1996.

Carr, Lois Green, Philip D. Morgan, and Jean B. Russo, eds. *Colonial Chesapeake Society.* Chapel Hill: University of North Carolina Press, 1988.

Carse, Mary Howell. "The Mohawk Iroquois." Archaeological Society of Connecticut *Bulletin* 23 (1949): 3–53.

Carsten, Janet, ed. *Cultures of Relatedness: New Approaches to the Study of Kinship.* Cambridge: Cambridge University Press, 2000.

Carter, Paul. *The Road to Botany Bay: An Essay in Spatial History.* London: Faber & Faber, 1987.

Carter, William Howard. "Chains of Consumption: The Iroquois and Consumer Goods, 1550–1800." Ph.D. diss. Princeton University, 2008.

Cassedy, Daniel F., Paul A. Webb, and J. Bradley. "The Vanderwerken Site: A Protohistoric Iroquois Occupation on Schoharie Creek." *BJNYSAA* 111/112 (1996): 21–34.

Catalogne, Gédéon de. "Recueil de ce qui s'est passé en Canada au sujet de la guerre tant des Anglais et que des Iroquois, depuis l'année 1682." 1716. Reprint, LHSQ *Historical Documents,* ser. 3, vol. 3, 3–82, Quebec: Middleton & Dawson, 1871.

Catalogue of the Manuscript Maps, Charts, and Plans of the Topographical Drawings in the British Museum. 3 vols. London: British Museum, 1844–61.

Ceci, Lynn. "The Value of Wampum among the New York Iroquois." *Journal of Anthropological Research* 38 (1982): 97–107.

Chacon, Richard J., and Ruben J. Mendoza, eds. *North American Indigenous Warfare and Ritual*

Violence. Tucson: University of Arizona Press, 2007.

Chadwick, Edward M. *The People of the Longhouse.* Toronto: Church of England, 1897.

Chambers, Ian. "Spatial Personas: A New Technique for Interpreting Colonial Encounters in Colonial North America." *History Compass* 6 (2008): 1164–72.

Champlain, Samuel E. *The Works of Samuel de Champlain.* 6 vols. Ed. H. P. Biggar. Toronto: Champlain Society, 1922–36.

Chandler, Alfred D., Jr., and James W. Cortada, eds. *A Nation Transformed by Information: How Information Has Shaped the United States from Colonial Times to the Present.* New York: Oxford University Press, 2000.

Chapdelaine, Claude. "The Mandeville Site and the Definition of a New Regional Group within the Saint Lawrence Iroquoian World." *MIN* 39 (1990): 43–63.

——. "The Sedentarization of the Prehistoric Iroquoians: A Slow or Rapid Transformation?" *Journal of Anthropological Archaeology* 12 (1993): 173–209.

——. "La Transhumance et les Iroquoiens du Saint-Laurent." *RAQ* 23.4 (1993): 23–38.

Chapdelaine, Claude, Norman Clermont, and Robert Marquis, eds. *Étude du reseau d'interactions des Iroquoiens préhistoriques du Québec méridional par les analyses physiochimiques.* Montreal: Recherches Amérindiennes au Québec, 1995.

Chapdelaine, Claude, and Gregory G. Kennedy. "The Origin of the Iroquoian Rim Sherd from Red Bay." *MIN* 40 (1990): 41–43.

Chapin, Howard M. *Sachems of the Narragansetts.* Providence: Rhode Island Historical Society, 1931.

Chardon, Roland. "The Linear League in North America." *Annals of the Association of American Geographers* 70 (1980): 129–53.

Charlevoix, Pierre F. X. de. *History and General Description of New France.* 1870. Reprint, 6 vols., trans. John Gilmary Shea, Chicago: Loyola University Press, 1962.

——. *Journal of a Voyage to North-America.* 1761. Reprint, 2 vols., Ann Arbor, Mich.: University Microfilms, 1966.

Charlton, Thomas. "On Iroquois Incest." *Anthropologica* 10 (1968): 29–44.

Chevalier, Jacques. "Myth and Ideology in 'Traditional' French Canada: Dollard; The Martyred Warrior." *Anthropologica* 21 (1979): 143–75.

Cheves, Langdon, ed. "The Shaftesbury Papers and other Records Relating to Carolina and the First Settlement on the Ashley River Prior to the Year 1676." *South Carolina Historical Society Collections* (Charleston) 5 (1897).

Chilton, Elizabeth, ed. *Material Meanings: Critical Approaches to the Interpretation of Material Culture.* Salt Lake City: University of Utah Press, 1999.

Christoph, Peter R., ed. *Administrative Papers of Governors Richard Nicolls and Francis Lovelace, 1664–1673.* Baltimore: Genealogical Publishing, 1980.

——. *The Dongan Papers, 1683–1688.* Pt. 1. *Admiralty Court and Other Records of the Administration of New York Governor Thomas Dongan.* Syracuse, N.Y.: Syracuse University Press, 1993.

Christoph, Peter R., and Florence A. Christoph, eds. *The Andros Papers: Files of the Provincial Secretary of New York during the Administration of Governor Sir Edmund Andros, 1674–1680.* 3 vols. Syracuse, N.Y.: Syracuse University Press, 1989–91.

——. *Books of General Entries of the Colony of New York.* Vol. 1, *Orders, Warrants, Letters, Commissions, Passes, and Licenses Issued by Governors Richard Nicolls and Francis Lovelace, 1664–1673.* Baltimore: Genealogical Publishing, 1982.

——. *Books of General Entries of the Colony of New York.* Vol. 2, *Orders, Warrants, Letters, Commissions, Passes and Licenses Issued by Governors Sir Edmund Andros and Thomas Dongan, and Deputy Governor Anthony Brockholls, 1674–1688.* Baltimore: Genealogical Publishing, 1982.

Christoph, Peter R., Kenneth Scott, and Kenn Stryker-Rodda, eds. *Kingston Papers.* 2 vols. Baltimore:

Genealogical Publishing, 1976.

Church, Benjamin. *Diary of King Philip's War, 1675–76.* Ed. Alan Simpson and Mary Simpson. Chester, Conn.: Pequot Press, 1975.

Claasen, Cheryl, and Rosemary A. Joyce, eds. *Women in Prehistory: North America and Mesoamerica.* Philadelphia: University of Pennsylvania Press, 1996.

Claassen, Cheryl, and Samuella Sigmann. "Sourcing Busycon Artifacts of the Eastern United States." *American Antiquity* 58 (1993): 333–47.

Clark, Douglas, and Allen Owen. "Recent Excavations on the Cody Site, Ond 5–4." NYSAA Chenango Chapter *Bulletin* 16.3 (March 1976): 1–10.

Clark, Lynn. "Gender at an Early Seventeenth Century Oneida Village." Ph.D. diss., Binghamton University, 2004.

Clarke, G. N. G. "Taking Possession: The Cartouche as a Cultural Text in Eighteenth-Century Maps." *Word & Image* 4.2 (1988): 455–74.

Cleland, Charles E., ed. *For the Director: Essays in Honor of James B. Griffin.* University of Michigan Museum of Anthropology *Anthropological Papers* No. 61. Ann Arbor, Mich., 1967.

———. *Rites of Conquest: The History and Culture of Michigan's Native Americans.* Ann Arbor: University of Michigan Press, 1992.

Clément, Daniel, ed. *The Algonquins.* Canadian Museum of Civilization *Mercury Series* No. 130. Ottawa, Ont., 1996.

Clermont, Norman. "L'Importance de la Pêche en Iroquoisie." *RAQ* 14 (1984): 17–23.

———. "Une Figure Iroquoise: Garakontié." *RAQ* 7 (1978): 101–7.

Clifford, James. *Routes: Travel and Translation in the Late Twentieth Century.* Cambridge, Mass.: Harvard University Press, 1997.

Clifton, James. *The Prairie People: Continuity and Change in Potawatomi Indian Culture, 1665–1965.* 1977. Reprint, Iowa City: University of Iowa Press, 1998.

Coates, Colin M., and Cecilia Morgan. *Heroines and History: Representations of Madeleine de Verchères and Laura Secord.* Toronto: University of Toronto Press, 2002.

Codignola, Luca. "The Battle Is Over: Campeau's *Monumenta* vs. Thwaites's *Jesuit Relations.*" *European Review of Native American Studies* 10.2 (1996): 3–10.

Cohen, Ronald D. "The Hartford Treaty of 1650: Anglo-Dutch Cooperation in the Seventeenth Century." *New-York Historical Society Quarterly* 53 (1969): 311–32.

Colden, Cadwallader. *The History of the Five Indian Nations Depending on the Province of New-York in America.* 1727. Reprint, 2 vols. in one, Ithaca, N.Y.: Cornell University Press, 1964.

———. *The History of the Five Indian Nations which are dependent on the Province of New-York and which are a barrier between the English and the French in that part of the world.* 1747. Reprint, 2 vols., New York: Allerton, 1922.

Coley, Robert L., James A. Jolly, and Carole L. Slotter, eds. *Millersville-Penn Manor Community History.* Millersville, Pa.: Millersville Bicentennial Committee, 1976.

Collection de Manuscrits contenant Lettres, Mémoires, et autres Documents Historiques Relatifs a la Nouvelle-France. 4 vols. Quebec: A. Coté, 1883–85.

Collections of the Illinois State Historical Library. 32 vols. Springfield, Ill.: State Historical Library, 1915–40.

Collections of the New-York Historical Society. Third Series. 64 vols. New York: New-York Historical Society, 1869–1931.

Collections of the State Historical Society of Wisconsin. 31 vols. Madison: State Historical Society of Wisconsin, 1855–1931.

The Colonial Laws of New York from the Year 1664 to the Revolution, Including the Charters to the Duke of York, the Commissions and Instructions to Colonial Governors, the Duke's Laws, the

Laws of the Dongan and Leisler Assemblies, the Charters of Albany and New York, and the Acts of the Colonial Legislatures from 1691 to 1775 Inclusive. 5 vols. Albany, N.Y.: J. B. Lyon, 1894–96.

Comaroff, Jean. *Body of Power, Spirit of Resistance: The Culture and History of a South African People.* Chicago: University of Chicago Press, 1985.

Connelly, Kevin. "The Textual Function of Onondaga Aspect, Mood, and Tense: A Journey into Onondaga Conceptual Space." Ph.D. diss., Cornell University, 1999.

Conway, Thor. "Ojibwa Oral History Relating to 19th Century Rock Art." *American Indian Rock Art* 15 (1992): 11–26.

Cook, James W., Lawrence B. Glickman, and Michael O'Malley, eds. *The Cultural Turn in U.S. History.* Chicago: University of Chicago Press, 2008.

Cook, Ramsey, ed. *The Voyages of Jacques Cartier.* Toronto: University of Toronto Press, 1993.

Cooke, Charles A. "Iroquois Personal Names: Their Classification." *APSP* 96 (1952): 427–38.

Coolidge, Guy O. "French Occupation of the Champlain Valley, from 1609 to 1759." Vermont Historical Society *Proceedings* 6.3 (1938): 143–313.

Cornelius, Carol. *Iroquois Corn in a Culture-Based Curriculum: A Framework for Respectfully Teaching about Cultures.* Albany, N.Y.: SUNY Press, 1999.

Cornwell, W. S. "An Artificially Deformed Skull from the Dann Site." *BJNYSAA* 17 (1959): 10–12.

Cosgrove, Denis, and Stephen Daniels, eds. *The Iconography of Landscape: Essays on the Symbolic Representation, Design, and Use of Past Environments.* Cambridge: Cambridge University Press, 1988.

Coupland, Gary, and E. B. Banning, eds. *People Who Lived in Big Houses. Monographs in World Prehistory* No. 27. Madison, Wis.: Prehistory Press, 1996.

Cowan, William, ed. *Papers of the Twenty-second Algonquian Conference.* Ottawa, Ont.: Carleton University, 1991.

Cowin, Verna L. "Shell Ornaments from Cayuga County, New York." *AENA* 28 (2000): 1–14.

Cox, Bruce A., ed. *Native People, Native Lands: Canadian Indians, Inuit, and Métis.* Ottawa, Ont.: Carleton University Press, 1987.

Cox, Isaac J., ed. *The Journeys of Réné Robert Cavelier, Sieur de la Salle.* 2 vols. New York: A. S. Barnes, 1905.

Coyne, James H., trans. and ed. "Exploration of the Great Lakes, 1669–1670, by Dollier de Casson and de Bréhant de Galinée." Ontario Historical Society *Papers and Records* 4 (1903): 1–89.

———. "The Jesuits' Mill or Mortar: The Great Dispersion of the Hurons, 1649 to 1651." *RSCT* ser. 3, vol. 20 (1926): 9–14.

Crawford, Gary W., David G. Smith, and Vandy E. Bowyer. "Dating the Entry of Corn (*Zea mays*) into the Lower Great Lakes Region." *American Antiquity* 62 (1997): 112–119.

Cresswell, Tim. *On the Move: Mobility in the Modern Western World.* New York: Routledge, 2006.

Crouse, Nellis. "Contributions of the Canadian Jesuits to the Geographical Knowledge of New France, 1632–1675." Ph.D. diss., Cornell University, 1924.

Cushner, Nicholas P. *Why Have You Come Here? The Jesuits and the First Evangelization of Native America.* New York: Oxford University Press, 2006.

Cusick, James G., ed. *Studies in Culture Contact.* Center for Archaeological Investigations *Occasional Paper* No. 25. Carbondale: Southern Illinois University, 1995.

Custer, Jay F. "Analysis of Grave Good Assemblages from the Strickler Site: A Contact Period Susquehannock Site in Lancaster County, Pennsylvania." *Journal of Middle Atlantic Archaeology* 1 (1985): 33–41.

Dabulskis-Hunter, Susan. *Outsider Research: How White Writers "Explore" Native Issues, Knowledges, and Experiences.* Bethesda, Md.: Academic Press, 2002.

Darnell, Regna, and Michael K. Foster, eds. *Native North American Interaction Patterns.* Canadian

Museum of Civilization *Mercury Series* No. 112. Ottawa, Ont., 1988.

Darnton, Robert. *The Great Cat Massacre and Other Episodes in French Cultural History.* New York: Basic Books, 1984.

Day, Gordon M. "The Identity of the Sokokis." *Ethnohistory* 12 (1965): 237–49.

———. *The Identity of the St. Francis Indians.* National Museum of Man *Mercury Series* No. 71. Ottawa, Ont., 1981.

Deagan, Kathleen. *Spanish St. Augustine: The Archaeology of a Colonial Creole Community.* New York: Academic Press, 1983.

Deale, Valentine B. "The History of the Potawatomis before 1722." *Ethnohistory* 5 (1958): 305–60.

Dechêne, Louise. *Habitants and Merchants in Seventeenth Century Montreal.* Trans. Liana Vardi. Montreal: McGill-Queen's University Press, 1992.

de Costa, Ravi. "Cosmology, Mobility, and Exchange: Indigenous Diplomacies before the Nation-State." *Canadian Foreign Policy* 13.3 (2007): 13–28.

Deer, A. Brian. "La 'loi des condoléances' et la structure de la Ligue: Commentaire sur *The Great Law and the Longhouse: A Political History of the Iroquois Confederacy* de William N. Fenton." Trans. Pierre Dumais and Roland Tremblay. *RAQ* 29.2 (1999): 63–76.

Deloria, Philip. *Indians in Unexpected Places.* Lawrence: University Press of Kansas, 2004.

———. *Playing Indian.* New Haven, Conn.: Yale University Press, 1998.

DeMallie, Raymond J., ed. *Plains.* Vol. 13 of *Handbook of North American Indians.* Washington, D.C.: Smithsonian Institution, 2001.

Demers, Paul. "The French Colonial Legacy of the Canada-United States Border in Eastern North America, 1650–1783." *French Colonial History* 10 (2009): 35–54.

Dennis, Matthew. *Cultivating a Landscape of Peace: Iroquois-European Encounters in Seventeenth-Century America.* Ithaca, N.Y.: Cornell University Press, 1993.

Denton, Daniel. *A Brief Description of New York.* 1670. Reprint, Ann Arbor, Mich.: University Microfilms, 1966.

DeOrio, Robert. "A Preliminary Sequence of the Historic Cayuga Nation within the Traditional Area." NYSAA Beauchamp Chapter *Newsletter* 9.4 (1978): n.p.

Desrosiers, Léo-Paul. "Les Trois Rivières (1535–1634)." *Les Cahiers des Dix* 11 (1946): 63–95.

Devine, E. J. *Historic Caughnawaga.* Montréal: Messenger Press, 1922.

Dickinson, John A. "Annaotaha et Dollard vus de l'autre côté de la palisade." *RHAF* 35.2 (1981): 163–78.

———. "La Guerre Iroquoise et la Mortalité en Nouvelle-France, 1608–1666." *RHAF* 36 (1982): 31–54.

Dickinson, John A., and Jan Grabowski. "Les Populations Amérindiennes de la Vallée Laurentienne, 1608–1765." *Annales de Démographie Historique* (1993): 51–65.

Divale, William M. *Matrilocal Residence in Pre-Literate Society.* Ann Arbor, Mich.: UMI Press, 1974.

Dixon, Heriberto. "A Saponi by Any Other Name is Still a Siouan." *AICRJ* 26.3 (2002): 65–84.

Dobyns, Henry F. "More Methodological Perspectives on Historical Demography." *Ethnohistory* 36 (1989): 285–99.

Dodge, Martin, and Rob Kitchin. "Code and the Transduction of Space." *Annals of the Association of American Geographers* 95 (2005): 162–80.

Dollier de Casson, François. "Histoire de Montréal, 1640–1672." 1868. Reprint, LHSQ *Historical Documents,* ser. 3, vol. 1, Montreal: Eusèbe Senecal, 1871.

Donnelly, Joseph P., trans. and ed. "Belmont's History of Brandy." *Mid-America* 34 (1952): 42–63.

Doolittle, William E. *Cultivated Landscapes of Native North America.* New York: Oxford University Press, 2000.

Doran, Kwinn H. "Ganienkeh: Haudenosaunee Labor-Culture and Conflict Resolution." *AIQ* 26 (Winter 2002): 1–23.

Douglass, William A., and Jon Bilbao. *Amerikanuak: Basques in the New World.* 1975. Reprint, Reno:

University of Nevada Press, 2005.

Dowd, Gregory E. "The Panic of 1751: Rumors on the Cherokee-South Carolina Frontier." *WMQ* 53 (1996): 527–60.

Doxtator, Deborah. "What Happened to the Iroquois Clans? A Study of Clans in Three Nineteenth Century Rotinonhsyionni Communities." Ph.D. diss., University of Western Ontario, 1996.

Drake, James. *King Philip's War: Civil War in New England, 1675–1676.* Amherst: University of Massachusetts Press, 1999.

Drake, Samuel G., ed. *The History of the Indian Wars in New England.* 2 vols. Roxbury, Mass.: Elliot Woodward, 1865.

———, ed. *Indian Captivities, or Life in the Wigwam.* Auburn, N.Y.: Derby and Miller, 1850.

Drooker, Penelope B. "Two Noded Pipes from West Virginia." *West Virginia Archaeologist* 54.1–2 (2002): 47–50.

———. *The View from Madisonville: Protohistoric Western Fort Ancient Interaction Patterns.* University of Michigan Museum of Anthropology *Memoirs* No. 21. Ann Arbor, Mich., 1997.

Dubé, Jean-Claude. *The Chevalier de Montmagny (1601–1657): First Governor of New France.* Trans. Elizabeth Rapley. Ottawa, Ont.: University of Ottawa Press, 2005.

Dubé, Pauline, ed. *La Nouvelle France Sous Joseph-Antoine Le Febvre de La Barre, 1682–1685: Lettres, Mémoires, Instructions, et Ordonnances.* Sillery, Queb.: Les Éditions du Septentrion, 1993.

Du Creux, François. *The History of Canada or New France.* 1664. Reprint, 2 vols., trans. Percy J. Robinson, Toronto: Champlain Society, 1951–52.

Dunn, Mary Maples, and Richard S. Dunn, eds. *The Papers of William Penn.* 5 vols. Philadelphia: University of Pennsylvania Press, 1981–87.

Dunn, Richard S., James Savage, and Laetitia Yaendle, eds. *The Journal of John Winthrop, 1630–1649.* Cambridge, Mass.: Harvard University Press, 1996.

Dunnigan, Brian L. *Frontier Metropolis: Picturing Early Detroit, 1701–1838.* Detroit, Mich.: Wayne State University Press, 2001.

———. "Portaging Niagara." *Inland Seas* 42 (1986): 177–83, 216–23.

DuVal, Kathleen. *The Native Ground: Indians and Colonists in the Heart of the Continent.* Philadelphia: University of Pennsylvania Press, 2006.

Eccles, William J. *Essays on New France.* Toronto: Oxford University Press, 1987.

———. *Frontenac: The Courtier Governor.* 1959. Reprint, Toronto: McClelland and Stewart, 1965.

———. "St. Malo's Sailor." *Literary Review of Canada* (February 1994): 21–22.

Ecclesiastical Records of the State of New York. 7 vols. Albany, N.Y.: J. B. Lyon, 1901–16.

Echo-Hawk, Roger C. "Ancient History in the New World: Interpreting Oral Traditions and the Archaeological Record." *American Antiquity* 65 (2000): 267–90.

Eekhof, A. *Jonas Michaëlius: Founder of the Church in New Netherland.* Leiden: A. W. Sijthoff's, 1926.

Ehrenreich, Robert M., ed. *Metals in Society: Theory Beyond Analysis.* University of Pennsylvania Museum of Archaeology and Anthropology, *Research Papers in Science and Archaeology* No. 8, Part 2. Philadelphia, 1991.

Ehrhardt, Kathleen L. *European Metals in Native Hands: Rethinking the Dynamics of Technological Change, 1640–1683.* Tuscaloosa: University of Alabama Press, 2005.

Eid, Leroy V. "The Ojibwa-Iroquois War: The War the Five Nations Did Not Win." *Ethnohistory* 26 (1979): 297–324.

Eldridge, Larry D., ed. *Women and Freedom in Early America.* New York: New York University Press, 1999.

Eliade, Mircea. *The Myth of the Eternal Return: Cosmos and History.* 1954. Reprint, trans. Willard R. Trask, ed. Jonathan Z. Smith, Princeton, N.J.: Princeton University Press, 2005.

Ellis, Chris J., and Neal Ferris, eds. *The Archaeology of Southern Ontario to A.D. 1650.* Ontario

Archaeological Society, London Chapter. *Occasional Publications* No. 5. London, Ont., 1990.

Ellis, Douglas, ed. *Âtalôhkâna nesta tipâcimôwina: Cree Legends and Narratives from the West Coast of James Bay.* Winnipeg: University of Manitoba Press, 1995.

Engelbrecht, William. "Erie." *BJNYSAA* 102 (1991): 2–12.

——. *Iroquoia: The Development of a Native World.* Syracuse, N.Y.: Syracuse University Press, 2003.

——. "The Iroquois: Archaeological Patterning on the Tribal Level." *World Archaeology* 6 (1974): 52–65.

Engelbrecht, William, and Donald K. Grayson, eds. *Essays in Northeastern Anthropology in Memory of Marian E. White. Occasional Publications in Northeastern Anthropology* No. 5. Rindge, N.H.: Franklin Pierce College Department of Anthropology, 1978.

Ericson, Jonathan E., and Timothy K. Earle, eds. *Contexts for Prehistoric Exchange.* New York: Academic Press, 1982.

Ethridge, Robbie, and Charles Hudson, eds. *The Transformation of the Southeastern Indians, 1540–1760.* Jackson: University Press of Mississippi, 1998.

Ewen, Charles R. "Continuity and Change: De Soto and the Apalachee." *Historical Archaeology* 30.2 (1996): 41–53.

Ewers, John C. "Iroquois Indians in the Far West." *Montana: The Magazine of Western History* 13.2 (1963): 2–10.

Faillon, Étienne-Michel. *Histoire de la colonie française en Canada.* 3 vols. Montreal: Bibliothèque Paroissale, 1865–66.

Falk, Lisa, ed. *Historical Archaeology in Global Perspective.* Washington, D.C.: Smithsonian Institution, 1991.

Fanon, Frantz. *The Wretched of the Earth.* Trans. Constance Farrington. New York: Grove Press, 1968.

Feifel, Herman, ed. *The Meaning of Death.* New York: McGraw-Hill, 1959.

Feister, "Linguistic Communication between the Dutch and Indians in New Netherland." *Ethnohistory* 20 (1973): 25–38.

Feld, Steven, and Keith M. Basso, eds. *Senses of Place.* Santa Fe, N.M.: School of American Research Press, 1996.

Fenton, William N. "Captain Hyde's 'Observations of the Five Nations of Indians at New York, 1698.'" *American Scene Magazine* 6.2 (1965): n.p.

——. "Contacts between Iroquois Herbalism and Colonial Medicine." Smithsonian Institution *Annual Report for 1941.* Washington, D.C., 1942, 503–26.

——. "Cultural Stability and Change in American Indian Societies." *Journal of the Royal Anthropological Institute of Great Britain and Ireland* 83 (1953): 169–74.

——. *The False Faces of the Iroquois.* Norman: University of Oklahoma Press, 1987.

——. "Fish Drives among the Cornplanter Senecas." *Pennsylvania Archaeologist* 12 (1942): 48–52.

——. *The Great Law and the Longhouse: A Political History of the Iroquois Confederacy.* Norman: University of Oklahoma Press, 1998.

——. "Howard Sky, 1900–1971: Cayuga Faith-Keeper, Gentleman, and Interpreter of Iroquois Culture." *American Anthropologist* 74 (1972): 758–62.

——. "Huronia: An Essay in Proper Ethnohistory." *American Anthropologist* 80 (1978): 923–35.

——. "An Iroquois Condolence Council for Installing Cayuga Chiefs in 1945." *Journal of the Washington Academy of Sciences* 36 (April 1946): 110–27.

——. "The Iroquois Confederacy in the Twentieth Century: A Case Study in the Theory of Lewis H. Morgan in *Ancient Society.*" *Ethnology* 4.3 (1965): 251–65.

——. *The Iroquois Eagle Dance: An Offshoot of the Calumet Dance.* 1953. Reprint, Syracuse, N.Y.: Syracuse University Press, 1991.

——. "Iroquois Suicide: A Study in the Stability of a Cultural Pattern." Bureau of American Ethnology *Bulletin* 128. Washington, D.C.: Smithsonian Institution, 1941, 80–137.

——. *The Little Water Medicine Society of the Senecas.* Norman: University of Oklahoma Press, 2002.

——. "The Lore of the Longhouse: Myth, Ritual, and Red Power." *Anthropological Quarterly* 48 (1975): 131–47.

——, ed. *Parker on the Iroquois.* Syracuse, N.Y.: Syracuse University Press, 1968.

——. "Problems Arising from the Historic Northeastern Position of the Iroquois." Smithsonian Institution *Miscellaneous Collections* 100. Washington, D.C., 1940, 159–252.

——. "The Roll Call of the Iroquois Chiefs: A Study of a Mnemonic Came from the Six Nations Reserve." Smithsonian Institution *Miscellaneous Collections* 111, No. 15. Washington, D.C., February 1950, 1–73.

——. "Seth Newhouse's Traditional History and Constitution of the Iroquois Confederacy." *APSP* 93 (1949): 141–58.

——. "Simeon Gibson: Iroquois Informant, 1889–1943." *American Anthropologist* 46 (1944): 231–34.

——. *Symposium on Local Diversity in Iroquois Culture.* Bureau of American Ethnology *Bulletin* 149. Washington, D.C.: Smithsonian Institution, 1951.

——. "This Island, the World on a Turtle's Back." *Journal of American Folklore* 75 (1962): 283–300.

——. "Tonawanda Longhouse Ceremonies: Ninety Years After Lewis Henry Morgan." Bureau of American Ethnology *Bulletin* 128. Washington, D.C.: Smithsonian Institution, 1941. 140–65.

——. "Toward the Gradual Civilization of the Indian Natives: The Missionary and Linguistic Work of Asher Wright (1803–75) among the Senecas of Western New York." *APSP* 100 (1956): 567–81.

——. "The Training of Historical Ethnologists in America." *American Anthropologist* 54 (1952): 328–39.

——. "Twi'-Yendagon' (Woodeater) Takes the Heavenly Path: On the Death of Henry Redeye (1864–1946), Speaker of the Coldspring Seneca Longhouse." *American Indian* 3.3 (1946): 11–15.

Fenton, William N., and Merle L. Deardorff. "The Last Passenger Pigeon Hunts of the Cornplanter Senecas." *Journal of the Washington Academy of Sciences* 33 (1943): 289–315.

Fenton, William N., and Ernest Stanley Dodge. "An Elm Bark Canoe in the Peabody Museum of Salem." *American Neptune* 9.3 (1949): 185–206.

Fenton, William N., and John Gulick, eds. *Symposium on Cherokee and Iroquois Culture.* Bureau of American Ethnology *Bulletin* 180. Washington, D.C.: Smithsonian Institution, 1961.

Ferdais, Marie. "Matrilinealité et/ou matrilocalité chez les Iroquoiens: Remarques critiques et méthodologiques à l'usage des archéologues." *RAQ* 10.3 (1980): 181–88.

Ferguson, John P. "The Schoharie Iroquois?" *Schoharie County Historical Review* (Fall–Winter 1984): 14–18.

——. *The Schoharie Mohawks.* Howes Cave, N.Y.: Iroquois Indian Museum, 2009.

——. *The Search for the Schoharie Mohawk.* CD-ROM. Cobleskill, N.Y.: Iroquois Indian Museum, 2000.

Ferguson, R. Brian, and Neil L. Whitehead, eds. *War in the Tribal Zone: Expanding States and Indigenous Warfare.* Santa Fe, N.M.: School of American Research Press, 1992.

Ferland, Jean-Baptiste Antoine. *Cours d'Histoire du Canada.* 2 vols. Quebec: A. Coté, 1861–65.

Ferris, Neal. *The Archaeology of Native-Lived Colonialism: Challenging History in the Great Lakes.* Tucson: University of Arizona Press, 2009.

——. "Beyond the Frontier: An Early Historic Trade Axe from Kent County." *KEWA: Bulletin of the London Chapter, Ontario Archaeological Society* 86.7 (1986): 19–23.

——. "In Their Time: Archaeological Histories of Native-Lived Contacts and Colonialisms in Southwestern Ontario, A.D. 1400–1900." Ph.D. diss., McMaster University, 2006.

Finlayson, William D. *Iroquoian People of the Land of Rocks and Water, A.D. 1000–1650: A Study in Settlement Archaeology.* London Museum of Archaeology *Special Publication* No. 1. 4 vols. London, Ont., 1998.

"First Publication of a Jesuit Letter, Written by Father Jean Pierron, August 12, 1667." *BJNYSAA* 6 (March 1956): 5–10.

Fischer, David H. *Champlain's Dream: The European Founding of North America.* New York: Simon and Schuster, 2008.

Fisher, Charles L., ed. *Peoples, Places, and Material Things: Historical Archaeology of Albany, New York.* NYSM *Bulletin* (University of the State of New York, State Education Department, Albany) 499 (2003).

Fitzgerald, William R. *Lest the Beaver Run Loose: The Early 17th Century Christianson Site and Trends in Historic Neutral Archaeology.* National Museum of Man *Mercury Series* No. 111. Ottawa, Ont., 1982.

———. "A Refinement of Historic Neutral Chronologies: Evidence from Shaver-Hill, Christianson, and Robertson-Dwyer." *OA* 38 (1982): 31–46.

Fixico, Donald L. "The Alliance of the Three Fires in Trade and War, 1630–1812." *Michigan Historical Review* 20.2 (1994): 1–23.

———. "Ethics and Responsibilities in Writing American Indian History." *AIQ* 20 (Winter 1996): 29–39.

Foley, Denis. "The Iroquois Condolence Business." *MIN* 5 (1973): 47–53.

Follett, Harrison C. "Chronology of Indian Affairs in Cayuga County." Archaeological Society of Central New York *Bulletin* 2.6 (1947): 38–40.

———. "Following the Cayuga Iroquois Migration (1550–1800) in Cayuga County, New York." Archaeological Society of Central New York *Bulletin* 1.5 (July 1946); 1.6 (August 1946); 1.7 (September 1946); 1.8 (October 1946); 1.9 (November 1946); 1.10 (December 1946); 2.1 (January 1947).

Forbes, Allan, Jr. "Two and a Half Centuries of Conflict: The Iroquois and the Laurentian Wars." *PAA* 40 (3–4) (1970): 1–20.

Force, Peter, ed. *Tracts and Other Papers, Relating Principally to the Origin, Settlement, and Progress of the Colonies of North America, From the Discovery of the Country to the Year 1776.* 1836–46. Reprint, 4 vols., Gloucester, Mass.: Peter Smith, 1963.

Foreman, Carolyn T. *Indians Abroad, 1493–1938.* Norman: University of Oklahoma Press, 1943.

Foster, Michael K. "Jacob Ezra Thomas: Educator and Conservator of Iroquois Culture." *Histories of Anthropology Annual* 1 (2005): 219–45.

———, ed. *Papers in Linguistics from the 1972 Conference on Iroquoian Research.* National Museum of Man *Mercury Series* No. 10. Ottawa, Ont., 1974.

Foster, Michael K., Jack Campisi, and Marianne Mithun, eds. *Extending the Rafters: Interdisciplinary Approaches to Iroquoian Studies.* Albany, N.Y.: SUNY Press, 1984.

Foster, Michael K., and William Cowan, eds. *In Search of New England's Native Past: Selected Essays by Gordon M. Day.* Amherst: University of Massachusetts Press, 1998.

Fournier, Martin. *Pierre-Esprit Radisson: Aventurier et Commerçant, 1636–1710.* Sillery, Queb.: Septentrion, 2001.

Fowke, Gerard. *Archeologic Investigations in James and Potomac Valleys.* Bureau of American Ethnology *Bulletin* 23. Washington, D.C.: Smithsonian Institution, 1894.

Fox, William A. "The North-South Copper Axis." *Southeastern Archaeology* 23 (2004): 85–97.

———. "*Thaniba Wakondagi* among the Ontario Iroquois." *CJA* 26 (2002): 130–51.

Franklin, Benjamin. *The Bagatelles from Passy by Benjamin Franklin.* New York: Eakins Press, 1967.

Franquet, Louis. *Voyages et Mémoires sur le Canada.* 1752. Reprint, Montreal: Éditions Élysée, 1974.

Freidel, Frank, ed. *Harvard Guide to American History.* Rev. ed. 2 vols. Cambridge, Mass.: Belknap Press of Harvard University Press, 1974.

Frese, Joseph R., and Jacob Judd, eds. *Business Enterprise in Early New York.* Tarrytown, N.Y.: Sleepy Hollow Press, 1979.

Frijhoff, Willem. "Jesuits, Calvinists, and Natives: Attitudes, Agency, and Encounters in the Early Christian Missions in the North." *De Halve Maen* 81.3 (2008): 47–54.

Funk, Robert E. *Archaeological Investigations in the Upper Susquehanna Valley, New York State.* 2

vols. Buffalo, N.Y.: Persimmon Press, 1993.

Funk, Robert E., and Charles F. Hayes III, eds. *Current Perspectives in Northeastern Archaeology: Essays in Honor of William A. Ritchie.* NYSAA *Researches and Transactions* No. 17. Rochester, N.Y., 1977.

Funk, Robert E., and Robert D. Kuhn. *Three Sixteenth Century Mohawk Iroquois Village Sites.* NYSM *Bulletin* (University of the State of New York, State Education Department, Albany) 503 (2003).

Fur, Gunlög. *Colonialism in the Margins: Cultural Encounters in New Sweden and Lapland.* Boston: Brill, 2006.

Gabriel-Doxtator, Brenda Katlatont, and Arlette Kanawatie Van Den Houde, eds. *At the Wood's Edge: An Anthology of the History of the People of Kanehsatà:ke.* Kanesatake, Quebec: Kanesatake Education Center, 1995.

Gallay, Alan, ed. *Colonial Wars of North America, 1512–1763: An Encyclopedia.* New York: Garland, 1996.

Gallivan, Martin D. *James River Chiefdoms: The Rise of Social Inequality in the Chesapeake.* Lincoln: University of Nebraska Press, 2003.

Galloway, Patricia. *Choctaw Genesis, 1500–1700.* Lincoln: University of Nebraska Press, 1995.

Gallup, Andrew, ed. *Memoir of a French and Indian War Soldier: "Jolicoeur" Charles Bonin.* Bowie, Md.: Heritage Books, 1993.

Ganter, Granville, ed. *The Collected Speeches of Sagoyewatha, or Red Jacket.* Syracuse, N.Y.: Syracuse University Press, 2006.

——. "'Make Your Minds Perfectly Easy': Sagoyewatha and the Great Law of the Haudenosaunee." *Early American Literature* 44 (2009): 121–46.

Garrad, Charles. "The Attack on Ehwae in 1640." *OH* 65.2 (1973): 107–11.

——. "Chabanel and Honare,enhak." Petun Research Institute *Bulletin* 22 (November 1998). http://www.wyandot.org/petun.

——. "Commemorating the 350th Anniversary of the Dispersal of the Wyandots from Ontario, and Celebrating Their Return." Petun Research Institute *Bulletin* 36 (June 2003). http://www.wyandot.org/petun.

——. "The Survival of the Wenro and How I Became One." *KEWA: Bulletin of the London Chapter, Ontario Archaeological Society* 98.4 (1998): 2–9.

Gehring, Charles T. *Correspondence, 1647–1653.* Syracuse, N.Y.: Syracuse University Press, 2000.

——. *Council Minutes, 1652–1654.* Syracuse, N.Y.: Syracuse University Press, 1983.

——. *Delaware Papers (Dutch Period): A Collection of Documents Pertaining to the Regulation of Affairs on the South River of New Netherland, 1648–1664.* Baltimore: Genealogical Publishing, 1981.

——. *Delaware Papers (English Period): A Collection of Documents Pertaining to the Regulation of Affairs on the Delaware, 1664–1682.* Baltimore: Genealogical Publishing, 1977.

——. "The Dutch among the People of the Long River." *Annals of New Netherland* (2001). http://www.nnp.org.

——. *Fort Orange Court Minutes, 1652–1660.* Syracuse, N.Y.: Syracuse University Press, 1990.

——, ed. "An Undiscovered van Rensselaer Letter." *de Halve Maen* 54.3 (1979): 13, 28.

Gehring, Charles T., trans., and Robert S. Grumet, ed. "Observations of the Indians from Jasper Danckaerts's Journal, 1679–1680." *WMQ* 44 (1987): 104–20.

Gehring, Charles, and William A. Starna. "A Case of Fraud: The Dela Croix Letter and Map of 1634." *NYH* 66 (1984): 249–61.

——. "Dutch and Indians in the Hudson Valley: The Early Period." *Hudson Valley Regional Review* 9.2 (1992): 1–25.

Gehring, Charles T., trans., and William A. Starna, ed. *A Journey into Mohawk and Oneida Country, 1634–1635: The Journal of Harmen Meyndertsz van den Bogaert.* Syracuse, N.Y.: Syracuse University Press, 1988.

Gehring, Charles, William A. Starna, and William N. Fenton. "The Tawagonshi Treaty of 1613: The Final Chapter." *NYH* 60 (1987): 373–93.

Gélinas, Claude. "La Nature des Attaques Iroquoises Contre Ville-Marie (1642–1667)." *RAQ* 24.1–2 (1994): 119–27.

Gélinas, Cyrille. *The Role of Fort Chambly in the Development of New France, 1665–1760.* Ottawa, Ont.: Parks Canada, 1983.

Gendron, Nicolas. *Quelques Particularitez du pays des Hurons en la Nouvelle France, Remarquées par le Sieur Gendron, Docteur en Medicine, qui a demeuré dans ce Pays-là fort long-temps.* 1660. Reprint, Albany, N.Y.: J. Munsell, 1868.

Genheimer, Robert A., ed. *Cultures Before Contact: The Late Prehistory of Ohio and Surrounding Regions.* Columbus: Ohio Archaeological Council, 2000.

George-Kanentiio, Doug. *Iroquois Culture and Commentary.* Santa Fe, N.M.: Clear Light, 2000.

Gervais, Diane, and Serge Lusignan. "De Jeanne d'Arc à Madeleine de Verchères: La Femme Guerrière dans la Société d'Ancien Régime." *RHAF* 53 (1999): 171–205.

Gibson, John Arthur. *Concerning the League: The Iroquois League Tradition as Dictated in Onondaga.* Ed. and trans. Hanni M. Woodbury, in collaboration with Reg Henry and Harry M. Webster. *Algonquian and Iroquoian Linguistics Memoir* No. 9. Winnipeg: University of Manitoba, 1992.

Giddens, Anthony. *The Consequences of Modernity.* Stanford, Calif.: Stanford University Press, 1990.

Girard, Camil, and Édith Gagné. "Première Alliance Interculturelle: Rencontre entre Montagnais et Français à Tadoussac en 1603." *RAQ* 25.3 (1995): 3–14.

Girouard, Désiré. *Lake St. Louis: Old and New.* Montreal: Poirier and Bessette, 1893.

Given, Brian J. *A Most Pernicious Thing: Gun Trading and Native Warfare in the Early Contact Period.* Ottawa, Ont.: Carleton University Press, 1994.

Glatthaar, Joseph T., and James K. Martin. *Forgotten Allies: The Oneida Indians and the American Revolution.* New York: Hill and Wang, 2006.

Goddard, Ives, ed. *Languages.* Vol. 17 of *Handbook of North American Indians.* Washington, D.C.: Smithsonian Institution, 1996.

Godi'Nigoha: The Women's Mind. Brantford, Ont.: Woodlands Cultural Center, 1997.

Goldenweiser, Alexander A. "The Clan and Maternal Family of the Iroquois League." *American Anthropologist* 15 (1913): 696–97.

———. "The Death of Chief John A. Gibson." *American Anthropologist* 14 (1912): 692–94.

———. "On Iroquois Work, 1912." Geological Survey of Canada *Summary Reports for 1912* (Ottawa, Ont.), (1913), 464–75.

———. "On Iroquois Work, 1913–14." Geological Survey of Canada, *Summary Reports for 1913* (Ottawa, Ont.), (1914), 365–72.

Goldsmith, Sean, et al., eds. *Ancient Images, Ancient Thought—The Archaeology of Ideology: Proceedings of the 23rd Annual Chacmool Conference.* Calgary: Archaeological Association of the University of Calgary, 1990.

Goldstein, Alyosha. "Where Nation Takes Place: Proprietary Regimes, Antistatism, and U.S. Settler Colonialism." *South Atlantic Quarterly* 107 (2008): 833–61.

Goldstein, Robert A. *French-Iroquois Diplomatic and Military Relations, 1609–1701.* The Hague: Mouton, 1969.

Goodenough, Ward H. "Residence Rules." *Southwestern Journal of Anthropology* 12 (1956): 22–37.

Gookin, Daniel. *Historical Collections of the Indians in New England, of Their Several Nations, Numbers, Customs, Manners, Religion and Government, before the English Planted There.* 1792.

Reprint, ed. Jeffrey H. Fiske, Towtaid, Mass.: n.p., 1970.

Gordon, Colin, ed. *Power/Knowledge: Selected Interviews and Other Writings, 1972–1977.* New York: Pantheon Books, 1980.

Gordon, Jeffrey J. "Onondaga Iroquois Place-Names: An Approach to Historical and Contemporary Indian Landscape Perception." *Names* 32 (1984): 218–33.

Gosden, Chris. *Archaeology and Colonialism.* Cambridge: Cambridge University Press, 2004.

Gough, Barry, and Laird Christie, eds. *New Dimensions in Ethnohistory: Papers of the Second Laurier Conference on Ethnohistory and Ethnology.* Canadian Museum of Civilization *Mercury Series* No. 120. Ottawa, Ont., 1991.

Graeber, David. *Toward an Anthropological Theory of Value: The False Coin of Our Own Dreams.* New York: Palgrave, 2001.

Gramly, Richard Michael. *Two Early Historic Iroquoian Sites in Western New York.* Buffalo, N.Y.: Persimmon Monographs in Archaeology, 1996.

Granger, Joseph. "The Orchid Site, Area B, Fort Erie, Ontario." *BJNYSAA* 67 (1976): 1–39.

Grant, W. L., and J. Munro, eds. *Acts of the Privy Council of England, Colonial Series.* 6 vols. Hereford, U.K.: Her Majesty's Stationery Office, 1908–12.

Grassmann, Thomas. *The Mohawk Indians and Their Valley, Being a Chronological Documentary Record to the End of 1693.* Schenectady, N.Y.: Eric Hugo Photography and Print, 1969.

Gray, Linda Breur. "Narratives and Identities in the St. Lawrence River Valley, 1667–1720." Ph.D. diss., McGill University, 1999.

Graymont, Barbara. *The Iroquois in the American Revolution.* Syracuse, N.Y.: Syracuse University Press, 1972.

Greer, Allan. *Mohawk Saint: Catherine Tekakwitha and the Jesuits.* New York: Oxford University Press, 2005.

Grenoble, Lenore A., and Lindsay A. Whaley, eds. *Endangered Languages: Language Loss and Community Response.* New York: Cambridge University Press, 1998.

Gronim, Sara Sidstone. "Geography and Persuasion: Maps in British Colonial New York." *WMQ* 58 (2001): 373–402.

Grounds, Richard A., George E. Tinker, and David E. Wilkins, eds. *Native Voices: American Indian Identity and Resistance.* Lawrence: University Press of Kansas, 2003.

Grumet, Robert S. *Historic Contact: Indian People and Colonists in Today's Northeastern United States in the Sixteenth through Eighteenth Centuries.* Norman: University of Oklahoma Press, 1995.

Guillard, Yann, Denys Delâge, and Mathieu d'Avignon. "Les signatures amérindiens: Essai d'interprétation des traités de paix de Montréal de 1700 et de 1701." *RAQ* 31.2 (2001): 21–41.

Guldenzopf, David B. "The Colonial Transformation of Mohawk Iroquois Society." Ph.D. diss., State University of New York at Albany, 1987.

Guthe, Alfred K. *The Late Prehistoric Occupation in Southwestern New York: An Interpretive Analysis.* NYSAA *Researches and Transactions* No. 14. Albany, N.Y., 1958.

Haas, Angela M. "Wampum as Hypertext: An American Indian Intellectual Tradition of Multimedia Theory and Practice." *Studies in American Indian Literatures* 19.4 (2007): 77–100.

Haas, Jonathan, ed. *From Leaders to Rulers.* New York: Kluwer Academic/Plenum, 2001.

Hacquebord, Louwrens, and Richard Vaughan, eds. *Between Greenland and America: Cross-Cultural Contacts and the Environment in the Baffin Bay Area.* The Netherlands: University of Groningen Arctic Center, 1987.

Haddad, Yvonne Y., and Ellison B. Findly, eds. *Women, Religion, and Social Change.* Albany, N.Y.: SUNY Press, 1985.

Haefeli, Evan. "On First Contact and Apotheosis: Manitou and Men in North America." *Ethnohistory* 54 (2007): 407–43.

Haefeli, Evan, and Kevin Sweeney. *Captors and Captives: The 1704 French and Indian Raid on Deerfield.* Amherst: University of Massachusetts Press, 2003.

Hagedorn, Nancy L. "Brokers of Understanding: Interpreters as Agents of Cultural Exchange in Colonial New York." *NYH* 76 (1995): 379–408.

Hagerty, Gilbert. "The Iron Trade Knife in Oneida Territory." *PAA* 33 (1963): 93–114.

——. *Wampum, War, and Trade Goods West of the Hudson.* Interlaken, N.Y.: Heart of the Lakes Publishing, 1985.

Hale, Horatio. *The Iroquois Book of Rites and Hale on the Iroquois.* 1883. Reprint, Ohsweken, Ont.: Iroqrafts, 1989.

——. "An Iroquois Condoling Council." *RSCT* ser. 2, vol. 1 (1895): 48–59.

Hall, Anthony J. *The American Empire and the Fourth World.* Montreal: McGill-Queen's University Press, 2003.

Hall, Clayton Coleman, ed. *Narratives of Early Maryland, 1633–1684.* 1910. Reprint, New York: Barnes and Noble, 1953.

Hall, Robert L. *An Archaeology of the Soul: North American Indian Belief and Ritual.* Urbana: University of Illinois Press, 1997.

Hall, Roger, William Westfall, and Laurel S. McDowell, eds. *Patterns of the Past: Interpreting Ontario's History.* Toronto: Dundurn Press, 1988.

Halpenny, Frances, et al., eds. *Dictionary of Canadian Biography.* 14 vols. to date. Toronto: University of Toronto Press, 1966–.

Halsey, John R., and Michael D. Stafford, eds. *Retrieving Michigan's Buried Past: The Archaeology of the Great Lakes State.* Bloomfield Hills, Mich.: Cranbrook Institute of Science, 1999.

Hamell, George L. "The Iroquois and the World's Rim: Speculations on Color, Culture, and Contact." *AIQ* 16 (Autumn 1992): 451–69.

——. "Strawberries, Floating Islands, and Rabbit Captains: Mythical Realities and European Contact in the Northeast during the Sixteenth and Seventeenth Centuries." *Journal of Canadian Studies* 21.4 (1987): 72–94.

Hamilton, Edward P., ed. *Adventure in the Wilderness: The American Journals of Louis Antoine de Bougainville, 1756–1760.* 1964. Reprint, Norman: University of Oklahoma Press, 1990.

Hamilton, Raphael. "Who Wrote *Premier Établissement de la Foy dans Nouvelle France?*" *CHR* 57 (1976): 265–88.

Hamori-Torok, Charles. *Tyendinaga: From Confederacy to Local Autonomy.* Trent University *Occasional Papers in Anthropology* No. 6. Peterborough, Ont., 1988.

Hamori-Torok, Charles, and Joanne Heath-Manger. *Unity and Sovereignty? The Gibson (Oka) Mohawk.* Trent University *Occasional Papers in Anthropology* No. 7. Peterborough, Ont., 1991.

Harrington, C. R. "Marine Mammals in the Champlain Sea and the Great Lakes." New York Academy of Sciences *Annals* 288 (1977): 508–37.

Harris, R. Cole, ed. *Historical Atlas of Canada.* Vol. 1, *From the Beginning to 1800.* Toronto: University of Toronto Press, 1987.

——. "How Did Colonialism Dispossess? Comments from an Edge of Empire." *Annals of the Association of American Geographers* 94 (2004): 165–82.

——. *The Seigneurial System in Early Canada: A Geographical Study.* Madison: University of Wisconsin Press, 1966.

Hart, John P., ed. *Current Northeast Paleobotany.* NYSM *Bulletin* (University of the State of New York, State Education Department, Albany) 494 (1999).

——. "Maize, Matrilocality, Migration, and Northern Iroquoian Evolution." *Journal of Archaeological Method and Theory* 8 (2001): 151–82.

——. "Rethinking the Three Sisters." *Journal of Middle Atlantic Archaeology* 19 (2003): 73–82.

Hart, John P., and Hetty Jo Brumbach. "The Death of Owasco." *American Antiquity* 68 (2003): 737–52.

Hartig, John H., ed. *Honoring Our Detroit River, Caring for Our Home.* Bloomfield Hills, Mich.: Cranbrook Institute of Science, 2003.

Hasenstab, Robert J. "Agriculture, Warfare, and Tribalization in the Iroquois Homeland of New York: A G.I.S. Analysis of Late Woodland Settlement." Ph.D. diss., University of Massachusetts, 1990.

———. "Canoes, Caches, and Carrying Places: Territorial Boundaries and Tribalization in Late Woodland Western New York." *BJNYSAA* 95 (1987): 39–49.

Hatfield, April Lee. *Atlantic Virginia: Intercolonial Relations in the Seventeenth Century.* Philadelphia: University of Pennsylvania Press, 2004.

Haudenosaunee Environmental Task Force. *Words That Come Before All Else: Environmental Philosophies of the Haudenosaunee.* Akwesasne Mohawk Territory: Native North American Traveling College, 2000.

Hauptman, Laurence. *Conspiracy of Interests: Iroquois Dispossession and the Rise of New York State.* Syracuse, N.Y.: Syracuse University Press, 1999.

———. *The Iroquois and the New Deal.* Syracuse, N.Y.: Syracuse University Press, 1981.

———. "The Two Worlds of Aunt Dinah John (1774?-1883), Onondaga Indian." *NYH* 87 (2006): 5–27.

Hauptman, Laurence, and Jack Campisi, eds. *Neighbors and Intruders: An Ethnohistorical Exploration of the Indians of Hudson's River.* National Museum of Man *Mercury Series* No. 39. Ottawa, Ont., 1978.

Hauptman, Laurence, and L. Gordon McLester III, eds. *The Oneida Indian Journey from New York to Wisconsin, 1784–1860.* Madison: University of Wisconsin Press, 1999.

Havard, Gilles. *The Great Peace of 1701: French-Native Diplomacy in the Seventeenth Century.* Trans. Phyllis Aronoff and Howard Scott. Montreal: McGill-Queen's University Press, 2001.

Havard, Gilles, and Cécile Vidal. *Histoire de l'Amérique Française.* Paris: Éditions Flammarion, 2003.

Hawkins, Alicia L. "Recreating Home? A Consideration of Refugees, Microstyles, and Frilled Pottery in Huronia." *OA* 77/78 (2004): 62–79.

Hawley, Charles. *Early Chapters of Cayuga History: Jesuit Missions in Goi-o-gouen, 1656–1684.* Auburn, N.Y.: Knapp & Peck, 1879.

Hayden, Brian. "Corporate Groups and the Late Ontario Iroquoian Longhouse." *OA* 28 (1976): 3–16.

Hayes, Charles F., III, ed. *Proceedings of the 1982 Glass Trade Bead Conference.* RMSC *Research Records* No. 16. Rochester, N.Y., 1983.

———. *Proceedings of the 1984 Trade Gun Conference.* RMSC *Research Records* No. 18. Rochester, N.Y., 1985.

Hayes, Charles F., III, and Lynn Ceci, eds. *Proceedings of the 1986 Shell Bead Conference: Selected Papers.* RMSC *Research Records* No. 20. Rochester, N.Y., 1989.

Hayes, Charles F., III, Connie Cox Bodmer, and Lorraine P. Saunders, eds. *Proceedings of the 1992 People to People Conference: Selected Papers.* RMSC *Research Records* No. 23. Rochester, N.Y., 1994.

Hayes, Charles F., III, Connie Cox Bodmer, and Martha L. Sempowski, eds. *Proceedings of the 1989 Smoking Pipe Conference.* RMSC *Research Records* No. 22. Rochester, N.Y., 1992.

Hazard, Samuel, ed. *Minutes of the Provincial Council of Pennsylvania.* 16 vols. Harrisburg, Pa.: Theo. Fenn, 1838–53.

Hazard, Samuel, et al., eds. *Pennsylvania Archives.* 9 series. 138 vols. Philadelphia and Harrisburg: Joseph Severns, 1852–1949.

Headrick, Daniel R. *When Information Came of Age: Technologies of Knowledge in the Age of Reason and Revolution, 1700–1850.* New York: Oxford University Press, 2000.

Heckewelder, John. *History, Manners, and Customs of the Indian Nations Who Once Inhabited Pennsylvania and the Neighboring States.* 1876. Reprint, New York: Arno Press, 1971.

Heidenreich, Conrad. "An Analysis of the 17th Century Map 'Novvelle France.'" *Cartographica* 25.3

(1988): 67–111.

———. "The Changing Role of Natives in the Exploration of Canada: Cartier (1534) to Mackenzie (1793)." *Terrae Incognitae* 37 (2005): 28–40.

———. *Huronia: A History and Geography of the Huron Indians, 1600-1650.* Toronto: McClelland and Stewart, 1971.

———. "Measures of Distance Employed on 17th and Early 18th Century Maps of Canada." *Canadian Cartographer* 12.2 (1975): 121–37.

———. "Seventeenth Century Maps of the Great Lakes: An Overview and Procedures for Analysis." *Archivaria* 6 (Summer 1978): 83–112.

Heisey, Henry W., and J. Paul Witmer. "Of Historic Susquehannock Cemeteries." *PAA* 32 (1962): 99–130.

Hele, Karl S. *Lines Drawn Upon the Water: First Nations and the Great Lakes Borders and Borderlands.* Waterloo, Ont.: Wilfrid Laurier University Press, 2008.

Helm, June. *Subarctic.* Vol. 6 of *Handbook of North American Indians.* Washington, D.C.: Smithsonian Institution, 1981.

Helms, Mary W. "Matrilocality, Social Solidarity, and Culture Contact: Three Case Histories." *Southwestern Journal of Anthropology* 26 (1970): 197–212.

Henderson, John S., and Patricia J. Netherly, eds. *Configurations of Power: Holistic Anthropology in Theory and Practice.* Ithaca, N.Y.: Cornell University Press, 1993.

Hendricks, Margo, and Patricia Parker, eds. *Women, "Race" and Writing in the Early Modern Period.* New York: Routledge, 1994.

Hennepin, Louis. *A Description of Louisiana.* 1880. Reprint, Ann Arbor, Mich.: University Microfilms, 1966.

———. *A New Discovery of a Vast Country in America.* 1698. Reprint, 2 vols., ed. Reuben G. Thwaites, Chicago: A. C. McClurg, 1903.

Henry, Dixie Lee. "Cultural Change and Adaptation among the Oneida Iroquois, A.D. 1000–1700." Ph.D. diss., Cornell University, 2001.

Herbstritt, James T. "Foley Farm: The Importance of Architecture and the Demise of the Monongahelans." *PAA* 73 (2003): 33–40.

Herrick, James W. *Iroquois Medical Botany.* Syracuse, N.Y.: Syracuse University Press, 1995.

Hertzberg, Hazel W. *The Great Tree and the Longhouse: The Culture of the Iroquois.* New York: Macmillan, 1966.

Hewitt, J. N. B. "A Constitutional League of Peace in the Stone Age of America: The League of the Iroquois and Its Constitution." Smithsonian Institution *Annual Report for 1918.* Washington, D.C., 1920. 527–45.

———. "The Culture of the Indians of Eastern Canada." *EFWSI 1928* (1929), 179–82.

———. "Field Researches among the Six Nations of the Iroquois." *EFWSI 1930* (1931), 201–6.

———. "Field Studies among the Iroquois Tribes." *EFWSI 1931* (1932), 175–78.

———. "Field Studies of the Iroquois in New York State and in Canada." *EFWSI 1936* (1937), 83–86.

———. "Field-Work among the Iroquois Indians of New York and Canada." *EFWSI 1932* (1933), 81–84.

———, ed. "Iroquoian Cosmology, Part I." Bureau of American Ethnology *Annual Report for 1899-1900,* 127–339. Washington, D.C.: Smithsonian Institution, 1903.

———, ed. "Iroquoian Cosmology, Part II." Bureau of American Ethnology *Annual Report for 1925-1926,* 449–819. Washington, D.C.: Smithsonian Institution, 1928.

———. "The 'League of Nations' of the Iroquois in Canada." *EFWSI 1929* (1930), 201–6.

———. "Legend of the Founding of the Iroquois League." *American Anthropologist* 5 (1892): 132–43.

———. *A Mohawk Form of Ritual Condolence, 1782, by John Deserontyon.* Museum of the American Indian, Heye Foundation, *Indian Notes and Monographs* 10.8 (1928): 83–122.

———. "The Requickening Address of the Iroquois Condolence Council." *Journal of the Washington*

Academy of Sciences 34 (March 1944): 65–84.

——. "The Requickening Address of the League of the Iroquois." *Holmes Anniversary Volume.* Washington, D.C.: Bryan Press, 1916. 65–85.

——. "Review of *The Constitution of the Five Nations, Traditional History of the Confederacy of the Six Nations, Civil, Religious, and Mourning Councils and Ceremonies of Adoption of the New York Indians.*" *American Anthropologist* 19 (1917): 429–38.

——. "Some Esoteric Aspects of the League of the Iroquois." *Proceedings of the Nineteenth International Congress of Americanists Held at Washington, December 27–31, 1915.* Washington, D.C., 1917. 322–26.

Heye, George G. "Wampum Collection." Museum of the American Indian, Heye Foundation, *Indian Notes* 7 (1930): 320–23.

Hill, Asa R. "The Historical Position of the Six Nations." Ontario Historical Society *Papers and Records* 19 (1922): 103–9.

Hill, Bruce, Ian Gillen, and Glenda MacNaughton. *Six Nations Reserve.* Toronto: Fitzhenry and Whiteside, 1987.

Hill, Carole E., ed. *Symbols and Society: Essays on Belief Systems in Action.* Southern Anthropological Society *Proceedings* No. 9. Athens: University of Georgia Press, 1975.

Hill, Jane H., and Judith T. Irvine, eds. *Responsibility and Evidence in Oral Discourse.* Cambridge: Cambridge University Press, 1993.

Hill, Richard, Sr. "Continuity of Haudenosaunee Government." *Northeast Indian Quarterly* 4 (Autumn 1987): 10–14.

——. "Oral Memory of the Haudenosaunee: Views of the Two Row Wampum." *Northeast Indian Quarterly* 7 (Spring 1990): 21–30.

Hill, Susan M. "The Clay We Are Made Of: An Examination of Haudenosaunee Land Tenure on the Grand River Territory." Ph.D. diss., Trent University, 2005.

Hinderaker, Eric. *Elusive Empires: Constructing Colonialism in the Ohio Valley, 1673–1800.* Cambridge: Cambridge University Press, 1997.

"Histoire du Canada, par M. l'Abbé de Belmont." 1840. Reprint, LHSQ *Transactions* 18 (1886): 21–56.

History of Montgomery and Fulton Counties, N.Y. New York: F. W. Beers, 1878.

Hodder, Ian, ed. *The Meaning of Things: Material Culture and Symbolic Expression.* London: Unwin Hyman, 1989.

——. *The Spatial Organisation of Culture.* Pittsburgh: University of Pittsburgh Press, 1978.

Hodge, Frederick Webb, ed. *Handbook of American Indians North of Mexico.* Bureau of American Ethnology *Bulletin* 30. 2 vols. Washington, D.C.: Smithsonian Institution, 1907–10.

——. *Proceedings of the Nineteenth International Congress of Americanists, Held at Washington, December 27–31, 1915.* Washington, D.C., 1917.

Hoffecker, Carol E., et al., eds. *New Sweden in America.* Newark: University of Delaware Press, 1995.

Hoffer, Peter Charles. *Sensory Worlds in Early America.* Baltimore: Johns Hopkins University Press, 2003.

Hoffman, Albert J. "The McClintock Burial Site." *BJNYSAA* 7 (1956): 3–5.

Hoffman, Bernard G., ed. "Account of a Voyage Conducted in 1529 to the New World, Africa, Madagascar, and Sumatra, Translated from the Italian, with Notes and Comments." *Ethnohistory* 10 (1963): 1–79.

——. "Ancient Tribes Revisited: A Summary of Indian Distribution and Movement in the Northeastern United States from 1534 to 1779." *Ethnohistory* 14 (1967): 1–46.

——. *Cabot to Cartier: Sources for a Historical Ethnography of Northeastern North America, 1497–1550.* Toronto: University of Toronto Press, 1961.

——. *Observations on Certain Ancient Tribes of the Northern Appalachian Province.* Bureau of

American Ethnology *Bulletin* 191. Washington, D.C.: Smithsonian Institution, 1964.

Hoffman, Ronald, Mechal Sobel, and Frederika J. Teute, eds. *Through a Glass Darkly: Reflections on Personal Identity in Early America.* Chapel Hill: University of North Carolina Press, 1997.

Hofstra, Warren R., ed. *Cultures in Conflict: The Seven Years' War in North America.* Lanham, Md.: Rowman and Littlefield, 2007.

Holmes, Paula E. "The Narrative Repatriation of Blessed Kateri Tekakwitha." *Anthropologica* 43 (2001): 87–103.

Hook, Duncan R., and David R. M. Gaimster, eds. *Trade and Discovery: The Scientific Study of Artefacts from Post-Medieval Europe and Beyond.* British Museum *Occasional Paper* No. 109. London, 1995.

Hopkins, Kelly. "The Impact of European Material Culture on New York Iroquois Ecologies, Economies, and Diplomacy, 1700–1730." *New England Journal of History* 62 (Fall 2005–2006): 40–72.

Horn-Miller, Kahente. "Otiyaner: The 'Women's Path' through Colonialism." *Atlantis* 29.2 (2005): 57–68.

Horr, David A., ed. *Indians of Northeastern Illinois.* New York: Garland, 1974.

Hosbach, Richard, and Stanford Gibson. "The Wilson Site: A Protohistoric Oneida Village." NYSAA Chenango Chapter *Bulletin* 18.4 (1980): 23–92.

Hosbach. Richard, et al. "The Dungey Site (MSV-6): An Historic Oneida Village—A Short Longhouse." NYSAA Chenango Chapter *Bulletin* 29.1 (December 2006): 37–72.

Hosmer, James K., ed. *Winthrop's Journal "History of New England," 1630–1649.* 2 vols. New York: Barnes and Noble, 1908.

Houghton, Frederick. *The Archeology of the Genesee Country.* NYSAA *Researches and Transactions* No. 3.2. Rochester, N.Y., 1922.

——. "The Seneca Nation from 1655 to 1687." Buffalo Society of Natural Sciences *Bulletin* 10.2 (1910): 363–476.

Hoxie, Frederick E. "Retrieving the Red Continent: Settler Colonialism and the History of American Indians in the U.S." *Ethnic and Racial Studies* 31 (2008): 1153–67.

Hsu, Francis K., ed. *Kinship and Culture.* Chicago: Aldine, 1971.

Hudson, Charles, ed. *Black Drink: A Native American Tea.* 1979. Reprint, Athens: University of Georgia Press, 2004.

Hudson, Charles, and Carmen Chaves Tesser, eds. *The Forgotten Centuries: Indians and Europeans in the American South, 1521–1704.* Athens: University of Georgia Press, 1994.

Huey, Paul R. "Archaeological Testing for an Electrical Line at Ganondagan State Historic Site, July 12, 1994." *BJNYSAA* 108 (1994): 11–17.

——. "The Archaeology of 17th Century New Netherland since 1985: An Update." *Northeast Historical Archaeology* 34 (2005): 95–118.

——. "Schuyler Flatts Archaeological District National Historic Landmark." *BJNYSAA* 114 (1998): 24–31.

Hulbert, Archer B., and William N. Schwarze, eds. *David Zeisberger's History of the Northern American Indians.* 1910. Reprint, Columbus: Ohio Historical Society, 1991.

Hulsebosch, Daniel J. *Constituting Empire: New York and the Transformation of Constitutionalism in the Atlantic World, 1664–1830.* Chapel Hill: University of North Carolina Press, 2005.

Hunter, Charles E. "A Susquehanna Indian Town on the Schuylkill." *PAA* 53.3 (1983): 17–19.

Hunter, Jamie. "Erie Stone: A Seventeenth Century Iroquoian Trading Commodity." *KEWA: Newsletter of the London Chapter, Ontario Archaeological Society* 85.2 (1985): 2–8.

Hunter, William A. "Refugee Fox Settlements among the Senecas." *Ethnohistory* 3 (1956): 11–20.

Huntington, Richard, and Peter Metcalf, eds. *Celebrations of Death: The Anthropology of Mortuary Ritual.* Cambridge: Cambridge University Press, 1979.

Hurtado, Albert L. *Reflections on American Indian History: Honoring a Past, Building a Future.* Norman: University of Oklahoma Press, 2008.

Hutchins, Peter W., and Anjali Choksi. "From *Calder* to *Mitchell:* Should the Courts Patrol Cultural Borders?" *Supreme Court Law Review* 16 (2002): 242–83.

Idle, Dunning. *The Post of the St. Joseph River during the French Régime, 1679–1761.* Niles, Mich.: Support the Fort, Inc., 2003.

Ingersoll, Daniel W., Jr., and Gordon Bronitsky, eds. *Mirror and Metaphor: Material and Social Constructions of Reality.* Lanham, Md.: University Press of America, 1989.

Ingersoll, Thomas N. *To Intermix with Our White Brothers: Indian Mixed Bloods in the United States from Earliest Times to the Indian Removals.* Albuquerque: University of New Mexico Press, 2005.

Irwin, Lee. "Contesting World Views: Dreams among the Huron and Jesuits." *Religion* 22 (1992): 259–69.

Isaac, Erich. "Kent Island." *Maryland Historical Magazine* 52 (1957): 93–119, 210–32.

Jackson, L. J., et al. "A Winter of Discontent: The Charity Site, 1991." *Arch Notes* 92.6 (1992): 5–8.

Jacobs, Jaap. *New Netherland: A Dutch Colony in Seventeenth-Century America.* Leiden: Brill, 2005.

———. "Truffle Hunting with an Iron Hog: The First Dutch Voyage up the Delaware River." Paper presented at the McNeil Center for Early American Studies, Philadelphia, Pa., April 20, 2007.

Jaenen, Cornelius J. "Missionaries as Explorers: The Récollets of New France." *Journal of the Canadian Church Historical Society* 22 (October 1980): 32–45.

Jaenen, Cornelius J., ed. *The French Regime in the Upper Country of Canada during the Seventeenth Century.* Toronto: Champlain Society, 1996.

James, Bartlett B., and J. Franklin Jameson, eds. *Journal of Jasper Danckaerts, 1679–1680.* New York: Charles Scribner's Sons, 1913.

Jameson, J. Franklin, ed. *Narratives of New Netherland, 1609–1664.* 1909. Reprint, New York: Barnes and Noble, 1959.

Jamieson, James B. "An Examination of Prisoner Sacrifice and Cannibalism at the St. Lawrence Iroquoian Roebuck Site." *CJA* 7 (1983): 159–75.

———. "Place Royale: A Prehistoric Site from the Island of Montreal." *OA* 47 (1987): 59–71.

Jamieson, Susan M. "Regional Interaction and Ontario Iroquois Evolution." *CJA* 16 (1992): 70–88.

Jefferson, Thomas. *Notes on the State of Virginia.* 1787. Reprint, ed. William Peden, New York: W. W. Norton, 1954.

Jemison, G. Peter. "Ganondagan Lives On." *Turtle Quarterly* 1 (1986): 3.

Jemison, G. Peter, and Anna M. Schein, eds. *Treaty of Canandaigua 1794: 200 Years of Treaty Relations between the Iroquois Confederacy and the United States.* Santa Fe, N.M.: Clear Light, 1996.

Jennings, Francis. *The Ambiguous Iroquois Empire: The Covenant Chain Confederation of Indian Tribes with English Colonies from Its beginnings to the Lancaster Treaty of 1744.* New York: W. W. Norton, 1984.

Jennings, Francis, et al., eds. *The History and Culture of Iroquois Diplomacy: An Interdisciplinary Guide to the Treaties of the Six Nations and Their League.* Syracuse, N.Y.: Syracuse University Press, 1985.

Jensen, Joan M. "Native American Women and Agriculture: A Seneca Case Study." *Sex Roles* 3 (1977): 423–41.

Jeske, Robert J., and Douglas K. Charles, eds. *Theory, Method, and Practice in Modern Archaeology.* Westport, Conn.: Praeger, 2003.

"The Jesuit Mission Site of St. Joseph." NYSAA Lewis Henry Morgan Chapter *The Iroquoian* 19 (Spring 1991): 11–19.

"John Paine's Journal, 1672." Colonial Society of Massachusetts *Publications* 18 (January 1916): 188–92.

Johnson, Amandus, ed. *The Instruction for Johan Printz, Governor of New Sweden.* 1930. Reprint, Port Washington, N.Y.: Ira J. Friedman, 1969.

Johnson, Elden, ed. *Aspects of Upper Great Lakes Anthropology: Papers in Honor of Lloyd A. Wilford.* St. Paul: Minnesota Historical Society, 1974.

Johnson, Lawrence. "Les lieux de la Paix de 1701, et autres considerations sur les campements amérindiens à Montréal." *RAQ* 31.2 (2001): 9–19.

Johnston, A. J. B., ed. *Essays in French Colonial History: Proceedings of the 21st Annual Meeting of the French Colonial Historical Society.* East Lansing: Michigan State University Press, 1997.

Johnston, Louise, ed. *Aboriginal People and the Fur Trade: Proceedings of the 8th North American Fur Trade Conference, Akwesasne.* Ottawa, Ont.: Dollco, 2001.

———. "The Covenant Chain of Peace: Metaphor and Religious Thought in Seventeenth Century Haudenosaunee Council Oratory." Ph.D. diss., McGill University, 2004.

Jones, David S. *Rationalizing Epidemics: Meanings and Uses of American Indian Mortality since 1600.* Cambridge, Mass.: Harvard University Press, 2004.

Jones, Eric E. "Iroquois Population History and Settlement Ecology, A.D. 1500–1700." Ph.D. diss. Pennsylvania State University, 2008.

———. "Using Viewshed Analysis to Explore Settlement Choice: A Case Study of the Onondaga Iroquois." *American Antiquity* 71 (2006): 523–38.

Jones, P. D., et al. "The Evolution of Climate over the Last Millennium." *Science Magazine* 292 (April 27, 2001): 662–67.

Jordan, Kurt A. "Seneca Iroquois Settlement Pattern, Community Structure, and Housing, 1677–1779." *Northeast Anthropology* 67 (2004): 23–64.

———. *The Seneca Restoration, 1715–1754: An Iroquois Local Political Economy.* Gainesville: University Press of Florida, 2008.

A Journal Kept by Coll. Stephen Courtland and Coll. Nich. Beyard, of Their Majesties Council for the Province of New-York, being appointed by the Council to attend His Excellency Benjamin Fletcher to Albany in treating with the Indians of the Five Nations, and River Indians of that Province, in the months of June and July 1693. New York: William Bradford, 1693.

Judd, Carol M., and Arthur J. Ray, eds. *Old Trails and New Directions: Papers of the Third North American Fur Trade Conference.* Toronto: University of Toronto Press, 1980.

Jugements et Déliberations du Conseil Souverain de la Nouvelle-France. 6 vols. Quebec: A. Coté, 1885–91.

Junker-Anderson, C. "The Eel Fisheries of the St. Lawrence Iroquoians." *NAA* 9.2 (1988): 97–121.

Jury, Wilfrid, and Elsie McLeod Jury. *Sainte-Marie among the Hurons.* Toronto: Oxford University Press, 1954.

Kammen, Michael. *Colonial New York: A History.* 1975. Reprint, New York: Oxford University Press, 1996.

Kapches, Mima T. "Invisible Women." *Rotunda* 35 (Spring 2003): 12–19.

———. "The Spatial Dynamics of Ontario Iroquois Longhouses." *American Antiquity* 55 (1990): 49–67.

Kelsey, Harry. *Sir Francis Drake: The Queen's Pirate.* New Haven: Yale University Press, 1998.

Kelton, Paul. "Avoiding the Smallpox Spirits: Colonial Epidemics and Southeastern Indian Survival." *Ethnohistory* 51 (2001): 45–71.

Kent, Barry C. *Susquehanna's Indians.* 1984. Reprint, Harrisburg: Pennsylvania Historical and Museum Commission, 1993.

Kenyon, Ian, and William Fitzgerald. "Dutch Glass Beads in the Northeast: An Ontario Perspective." *MIN* 32 (1986): 1–34.

Kenyon, W. A. *The Grimsby Site: A Historic Neutral Cemetery.* Toronto: Royal Ontario Museum, 1982.

Keppler, Joseph. "The Peace Tomahawk Algonkian Wampum." Museum of the American Indian, Heye Foundation, *Indian Notes* 6 (1929): 130–38.

Kerber, Jordan E., ed. *Archaeology of the Iroquois: Selected Readings and Resarch Resources.* Syracuse, N.Y.: Syracuse University Press, 2007.

———. *Cross-Cultural Collaboration: Native Peoples and Archaeology in the Northeastern United States.* Lincoln: University of Nebraska Press, 2006.

Ketchum, William. *An Authentic and Comprehensive History of Buffalo.* 2 vols. Buffalo, N.Y.: Rockwell, Baker, and Hill, 1864–65.

Kidd, Kenneth E. *The Excavation of Ste.-Marie I.* Toronto: University of Toronto Press, 1949.

Kim, Sung Bok. *Landlord and Tenant in Colonial New York: Manorial Society, 1664–1775.* Chapel Hill: University of North Carolina Press, 1978.

Kimball, Solon T., and James B. Watson, eds. *Crossing Cultural Boundaries: The Anthropological Experience.* San Francisco: Chandler, 1972.

King, J. C. H. *Thunderbird and Lightning: Indian Life in Northeastern North America, 1600–1900.* London: Trustees of the British Museum, 1982.

King, J. C. H., and Christian Feest, eds. *Three Centuries of Woodlands Indian Art: A Collection of Essays.* Aldenstadt, Germany: ZKF Publishers, 2007.

King, Joyce Tekahnawiiaks. "The Value of Water and the Meaning of Water Law for the Native Americans Known as the Haudenosaunee." *Cornell Journal of Law and Public Policy* 16 (2001): 449–72.

King Philip's War Narratives. Ann Arbor, Mich.: University Microfilms, 1966.

Kinietz, W. Vernon. *The Indians of the Western Great Lakes, 1615–1760.* 1940. Reprint, Ann Arbor: University of Michigan Press, 1991.

Kip, William I., ed. *The Early Jesuit Missions in North America.* New York: Wiley and Putnam, 1846.

Klinck Carl F., and James J. Talman, eds. *The Journal of Major John Norton, 1816.* Toronto: Champlain Society, 1970.

Kloos, Peter. "Matrilocal Residence and Local Endogamy: Environmental Knowledge or Leadership?" *American Anthropologist* 65 (1963): 854–62.

Knowles, Nathaniel. "The Torture of Captives by the Indians of Eastern North America." *APSP* 82 (1940): 151–225.

Koch, Erec R., ed. *Classical Unities: Space, Time, Action; Actes du 32e congrès annuel de la North American Society for Seventeenth Century French Literature, Tulane University, 13–15 avril 2000.* Tubingen, Germany: Gunter Narr Verlag, 2002.

Konrad, Victor. "An Iroquois Frontier: The North Shore of Lake Ontario during the Late Seventeenth Century." *Journal of Historical Geography* 7.2 (1981): 129–44.

Koppedrayer, K. I. "The Making of the First Iroquois Virgin: Early Jesuit Biographies of the Blessed Kateri Tekakwitha." *Ethnohistory* 40 (1993): 277–306.

Kraft, Herbert C. *The Lenape-Delaware Indian Heritage: 10,000 B.C.–A.D. 2000.* Elizabeth, N.J.: Lenape Books, 2001.

———. "Sixteenth and Seventeenth Century Indian/White Trade Relations in the Middle Atlantic and Northeast Regions." *AENA* 17 (1989): 1–29.

Krech, Shepard. *The Ecological Indian.* New York: W.W. Norton, 1999.

Kuhn, Robert D. "The Cromwell Site (NYSM 1121): Including a Brief Treatise on Early Seventeenth Century Mohawk Pottery Trends." *BJNYSAA* 108 (1994): 29–38.

Kuhn, Robert D., and Robert E. Funk. "Boning Up on the Mohawk: An Overview of Mohawk Faunal Assemblages and Subsistence Patterns." *AENA* 28 (2000): 29–62.

Kuhn, Robert D., Robert E. Funk, and James F. Pendergast. "The Evidence for a St. Lawrence Iroquoian Presence on Sixteenth Century Mohawk Sites." *MIN* 45 (1993): 77–86.

Kuhn, Robert D., and Martha L. Sempowski. "A New Approach to Dating the League of the Iroquois." *American Antiquity* 66 (2001): 301–14.

Kuhn, Robert D., and Dean Snow, eds. *The Mohawk Valley Project: 1983 Jackson-Everson Excavations.* Albany: Institute for Northeast Anthropology, State University of New York at Albany, 1986.

Kupp, Jan. "Dutch Influences in Canada II." *De Halve Maen* 56.2 (1981): 14–16, 25.

——. "Dutch Influences in Canada, III" *De Halve Maen* 56.3 (1982): 13–16, 18.

Kupperman, Karen O. *Roanoke: The Abandoned Colony.* Totowa, N.J.: Rowman and Allenheld, 1984.

Kurath, Gertrude P. *Iroquois Music and Dance: Ceremonial Arts of Two Seneca Longhouses.* Bureau of American Ethnology *Bulletin* 187. Washington, D.C.: Smithsonian Institution, 1962.

Labaree, Leonard Woods, ed. *Royal Instructions to British Colonial Governors, 1670–1776.* 1935. Reprint, 2 vols., New York: Octagon Books, 1967.

Labourdette, Jean-François, Jean-Pierre Possou, and Marie-Catherine Vignal, eds. *Le Traité de Vervins.* Paris: Presses de l'Université de Paris-Sorbonne, 2000.

Lacroix, Yvan. *Les Origines de La Prairie (1667–1697).* Montreal: Bellarmin, 1981.

Lafitau, Joseph-François. *Customs of the American Indians Compared with the Customs of Primitive Times.* 1724. Reprint, 2 vols., ed. William N. Fenton, trans. Elizabeth L. Moore, Toronto: Champlain Society, 1974–77.

Lahontan, Louis-Armand de Lom d'Arce de. *New Voyages to North America.* 1703. Reprint, 2 vols., ed. Reuben G. Thwaites, Chicago: A. C. McClurg, 1905.

Lamarche, Hélène. "Les habitants de Lachine et le massacre de 1689." *Mémoires de la Société Généalogique Canadienne-Française* 50.3 (1999): 189–228.

Lamontagne, Leopold, ed., and Richard A. Preston, trans. *Royal Fort Frontenac.* Toronto: Champlain Society, 1958.

Lanctot, Gustave. *Montréal under Maisonneuve, 1642–1665.* Trans. Alta Lind Cook. Toronto: Clarke, Irwin, 1969.

Landis, David H. "The Location of the Susquehannock Fort." Lancaster County Historical Society *Papers* 14 (1910): 81–113.

Landry, Yves. *Pour Le Christ et Le Roi: La vie au temps des premiers Montrealais.* Montreal: Éditions Libre Expression, 1992.

Landsman, Gail. "Anthropology, Theory, and Research in Iroquois Studies, 1980–1990: Reflections from a Disability Studies Perspective." *Histories of Anthropology Annual* 2 (2006): 242–63.

——. *Sovereignty and Symbol: Indian-White Conflict at Ganienkeh.* Albuquerque: University of New Mexico Press, 1988.

Landsman, Gail, and Sara Ciborski. "Representation and Politics: Contesting Histories of the Iroquois." *Current Anthropology* 7 (1992): 425–47.

Latta, Martha A. "Identification of the 17th Century French Missions in Eastern Huronia." *CJA* 9.2 (1985): 147–71.

——. "The Search for St. Ignace II." *OA* 48 (1988): 3–16.

Lauria, Lisa M. "Mythological Giants of the Chesapeake: An Evaluation of the Archaeological Constructions of 'Susquehannock.'" *Journal of Middle Atlantic Archaeology* 20 (2004): 21–28.

Leavelle, Tracy Neal. "Geographies of Encounter: Religion and Contested Spaces in Colonial North America." *American Quarterly* 56 (2004): 913–43.

Le Blant, Robert, and René Beaudry, eds. *Nouveau Documents sur Champlain et son époque, Volume I (1560–1622).* Public Archives of Canada *Publication* No. 15. Ottawa, Ont., 1967.

Le Clercq, Christian. *First Establishment of the Faith in New France.* 1691. Reprint, ed. John G. Shea, 2 vols., New York: John G. Shea, 1881.

Leder, Lawrence H., ed. *The Livingston Indian Records, 1666–1723.* Gettysburg: Pennsylvania Historical Association, 1956.

Lee, Thomas E. "The Long Sault of the Ottawa Gives Up Its Secrets." *PAA* 31 (1961): 97–105.

Le Journal des Jesuites, Publié d'après le Manuscrit Original Conservé aux Archives du Seminaire de

Québec. 1871. Reprint, Montreal: Éditions François-Xavier, 1973.

Lemay, J. A. Leo. *The Life of Benjamin Franklin.* Vol. 2. *Printer and Publisher, 1730–1747.* Philadelphia: University of Pennsylvania Press, 2006.

Lenig, Wayne. "*In Situ* Thought in Eastern Iroquois Development: A History." *BJNYSAA* 116 (2000): 58–70.

———. "Patterns of Material Culture during the Early Years of the New Netherland Trade." *Northeast Anthropology* 58 (1999): 47–74.

———. "The Swart Collection and Mohawk Archaeology." Unpublished paper in author's possession, 2003.

Lenik, Edward J. *Picture Rocks: American Indian Rock Art in the Northeast Woodlands.* Hanover, N.H.: University Press of New England, 2002.

Lennox, Paul. *The Bogle I and Bogle II Sites: Historic Neutral Hamlets of the Northern Tier.* National Museum of Man *Mercury Series* No. 121. Ottawa, Ont., 1984.

———. *The Hood Site: A Historic Neutral Town of 1640 A.D.* National Museum of Man *Mercury Series* No. 121. Ottawa, Ont., 1984.

Le Roy, Claude-Charles, *dit* Bacqueville de la Potherie. *Histoire de l' Amérique Septentrionale: Relation d'un Séjour en Nouvelle-France.* 1722. Reprint, 4 vols. in two, Monaco: Éditions du Rocher, 1997.

Lescarbot, Marc. *The History of New France.* 1609. Reprint, 3 vols., trans. W. L. Grant, ed. H. P. Biggar, Toronto: Champlain Society, 1907–14.

Lestringant, Frank, ed. *La France-Amérique (XVIe–XVIIe siècles: Actes du XXXVe colloque internationale d'études humanists.* Paris: Honoré Champion Éditeur, 1998.

Le Sueur, Jacques. "History of the Calumet and of the Dance." Museum of the American Indian, Heye Foundation, *Contributions* 12.5 (1952): 1–22.

Le Tac, Sixte. *Histoire Chronologique de la Nouvelle France ou Canada.* 1689. Reprint, ed. Eugene Réveillaud, Paris: G. Fischbacher, 1888.

"Letter of Joseph-Marie Chaumonot to Father Philippe Nappi, [August 1641]." Trans. Elizabeth Revel. *KEWA: Bulletin of the London Chapter, Ontario Archaeological Society* 82.2 (1982): 4–7.

Levy, Philip. *Fellow Travelers: Indians and Europeans Contesting the Early American Trail.* Gainesville: University Press of Florida, 2007.

Lewandowski, Stephen. "Diohe'ko: The Three Sisters in Seneca Life: Implications for a Native Agriculture in the Finger Lakes Region." *Agriculture and Human Values* 4.2 (1987): 76–93.

Lewis, G. Malcolm, ed. *Cartographic Encounters: Perspectives on Native American Mapmaking and Map Use.* Chicago: University of Chicago Press, 1998.

———. "First Nations Mapmaking in the Great Lakes Region in Intercultural Contexts: A Historical Review." *Michigan Historical Review* 30.2 (2004): 1–34.

———. "Intracultural Mapmaking by First Nations Peoples in the Great Lakes Region: A Historical Review." *Michigan Historical Review* 32.1 (2006): 1–17.

Lewis, Michael, ed. *American Wilderness: A New History.* New York: Oxford University Press, 2007.

Lewis-Lorentz, Alexandra J. "From Gannagaro to Ganondagan: A Process and Reality of Seneca Iroquois Identity." Ph.D. diss., University of Washington, 1990.

Liberty, Margot, ed. *American Indian Intellectuals, 1976 Proceedings of the American Ethnological Society.* St. Paul, Minn.: West, 1978.

Lightfoot, Kent G. *Indians, Missionaries, and Merchants: The Legacy of Colonial Encounters on the California Frontiers.* Berkeley: University of California Press, 2005.

Lincoln, Charles H., ed. *Narratives of the Indian Wars, 1675–1699.* New York: Barnes and Noble, 1913.

Lipman, Andrew. "'A Meanes to Knitt Them Togeather': The Exchange of Body Parts in the Pequot War." *WMQ* 65 (2008): 3–28.

Litalien, Raymonde, and Denis Vaugeois, eds. *Champlain: The Birth of French America.* Trans. Käthe Roth. Montreal: McGill-Queen's University Press, 2004.

Little, Elizabeth A. "Inland Waterways in the Northeast." *Midcontinental Journal of Archaeology* 12 (1987): 55–76.

Livi-Bacci, Massimo. *A Concise History of World Population.* Trans. C. Ipsen. Cambridge: Blackwell, 1992.

Lockhart, James. *Of Things of the Indies: Essays Old and New in Early Latin American History.* Stanford, Calif.: Stanford University Press, 1999.

Locock, Martin, ed. *Meaningful Architecture: Social Interpretations of Buildings.* Aldershot, U.K.: Avebury, 1994.

London Chapter of the Ontario Archaeological Society, Inc. *Onoyota'a:ka: People of the Standing Stone.* London, Ont., 1987.

Long, John. *Voyages and Travels of an Indian Interpreter and Trader, Describing the Manners and Customs of North American Indians.* 1791. Reprint, Toronto: Coles Publishing, 1971.

Lounsbury, Floyd G. *Iroquois Place-Names in the Champlain Valley.* Albany: University of the State of New York, 1960.

Lowensteyn, Pieter. "The Role of the Dutch in the Iroquois Wars." *De Halve Maen* 58.3 (1984): 1–9, 23.

Lozier, Jean-François. "Lever des chevelures en Nouvelle-France: La politique française du paiement des scalps." *RHAF* 56.4 (2003): 513–42.

Lutz, Donald S. "The Iroquois Confederation Constitution: An Analysis." *Publius: The Journal of Federalism* 28.2 (1998): 99–127.

Lyford, Carrie. *Iroquois: Their Arts and Crafts.* 1945. Reprint, Surrey, B.C.: Hancock House, 1989.

Lynch, James. "The Iroquois Confederacy and the Adoption and Administration of Non-Iroquoian Individuals and Groups Prior to 1756." *MIN* 30 (1985): 83–99.

Lyons, Oren, et al., eds. *Exiled in the Land of the Free: Democracy, Indian Nations, and the U.S. Constitution.* Santa Fe, N.M.: Clear Light, 1992.

MacCord, Howard A. "Ricahecrian Identity: One of Virginia's Many Archaeological Challenges." Archeological Society of Virginia *Quarterly Bulletin* 48 (December 1993): 187–88.

———. "The Susquehannock Indians in West Virginia." *West Virginia Archaeologist* 13 (1952): 239–53.

MacDonald, John D. A. "The Neutral Freelton Village Site." *KEWA: Newsletter of the London Chapter, Ontario Archaeological Society* 91.3 (1991): 3–22.

Macdonald, Robert I., and Ronald F. Williamson. "Sweat Lodges and Solidarity: The Archaeology of the Hubbert Site." *OA* 71 (2001): 29–78.

MacEachern, Scott, David J. W. Archer, and Richard D. Garvin, eds. *Households and Communities: Proceedings of the Twenty-First Annual Conference of the Archaeological Association of the University of Calgary.* Calgary, 1989.

MacLeod, D. Peter. "The Anishnabeg Point of View: The History of the Great Lakes Region to 1800 in Nineteenth-Century Mississauga, Odawa, and Ojibwa Historiography." *CHR* 73 (1992): 194–210.

MacNeish, Richard S. *Iroquois Pottery Types: A Technique for the Study of Iroquois Prehistory.* National Museum of Canada *Bulletin* No. 124. Ottawa, Ont.: Canadian Department of Resources and Development, National Parks Branch, 1952.

Magee, Kathryn. "'They Are the Life of the Nation': Women and War in Traditional Nadouek Society." *Canadian Journal of Native Studies* 28 (2008): 119–38.

Maine Historical Society. *Collections.* Series 2. 19 vols. Portland: Maine Historical Society, 1889–1916.

Majewski, Teresita, and David Gaimster, eds. *International Handbook of Historical Archaeology.* New York: Springer, 2009.

Major, Rachel. "Les Jésuites chez les Hurons en 1648–49." *Canadian Journal of Native Studies* 26

(2006): 53–69.

Malkki, Lisa. "National Geographic: The Rooting of Peoples and the Territorialization of Identity among Scholars and Refugees." *Cultural Anthropology* 7 (1992): 24–43.

Mallery, Garrick. "Sign Language among North American Indians." United States Bureau of Ethnology *Annual Report, 1879–80*. Washington, D.C.: United States Government Printing Office, 1881, 263–552.

Mancall, Peter, ed. *The Atlantic World and Virginia, 1550–1624*. Chapel Hill: University of North Carolina Press, 2007.

Mandzy, Adrian. "History of Cayuga Acculturation: An Examination of the 17th Century Cayuga Iroquois Archaeological Data." M.A. thesis, Michigan State University, 1992.

———. "The Rogers Farm Site: A Seventeenth Century Cayuga Site." *BJNYSAA* 100 (1990): 18–25.

Mann, Barbara Alice. *Iroquoian Women: The Gantowisas*. New York: Peter Lang, 2000.

Mann, Charles C. *1491: New Revelations of the Americas before Columbus*. New York: Alfred A. Knopf, 2005.

Margry, Pierre, ed. *Découvertes et Établissements des Français dans l'Ouest et dans le Sud de l'Amérique Septentrionale, 1614–1754*. 6 vols. Paris: Maisonneuve Frères et Ch. Leclerc, 1879–88.

Marshall, Joyce, ed. *Word from New France: The Selected Letters of Marie de l'Incarnation*. Toronto: Oxford University Press, 1967.

Marshall, Orsamus H., ed. *The Historical Writings of Orsamus H. Marshall Relating to the Early History of the West*. Albany, N.Y.: Joel Munsell's Sons, 1887.

———. *Narrative of the Expedition of the Marquis De Nonville against the Senecas in 1687*. New York: Bartlett and Welford, 1848.

Martelle, Holly. "Some Thoughts on the Impact of Epidemic Disease and European Contact on Ceramic Production in Seventeenth Century Huronia." *OA* 77/78 (2004): 22–43.

Martijn, Charles A. "The Iroquoian Presence in the Estuary and Gulf of the Saint Lawrence Valley: A Reevaluation." *MIN* 40 (1990): 45–63.

Martijn, Charles, Selma Barkham, and Michael M. Barkham. "Basques? Beothuk? Inuit? or St. Lawrence Iroquoians? The Whalers on the 1546 Desceliers Map, Seen through the Eyes of Different Beholders." *Newfoundland Studies* 19 (2003): 187–206.

Martin, Scott W. J. "Languages Past and Present: Archaeological Approaches to the Appearance of the Northern Iroquoian Speakers in the Lower Great Lakes Region of North America." *American Antiquity* 73 (2008): 441–63.

———. "Lower Great Lakes Region Maize and Enchainment in the First Millennium A.D." *OA* 77/78 (2004): 135–58.

Mason, Ronald J. *Inconstant Companions: Archaeology and North American Indian Oral Traditions*. Tuscaloosa: University of Alabama Press, 2006.

———. *Rock Island: Historical Indian Archaeology in the Northern Lake Michigan Basin*. Midcontinental Journal of Archaeology *Special Paper* No. 6. Kent, Ohio: Kent State University Press, 1986.

Massachusetts Historical Society. *Collections*. 7 series. 89 vols. to date. Boston: Massachusetts Historical Society, 1792–.

Massey, Doreen. *For Space*. London: Sage, 2005.

Massicotte, E. Z. "La Foire des Pelleteries a Montréal au XVIIe Siècle." *BRH* 28 (1922): 373–80.

———. "La Milice de 1663." *BRH* 32 (1926): 405–18.

Masterson, James A. "A Foolish Oneida Tale." *American Literature* 10 (1938–39): 53–65.

Mathur, Mary E. Fleming. "The Iroquois in Ethnography." *Indian Historian* 2.3 (1969): 12–18.

Matson, Cathy. *Merchants and Empire: Trading in Colonial New York*. Baltimore: Johns Hopkins University Press, 1998.

Maud, John. *Visit to the Falls of Niagara in 1800*. London: Longman, Rees, Orme, Brown, and Green,

1826.

Mayer, Robert G. "The Oneida of the Thames Archaeological Survey." *KEWA: Bulletin of the London Chapter, Ontario Archaeological Society* 86.6 (1986): 3–18.

Mayer-Oakes, William J. *Prehistory of the Upper Ohio Valley.* Carnegie Museum *Annals* No. 34. Pittsburgh, 1955.

McCaffrey, Moira T., et al., eds. *Wrapped in the Colours of the Earth: Cultural Heritage of the First Nations.* Montreal: McCord Museum of Canadian History, 1992.

McCarthy, Richard L. "The Lewiston Portage Site." *Niagara Frontier* 8 (Spring 1961): 8–12.

McCarthy, Richard L., and Harrison Newman. "A Seneca Indian Find." *Niagara Frontier* 7.4 (1961): 136–38.

McCarthy, Theresa L. "Iroquoian and Iroquoianist: Anthropologists and the Haudenosaunee at Grad River." *Histories of Anthropology Annual* 4 (2008): 135–71.

McCashion, John H. "The Clay Tobacco Pipes of New York State, Part I: Caughnawaga, 1667–1693." *BJNYSAA* 65 (November 1975): 1–19.

———. "The Clay Tobacco Pipes of New York State, Part III: Stone Quarry Oneida—MSV 4–2." NYSAA Chenango Chapter *Bulletin* 24.4 (November 1991): 1–77.

———. "The Clay Tobacco Pipes of New York State, Part V: An Analysis of the Clay Tobacco Pipes from the White Orchard Mohawk Site (CNJ-3)." NYSAA Beauchamp Chapter *Bulletin* 6.1 (Fall 1994): 1–81.

———. "An Unique Dutch Clay Tobacco Pipe from the Blowers Oneida Site and a Preliminary Statement on the Seventeenth Century Oneida Site Sequence Based on the Pipe Data." NYSAA Chenango Chapter *Bulletin* 18.1 (July 1979): 1–25.

McConville, Brendan. *The King's Three Faces: The Rise and Fall of Royal America, 1688–1776.* Chapel Hill: University of North Carolina Press, 2006.

McCracken, Richard J. "Susquehannocks, Brûlé, and Carantouannais: A Continuing Research Problem." *BJNYSAA* 91 (1985): 39–51.

McDowell-Loudan, Ellis. "Ste-Marie de Gannentaha." http://www.otsiningo.com/stemarie.htm.

McElrath, Dale L., Thomas E. Emerson, and Andrew C. Fortier, eds. *Late Woodland Societies: Tradition and Transformation Across the Midcontinent.* Lincoln: University of Nebraska Press, 2000.

McElwain, Thomas. *Mythological Tales and the Allegany Seneca: A Study of the Socio-Religious Context of Traditional Oral Phenomena in an Iroquois Community.* Västervick, Sweden: Eckblads Tryckeri, 1978.

McIlwaine, H. R., ed. *Executive Journals of the Council of Colonial Virginia.* 6 vols. Richmond, Va.: D. Bottom, 1925–66.

———. *Journals of the House of Burgesses of Virginia.* 13 vols. Richmond, Va.: E. Waddey, 1905–15.

McLaren, John A., A. R. Buck, and Nancy E. Wright, eds., *Despotic Dominion: Property Rights in British Settler Societies.* Vancouver: University of British Columbia Press, 2005.

McLay, K. A. J. "Wellsprings of a 'World War': An Early English Attempt to Conquer Canada during King William's War, 1688–1697." *Journal of Imperial and Commonwealth History* 34 (2006): 155–75.

Mead, Margaret, ed. *Cooperation and Competition among Primitive Peoples.* New York: McGraw-Hill, 1937.

Means, Bernard K. *Circular Villages of the Monongahela Tradition.* Tuscaloosa: University of Alabama Press, 2007.

"Memoires de Feu Monsieur Boucher, Seigneur de Boucherville et Ancien Gouverneur de Trois-Rivières." *BRH* 32 (1926): 398–404.

"Memorandum Relating to the Surrender of Québec." In A. G. Doughty, ed., *Public Archives of Canada Report for 1912,* Appendix D. Ottawa, Ont.: Public Archives of Canada, 1913.

Merlan, Francesca. "Indigeneity: Global and Local." *Current Anthropology* 50 (2009): 303–33.

Merrell, James H. *Into the American Woods: Negotiators on the Pennsylvania Frontier.* New York: W. W. Norton, 1999.

Merwick, Donna. *Possessing Albany, 1630–1710: The Dutch and English Experiences.* Cambridge: Cambridge University Press, 1990.

———. *The Shame and the Sorrow: Dutch-Amerindian Encounters in New Netherland.* Philadelphia: University of Pennsylvania Press, 2006.

Metz, Elizabeth. *Sainte Marie among the Iroquois: A Living History Museum of the French and Iroquois at Onondaga in the 17th Century.* 3rd ed. Syracuse, N.Y.: Friends of Historic Onondaga Lake, 1995.

Meuwese, Marcus P. "'For the Peace and Well-Being of the Country': Intercultural Mediators and Dutch-Indian Relations in New Netherland and Dutch Brazil, 1600–1664." Ph.D. diss., University of Notre Dame, 2003.

Meyer, Daniel A., Peter C. Dawson, and Donald T. Hanna, eds. *Debating Complexity: Proceedings of the 26th Annual Conference of the Archaeological Association of the University of Calgary.* Calgary, 1996.

Meyer, William E. "Indian Trails of the Southeast." Bureau of American Ethnology *Annual Report for 1924–25.* Washington, D.C.: Smithsonian Institution, 1928, 749–65.

Michaelsen, Scott. "Ely S. Parker and Amerindian Voices in Ethnography." *American Literary History* 8 (1996): 615–38.

———. *The Limits of Multiculturalism: Interrogating the Origins of American Anthropology.* Minneapolis: University of Minnesota Press, 1999.

Michelaki, Kostalena. "More than Meets the Eye: Reconsidering Variability in Iroquoian Ceramics." *CJA* 31 (2007): 143–70.

Michelsen, Gunther. "An Account of an Iroquois Condolence Council." *MIN* 36 (1988): 61–75.

———. "Iroquois Population Statistics." *MIN* 14 (1977): 3–17.

Michigan Pioneer and Historical Society. *Collections.* 40 vols. Lansing, Mich.: Robert Smith, 1874–1929.

Miller, John. *A Description of the Province and City of New York, with Plans of the City and Several Forts as they Existed in the Year 1695.* 1695. Reprint, London: Thomas Rodd, 1843.

Miller, J. R. *Compact, Contract, Covenant: Aboriginal Treaty-Making in Canada.* Toronto: University of Toronto Press, 2009.

Miller, Susan A. "Native Historians Write Back: The Indigenous Paradigm in American Indian Historiography." *Wicazo Sa Review* 24 (Spring 2009): 25–45.

Milner, George R. "Warfare in Prehistoric and Early Historic Eastern North America." *Journal of Archaeological Research* 7.2 (1999): 105–51.

Miroff, Laurie E., and Timothy D. Knapp, eds. *Iroquoian Archaeology and Analytic Scale.* Knoxville: University of Tennessee Press, 2009.

Mithun, Marianne. "Stalking the Susquehannocks." *International Journal of American Linguistics* 47 (1981): 1–26.

Mithun, Marianne, and Hanni M. Woodbury, eds. *Northern Iroquoian Texts.* International Journal of American Linguistics Native American Texts Series, Monograph No. 4. Chicago: University of Chicago Press, 1980.

Mohawk, John. *War against the Seneca: The French Expedition of 1687.* Ganondagan State Historic Site. New York State Office of Parks, Recreation, and Historic Preservation, 1987.

Mohawk River Valley Project. *Kanatsiohareke (Ganajohalaygay) = The Clean Pot: Longhouse People Return to the Mohawk River Valley.* New York, 1993.

Moloney, Francis X. *The Fur Trade in New England, 1620–1676.* Cambridge, Mass.: Harvard University Press, 1931.

Monture-Angus, Patricia. *Journeying Forward: Dreaming First Nations Independence.* Halifax, N.S.: Fernwood, 1999.

Moody, Kevin, and Charles L. Fisher. "Archaeological Evidence of the Colonial Occupation at Schoharie Crossing State Historic Site, Montgomery County, New York." *BJNYSAA* 99 (1989): 1–13.

Moore, Alexander, ed. *Nairne's Muskohogean Journals: The 1708 Expedition to the Mississippi River.* Jackson: University of Mississippi Press, 1988.

Moore, James A., and Michael S. Keene, eds. *Archaeological Hammers and Theories.* New York: Academic Press, 1983.

Morgan, Lewis Henry. *Ancient Society.* 1877. Reprint, Tucson: University of Arizona Press, 1985.

——. *Houses and House-Life of the American Aborigines.* 1881. Reprint, Chicago: University of Chicago Press, 1965.

——. *League of the Iroquois.* 1851. Reprint, New York: Corinth Books, 1962.

Morin, Eugene. "Early Late Woodland Social Interaction in the St. Lawrence River Valley." *AENA* 29 (2001): 69–94.

Morrison, A. J. "The Virginia Indian Trade to 1673." William and Mary College *Quarterly Historical Magazine* ser. 2, 1 (October 1921): 217–36.

Morse, Jedediah. *Report to the Secretary of War on Indian Affairs.* New Haven, Conn.: S. Converse, 1822.

Moulton, Gary, ed. *The Papers of Chief John Ross.* 2 vols. Norman: University of Oklahoma Press, 1985.

Mourin, Samuel. "Porter la Guerre Chez Les Iroquois: Les Expéditions Françaises Contre Les Villages Des Cinq Nations à la Fin du XVIIe Siècle." *Études Canadiennes* 63 (2007): 7–26.

Moussette, Marcel. "An Encounter in the Baroque Age: French and Amerindians in North America." *Historical Archaeology* 37.4 (2003): 29–39.

——. "1655: Raid Agnier sur l'île aux Oies." *Les Cahiers de Dix* 57 (2003): 273–95.

Muller, Kathryn V. "The Two 'Mystery' Belts of Grand River: A Biography of the Two Row Wampum and the Friendship Belt." *AIQ* 31 (Winter 2007): 129–64.

Munro, William Bennett. *Documents Relating to the Seigniorial Tenure in Canada, 1598-1854.* Toronto: Champlain Society, 1908.

Munsell, Joel, ed. *The Annals of Albany.* 10 vols. Albany, N.Y.: Munsell and Rowland, 1850–59.

Murray, Jean. "The Early Fur Trade in New France and New Netherland." *CHR* 19 (1938): 365–77.

Murray, Louise Wells. *Selected Manuscripts of General John S. Clark.* Athens: Society for Pennsylvania Archaeology, 1931.

Myers, Albert Cook, ed. *Narratives of Early Pennsylvania, West New Jersey, and Delaware, 1630-1707.* New York: Charles Scribner's Sons, 1912.

Myers, Andrew J. "An Examination of Late Prehistoric McFate Trail Locations." *PAA* 67 (1997): 45–53.

Myers, Merlin G. *Households and Families of the Longhouse Iroquois at Six Nations Reserve.* Lincoln: University of Nebraska Press, 2006.

Nabokov, Peter. *Indian Running.* Santa Barbara, Calif.: Capra Press, 1981.

Naroll, Raoul. "The Causes of the Fourth Iroquois War." *Ethnohistory* 16 (1969): 51–81.

Nassaney, Michael S., et al. "The Search for Fort St. Joseph (1691-1781) in Niles, Michigan." *Midcontinental Journal of Archaeology* 28.2 (2003): 107–44.

A Narrative of an Attempt made by the French of Canada Upon the Mohaques Country, Being Indians under the Protection of their Majesties Government of New-York. New York: William Bradford, 1693.

Neill, Alexander B., et al. "The Dungey Site (MSV-6): An Historic Oneida Village—Iron Knives and Trade Axes." NYSAA Chenango Chapter *Bulletin* 29.1 (December 2006): 73–78.

Neill, Edward D., ed. *The Founders of Maryland, as Portrayed in Manuscripts, Provincial Records, and Early Documents.* Albany, N.Y.: J. Munsell, 1876.

——. *Virginia Carolorum: The Colony Under the Rule of Charles the First and Second,* A.D. *1625–*A.D. *1685, Based Upon Manuscripts and Documents of that Period.* Albany, N.Y.: Joel Munsell's Sons, 1886.

New York (Colony) Council Minutes, 1668–1783. 31 vols. Series A1895. New York State Archives, Albany.

New York (Colony) Council Papers, 1664–1781. 103 vols. Series A1894. New York State Archives, Albany.

Newhouse, David. "Indigenous Knowledge in a Multicultural World." *Native Studies Review* 15.2 (2004): 139–54.

Nichols, John W., ed. *Actes du Trente-Deuxième Congrès des Algonquinistes.* Winnipeg: L'Université du Manitoba, 2001.

Niemczycki, Mary Ann Palmer. "Cayuga Archaeology: Where Do We Go From Here?" *BJNYSAA* 102 (1991): 27–33.

——. "The Genesee Connection: The Origins of Iroquois Culture in West-Central New York." *NAA* 7 (1986): 15–44.

——. *The Origin and Development of the Seneca and Cayuga Tribes of New York State.* RMSC *Research Records* No. 17. Rochester, N.Y., 1984.

——. "Seneca Tribalization: An Adaptive Strategy." *MIN* 36 (1988): 77–87.

Noble, William C. "Tsouharissen's Chiefdom: An Early Historic 17th Century Neutral Iroquoian Ranked Society." *CJA* 9.2 (1985): 131–46.

Noon, John A. *Law and Government of the Grand River Iroquois.* Viking Fund *Publications in Anthropology* No. 12. New York: Viking Fund, 1929.

Norton, Thomas Elliott. *The Fur Trade in Colonial New York.* Madison: University of Wisconsin Press, 1974.

Novak, M., et al., eds. *Wild Furbearer Management and Conservation in North America.* Toronto: Ontario Ministry of Natural Resources, 1987.

Oberg, Michael Leroy. *Uncas: First of the Mohegans.* Ithaca, N.Y.: Cornell University Press, 2003.

O'Brien, Michael J. *Paradigms of the Past: The Story of Missouri Archaeology.* Columbia: University of Missouri Press, 1996.

O'Callaghan, E. B., ed. *Calendar of Historical Manuscripts in the Office of the Secretary of State, Albany, New York.* Vol. 2, *English Historical Manuscripts, 1664–1775.* Albany, N.Y.: Weed, Parsons, 1866.

——. *Documentary History of the State of New York.* 4 vols. Albany, N.Y.: Weed, Parsons, 1849–51.

——. *History of New Netherland, or, New York under the Dutch.* 2 vols. New York: D. Appleton, 1845–48.

——. *Laws and Ordinances of New Netherland, 1638–1674.* Albany, N.Y.: Weed, Parsons, 1868.

O'Callaghan, E. B., and Berthold Fernow, eds. *Documents Relative to the Colonial History of the State of New York.* 15 vols. Albany, N.Y.: Weed, Parsons, 1853–87.

Odato, James M. "Federal Ruling Rejects Plans for Catskills Casinos." *Albany (New York) Times-Union,* January 5, 2008.

O'Donnell, James H., III. *Ohio's First Peoples.* Athens: Ohio University Press, 2004.

Oetelaer, Gerald A., and David Meyer. "Movement and Native American Landscapes: A Comparative Approach." *Plains Anthropologist* 51 (2006): 355–74.

Oldmixon, John. *The British Empire in America, Containing the History of the Discovery, Settlement, Progress, and State of the British Colonies on the Continent and Islands of America.* 1741. Reprint, 2 vols., New York: Augustine M. Kelley, 1969.

Olds, Nathaniel S., ed. and trans. "Journal of the Expedition of the Marquis de Denonville, against the Iroquois, 1687, by the Chevalier de Baugy." Rochester Historical Society *Publication Fund Series* 9 (Rochester, N.Y., 1930): 3–56.

Onondaga Nation. http://www.onondaganation.org/culture/wpm_tworow.html.

Orchard, William C. "Mohawk Burden Straps." Museum of the American Indian, Heye Foundation,

Indian Notes 6 (1929): 351–58.

Orlandini, John B. "The Passenger Pigeon: A Seasonal Native American Food Source." *Pennsylvania Archaeologist* 66.2 (1996): 71–77.

Orr, David G., and Daniel G. Crozier, eds. *The Scope of Historical Archaeology: Essays in Honor of John L. Cotter.* Philadelphia: Temple University Department of Anthropology, 1984.

Ortner, Sherry B. "Theory in Anthropology since the Sixties." *Comparative Studies in Society and History* 26 (1984): 126–66.

Osborne, Brian, and Michael Ripmeester. "The Mississaugas Between Two Worlds: Strategic Adjustments to Changing Landscapes of Power." *Canadian Journal of Native Studies* 17 (1997): 259–91.

O'Shea, Marty. "Springfield's Puritans and Indians, 1636–1655." *Historical Journal of Massachusetts* 26 (Winter 1998): 46–72.

Oto and Missouri Indians. New York: Garland, 1974.

Otterbein, Keith F. "Huron vs. Iroquois: A Case Study in Intertribal Warfare." *Ethnohistory* 26 (1979): 141–52.

——. "Why the Iroquois Won: An Analysis of Iroquois Military Tactics." *Ethnohistory* 11 (1964): 56–63.

Otto, Paul. *The Dutch-Munsee Encounter in America: The Struggle for Sovereignty in the Hudson Valley.* New York: Berghahn Books, 2006.

Oury, Dom Guy, ed. *Marie de l'Incarnation, Ursuline (1599–1672): Correspondance.* Solesmes, France: Abbaye St.-Pierre, 1971.

Overstreet, David F. "Oneota Prehistory and History." *Wisconsin Archeologist* 78 (1–2) (1997): 250–97.

Paine, Richard L., ed. *Integrating Archaeological Demography: Multidisciplinary Approaches to Prehistoric Population.* Southern Illinois University Center for Archaeological Investigations Occasional Paper No. 24. Carbondale, Ill., 1997.

Palmer, William P., ed. *Calendar of Virginia State Papers and Other Manuscripts.* 11 vols. Richmond, Va.: R. F. Walker, 1875–93.

Paltsits, Victor Hugo, ed. *Minutes of the Executive Council of the Province of New York: Administration of Francis Lovelace, 1668–1673.* 2 vols. Albany, N.Y.: J. B. Lyon 1910.

Parker, Arthur C. *An Analytical History of the Seneca Indians.* NYSAA Lewis Henry Morgan Chapter Researches and Transactions 6.1–5. Canandaigua, N.Y.: Times Presses, 1926.

——, ed. *The Archeological History of New York.* NYSM *Bulletin* (University of the State of New York, Albany) 235–36 (1920).

——. *A Contact Period Seneca Site Situated at Factory Hollow, Ontario County, N.Y.* NYSAA *Researches and Transactions* 1.2. Canandaigua, N.Y.: Press of C. F. Milliken, 1919.

——. *Life of General Ely S. Parker, Last Grand Sachem of the Iroquois and General Grant's Military Secretary.* Buffalo Historical Society Publications 23. Buffalo, N.Y., 1919.

——. "Secret Medicine Societies of the Seneca." *American Anthropologist* 11 (1909): 113–30.

——. *Seneca Myths and Folk Tales.* 1923. Reprint, Lincoln: University of Nebraska Press, 1989.

Parker, Ely S. "The Political Condition of the Ag-wa-nar-she-one [ca. 1845]." PA 49. Ely S. Parker Collection, HEHL.

Parmenter, Jon W. "After the Mourning Wars: The Iroquois as Allies in Colonial North American Campaigns, 1676–1760." *WMQ* 64 (2007): 39–82.

Pasternak, Burton, Carol R. Ember, and Melvin Ember. "On the Conditions Favoring Extended Family Households." *Journal of Anthropological Research* 32.2 (1976): 109–23.

Pearce, Robert J. "Turtles from Turtle Island: An Archaeological Perspective from Iroquoia." *OA* 79/80 (2005): 88–108.

Pearson, Jonathan, ed. *Early Records of the City and County of Albany, and Colony of Rensselaerswyck, 1656–1675.* Albany, N.Y.: J. Munsell, 1869.

——. *A History of the Schenectady Patent in the Dutch and English Times, Being Contributions Toward a History of the Lower Mohawk Valley.* Albany, N.Y.: J. Munsell's Sons, 1883.

Pencak, William A., and C. E. Wright, eds. *Authority and Resistance in Early New York.* New York: New-York Historical Society, 1988.

Pencak, William A., and Daniel K. Richter, eds. *Friends and Enemies in Penn's Woods: Indians, Colonists, and the Racial Construction of Pennsylvania.* University Park: Pennsylvania State University Press, 2004.

Pendergast, James F. "The Confusing Identities Attributed to Stadacona and Hochelaga." *Journal of Canadian Studies* 32.4 (1998): 53–87.

——. "The Kakouagoga or Kahkwas: An Iroquoian Nation Destroyed in the Niagara Region." *APSP* 138 (1994): 96–144.

——. *The Massawomecks: Raiders and Traders of the Chesapeake Bay in the Seventeenth Century.* APS *Transactions* No. 81, Part 2. Philadelphia, 1991.

——. "Native Encounters with Europeans in the Sixteenth Century in the Region Now Known as Vermont." *Vermont History* 58 (1990): 99–124.

——. "The Ottawa River Algonquin Bands in a St. Lawrence Iroquoian Context." *CJA* 23 (1999): 63–136.

——. "Were the French on Lake Ontario in the Sixteenth Century?" *MIN* 29 (1985): 71–85.

Pendergast, James F., and Bruce G. Trigger. *Cartier's Hochelaga and the Dawson Site.* Montreal: McGill-Queen's University Press, 1972.

Pendergast, James F., and Claude Chapdelaine, eds. *Essays in St. Lawrence Iroquoian Archaeology Dedicated to James V. Wright.* Dundas, Ont.: Copetown Press, 1993.

Pentland, David H., ed. *Papers of the Twenty-eighth Algonquian Conference.* Winnipeg: University of Manitoba, 1997.

Peregrine, Peter. "Matrilocality, Corporate Strategy, and the Organization of Production in the Chacoan World." *American Antiquity* 66 (2001): 36–46.

Peregrine, Peter N., and Melvin Ember, eds. *Encyclopedia of Prehistory.* Vol. 6, *North America.* New York: Kluwer Academic/Plenum, 2001.

Pestana, Carla G. *The English Atlantic in an Age of Revolution, 1640–1661.* Cambridge, Mass.: Harvard University Press, 2004.

Pestana, Carla G., and Sharon V. Salinger, eds. *Inequality in Early America.* Hanover, N.H.: University Press of New England, 1999.

Petrovich, Alisa V. "Perception and Reality: Colbert's Native American Policy." *Louisiana History* 39 (1998): 73–83.

Peyser, Joseph, ed. *Letters from New France: The Upper Country, 1686–1783.* Urbana: University of Illinois Press, 1992.

Peyser, Joseph, trans., and José Antonio Brandão, ed. *Edge of Empire: Documents of Michilimackinac, 1671–1716.* East Lansing: Michigan State University Press, 2008.

Piddington, Ralph, ed. *Kinship and Geographical Mobility.* Leiden: E. J. Brill, 1965.

Pilkington, Walter, ed. *The Journals of Samuel Kirkland: 18th Century Missionary to the Iroquois, Government Agent, Father of Hamilton College.* Clinton, N.Y.: Hamilton College, 1980.

Pomedli, Michael M. "Eighteenth-Century Treaties: Amended Iroquois Condolence Rituals." *AIQ* 19 (Summer 1995): 319–39.

Porter, Tom Sakokwenionkwas. *Kanatsiohareke: Traditional Mohawk Indians Return to Their Ancestral Homeland.* Greenfield Center, N.Y.: Bowman Books, 2006.

Postma, Johannes, and Victor Enthoven, eds. *Riches from Atlantic Commerce: Dutch Transatlantic Trade and Shipping, 1585–1817.* Leiden: Brill, 2003.

Potter, Stephen R. *Commoners, Tribute, and Chiefs: The Development of Algonquian Culture in the Potomac Valley.* Charlottesville: University of Virginia Press, 1993.

Pouchot, Pierre. *Memoirs on the Late War in North America between France and England.* 1781. Reprint, ed. Brian L. Dunnigan and trans. Michael Cardy, Youngstown, N.Y.: Old Fort Niagara Association, 1994.

Poulton, Dana R. "Report on the 1991 Archaeological Investigations of the Bead Hill Site, City of Scarborough, Ontario." Ms. on file, Ontario Service Centre, Parks Canada, Cornwall, Ont.

Pratt, Marjorie K. "The St. Lawrence Iroquoians of Northern New York." *BJNYSAA* 102 (1991): 43–46.

Pratt, Mary Louise. *Imperial Eyes: Travel Writing and Transculturation.* New York: Routledge, 1992.

Pratt, Peter. *Archaeology of the Oneida Iroquois.* Vol. 1. *Occasional Publications in Northeastern Anthropology* No. 1. George's Mills, N.H.: Man in the Northeast, 1976.

Prazniak, Roxanne, and Arif Dirlik, eds. *Places and Politics in an Age of Globalization.* Lanham, Md.: Rowman and Littlefield, 2001.

Preston, David L. "The Texture of Contact: European and Indian Settler Communities on the Iroquoian Borderlands, 1720–1780." Ph.D. diss., College of William and Mary, 2002.

Prins, Anneke, et al., eds. *The Low Countries and the New World(s).* Lanham, Md.: University Press of America, 2000.

Pritchard, James S. "For the Glory of God: The Quinte Mission, 1668–1680." *OH* 65 (1973): 133–48.

Propositions Made by the Five Nations of Indians, viz., The Mohaques, Oneydes, Onnondages, Cayouges, and Sinnekes, to his Excellency Richard, Earl of Bellomont, Capt. General and Governour in Chief of his Majesties Province of New-York, &c. in Albany, the 20th of July, Anno. Dom. 1698. New York: William Bradford, 1698.

Quaife, Milo Milton, ed. *The Western Country in the Seventeenth Century: The Memoirs of Lamothe Cadillac and Pierre Liette.* Chicago: Lakeside Press, 1947.

Quinn, David B., ed. *Early Maryland in a Wider World.* Detroit: Wayne State University Press, 1982.

——. "Henri Quatre and New France." *Terrae Incognitae* 22 (1990): 13–28.

——, ed. *New American World: A Documentary History of North America to 1612.* 5 vols. New York: Arno Press, 1979.

——. *North America from the Earliest Discovery to First Settlements: The Norse Voyages to 1612.* New York: Harper and Row, 1977.

——, ed. *The Roanoke Voyages, 1584–1590.* 1955. Reprint, 2 vols., New York: Dover Publications, 1991.

——. *Sources for the Ethnography of Northeastern North America to 1611.* National Museum of Man Mercury Series No. 76. Ottawa, Ont., 1981.

Quinn, David B., and Alison M. Quinn, eds. *The English New England Voyages, 1602–1608.* Cambridge: Cambridge University Press, 1983.

Rafert, Stewart. *The Miami Indians of Indiana: A Persistent People, 1654–1994.* Indianapolis: Indiana Historical Society, 1996.

Rafferty, Sean, and Rob Mann, eds. *Smoking and Culture: The Archaeology of the Tobacco Pipe in Eastern North America.* Knoxville: University of Tennessee Press, 2004.

Raibmon, Paige. *Authentic Indians: Episodes of Encounter from the Late Nineteenth Century Northwest Coast.* Durham, N.C.: Duke University Press, 2005.

Ramenofsky, Ann F. *Vectors of Death: The Archaeology of European Contact.* Albuquerque: University of New Mexico Press, 1987.

Ramsden, Peter. "The Current State of Huron Archaeology." *Northeast Anthropology* 51 (1996): 101–12.

——. "Palisade Extension, Village Expansion, and Immigration in Trent Valley Huron Villages." *CJA* 12 (1988): 177–83.

Rankin, Lisa, and Peter Ramsden, eds. *From the Arctic to Avalon: Papers in Honour of Jim Tuck.* British Archaeological Reports International Series No. 1507. Oxford: John and Erica Hedges, 2006.

Ransom, James W., and Kreg T. Ettenger. "Polishing the Kaswentha: A Haudenosaunee View of Environmental Cooperation." *Environmental Science and Policy* 4 (2001): 219–28.

Rapport de l'Archiviste du Province de Québec. 42 vols. Quebec: Archives Nationales du Québec, 1921–69.

Rasmussen, Birgit Brander. "Negotiating Peace, Negotiating Literacies: A French-Iroquois Encounter and the Making of Early American Literature." *American Literature* 79 (2007): 445–73.

Rath, Richard C. *How Early America Sounded.* Ithaca, N.Y.: Cornell University Press, 2003.

Raudzens, George C., ed. *Technology, Disease, and Colonial Conquests, Sixteenth to Eighteenth Centuries.* Leiden: Brill, 2006.

Rayner-Herter, Nancy. "The Niagara Frontier Iroquois: A Study of Sociopolitical Development." Ph.D. diss. State University of New York at Buffalo, 2001.

Recht, Michael. "The Role of Fishing in the Iroquois Economy, 1600–1792." *New York History* 76 (1995): 4–30.

Records of the Society for the Propagation of the Gospel in Foreign Parts. Microfilm ed. London, 1964.

Redington, Joseph, and William A. Shaw, eds. *Calendar of Treasury Books and Papers, 1556/7–1745, Preserved in Her Majesty's Public Record Office.* 11 vols. London: Her Majesty's Stationery Office, 1865–1943.

Redmond, Brian G., and Katharine C. Ruhl. "Rethinking the 'Whittlesley Collapse': Late Prehistoric Pottery Migrations in Eastern Ohio." *AENA* 30 (2002): 59–80.

Répertoire des actes de baptême, mariage, et sépulture du Québec ancien, 1621–1799. CD-ROM. Montreal: Gaëtan Morin, 2002.

Resek, Carl. *Lewis Henry Morgan: American Scholar.* Chicago: University of Chicago Press, 1960.

Reynolds, Cuyler. *Albany Chronicles: A History of the City Arranged Chronologically, From the Earliest Settlement to the Present Time.* Albany, N.Y.: J.B. Lyon, 1906.

Reynolds, Wynn R. "Persuasive Speaking of the Iroquois Indians at Treaty Councils." Ph.D. diss., Columbia University, 1957.

Rhode Island Historical Society. *Collections.* 34 vols. Providence: Rhode Island Historical Society, 1827–1941.

Rice, James D. *Nature and History in the Potomac Country: From Hunter-Gatherers to the Age of Jefferson.* Baltimore: Johns Hopkins University Press, 2008.

Richardson, James B. III, David A. Anderson, and Edward R. Cook. "The Disappearance of the Monongahela: Solved?" *AENA* 30 (2002): 81–90.

Richter, Daniel K. *Facing East from Indian Country: A Native History of Early America.* Cambridge, Mass.: Harvard University Press, 2001.

——. "Iroquois versus Iroquois: Jesuit Missions and Christianity in Village Politics." *Ethnohistory* 32 (1985): 1–16.

——. *The Ordeal of the Longhouse: The Peoples of the Iroquois League in the Era of European Colonization.* Chapel Hill: University of North Carolina Press, 1992.

——, ed. "Rediscovered Links in the Covenant Chain: Previously Unpublished Transcripts of New York Indian Treaty Minutes, 1677–1691." American Antiquarian Society *Proceedings* 92 (1982): 45–85.

——. "'Some of Them . . . Would Always Have a Minister with Them': Mohawk Protestantism, 1683–1719." *AIQ* 16 (Autumn1992): 474–84.

——. "Up the Cultural Stream: Three Recent Works in Iroquois Studies." *Ethnohistory* 32 (1985): 363–69.

——. "War and Culture: The Iroquois Experience." *WMQ* 40 (1983): 528–59.

Richter, Daniel K., and James H. Merrell, eds. *Beyond the Covenant Chain: The Iroquois and Their Neighbors in Indian North America, 1600–1800.* Syracuse, N.Y.: Syracuse University Press, 1987.

Ridley, Frank. "The Wenro in Huronia." *Anthropological Journal of Canada* 11 (1973): 10–20.

Rink, Oliver A. *Holland on the Hudson: An Economic and Social History of Dutch New York.* Ithaca, N.Y.: Cornell University Press, 1986.

Rioux, Marcel. "Relations between Religion and Government among the Longhouse Iroquois of Grand River, Ontario." *Annual Report of the National Museum of Canada for the Fiscal Year 1950–51.* National Museum of Canada *Bulletin* No. 126. Ottawa, Ont., 1952, 94–98.

Ritchie, William A. *The Archaeology of New York State.* Rev. ed. Harrison, N.Y.: Harbor Hill Books, 1980.

Ritchie, William A., and Robert E. Funk. *Aboriginal Settlement Patterns in the Northeast.* New York Museum and Science Service *Memoir* No. 20. Albany: University of the State of New York, State Education Department, 1973.

Ritzenthaler, Robert. "The Oneida Indians of Wisconsin." *Bulletin of the Public Museum of the City of Milwaukee* 19 (1950): 1–52.

Roberts, Robert B. *Encyclopedia of Historic Forts: The Military, Pioneer, and Trading Posts of the United States.* New York: Macmillan, 1988.

Robertson, David A. "Mourning, Curing, Feasting, or Industry? The Interpretation of the Quinte and Perch Lake Mounds." *OA* 72 (2001): 38–63.

Robie, Harry W. "Kiotsaeton's Three Rivers Address: An Example of 'Effective' Iroquois Oratory." *AIQ* 6 (Autumn–Winter 1982): 238–53.

Robinson, Percy J. "Montreal to Niagara in the Seventeenth Century." *RSCT* ser. 3, vol. 38 (1944), part 2, 137–53.

——. *Toronto during the French Regime: A History of the Toronto Region from Brûlé to Simcoe.* 1933. Reprint, Toronto: University of Toronto Press, 1965.

Robinson, W. Stitt. *Maryland Treaties, 1632–1775.* Vol. 6 of *Early American Indian Documents: Treaties and Laws, 1607–1789.* Frederick, Md.: University Publications of America, 1987.

——. "Tributary Indians in Colonial Virginia." *VMHB* 67 (1959): 49–64.

Rochemonteix, Camille de. *Les Jésuites et la Nouvelle-France au XVIIe Siècle.* 3 vols. Paris: Letouzey et Ané, 1895–96.

Rogers, Edward S., and Donald B. Smith, eds. *Aboriginal Ontario: Historical Perspectives on the First Nations.* Toronto: Dundurn, 1994.

Rogers, J. Daniel, and Samuel M. Wilson, eds. *Ethnohistory and Archaeology: Approaches to Postcontact Change in the Americas.* New York: Plenum Press, 1993.

Ronda, James. "The Sillery Experiment: A Jesuit-Indian Village in New France, 1637–1663." *AICRJ* 3 (1979): 1–18.

Roper, Louis H., and Bertrand van Ruymbeke, eds. *Constructing Early Modern Empires: Proprietary Ventures in the Atlantic World, 1500–1750.* Leiden: Brill, 2007.

Rosenblatt, Paul C., R. Patricia Walsh, and Douglas A. Jackson. *Grief and Mourning in Cross-Cultural Perspective.* New Haven, Conn.: Human Relations Area Files Press, 1976.

Ross, Thomas E., and Tyrel G. Moore, eds. *A Cultural Geography of North American Indians.* Boulder, Colo.: Westview Press, 1987.

Rothschild, Nan. *Colonial Encounters in a Native American Landscape: The Spanish and Dutch in North America.* Washington, D.C.: Smithsonian Institution, 2003.

Rotstein, Abraham. "Trade and Politics: An Institutional Approach." *Western Canadian Journal of Anthropology* 3 (1972): 1–28.

Rountree, Helen C. *Pocahontas, Powhatan, Opechancanough: Three Indian Lives Changed by Jamestown.* Charlottesville: University of Virginia Press, 2005.

——, ed. *Powhatan Foreign Relations, 1500–1722.* Charlottesville: University of Virginia Press, 1993.

Rountree, Helen C., and Thomas E. Davidson. *Eastern Shore Indians of Virginia and Maryland.* Charlottesville: University of Virginia Press, 1997.

Rumney, George R. "The Ottawa-Nipissing Canoe Route in Early Western Travel." *Canadian*

Geographical Journal 42 (1951): 26–33.

Rumrill, Donald. "An Interpretation and Analysis of the Seventeenth Century Mohawk Nation: Its Chronology and Movements." *BJNYSAA* 90 (1985): 1–39.

———. "The Mohawk Glass Trade Bead Chronology, ca. 1560–1785." *Beads: Journal of the Society of Bead Researchers* 3 (1991): 5–45.

Rushforth, Brett. "'A Little Flesh We Offer You': The Origins of Indian Slavery in New France." *WMQ* 60 (2003): 777–808.

Rutsch, Edward S. *Smoking Technology of the Aborigines of the Iroquois Area of New York State.* Rutherford, N.J.: Fairleigh Dickinson University Press, 1973.

Ruttenber, E. M. *History of the Indian Tribes of Hudson's River.* Albany, N.Y.: Joel Munsell, 1872.

Ryan, Beth, and Adam Dewbury. "The Eugene Frost Collection: Artifacts from the Seneca Iroquois Dann Site, *circa* 1655–1675." Cornell University Archaeological Collections Documentation Project, Report No. 1. Department of Anthropology, Cornell University, October 2007.

Rydjord, John. *Indian Place-Names.* Norman: University of Oklahoma Press, 1968.

Safford, L. O., John C. Bjorkborn, and John C. Zasada. "*Betula papyrifera* Marsh." http://www.na.fs.fed.us/spfo/pubs/silvics_manual/volume_2/betula/papyrifera.htm.

Sagard, Gabriel. *Histoire du Canada et Voyages Que Les Frères Mineurs Recollects y Ont Faicts Pour La Conversion des Infidèles, Depuis l'An 1615.* 4 vols. Paris: Edwin Tross, 1866.

———. *The Long Journey to the Country of the Hurons.* 1632. Reprint, ed. George M. Wrong, trans. H. H. Langton, Toronto: Champlain Society, 1939.

Sainsbury, W. N., et al., eds. *Calendar of State Papers, Colonial Series: America & West Indies.* 45 vols. to date. London: Her Majesty's Stationery Office, 1860–.

Salley, Alexander S., Jr., ed. *Narratives of Early Carolina, 1650-1708.* 1911. Reprint, New York: Barnes and Noble, 1953.

Sanday, Peggy R. *Divine Hunger: Cannibalism as a Cultural System.* Cambridge: Cambridge University Press, 1986.

Sanson, Nicolas. *America: 1667.* Ed. Louis M. Bloch Jr., trans. Pauline Carson Bloch and Robert Martinon. Cleveland: Bloch, 1959.

Santiemma, Adriano. "La Ligue des Iroquois: Une 'Paix' d'espace, de temps, et de parenté." *RAQ* 31.2 (2001): 87–97.

Saunders, Barbara, and Lea Zuyderhoudt, eds. *The Challenges of Native American Studies: Essays in Celebration of the Twenty-fifth American Indian Workshop.* Leuven, Germany: Leuven University Press, 2004.

Saunders, Shelley R., Dean Knight, and Michael Gates. "Christian Island: A Comparative Analysis of Osteological and Archaeological Evidence." Canadian Archaeological Association *Bulletin* 6 (1974): 121–62.

Sayers, William. "The Etymology of *Iroquois:* 'Killer People' in a Basque-Algonquian Pidgin or an Echo of Norse *Irland et Mikla:* 'Greater Ireland'?" *Onomastica Canadiana* 88 (2006): 43–56.

Schlesinger,Roger, and Arthur P. Stabler, eds. *André Thevet's North America: A Sixteenth-Century View.* Kingston, Ont.: McGill-Queen's University Press, 1986.

Schmalz, Peter S. *The Ojibwa of Southern Ontario.* Toronto: University of Toronto Press, 1991.

Schmidt, Benjamin. "Mapping an Empire: Cartographic and Colonial Rivalry in Seventeenth-Century Dutch and English North America." *WMQ* 54 (1997): 549–78.

Schoolcraft, Henry Rowe. *Notes on the Iroquois.* 1847. Reprint, ed. Philip P. Mason, East Lansing: Michigan State University Press, 2002.

Schutt, Amy C. *Peoples of the River Valleys: The Odyssey of the Delaware Indians.* Philadelphia: University of Pennsylvania Press, 2007.

Scott, Duncan C. "Traditional History of the Confederacy of the Six Nations, Prepared by a Committee of Chiefs." *RSCT* ser. 3, vol. 5 (1911), part 2, 199–213.

Scott, Patricia Kay. "Historic Contact Archaeological Deposits within the Old Fort Niagara National Historic Landmark." *BJNYSAA* 114 (1998): 45–57.

Scott, Stuart D., and Patricia Kay Scott. "Lower Landing Archaeological District National Historic Landmark." *BJNYSAA* 114 (1998): 58–72.

Seaton, S. Lee, and Henri J. M. Claessen, eds. *Political Anthropology: The State of the Art.* The Hague: Mouton, 1979.

Seed, Patricia. *Ceremonies of Possession in Europe's Conquest of the New World, 1492–1640.* Cambridge: Cambridge University Press, 1995.

Selden, George B. "Denonville's Army and Its Bivouac at Mendon Ponds." *RHS-PFS* 9 (1930): 227–32.

Semmes, Raphael. *Captains and Mariners of Early Maryland.* Baltimore: Johns Hopkins University Press, 1937.

Sempowski, Martha L. "Differential Mortuary Treatment of Seneca Women: Some Social Inferences." *AENA* 14 (1986): 35–44.

Sempowski, Martha L., and Lorraine P. Saunders. *Dutch Hollow and Factory Hollow: The Advent of Dutch Trade among the Seneca.* RMSC *Research Records* No. 24. Rochester, N.Y., 2001.

Shannon, Timothy J. *Iroquois Diplomacy on the Early American Frontier.* New York: Viking Penguin, 2008.

Shea, John G., ed. *Discovery and Exploration of the Mississippi Valley, with the Original Narratives of Marquette, Allouez, Membré, Hennepin, and Anastase Douay.* New York: Redfield, 1852.

Shimony, Annemarie. *Conservatism among the Iroquois at Six Nations Reserve.* 1961. Reprint, Syracuse, N.Y.: Syracuse University Press, 1994.

Shoemaker, Nancy, ed. *Clearing a Path: Theorizing the Past in Native American Studies.* New York: Routledge, 2002.

———. *Negotiators of Change: Historical Perspectives on Native American Women.* New York: Routledge, 1995.

———. *A Strange Likeness: Becoming Red and White in Eighteenth Century North America.* New York: Oxford University Press, 2004.

Shomette, Donald G., and Robert D. Haslach. *Raid on America: The Dutch Naval Campaign of 1672–1674.* Columbia: University of South Carolina Press, 1988.

Shurtleff, Nathaniel B., ed. *Records of the Governor and Company of the Massachusetts Bay in New England.* 5 vols. Boston: William White, 1853–54.

Shurtleff, Nathaniel B., and David Pulsifer, eds. *Records of the Colony of New Plymouth in New England.* 12 vols. Boston: William White, 1855–61.

Shweder, Richard A., and Robert A. Levine, eds. *Culture Theory: Essays on Mind, Self, and Emotion.* Cambridge: Cambridge University Press, 1984.

Sibley, David. *Geographies of Exclusion: Society and Difference in the West.* London: Routledge, 1995.

Sider, Gerald. *Living Indian Histories: Lumbee and Tuscarora People in North Carolina.* Chapel Hill: University of North Carolina Press, 2003.

Silliman, Stephen. "Culture Contact or Colonialism: Challenges in the Archaeology of Native North America." *American Antiquity* 70 (2005): 55–74.

Simms, Jeptha R. *History of Schoharie County and Border Wars of New York.* Albany, N.Y.: Munsell & Tanner, 1845.

Simpson, Audra. "On Ethnographic Refusal: Indigeneity, 'Voice,' and Colonial Citizenship." *Junctures: The Journal for Thematic Dialogue* 9 (2007): 67–80.

———. "To the Reserve and Back Again: Kahnawake Mohawk Narratives of Self, Home, and Nation." Ph.D. diss. McGill University, 2004.

Simpson, Leanne. "Looking After *Gdoo-naaganinaa:* Precolonial Nishnaabeg Diplomatic and Treaty

Relationships." *Wicazo Sa Review* 23 (Fall 2008): 29–42.

Sinclair, A. T. "Tattooing of the North American Indians." *American Anthropologist* 11 (1909): 362–400.

Sioui, Georges A. *For an Amerindian Autohistory.* Trans. Sheila Fischman. Montreal: McGill-Queen's University Press, 1992.

———. *Histoires de Kanatha: Vues et Contées.* Ottawa: Presses de l'Université d'Ottawa, 2008.

———. *Huron-Wendat: The Heritage of the Circle.* Trans. Jane Brierley. Vancouver: University of British Columbia Press, 1999.

———. *Les Wendats: Une civilisation méconnue.* Sainte-Foy, Queb.: Les Presses de l'Université Laval, 1994.

Sivertsen, Barbara J. *Turtles, Wolves, and Bears: A Mohawk Family History.* Bowie, Md.: Heritage Books, 1997.

Skinner, Alanson. *Notes on Iroquois Archeology.* Museum of the American Indian, Heye Foundation, *Indian Notes and Monographs* No. 18 (1921).

Skinner, Claiborne. *The Upper Country: French Colonial Enterprise in the Great Lakes.* Baltimore: Johns Hopkins University Press, 2008.

Slotkin, Richard, and James K. Folsom, eds. *"So Dreadfull a Judgment": Puritan Responses to King Philip's War.* Middletown, Conn.: Wesleyan University Press, 1978.

Sluyter, Andrew. *Colonialism and Landscape: Postcolonial Theory and Applications.* Lanham, Md.: Rowman and Littlefield, 2002.

Smith, Eleazer Y. "Captain Thomas Willett: First Mayor of New York." *NYH* 21 (1940): 404–17.

Smith, Erminnie A. "Myths of the Iroquois." Bureau of American Ethnology *Annual Report for 1880–1881.* Washington, D.C.: Smithsonian Institution, 1883. 47–116.

Smith, Jonathan Z. *To Take Place: Toward Theory in Ritual.* Chicago: University of Chicago Press, 1987.

Smith, Mark M. "Culture, Commerce, and Calendar Reform in Colonial America." *WMQ* 55 (1998): 557–84.

Smith, William, Jr. *The History of the Province of New York.* 1757. Reprint, 2 vols., ed. Michael Kammen, Cambridge, Mass.: Belknap Press of Harvard University Press, 1972.

Snow, Dean, ed. *Foundations of Northeast Archaeology.* New York: Academic Press, 1981.

———. *The Iroquois.* Malden, Mass.: Blackwell, 1994.

———. "Mohawk Demography and the Effects of Exogeneous Epidemics on American Indian Populations." *Journal of Anthropological Archaeology* 15 (1996): 160–82.

———. *Mohawk Valley Archaeology: The Sites.* Matson Museum of Anthropology, Pennsylvania State University, *Occasional Papers in Anthropology* No. 23. University Park, Pa., 1995.

———. *The Mohawk Valley Project: 1982 Field Season Report.* Albany, N.Y.: Institute for Northeast Anthropology, State University of New York at Albany, 1985.

Snow, Dean R., Charles T. Gehring, and William A. Starna, eds. *In Mohawk Country: Early Narratives about a Native People.* Syracuse, N.Y.: Syracuse University Press, 1996.

Snow, Dean, and Kim H. Lanphear. "European Contact and Indian Depopulation in the Northeast: The Timing of the First Epidemics." *Ethnohistory* 35 (1988): 15–33.

———. "Rejoinder to Dobyns." *Ethnohistory* 36 (1989): 299–304.

Snow, Dean, and William A. Starna. "Sixteenth-Century Depopulation: A View from the Mohawk Valley." *American Anthropologist* 91 (1989): 142–49.

Soderlund, Jean R., and Catherine S. Parzynski, eds. *Backcountry Crucibles: The Lehigh Valley from Settlement to Steel.* Bethlehem, Pa.: Lehigh University Press, 2008.

Sohrweide, Gregory. "Onondaga Longhouses in the Late Seventeenth Century on the Weston Site." *BJNYSAA* 117 (2001): 1–24.

Sorg, David J. "Linguistic Affiliations of the Massawomeck Confederacy." *PAA* 73 (2003): 1–7.

Sowter, T. W. E. "Algonkin and Huron Occupation of the Ottawa Valley." *Ottawa Naturalist* 23 (1909):

61–68, 92–104.

Speck, Frank G. "Boundaries and Hunting Groups of the River Desert Algonquin." Museum of the American Indian, Heye Foundation, *Indian Notes* 6.2 (1929): 97–120.

———. *The Iroquois: A Study in Cultural Evolution.* 1945. Reprint, Cranbrook Institute of Science *Bulletin* No. 23, Bloomfield Hills, Mich., 1955.

———. "Montagnais and Naskapi Tales from the Labrador Peninsula." *Journal of American Folklore* 38 (1925): 1–32.

Spencer, Robert F., ed. *Forms of Symbolic Action.* Seattle: University of Washington Press, 1971.

Spoehr, Alexander. "Changing Kinship Systems." Field Museum of Natural History *Anthropological Series* 33.4 (1947): 151–235.

St. George, Robert B., ed. *Possible Pasts: Becoming Colonial in Early America.* Ithaca, N.Y.: Cornell University Press, 2000.

St. John, Donald P. "The Dream-Vision Experience of the Iroquois: Its Religious Meaning." Ph.D. diss., Fordham University, 1981.

St.-Arnaud, Daniel. *Pierre Millet en Iroquoisie au XVIIe Siècle.* Sillery, Queb.: Les Éditions du Septentrion, 1998.

Staffa, Susan J. *Schenectady Genesis: How a Dutch Colonial Village Became an American City, ca. 1661-1800.* Vol. 1, *The Colonial Crucible, ca. 1661-1774.* Fleischmanns, N.Y.: Purple Mountain Press, 2004.

Staller, John E., Robert H. Tykot, and Bruce F. Benz, eds. *Histories of Maize.* Boston: Elsevier Academic Press, 2006.

Standen, Dale, and David McNabb, eds. *Gin Das Winan: Documenting Aboriginal History in Ontario.* Champlain Society *Occasional Papers* No. 2. Toronto, 1996.

Stanley, George F. G. "The Policy of 'Francisation' as Applied to the Indians during the Ancient Regime." *RHAF* 3 (1949): 333–48.

Stark, William T., ed. *The Archaeology of Social Boundaries.* Washington, D.C.: Smithsonian Institution, 1998.

Starna, William A. "The Biological Encounter: Disease and the Ideological Domain." *AIQ* 16 (Autumn 1992): 511–19.

———. "Retrospecting the Origins of the League of the Iroquois." *APSP* 152 (2008): 279–321.

———. "Review Essay: Early Encounters in New Netherland." *NYH* 88.3 (2007): 321–34.

———. "Seventeenth-Century Dutch-Indian Trade: A Perspective from Iroquoia." *De Halve Maen* 59.3 (1986): 5–8, 21.

Starna, William A., and José A. Brandão. "From the Mohawk-Mahican War to the Beaver Wars: Questioning the Pattern." *Ethnohistory* 51 (2004): 725–50.

Starna, William A., George R. Hamell, and William L. Butts. "Northern Iroquoian Horticulture and Insect Infestation: A Cause for Village Removal." *Ethnohistory* 31 (1984): 197–207.

Starna, William A., and Ralph Watkins. "Northern Iroquoian Slavery." *Ethnohistory* 38 (1991): 34–57.

Steckley, John L. "The Clans and Phratries of the Hurons." *OA* 37 (1982): 29–34.

———, ed. *De Religione: Telling the Seventeenth-Century Jesuit Story in Huron to the Iroquois.* Norman: University of Oklahoma Press, 2004.

———. "The Early Map 'Novvelle France': A Linguistic Analysis." *OA* 51 (1990): 17–29.

———. "Finding a Home for Two Tribes." *Michigan Archaeologist* 31.4 (1985): 123–29.

———. "Huron Kinship Terminology." *OA* 55 (1993): 35–59.

———. "A Tale of Two Peoples." *Arch Notes* 85 (July/August 1985): 9–12.

———. "Wendat Dialects and the Development of the Huron Alliance." *Northeast Anthropology* 54 (1997): 23–36.

Steele, Ian K. *The English Atlantic, 1675-1740: An Exploration of Communication and Community.* New

York: Oxford University Press, 1986.

Stewart, Frances L. "Faunal Findings from Three Longhouses of the McKeown Site (BeFv-1), a St. Lawrence Iroquoian Village." *OA* 54 (1992): 17–36.

Stewart, Frances L., and Ellen Cowie. "Dietary Indications for a St. Lawrence Iroquoian Site in Northern New England." *AENA* 35 (2007): 21–36.

Stewart, T. D., and W. R. Wedel. "The Finding of Two Ossuaries on the Site of the Indian Village of Nacotchtanke (Anacostia)." *Journal of the Washington Academy of Sciences* 27.5 (1937): 213–19.

Stock, Leo Francis, ed. *Proceedings and Debates of the British Parliaments Respecting America.* 5 vols. Washington, D.C.: Carnegie Institution, 1924–41.

Stokes, I. N. Phelps. *The Iconography of Manhattan Island, 1498–1909.* 6 vols. New York: Robert H. Dodd, 1915–28.

Story, G. M., ed. *Early European Settlement and Exploitation in Atlantic Canada: Selected Essays.* St. John's, Newf.: Memorial University, 1982.

Strawn, Robertson. "Public Speaking in the Iroquois League." Ph.D. diss., University of Michigan, 1940.

Strong, John A. "The Imposition of Colonial Jurisdiction over the Montauk Indians of Long Island." *Ethnohistory* 41 (1994): 561–90.

——. "Mohawk Sovereignty Over the Long Island Indians: Fact or Fiction? A Re-examination of Primary and Secondary Sources." *Long Island Historical Journal* 14 (2002): 15–26.

Sublett, Audrey J., and C. F. Wray. "Some Examples of Accidental and Deliberate Human Skeletal Modification in the Northeast." *BJNYSAA* 50 (November 1970): 14–26.

Sullivan, Dennis. *The Punishment of Crime in Colonial New York: The Dutch Experience in Albany during the Seventeenth Century.* New York: Peter Lang, 1997.

Sullivan, James, et al., eds. *The Papers of Sir William Johnson.* 14 vols. Albany: University of the State of New York, 1921–65.

Sullivan, Lawrence E., ed. *Native American Religions: North America.* New York: MacMillan, 1987.

Sullivan, Lynne P., ed. *Reanalyzing the Ripley Site: Earthworks and Late Prehistory on the Lake Erie Plain.* NYSM *Bulletin* (University of the State of New York, State Education Department, Albany) 489 (1996).

Sullivan, Lynne P., and Susan C. Prezzano, eds. *Archaeology of the Appalachian Highlands.* Knoxville: University of Tennessee Press, 2001.

Sulte, Benjamin. "Trois-Rivières d'Autrefois." *Mélanges Historiques* ser. 4, no. 18 (1931): 26–44.

The Sun King: Louis XIV and the New World. New Orleans: Louisiana Museum Foundation, 1984.

Swartz, Deborah. "A Reevaluation of Late Woodland Cultural Relationships in the Susquehanna Valley in Pennsylvania." *MIN* 29 (1985): 29–54.

Tanguay, Jean. "Les Règles d'alliance et l'occupation huronne de territoire." *RAQ* 30.3 (2000): 21–34.

Tanner, Tyree. "The Indian Castle Site." NYSAA William M. Beauchamp Chapter *Bulletin* 8 (2001): 1–50.

——. "The Lot 18 Site." NYSAA William M. Beauchamp Chapter *Bulletin* 3 (Spring 1978): 1–12.

Taylor, Alan. *American Colonies.* New York: Viking Penguin, 2001.

——. *The Divided Ground: Indians, Settlers, and the Northern Borderlands of the American Revolution.* New York: Alfred A. Knopf, 2006.

Taylor, William E. "The Fort Hill Bluff Site." Massachusetts Archaeological Society *Bulletin* 38.1–2 (1976): 7–12.

Tehanetorens, ed. *Tales of the Iroquois, Volumes 1 and 2.* 1976. Reprint, Ohsweken, Ont.: Iroqrafts, 1992.

——. *Wampum Belts.* Ohsweken, Ont.: Iroqrafts, 1983.

Tehariolina, Margeurite Vincent. *La Nation Huronne: Son histoire, Sa Culture, Son Esprit.* Quebec: Éditions du Pélican, 1984.

Thomas, Edward H. "In Search of Etharita or St. Jean." *PAA* 29 (1959): 93–97.

Thomas, Jacob. "Articles of Kariwiio." Trans. Richard Aroniateka Mitchell. In *Traditional Teachings*, 73–101. Cornwall Island, Ont.: North American Indian Travelling College, 1984.

Thomas, M. Halsey, ed. *The Diary of Samuel Sewall*. 2 vols. New York: Farrar, Strauss, and Giroux, 1973.

Thomas, Peter Allen. "In the Maelstrom of Change: The Indian Trade and Cultural Process in the Middle Connecticut River Valley, 1635–1665." Ph.D. diss., University of Massachusetts, 1979.

Thompson, John H., ed. *Geography of New York State*. Syracuse, N.Y.: Syracuse University Press, 1966.

Thompson, Robert G., John P. Hart, Hetty Jo Brumbach, and Robert Lusteck. "Phytolith Evidence for Twentieth Century B.P. Maize in Northern Iroquoia." *Northeast Anthropology* 68 (2004): 25–35.

Thornton, Russell, Tim Miller, and Jonathan Warren. "American Indian Population Recovery Following Smallpox Epidemics." *American Anthropologist* 93 (1991): 28–45.

Thwaites, Reuben G., ed. *The Jesuit Relations and Allied Documents: Travels and Explorations of the Jesuit Missionaries in New France, 1610–1791*. 73 vols. Cleveland: Burrows Brothers, 1896–1901.

Tilley, Christopher. *A Phenomenology of Landscape: Places, Paths, and Monuments*. Oxford: Berg, 1994.

Tinling, Marion, ed. *The Correspondence of the Three William Byrds of Westover, Virginia: 1684–1776*. 2 vols. Charlottesville: University of Virginia Press, 1977.

"Tionnontates: The Petuns or Tobacco Nation of the Nottawasaga Lowlands." *26th Annual Archaeological Report for 1914, Being Part of Appendix to the Report of the Minister of Education, Ontario*. Toronto, 1914, 7–18.

Tiro, Karim, ed., and Cesare Marino, trans. *Along the Hudson and Mohawk: The 1790 Journey of Count Paolo Andreani*. Philadelphia: University of Pennsylvania Press, 2006.

Todorov, Tzvetan. *The Conquest of America: The Question of the Other*. Trans. Richard Howard. New York: Harper and Row, 1984.

Tooker, Elisabeth M. "Clans and Moieties in North America." *Current Anthropology* 12 (1971): 357–76.

——. *An Ethnography of the Huron Indians, 1615–1649*. 1964. Reprint, Syracuse, N.Y.: Syracuse University Press, 1991.

——. *The Iroquois Ceremonial of Midwinter*. 1970. Reprint, Syracuse, N.Y.: Syracuse University Press, 2000.

——, ed. *Iroquois Culture, History, Prehistory: Proceedings of the 1965 Conference on Iroquois Research*. 1967. Reprint, Albany: University of the State of New York, New York State Education Department, and New York State Museum and Science Service, 1970.

——. "The Iroquois Defeat of the Hurons: A Review of the Causes." *PAA* 33 (1963): 115–23.

——, ed. *An Iroquois Source Book*. 3 vols. New York: Garland Publishers, 1985–86.

——. "The League of the Iroquois: Its History, Politics, and Ritual." In Bruce G. Trigger, ed., *Northeast*, vol. 15 of *Handbook of North American Indians*. Washington, D.C.: Smithsonian Institution Press, 1978.

——. *Lewis H. Morgan on Iroquois Material Culture*. Tucson: University of Arizona Press, 1994.

——. "Masking and Matrilineality in North America." *American Anthropologist* 70 (1968): 1170–76.

——. *Naming Systems: 1980 Proceedings of the American Ethnological Society*. Washington, D.C.: American Ethnological Society, 1984.

——. "Northern Iroquoian Social Organization." *American Anthropologist* 72 (1970): 90–97.

——. "On the Development of the Handsome Lake Religion." *APSP* 133 (1989): 35–50.

——. "On the New Religion of Handsome Lake." *Anthropological Quarterly* 41 (1968): 189–99.

——. "The United States Constitution and the Iroquois League." *Ethnohistory* 35 (1988): 305–36.

Traphagan, John W. "Embodiment, Ritual Incorporation, and Cannibalism among the Iroquoians after 1300 C.E." *Journal of Ritual Studies* 22.2 (2008): 1–12.

Trautmann, Thomas R. *Lewis Henry Morgan and the Invention of Kinship*. Berkeley: University of California Press, 1987.

Trelease, Allen W. *Indian Affairs in Colonial New York: The Seventeenth Century.* 1960. Reprint, Lincoln: University of Nebraska Press, 1997.

Tremblay, Louise. "La Politique Missionaire des Sulpiciens au XVIIe et debut de XVIIIe Siècle, 1668–1735." Mémoire de Maitre des Arts, Université de Montréal, 1981.

Tremblay, Roland ed. *The St. Lawrence Iroquoians: Corn People.* Montreal: Pointe-à-Callière, Montreal Museum of Archaeology, 2006.

Trigger, Bruce G. *The Children of Aataentsic: A History of the Huron People to 1660.* 1976. Reprint, Montreal: McGill-Queen's University Press, 1987.

——. "Early Native North American Responses to European Contact: Romantic versus Rationalistic Interpretations." *Journal of American History* 77 (1991): 1195–1215.

——. "Iroquoian Matriliny." *PAA* 48 (1978): 55–65.

——. "The Liberation of Wendake" *OA* 72 (2001): 3–14.

——. "The Mohawk-Mahican War (1624–28): The Establishment of a Pattern." *CHR* 52 (1971): 276–86.

——. *Natives and Newcomers: Canada's "Heroic Age" Reconsidered.* Montreal: McGill-Queen's University Press, 1985.

——, ed. *Northeast.* Vol. 15 of *Handbook of North American Indians.* Washington, D.C.: Smithsonian Institution Press, 1978.

——. "Sixteenth Century Ontario: History, Ethnohistory, and Archaeology." *OH* 71 (1979): 205–23.

Trigger, Bruce G., and Wilcomb E. Washburn, eds. *The Cambridge History of the Native Peoples of the Americas.* Vol. 1. *North America.* Part 1. New York: Cambridge University Press, 1996.

Trigger, Bruce G., Toby Morantz, and Louise Dechêne, eds. *Le Castor Fait Tout: Selected Papers of the Fifth North American Fur Trade Conference, 1985.* Montreal: Lake St. Louis Historical Society, 1987.

Trowbridge, Charles C., ed. *Meearmeear Traditions.* University of Michigan Museum of Anthropology *Occasional Contributions* No. 7. Ann Arbor, Mich., 1938.

Trudel, Marcel. *The Beginnings of New France, 1524–1663.* Trans. Patricia Claxton. Toronto: McClelland and Stewart, 1973.

——. *Histoire de la Nouvelle-France.* Vol. 4, *La Seigneurie de la Compagnie des Indes Occidentales, 1663–1674.* Montreal: Fides, 1997.

Tuck, James A. *Onondaga Iroquois Prehistory: A Study in Settlement Archaeology.* Syracuse, N.Y.: Syracuse University Press, 1971.

Turgeon, Laurier. "Basque-Amerindian Trade in the St. Lawrence during the Sixteenth Century: New Documents, New Perspectives." *MIN* 40 (1990): 81–87.

——. "French Beads in France and Northeastern North America during the Sixteenth Century." *Historical Archaeology* 35.4 (2001): 58–82.

——. "French Fishers, Fur Traders, and Amerindians during the Sixteenth Century: History and Archaeology." *WMQ* 55 (1998): 585–610.

——. "The Tale of the Kettle: Odyssey of an Intercultural Object." *Ethnohistory* 44 (1997): 1–29.

Turnbaugh, William A. *Man, Land, and Time: The Cultural Prehistory and Demographic Patterns of North-Central Pennsylvania.* Evansville, Ind.: Unigraphic, 1977.

Turnbull, J. H., and C. H. Hoadly, eds. *Public Records of the Colony of Connecticut.* 15 vols. Hartford, Conn.: Case, Lockwood, and Brainard, 1850–90.

Turner, Victor. *Dramas, Fields, and Metaphors: Symbolic Action in Human Society.* Ithaca, N.Y.: Cornell University Press, 1974.

Twigg, Deb. "Revisiting the Mystery of 'Carantouan' and 'Spanish Hill.'" *PAA* 75.2 (2005): 24–33.

University of the State of New York, Division of Archives and History. *The Sullivan-Clinton Campaign in 1779: Chronology and Selected Documents.* Albany, N.Y., 1929.

Upham, Steadman, ed. *The Evolution of Political Systems: Sociopolitics in Small-Scale Sedentary*

Societies. Cambridge: Cambridge University Press, 1990.

van der Donck, Adriaen. *Description of New Netherland.* 1655. Reprint, ed. Thomas F. O'Donnell, Syracuse, N.Y.: Syracuse University Press, 1968.

van Dongen, Alexandra, et al., eds. *One Man's Trash Is Another Man's Treasure: The Metamorphosis of the European Utensil in the New World.* Rotterdam: Museum Boymans-van Beunigen, 1996.

van Gastel, Ada. "Van der Donck's Description of the Indians: Additions and Corrections." *WMQ* 47 (1990): 411–21.

van Gennep, Arnold. *The Rites of Passage.* 1908. Reprint, trans. Monika K. Vizedom and Gabrielle L. Caffee, Chicago: University of Chicago Press, 1961.

van Laer, A. J. F., ed. "Albany Notarial Papers, 1666–1693." Dutch Settlers' Society of Albany *Yearbook* 13 (1937–38): 1–18.

———. "Albany Notarial Papers, 1667–1687." Dutch Settlers' Society of Albany *Yearbook* 14 (1938–39): 1–18.

———. "Arent van Curler and His Historic Letter to the Patroon [June 16, 1643]." Dutch Settlers' Society of Albany *Yearbook* 3 (1927–28): 11–29.

———. *Correspondence of Jeremias van Rensselaer, 1651–1674.* Albany: University of the State of New York, 1932.

———. *Council Minutes, 1638–1649.* Baltimore: Genealogical Publishing, 1974.

———. "Documents Relating to Arent van Curler's Death." Dutch Settlers' Society of Albany *Yearbook* 3 (1927–28): 30–34.

———. *Documents Relating to New Netherland, 1624–1626 in the Henry E. Huntington Library.* San Marino, Calif.: Henry E. Huntington Library and Art Gallery, 1924.

———. "Early Dutch Manuscripts." *NYH* 3 (1922): 221–33.

———. *Minutes of the Court of Albany, Rensselaerswyck, and Schenectady, 1668–1685.* 3 vols. Albany: University of the State of New York, 1926–32.

———. *Minutes of the Court of Rensselaerswyck, 1648–1652.* Albany: University of the State of New York, 1922.

———. *Van Rensselaer-Bowier Manuscripts, Being the Letters of Kiliaen van Rensselaer, 1630–1643.* Albany: University of the State of New York, 1908.

van Loon, L. G., ed. "Letter from Jeronumus de la Croix to the Commissary at Fort Orange and a Hitherto Unknown Map Relating to Surgeon Van den Bogaert's Journey into the Mohawk Country." Dutch Settlers' Society of Albany *Yearbook* 15 (1939–40): 1–10.

———. "Tawagonshi: Beginning of the Treaty Era." *Indian Historian* 1.3 (1968): 23–26.

van Schaick, John H. "Showdown at Fort Orange." *De Halve Maen* 65.3 (1992): 37–45.

Van Zandt, Cynthia J. *Brothers among Nations: The Pursuit of Intercultural Alliances in Early America, 1580–1660.* New York: Oxford University Press, 2008.

Vaughan, Alden T. *New England Frontier: Puritans and Indians, 1620–1675.* 3rd ed. Norman: University of Oklahoma Press, 1995.

Vecsey, Christopher L. *The Paths of Kateri's Kin.* Notre Dame, Ind.: University of Notre Dame Press, 1997.

———. "The Story and Structure of the Iroquois Confederacy." *Journal of the American Academy of Religion* 54 (1986): 79–106.

Vecsey, Christopher L., and William A. Starna, eds. *Iroquois Land Claims.* Syracuse, N.Y.: Syracuse University Press, 1988.

Venema, Janny. *Beverwijck: A Dutch Village on the American Frontier, 1652–1664.* Albany: State University of New York Press, 2003.

———. "The Court Case of Brant Aertz van Slichtenhorst against Jan Van Rensselaer." *De Halve Maen* 74 (2001): 3–8.

Verano, John W., and Douglas H. Ubelaker, eds. *Disease and Demography in the Americas.* Washington, D.C.: Smithsonian Institution Press, 1992.

Verney, Jack. *The Good Regiment: The Carignan-Salières Regiment in Canada, 1665–1668.* Montreal: McGill-Queen's University Press, 1991.

"Vers Burlesque."*BRH* 33 (1927): 264–82.

Vest, Jay Hansford C. "An Odyssey among the Iroquois: A History of Tutelo Relations in New York." *AIQ* 29 (Winter/Spring 2005): 124–55.

Viele, Kathlyne Knickerbocker. *Viele Records, 1613–1913.* New York: Tobias A. Wright, 1913.

Walde, Dale, and Noreen D. Willows, eds. *The Archaeology of Gender.* Calgary: Archaeological Association of the University of Calgary, 1991.

Walker, William H., and Michael Brian Schiffer. "The Materiality of Social Power: The Artifact-Acquisition Perspective." *Journal of Archaeological Method and Theory* 13.2 (2006): 67–88.

Wall, Robert, and Heather Lapham. "Material Culture of the Contact Period in the Upper Potomac Valley: Chronological and Cultural Implications." *AENA* 31 (2003): 151–77.

Wallace, Anthony F. C. *The Death and Rebirth of the Seneca.* New York: Vintage Books, 1969.

——. "The Dekanawideh Myth Analyzed as the Record of a Revitalization Movement." *Ethnohistory* 5 (1958): 118–30.

Wallace, Paul A. W. *The Iroquois Book of Life: White Roots of Peace.* 1946. Reprint, Santa Fe, N.M.: Clear Light, 1994.

Walthall, John A., and Thomas E. Emerson, eds. *Calumet and Fleur-de-Lys: Archaeology of Indian-French Contact in the Midcontinent.* Washington, D.C.: Smithsonian Institution Press, 1992.

Ward, Harry M. *The United Colonies of New England, 1643–1690.* New York: Vantage Press, 1961.

Warkentin, Germaine. "In Search of the 'The Word of the Other': Aboriginal Sign Systems and the History of the Book in Canada." *Book History* 2.1 (1999): 1–27.

Warkentin, Germaine, and Carolyn Podruchny, eds. *Decentering the Renaissance: Canada and Europe in Multidisciplinary Perspective, 1500–1700.* Toronto: University of Toronto Press, 2001.

Warren, Stephen. *The Shawnees and Their Neighbors, 1795–1870.* Urbana: University of Illinois Press, 2005.

Warrick, Gary. "European Infectious Disease and Depopulation of the Wendat-Tionontate (Huron-Petun)." *World Archaeology* 35 (2003): 258–75.

——. *A Population History of the Huron-Petun,* A.D. *500–1650.* Cambridge: Cambridge University Press, 2008.

——. "The Precontact Iroquoian Occupation of Southern Ontario." *Journal of World Prehistory* 14 (2000): 415–66.

Waterman, Kees-Jan, trans. and ed. *"To Do Justice to Him and Myself": Evert Wendell's Account Book of the Fur Trade with Indians in Albany, New York, 1695–1726.* Philadelphia: American Philosophical Society, 2008.

Waugh, Frederick W. *Iroquis [sic] Foods and Food Preparation.* Ottawa, Ont.: Government Printing Bureau, 1916.

Webb, Stephen Saunders. *1676: The End of American Independence.* New York: W. W. Norton, 1984.

Webster, Gary Stewart. "Susquehannock Animal Economy." *NAA* 6 (1984–85): 41–62.

——."Northern Iroquoian Hunting: An Optimization Approach." Ph.D. diss., Pennsylvania State University, 1983.

Weslager, Clinton A. *The Nanticoke Indians—Past and Present.* Newark: University of Delaware Press, 1983.

Wesley, Norman, and Andy Faries, eds. *Stories from the James Bay Coast.* Cobalt, Ont.: Highway Book Shop, 1993.

Westra, Haijo J. "A New Version of Lahontan's 'Hieroglypic' Message." *European Review of Native*

American Studies 7 (1993): 21–26.

White, Ed. "Early American Nations as Imagined Communities." *American Quarterly* 56 (2001): 49–81.

White, Ed, and Michael Drexler. "Colonial Studies." *American Literary History* 16 (2004): 728–57.

White, Kevin J. "Haudenosaunee Worldviews through Iroquoian Cosmologies: The Published Narratives in Historical Context." Ph.D. diss. State University of New York at Buffalo, 2007.

White, Marian E. "Ethnic Identification and Iroquois Groups in Western New York and Ontario." *Ethnohistory* 18 (1971): 29–38.

——. *Iroquois Culture History in the Niagara Frontier Area of New York State.* University of Michigan Museum of Anthropology *Anthropological Papers* No. 16. Ann Arbor, Mich., 1961.

——. "On Delineating the Neutral Iroquois of the Eastern Niagara Peninsula of Ontario." *OA* 17 (1972): 62–74.

——. "The Orchid Site Ossuary, Fort Erie, Ontario." *BJNYSAA* 38 (1966): 1–35.

White, Richard. *The Middle Ground: Indians, Empires, and Republics in the Great Lakes Region, 1650–1815.* Cambridge: Cambridge University Press, 1991.

Whiteley, Peter. *Deliberate Acts: Changing Hopi Culture through the Oraibi Split.* Tucson: University of Arizona Press, 1988.

——. "Why Anthropology Needs More History." *Journal of Anthropological Research* 60 (2004): 487–514.

Whitmore, W. H., ed. *The Andros Tracts.* Prince Society *Publications* Nos. 5–7. Boston: T. R. Marvin & Son, 1868–74.

Widlok, Thomas. "Mapping Spatial and Social Permeability." *Current Anthropology* 40 (1999): 392–400.

Wildcat, Daniel R. "Indigenizing the Future: Why We Must Think Spatially in the Twenty-First Century." *American Studies* 46 (Fall–Winter 2005): 417–40.

Williams, Brackette F. "A Class Act: Anthropology and the Race to Nation Across Ethnic Terrain." *Annual Review of Anthropology* 18 (1989): 401–44.

Williams, Samuel C., ed. *Adair's History of the American Indians.* 1775. Reprint, Johnson City, Tenn.: Watauga Press, 1930.

Williamson, Margaret Holmes. *Powhatan Lords of Life and Death.* Lincoln: University of Nebraska Press, 2003.

Williamson, Ronald F., and Susan Pfeiffer. *Bones of the Ancestors: The Archaeology and Osteobiography of the Moatfield Site.* Archaeological Survey of Canada Mercury Series *Paper* No. 163. Ottawa: Canadian Museum of Civilization, 2003.

Williamson, Ronald F., and David A. Robertson. "Peer Polities Beyond the Periphery: Early and Middle Iroquoian Regional Interaction." *OA* 58 (1994): 27–48.

Williamson, Ronald F., and Christopher M. Watts, eds. *Taming the Taxonomy: Toward a New Understanding of Great Lakes Archaeology.* Toronto: Eastend Books, 1999.

Williamson, Ronald F., and Annie Veilleux. "A Review of Northern Iroquoian Decorated Bone and Antler Artifacts: A Search for Meaning." *OA* 79/80 (2005): 3–37.

Williams-Shuker, Kimberley Louise. "Cayuga Iroquois Households and Gender Relations during the Contact Period: An Investigation of the Rogers Farm Site, 1660s-1680s." Ph.D. diss., University of Pittsburgh, 2005.

Willoughby, C. C. "A Mohawk (Caughnawaga) Halter for Leading Captives." *American Anthropologist* 40 (1938): 48–50.

Winthrop Papers. 6 vols. to date. Boston: Massachusetts Historical Society, 1929–.

Wiseman, Frederick. *Reclaiming the Ancestors: Decolonizing a Taken Prehistory of the Far Northeast.* Hanover, N.H.: University Press of New England, 2005.

——. *The Voice of the Dawn: An Autohistory of the Abenaki Nation.* Hanover, N.H.: University Press of New England, 2001.

Wishart, David J. "The Selectivity of Historical Representation." *Journal of Historical Geography* 23 (1997): 111–18.

Witgen, Michael. "The Rituals of Possession: Native Identity and the Invention of Empire in Seventeenth-Century Western North America." *Ethnohistory* 54 (2007): 639–68.

Witthoft, John. *Green Corn Ceremonialism in the Eastern Woodlands.* University of Michigan Museum of Anthropology *Occasional Contributions* No. 13. Ann Arbor, Mich., 1949.

Witthoft, John, and W. Fred Kinsey III, eds. *Susquehannock Miscellany.* Harrisburg: Pennsylvania Historical and Museum Commission, 1959.

Wolf, Eric R. *Europe and the People without History.* Berkeley: University of California Press, 1982.

——. "Facing Power—Old Insights, New Questions." *American Anthropologist* 92 (1990): 586–96.

Wolf, Morris. *Iroquois Religion and Its Relation to Their Morals.* New York: Columbia University Press, 1919.

Wolfe, Patrick. "Settler Colonialism and the Elimination of the Native." *Journal of Genocide Research* 8 (2006): 387–409.

——. *Settler Colonialism and the Transformation of Anthropology: The Politics and Poetics of an Ethnographic Event.* London: Cassell, 1999.

Womack, Craig S. *Red on Red: Native American Literary Separatism.* Minneapolis: University of Minnesota Press, 1999.

Wonderley, Anthony. "Archaeological Research at the Oneida Vaillancourt Site." *BJNYSAA* 122 (2006): 1–26.

——. *At the Font of the Marvelous: Exploring Oral Narrative and Mythic Imagery of the Iroquois and Their Neighbors.* Syracuse, N.Y.: Syracuse University Press, 2009.

——. "Effigy Pipes, Diplomacy, and Myth: Exploring Interaction between St. Lawrence Iroquoians and Eastern Iroquois in New York State." *American Antiquity* 70 (2005): 211–40.

——. "Iroquois Ceramic Iconography: New Evidence from the Oneida Vaillancourt Site." *OA* 79/80 (2005): 73–87.

——. "The Iroquois Creation Story Over Time." *Northeast Anthropology* 62 (2001): 1–16.

——. "Oneida Ceramic Effigies: A Question of Meaning." *Northeast Anthropology* 63 (2002): 23–48.

——. "An Oneida Community in 1780: Study of an Inventory of Iroquois Property Losses during the Revolutionary War." *Northeast Anthropology* 56 (1998): 19–41.

——. *Oneida Iroquois Folklore, Myth, and History: New York Oral Narratives from the Notes of H. E. Allen and Others.* Syracuse, N.Y.: Syracuse University Press, 2005.

Wonderley, Daryl E. "The Importance of Cloth Seals Found on Two 17th-Century Oneida Occupations (MSV 4 and MSV 6)." NYSAA Chenango Chapter *Bulletin* 28 (July 2001): 15–27.

Woodward, Arthur. "The Metal Tomahawk: Its Evolution and Distribution in North America." Fort Ticonderoga Museum *Bulletin* 8 (January 1946): 2–42.

Woodward, David, and G. Malcolm Lewis, eds. *The History of Cartography.* 3 vols. Chicago: University of Chicago Press, 1987.

Wraxall, Peter. *An Abridgment of the Indian Affairs Contained in Four Folio Volumes, Transacted from the Colony of New York, from the Year 1678 to the Year 1751.* Ed. C. H. McIlwain. Cambridge, Mass.: Harvard University Press, 1915.

Wray, Charles F. "The Volume of Dutch Trade Goods Received by the Seneca Iroquois, 1600–1687 A.D." *New Netherland Studies: An Inventory of Current Research and Approaches. Bulletin KNOB: Tijdschrift van de Koninklinke Nederlandse Oudheide Kundige* 84.2–3 (June 1985): 100–112.

Wray, Charles F., and Robert Graham. "New Discoveries On an Old Site: The Bunce Site I." *BJNYSAA* 18 (1960): 1–4.

Wray, Charles F., Martha L. Sempowski, and Lorraine P. Saunders. *Tram and Cameron: Two Early Contact Era Seneca Sites.* RMSC *Research Records* No. 21. Rochester, N.Y., 1991.

Wray, Charles F., et al. *The Adams and Culbertson Sites.* RMSC *Research Records* No. 19. Rochester, N.Y., 1987.

Wright, Bruce. *A Proxemic Analysis of the Iroquoian Settlement Pattern.* Calgary: Western, 1979.

Wright, Gordon K. *The Neutral Indians: A Sourcebook.* NYSAA *Occasional Papers* No. 4. Rochester, N.Y., 1963.

Wright, James V., and Jean-Luc Pilon, eds. *A Passion for the Past: Papers in Honour of James F. Pendergast.* Canadian Museum of Civilization *Mercury Series* No. 164. Gatineau, Queb., 2004.

Wright, Joyce M. "Ceramic Vessels of the Wendat Confederacy: Indicators of Tribal Affiliation or Mobile Clans?" *CJA* 30 (2006): 40–72.

Wright, Milton J. *The Walker Site.* National Museum of Man *Mercury Series* No. 103. Ottawa, Ont., 1981.

Wykoff, M. William. "The Land of the Eries in 1653: An Analysis of Radisson's Captivity Voyage." *Terrae Incognitae* 27 (1995): 15–45.

INDEX

A

Abenakis: French alliance with, 18–19; Iroquois conflicts with, 111, 115, 118; Laurentian Iroquois among, 15–16; scalp-collecting of, 239; Seneca offensives against, 200

Abrams, George, 306 (n. 75)

Achkameg, Pierre, 70

adoptees: Algonquin widow's story as, 17–18; assimilative and associative types of adoption, 103, 312 (n. 26); benefits brought by Laurentian Iroquois as, 15–16; captives integrated as, 57–62; captives treated as, 52–53; competition for and conflicts over, 77, 80–89, 93, 94–100, 329–30 (n. 3); continuing importance of, 200–201; daily lives of, 102; diplomatic efforts concerning, 96–100; disease epidemic as rekindling search for, xxxiv–xxxv, 45–46; distribution and integration of, 102–3, 155; Illinois and Westos as, 165; in Iroquois siege against Zachariah fort, 166; Jesuits on, 102–5; military and diplomatic efforts to integrate, 77, 80–86, 329–30 (n. 3); non-Natives as, 18, 58, 83–84, 85–86, 105, 108, 119, 206, 332 (n. 15); number of nations represented by, 102, 336 (n. 76); relocation and expanding territory in assimilation of, 128, 130–36, 138–40, 142; reproductive potential of, 71; as "requickening" population, 41–42, 77, 80–86, 100–105, 124–25; spatial segregation of Wendat, 343 (n. 5); war parties in search of, 115, 340 (n. 121)

Agariata (Neutral adoptee), 121, 131

Agheroense (Mohawk headman), 64, 65

Agojoudas (likely Iroquois), 309 (n. 11)

Agona ("captain" of Stadacona), 10

agriculture: Denonville's destruction of crops, 194–95; innovative techniques in, 145; maize crop, xxxvii, 311 (n. 23); origin of, 300 (n. 33); overemphasis on, xxxvii–xxxviii; plant, animal, and aquatic resources as supplement to, xxxix. *See also* natural resources; subsistence patterns

Ahrendahronon Wendats: in French military expedition, 19–20, 25, 27; Iroquet allies of, 51; peace overtures of, 71; relocations of, 15, 99

Ailleboust, Louis d', 104, 106

Albany: Anglo-American relations with Iroquois centralized at, 150–52; Anglo-French trade controversy increased at, 198–99; condolences for Hannonsache offered at, 163; corrupt officials in, 264–65; downturn in trade at (1689), 207–8; English protocols at, 135; firearms obtained at, 130; French view of trading at, 166–67; Iroquois control of, 211–12; Iroquois defiance of, 189, 199–200; Iroquois-English negotiations at, ix, 121, 159–60, 209, 293 (n. 1); Iroquois formal peace negotiations at (1694), 236–37; Iroquois mobility as challenge for, 140–41, 147–52, 162, 256–57; Iroquois preliminaries to peace at, 260–62; Iroquois-Susquehannock conflict and, 148–49; Iroquois treaties with

G

treaties of, 266–71; placenames at time of, 265; preliminaries to, 257–66; signatories to, 268–69, 365–66 (n. 107), 366 (n. 108), 366 (nn. 111–12); underlying background to, 271

Grassmann, Thomas, 325 (n. 37)

Greysolon du Lhut, Daniel, 176, 186

Griffon (ship), 157–58

H

Hagerty, Gilbert, 322 (n. 7)

Hamilton, Raphael, 319 (n. 60)

Hamilton (Ontario), Neutral town near, 82

Handsome Lake revival movement, xxx–xxxi

Hannonsache (Seneca headman), 163–64, 169, 184–85, 203

Hansen, Hendrick, 263

Heidenreich, Conrad, 309 (n. 11)

Hendricksen, Cornelis, 25

Hennepin, Louis: attack on Tamaroa and, 160; on calumet pipe, 352 (n. 143); on Cayugas, 155–56; on Jesuit role in Iroquoia, 128; La Salle's mission for, 157–58; report concerning Seneca attack, 163

Henri IV (king of France), 18

Hewitt, J. N. B., 319 (n. 71)

Hewitt, John Napoleon Brinton, 38

Hiawatha (Deganawidah's follower), xlv

Hill, Richard W., Sr., 299 (n. 30)

historiography: assumptions in, xxviii–xxix; conception of space in, 276; dismissive view of Iroquois in, xxviii–xxxv; Morgan's influence on, xxix–xxxi. *See also* methodology

Hochelaga: Cartier's entry into, 3, 9; descendants of, 66; dispersal of, 14–15; layout of, 4; location of, 6, 308 (n. 1); navigational knowledge in, 10; population of, 308 (n. 1)

Hontom, Hans Jorisz, 28, 32, 37

hospitality: equitable, clan-based distribution in, xxxix; as evidence of control, 157; image of kettle as, xliii; Jesuits' interpretation of, 168; mobility and travel sustained by, ix–xi, xlii, xliii; peace negotiations and, 65; for winter hunting parties, 145, 155

"Hot Powder" (Kahnawake headman), 154

Howard, Lord Francis (Baron Howard of Effingham), 184

Hudson, Henry, 22

Hudson River valley: Dutch and French competition over, 25–27, 28; Mohawk presence and trade in, 22–24; Peach Tree War in, 94, 106. *See also* Albany; Fort Orange; New York

hunting expeditions: as detrimental to proselytizing, 156; family ties renewed via, 238, 251; French fears of, 258; joint efforts in, 14–15, 144, 154; mixed parties and attacks on, 243–45; territorial claims based on, 308 (n. 1); women's and men's roles in, xl

Huron language (*Hotinnonchiendi*), 89

Hurons: Iroquois attacks on, 84; in Iroquois war parties, 74; limits to mobility of, 305 (n. 66). *See also* Wendats

I

identities: adaptability of, xii; of adoptees, as Iroquois vs. Christian, 102–3; "authentic" and "inauthentic," xxxiii; of Mohawks as Iroquois, 14–15; spatial mobility embedded in, xxxv–xxxvi. *See also* clans and moieties; culture and cultural values; epistemology

Illinois country, 172, 178

Illinois people: access to military stores, 158, 169; hunting practices of, 178; Iroquois captives of, 200; Iroquois conflicts with, 79, 156, 160–61, 163, 165, 204, 216, 236; repatriated women of, 195

infant burials, xlii

information conduits: on Denonville's expedition's whereabouts and doings, 190, 192–94; mobility, surveillance, and exclusion linked in, xliii, xlviii–xlix; speed of, 307 (n. 84). *See also* communication networks; reconnaissance and surveillance

Ingoldsby, Richard, 220, 222

Iowas, 79

Irondequoit Bay: Denonville's expedition at, 190, 192, 193, 195; La Salle's expedition at, 136, 138

Iroquets: Algonquins known as, 14–15, 17, 19, 25–26, 27, 28, 32, 51; leader known as, 19–20

Iroquoia: in 1534–1634, 5–6; in 1697, ix; in 1851, xxxi–xxxii; in 2008, 278; Anglo-American claims to, 174–75; arguments for peace with New France in, 222–23; assigned New York

Matson, Cathy, 321 (n. 86)

"Memoir in Proof" (French, 1686), 188, 353 (n. 15)

methodology: "downstreaming" and integrative analysis in, xxxv; expanded evidentiary base in, xxviii; "sedentarist metaphysics" in, xxix–xxxi; terminology, dating, and citations, xv–xvi; "upstreaming" (projecting) in, xxxi–xxxiv, 298 (n. 23). *See also* historiography

Meulles, Jacques de, 173, 174, 176, 179

Miamis: decline to assist French, 208; hunting practices of, 178; Iroquois captives of, 240; Iroquois conflicts with, 79, 167, 204, 216, 236; Onondaga attacks on, 200; repatriated women of, 195, 200–201; Seneca offensives against, 186, 200; Seneca outreach to, 158; in Seneca war party, 160–61

Michelaki, Kostalena, 330–31 (n. 9)

Michilimackinac. *See* Fort Michilimackinac

"migration hypothesis" (Snow), 299 (n. 30)

military tactics: captives as shields attached to war parties, 53, 57–62, 119; *cavalier* (elevated platform) in, 26–27; Iroquois access to firearms and, 48–49, 48–50, 56–57, 60–61, 72, 110, 114, 118, 130; Jesuit missions as refuge from, 51; shift from large to small war parties, 56–57. *See also* mourning rituals and wars

Millet, Pierre: communications from, 227, 228; on condolences, 147; as Denonville's emissary, 185; face painted red and black after capture, 325 (n. 37); Frontenac-Tareha negotiations and, 229; as guide for French, 247; Iroquois capture and adoption of, 205; on Iroquois military strength, 206; on La Prairie, 214; Oneidas' preservation of, 212–13; Tareha's repatriation of, 239, 248

Mississaugas, 88

Mississippi River valley, 266. *See also* Fort St. Louis

Mitchell v. Minister of National Revenue (Canada, 2001), 275

mobility: Anglo-American fears of, 140–41, 147–52, 162, 256–57; asserting right of, 115, 130–40, 161–62, 178, 189, 260–61; centrality of, xl, xlii–xlix, 266–71, 276–77; characteristics of, xxxvi–xxxvii, 5; Courcelles's threats

against, 138–41; critical problems in understanding, xxxvii–xxxviii; cultural values strengthened by, xi–xv; Denonville's report on, 188; diplomatic goal of ensuring, 54–55; evidence for, ix–xi; formal, public representations of, 3, 9; French fears of, 148, 152–54, 162; generative power of, xxxv–xxxvi, xlviii–xlix; Jesuit residents in Iroquoia as ensuring, 128; La Salle's ship as challenge to, 158; military campaigns as demonstrations of, 152; Morgan's assumptions about, xxxi; nonlinear nature of, xxxvi; parallel treaties as reflecting role of, 266–71; postcolonial struggles over, 275; post-epidemic population recovery via, xxxiv–xxxv; Quebec visit as manifestation of, 259; range and extent of, xlvii–xlviii, xlviii–xlix; ritualized regulation of, xxvii–xxviii; subsistence patterns balanced with, xxxvii–xxxviii. *See also* captive-taking; diplomacy; information conduits; spatial consciousness; trade and exchange; war parties and warfare

Mohawk-Mahican War (so-called), 32–35

Mohawk River valley: battles in, 137; in metaphorical longhouse, xlviii; number of warriors in, 146; relocations across, 32; relocations encouraged to, 201; reorganizing towns of, 227

Mohawks: Algonquin conflicts with, 18–19, 36, 53, 55–56, 64–65, 70–75; in Anglo-American attack on French, 218–19; Anglo-American negotiations with, 159, 161–62, 167–68, 217; Anglo-Americans and Tree of Peace with, 204–5, 217; Anglo-Americans attacked by, 137, 160; decline to participate in Anglo-American attack on French, 213; depopulation from epidemics, 322 (n. 9); detained then released at Albany, 197; dissatisfaction with prices at Fort Orange, 46, 333–34 (n. 34); Dutch assistance requested by, 99–100, 105, 106, 109; Dutch negotiations with, 22–24, 58–59, 94–95, 108–9, 113–14; Dutch relationships with Mahicans and, 109, 316–17 (n. 46), 333–34 (n. 34); firearms acquired by, 48–50; French and Laurentians pursued by, 211; French expeditions against, 6, 19–21, 224–26; French negotiations with, 28–31, 52–55, 62–70, 121–22, 130–31; French